CRIMINOLOGY

This fully comprehensive general introduction to criminology from a sociological perspective provides a much-needed textbook for an increasingly popular area of study. Written by a team of authors with a broad range of teaching and research experience, it covers most modules offered in UK criminology courses and will be valuable to students of criminology worldwide. It covers:

• The key traditions in criminology, their critical assessment and more recent developments • New ways of thinking about crime and control, including crime and emotions, drugs and alcohol from a public health perspective • Different dimensions of the problem of crime and misconduct, including crime and sexuality, crimes against the environment, crime and human rights, organisational deviance • Key debates in criminological theory • The criminal justice system • New areas such as the globalisation of crime and crime in cyberspace.

Specially designed to be user-friendly, each chapter includes:

• Introductory key issues summarising the chapter content
• A clear and accessible structure
• Superb illustrations and tables
• Glossary of terms and key words highlighted in each chapter
• Supporting case studies and examples, boxed throughout
• Chapter summaries and critical thinking questions
• Annotated further reading sections
• Additional resource information as Web links
• A support Website at **http://www.routledge.com/textbooks/0415281687**

Eamonn Carrabine, Paul Iganski, Maggy Lee, Ken Plummer and **Nigel South** all work in the Department of Sociology at the University of Essex.

CRIMINOLOGY

A sociological introduction

Eamonn Carrabine,
Paul Iganski,
Maggy Lee,
Ken Plummer,
Nigel South

Routledge
Taylor & Francis Group

LONDON AND NEW YORK

First published 2004
by Routledge
11 New Fetter Lane, London EC4P 4EE

Simultaneously published in the USA and Canada
by Routledge
29 West 35th Street, New York, NY 10001

Routledge is an imprint of the Taylor & Francis Group

© 2004 Eamonn Carrabine, Paul Iganski, Maggy Lee,
Ken Plummer, Nigel South

Designed and typeset in Garamond by Keystroke, Jacaranda Lodge,
Wolverhampton
Printed and bound in Great Britain by TJ International Ltd, Padstow,
Cornwall

British Library Cataloguing in Publication Data
A catalogue record for this book is available from the British Library

Library of Congress Cataloging in Publication Data
A catalog record for this book has been requested

ISBN 0–415–28167–9 (hbk)
ISBN 0–415–28168–7 (pbk)

CONTENTS

PART 5 GLOBALISING CRIME   311

17 The Greening of Criminology   313

18 Crime and the Media   331

LIST OF ILLUSTRATIONS

PLATES

■ FIGURES

■ TABLES

■ CASE STUDY AND EXAMPLE BOXES

NOTES ON THE AUTHORS

Eamonn Carrabine is a Lecturer in the Department of Sociology at the University of Essex. He has published in three broad areas: the sociology of imprisonment, youth culture and theoretical criminology. His work has appeared in *Punishment and Society*, *Theoretical Criminology* and *The Howard Journal of Criminal Justice* (1988). His books include *Crime in Modern Britian* (co-authored, 2002) and *Power, Discourse and Resistance: A Genealogy of the Strangeways Prison Riot* (2004). He is also contributing to a forthcoming Encyclopedia of Prisons and Correctional Facilities.

Paul Iganski is a Lecturer in the Department of Sociology at the University of Essex. He trained and worked as a psychiatric nurse in Cheshire and the community before enrolling at university as a mature student. His main areas of research are hate, violence, rights, racial stratification and equal opportunities. Since 1998 he has been a Visiting Scholar at the Brudnick Center for the Study of Conflict and Violence at Northeastern University, Boston. In 2000 he was appointed Civil Society Fellow of the Institute for Jewish Policy Research. He is co-author of the book *Ethnicity, Equality of Opportunity and the British National Health Service* (2002, with David Mason), editor of *The Hate Debate: Should Hate be Punished as a Crime?* (2002) and *A New Antisemitism? Debating Judeophobia in 21st-Century Britain* (2003, with Barry Kosmin).

Maggy Lee is a Lecturer in the Department of Sociology at the University of Essex. She worked as a criminal justice researcher at the Institute for the Study of Drug Dependence and lectured at Birkbeck College, University of London, from 1992 to 1996 before joining the Department of Sociology, University of Essex. Her main areas of research are policing, drug policy and enforcement, juvenile delinquency, migration and human rights. Recent publications include *Youth, Crime and Police Work* (1998), *Crime in Modern Britain* (2002) with Eamonn Carrabine, Pamela Cox and Nigel South, all in the department at Essex, and 'Drugs policing' (with Nigel South) in T. Newburn (ed.) *Handbook of Policing* (2003).

Ken Plummer is Professor of Sociology University of Essex, and a Visiting Professor of Sociology at the University of California at Santa Barbara. His main teaching interests are in areas of social psychology, sexuality, crime and stigma, and introductory sociology. He has published prolifically, including *Sexual Stigma* (1975), *Documents of Life* (1983), *Telling Sexual Stories* (1995), *The Making of the Modern Homosexual* (1981), *Modern Homosexualities* (1992), *Symbolic Interactionism* (1990), *The Chicago School* (Routledge, 1997, 4 vols), *Documents of Life – 2: An Invitation to a Critical Humanism* (2001), *Sexualities: Critical Assessments* (2002) and *Intimate Citizenship* (2003).

Nigel South is Professor in the Department of Sociology and Research Professor in the Department of Health and Human Sciences at Essex University. He has taught at various universities in London and New York, and between 1981 and 1990 worked as a Research Sociologist at the Institute for the Study of Drug Dependence in London. His current research interests include inter-agency initiatives across the health, welfare and criminal justice systems, drug prevention initiatives, environmental health and environmental crime; crime, social order and policy in Britain and, comparatively, drug distribution and controls in Britain, wider Europe and North America; and theoretical and comparative criminology. His recent books include *Youth, Crime, Deviance and Delinquency* (ed.) (1999), *Crime in Modern Britain* (co-author) (2000), *Drugs, Cultures, Controls and Everyday Life* (ed.) (1999) and *The New European Criminology* (co-editor 1998).

ACKNOWLEDGEMENTS

We are indebted to the people and organisations mentioned below and in the text for the kind permision given to reproduce the plates and illustrations in this book. Every effort has been made to contact copyright holders; any ommissions brought to our attention will be amended in future editions.

For those interested in the natural history of the texts they hold in their hands – a few words. The idea for this book emerged as we succumbed to the persuasive powers of Mari Shullaw, then commissioning editor at Routledge. It was originally conceived as a text to be called *The Criminological Imagination* (but the publisher didn't like this title) and to be even more widely encompassing than the version here (but the authors didn't like the amount of work involved). Amidst all the other demands on our time – teaching, administration, research commitments, the joys of programme specifications and preparing for Audits, as well as attempts to 'have a life', progress on the book was initially slow. But, as happens whether you are an undergraduate or a lecturer, faced with multiple priorities and attractive displacement activities, two things can help get the writing job done. First, it gets easier as the project shapes up and begins to look 'ok'. Second, it is valuable if someone – say, a teacher or production editor – manages to combine helpful encouragement with stern warnings.

This has been a major project incurring various debts. At a personal level we thank Chris Ellis, Alison Inman, Everard Longland, Christine Rogers, Daniel South, and Caroline Thomas. Agnes Skamballis deserves special mention for outstanding support and expert research assistance. Thanks also to Natalie Mann and Ray Plummer for additional research assistance. As ever, the Department of Sociology provided a congenial and supportive environment for our work.

Our thanks for initiating and taking the project to completion to colleagues at Routledge, especially Moira Taylor and Nicola Cooper. Thanks also to our anonymous reviewers for valuable suggestions and criticisms, and to the named readers who have provided 'product endorsements'. Inevitably we have drawn upon our previous work in preparing this text and we acknowledge copyright holders, collaborators and editors, for permission to revise such work. Data and tables from the Home Office are reproduced by permission.

Finally, this has been a collaborative effort and we have all, in some way or another, helped to shape each other's chapters. Nonetheless, if there are any parts of the book that you don't like then the blame undoubtedly lies with 'someone else'.

EC, PI, ML, KP, NS.
Colchester, January 2004.

PART 1 THE CRIMINOLOGICAL IMAGINATION

In this section, we explain what a sociological approach to crime is all about, provide a basic timeline, and raise some of the methodological issues in looking at criminological data.

Introductory Timeline

The early period	Demonism, witchcraft
Late eighteenth century onwards	The Classical School and Beccaria
France, 1820s	Creation of criminal statistics
1870s	The Italian or Positivist School
Early twentieth century	Heredity and criminal families: the Jukes, the Kallikaks
1914 etc.	Theories of feeble-mindedness (intelligence theories)
	Twin research
	Somatotypes theory
	Endocrinology
1920s	Psychoanalytic theories
1920s	Life story research
1910 onwards	Durkheim and functionalist criminology
1930s onwards	Anomie theory
1920s/1930s	The Chicago tradition
1920s/1930s	Zonal theory
1930s/1940s	Differential association
1960s/1970s	Subcultural theory
1960s/1970s	Labelling theory
1970s onwards	Moral panic theory
1960s	The Neo- Chicagoan School
1960s onwards	Control theory
	Marxist/conflict criminologies
1973	New Criminology
1970s	Critical criminology
1970s	Birmingham Centre for Contemporary Cultural Studies (BCCCS)
1970s	The political economy of crime
1976	The justice model
	Administrative/actuarial criminology
1970s onwards	Feminist criminology
Late 1970s onwards	Black and anti-racist criminology
Late 1970s onwards	Foucauldian genealogies and governance
1980s	Left realism
1980s	Resurgence of radical right
1990s	Reintegrative shaming theory
1990s	Cultural criminology and the seductions of crime
1990s	Postmodern criminology
1990s	Green criminology
2000s	Globalisation of crime
2000s	Risk criminology
2000s	Criminologies of war and terrorism
2000s	Human rights

CHAPTER 1

KEY ISSUES

▌ What is criminology?

▌ What is sociology?

▌ Why a sociological introduction to criminology?

▌ Why are 'social divisions' important?

▌ What is the structure of this book?

Introduction

▌ AN INTRODUCTION: THE VARIED MEANINGS OF CRIMINOLOGY

Criminology has many meanings but at its widest and most commonly accepted it is taken to be the scientific understanding of crime and criminals. But such a definition will really not get us very far. For hidden within the term there come many different topics, different approaches to 'science' and different disciplines.

▌ WHAT KIND OF TOPICS?

Much criminology stays firmly within the existing confines of the criminal law. Criminology explores the bases and implications of criminal laws - how they emerge, how they work, how they get violated and what happens to violators. But we know that laws vary from time to time and from place to place. Laws are relative, and always historically shaped. Even something as seemingly universally condemned as killing others has its moments when it is acceptable (e.g. in war). Many criminologists believe therefore that they should not be confined by the bounds of law - this would make criminology a very traditional, orthodox and even conservative discipline. Rather, criminologists should also be able and willing to take on wider matters. As you will see, although our main focus in this book is indeed the existing laws, we also include an array of areas that are not quite so clearly defined by the current law: crimes against human rights, environmental crimes, and hate crimes. These are often not crimes in a strict sense of the word. But they are included here.

WHAT KIND OF STUDY?

Some criminologists make very orthodox claims to be scientists: observing, testing, measuring and trying to produce law like statements around crime. We will meet some of this work in Chapter 3, where we introduce the ideas of positivism and of Lombroso and his followers. However, other criminologists do not claim to be scientific in this way. For instance, in 1956, Vold published a text called *Theoretical Criminology*. In this text, he was simply considering laying out major ways of thinking and theorizing about crime- and not necessarily with their testing (but he did adopt a particular perspective – conflict theory – which we shall return to in Chapter 5). Likewise, when Ian Taylor, Paul Walton and Jock Young published *The New Criminology* in 1975 (also discussed in Chapter 5), their aim was not to make a scientific study but rather to highlight a stance which was critical. So, as we shall see, there are a range of different versions of knowledge (or epistemologies) that can be adopted in the study of crime

WHAT SORT OF ACADEMIC DISCIPLINE?

Most frequently criminology is seen to combine disciplines – it is multidisciplinary or inter-disciplinary. Thus for example it is not unusual to find criminology drawing upon the work of legal scholars, philosophers, biologists, psychiatrists, and psychologists. Although we will have recourse to other disciplines, in this book our prime focus is with the sociologists – all the authors are sociologists, and work in a sociology department.

SO WHAT IS SOCIOLOGY?

Sociology can be seen as the *systematic study of human society*. But it is much more than a listing of facts and theories about society. Instead it becomes a form of consciousness, a way of thinking, a critical way of seeing. For as Peter Berger (1963: 34) says: 'The first wisdom of sociology is this; things are not what they seem.'

Thus, in criminology, the sociological approach does not take for granted common sense discussions of crime - as found for example in the media, popular film or even the news. Nor does it presume such things as the 'biological criminal'. Instead, it always challenges the taken for granted, asks questions about what we believe to be true about crime, and attempts to lay out how crime is shaped by wider social factors.

Some fifty years ago, C. Wright Mills claimed that developing what he called the 'sociological imagination' would help people to become more active citizens. Charles Wright Mills (1916–62) was a US sociologist who held up sociology as an escape from the 'traps' of our lives. It can show us that society – not our own foibles or failings – is responsible for many of our problems. In this way, Mills maintained, sociology transforms *personal problems* (like criminal behaviour) into *public and political issues* (like 'the crime problem'). For Mills 'The sociological imagination enables us to grasp history and biography and the relations between the two within society. That is its task and its promise . . .' (Mills, 1967: 4).

WHY A 'SOCIOLOGICAL INTRODUCTION' TO CRIMINOLOGY?

In this book we aim to provide a sociological introduction to criminology. Sociology is about seeing the human world with a critical eye – realising that there are general patterns of social life that shape people's life experiences, their attitudes, beliefs, behaviour and their identity. The human world that sociologists are interested in is broad and diverse in scope, ranging from day-to-day interactions between people to historical and global social phenomena. Taking a sociological perspective on that world involves trying to step outside society, becoming a stranger, so that the familiar becomes a field of adventure, not a refuge of common sense. It involves trying to look at society as a newcomer, if you like. It means that we must challenge our common sense. This way of looking at the social world involves nurturing and applying the 'sociological imagination'. In particular, it involves developing our minds to see that many personal troubles experienced by individuals – unemployment, poverty, crime victimization, to name just a few – are also public issues and that, in turn, these are interrelated with wider social forces.

In this book we aim to apply and hopefully nurture, a 'criminological imagination'. In outline, this involves appreciating that:

- Crime is a truly sociological concept. It does not exist as some autonomous entity but is socially constructed. While there is much agreement, what is regarded as crime also varies across time, place and people.
- The criminal is also a social construct, defined as such by the same social processes that define certain acts as crimes and others not.
- Crime control and punishment are also shaped by social influences that determine the seriousness of acts defined as criminal, and the priority with which they are to be addressed.

SOCIOLOGY, SOCIAL DIVISIONS AND CRIME

The analysis of social divisions is central to the sociological enterprise. For a long time though, sociologists focused primarily upon one major system of social division: inequalities associated with social and economic positions. Such a focus looks at how people are ranked in terms of their economic situation, their power and their prestige. It focuses especially on social class (and on caste and slavery in some kinds of societies). But more recently, sociologists have recognised that such divisions can be organised through other key social processes such as gender, ethnicity, sexuality, disability and age. In relation to crime, we can therefore identify hierarchies and social divisions that have received more recent recognition:

- social and economic divisions: here a person's labour, wealth and income play a key role in crime;
- gender and sexuality divisions: here a person's position as a man or as a woman plays a key role in crime;
- ethnic and racialised divisions: here a person's 'race' and ethnicity plays a key role in crime;
- age divisions: here a person's age plays a key role in crime.

Each of these areas of inequality and social division are addressed in this book. In particular, Chapter 4 discusses the work of criminologists who have argued that understanding of the causes and the experience of crime needs to be looked for in entrenched structural – social and economic – inequalities. Conflict analyses of crime, for instance, have drawn attention to how the crimes that poor people commit are subject to disproportionate attention by criminal justice systems.

However, it is an odd irony that conflict analyses – concerned about class and power differences – for so long neglected the importance of gender despite their focus on social inequality. If, as conflict theory suggests, economic disadvantage is a primary cause of crime, why do women (whose economic position is, on average, much worse than that of men) commit far fewer crimes than men do?

Up until the 1970s, the study of crime and deviance was very much a male province. British sociologist Carol Smart in her book *Women, Crime and Criminology*, published in 1977, documented the neglect of women in such study. She also showed that when women had been included, the approach had usually been highly sexist or outrightly misogynist.

The contributions of feminist scholars to the study of crime raised some fundamental questions. One question is what Kathy Daly and Meda Chesney Lind (1988) have called 'the generalisability problem'. This refers to whether theories generated to explain male offending can be used to explain female offending. Can women simply be inserted into theories that explain male offending, or are new theoretical developments necessary to explain female crime?

In redressing the omissions of criminology, feminist scholars saw an additional – but also an obvious – neglect of a focus upon men as men. Although crime is indeed largely – although not exclusively – committed by men, this dimension of analysis had been largely ignored: it was a key missing link. Hence, feminist criminologists began to raise the issue of masculinity and crime. They have suggested that since more men are involved in crimes, there may be a link between forms of masculinity and forms of crime. It is only relatively recently, then, that the obvious fact that crime is in some way bound up with masculinity has been taken up as in any way problematic. Much of the subsequent relevant research to date has tended to concentrate on the two areas of domestic violence and youth crime.

We address gender, sexuality and masculinity centrally in Chapter 4, but relevant issues are also raised elsewhere throughout the book. A further social division addressed in the book concerns 'race' and ethnicity. In Britain, as well in North America, some minority ethnic groups, and especially black communities, are over-represented in the criminal justice process – in police stops, in appearances in court, and in the prison population. Many commentators give the impression – especially in elements of the popular press – that some minority ethnic communities are somehow more criminally inclined than others. Such an impression both reflects and reinforces racist ideologies. Various factors are at work that account for crime. Crime is not evenly distributed across the social spectrum, and age, location, gender and socio-economic position are important variables in accounting for offending and victimization.

Analysing the relationship between 'race' and crime seriously also means taking account of discrimination in the criminal justice system. In Britain, the racist murder of black teenager Stephen Lawrence by a gang of white youths at a bus stop in London in 1993 – and the inquiry into the police investigation that followed – thrust the tragedy of violent racism into the public consciousness with a potency never present before. The flawed police investigation into the murder became, for many, symbolic of the character of relations between the police and minority ethnic communities in Britain. Fundamentally, using the language of 1960s Black Power activists in the United States, the 'Macpherson Inquiry' (1999) observed that the police investigation was characterised by *institutional racism*. Prior to the investigation, researchers had been producing evidence of racial prejudice and discrimination among some police officers for over two decades. We focus further on issues of 'race' and criminal justice in Part 4 of this book, 'Controlling Crime'. However, the salience of focusing on 'race' and ethnicity in criminological inquiry is observed in a number of other places in the book.

To this point, we have discussed social divisions around class, gender, sexuality and 'race' as if they are discrete categories in which people live their lives. Yet in practice they are experienced 'as a totality' by individuals (Allen, 1987: 169–70). Any one person's experience at any one moment in time is a product of interacting divisions. One response to this reality, which has been put forward by Kathy Daly (1997), is the 'multiple inequalities' approach around the class–race–gender axis of investigation. She suggests that everyone is located in a matrix of multiple social relations. This means that race and gender are just as relevant to the analysis of white men as they are to that of black women.

STRUCTURE OF THE BOOK

The book is organised into five parts. Following this introduction and the next chapter on 'Methodology and Measurement in Criminology', Part 2 – 'Thinking about Crime' – introduces the major movements in criminological thought and theory, organised – to help you make sense of it all – as a chronological narrative of the key theoretical developments. The timeline at the start of this chapter shows the major movements in criminological thinking covered by the book as a whole. The third part – 'Doing Crime' – focuses on developing an understanding of experiences and patterns of criminal activity and crime victimisation. Part 4 – 'Controlling Crime' – focuses on processes, theories and problems about crime control and punishment. The fifth and final section – 'Globalising Crime' – introduces perspectives on how global forces impact upon crime and crime control. We also look to the dynamic boundaries of the criminological imagination.

HOW TO USE THE BOOK

We would like you to use the book in the same way that we encourage students to use our university lectures – as a path to learning. Our lectures provide a guide to key issues – a road map of ideas, if you like – and a route through the maze of reading material. The chapters in this book serve in the same way. We try to guide you through the key topics, debates and research relevant to taking a sociological approach to criminology. However, in no way do we claim to provide the definitive, or final, word by any means! Learning comes through a process of exploration, and especially through the struggle to comprehend. We will not serve you well by removing the need for that struggle. Therefore, we aim to point you in the right direction but you must take the next steps yourself. Hence, reading this book alone will not suffice. We try to guide you to the reading that we have found to be the most informative and influential for the issues in criminology we deal with. But we provide only an outline. We hope that you will use our guide to select your further study and engage with it yourself. After all, in thinking critically, we are providing only our perspectives. You may develop your own. Consequently, as with all journeys there is more than one way of reaching your destination. Some paths are obviously the best way; for others, you must make your own informed judgement.

SPECIAL FEATURES

Chapter summaries

At the end of each chapter you will find a summary listing the key points. They are intended not to provide a full summary of the chapter, but to serve as a reminder about the key issues raised. So they probably won't make much sense until you read the whole chapter first!

Critical thinking questions

You will also find a number of 'critical thinking questions' at the end of each chapter. These are not examination questions. They are intended to get you thinking about what we see as some of the most important issues raised in the chapters. You will see that they are not questions to which you can give a 'yes' or 'no' answer. Instead, you will need to think carefully about them, revisit some of the points made in the chapter in question and in some cases consult the further reading recommended for that chapter.

Suggestions for further study

At the end of each chapter you will also see a section labelled 'Further Study'. This section has a number of purposes. In general, it is hoped that it will serve as a resource for you for future use – something that you can return to as a guide for your reading. Under this section we list key books – and articles in some cases – that we think make the most valuable contribution to understanding the issues covered by the chapter. The reading listed ranges from books that are suitable for the new student to criminology in general, for those new to the topic of the chapter in particular, and to the student (or tutor!) who wishes to develop their understanding in a greater depth than is covered in the chapter.

Suggestions about more information

Finally, at the end of each chapter, under the heading 'More Information', we list some Websites that provide useful information. These are also listed on the Website that accompanies this book and as this site is updated with additional Web resources and Internet links we hope it will also be a valuable resource for you and your studies.

Glossary

A glossary of key concepts used is provided at the end of the book. Concepts – abstract representations, or mental images of things observed and experienced in the real world – provide the foundations of sociological thinking. They are therefore fundamental to a sociological approach to the study of crime, deviance and social control. 'Crime' itself is a concept. We don't witness, hear, or read about 'crime' when it happens. What we do see or learn are things that we have come to think of – or conceptualise – as crime. Those things are taken to be indicators of crime, if you like, not crime itself.

In the glossary we provide a short definition of the key concepts used. While the glossary is intended to help you, do think, with a critical, inquiring mind, about the definitions provided. Concepts don't just exist 'out there' somewhere; they are made up as abstract representations of things.

In thinking about the meaning of concepts you may find it useful to consult a good encyclopaedia of sociology and a good criminological dictionary where you might find the particular concept you are interested in discussed in much more detail than provided in our glossary.

CHAPTER 2

Methodology and Measurement in Criminology

KEY ISSUES

▌ Why is it necessary to think critically about crime statistics?

▌ What moral questions concern research on the lived experience of crime?

▌ Is it inevitable that criminological researchers must 'take sides'?

▌ In what ways is criminological research distinctive from other areas of sociological research?

INTRODUCTION

Specialist texts on research methodology and methods have proliferated in the social sciences. In some subjects, such as sociology, the study of 'methodology' – the theoretical principles and framework behind different ways of carrying out research – and research 'methods' – the tools or instruments used by researchers to gather their evidence – has virtually become a discipline on its own, spawning a number of specialist scholarly journals and a multitude of general texts and specialist books.

Criminological researchers – coming from a variety of disciplines – draw from research techniques used in sociology, psychology, political science and history, to name just a few. In recent years, though, criminologists too have become more reflective about research issues affecting their own subject relative to others, resulting in a number of specialist texts (Jupp, 1989; Maxfield and Babbie, 1995; Sapsford, 1996; Jupp *et al.* 2000; King and Wincup, 2000; Champion, 2000). A question that students, teachers and researchers in criminology often grapple with is whether there is anything distinctive about criminological research compared with research in other disciplines in the human and social sciences. This question provides the foundation for this chapter, which unfolds around three key topics: the construction and interpretation of statistics; the ethical, legal and moral dilemmas faced by researchers when they try to study the lived experience of crime and crime control; and questions about whose side criminological researchers are on.

THINKING CRITICALLY ABOUT STATISTICS

Many people are 'awestruck' by statistics; so says Joel Best in his book *Damned Lies and Statistics* (2001). They treat them with reverence, as if they have magical qualities and represent 'the truth'. Other people, according to Best, are a little more thoughtful about statistics, but they remain naïve. They can make judgements about the extent of a phenomenon represented by statistics, but generally they too accept statistics as 'hard facts', believing in the sincerity of how social problems are defined by the data. They generally do not suspect that statistics might be flawed. In sharp contrast, the 'cynical', as Best calls them, are deeply suspicious about statistics, believing that they are likely to be flawed, and, even worse, part of a deliberate attempt to mislead and deceive. This view is epitomised by Benjamin Disraeli's oft-quoted claim that 'there are three kinds of lies: lies, damned lies and statistics'. Believing that statistics can be used to prove anything, the cynical dismiss them as worthless.

However, Best exhorts us to be neither awestruck, naïve nor cynical. Instead, we need to think critically. Thinking critically involves a thoughtful approach that evaluates the merits and limitations of the particular statistics in question. The critical appreciate that in summarising complex information, statistics lose some of that complexity. Simplifications and omissions result: choices are made about how to define the problem being measured, and how to go about measuring it. In evaluating these choices, the critical make an informed judgement about how useful the statistics remain. The aim of this section is to encourage a critical approach to crime statistics and to indicate and apply some of the questions characteristic of such an approach. Such questions should be applied when interpreting social statistics generally. However, arguably the pitfalls and problems affecting crime statistics – even though they affect other statistics – are particularly acute, and require a constant state of vigilance.

Recorded crime

It is vital to measure crime accurately if we are to tackle it effectively.
(Rt Hon. David Blunkett MP, Home Secretary, July 2001)

The main source of official recorded crime statistics for Britain is the annual publication *Criminal Statistics*, which has separate volumes for England and Wales, Scotland, and Northern Ireland. Data are published on the Internet and so are readily accessible for students, the general public, journalists, and anybody else with an interest. The crimes recorded by no means reflect the full extent of unlawful activity. To take the case of England and Wales, there are a number of omissions in terms of the scope of their coverage. The figures do not include data from police forces for which the Home Office is not responsible – for instance, the British Transport Police, Ministry of Defence Police, and the UK Atomic Energy Police, who publish their own statistics. Nor do they include cases of tax and benefit fraud known to agencies such as the Inland Revenue, Customs and Excise, and the Department of Social Security, which have their own investigative and prosecutorial functions. They do not

Plate 2.1 Graham cartoon from the *Manchester Evening News*.
Source: © Guardian Media Group plc.

include environmental crime and corporate crime. And for all categories of crime recorded, many crimes committed simply do not end up in police records. (A clear overview of the omissions is provided by Muncie, 2001: 25–39.)

Recorded crime statistics are not the product of a neutral fact-collecting process. As stated in the appendix to *Criminal Statistics England and Wales*, 'the recording process starts when someone reports to the police that an offence has been committed or when the police observe or discover an offence'. Under the National Crime Reporting Standard introduced on 1 April 2002, any incident – whether or not classified as a crime – must be recorded. The police make an initial examination of the facts to determine if there is prima facie evidence that an offence has been committed; a crime report may then be made out. However, for a crime to be registered in the official data, a number of things need to happen:

- There needs to be a recognition by victims (who initiate the vast majority of recorded crimes), or possibly a witness, that a crime has actually taken place.
- It must then be notified to the police.
- The police must acknowledge that a crime has allegedly occurred and record it as such.

There are many impediments along the way to prevent a crime being recorded – the process has been called 'the crime funnel' (see also Chapter 14 in this book). It is

BOX 2.1 SOURCES OF OFFICIAL STATISTICS ON THE INTERNET

Statistics Canada:
www.statcan.ca
Key words: justics and crime

The UK Home Office:
www.homeoffice.gov.uk
Key words: criminal statistics England and Wales

Justice website Federal Bureau of Investigation:
www.fbi.gov
Key words: Uniform Crime Reports

Scottish Executive:
www.scotland.gov.uk
Key words: recorded crime, crime statistics

Australian Bureau of Statistics:
www.abs.gov.au
Key words: recorded crime

Sources: the individual government departments

well known, consequently, that only a small proportion of incidents that would be classified as crime are recorded by official statistics. The statistics represent only the tip of the iceberg. Early local crime surveys – to be discussed on p. 16 – revealed that many victims do not report crimes to the police. These survey findings are supported by anecdotal accounts from victims. For instance, a victim's perception about how seriously their allegation will be taken by the police will affect the reporting of crime. Once it has been reported, there is a great deal of discretion on the part of the police officers about whether to record offences that come to their attention. Complaints from victims may be disbelieved, or they may be thought to be too trivial and not to be crimes at all. They may even be excluded to avoid work and improve the clear-up rate. Other factors affect crime records: reporting requirements for insurance claims, for instance, result in a high level of reporting of property crimes; and changing patterns of policing and targeting of crimes will affect the numbers of particular crimes that come to the attention of the police (Bottomley and Coleman, 1981; Maguire, 1997). In short, the recording of crime involves a complex process of interpretation and interaction. It is certainly not a straightforward process, hence the 'critical' (to use Joel Best's term again) will not interpret official crime data for any particular crime without a good understanding first of how the statistics were compiled.

Racist incidents: an exemplar of thinking critically about recorded crime

One type of crime, racist crime – crimes in which victims are targeted because of their 'race' or ethnicity – provides a very useful exemplar to illustrate some of the limitations of recorded crime data. Data on racist incidents for England and Wales can be found in *Statistics on Race and the Criminal Justice System*, published by the Home Office, the ministry responsible for crime and policing policy, immigration and nationality. Britain has a long history of racist crime (Bowling, 1998; Witte,

1996), but in statistical terms it simply did not exist before 1979, as it was not recorded in official statistics until then.

There has since been a huge increase in the number of recorded incidents, especially in the late 1990s (see Figure 2.1). The data seem to suggest that racist crime has escalated: certainly the awestruck and the naïve – to use Joel Best's categories – would think so. But is this really the case?

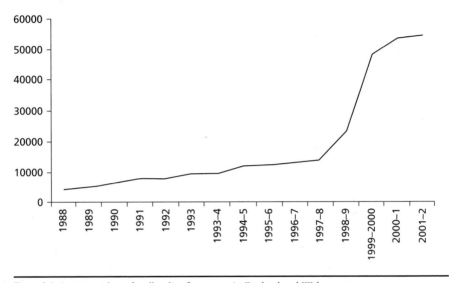

Figure 2.1 Racist incidents for all police force areas in England and Wales.

Sources: 1988 to 1996–7, *Racial Violence and Harassment: A Consultation Document*, London: Home Office (1997); 1997–8 to 1999, *Statistics on Race and the Criminal Justice System*, London: Home Office (2000); 2000–1 and 2001–2, *Statistics on Race and the Criminal Justice System*, London: Home Office (2002).

To think critically about the statistics, we would need to bear in mind the observation made above that not all crimes appear in police records. In the case of racist incidents it is clear that in the past there has been significant under-reporting by victims due – to some extent – to dissatisfaction with the police handling of reported incidents. A number of common allegations have been made by victims. Often, they have complained about considerable delays before police attend incidents (Gordon, 1990: 13). It has also been alleged that the police have frequently refused to acknowledge the racial motives behind incidents, often explaining them away as minor disputes between neighbours (Dunhill, 1989: 70). Victims of racist incidents have also complained that the police are reluctant to prosecute the perpetrators, and on occasion the victims themselves have been subject to hostile treatment from the police (Gordon, 1990: 20–1; see also Chapter 7 of this book); fear of such hostility has served as a deterrent to reporting incidents.

In taking a critical view of the number of recorded racial incidents, the apparent increase over time could quite conceivably reflect changes in police recording practices and also perhaps a greater motivation by victims to report crimes. The sharp rise in the number of recorded incidents in the late 1990s following the publication of the report of the Stephen Lawrence inquiry in 1999 (Macpherson, 1999) supports such an observation. The report not only drew widespread public attention to the problem of racist crime, but in labelling the Metropolitan Police Service as 'institutionally racist' it led to a major examination by police forces concerning how they respond to racist incidents. The definition of an incident was also broadened to include *any incident which is perceived to be racist by the victim or any other person* – previously, it was limited to the perception of the victim and the police. It is also likely that the establishment of racially aggravated offences for the first time in Britain under the 1998 Crime and Disorder Act made police forces more alert to such offences.

As this exemplar shows, a comparison of recorded crime data over time can be hazardous and it is perhaps impossible to represent the historical reality. Comparing official crime data between countries can be even more problematic. Again, data on racist incidents provide a good exemplar. If one looks at data for the United States recorded by the Federal Bureau of Investigation's (FBI) Uniform Crime Reports, then curiously, given the different size of the populations involved, and the greater ethnic diversity in the US population, the data for England and Wales show a much higher level of incidents. The number of recorded racist incidents in England and Wales for the year 2001–2 was 54,351, compared with 4,367 so-called hate crime incidents recorded by the FBI for 2001 in which the victims were targeted because of their 'race'. The criteria used by the FBI for defining hate crimes are far more stringent than the criteria used by police services in England and Wales. For the FBI, there must be 'sufficient objective facts . . . to lead a reasonable and prudent person to conclude that the offender's actions were motivated, in whole or in part, by bias (US Federal Bureau of Investigation, 1999). In contrast, as discussed in the previous paragraph, police services in England and Wales define racial incidents more broadly as *any incident which is perceived to be racist by the victim or any other person* – recorded incidents do not even have to be identifiable offences, and it is not possible from the regularly published data to determine which incidents were recorded as crimes. It is clear, too, that there are many omissions from the FBI's 'hate crime' data. According to the Southern Poverty Law Center – a leading non-profit organisation tackling hate, intolerance and discrimination in the United States – and to research commissioned by the United States Bureau of Justice Assistance (McDevitt *et al.*, 2000), the reporting system is 'full of holes'. Not all law enforcement agencies submit data, and the Southern Poverty Law Center, in an intelligence report dated Winter 2001, estimates the number of hate crimes to be six times greater than the number reported by the FBI.

National crime victimization surveys

Given the well-known limitations to police recorded crime statistics, many countries have established official crime victimization surveys. They attempt to shed light on the 'dark figure' of crime by asking samples of people directly about their experiences of crime victimization. In the United States, the National Crime Victimization Survey was established in 1972 and is now conducted annually. The first national crime victimization survey in Britain, the British Crime Survey (BCS), was carried out in

1982, with further surveys in 1984, 1988, 1992, 1996 and 1998. In the 2000 British Crime Survey, close to 23,000 people aged 16 and over were interviewed. From 2001 the BCS moved to an annual cycle, with 40,000 respondents to be interviewed per year. The BCS measures the amount of crime in England and Wales by asking people about crimes they have experienced in the past year. It asks about people's attitudes to crime, such as how much they fear crime and what measures they take to avoid it. It also asks about people's attitudes to the criminal justice system, including the police and the courts. The survey findings are published in a variety of specialist reports available online on the Home Office Website, and complete datasets of pri-mary data are available for secondary analysis and can be obtained from the University of Essex data archive. The questions used in the British Crime Survey are also published online by the Question Bank at the University of Surrey.

For some crimes, the BCS estimates of their extent far exceed the numbers recorded in police statistics. Again, racist incidents provide a useful exemplar to illus-trate the point. For 1999, the British Crime Survey estimated that there had been nearly six times as many racially motivated incidents as the number recorded by the police. Most interestingly, while the police statistics show a sharp increase in the number of racist incidents in the 1990s, a comparison of the estimates for the 1995 and 1999 British Crime Surveys actually shows a decline (Figure 2.2), suggesting that the increase in recorded racial incidents recorded by the police is a combination of the increased willingness by victims to report them and improved police recording practices (Clancy *et al.*, 2001).

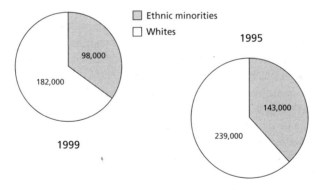

Figure 2.2 Estimates from the 1999 and 1995 British Crime Surveys on the number of incidents considered by the victim to be racially motivated.

Source: British Crime Surveys, 1999, 1995.

Comparison of BCS estimates of other crimes from 2002–3 interviews with recorded crime statistics for 2002 reveals varying levels of difference (Simmons and Dodd, 2003). According to the British Crime Survey, there were:

•   over twice as many woundings;
•   twice as many bicycle thefts;
•   three times as many offences of vandalism;
•   three times as many thefts from the person.

For thefts of vehicles, BCS and police recorded figures are relatively similar, because victims more readily report such thefts to the police in order to obtain help in recovering their vehicles and for insurance purposes.

As discussed in Chapter 7, crime victimization surveys have helped to redress imbalance in early criminological works, by providing insights into under-reported and under-recorded crime and to sensitise policymakers to the range and diversity of victim experiences. However, crime victimization surveys also have serious limitations. In almost all cases, victim surveys are confined to individual and household victimization. Crime victimization surveys therefore provide very limited notions about what crime is and who the victims are. They have a tendency to focus on the 'conventional' crimes while other equally harmful acts (and victims) remain hidden.

Large-scale international victim surveys have also been carried out so that some international comparisons can be made. For example, the International Crime Victim Survey (ICVS) series funded by the Ministry of Justice of the Netherlands was initiated in 1988 and has since been carried out in some fifty-five different countries. The project was set up to fill the gap in adequate recording of offences by the police for purposes of comparing crime rates in different nations and to provide a crime index independent of police statistics as an alternative standardised measure. The ICVS is the most far-reaching programme of standardised sample surveys to look at householders' experience of crime, policing, crime prevention and feelings of insecurity in a large number of nations.

Again, as discussed in Chapter 7, there are also specific problems, though, with using international victimization reports to measure crime. The cultural perception of crime in different countries may affect the respondents (Newman 1999: 25). It is clear that findings from victimization surveys need to be interpreted very carefully, with the knowledge that apparent differences may reflect definitional variations as much as variations in the incidence of crime.

Local victim surveys with a narrower geographical focus have also made a significant contribution to knowledge about crime. They have highlighted the uneven distribution of risks of victimization, showing that certain age or social groups are more frequently subjected to crime than others. For example, by focusing on particular localities, local victim surveys (notably in Islington, Merseyside, Edinburgh and Rochdale) have shown the higher levels of crime prevailing in socially deprived areas and the disproportionate victimization of women, of minority ethnic groups and of the poor (Crawford et al., 1990; Kinsey, 1984; Mooney, 1993; Forrester et al., 1988). In particular, local victim surveys have revealed levels of violence and sexual crime against women higher than those revealed by mass victimization surveys, and certainly far higher than those indicated by police records (Hanmer and Saunders, 1984; Radford, 1987; Painter and Farrington, 1998). Indeed, the highest estimates of domestic violence have come from local victimization surveys, which probably reflects the problems of using narrow legal definitions in understanding sexual victimization and interviewers' insensitivity to women's personal and often painful experiences in earlier national crime surveys. For example, the first two British Crime Surveys revealed only one (unreported) case of attempted rape and seventeen and eighteen cases of sexual assault respectively in the 1983 and 1985 reports. By contrast, the first Islington Crime Survey (Jones *et al.*, 1986) showed that one-third of the households in that area contained people who had been sexually assaulted during the previous year, and that young white women were twenty-nine times more likely to be assault victims than women aged over 45.

Not all victim surveys are directed at individual victims. Commercial victimization surveys ask both retail and manufacturing premises about the crime they have experienced in a particular period of time. Such surveys can provide an alternative measure of the crime problem and the extent of **repeat victimization** of the same premises (see Chapter 8). Results from the 1993 survey of commercial premises in England and Wales highlight the prevalence of crime in the commercial sector, although offences such as some types of theft (theft by staff) and fraud are more difficult to detect and are therefore more likely to be undercounted. Eight out of ten retailers and two-thirds of manufacturing premises experienced one or more of the crimes covered by the survey. Some premises also suffered a disproportionate amount of crime: 3 per cent of retailers accounted for over half of the crime recorded by the survey and 8 per cent of manufacturers accounted for two-thirds of the crime in the survey (Mirrlees-Black and Ross, 1995).

Thinking positively about crime statistics

The critical perspective applied to official crime statistics to this point perhaps suggests that the statistics provide more of an insight into official definitions of crime, crime recording and policing practice than into the actual level of unlawful activity. Thinking critically about crime statistics, though, also involves thinking about the potential they offer. While the statistics may not provide the reliable measures of crime that policymakers, academics and journalists, for instance, would wish for, at the local level crime data collected by police forces and not routinely published provide a sound basis for evidence-based policing. A major aim behind the recording of all incidents reported to the police – even if some may not be subsequently classified as a crime – as set down by the national crime reporting standard introduced in 2002, is to provide more accurate intelligence for policing at the local level, and for intervention by other agencies. In the case of so-called hate crime statistics, Elizabeth Stanko and colleagues argue that:

> We are convinced that police information on hate crimes and domestic violence can provide a grounded, evidence-based approach to challenging public understanding and agency responses in this area. The information offered by those who contact the police for help and *recorded by the police as criminal incidents* is an invaluable source of knowledge. This information, when analysed, can lead to the thinking around what officers need to know (in training or in management), document the network of overlapping interests and support systems within a community essential for victims' safety, and inform strategic planning for community safety.
>
> (Stanko *et al.*, 2002: 123)

The analysis of 'hate crime' data collected by police forces – to which Stanko and colleagues refer – has been invaluable in challenging common stereotypes of hate crime offenders and the contexts in which they occur.

Hate crime is discussed further in Chapter 10.

GETTING INSIDE THE IMMEDIACY OF CRIME

While the limitations of official crime statistics frustrate criminologists, the potential of researching criminal activity first-hand has excited the criminological imagination. In a much-quoted phrase, Robert E. Park, chair of the Department of Sociology at the University of Chicago in the 1920s, exhorted research students to 'go get the seat of your pants dirty in real research' – in short, to go and get acquainted first-hand with the social world around them.

While anthropologists at the time were still studying exotic cultures in far-flung places, Park believed that anthropological methods could be used in urban research – that is, people should be studied in their natural environments. The city was seen as a 'social laboratory' in which social processes and human nature could be studied *in situ*. With this way of thinking, a distinctive mix of research styles was used to understand social life by what has come to be known as the 'Chicago School'. It was highly influential for the future development of sociology (as discussed in Chapter 4 of this book). A variety of research methods were used to capture the complexity of social life: interviews, the study of personal documents, and, famously, observational methods. For real understanding, imaginative participation in the lives of others was required; empathy, as well as an acute eye, was the key (Bulmer, 1984). Ethnographic research was a major research style employed during this period. It is an approach in which the researcher participates in a social setting, 'amid the action' for an extended period of time; makes regular observations of people and events in that setting; listens to people and engages in conversations; interviews informants about issues that cannot be observed directly by the researcher; collects documents about the group under study; and writes up a faithful representation of what they have discovered in a detailed account of their study.

Major studies of crime and deviance carried out under the Chicago School during this period were Nels Anderson's *The Hobo: The Sociology of the Homeless Man* (1923), Frederic Thrasher's *The Gang* (1927), John Landesco's *Organized Crime in America* (1929), Clifford Shaw's *The Jack Roller* (1930) and Paul G. Cressey's *The Taxi-Dance Hall* (1932). Paul Cressey stated that his first objective 'was to give an unbiased and intimate picture of the social world of the typical taxi-dance hall' (a hall where customers paid to dance with young women). According to Cressey, and characteristic of an ethnographic approach:

> Observers were sent into the taxi-dance halls. They were instructed to mingle with the others and to become as much a part of this social world as ethically possible. . . . The investigators functioned as anonymous strangers and casual acquaintances . . . without encountering the inhibitions and resistance usually met in formal interviews.
>
> (Cressey, 1932: xxxiv)

Ethnographic research in the United States lost some of its momentum from the mid-1930s with the growth in interest in survey research. It achieved a renaissance immediately after the Second World War in the 'Second Chicago School' (discussed on p. 21), and then in the 1960s the heart of the ethnographic endeavour moved to California, with a focus on counter-cultural, deviant and alternative groups. Adler and Adler (1998: xiii) observe that:

> Free to go out and study those groups in close proximity, these ethnographers realized that the only sensible way to get information about hidden populations was to study them naturistically. Disdaining the research endeavors that analyzed criminals as captured populations, these sociologists and criminologists went into bars, inside gangs, and into the inner sanctums of deviant populations to find out what constituted their realities.

Some of the noted studies of this period included John Lofland's *Doomsday Cult* (1966), Marvin Scott's *The Racing Game* (1968), Jacqueline P. Wiseman's *Stations of the Lost* (1970), and Jack Douglas and Paul Rasmussen's *The Nude Beach* (1977).

Adler and Adler argue that the late 1970s to the early 1990s were the 'Dark Ages' of ethnographic research. During this period, university ethics committees, cautious of the moral, ethical and legal implications of fieldwork on crime and deviance (discussed in the next subsection), inhibited ethnographic research.

The tradition of the ethnographic study of deviance, crime and control has not been as strong in Britain as it has in the United States. Nevertheless, there have been outstanding works such as James Patrick's study of gang life in Glasgow (1973), Howard Parker's study of 'joy-riding' in the inner city (1974), Jason Ditton's study of fiddling and pilfering in a bakery (1977), Anne Campbell's study of violence among female gangs (1988) and Dick Hobbs's study of crime and policing in east London (1988), to name a few.

Moral, ethical and legal difficulties of getting inside the immediacy of crime

When researchers study those who engage in criminal activity they face, in the words of Soloway and Walters, 'a true moral, ethical, and legal existential crisis' (1977: 161). One dilemma is whether researchers themselves should engage in criminal activity. Taken to its extreme, the logic of the ethnographic study of criminality suggests that they should. Jeff Ferrell, one advocate of researchers crossing the line into certain areas of criminality, argues that 'For the dedicated field researcher who seeks to explore criminal subcultures and criminal dynamics, obeying the law may present as much of a problem as breaking it' (1998: 26). Drawing from Max Weber's notion of *verstehen*, Ferrell argues that to achieve criminological *verstehen* – that is, an appreciation of the lived experience of criminals, the situated meanings, emotions, and the logic of crime – researchers must be prepared to participate in the immediacy of crime, to share the lived experience themselves. If they are prepared to do so, however, they will need to make some ethical decisions about how far they are prepared to go, what criminal acts they are prepared to participate in, and what criminal acts are inappropriate for study. They will also need to evaluate what responsibilities they might have to victims, to criminals, to those involved in crime control, to themselves and to their profession.

The dilemmas faced by field researchers when studying criminality have been debated for many years. The question of participation in criminal activity is perhaps one of the most dramatic dilemmas, but is not the only one. One notable contributor to the debate, Ned Polsky, was scathing in his critique of what he called 'jailhouse' sociology, arguing that 'Sociology isn't worth much if it is not ultimately about real live people in their ordinary life-situations' (1967: 133). Polsky argued:

> If one is effectively to study adult criminals in their natural settings, he must make the moral decision that in some ways he will break the law himself. He need not be a 'participant' observer and commit the criminal acts under study, yet he has to witness such acts or be taken into confidence about them and not blow the whistle. That is, the investigator has to decide that when necessary he will 'obstruct justice' or have 'guilty knowledge' or be an 'accessory' before and after the fact, in the full legal sense of those terms. He will not be enabled to discern some vital aspects of criminal lifestyles and subcultures unless he (1) makes such a moral decision, (2) makes the criminals believe him, and (3) convinces them of his ability to act in accord with his decision.
>
> (1967: 133–4)

Numerous field researchers of criminality have either witnessed, or been told about, criminal activity. Some have even inadvertently become involved in criminal acts. Soloway and Walters (1977), for instance, relate a situation in which the researcher was unwittingly involved in an armed robbery, as it occurred while he was waiting for the perpetrators to return to their car in which he was being given a ride, which subsequently became the getaway car. James Inciardi, in one of a number of fieldwork adventures, accidentally participated in a convenience store hold-up (1977).

Codes of professional ethics such as the one established by the British Sociological Association advise researchers that 'Research data given in confidence do not enjoy legal privilege, that is they may be liable to subpoena by a court, and research parti-cipants should be informed about this.' This has in fact occurred (Brajuha and Hallowell, 1986; Leo, 1995), and in one noted case, doctoral student Rik Scarce was jailed for 159 days for refusing to disclose information about the alleged criminal activity of his research subjects (Scarce, 1994, 1995). Scarce argued that he was abid-ing by the code of ethics of his professional association – the American Sociological Association – which at the time stated that 'Confidential information provided by research participants must be treated as such by sociologists, even when this information enjoys no legal privilege and legal force is applied' (Scarce, 1995: 88).

Criminal transgressions arguably on occasion have a sensual attraction and excitement for researchers as they do for the offenders. Lewis Yablonsky famously argued:

> Many criminologists have an intense (and perhaps vicarious) personal interest in the criminal exploits of their subjects. Many are intrigued voyeurs of the

criminal world. . . . In my judgement, the 'applied sociologist' working in the criminal community must proceed with caution. He should avoid: (1) being considered a 'foolish buff,' a crime fan, or a voyeur intrigued by 'cute' crime patterns; (2) becoming a tool in any illegal activity; and (3) reinforcing the criminal motivations of his clients by his neutrality about their behaviour.

(1965: 71, 72)

In short, Yablonsky believed that the interest of researchers in criminals served to glamorise and reinforce criminal activity.

Despite its potential attractions, researching crime and deviance does have its costs, for as Jeff Ferrell and Mark Hamm argue:

[I]f criminological and sociological field researchers are the beneficiaries of their field research, if they find there perhaps some measure of professional success and personal, thrill-seeking satisfaction, they are equally victims of this enterprise. In trouble with legal authorities and academic gatekeepers alike, vulnerable to charges of immodest behavior and outright immorality, forced into bad moments of personal and professional doubt, field researchers all too regularly confront the limits of methodology and identity in the course of their work.

(1998: 7–8)

TAKING SIDES IN CRIMINOLOGICAL RESEARCH

Many sociologists, including those working in the field of criminology, have liberal leanings: they are particularly concerned about inequality and injustice. Many aim for their research to be more than an academic exercise; they want it to contribute to social change. Debate about the sympathies of sociologists who study crime and deviance was fuelled by the perspectives of scholars working in the Chicago School of Sociology directly after the Second World War – what has been labelled by some as the 'Second Chicago School'. The school was characterised by a divergent range of perspectives, but one dominant perspective characterising the work of the eminent sociologists Howard Becker, Erving Goffman, William Westley, Joseph Gusfield and Harold Finestone was to take the perspective of the 'underdog' (Galliher, 1995), and indeed it was labelled 'underdog sociology' (Gouldner, 1973).

Howard Becker's presidential address in 1966 to the Society for the Study of Social Problems, published in his widely cited and famous essay 'Whose Side Are We On?' (1967), is emblematic of the approach. Although it was published nearly four decades ago, it is still debated in the scholarly literature, and as Martin Hammersley has recently argued, 'it continues to have relevance for us today, not least in posing fundamental questions that still need answering' (2001: 107).

A radical interpretation of Becker's essay is that he is exhorting a partisan sociology in the study of deviance: for sociologists to take the sides against authority and in favour of the less powerful. Indeed, the title of Becker's essay appears to assume that researchers have no choice but to take sides, and this is evident in the opening paragraphs. In Becker's words,

> [O]ne would have to assume, as some apparently do, that it is indeed possible to do research uncontaminated by personal and political sympathies. I propose to argue that it is not possible and, therefore, that the question is not whether we should take sides, since we inevitably will, but rather whose side are we on.
>
> (1967: 239)

Martin Hammersley suggests that the 'radical reading of Becker's article probably accounts for much of its continuing popularity: it is consonant with the growing influence in many areas of the social sciences of both political and epistemological radicalism' (2001: 92).

However, a partisan sociology was not Becker's apparent intent. His argument must be read in the context of the development of labelling theory of deviance, as he argues that the perspective of those in authority comes to dominate the definition of what is deviance and to frame the understanding of it:

> Credibility and the right to be heard are differentially distributed across the hierarchy – across the ranks of the system. . . . In any system of ranked groups, participants take it as given that members of the highest group have the right to define things the way they are.
>
> (1967: 241)

He further argues that

> In the case of deviance, the hierarchical relationship is a moral one. The super-ordinate parties in the relationship are those who represent the forces of approved and official morality; the subordinate parties are those who, it is alleged, have violated that morality.
>
> (1967: 240)

Becker's argument is an epistemological one: to achieve a more thorough understanding of deviance, and social problems more broadly, more than one perspective must be taken into account. But it is impossible for any one single researcher at any one point in time to achieve a balanced view – from the perspective of all sides concerned – about a social problem, so inevitably a side has to be chosen. In the context of the prevailing hierarchy of credibility, therefore, to achieve a more complete understanding of what has been labelled a social problem, it is essential that the researcher takes the perspective of the oppressed, rather than the oppressor.

Becker's argument is inevitably radical. When a researcher tells the story from the perspective of the underdog and challenges the conventional, established, official view of the problem, and perhaps reveals the shortcomings, limitations and failures of responsible officials in the police, courts and prisons, for instance, that story is inherently subversive in effect as it challenges the dominant power structure. Consequently, when researchers study a social problem from the perspective of the relatively powerless, they may be inclined to accuse themselves, and be accused by others, of bias. The charge, according to Becker, will be that

In the course of our work and for who knows what private reasons, we fall into deep sympathy with the people we are studying, so that while the rest of the society views them as unfit in one or another respect for the deference ordinarily accorded a fellow citizen, we believe that they are at least as good as anyone else, more sinned against than sinning. Because of this we do not give a balanced picture. We focus too much on questions whose answers show that the supposed deviant is morally in the right and the ordinary citizen morally in the wrong. We neglect to ask those questions whose answers would show that the deviant, after all, has done something pretty rotten and, indeed, pretty much deserved what he gets.

(1967: 240)

Becker further argues that

We provoke the suspicion that we are biased in favor for the subordinate parties . . . when we tell the story from their point of view. We may, for instance, investigate their complaints, even though they are subordinates, about the way things are run just as though one ought to give their complaints as much credence as the statements of responsible officials. We provoke the charge when we assume, for the purposes of our research, that subordinates have as much right to be heard as superordinates, that they are as likely to be telling the truth as they see it as superordinates, that what they say about the institution has a right to be investigated and have its truth or falsity established, even though responsible officials assure us that it is unnecessary because the charges are false.

(1967: 241)

Even though researchers might be accused of bias, this does not necessarily mean that they will actually be biased or partisan in their approach. Indeed, Becker adheres to a commitment to value neutrality, arguing that the researcher must aim for unbiased research. He certainly does not advocate researchers choosing which side they are on and then doing research in such a way as to serve it. As Becker argued, 'whatever side we are on, we must use our techniques impartially enough that a belief to which we are especially sympathetic could be proved untrue'.

Becker's call to take the side of the underdog in the study of deviance has been accused of 'romanticism'. In a famous critique, Alvin Gouldner, in his essay 'The Sociologist as Partisan', argues that

the pull to the underdog's exotic difference takes the form of 'essays on quaintness'. The danger is, then, that such an identification with the underdog becomes the urban sociologist's equivalent of the anthropologist's (one-time) romantic appreciation of the noble savage.

(1973: 37)

For Gouldner, Becker's approach 'expresses the satisfaction of the Great White Hunter who has barely risked the perils of the urban jungle to bring back an exotic specimen. It expresses the romanticism of the zoo curator who preeningly displays his rare specimens' (1973: 38). Gouldner argues that in fact, the agenda of 'radical sociologists' should be to study the 'overdog', the 'power elites' who shape the legal system and law enforcement and penal practice, rather than the underdog studied by liberal sociologists – among whom he includes Becker – and how they are victimized by 'bureaucratic caretakers' such as police officers and social workers.

Both approaches shaped future directions of criminological research and theorising. The radical approach underpins 'conflict criminology' (discussed in Chapter 5 of this book), which addresses how legal systems, law enforcement policy and penal practices are shaped to the advantage of political and economic elites. The influence of both the liberal and radical approaches can be seen in the research agenda of 'left-idealism' (a movement in criminology also discussed in Chapter 5), which focused on the role of the state and major institutions such as the criminal justice system and the media in shaping the meaning of crime and crime control.

SUMMARY

1   It seems fairly safe to suggest that there is no distinctive methodology or set of methods used in criminological research. However, while there are some concerns that criminological researchers share with researchers in other subjects, they arguably have a greater significance in the study of crime, deviance and crime control.
2   Researchers and students alike need to cast a particularly critical eye when they use crime statistics.
3   When one is engaged in criminological research, the moral, legal and ethical implications require very careful consideration
4   When researching crime, students and researchers alike need to reflect about how their particular sympathies – in whatever direction they may lie – potentially affect their research.

CRITICAL THINKING QUESTIONS

1   What questions might be asked when thinking critically about crime statistics?
2   To understand crime, is it really necessary for researchers to become criminals?
3   When criminological researchers 'take sides', are they biased in the way they approach their research?

FURTHER STUDY

Cromwell, P. F. (ed.) (2003) *In Their Own Words: Criminals on Crime*, (Third Edition), Los Angeles: Roxbury. Fieldwork accounts of crime uniquely from the prospects of offenders.

Ferrell, J. and Hamm, M. (eds) (1998) *Ethnography at the Edge: Crime, Deviance, and Field Research*, Boston: Northeastern University Press. A valuable collection of essays that provides methodological, political and theoretical reflections of fieldwork on crime and deviance.

King, R. D. and Wincup, E. (eds) (2000) *Doing Research on Crime and Justice*, Oxford: Oxford University Press. A comprehensive collection of essays on the practicalities and problems of doing criminological research.

MORE INFORMATION

Statistics Canada
http://www.statcan.ca/start.html
Produces national statistics on the population, resources, economy, society and culture of Canada.

Federal Bureau of Investigation
http://www.fbi.gov/homepage.htm
The FBI is the principal investigative arm of the United States Department of Justice.

FBI: Hate Crime Data Collection Guidelines
http://www.fbi.gov/ucr/hatecrime.pdf
FBI: National Incident-Based Reporting System on Hate Crimes

Australian Bureau of Statistics
http://www.abs.gov.au/
The Australian Bureau of Statistics is Australia's official statistical organisation.

The Home Office
http://www.homeoffice.gov.uk/
The Home Office is the government department responsible for internal affairs in England and Wales.

The Scottish Executive
http://www.scotland.gov.uk
The Scottish Executive is the devolved government for Scotland. It is responsible for most of the issues of day-to-day concern to the people of Scotland, including health, education, justice, rural affairs, and transport.

UK Data Archive at the University of Essex:
http://www.data-archive.ac.uk/
The UKDA provides resource discovery and support for secondary use of quantitative and qualitative data in research.

The Question Bank
http://qb.soc.surrey.ac.uk/
Questions from the British Crime Survey can be read online at the Question Bank, University of Surrey.

PART 2 THINKING ABOUT CRIME

In this section, we outline a wider range of different ways of thinking about crime – from some of the earliest 'scientific traditions' to more recent developments that link crime to conditions of late modern society. Many key terms and ideas are introduced along the way.

CHAPTER 3

KEY ISSUES

▌ What traditions emerged from the Enlightenment?

▌ What is the classical inheritance?

▌ What is the positivist inheritance?

▌ What are their key differences?

The Enlightenment and Early Traditions

INTRODUCTION

The received history of criminology as a discipline of study often starts with influential figures such as 'Beccaria' and 'Lombroso', and their links with landmark theoretical perspectives such as classicism in the eighteenth century and positivism in the nineteenth. This indeed will be our task in this chapter: to provide a basic introduction and fairly standard account of criminology's history which begins with the writings of criminal law reformers in the eighteenth century, particularly in the work of Cesare Beccaria, Jeremy Bentham and John Howard. These writers are said to draw upon Enlightenment ideals and characterise the offender as a rational, free-willed actor who engages in crime in a calculated way and is responsive to the deterrent penalties that these reformers advocated. This classical school of criminology is then challenged in the late nineteenth century by writers of the positivist school, which typically includes the writings of Cesare Lombroso, Enrico Ferri and Francis Galton, who adopted a more empirical, scientific approach to the subject and investigated the criminal using the techniques of psychiatry, anthropology and other new human sciences. The positivist school claimed to have discovered the existence of 'criminal types' whose behaviour was determined rather than chosen, and for whom treatment rather than punishment was appropriate. Subsequent work has refuted many of the claims of Lombroso, but the project of a 'scientific criminology' continues to this day.

A caution

One of the immediate problems with this characterisation is that it implies that people only began to think about crime in a sensible fashion from the middle of the eighteenth century. This is seriously misleading, not least since breaking social rules is an intrinsic element of social organisation. In other words, crime is an inevitable feature of society, a point that Durkheim made in the late nineteenth century (see Chapter 4). Discourses on crime and criminals are as old as human civilisation. For instance, there are various propositions about crime put forward in the writings of ancient and medieval philosophers, and the theology of the Church of Rome, the theology of the Protestant reform tradition and early modern legal thought all contain understandings of criminality. In fact, what we need to recognise is that there are a variety of ways of 'thinking about crime', and that criminology is only one version among others.

It should also be emphasised that this is not to say that criminology is our modern response to a timeless and unchanging set of questions, not least because in earlier times the mental structures and cultural sensibilities that governed thinking about crime in earlier periods were very different from our own. For instance, if we take Christianity, it is clear that this system of thought did not separate out the law-breaker as different or abnormal, but rather understood his or her behaviour as a manifestation of universal human depravity and the sinful state of all humankind. This is clearly a very different way of thinking about crime from that espoused by criminology.

Nevertheless, traditional accounts of crime, whether these be Christian or otherwise, are not entirely remote from present thinking about the subject. For instance, if we look at the diverse literature of the early modern period, which includes criminal biographies and broadsheets, accounts of the Renaissance underworld, Tudor rogue pamphlets, Elizabethan dramas and Jacobean city comedies, we can see rudimentary versions of our present understandings of how one becomes deviant. Perhaps the most famous example is Daniel Defoe's novel *Moll Flanders*, which was published in 1722. On one level, it is a Puritan's tale of sin and repentance, but it is nevertheless rich in the features with which modern criminological theories are cast. For instance, the story tells us how the offender fell in with bad company, was sorely tried by temptation, became too fond of drink, lost her reputation and was driven to crime by lust – but if we use a more neutral language to tell the tale, then we are not that far removed from contemporary criminology.

So when we think of the seventeenth- and eighteenth-century understandings of crime, what becomes clear is that crime was regarded as omnipresent temptation to which all humankind was vulnerable, but when it became a question of why some succumbed and others resisted, the explanations trailed off into the unknowable, resorting to fate, or the will of God.

There are two points that need to be emphasised in these opening remarks. The first is that we need to be cautious of histories of criminology that begin with classicism and suggest that no one had seriously thought about crime before, even though we are going to do just that! The second is that other ways of thinking about crime did not disappear with the coming of the modern, scientific age. In fact, it is more accurate to say that criminology operates in a culture that combines many (traditional and scientific) modes of thought and action. In fact, these intuitive and instinctive understandings are often still more persuasive than criminological research.

ENLIGHTENMENT THINKING ABOUT CRIME

It may be useful to start our understanding of recent ways of thinking about crime through a simple contrast between a public execution, staged as a spectacle, in the mid-eighteenth century and a prison timetable in the early nineteenth. The example is given in the opening pages of Michel Foucault's *Discipline and Punish: The Birth of the Prison* (1977) – a classic study to which we return later.

In a long paragraph, he describes an execution in 1757:

> on a scaffold that will be erected [at the Place de Grève], the flesh will be torn from his breasts, arms, thighs and calves with red hot pincer, his right hand . . . burnt with sulphur, and, on those places where the flesh will be torn away, poured molten lead, boiling oil, burning resin, wax and sulphur melted together and then his body drawn and quartered by four horses and his limbs and body consumed by fire, reduced to ashes and thrown to the winds.
>
> (Foucault, 1977: 3)

This passage is followed by another long description, this time of a timetable. It is some eighty years on:

> Art. 17. The prisoners' day will begin at six in the morning in winter and at five in the summer . . . they will work for nine hours a day. . . .
> Art. 18. Rising. At the first drum-roll, the prisoners must rise and dress in silence . . . at the second drum-roll, they must be dressed and make their beds. At the third, they must line up and proceed to the chapel for morning prayer . . .
> Art. 19. The prayers are conducted by the chaplain and followed by a moral or religious reading. This exercise must not last more than half an hour . . .
>
> (Foucault, 1977: 6)

The differences in systems of control are clearly illustrated. In the striking opening pages, Foucault compares the earlier forms of brutal and chaotic punishment on *the body* with the more recent forms of *surveillance and imprisonment*, which are intensely rule governed. What we are seeing here is a shift from an understanding of crime based on non-rational thinking to one based upon the principles of Enlightenment thinking

The French *philosophes* were the cornerstone of such thinking, highlighting the importance of rationality. In matters of crime, they marked a distinctive move away from systems that were capricious and 'barbaric' to systems that were to become more and more rational, predictable and disciplining (as we see in many chapters throughout this book). They were a 'solid, respectable clan of revolutionaries' (Gay,

1973: 9), and included Montesquieu, Rousseau and Voltaire. Such thinking sign-posted the arrival of the 'modern world', and the sociologist Peter Hamilton (1996) has suggested ten hall marks of the Enlightenment mind:

- Reason became a key way of organising knowledge.
- Empiricism – facts that can be apprehended through the senses.
- Science – linked especially to experimental scientific revolution.
- Universalism – especially the search for general laws.
- Progress – the idea that 'the human condition' can be improved.
- Individualism – the starting point for all knowledge.
- Toleration – the view that beliefs of other nations and groups are not inherently inferior to European Christianity.
- Freedom.
- The idea of the uniformity of human nature.
- Secularism – often opposed to the Church.

THE CLASSICAL TRADITION IN CRIMINOLOGY

Enlightenment thinking was the cornerstone of the classical approach to crime. It aimed to introduce a much more rational and fair system for organising punishments and control. It had much less of a focus on the criminal *per se* and it had little concern with establishing the causes of crime. In general, its concern was to establish a more just social order.

Cesare Beccaria – 'the Rousseau of the Italians' (Beirne, 1993: 14) – is generally seen, at least symbolically, as the founder of this movement. He was born in Milan, Italy, on 15 March 1738. A humanist, he wanted more than anything to see the reform of the irrationality and unfairness of the judicial system that had existed for centuries (including the abolition of torture and capital punishment). His work draws freely from:

- Social contract theory – the theory of how imaginary individuals come together to make a society work (exemplified in the work of Jean-Jacques Rousseau).
- The view that human beings have 'free wills' – human actions are not simply determined by inside or outside 'forces' but can be seen as matters of free decisions.
- The idea of punishment as deterrent – rational beings will choose not to commit crimes if the punishment fits the crime.
- Utilitarianism – laws useful to the greatest number should be observed. Jeremy Bentham argued that their violation would open the door to anarchy.
- Secularism – Beccaria wanted to build a humanist theory that avoided ideas of God's law, revelation or natural justice and that focused on the living, sentient human being, subject to pains and pleasures. He wanted law to be made by human beings, and rational.

At the heart of classic thought were ideas on the nature of punishment (see the more recent development of these ideas in Chapter 13). Punishments could deter only if they were 'proportional' to the crime. Proportionality means (1) that the severity of punishments corresponds to the severity of the harm done by the crime, so that more serious crimes receive more serious punishments; and (2) that the type of punishment resembles the crime, so that others in society can best associate the punishment with the crime. Punishment must be essentially public, prompt, necessary, the least possible in the given circumstances, proportionate to the crimes, and dictated by the laws.

Such ideas start to be developed in Beccaria's *Dei delitti e delle pene* (An Essay on Crimes and Punishments) of July 1764. This is one of the classics of Enlightenment thinking and early modern penology. Box 3.1 shows the range of themes he raised in this short but influential book.

BOX 3.1 CESARE BECCARIA'S *ESSAY ON CRIMES AND PUNISHMENTS*

Plate 3.1 Cesare Beccaria (1738–94), Italian legal theorist and political economist.
Source: Mary Evans Picture Library.

This key text of classical thinking is a very short book devoting brief chapters to such topics as:

- Of the origins of punishments
- Of the right to punish
- Of the proportion between crimes and punishments
- Of estimating the degree of crimes
- Of the divisions of crime
- Of crimes which disturb the public tranquillity
- Of torture
- Of pecuniary punishments
- Of the advantage of immediate punishments
- Of the punishment of nobles
- Of robbery
- Of banishment
- Of the punishment of death
- Of suicide
- Of smuggling
- Of bankrupts
- Of the sciences
- Of education

continued

Here are some of his views for discussion:

> By justice I understand nothing more than that bond which is necessary to keep the interests of individuals united; without which, men would return to their original state of barbarity. All punishments, which exceed the necessity of preserving this bond, are in their nature unjust.
>
> (chapter 2)

> A scale of crimes may be formed of which the first degree should consist of those which immediately tend to the dissolution of society and the last of the smallest possible injustice done to a private member of that society.
>
> (chapter 6)

> A punishment may not be an act of violence, of one, or of many against a private member of society; it should be public; immediate and necessary; the least possible in the case given; proportioned to the crime; and determined by the laws.
>
> (chapter 47)

Classical ideas may also be found in the work of the English utilitarian philosopher and penal reformer Jeremy Bentham (1748–1832). Building a moral calculus and arguing for the greatest happiness of the greatest number, he felt that punishments should be calculated to inflict pain in direct proportion to the damage done to the public interest. One of his ideas was the concept of prison design. He argued for a prison with a tower at the centre and a periphery building composed of cells from which every inmate could be observed (Figure 3.1). The cells would all have windows that would enable surveillance by prison guards. Whereas the old dungeons hurled an indiscriminate group of people together in large, dark and unmonitored cells, Bentham's principles were ones of visibility and inspection. Although Bentham's prison was never built, his views did encourage an increasingly rational system of penality in which prisons took on a new character (Bozovic, 1995).

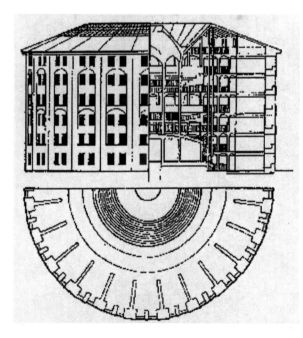

Figure 3.1 The Panopticon of Jeremy Bentham.

Source: After Barton and Barton (1993: 139).

Back to justice: some recent classical developments

It is important to realise that just as ideas never appear 'out of the blue' but emerge from historical change, so too do ideas rarely simply 'vanish'. They become modified, often being worked into new languages, but they are still around. This is very much true of classicism, which is a key to the justice system today. As we see in more detail in Chapter 13, in the latter years of the twentieth century there was a considerable revival of interest in classical thought.

In the early 1970s, the debate over what constitutes good sentencing policy was reopened. What is a just sentence? The 'Back to Justice' model suggested by Von Hirsch and his colleagues claimed that 'The severity of punishment should be commensurate with the seriousness of the wrong' (Von Hirsch, 1976 :66). They argued that:

1   The degree of likelihood that the offender might return to crime should be irrelevant to the choice of sentence. He should be sentenced on what he has done.
2   Indeterminate sentences should be abolished. Particular crimes merit particular punishments, and offenders should know what they will get.
3   Sentencing discretion should be sharply reduced. A system of standardised penalties should be introduced.
4   Imprisonment should be limited to serious offences – usually crimes leading to serious harm.
5   Milder penalties should not claim to rehabilitate, but simply be less severe punishments (Von Hirsch, 1976).

The problems with the classical model

- The classical model often believes in an overly rational vision of human nature, arguing that people behave in a purely self-interested and 'free' fashion. If they can see they will be punished, they will be deterred; if they think they can get away with crime, they will. It is a model that haunts social science (especially economics), and it is too simple.
- Unlike positivism, it views committing crime as making a free choice; but we may be left wondering just how really free crime is.
- It assumes that societies work in fair and just ways, whereas often it is not possible to have justice and fairness in societies that are themselves organised in ways that are neither just or fair. You cannot easily have 'justice in an unjust society'.

THE POSITIVIST MOVEMENT

The criminal type and Lombroso

Writing in the nineteenth century, Lombroso is usually seen as the founder of modern criminology and certainly achieved much fame or notoriety in the closing years of the twentieth century. (He is mentioned, for example, in the Sherlock Holmes and Dracula novels popular at the time.) For Lombroso, many criminals (not all) were atavistic throwbacks to an earlier form of species on the evolutionary scale. These stigmata could be found in all kinds of anomalies of the body. Many criminals, he said, may be found to have a distinctive physique: low foreheads, prominent jaws and cheekbones, protruding ears, excessive hairiness and unusually long arms that, taken together, cause them to resemble the apelike ancestors of human beings. He is often seen as inventing the idea of the criminal body (although he was not actually the first – ideas germinate less sharply than this), which he introduced in 1876 in his book *L'uomo delinquente* (The Criminal Man), which went through five editions. (No English translation has been published, but see Lombroso-Ferrero, 1911.) In this study, he observed the physical characteristics of Italian prisoners and compared them to Italian soldiers – contrasting such items as their heads, body, arms and skin. One was the brigand Vilella, whom he studied through a post-mortem examination. In a famous passage, he remarked:

> This was not merely an idea, but a revelation. At the sight of that skull, I seemed to see all of a sudden, lighted up as a vast plain under a flaming sky, the problem of the nature of the criminal – an atavistic being who reproduces in his person the ferocious instincts of primitive humanity and the inferior animals. Thus were explained anatomically the enormous jaws, high cheek-bones, prominent super-ciliary arches, solitary lines in the palms, extreme size of orbits, handle-shaped or sessile ears found in criminals, savages and apes, insensibility to pain, extremely acute sight, tattooing, excessive idleness, love of orgies, and the irresistible craving for evil for its own sake, the desire not only to extinguish life in the victim, but to mutilate the corpse, tear its flesh, and drink its blood.
>
> (quoted in Wolfgang, 1960: 248)

But Lombroso's work was flawed. Had he looked beyond prison walls, he would have realised that the physical features he attributed exclusively to prisoners were actually found throughout the entire population. We now know that no physical attributes, of the kind described by Lombroso, simply distinguish criminals from non-criminals (Goring, 1913/1972). Yet although his work had many failings, he is usually credited with turning interest away from simply the criminal law to an understanding of the criminal type.

There were several others who were engaged with Lombroso in the search for the causes of crime, such as Raffaele Garofalo (1852–1934) and Enrico Ferri (1856–1928). Together they came to be identified as the Italian School. Ferri provided a view of the causes of crime under three main heads: the anthropological, telluric (physical) and social. He was against the view that any one factor could cause crime, and saw instead the need to take factors in combination. Lombroso's great contribution was to highlight the biological (or anthropological as it was often called in those days) – even though he recognised other factors. But for Ferri,

> [E]very crime from the smallest to the most atrocious, is the result of the interaction of these three causes, the anthropological condition of the criminal,

the telluric [literally, 'pertaining to the earth'] environment in which he is living, and the social environment in which he is born, living and operating.

(quoted in Muncie *et al.*, 2003: 36)

The anthropological component highlighted heredity and constitution; the physical factors highlighted issues such as climate and season; and the social element stressed population, religion, education and the like. Ferri classified criminals under five basic types: criminal lunatics, the born incorrigibles, habitual criminals, occasional criminals and emotional criminals.

Researchers on crime began to examine its link with such factors as 'mental subnormality', IQ, twins, criminal families and body build. Along the way, this meant introducing a range of 'scientific tools of measurement' – from IQ tests to criminal photography.

Statistical regularity and positivism

Another early 'scientist of crime' was Quetelet (1796–1874), who was a leading statistician of the nineteenth century. Developing a theory of social mechanics, he believed that statistical research could outline the average features of a population, and that it would hence be possible to discover the underlying regularities for both normal and abnormal behaviour. In 1835 he published *Treatise on Man, and the Development of His Faculties*, in which he depicted 'average man', against which abnormal man could be measured. (He found the average man through bell-shaped curves.) Crime, then, could be studied systematically.

The publication of early criminal statistics in France (in the 1820s) meant that regularities could be spotted in such features as sex, age, climate and economic conditions. Likewise, the French sociologist Émile Durkheim (1858–1917) could study suicide rates (at that time suicide was a crime in most countries) to show that suicides also had a very definite pattern. By examining suicide records in and around his native France, he could show that some categories of people were more likely than others to choose to take their own lives. He found, for instance, that men, Protestants, wealthy people and the unmarried each had significantly higher suicide rates than women, Roman Catholics and Jews, the poor, and married people. Durkheim deduced that these differences corresponded to people's degree of *social integration*. Low suicide rates characterised categories of people with strong social ties; high suicide rates were found among those who were more socially isolated and individualistic. In the male-dominated societies, men certainly had more autonomy than women; individualistic Protestants were more prone to suicide than Catholics and Jews, whose rituals foster stronger social ties; the wealthy clearly have much more freedom of action than the poor but, once again, at the cost of a higher suicide rate. Finally, single people, with weaker social ties than married people, are also at greater risk of suicide.

BOX 3.2 CESARE LOMBROSO (1836–1909) AND HIS PHOTOS OF CRIMINAL TYPES

The man

Born on 6 November 1835 in Verona, perhaps more than anyone else Cesare Lombroso is 'the founder of modern criminology'. An Italian physician who worked in prisons, he was director of a mental asylum in Pesaro, Italy, and professor of psychiatry and criminal anthropology at the University of Turin. Writing at a time where there was a widespread interest in social Darwinism and eugenics, he drew his ideas in part from phrenology, and they were also linked to craniology and physiognomy – which look at the structures of the brain and the mind. He was an early criminal anthropologist, founder of the positivist school of penal jurisprudence. Lombroso was a socialist, and much of his work advocated more humane treatment of criminals. He was an early advocate of the indeterminate sentence, as well as the reduction of the death penalty.

Plate 3.2 Cesare Lombroso (1836–1909), Italian physician and criminologist. Lombroso is considered the founder of modern criminology, though many dispute this.

Source: Elliot and Fry in *Nos Maîtres*, Mary Evans Picture Library.

Reading Lombroso: some extracts from his writing capture his concerns

Spot the criminal through differences

> . . . deviation in head size and shape from the type common to the race and religion from which the criminal came; asymmetry of the face; excessive dimensions of the jaw and cheek bones; eye defects and peculiarities; ears of unusual size, or occasionally very small, or standing out from the head as do those of the chimpanzee; nose twisted, upturned, or flattened in thieves, or swollen nostrils; lips fleshy, swollen, and protruding; pouches in the cheek like those of some animals; peculiarities of the palate, such as a large central ridge, a series of cavities and protuberances such as are found in some reptiles, and a cleft palate; abnormal dentition; chin receding, or excessively long or short and flat, as in apes; abundance, variety, and precocity of wrinkles, anomalies of the hair, marked by characteristics of the hair of the opposite sex; defects of the thorax, such as too many or too few ribs, or super-numerary nipples; inversion of sex characteristics in the pelvic organs; excessive length of arms; supernumerary fingers and toes; imbalance of the hemispheres of the brain (asymmetry of cranium)
>
> (Wolfgang, 1960: 250)

Types of criminal by physical characteristics

... as a rule, the *thieves* have mobile hands and face; small, mobile, restless, frequently oblique eyes; thick and closely set eyebrows; flat or twisted nose; thin beard; hair frequently thin; almost receding brow. Both they and those committing *rape* frequently have ears *ad ansa*. The latter often have brilliant eyes, delicate faces, tumid lips and eyelids; as a rule they are of delicate structure and sometimes hunchbacked. . . . The *habitual homicides* have cold, glassy eyes, immobile and sometimes sanguine and inflamed; the nose, always large, is frequently aquiline or, rather, hooked; the jaws are strong, the cheekbones large, the hair curly, dark and abundant; the beard is frequently thin, the canine teeth well developed and the lips delicate; frequent nystagmus and unilateral facial contractions, with a baring of the teeth and a contraction of the jaws. . . . In general *all criminals* have ears *ad ansa*, abundant hair, thin beard, prominent fronat sinuses, protruding chin, large cheekbones, etc.

(Wolfgang, 1960: 251)

Plate 3.3 Criminal types – an example from Lombroso's study that claimed to relate physiognomy to criminal nature. This plate shows young and female murderers. Lombroso's research involved the measurement and frequently the photographing of body and facial types.

Source: Reproduced in Lombroso, '*L'Homme criminel*', plate lxiv, Mary Evans Picture Library.

The positivist inheritance

Positivism was one of the earliest strands of criminological thinking and it is still very much alive today. A major account of positivistic criminology has been provided by the sociologist David Matza (1964). In a brilliant opening chapter of his book *Delinquency and Drift*, he summarised it as having three major characteristics:

1 The criminal is a specific type of person. Thus, criminology started to draw up long classification systems of different kinds of offenders. Lombroso, for example, identified not just the born criminal, but also the emotional criminal, the morally insane criminal and the masked epileptic criminal.

2 The criminal differs from others. The focus is upon finding the different characteristics – which may range from body parts (e.g. the size and weight of

skulls), body types (as in Sheldon's work) and on to personality types (as with the work of Walter Reckless). Long lists of ways in which offenders differ from non-offenders can be drawn up. This process was advanced greatly by new technologies such as photography (which could record bodily and facial features) in the nineteenth century and fingerprint testing in the twentieth century. Most recently, chromosome typing (the XYY chromosome is said to be linked to violent offences) and DNA testing have become the focus of attention. The police now make regular use of 'criminal profiling'.

3   The criminal is 'driven' into crime through factors outside his or her control. Positivism seeks out explanations for criminal conduct as in some way out of the control of the criminal who perpetrates criminal acts. Thus, crime is caused by 'feeble-mindedness', 'atavistic regression', 'unsuccessful socialisation' or 'XYY chromosomes'. Crime, says Matza, is not a free choice but is determined. Positivism is a deterministic theory.

These features can still be found in a great deal of criminological research. One major strand of such work, linked to the celebrated criminologists Sheldon and Eleanor Glueck, has been identified as the multi-factor approach. This entails sampling a large number of delinquents or criminals to see whether they present characteristics in common that are found less frequently in a general population. Often these are prospective longitudinal surveys.

The criminal career approach brings together a number of these key factors and shows how they develop over time. It looks at such issues as why people start offending (onset), why they continue (persistence), whether their behaviour becomes more serious or not (escalation) and why people stop (desistance). The major risk factors ('factors that increase the risk of occurrence of events such as the onset, frequency, persistence, duration of offending'; Farrington, 1997) include impulsivity (now often called HIA – hyperactivity impulsivity attention deficit), low intelligence, poor parental supervision, broken homes, convicted parents, socioeconomic deprivation, poor schooling, and 'situational factors' (Farrington, 1997). These factors are highly correlated with crime.

BOX 3.3 SUMMARY OF SOME BIOLOGICALLY BASED THEORIES OF CRIME

William Sheldon's Theory of Somatotypes (based on early work of Kretschmer) links crime to body types:

- endomorph – chubby, round, not criminal;
- ectomorph – skinny, frail, not criminal.
- mesomorph – heavy, muscular, criminal.

Kallikak and Juke families. The descendants of Martin Kallikak's illegitimate son exhibited a remarkably high degree of criminality across several generations, and the descendants of Ada Juke included seven murderers, sixty thieves, fifty prostitutes, etc. These two cases contributed to early view that crime and deviance were inheritable.

Twin studies compare criminality of identical twins with criminality of fraternal twins. Generally, twin studies have shown higher rate of similar criminality (concordance) (60–70 per cent) for identical twins than for fraternal twins (15–30 per cent), although some say that these percentages are exaggerated. This provides some support for the idea that genetics may play a role in criminal behaviour. Perhaps the most famous case of twin studies is to be found in the work of Karl Christiansen, who examined 3,586 sets of twins born between 1881 and 1910. In 35 per cent of the cases, both identical twins would have criminal convictions. In only 12 per cent of fraternal twins would both have criminal convictions, which provides some support for a genetic link.

XYY chromosome research. This became a particular controversy in the 1960s. 'Normal' males have an XY sex-chromosome configuration, but some males (1 in 1,000) have an extra Y chromosome, giving them an XYY configuration. Research in the 1960s found a slight suggestion of an association between XYY configuration and criminality. This led to the idea of the 'super-male criminal', full of aggression. More recent studies have refuted the idea that having the XYY configuration 'causes' men to commit crimes.

Biochemical factors. Serotonin deficiency may be related to impulsiveness, crime and violence An imbalance involving dopamine, noradrenaline and serotonin may be conducive to deviant/criminal behaviour.

Brain dysfunction. There is some evidence that neurological defects are more common among excessively violent people than among the general population. EEG readings on some adult criminals are similar to those of normal people at younger ages (brain immaturity)

Also, old concerns like learning disabilities and new problems like attention deficit hyperactivity disorder (ADHD) may be linked to crime.

Potential criticisms

- Crime is probably the result of a combination of factors, including social, psychological, political, economic and geographic ones – rarely, if ever, biology on its own.
- Unrepresentative samples are very common in such research. Generally, such research raises severe methodological problems (how do you separate out biological from social factors?).
- Causation is often muddled with correlation: an association between bodily features and criminal behaviour does not mean that biology caused the behaviour.
- Sometimes there may be a labelling effect: society reacts to certain types, and this may generate response that are criminal.
- In general, the evidence for such research is at best limited.

See Fishbein (2000).

The problems with the positivist model

- In contrast with the classical model, the positivist model often assumes that people are driven into crime by forces largely out of their control. It may hence argue that people are not free and not responsible for their actions. It is too prone to deny the meanings of crime in people's lives. In some ways it is a mirror image of the classical position, and what is required is a way of approaching crime which allows for both choice and determinism.
- It exaggerates the differences between criminal and non-criminals. By focusing upon what makes a criminal different from the population, it tends to suggest an image of the normal and the abnormal, of them and us. In fact, many criminals overlap with the population – are indeed just like you and me; indeed are you and me.
- It has a tendency to neglect the workings of the penal system: the law or its aspects by which crimes come to be invented and/or regulated. Crimes are assumed as givens, as unproblematic categories.

THE TENSIONS BETWEEN POSITIVISM AND CLASSICAL THINKING

Both the classical tradition and positivism come in many different varieties, and although they have their roots in the past, they are both still alive and well in the criminal justice system today. As you read this book, you may like to identify aspects of the reappearance of each. They have been extremely influential and can be seen as master moulds that organise many ways of thinking about crime. Table 3.1 opposite suggests some of the key contrasts to be clear about.

SUMMARY

1 There is no straightforward history of criminology. Although it is a convention in textbooks to suggest the importance of classical theory and positivism as the founding ideas, there are many earlier ways of thinking about crime linked to demonism, religions, witchcraft, and the like.

2 The classical school symbolised by Beccaria is linked to Enlightenment ideas of rationality, free will, choice, progress.

3 The positivist school symbolised by Lombroso and Ferri usually focuses on the criminal as a particular type, stresses determinism, and looks at the characteristics that mark out the criminal from the normal. There can be social differences as well as biological ones.

4 Classical and positivist theories suggest mutually contradictory images of crime and criminal justice. But both are alive and well today, exist in modern versions and continue to influence the workings of penal policy.

Table 3.1 Comparison of classical and positivist schools

ISSUE	CLASSICAL SCHOOL	POSITIVE SCHOOL
Roots	Enlightenment	Modern science
Focus	Criminal administration	Criminal person
Approach	Philosophical – social contract theory, utilitarianism	Scientific, positivism Laws Measurements
View of human nature	Free will Hedonism Morally responsible for own behaviour	Determined by biological, psychological, and social environment Moral responsibility obscured
View of justice system	Social contract; exists to protect society; due process and concern with civil rights; restrictions on system Definite sentence	Scientific treatment system to cure pathologies and rehabilitate offenders; no concern with civil rights Indefinite sentence
Form of law	Statutory law; exact specification of illegal acts and sanctions	Social law; illegal acts defined by analogy; scientific experts determine social harm and proper form of treatment
Purpose of sentencing	Punishment for deterrence; sentences are determinate (fixed length)	Treatment and reform; sentences are indeterminate (variable length until cured)
Criminological experts	Philosophers; social reformers	Scientists; treatment experts

CRITICAL THINKING QUESTIONS

1   What was the Enlightenment? Consider some of the key intellectual contributions it made and then consider the different ways in which people may have thought about crime before the Enlightenment.
2   Examine the idea of a criminal type of person. How far does this idea mirror common sense? What are the most recent accounts of such a criminal?
3   Clarify what you understand by a just deserts model (tip: read Von Hirsch, 1976, chs 27 and 28) and ponder your own penal tariff. What are the limits and difficulties of such an approach?
4   Look at the contradictory tensions found between positivism and classical thought. How do you see them at work in the modern criminal justice system?

FURTHER STUDY

Beccaria, C. *Beccaria: On Crimes and Punishments and Other Writings*, edited by Richard Bellamy (1995), Cambridge: Cambridge University Press. A short selection of Beccaria's original writings.

Beirne, P. (1993) *Inventing Criminology: Essays on the Rise of 'Homo Criminalis'*, Albany: State University of New York Press.

Looks at the intellectual history of criminology from Beccaria to Goring.

Garland, D. (2003) 'Of Crime and Criminals: The Development of Criminology in Britain', in M. Maguire, R. Morgan and R. Reiner (eds) *The Oxford Handbook of Criminology*, 3rd edn, Oxford: Oxford University Press.

An article which critically looks at the growth of criminology (mainly in the UK).

Gould, S. J. (1981) *The Mismeasure of Man*, New York: W.W. Norton. A classic statement of the misuse of biological theories and measurements.

Rafter, N. H. (1997) *Creating Born Criminals*, Chicago: University of Illinois Press.

A social history of biologically founded theories of crime in the United States, the study shows their influence on theories today.

Von Hirsch, A. (1976) *Doing Justice: The Choice of Punishments*, New York: Hill and Wang. A clear and useful account of justifications for punishment, heavily derived from classical thinking.

MORE INFORMATION

For more general guides to theory, see:

Burke, R. H. (2001) *An Introduction to Criminological Theory*, Cullompton, Devon: Willan. A comprehensive yet short introduction to the main criminological theories.

Downes, D. and Rock, P. (1998) *Understanding Deviance: A Guide to the Sociology of Crime and Rule Breaking*, 3rd edn (2003, 4th edn), Oxford: Oxford University Press. For a long while this has been the most sophisticated general treatment of the full range of theories of crime discussed in this and other chapters. Regularly updated, it also provides a bibliography that signposts all the major books in the field.

Muncie, J., McLaughlin, E. and Langan, M. (eds) (2003) *Criminological Perspectives: A Reader*, 2nd edn, London: Sage/Open University. An exceptionally valuable collection of around fifty readings extracted from all the major positions and perspectives on crime ranging from Beccaria and Lombroso to Braithwaite and Smart.

Cullen, F. T. and Agnew, R. (2003) *Criminological Theory: Past to Present (Essential Readings)*, 2nd edn, Los Angeles: Roxbury Park. There are many readers in criminology but this one stands out as an excellent collection of classic statements. Useful for the whole of Part 2 of this book.

Crimetheory.Com
www.crimetheory.com
A Website that provides a brief introduction to a number of theories and theorists.

KEY ISSUES

▌ How did the early sociologists study crime?

▌ What is the functionalist approach to crime?

▌ What role did the Chicago School play in developing criminology?

▌ What are the strengths and weaknesses of each theory?

Early Sociological Thinking about Crime

INTRODUCTION

In this chapter we turn to some of the major ways of thinking about crime introduced by sociologists, largely – but not exclusively – during the twentieth century, and with a key concern about delinquency and youthful gangs and crime. Although much of their work has been criticised and subsequently modified, it does still provide very useful road maps into contemporary thinking about crime. We live on its shoulders.

Six major images capture the basics of these theories, and they are not mutually exclusive – indeed, they benefit from merging with each other, as they each have somewhat different emphases. (And indeed today, criminologists would rarely be happy with just one theory.) These images are as follows:

1   Crime is 'normal' in all societies – it serves certain functions and may even help keep a society orderly. It cannot, therefore, be easily eliminated. Crime may be usefully understood in mapping these functions.

2   Crime is bound up with conflict, often of a class based nature in which crimes of the powerful are much less noticed than the crimes of the weak. Crime may be usefully understood in terms of social divisions and interests, especially economic interests.

3   Crime is bound up with tension, stresses and strains within societies. Most commonly there is a breakdown of the smooth workings of society – often called anomie (or normlessness) and sometimes referred to as social pathology or social disorganisation (especially in earlier studies). Crime may usefully be understood by looking at the tensions and strains that exist within a society.

4 Crime is strongly (but far from exclusively) linked to city life. Modern cities bring with them cultural enclaves that seem more prone to generating criminal/ delinquent styles of life with their own values, languages, norms, dress codes, etc. Crime may usefully be understood through mapping these 'criminal areas'.

5 Crime is learned in ordinary everyday situations. There is a process of cultural transmission, and crime may be usefully understood through looking at life histories and how people learn their everyday meanings and values.

6 Crime comes about through a lack of attachment to groups valuing law abiding behaviour. Controls and regulations break down. Crime here may be usefully understood through the breakdown of social controls.

There are other ways of thinking about the social foundations of crime, and there have been accounts that create bridges between the positions (especially in the work of 'delinquency opportunity' theory – which attempts to synthesise positions 2, 3 and 4). In what follows, each of these ways of thinking will be briefly introduced.

THE NORMALITY OF CRIME

In his pioneering study of deviance, Émile Durkheim made the curious claim that there is nothing abnormal about deviance; in fact, it is to be found in all societies and must therefore be seen as a normal part of society. He adopted a **functionalist perspective**: the theory that looks at the ways in which societies become integrated as their various parts perform various functions. At base, Durkheim suggests that crime and deviance perform four functions essential to society:

1 Culture involves moral choices over the good and bad life. Unless our lives and societies are to dissolve into chaos, there will usually be a preference for some values and some behaviours over others. Yet the very conception of 'the good' rests upon an opposing notion of 'the bad'; you cannot have one without the other. And just as there can be no good without evil, so there can be no justice without crime. Deviance, in short, is indispensable to the process of generating and sustaining morality.

2 This also means that 'deviance' tends to clarify and mark out moral boundaries. By defining some individuals as deviant, people draw a social boundary between right and wrong. For example, a university marks the line between academic honesty and cheating by disciplining those who commit plagiarism. In all spheres of life – sexuality, religion, family life, work – people draw up codes of conduct and police 'the good'. Drawing attention to the bad may serve to highlight the good.

3 In fact, Durkheim argues that responding to deviance actually promotes social unity. People typically react to serious deviance with collective outrage. In doing so, Durkheim explained, they reaffirm the moral ties that bind them. Deviance brings people together, creating a moral unity – often built from outrage. In the past, for instance, people would gather at executions to express their common hostility to the criminal; more recently, they often express this rage through the newspapers and the media generally.

4   On top of this, deviance may also encourage social change. Deviant people, Durkheim claimed, push a society's moral boundaries, suggesting alternatives to the status quo and encouraging change. Moreover, he declared, today's deviance sometimes becomes tomorrow's morality (1895/1988: 71). In the 1950s, for example, many people denounced rock-and-roll music as a threat to the morals of youth and an affront to traditional musical tastes. Since then, however, rock-and-roll has been swept up in the musical mainstream, becoming a multi-billion-dollar industry. Protest movements of one generation may be seen as deviants, but they often bring about change that becomes the norm for subsequent generations.

Functionalist theory, then, teaches us a great paradox about crime and deviance: that far from always being disruptive, it may contribute to a social system and underlie the operation of society. We will always have to live with deviance, suggests Durkheim, because it is bound up with the very conditions of social order. For as long as we want notions of the good and for as long as we want social change, deviance will be necessary.

The problems with functionalism

- It is indeed likely that most societies do have crime, but we know that they differ enormously in their rates of crime. Thus, for example, the United States has extremely high crime rates – whereas some other societies, such as Japan or Iran, seem to have very low crime rates. This account does not really help us see just why these rates are so different. That said, functionalists such as Durkheim might argue that crime rates soar when societies are under stress (as we will see in the next section), and the responses of others to crime – from media reporting to public concern – serve to strengthen the society by bringing together citizens in common opposition. There is a strong connection here to contemporary moral panic theory which is discussed in Chapter 5.
- But the abiding problem with functionalism is the way in which it highlights how societies are integrated, how there are shared values, how there is consensus. This may be true of relatively simple societies, but as societies become more indus-trialised, more fragmented, more postmodern, so it is hard to see that there is shared agreement on morality in society. Durkheim's theory may have elements of truth; but it is far from being the whole story.

THE EGOISM OF CRIME IN CAPITALIST SOCIETY

Quite an opposite story is told from Marxist theory and conflict theory. As Box 4.1 shows, although Karl Marx (1818–83) and his collaborator Friedrich Engels were a long way from being criminologists, their observations about the workings of capitalism often highlighted how it was a system that generated relatively high levels of crime.

BOX 4.1 MARX AND ENGELS ON CRIME

Engels

Immorality is fostered in every possible way by the conditions of working class life. The worker is poor; life has nothing to offer him; he is deprived of virtually all pleasures. Consequently, he does not fear the penalties of the law. Why should he restrain his wicked impulses? Why should he leave the rich man in undisturbed possession of his property? Why should he not take at least a part of this property for himself? What reason has the worker for *not* stealing?

. . . Distress due to poverty gives the worker only the choice of starving slowly, killing himself quickly or taking what he needs where he finds it – in plain English – stealing. And it is not surprising that the majority prefers to steal rather than starve to death or commit suicide.

. . . The clearest indication of the unbounded contempt of the workers for the existing social order is the wholesale manner in which they break its laws. If the demoralisation of the worker passes beyond a certain point then it is just as natural that he will turn into a criminal – as inevitably as water turns into steam at boiling point. Owing to the brutal and demoralising way in which he is treated by the bourgeoisie, the worker loses all will of his own and, like water, he is forced to follow blindly the laws of nature. There comes a point when the worker loses all power [to withstand temptation]. Consequently, the incidence of crime has increased with the growth of the working-class population and there is more crime in Britain than in any other country in the world. The annual statistics of crime issued by the Home Office show that there has been an extraordinarily rapid growth of crime. The number of those committed for trial on criminal charges in England and Wales alone has increased sevenfold in thirty-seven years. . . .

. . . There can be no doubt that in England the social war is already being waged. Everyone looks after his own interests and fights only for himself against all comers. Whether in doing so he injures those who are his declared enemies is simply a matter of selfish calculation as to whether such action be to his advantage or not. It no longer occurs to anybody to come to a friendly understanding with his neighbours. All differences of opinion are settled by threats, by invoking the courts, or even by taking the law into one's own hands. In short, everyone sees in his neighbour a rival to be elbowed aside, or at best a victim to be exploited for his own ends.

(Engels, 1845/1958: 130, 145–6, 149, 242, 243)

Marx

Present-day society, which breeds hostility between the individual man and everyone else, thus produces a social war of all against all which inevitably in individual cases, notably among uneducated people, assumes a brutal, barbarously violent form – that of crime. In order to protect itself against crime, against direct acts of violence, society requires an extensive, complicated system of administrative and judicial bodies which requires an immense labour force. In communist society this would likewise be vastly simplified and precisely because – strange though it may sound – the administrative body in this society would have to manage not merely individual aspects of social life, but the whole of social life, in all its various activities, in all its aspects. We eliminate the contradiction between the individual man and all others, we counter-pose social peace to social war, we put the axe to the *root* of crime – and thereby render the greatest, by far the greatest part of the present activity of the administrative and judicial bodies superfluous. Even now crimes of passion are becoming fewer and fewer in comparison with calculated crimes, crimes of interest – crimes against *persons* are declining, crimes against *property* are on the increase. Advancing civilisation moderates violent out-breaks of passion even in our present-day society, which is on a war footing; how much more will this be the case in communist, peaceful society! Crimes against property cease of their own accord where everyone receives what he needs to satisfy his natural and his spiritual urges, where social gradations and distinctions cease to exist.

(Marx and Engels, 1845/1975: 248–9)

Willem Adrian Bonger (1876–1940) was a Marxist Dutch sociologist/criminologist who committed suicide rather than submit to the Nazis, and whose PhD thesis was published in 1916 as 'Criminality and Economic Conditions'. He suggested that major shifts in crime come with the emergence of capitalism, and after an exposition of the working of capitalism, Bonger concluded that the present economic system 'weaken[s] the social feelings . . . breaks social bonds and makes social life much more egoistic'. For him, it was capitalism that generated an egoistic culture – with capitalists being greedy and workers becoming demoralised. It brutalises many, and helps create an 'insensibility to the ills of others'. As he writes,

Long working hours and monotonous labor brutalize those who are forced into them: bad housing conditions contribute also to debase the moral sense, as does [sic] the uncertainty of existence, and finally absolute poverty, the frequent consequence of sickness and unemployment, ignorance and lack of any training of any kind contribute their quota . . . the demoralizing of all is the status of the lower proletariat.

(quoted in Muncie *et al.*, 1996: 43)

From this he goes on to discuss four different types of crime all linked to economic conditions. These were (a) vagrancy and mendacity; (b) theft; (c) robbery and homicide for economic reasons (mainly by poor people); and (d) fraudulent bancruptcy, adulteration of food, etc.

This theory can also be seen in strands of the underclass theory, and in many aspects of Marxist theory which are still alive today.

The problems with Marxism

- As is well known, many of Marx's major predictions have simply not come true, and in the eyes of many, the whole theory has been discredited. All the same, Marxists criminologists do see a number of key ideas in Marx's ideas that can help in the study of crime. Those ideas have led to the broader arguments of conflict theory and new left realism, both of which will be discussed later.
- Again, there is too strong a deterministic streak in the theory. It is as if being poor would necessarily drive you into crime – whereas we know that the vast majority of poor people never commit serious crimes.
- There is also a lurking pejorative sense that working-class life is miserable, wretched and immoral; a lot of value claims are imported into the theory, and most contemporary theories of class would find this suspect.

CULTURAL TRANSMISSION, CITY LIFE AND THE CHICAGO SCHOOL

As is shown in Chapter 2, a major tradition for approaching crime and delinquency started to emerge at the University of Chicago in the first four decades of the twentieth century. Chicago was itself a leading centre for the study of sociology. It was the first major department of sociology; it produced the first major textbook; it trained a large number of graduate students; and it produced many monographs on the nature of city life at that time – including tramps, dance halls, prostitution, organised crime, mental illness, slums. Indeed, it has been said that Chicago in the 1920s is the most studied city of all time. Although inspired by European theorists such as Tonnies, Durkheim and Simmel, the unique contribution of the Chicago sociologists was in making the city itself a social laboratory for actual research. And the study of cities and crime has remained important for criminology.

Chicago itself was an extraordinary city: a new metropolis exploding with new populations, mass migration from all over Europe and the southern states of America, growing from a few hundred people in the mid-1880s to over 3 million in the 1930s. Its growth brought with it all the signs of modernity – from dance crazes, movies and cars to bootlegging, crime and unemployment. This was the Jazz Age.

Robert Ezra Park (1864–1944) was chair of the Department of Sociology and had a passion for walking the streets of the world's great cities, observing the full range of human turbulence and triumph. Throughout his thirty-year career at the University of Chicago, he led a group of dedicated sociologists in direct, systematic observation of urban life. In a classic line, he claimed that 'I suspect that I have actually covered more ground, tramping about in cities in different parts of the world, than any other living man' (quoted in Bulmer, 1984). At Park's urging, generations of sociologists at the University of Chicago rummaged through practically every part of their city.

From this research, Park came to understand the city as a highly ordered mosaic of distinctive regions, including industrial districts, ethnic communities and criminal/ delinquent/'vice' areas. These so-called natural areas all evolved in relation to one another, forming an urban ecology. To Park, the city operated like a living social organism. Urban variety was central: even though many people saw the city as disorganised and even dangerous, social life in the city was intoxicating. Walking the city streets, he became convinced that urban places offer a better way of life – the promise of greater human freedom and opportunity – than we can find elsewhere. But the downside may well be a growth in crime and dangerousness. These are all themes we recognise in current criminological debates, but they are far from new.

The Chicago School and crime

The Chicago sociologists borrowed from some earlier social work traditions. From the United States they were influenced by the work of Jane Adams (who ran a community project, Hull House, and also worked to map out the different parts of the city and its problems); and from the United Kingdom they had the example of the famous poverty studies of Charles Booth and others. From these opening ideas that parts of the city were perhaps more likely to harbour crime than others, the Chicago sociologists pioneered a range of approaches to the study of crime that may be briefly summarised as follows:

1   Crime may be more common in the city because the city generates a distinctive way of life. Indeed, the blasé attitude of city-dwellers and metropolitan styles – an urban way of living – bring greater tolerance for diversity and, in making the streets less communal and more anonymous, generate the possibility for a less controlling environment, but a more crimogenic one.

2   Crime can be found in 'natural habitats' or ecological zones. The city generates certain ways of life to be found in its various areas – and many of these could be linked to crime and deviance. In 1925 Ernest W. Burgess, a student and colleague of Robert Park, described land use in Chicago in terms of **concentric zones** that look rather like a bull's-eye. City centres, Burgess observed, are business districts bordered by a ring of factories, followed by residential rings with housing that becomes more expensive the further it stands from the noise and pollution of the city's centre.

3   Crime is basically learned in the same ways as everything else; it is normal learning. This idea of **differential association** was linked to the writings of Edwin Sutherland.

4   Crime is best studied through a range of different methodologies which when put together bring about a much richer understanding of crime than when only one single method is adopted. Thus, in his study of delinquency, Clifford

Shaw gathered detailed life histories of delinquent boys, and Burgess and Shaw examined the statistical records of delinquency for different parts of the city and spot-mapped them on to the 'ecological zones' that Robert Park had helped map out. Meanwhile, Frederic Thrasher was studying 1,313 gangs in their everyday life environments – an early and important instance of participant observation. And the backgrounds to delinquency in the city comes alive through studies of tramps (Anderson's *The Hobo*), dance halls (Cressey's *The Taxi-Dance Hall*), the slums (Zorbaugh) and organised crime.

5 Crime may be best dealt with through coordinated agencies: Chicago saw the start of Hull House through to the programmes of the Chicago Area Project.

The zonal theory of crime

At the heart of the Chicago theory was the idea of Park *et al.* (1925) that the urban industrial community of Chicago may be described as consisting of five successive zones (Figure 4.1):

I.   The central business district tends in American cities to be at once the retail, financial, recreational, civic, and political centres. The skyscrapers and canyon-like streets of this downtown district are thronged with shoppers, clerks, and office workers. Few people live there.

II. The zone in transition. This is an interstitial area where change is rapidly taking place. Here are to be found the slum or semi-slum districts. . . .

III. The zone of the workingmen's homes. This lies beyond the factory belt surrounding the central business district. It remains accessible, and is often within walking distance for the workers.

IV. The better residential zone is inhabited chiefly by the families engaged in professional and clerical pursuits. They are likely to have high school if not college education. This is the home of the middle class.

V.   The commuters' zone comprises the suburban districts.

Each of these zones could be studied in terms of the kinds of lifestyles that appeared there. This could be done partly through ethnographic research but also through looking at detailed statistical records (see Chapter 2). Thus, parts of the city could be analysed in terms of their crime rates, or the rates of mental illness measured. Of course, as we have seen, there are serious issues in measuring crime and deviance, and figures may only be approximations. Nevertheless, what the Chicago sociologists found was that there were distinctive areas where crime rates were much higher (the zone of transition). Here ethnic cultures conflicted, housing was run down, poverty was more widespread. *Certain parts of the city are more prone to crime.*

The work of Chicago sociologists has been transformed in recent years – much of it now passing under the title 'environmental criminology'. The old concentric zones model may no longer be considered valid, but other models of the city and new maps of the community have appeared (e.g. for Sheffield or Los Angeles) (Bottoms and Wiles, 2003).

BOX 4.2 SOME CLASSIC CHICAGO STUDIES

Edwin Sutherland (1883–1950): differential association theory

Source: University of Indiana Archive.

Edwin Sutherland has been called 'the Dean of American Criminology' . He was at Chicago only for a relatively brief time, but he wrote his study *24,000 Homeless Men* (Sutherland with Locke, 1936) and *The Professional Thief* (1937) there – the latter being a classic life story research of a thief, Chic Conwell. He moved on to Indiana University in 1936. *White Collar Crime* (1949) was published just before his death in 1950.

Frederic M. Thrasher (1892–1962) The Gang: A Study of 1,313 Gangs

Source: New York University Archives.

Thrasher's classic study took many years to complete, and concluded that there were roughly 25,000 or so members of gangs in Chicago. The gang underwent a kind of evolution from a loose grouping into a more structured form with a strong 'we' identity. It tended to emerge from play groups in the poorer part of the city. All the gangs were of boys; there was a general hostility towards girls in general because they were seen to weaken loyalty. Thrasher identified several types of gang (which we can still roughly identify today):

- the diffuse gang – never gets a proper organisation;
- the solidified gang – with a high degree of morale and solidarity, and usually with a clear name;
- the conventionalised gang – the athletic club (these made up about a quarter of all the gangs he observed);
- the criminal gang – can drift into habitual crime.

Later Thrasher moved to New York University and studied the Boys' Club of New York City.

continued

Edward Franklin Frazier (1894–1962)

A leading black sociologist who pioneered the study of black youth as well as the study of the black bourgeoisie, the black church and black families in the United States. He did his PhD at Chicago but later went on to become a leading professor in social work at Howard University.

Source: E. Franklin Frazier Papers/Moorland-Springarn Research Center, Howard University.

Clifford Shaw (1895–1957) and Henry D. McKay (1899–1980)

Both were graduate students at Chicago during the 1920s and later worked as a team for the Institute for Juvenile Research near the Chicago loop for thirty years. McKay was the statistician, Shaw (pictured left) was the fieldworker and activist (Snodgrass, 1982). They established the Chicago Area Project in 1932 which worked with the local community in an atempt to resolve the 'delinquency problem'.

Source: Courtesy of the Chicago Area Project, Chicago.

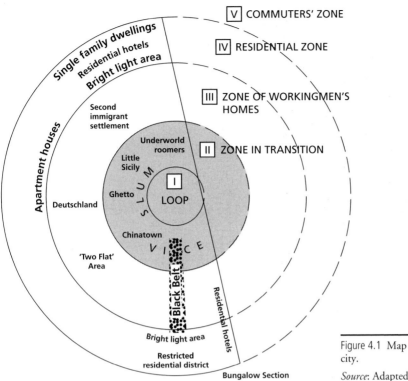

Figure 4.1 Map of the zonal theory of the city.

Source: Adapted from Park *et al.* (1925).

BOX 4.3 EARLY THEORIES OF CRIME AND SOCIAL POLICIES

Most sociological theories of crime bring with them implications for social policy and action. Both the Chicago School and anomie theory led to some major responses to crime in the twentieth century.

Chicago sociology led in part to the setting up of the Chicago Area Project (CAP), which was inaugurated by Shaw and McKay in 1934 and is one foundation for community and neighbourhood work. Here, the focus is on community change (which can include schools, family, street) and which sees the need to integrate values and enhance the capacities of local residents. If the community supports and fosters delinquent or criminal ways of life, then the proper focus of concern is the community. These days it may also be linked to community surveillance, neighbourhood watch community crime prevention campaigns.

Mobilization for Youth (MFY) was a project that grew in part out of anomie theory. It was part of the Kennedy administration's reforms in the early 1960s and led to an expansion of opportunity in education and work for young people.

continued

Both these projects have had limited success. Certainly some useful changes were made, and they have often served as models for other countries to follow,. But because they deal with middle-range change – at the level of community – it has been argued by critics that they fail to deal with the root of such problems in the wider society. The term 'community' itself, for example has been much criticised as being too romantic and imprecise.

CRIME AS LEARNED: DIFFERENTIAL ASSOCIATION THEORY

Edwin Sutherland is also identified with Chicago, and his key contribution to criminology is generally seen to be the theory of differential association, which he developed in various editions of his textbook *Principles of Criminology* (it first appeared in the 1939 edition). For Sutherland, crime was a normal learning process; we learn crime in much the same way as we learn everything else. Far from being genetic or biological, it was also not a matter of pathology or abnormal learning. Learning any social patterns – whether conventional or deviant – is a process that takes place in groups. According to Sutherland (1956), any person's tendency towards conformity or deviance depends on the relative frequency of association with others who encourage conventional behaviour or, as the case may be, norm violation.

1   Criminal behaviour is learned.
2   Criminal behaviour is learned in interaction with other persons in a process of communication.
3   The principal part of the learning of criminal behaviour occurs within intimate personal groups.
4   When criminal behaviour is learned, the learning includes (a) techniques of committing the crime, which are sometimes very complicated, sometimes very simple; and (b) the specific direction of motives, drives, rationalisations and attitudes.
5   The specific direction of motives and drives is learned from definitions of legal codes as favourable and unfavourable.
6   A person becomes delinquent because of an excess of definitions favourable to violation of law over definitions unfavourable to violation of law.
7   Differential associations may vary in frequency, duration, priority and intensity.
8   The process of learning criminal behaviour by association with criminal and anti-criminal patterns involves all the mechanisms that are involved in any other learning.
9   Though criminal behavior is an expression of general needs and values, it is not explained by those general needs and values since non-criminal behaviour is an expression of the same needs and values.

The problems with the Chicago School

- Although the Chicago School provided many of the foundational ideas of the sociology of crime, many of them are now not far short of a century old – and have been open to much refinement. Thus, although the city is still known to harbour 'natural areas' of crime, the concentric zones model is usually seen to be only one special case.
- There is also a problem with what is called 'the ecological fallacy'. We cannot assume that because certain areas are more 'criminal', everybody within those areas is likely to be a criminal; this is simply not true. So the theory is not strong at explaining why some people become criminal and others do not.

ANOMIE AND THE STRESSES AND STRAINS OF CRIME

Early social models of crime often assumed a certain harmony or fit between the parts of a society and its overall working. Societies functioned; and the institutions in them (from work and school to family and religion) worked to perform certain functions to keep a society balanced. How then can crime and deviance happen?

Drawing from the traditions established both by Marx and Durkheim, the US sociologist Robert K. Merton (1910–2003) saw crime and deviance emerging as an individual adaptation to pressures flowing from the social structure. In one of the most cited discussions of the twentieth century, Merton's *Social Structure and Anomie* (1938), modern capitalist society was seen as being under pressure, and the strains and tensions within it, Merton thought, led to crime and deviance. Distinguishing between a social structure (which provided economic roots to success) and a culture (which provided norms, values and goals – the 'American Dream'), Merton argued that deviance occurred where there was an imbalance between social structure (approved social means) and culture (approved goals). The tension or norm break-down he called **anomie**. His model was effectively what has been called a materialist one. He looked at just how important the American Dream of making it to the top through hard work and earning money was, and found that some people were so placed within society that they were unable to achieve this dream. He argued that this inability opened up a series of responses or adaptations (Table 4.1). He borrowed from Durkheim the notion of social integration and anomie.

Writing originally about North American society in the 1930s, Merton argued that the path to *conformity* was to be found in pursuing conventional goals by approved means. The true 'success story', in other words, is someone who gains wealth and prestige through talent and hard work. But not everyone who desires conventional success has the opportunity to attain it. Children raised in poverty, for example, may see little hope of becoming successful if they 'play by the rules'. As a result, they may seek wealth through one or another kind of crime – say, by dealing in cocaine. Merton called this type of deviance *innovation* – the attempt to achieve a culturally approved goal (wealth) by unconventional means (drug sales). Table 4.1 characterises innovation as accepting the goal of success while rejecting the conventional means of becoming rich.

Table 4.1 Merton's modes of individual adaptation to anomie		
	CULTURE GOALS	INSTITUTIONALISED MEANS
Conformity	+	+
Innovation	+	−
Ritualism	−	+
Retreatism	−	−
Rebellion	+/−	+/−

Key:

+ = acceptance

− = rejection

+/− = reject old and substitute new

The inability to become successful by normative means may also prompt another type of deviance that Merton calls *ritualism*. Ritualists resolve the strain of limited success by abandoning cultural goals in favour of almost compulsive efforts to live 'respectably'. In essence, they embrace the rules to the point where they lose sight of their larger goals. Lower-level bureaucrats, Merton suggests, often succumb to ritualism as a way of maintaining respectability.

Merton noted other adaptations. *Retreatism* was the rejection of both cultural goals and means so that one, in effect, 'drops out': some alcoholics, drug addicts and street people are examples. *Rebellion* involves the rejection of both the cultural definition of success and the normative means of achieving it. Those who adopt this response advocate radical alternatives to the existing social order, typically calling for a political transformation of society.

What is important in this kind of explanation is that it looks at society as a whole and finds stresses and strains within the system that seem to generate 'weak spots' – crime is induced through a system that has potentials for contradiction and conflict. Merton's theory has been extremely influential in the development of 'delinquent gang theory'.

The problems with anomie theory

- The problem with Merton's ideas is the presumption of goals and values. It is just possible that life was like this in 1930s America (though we doubt it), but it is certainly not like this in the early twenty-first century – which, as we see throughout this book, is often characterised as a postmodern, risk society. Societies are just too complex, have too many competing values systems and generate too much conflict for this simple unitary idea to be valid.
- Nor can we assume that people are simply socialised to a common set of values: quite the contrary, much evidence points to different socialisation patterns among different groups.

- And more: the theory also largely seems to assume that people are driven into crime through tensions, through grim necessity. As Jack Katz and others have pointed out (see Chapter 13), we do not necessarily need to see crime as motivated by painful sources. For many crime may be fun and exciting, and it may hold its own pleasures. This is not a very fashionable theory among many criminologists, but it is one that we consider elsewhere in the book.

We do not wish to make Merton's theory sound too facile and simply wrong. Its influence lies in that it pointed sharply to the role of economic factors in shaping crime, and to producing a genuinely social account that found the roots of crime to lie not in individual people, but in the organisation and workings of the wider society. It has had many ardent followers, and it still has many adherents today.

Gangs, youth and deviant subcultures

One of these followers is Albert Cohen (1918–), who has been influenced by Merton and Sutherland, who both taught him. His *Delinquent Boys* (1955) became an influential classic. In this study, Cohen notes that delinquent boys stole for the hell of it. They engaged in short-run hedonism and in what he called a 'reaction formation' to the frustration experienced as part of a class system, especially in school. They did not steal to gain goods or property, instead, they gained status among their peers through adopting malicious, negative values – the antithesis of the middle-class values taught in middle-class educational worlds.

Cohen's study of delinquent boys pioneered the idea that boys become delinquent because of what he termed 'status frustration', the process by which people feel thwarted when they aspire to a certain status. In schools especially, Cohen noted that boys from more deprived backgrounds often found school life an alienating and frustrating experience. They were being judged by what Cohen called the 'middle-class measuring rod'. They initially wanted to be successes, but found that they had not developed the skills to do this in their family and community life. For example, reading books was alien, and being polite and well-spoken hard. Their cultural differences had poorly equipped them for school life. Cohen suggests that in their frustration they inverted the values of the school – achievement, hard work and planning for the future – and developed instead a contra culture in which values of non-achievement, playing around and not thinking of the future become deliberately – almost perversely – their goals. Activities become non-utilitarian (they steal 'for the hell of it'), negativistic (opposing the values of adult society), malicious, versatile and characterised by short-run hedonism and group autonomy.

Cohen asserted that delinquency was most pronounced among lower-class youths because it is they who contend with the least opportunity to achieve success in conventional ways. Sometimes those whom society neglects seek self-respect by building a deviant subculture that 'defines as meritorious the characteristics they do possess, the kinds of conduct of which they are capable' (1971: 66). Having a notorious street reputation, for example, may win no points with society as a whole, but it may satisfy a youth's gnawing desire to 'be somebody'.

Unlike most of the Chicago sociologists, he did discuss girls – though in very stereotypical terms.

Synthesising the theories?

The prominent work of Richard A. Cloward (1926–) and Lloyd E. Ohlin (1918–), *Delinquency and Opportunity* (1960), can be seen as an attempt to form a bridge between the Chicago tradition (especially Sutherland's learning theory) and the strain tradition (especially Merton's anomie theory). They suggest that the delinquent subculture has its own opportunity structures. That is, young people have access to different kinds of youthful cultures. While they may aspire to the goals set by conventional society, working-class youth – as in Merton's and Cohen's model – can easily be thwarted and can not get ahead. But they also find that they have differential access to youth cultures too. In their own work, Cloward and Ohlin suggest that there were three major kinds of these cultures:

1 Criminal. The criminal youth culture is at the top of the hierarchy and means that alternative means to financial success become available. Here there are 'close bonds between different age levels of offender and between criminal and conventional elements' (Cloward and Ohlin, 1960: 171), so there is rapid integration between young and old into lives of crime.

2 Violent/conflict. Here there is not only little access to the legitimate opportunity structure, but also little access to the illegitimate/criminal one. Such youth may live in very unstable areas, and violence becomes the means therefore by which they seek to resolve their frustrations and problems. Violence becomes their source of status.

3 Retreatist/drug. Those who have neither access to the criminal culture nor the means to seek violent responses become 'double failures', and they are the most likely simply to 'drop out'. They become retreatists and turn to drink, drugs, sex and other forms of withdrawal from the wider social order.

Thus, Cloward and Ohlin maintain that criminal deviance results not simply from limited legitimate opportunity but also from available illegitimate opportunity. In short, deviance or conformity grows out of the relative opportunity structure that frames young people's lives. It was the nature of these opportunity structures and how they provide opportunities to learn deviant ways that fascinated the Chicago School. In its day – nearly fifty years ago – this was seen as a very elegant way of thinking about crime, bridging as it did the anomie tradition of Merton and the Chicago tradition of Shaw and Sutherland. To modern eyes, however, the theory looks somewhat contrived – and does not take into account a much wider range of forms of youthful culture.

There are more problems with the various Chicago theories:

• They fall short by assuming that everyone shares the same cultural standards for judging right and wrong.

- We must be careful not to define deviance in ways that unfairly focus attention on poor people. If crime is defined to include stock fraud as well as street theft, offenders are more likely to include affluent individuals.
- All structural-functional theories imply that everyone who violates conventional cultural standards will be branded as deviant. Becoming deviant, however, is actually a highly complex process.

CONTROL THEORIES

The term 'social control', initially linked to the work Edward Ross, who first used the term in the *American Journal of Sociology* in 1896, and linked to the classical school of Durkheim and Mead, started to develop as a broad theory of self control in the 1950s. Like the other broad ideas already considered, it does come in many guises.

Neutralisation theory

One of social control's earliest formulations is to be found in the work of Sykes and Matza. They argue that boys can commit delinquent acts when their commitment to the moral order is weakened, and that they can do this through what Sykes and Matza term techniques of neutralisation. These techniques are stories they tell themselves which break bonds through such devices as blaming others or denying responsibility.

Sykes and Matza suggest five major techniques that enable delinquents to break 'the moral bind to law' (Matza, 1964: 181):

1   *The denial of personal responsibility*. Here the delinquent uses a kind of social word play. 'Of course I'm delinquent. Who wouldn't be, coming from my background?' He then can neutralise personal responsibility by detailing the background of a broken home, lack of love, and a host of other factors.
2   *The denial of harm to anyone*. In this pattern of neutralisation, stealing a car is only borrowing it; truancy harms no one; and drug use 'doesn't hurt anyone but me'.
3   *The delinquent denies that the person injured or wronged is really a victim*. 'The [assaulted] teacher was unfair'; the victim of a mugging was 'only queer'; and the gang youth assaulted was 'out to get me'.
4   *The delinquent condemns the condemners*. 'Society is much more corrupt than I am.'
5   *Delinquent group or gang loyalties supersede loyalty to the norms of an impersonal society*. 'When I stabbed him, I was only defending my turf.' The youth places his gang or delinquent group above the law, the school and society.

Developing in close connection with this, *social bond theory* is effectively a theory of self-control. Walter Cade Reckless (1899–1988) and Simon Dinitz presented it as 'containment theory'. They looked at groups of boys to see what insulated some from crime of all kinds but not others – the techniques that neutralise 'good boys' from crime and foster 'bad boys' in it.

Social control theory

All this anticipated the general question later posed by Travis Hirschi. Most contemporary control theories effectively ask not 'Why do people become criminal and commit crime?' but the reverse and intriguing question: 'Why do most people not commit crime?'

In his earlier work, Hirschi argued that 'delinquent acts results when an individual's bond to society is weak or broken' (1969: 16). Hirschi asserts that conformity arises from four types of social controls that create a social bond (Table 4.2). The weaker they are, the more likely it is that criminal acts will happen.

Table 4.2	Hirschi's elements of the bond	
ELEMENT	EXAMPLES
Attachment	Identification with peers or parents, emotional bond between child and parent, concern and respect for parents' or peers' opinions, engaging in activities with peers, supervision by parents, intimate communications with parents, attitudes towards school, concern for teachers' opinions, general sensitivity to the opinions of others
Involvement	Time-consuming activity (work, sports, recreation, hobbies), time spent on homework, lack of boredom, amount of non-active leisure time, time spent talking with friends
Commitment	Investment in society (education, career, family), academic competence, educational aspirations and expectations, achievement orientation, expected occupation, importance of reputation
Belief	Respect for authorities, importance of and respect for law, absence of neutralisations

1   Attachment. Strong social attachments encourage conformity; weak relationships in the family, peer group and school leave people freer to engage in deviance.
2   Opportunity. The more one perceives legitimate opportunity, the greater the advantages of conformity. A young person bound for university, one with good career prospects, has a high stake in conformity. By contrast, someone with little confidence in future success drifts more towards deviance.
3   Involvement. Extensive involvement in legitimate activities – such as holding a job, going to school and completing homework, or pursuing hobbies – inhibits deviance. People with few such activities – those who simply 'hang out' waiting for something to happen – have time and energy for deviant activity.
4   Belief. Strong beliefs in conventional morality and respect for authority figures restrain tendencies towards deviance. By contrast, people with a weak conscience are more vulnerable to temptation.

Later, Gottfredson and Hirschi used this question as the basis for their more general theory of crime (1990), in which one issue matters above all others: that of self-control. Individuals with high self-control 'will be substantially less likely at all periods of life to engage in criminal acts' (ibid.: 89). This changes the theory a great deal, as all the other elements now go missing. Over the years, the theory has been much tested, and some criminologists now think it has been the most influential theory of delinquency over the past thirty years.

The problems with control theory

- Control theory is an odd theory of crime as it works from the assumption that most of us would commit crimes if we had the chance. It is only the social ties, bonds and attachments that prevent us from doing this. It is at least worth considering whether this is true.
- This also means that it neglects offenders' motivations: the cause is apparent – a lack of control. Again, we do not need special reasons to account for crime, except to note that the bonds have broken.
- More specifically, just how tight do these bonds have to be? Some argue that bonds may have to be too repressive, too overwhelming in modern societies.

REINTEGRATIVE SHAMING?

A theory that has developed more recently than Hirschi's and in many ways is connected is John Braithwaite's 're-integrative shaming'. In his influential book *Crime, Shame and Reintegration* (1989), Braithwaite highlights the importance of informal, rather than formal, sanctions in checking crime. As he says, 'It would seem that sanctions imposed by relatives, friends or a personally relevant collectivity have more effect on criminal behaviour than sanctions imposed by legal authority' (quoted in Muncie, 1999: 433). Closely allied to the work on shame by Thomas Scheff (which suggests that one of the central features of life is our search for honour and the ways in which shaming plays a role in that search), the emphasis on shaming can be seen to keep us in check. Shame is linked to taking the role of 'the other' (cf. Mead, 1934), and links to pangs of conscience when confronted with the possibility of wrongdoing. We want and need the social approval of others.

Shaming involves all social processes expressing disapproval that have the aim of inducing remorse in the offender. The shame that matters most is not that coming from officials such as the police or judges or courts but that from the people we care about most. It is not stigmatising in so far as it is aimed not at the offender *per se* but at the act the offender commits; the ultimate aim must be reintegration. The shaming itself creates outcasts, meaning that bonds of respect with the offender are not sustained. In contrast, reintegrative shaming is disapproval dispensed in a relationship with the offender that is based on respect, with the focus on the offence and where 'degradation ceremonies are followed by ceremonies to decertify deviance, where forgiveness, apology and repentance are culturally important' (Muncie *et al.*, 1996).

Braithwaite contends that reintegrative shaming is effective in complex urban societies as well as simpler ones. It is likely that those nations with low crime rates are those in which shaming has the greatest social power.

SUMMARY

1 The functionalist perspective on crime suggests that it is 'normal' in all societies – it serves certain functions and may even help keep a society orderly. Crime may be usefully understood in mapping these functions.
2 The Marxist theory of crime suggests that crime is bound up with conflict of a class-based nature in which crimes of the powerful are much less noticed than the crimes of the weak.
3 Anomie theory suggests crime is bound up with tension, stresses and strains within societies. Most commonly there is a breakdown of the smooth workings of society.
4 The Chicago School of sociology saw crime as being strongly linked to city life. Modern cities bring with them cultural enclaves that seem more prone to generating criminal/delinquent styles of life with their own values, languages, norms, dress codes, etc.
5 Differential association theory suggests that crime is learned in ordinary everyday situations through a process of cultural transmission.
6 Social control theory suggests that crime comes about through a lack of attachment to groups valuing law-abiding behaviour.
7 Reintegrative shaming involves all social processes expressing disapproval that have the aim of inducing remorse in the offender. The shame that matters most is not that coming from officials such as the police or judges or courts but that relating to the people we care about most.

CRITICAL THINKING QUESTIONS

1 Compare the following two views – one suggests that crime is normal, the other that capitalism generates crime.

There must be something rotten in the very core of a social system which increases its wealth without diminishing its misery, and increases in crimes even more rapidly than in numbers.

(Karl Marx, 'Population, Crime and Pauperism', *New York Daily Tribune*, 16 September 1859)

Crime is normal. . . . It is a factor in public health, an integral part of all healthy societies.

(Émile Durkheim, *Rules of Sociological Method*: 76)

2   Examine the different kinds of study of crime emanating from the Chicago School. Consider how they complement each other. Do they ultimately add up to a full understanding of delinquency and crime? If not, what is missing?

3   Look at your own home city or town. Can you map out the areas of greatest crime? How would you explain this concentration?

4   Critically discuss the factors that may weaken a person's bond to society. Is such weakening likely to lead to crime and deviance?

FURTHER STUDY

Bottoms, A. E. and Wiles, P. 'Environmental Criminology', Rock, P. 'Sociological Theories of Crime' and Taylor, I. 'The Political Economy of Crime' are all useful reviews to be found in Maguire, M., Morgan, R. and Reiner, R. (2003) *The Oxford Handbook of Criminology*, 3rd edn, Oxford: Oxford University Press.

Cloward, R. and Ohlin, L. E. (1960) *Delinquency and Opportunity: A Theory of Delinquent Gangs*, New York: Free Press.

Gabbidon, S., Greene, H. T. and Young, V. D. (2001) *African American Classics in Criminology and Criminal Justice*, Thousand Oaks, CA: Sage. Important volume examining the 'black' tradition of criminology in the United States.

Hirschi, T. (1969) *Causes of Delinquency*, Berkeley, CA: University of California Press. This is the classic statement of Hirschi's 'control theory'.

Matza, D. (1969) *Becoming Deviant*, Englewood Cliffs, NJ: Prentice Hall. Although old, this is one of the most sophisticated accounts of crime and deviance available. At its core it reviews the major traditions of anomie, cultural learning and labelling in the study of deviance; but it is highly original in its synthesis.

Merton, R. K. (1938) 'Social Structure and Anomie', *American Sociological Review*, 3 (October): 672–82. One of the most cited papers in the sociology of crime.

MORE INFORMATION

The Émile Durkheim Archive
http://durkheim.itgo.com/anomie.html
A comprehensive Website on Durkheim's life and works.

The University of Chicago: Department of Sociology
http://sociology.uchicago.edu/overview/history/html
Gives a brief history of the original Chicago School theorists.

The Chicago School of Pragmatism
http://www.pragmatism.org/genealogy/Chicago.htm
Provides a brief history of the foundation of the Chicago School of Pragmatism and its members.

The Society for Human Ecology (SHE).
http://www.societyforhumanecology.org/
This is an international interdisciplinary professional society that promotes the use of an ecological perspective in both research and application.

Radicalising Traditions: Labelling, New Criminologies and the Gender Issue

KEY ISSUES

▮ What is labelling theory?

▮ What was the significance and problems of the new deviancy theories and labelling theory?

▮ How did conflict theory arise and what are the questions of a new criminology?

▮ How did the Birmingham Centre for Contemporary Cultural Studies provide an advance over earlier subcultural theory?

▮ How did feminism and gender issues transform the nature of criminology?

▮ What has been the influence of Foucault?

INTRODUCTION

The social ways of thinking about crime discussed in Chapter 4 were very influential in shaping contemporary criminology and appeared predominantly in the first six decades of the twentieth century. In this chapter we look briefly at accounts of crime that came into prominence during the latter part of the twentieth century. Many of these can be seen in some way as a response to earlier theories – challenging them, debating them, extending them. Indeed, during this time there was a constant tendency to find new ways of thinking about crime – but often these new ways turned out to be little more than old ways updated, and often their newness was attacked very rapidly and they fell into decline as quickly as they appeared. But some of the theories had a more enduring impact. This chapter will briefly review these late-twentieth-century theories before turning in Chapter 6 to some of the most recent trends.

The 1960s was a time when everything came to be challenged. In criminology, the very idea of what crime and deviance was challenged. Claims from the past that we know what crimes are, we know what deviance is, that they are 'objective categories' – all these came under critical scrutiny. The thinking of the 1960s came to see such 'objective' definitions of crime and deviance as problematic. There was now a need to study the categories themselves – what they were, how they came about, and what they did to people. And much of this was political; suddenly, politics became a clear part of criminology.

This was at the time seen as quite a radical shift in emphasis and it gave rise to what was variously called the 'New Deviancy theorists', the 'Societal Reaction Perspective' or Labelling Theory. In the United Kingdom it generated an organisation – the National Deviancy Conference – that held regular conferences and discussions at York University between 1968 and 1973 (and resulted in several books: notably *Images of Deviance* (1971) and *Politics and Deviance* (1973)) (see Box 5.1). This grouping lasted a few years. It disbanded in the late 1970s but it had effectively come to an end much earlier. After this, a new series of divisions and schisms became apparent.

BOX 5.1 FROM THE NATIONAL DEVIANCY CONFERENCE TO THE RISE OF THE NEW CRIMINOLOGIES

Background

The National Deviancy Conference (NDC) was established in 1967 as a reaction against mainstream criminology. It held conferences at the University of York between 1967 and 1976 and thereafter turned for a while into a broader European organisation. Among its key founder members in the United Kingdom were Stanley Cohen, Laurie Taylor, Jock Young, Ian Taylor and Mary Macintosh.

What was the NDC responding against?

Its central position was a critique of mainstream criminology – as exemplified in work conducted at the Home Office or at the Institute for Criminology in Cambridge, which used traditional methods, lacked a firm sociological focus and was often rather conservative in outlook. Broadly, this was a time of student rebellion, growth in sociology and also a time for wider activism in various new penal reform and social change movements. These positions were brought together in a desire to radically rethink the problem of crime and deviance.

What theories did it draw from?

The NDC marked a strong concern with sociology and deviance – all its founders were sociologists, though it soon came to include radical practitioners too and members of radical change movements. It initially drew from the theories of symbolic interactionism, ethnomethodology, Marxism, appreciative ethnography, conflict theories, social movement activism, neo-functionalism, labelling theory and anarchistic criminology. Its members were writing before the arrival of a feminist criminology, though many of them were part of the newly emerging second-wave women's movement.

Examples of key texts

Jock Young, *The Drugtakers* (1971)
Stan Cohen, *Folk Devils and Moral Panics* (1972)
Laurie Taylor, *Deviance and Society* (1973)
Stan Cohen (ed.) *Images of Deviance* (1971)
Ian Taylor and Laurie Taylor (eds) *Politics and Deviance* (1973)

Plate 5.1 Stanley Cohen was one of the founders of the National Deviancy Conference. His initial work was on the mods and rockers, and he developed the idea of the moral panic. More recently he has looked at the workings of the control system (see Chapter 4) and at human rights.

Source: Stanley Cohen.

Demise and diffusion

The New Criminology (see Box 5.3, p. 78) eventually critiqued much of this new radicalism and itself unfolded into a number of other positions. Some of those involved left criminology altogether and developed other fields such as cultural studies or sexuality studies. Some remained with a particular theoretical orientation and developed it further – such as those who had initially applied ethnomethodology to the study of criminal statistics (they now went on to apply ethnomethodological reasoning to other areas of social life). And others went on to develop further criminologies – left realism, discourse theory, and feminist criminology – which will be discussed later in this chapter.

See Cohen (1971) and Taylor and Taylor (1973).

Briefly, the theories proposed:

- A turning away from conventional theories of crime which assumed the nature of criminal categories and control processes and asked questions about the causes of crime. Instead, it was argued that crime was a socially constructed category, that it differed throughout history and different cultures, and that there could not therefore be any 'criminal type' – since criminal types depended on who defined the laws at particular times. Instead, its focus moved to showing the societal reactions to crimes: the role of law, social control agencies, the media, etc. in shaping the nature of crime. Far from seeing crime control as solving the problem of crime, control may actually serve to shape and structure it. Crime was a political issue. There was a shift to social control, societal reaction and the labelling of crime.

- A turning away from views of crime that saw it as pathologies, disorganisation, strains, stresses and leakage within a consensual society which more or less agreed on values. Instead, its focus moved to pick up on the theme of conflict: to see crime (as some earlier criminologists such as Bonger had indeed done) as a special form of conflict.

- A much wider scope of questions within criminology. Labelling theory (which the above theory was usually called) had its merits in stretching the concerns of criminology away from offenders on to the role of social control. But it did this at the expense of examining the causes of crime. Some theorists started to suggest that all ways of thinking had their limits, and hence started to sketch out the questions that needed to be asked in developing a theory of crime.

- A re-examination of youth subcultural theories of crime, placing a much greater emphasis upon culture and cultural forms.

- A turning away from views of crime that ignored gender. It is curious how few theories of crime of the nineteenth and twentieth century recognised one of the most apparent facts about crime: that it is overwhelmingly committed by men. With the rise of modern (second-wave) feminism, the issue of gender was brought into criminology as a key element for thinking about crime.

- A move to see criminology as part of the very problem it tries to solve. Many interventions into the criminal sphere simply do not work in the way they are supposed to work. Instead, they tend to create wider concerns of surveillance and control.

■ 'DEVIANCE' AND LABELLING THEORY

For a short while during much of the late 1960s and the 1970s, labelling theory became the dominant sociological theory of crime. In one sense this was very odd, since it made few claims to try to understand what made people criminal. Quite the contrary: it tended to assume we would all be criminal if we could (in this, it had quite a lot in common with control theory, discussed in Chapter 4). Instead, it turned its focus on societal reactions to crime. Societal reactions could range from the informal responses of public opinion, families or the mass media to the more formal responses of police, courts and prisons.

Labelling theory highlights social reaction. In its narrowest version it asks what happens to criminals after they have been labelled; and suggests that crime may be heightened by criminal sanctions. Thus, sending an offender to prison may actually criminalise him or her further, and stigmatising minor infractions at too early an age may lead a young offender into a criminal career. In its broadest version, it suggests that criminology has given too much attention to criminals as types of people and insufficient attention to the panoply of social control responses – from the law and the police to media and public reactions – that help to give crime its shape.

The elementary understanding of the way in which criminal responses may shape crime goes back a long way: it is captured in popular phrases such as 'give a dog a bad name'. In the twentieth century the origins of the theory are usually seen to lie with Frank Tannenbaum in his classic study *Crime and the Community*. Here he argued that

> The process of making the criminal, therefore, is a process of tagging, defining, identifying, segregating, describing, emphasizing, evoking the very traits that are complained of. . . . The person becomes the thing he is described as being. . . . The way out is a refusal to dramatize the evil.
>
> (1938: 19–20)

The theory has a number of roots in earlier sociological traditions, but draws heavily on the idea of W. I. Thomas that 'when people define situations as real they become real in their consequences'. This is sometimes also known as the 'self-fulfilling prophecy' (see Janowitz, 1996).

Becker, Lemert and Cohen

The key labelling theorists are usually seen to be the North American sociologists Edwin Lemert and Howard S. Becker and the South African-born but UK-based criminologist Stanley Cohen.

Edwin Lemert (1951, 1967) argued that many episodes of norm violation – from truancy to under-age drinking – often provoke little reaction from others and have little effect on a person's self-concept. Lemert calls such passing episodes **primary deviance**. He asked what happens if other people take notice of someone's deviance and make something of it. If, for example, people begin to describe a young man as a 'boozer' or a 'drunk' or even an 'alcoholic' and then push him out of their group, he may become embittered, drink even more and seek the company of others who condone his behaviour. So the response to initial deviance can set in motion **secondary deviance**, by which an individual engages in repeated norm violations and begins to take on a deviant identity. The development of secondary deviance is one application of the Thomas theorem, which states that 'Situations defined as real become real in their consequences.'

The terms 'primary' and 'secondary deviance' capture the distinction between original and effective causes of deviance: primary deviation arises from many sources but 'has only marginal implications for the status and psychic structure of the person concerned', whereas secondary deviation refers to the ways in which stigma and punishment can actually make the crimes or deviance 'become central facts of existence for those experiencing them, altering psychic structure, producing specialised organisation of social roles and self regarding attitudes' (Lemert, 1967: 40–1). Deviant ascription became a pivotal or master status. It was Lemert who argued that rather than seeing crime as leading to control, it may be more fruitful to see the process as one in which control agencies structured and even generated crime.

Howard S. Becker was a second-generation Chicago sociologist (identified with the 1950s and 1960s) whose own work focused on marijuana use and its control. Studying the ways in which cultures and careers were transformed by negative sanctions against drug use, he outlined the broad problem of labelling when he asked:

> We [should] direct our attention in research and theory building to the questions: who applied the label of deviant to whom? What consequences does the application of a label have for the person so labelled? Under what circumstances is the label of a deviant successfully applied?
>
> (1963: 3)

In what became the canonical statement of labelling theory, he announced that

> Social groups create deviance by making the rules whose infraction constitutes deviance, and by applying those rules to particular people and labelling them as outsiders. . . . Deviance is *not* a quality of the act the person commits, but rather a consequence of the application by others of rules and sanctions to an 'offender'. The deviant is one to whom that label has successfully been applied: deviant behavior is behavior that people so label.
>
> (1963: 9)

BOX 5.2 BECKER'S TYPES OF DEVIANT BEHAVIOUR

	Obedient behaviour	Rule-breaking behaviour
Perceived as deviant	Falsely accused	Pure deviant
Not perceived as deviant	Conforming	Secret deviant

Source: Becker (1963: 20)

Becker challenged standard definitions of deviant behaviour. In his research on drug users he could show how sanctions against drug use led to distinctive subcultures and careers as drug users which, he claimed would not exist without the sanctions. Sanctions shaped the nature of drug use.

Stanley Cohen in his seminal work *Folk Devils and Moral Panics* (1972) looked at one of the first major youth phenomena in the United Kingdom. This was a study of the big English youth phenomenon of the 1960s: the rise of the so-called mods and rockers (see Plate 5.2, p. 75). Apart from the teddy boys of the 1950s, these were the first major youth phenomenon of the post-war era, and sparked off a great deal of controversy. They seemed to turn the local beaches of Clacton into a battleground. Cohen had an unusual take on all this: for him, the mods and rockers came into being, at least in part, because of the very responses of the media, the police and the courts – who helped define and shape them. The term **moral panic** is introduced to capture the heightened awareness of certain problems at key moments. The core idea of the book is that interventions – usually in the name of benevolence or 'doing good' – can sometimes actually make situations worse, not better. In his classic formulation:

> a condition, episode, person or group of persons emerges to become defined as a threat to societal values and interests: its nature is presented in a stylised and stereotypical fashion by the mass media; the moral barricades are manned by editors, bishops, politicians and other right thinking people.
>
> (1972: 9)

Moral panics have traditionally been short-lived and focused: a riot, a drug overdose, a violent crime, a pedophile murder. Yet, and maybe starting with AIDS, such isolated panics became almost pervasive and commonplace. As they spread out and generate higher levels of anxiety, society becomes constantly on edge about such 'problems' (McRobbie and Thornton, 1995: 560). Moral panics start to sign-post persistent ideological struggles over problems constructed on an almost daily basis. There is an 'endless overhead narrative of such [a] phenomenon as one panic gives way to another, or one anxiety is displaced across different panics' (Watney, 1997: 412). Yet as a strong sense of core values becomes less and less apparent, so the recognition of social problems becomes harder to define even as a more general social anxiety increases. Arguably, in late modern times with post-modern ideas, social problems have to become more extreme – or spoken about in extreme language – if they are to be noticed. (Some of these ideas are discussed further in Chapter 18.)

The wider contributions

Overall, the theory has covered a surprisingly wide range of issues and produced many classic studies. Thus, Edwin Schur's *Crime without Victims* (1963) looked at victimless crimes and showed how the legal response to the then criminalised homosexuality, abortion and drug use generated more problems than were solved. Erving Goffman's *Asylums* (1962) and Thomas J. Scheff's *Being Mentally Ill* (1966) developed a controversial theory of mental illness based upon labelling dynamics, suggesting that there was no such simple thing as mental illness; rather, the role of the mentally ill depended upon a major identification process. And the criminologist Lesley Wilkins's *Social Policy, Action and Research* (1967) used systems theory to show how a process of deviancy amplification works: how small deviations can through a process of feedback by control agencies become major patterns of deviance. (This latter idea was susbequently used to great effect by Jock Young in his study of Notting Hill drug use, *The Drugtakers* (1971).) All in all, this was a very productive period in the study of crime and deviance.

The labelling perspective brought political analysis into deviancy study. It recognised that labelling was a political act and that 'what rules are to be enforced, what behaviour regarded as deviant and which people labelled as outsiders must . . . be regarded as political questions' (Becker, 1963: 7). From this it went on to produce a series of empirical studies concerning the origins of deviancy definitions through political actions (in such areas as drug legislation, temperance legislation, delinquency definitions, homosexuality, prostitution and pornography) as well as the political bias in the apprehension and adjudication of deviants.

Labelling theory – with its rejection of so-called positivistic criminology – was closely allied to the development of the sociology of deviance. This sociology not only changed the theoretical base for the study of criminals, but also brought in its wake a dramatic restructuring of empirical concerns. Sociologists turned their interests to the world of expressive deviance: to the twilight, marginal worlds of tramps, alcoholics, strippers, dwarfs, prostitutes, drug addicts, nudists; to taxi-cab drivers, the blind, the dying, the physically ill and handicapped, and even to a motley array of problems in everyday life. It opened up the field of inquiry so that it was possible to discuss a range of areas hitherto neglected – blindness, subnormality, obesity, smoking and interpersonal relationships – thereby enabling both the foundations for a formal theory of deviance as a social property and a method for understanding the routine and the regular through the eyes of the ruptured and the irregular. Whatever these studies had in common, it was very clear by this stage that it was not conventional criminology.

The problems with labelling theory

Popular as the theory became, it was soon under attack. Among the most central criticisms made were the following:

- It is seen as a neo-liberal theory that gives too little attention to the state, power and the economy.
- From the political right, it is seen as overly sympathetic to the criminal and deviant – a proposal for going soft on crime.
- For rigorous positivist-minded social scientists, either it is untestable or, if it is tested, is found to be severely lacking in supportive evidence.
- Criminologists were usually unhappy about its neglect of the origins of deviance.
- More generally, labelling theory failed to provide any account of the initial motivations steering individuals towards deviance; it ignored the origins of deviant action.
- Closely linked to the above is the argument that labelling theorists had rescued the deviants from the deterministic constraints of biological, psychological and social forces only to enchain them again in a new determinism of societal reactions (Plummer, 1979).

Developments

Although labelling theory is always cited as one of the major sociological theories of crime and deviance, the original research and controversies that surrounded it during the 1970s have largely abated. The theory has become a quiet orthodoxy for some sociologists while being ignored by most criminologists. Yet several of its key themes have entered research under different guises. Three can be highlighted here.

The first is the theory of moral panics. An idea discussed by Howard Becker over the initial concern with drugs in the United States, it was developed further in the work of Stanley Cohen in his research on the panics concerning teenage mods and rockers in beach resorts on English bank holidays in the 1960s. The focus here becomes the exaggerated responses of control agencies (largely the media) in stirring up concern and anxiety. The study of moral panics has been applied to many areas and has become a staple feature of sociological research (Thompson, 1998; Critchley, 2003).

Plate 5.2 A youth lying on the sand at Margate, Kent, when mods and rockers clashed on the beach on 18 May 1964. The first major study of moral panics was that of this youth phenomenon of the 1960s.

Source: Associated Press.

The second is the theory of social constructionism. Much recent labelling theory has moved under this different name. This is an approach in sociology which argues that 'conditions must be brought to people's notice in order to become social problems' (Best, 1990: 11). Once again closely allied to Becker's notion of moral enterprise, it looks at the ways individuals, groups and societies come to label certain phenomena as problems and how others then respond to such claims. Joel Best, for instance, has traced the 'rhetoric and concern about child victims', while Joseph Gusfield (1981) has traced the drink-driving problem. Broadly, there is seen to be a 'social problems marketplace' in which people struggle to own social problems. This theory continues to examine the rhetorics, the claims and the power struggles behind such definitional processes.

A third area is the enhanced understanding of social control. Traditionally, many labelling theorists were concerned with the excessive encroachment of technology, bureaucracy and the state upon the personal life – often in its grossest forms such as the increasing medicalisation of deviance, the bureaucratisation of the control agencies and the concomitant dehumanisation of the lives of their 'victims', as well as the direct application of technology in the service of control. With the political shift to the right in many Western democracies in the 1980s, such concerns were co-opted as part of a market-based *laissez-faire* liberalism that aimed to roll back the state and introduce privatisation into social control. Despite this, labelling theorists have long been concerned with policies of decriminalisation, deinstitutionalisation, de-medicalisation, deprofessionalisation and the creation of social movements concerned with such activities (Cohen, 1985).

In sum: labelling theory highlights societal reactions to crime and deviance. It has a long history but became particularly prominent in the 1960s and 1970s. Since that time, and after a number of critiques, the theory has become something of an ortho-doxy. Currently, the theory of moral panics, social constructionist theories and theories of social control have become its modern day reincarnations.

CRIME AS CONFLICT

New deviancy theories returned power to the analysis of crime, and hence many sociologists also looked back to Marx and other conflict theorists to see the nature of crime. In the 1950s a major book by George Vold had already appeared, and had argued the need to focus more and more on inequalities and power. In his classic *Theoretical Criminology*, Vold claimed:

> The whole political process of law making, law breaking, and law enforcement becomes a direct reflection of deep seated and fundamental conflicts between interest groups and their more general struggles for the control of the police power of the state. Those who produce legislative majorities win control over the police power and dominate the policies that decide who is likely to be involved in the violation of the law.
>
> (1958: 208–9)

Many sociologists of crime came to adopt a conflict approach. We will just consider one brief example here.

Jeffrey Reiman and economic conflicts

One of the most accessible statements of the conflict theory of crime is Jeffrey Reiman's (1942–) *The Rich Get Richer and the Poor Get Prison*. Reiman shows how the poor are arrested and charged out of all proportion to their numbers for the kinds of crimes poor people generally commit: burglary, robbery, assault, and so forth. Yet when we look at the kinds of crimes poor people almost never have the opportunity to commit, such as antitrust violations, industrial safety violations, embezzlement and serious tax evasion, the criminal justice system shows an increasingly benign and merciful fate. The more likely it is for a particular form of crime to be committed by middle- and upper-class people, the less likely it is that it will be treated as a criminal offence (Reiman, 1979).

Ironically, for Reiman the criminal justice system is designed to fail – any success it achieves is a pyrrhic victory: it succeeds in its failures. As he says, 'On the whole, most of the system's practices make more sense if we look at them as ingredients to maintain rather than reduce crime' (Reiman, 2001: 4). It is a carnival mirror of crime: it reflects real dangers in our society, but it is a truly distorted image. We keep seeing and hearing about the wrong things in crime analysis, and the really serious crimes go missing. There are many other crimes that are far more costly and even dangerous but which never appear in the mirror. Much of his book is full of documentary evidence of the high cost of these crimes we neglect.

So for Rieman, the goals of a policy to eliminate crime are somewhat different. Most of his criteria are linked in various ways to establishing 'a more just distribution of wealth and income and mak[ing] equal opportunities a reality' (1979: 183). His work is often not discussed seriously by either criminologists or textbooks, but his book has been through six editions, has a major Website (provided at the end of this chapter), and seems to have become an idea that interests students more than it does the criminological profession. In part this may be a reflection of the fact that that very profession comes under attack in it!

THE NEW CRIMINOLOGY

Although there is a long history of conflict theories of crime (from at least Marx onwards), since the 1970s there has been a significant revitalisation of interest. A key book here was by the British sociologists of crime Ian Taylor, Paul Walton and Jock Young, called *The New Criminology* (1973; see Box 5.3). This was a substantial critique of all the theories outlined above, and more (each chapter takes a particular theory and dissects it). Broadly, they argued that most existing theories of crimes:

- had not looked at a wide enough range of questions (to take in the wider structural explanations of control as well as of crime, for instance);
- had often ignored wider material conflicts at the root of much of the criminal process;
- too frequently were deterministic in their assumptions and gave little role to the creative human actor willing to commit crimes;
- had inadequate epistemologies (theories of how we know the truth).

BOX 5.3 *THE NEW CRIMINOLOGY: FOR A SOCIAL THEORY OF DEVIANCE*

THE NEW CRIMINOLOGY

For a social theory of deviance

Ian Taylor, Paul Walton
and Jock Young

With a foreword by Alvin W. Gouldner

International Library of Sociology edited by John Rex

In this book, published in 1973, the authors, Ian Taylor, Paul Walton and Jock Young, review each of the major theories of criminology and find them lacking. They then argue that a series of key questions need to be addressed in any 'fully social theory of crime'. Their work is interesting both for its critique and for its framing of questions, and for over a decade it was one of the most influential books in British criminology. The questions it posed were:

1　The wider origins of the deviant act.
2　The immediate origins of the deviant act.
3　The actual act.
4　The immediate origins of social reaction.
5　The wider origins of deviant reaction.
6　The outcome of the social reaction on deviant's further action.
7　The nature of the deviant process as a whole.
8　The new criminology.

Plate 5.3　Cover of *The New Criminology*, published in 1973. It became a highly important watershed, taking stock of the old field of criminology and designating the requirements for a fully social theory of crime.

Source: © Routledge.

They argued that limitations were not just to be found in the early theories (positivism and classicism), but equally to be found in the so-called radical or sceptical theories of the 1970s (labelling, new deviance, etc.). These failed to do many things – and the whole field had become 'exhausted, except as a form of moral gesture' (Taylor *et al.*, 1973: 14). At the time of writing, all the authors were Marxists.

From their work, a new position started to appear that was based on the 'materiality' of crime, and was variously called critical criminology, working-class criminology or neo-Marxist criminology. Much of it borrowed from conflict theory and Marxism. For some of these writers, the problems of the poor and the working class were not the truly serious problems of crime. On the contrary, it was the crimes of the powerful (Pearce, 1976), that deserved focus; the wrong crimes and the wrong criminal were being focused upon. This was the basis of much of the first wave of radical criminology.

LEFT REALISM

Since the mid-1980s, one group of criminologists – from a conflict, Marxist background – have introduced the idea of left realism. Seeing crime as a serious problem, especially in inner-city areas, and one that has grown in recent years, they analyse what they call 'the square' of crime: the state, society and the public at large, offenders and victims (Figure 5.1). All four factors need to be looked at for all types of crime. Victims of crime are overwhelmingly poor, working-class people and, often, those who are marginalised and deprived because of their ethnicity. For example, unskilled workers are twice as likely to be burgled as other workers. *Much crime, then, is committed by the working class on the working class.* Young *et al.* argue that the causes of crime need to be looked for in deep structural inequalities. Crime is produced by **relative deprivation** – a perceived disadvantage arising from a specific comparison – and **marginalisation**, where people live on the edge of society and outside of the mainstream with little stake in society overall.

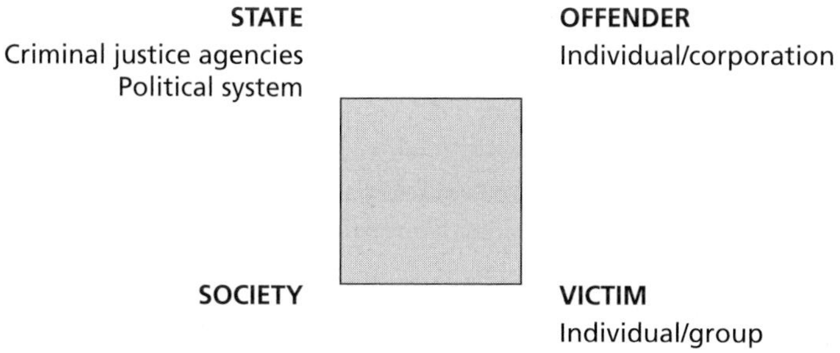

STATE
Criminal justice agencies
Political system

OFFENDER
Individual/corporation

SOCIETY

VICTIM
Individual/group

Figure 5.1 The square of crime.
Source: After Young (1997).

All this calls for the pursuit of justice at a wide level. The new realists argue for policies involving fundamental shifts in economic situations, enlightened prison policies, environmental design and accountable police. They stress that crime needs to be taken seriously and confronted by politicians, policymakers and academics – and the public's concerns listened to.

The stated aims of new left realists are to avoid over-general accounts of crime and to see crime in context. The specific shapes of crime, its causes and the way they are controlled change across the world as the society changes. New causes of crime and new patterns of crime appear worldwide. Ian Taylor, for example, argues that the strong shift to a 'market society' since the time of Margaret Thatcher and Ronald Reagan has not just tended to promote more 'ugly' crime, but also brought more 'brutish' penal responses. He sees a number of transitions that need to be dealt with in understanding current crime, including:

- The jobs crisis. New forms of work, as described in Chapter 6, have brought much less stable working conditions, together with underemployment and low pay. This provides a context for many young men especially to find better opportunities for a living in crime than in ordinary employment.
- The crisis of material poverty and social inequality. As we shall see, while most countries across the globe are experiencing some levels of prosperity, inequalities are widening. The marginalisation of whole groups of people makes crime an easier option.
- The fear of crime and 'the other'. The world appears to have become a dangerous place to live; there is a 'fear of crime' and a 'fortress mentality'. The heightened sense of insecurity makes many people unable to deal reasonably with the problem of crime.
- The crisis in the family and the wider culture.

LEFT IDEALISM?

With the arrival of a left realism, Jock Young (1975, 1979) and others could argue that critical criminology was fragmenting into a number of distinct strands, including what he identified as an 'idealist–realist' polarity. According to Young, the so-called left idealist position covers a range of perspectives on crime and the law – interactionism's micro-sociological approach (Downes and Rock, 1979), Marxism's macro-sociological approach (Sumner, 1976), abolitionism (Mathiesen, 1974) – and analyses of discipline and state power (Boyle *et al.*, 1975; Fitzgerald and Sim, 1979). Arguably, what unites them is an idealisation of the working-class criminal, a coercive conception of order, and an unwillingness to deal with aetiology, statistics and reform.

However, those identified as 'idealists' rejected the label and associated criticisms, and argued that their version of a 'criminology from below' against the authoritarian state and alliances with the radical penal lobby (e.g. the penal pressure group Radical Alternatives to Prison) was a response to the realities of life under Thatcherism. From their perspective there is a direct relationship between economic crises and political responses of the state and judiciary, leading to marginalisation and criminalisation of some groups and not others:

> [W]e are not saying that crime is not a problem for working-class people or that, contrary to the innuendo in some new realist writing, the terrible brutality suffered by many women is not a problem for them. Neither are we saying that the state cannot be reformed. . . . What we are saying is that the new realist position on law and order is theoretically flawed and, from a socialist perspective, it remains politically conservative in its conclusions about what can be done about the state.
>
> (Sim *et al.*, 1987: 59)

Divisions remain between the different strands of critical criminology. In recent years, many critical criminologists have also extended their work in different directions. For example, left realists have explored the socio-cultural context of law and order in a more reflexive fashion (Walton and Young, 1997), while others have oriented themselves towards a human rights discourse (Cohen, 2001; Scraton, 1999).

THE BIRMINGHAM CENTRE AND NEW SUBCULTURAL THEORY

Another important development that was taking place during the 1970s and early 1980s was the work based at the Birmingham Centre for Contemporary Cultural Studies (BCCCS), established in 1964 by Richard Hoggart (then a professor of English). It would be Hoggart's deputy, Stuart Hall, who would lead the Centre through its most influential period in the 1970s. Hall became director in 1968, before leaving in 1979 to take up the chair of Sociology at the Open University (Rojek, 2003). During his time there he encouraged many students to draw upon Marxist and critical thinking while still conducting empirical researches on crime and delinquency.

A good example of this was Phil Cohen's (1972) study of the emergence of 'mods' and 'skinheads' in the East End of London during the 1960s. In some respects it shared the Chicago School's emphasis on biography, place and change, but it also offered a distinctive class analysis of the destruction of working-class community and the erosion of its traditional culture. For Cohen (1972: 23), delinquent subcultures 'express and resolve, albeit "magically", the contradictions which remain hidden or unresolved in the parent culture'. In other words, the conflicts in adult culture are felt most acutely by the young and appear at various levels: at the ideological level, between 'traditional working class puritanism' and 'the new hedonism of consumption'; at the economic level, between a 'future as part of the socially mobile elite' or as 'part of the new lumpenproletariat' (Cohen, 1972: 23).

Youth style and delinquency do not solve the real crises in class relations. They are symbolic, or imaginary, attempts at resolving hidden problems, and examples of this, for Cohen, include the ways in which the original mod style was an attempt to realise the lifestyle of the socially mobile white-collar worker, as mods' dress and music reflected the hedonistic image of the affluent consumer. The later phenomenon of the skinhead he reads as a systematic inversion of the mods' pursuit of the upwardly mobile option. Instead, the skinheads followed the downwardly lumpen solution. Music and style were again the central focus of the action as they signified a reaction against the contamination of the parent culture by middle-class values, and the aggressive caricature of working-class values was regressively expressed through boots, braces and racism.

The Birmingham Centre refined this approach by explicitly drawing on Gramsci's (1971) work to locate subcultures not just in relation to parent cultures, but in a fully theorised understanding of class conflict. The conceptual framework is detailed in the chapter 'Subcultures, Cultures and Class' (Clarke *et al.*, 1976) from the collection *Resistance through Rituals* (Hall and Jefferson, 1976). Their argument is that 'cultural configurations will not only be subordinate to [the] dominant order: they will enter into struggle with it, seek to modify, resist or even overthrow its reign – its *hegemony*' (ibid.: 12; emphasis in original). The various post-war working-class youth subcultures discussed in the book are seen as movements that win back space, through issuing challenges to the status quo. However, these are not political solutions. Resistance is played out in the fields of leisure and consumption, rather than in the workplace. For Clarke *et al.* (1976), a key consequence of resistance through rituals and symbols is that it fails to challenge the broader structures of power.

One of the best examples of this approach is Paul Willis's *Learning to Labor* (1977), an ethnographic study of how school prepares young people for different positions in the labour market, as signalled very clearly in the title and the subtitle: *How Working Class Kids Get Working Class Jobs*. In his analysis of a Midlands secondary school he followed a group of working-class boys – the 'lads' – who opposed school authority and develop a subculture of nonconformity. Yet what he demonstrates is that the oppositional school culture of the lads offers only a limited resistance, and in fact prepares them for the shop floor culture of general labouring. In other words, having a laugh, skiving, being tough, sexism and racism are all forms of preparation for coping with work and will eventually trap them in dead-end jobs. The overall point is that symbolic resistance expresses the frustrations of working-class youth but will never develop into real power. In fact, as Willis's (1977) work tragically attests, the resistance reinforces inequality.

The Centre's most substantial work is *Policing the Crisis* (Hall *et al.*, 1978), in which Stuart Hall collaborated with Chas Critcher, Tony Jefferson, John Clarke and Brian Roberts to produce the most sophisticated statement of a 'fully social theory of deviance' (Taylor *et al.*, 1973) yet achieved. The book analyses the hegemonic crisis in the United Kingdom that began in the late 1960s and anticipates the victory of Margaret Thatcher's authoritarian 'law and order' programme in the 1979 general election. The first half of the book explores the moral panic that developed in Britain in the early 1970s over the phenomenon of mugging, and the authors demonstrate how the police, media and judiciary interact to produce ideological closure around the issue. Black youth are cast as the folk devil in police and media portrayals of the archetypal mugger – a scapegoat for all social anxieties produced by the changes to an affluent, but destabilised, society.

In the second half of the book they chart how the rapid deterioration of Britain's economic condition from the late 1960s meant that hegemony became increasingly difficult to sustain and the state turned from governance through consent to one based on coercion to control the crisis. The state's primary concern is to deflect the crisis away from class relations on to authority relations concerned with youth, crime and race – so that the white working class blame immigrants for the present conditions, rather than the faults contained in the capitalist system. In a discussion of the 'politics of "mugging"', Hall and his colleagues (1978) attempt to explain the rise in black criminality, which they see largely as the result of police labelling. But they do concede, within a broader consideration of black culture, consciousness and resistance, that some are forced into crime as a result of unemployment and a subcultural refusal to accept the lumpen role assigned to them under capitalism (see Chapter 18 of this book).

Some problems

Stanley Cohen (1980) (Plate 5.1, p. 69) developed a forceful critique of the Birmingham Centre's work in the introduction to the second edition of his *Folk Devils and Moral Panics*, which has become influential as it suggests the gap that had now developed between criminology and cultural studies. He begins by explaining how the new subcultural theory of the 1970s sought to radically distance itself, in both time and place, from the American functionalism of the 1950s via the 'the latest vocabulary imported from the Left Bank' (ibid.: xxviii). Yet for all the obscure Continental language, 'the new theory shares a great deal more with the old than it cared to admit' (ibid.: iv). The points of similarity are a focus on the same 'problematic':

- growing up in a class society;
- male urban working-class adolescents;
- delinquency as a collective solution to a structurally imposed problem.

Where the recent work does differ is through an 'over-facile drift to historicism' (Cohen, 1980: viii). What he means by this is that too much attention is given to contextualisation and historical development within Birmingham work, which often involves a particular emphasis on 'a single and one-directional historical trend' (ibid.: viii).

Cohen also raises a number of objections against reading resistance through rituals and symbols, which can be summarised as follows.

1   It is over-simplistic to understand resistance only in terms of opposition. Some actions will be conservative, irrational, inconsistent and 'simply wrong' (Cohen, 1980: xi).
2   There is a tendency to read the development of youth style as internal to the group, with commercialisation coming only later. This seriously underestimates the ways in which 'changes in youth culture are manufactured changes, dictated by consumer culture' (Cohen, 1980: xii).
3   Too often, subcultural activities are understood to be inherited from long traditions of working-class resistance which lead 'to the vexing issue of consciousness and intent' (Cohen, 1980: xiii) and the playing down of the meaning of style and subcultures to the members themselves.
4   He poses the question of why we should believe the interpretations offered of these subcultures and to what extent there is any sociological rigour in the conclusions drawn.

This is a formidable critique, and it is important to recognise that the Marxist emphasis on class was contested by feminists at the Centre in *Women Take Issue* (Centre for Contemporary Cultural Studies, 1980), and the relative neglect of 'race' was highlighted in *The Empire Strikes Back* (Centre for Contemporary Cultural Studies, 1983). Subsequent developments in cultural studies are too diverse to document here; but as we see in Chapter 6, there have been recent moves to take a cultural criminology further.

CULTURAL CRIMINOLOGY

The work of the BCCCS is often called a cultural criminology. But 'cultural criminology' more often refers to a hybrid of the 1990s that matched cultural studies with criminology. Its emphasis is on a critique of traditional motivational accounts of crime such as those of Merton or Lombroso, or even the new conflict theorists such as Jock Young who see the causes of crime as being in some ways pathological. Instead, the focus is upon much crime as fun, as being 'on the edge', as motivated by various pleasures and seductions. Graffiti, for example, or joyriding, some drugs, and even armed robbery bring an excitement often overlooked in classic accounts of crime. There is often a certain 'style', a 'cool image' that may be linked to them; and indeed a frisson of pleasure. Far from all crime being seen as pathological, some of it is now analysed as offering thrills, pleasures and subterranean (underground) values. In the words of one of its key books, these are the seductions of crime (Katz, 1988). These theories tend to focus upon particular kinds of crime and look intensely at the motivations and meanings for people who commit them. They often find pleasures involved in the act (see also Chapters 10 and 18).

Bakhtin (1984) suggested that there are moments in most societies when people are licensed to be irrational and offensive, and to transgress. Carnivals transgress and are an enjoyable part of everyday life. Consider the wild behaviour found at Mardi Gras carnivals in many countries. Most cultures have their own kind of carnival – think of the Notting Hill Carnival in London, or annual Gay Pride marches. When this idea is applied to crime, we have body modifications, joyriding, sadomasochism, drug use, raves, drinking, excess, risk taking, edgework.

A GENDER-AWARE CRIMINOLOGY

Another important development within radical traditions was the arrival of feminist criminology in the mid-1970s. It is an odd irony that the conflict analyses of crime we have discussed long neglected the importance of gender – despite their focus on social inequality. If, as conflict theory suggests, economic disadvantage is a primary cause of crime, why do women (whose economic position is, in general, much worse than that of men) commit far fewer crimes than men do?

Until the 1970s, the study of crime and deviance was very much a male province. But the influential work of British sociologist Carol Smart and others changed all that. In Smart's book *Women, Crime and Criminology* (Plate 5.4), published in 1997, she both documented the ways in which women had been neglected in the study of crime and deviance and showed that, when they had been included, the approach had usually been highly sexist or outright misogynist. Much later, Frances Heidensohn suggested that feminist scholarship over the past thirty years in criminology can be divided into two phases. First, there is the pioneering work that defined the agenda for the study of gender. Second, there has been consolidation, which has seen a range of studies produced in response to that agenda and debate over whether a feminist criminology is possible, or even desirable.

Plate 5.4 Cover of Carol Smart's *Women, Crime and Criminology*, published in 1976. Smart's path-breaking book brought women firmly into the sphere of criminological thinking.

Source: © Routledge.

Broadly, we can suggest three major contributions of the feminist approach:

- as a critique of existing malestream criminology – showing how women have been neglected, how they have been misrepresented, and how they may be brought back into existing theories;
- as a perspective to suggest new areas of study;
- as a way of bringing gender to the forefront and especially the role of men and masculinity in crime.

The critique of malestream criminology

In the 1970s, feminist criminology made its first contribution by making a major critique of the male bias inherent in the theories and writings of criminologists. Not only were nearly all leading theorists men, they also wrote almost exclusively about men – and when they did look at women offenders, it was usually with a set of assumptions that are at best called sexist. For instance, in one notorious case, a criminologist called Otto Pollak proposed that women are in fact *more* criminal than men: it is just they are also more devious and cunning and hence can 'cover up their crimes' better!

How does gender figure in some of the theories we have already examined? Robert Merton's anomie theory (see Chapter 4) defines cultural goals in terms of financial success, and this has traditionally had more to do with the lives of men, while women have been socialised to view success in terms of relationships, particularly marriage and motherhood (Leonard, 1982). A more woman-focused theory might point up the 'strain' caused by the cultural ideals of equality clashing with the reality of gender-based inequality. It could help us see that different forms of deviance may emerge for women: those that are linked to marriage and motherhood. Indeed, women who do not marry ('spinsters') and who do not have children ('childless') are often seen as 'problems'.

Labelling theory may offer greater insight into ways in which gender influences how we define deviance. To the extent that we judge the behaviour of females and males by different standards, the very process of labelling involves sex-linked biases. Further, because society generally places men in positions of power over women, men often escape direct responsibility for actions that victimize women. In the past, at least, men engaging in sexual harassment or other assaults against women have been tagged with only mildly deviant labels, if they have been punished at all.

New areas of study: bringing women back in

But feminist criminologists have gone much further than reappraising past theories and assumptions. They have opened up a whole field of new questions and issues. Among the issues have been the importance of the fear of crime in women's, and especially older women's, lives; the gendering of sexual violence, and especially the growth of awareness of domestic violence, rape and incest; and the gendering of social control.

One aspect of this has been the study of women in crime. Partly this meant the study of criminal women: girls in gangs, women prostitutes, shoplifters and other crimes with which women are more closely identified. But here we will just give two brief examples: the growing interest in the ways in which women are handled differently by the police, the courts and prisons (often through what is called a code of chivalry), and the centrality of sexual violence to much debate.

A code of chivalry

Much work has focused around what has been called a code of chivalry involving double standards at work. Some studies have been unable to come to cut-and-dried conclusions over the issue of whether men and women are treated in different ways by the courts. In fact, one study indicated that violent women offenders received more sympathetic and individualised justice for serious crimes, while men got no comparable understanding. But the majority of the research does tend to picture courts as places that have conventional and stereotyped views of gender roles, which they then reinforce in sentencing. For example, Carlen's study of Scottish courts found that distinctions were made between 'good' and 'bad' mothers, and the kind of sentence they received depended on the category into which they were perceived to fall.

What unites most authors on this topic of chivalry is that women coming before the courts experience what is known as the double bind of 'double deviance' and 'double jeopardy'. 'Double deviance', it is argued, arises primarily as a result of the fact that women's crime rates are so low. This has significant effects, because those women who do offend are seen to have transgressed not only social norms, but also gender norms. Or to put it another way, since courts are so unused to dealing with women offenders, those who do come before them are seen as both rule breakers and role defiant, and they may be treated accordingly. For example, in Edwards's study of female defendants before the Manchester City Magistrates' Court, she found that women were much more likely to be subject to an oppressive and paternalistic form of individualised justice. She argues that 'Female defendants are processed in accordance with the crimes which they have committed and the extent to which the commission of the act and its nature deviate from appropriate female behaviour' (1984: 213).

The argument is that double deviance leads to paternalism, protectiveness and excessive punishment for women offenders. As a result, many women offenders feel that they are placed in 'double jeopardy'. That is, they are actually punished twice. First, they face the usual sanctions of the criminal justice system, but in addition they may be more harshly treated because they are seen as deviant as women. Therefore, it is not entirely surprising to find that in most of the studies, women characterise their experience in the criminal justice system as one that is particularly unjust. It seems clear too that women also face informal systems of social control and justice.

For example, the stigma involved in the loss of reputation is particularly profound and damaging. Carlen (1983) found that a number of women offenders received beatings from their husbands, as well as the punishment meted out by the court sentence. Similarly, Heidensohn argues that much of the sense of injustice felt by women who come before the courts stems from their perceptions of such agencies as male-dominated and unsympathetic to them. She puts it rather nicely: 'chivalry appears to be a medieval concept neither practised nor cherished by the courts today' (1987: 103).

Violence against women

Another major area of debate opened by feminist criminologists has been the nature of sexual violence. Domestic violence, sexual harassment, child abuse and incest, and of course rape have all been placed formally on the agenda (they are discussed in Chapter 9). According to the United Nations, 'At least one in five of the world's female population has been physically or sexually abused by a man or men at some time in their life.' Figures vary across countries and for differing kinds of abuse; but that such abuse is both widespread and frequently condoned makes it a crucial area for understanding patriarchy.

Bringing gender to the forefront: masculinity theories and the problem of men

Having done this groundwork, feminists saw the obvious neglect of criminology in focusing upon men as men. Statistics repeatedly show that many more men than women commit crimes. Indeed, as Richard Collier notes, 'most crimes would remain unimaginable without the presence of men (Collier, 1998; see also Jefferson, 2002). This dimension had been ignored – it was a key missing link. One further contribution of feminist criminology has been to raise the issue of men, and masculinity.

If there is such a skew towards men, could this mean that the whole process of crime is connected to gender? It must be a strong probability. We are not of course saying that all men are criminal and all women are not; but we are suggesting that there is something about 'masculinity' – or at least certain forms of it – that makes it more probable that men will commit crimes. We need, for instance, to explain why it is that men commit more crimes and women fewer. And indeed, once we start to raise these issues, a whole new field of questions and problems arises.

One issue becomes the ways in which girls and women seem to be more regulated. For instance, in virtually every society in the world there would seem to be more stringent controls on women than men. Historically, our society has restricted the role of women to the home. The family is their domain. In many public spaces and bars, women remain decidedly unwelcome: these places are men's domains. And more, women on their own in public places may be looked upon with some suspicion. In some countries the normative constraints placed on women are really very great: in Saudi Arabia, women cannot vote or legally operate motor vehicles; in Iran, women who dare to expose their hair or wear make-up in public can be whipped. They are severely restricted in their access to public spaces. In this sense, in many countries women simply have less access to the possibilities of committing crimes.

But another issue is surely the expectation in many cultures of what it means to be a man. There is now a very considerable amount of research and writing on boys and men – on 'maculinities' – in sociology. The term 'masculinities' is used to denote that there are many ways of being and doing masculinity, and these change with different kinds of social order and society. At the same time, prominent theorists such as Connell also suggest that a key feature is that of patriarchy and the ways in which men come to dominate women (in most if not all societies). These are bound up with particular times and places, and hence are far from always being the same.

Researchers such as Messerschmidt (1993, 2000), Collier (1998), Jefferson (2002) and Mac an Ghaill (1994) have looked at boys and men in their variety to sense the processes involved in developing different kinds of masculinity. They tend to sense that there is a dominant mode of masculinity to be found in many societies (what is sometimes called hegemonic masculinity) that highlights such issues as power, dominance, aggressiveness, achievement, competition, status attainment, and the like. Masculinities are always worked at and always contested: they are never fixed and stable once and for all. And researchers also sense a variety of alternative masculinities that develop – sometimes linked to ethnicity, or being gay, or resisting common patterns (as in some versions of the men's movement). Their concerns suggest that men can be seen often as 'doing their gender' (i.e. performing as men) through various criminal activities such as football hooliganism, violence, road rage, rape and corporate crime. These crimes all have very different styles and meanings, but they can come to display men as certain kinds of men – congruently frequently with what it is expected to be in order 'to be a man'. This is an exciting new area of criminological thinking, and one in which more and more research is being conducted.

FOUCAULT AND DISCOURSE THEORY

One final influence on current thinking about crime and control must be mentioned here. For in many respects, the key inspiration behind many contemporary debates within criminology has to be seen as the influential French philosopher Michel Foucault (1926–84). And yet it is vital to know that not only was he not a criminologist, he was also firmly opposed to criminology! He is a philosopher of the history of ideas, and his work looks broadly at a number of institutions each with their accompanying knowledge – criminology and the prison may be one, but he also looks at 'the birth of the clinic' as a distinctly modern way of handling health, the development of the psychiatric discourse and modern approaches to madness, and the development of our modern languages around sexuality. Very wide-ranging, he even asks questions about the very idea of what it means to be an 'individual' human being in Western societies.

Plate 5.5 Michel Foucault (1926–84). Foucault was a leading critical thinker who debunked the notion of criminology as a science. His *Discipline and Punish* (1977) had a striking impact on criminological study, but in many ways, as a philosopher of the history of ideas, he was an anti-criminologist.

Source: Magnum Photos; *photo*: Martine Franck.

Foucault questions the roots and patterns of ideas found in social life and how they help construct what is going on in social worlds. He holds no simple view of cause and effect or of knowledge being linear and straightforward. Instead, he sees ideas as circulating in local complexes. They are disordered, contradictory, fragmentary. For Foucault, there is no scientific hierarchy any more. Instead, he traces genealogies. In general, he has looked at a number of major changes that mark out the distinctive ways we think in 'the modern world' when compared with past ones.

We have already seen a little of his work in the opening pages of Part 2 of the book (pp. 31–2) when he compares the transmission from forms of punishment in the *ancien régime* classical societies (which focus on the body, especially physical torture) to the micro-politics of modern, capitalist societies (which focus on surveillance, classification and normalisation – especially through the medium of prisons). He is concerned with the way in which criminology as a discipline grows at the same time as a whole new apparatus of crime control is brought into being. The whole profession of criminology, he suggests, is there not really to solve the problem of crime but to extend and organise power and surveillance.

Always a radical and critical thinker, he saw dramatic ruptures with the past and suggested that these modern developments are not signs of simple 'enlightened' progress, but rather evidence of extending power and increasing surveillance. For Foucault, power is everywhere and works its way through **discourses** – bodies of ideas and language, often backed up by institutions. Thus, criminology is a discourse that invents or produces its own set of ideas and languages about the criminal as an object to be studied, backed up by many institutions such as the prison and the courts. Power works its way distinctly through this discourse to help shape the whole society's view of crime. 'Knowledge' in this view may act as a way of keeping people under control.

Many of Foucault's ideas challenge common sense. Whereas we like to see criminology as a science that studies and helps us understand crime, Foucault sees it as a discourse that extends surveillance and power relations. Whereas we like to see prisons as means of reducing crime, he sees them as mechanisms for extending crime. He is very clear what he thinks of criminology:

> Have you read any criminological texts? They are staggering. And I say this out of astonishment, not aggressiveness, because I fail to comprehend how the discourse of criminology has been able to go on at this level. One has the impression that it is of such utility, is needed so urgently and rendered so vital for the working of the system, that it does not even need to seek a theoretical justification for itself, or even simply a coherent framework. It is entirely utilitarian. I think one needs to investigate why such a 'learned' discourse became so indispensable to the functioning of the nineteenth century penal system.
>
> (Foucault, 1975/1980: 47)

As you can see, his ideas are controversial, very influential and much discussed. Some say he was one of the most brilliant figures of twentieth-century thought. Others feel that his difficult writing and complexity have detracted from engagement with what is happening in the real world (see also Chapters 9, 13, and 16 for further amplification of Foucault's ideas.)

SUMMARY

1   Labelling theory focuses upon the societal reactions to crimes – the role of law, social control agencies, the media, etc. in playing their part in shaping the nature of crime. Far from crime control solving the problem of crime, control may actually serve to shape and structure it. Key theorists are Lemert, Becker and Cohen.

2   In the mid-1970s, the publication of *The New Criminology* generated a concern with a wider range of questions about crime and brought neo-Marxism and conflict theory to the fore.

3   The research of the BCCCS re-examined youth subcultural theories of crime, placing a much greater emphasis upon culture and cultural forms. It had clear links to Marxist theorising.

4   The issue of gender was brought into criminology as a key element for thinking about crime.

5   Foucault sowed the seeds of a major 'anti-criminology' movement, arguing that criminology was a discourse through which power–knowledge relations were enacted.

CRITICAL THINKING QUESTIONS

1   Discuss the ways in which criminology has become 'radicalised' in recent years. Has this radicalisation helped to provide a more satisfactory account of crime?

2   What are moral panics? Identify a recent one you have seen discussed in the media. Does such a panic differ very much from the ones studied by Stan Cohen and Jock Young over thirty years ago?

3   Identify a contemporary youth delinquent culture. Which of the theories outlined in this chapter seem best at helping you understand it?

4   Trace the emergence of feminist criminology and assess its impact on refining what criminology is.

5   How would you account for the fact that men seem much more likely to be criminal than women?

6   Given so much writing and talking about crime, why has there been so little success in its reduction?

FURTHER STUDY

Becker, H. S. (1963) *Outsiders: Studies in the Sociology of Deviance*, New York: Free Press.
Lemert, E. (1967) *Human Deviance, Social Problems and Social Control*, Englewood Cliffs, NJ: Prentice Hall.
Two classic studies of labelling.

Maguire, M., Morgan, R. and Reiner, R. (2002) *The Oxford Handbook of Criminology*, 3rd edn, Oxford: Clarendon Press. This has become the key text: very comprehensive coverage of the whole field of crime and control by specialist writers. It is, however, expensive.

Messerschmidt, J. (1993) *Masculinities and Crime: Critique and Reconceptualization of Theory*, Lanham, MD: Rowman and Littlefield. Both are valuable introductions to the issue of gender.

Taylor, I. (1999) *Crime in Context: A Critical Criminology of Market Societies*, Oxford: Polity.

Walkgate, S. (1995) *Gender and Crime: An Introduction*, London: Prentice Hall.

Young, J. (2000) *The Exclusive Society: Social Exclusion, Crime and Difference in Late Modernity*, London, Sage. Two lively studies that examine the crime problem from a critical perspective.

MORE INFORMATION

Howard S. Becker Homepage
http://home.earthlink.net/~hsbecker/.
A comprehensive site with a selection of published papers and links.

Allyn & Bacon Publishers
http://www.ablongman.com/signup
Jeffrey Reiman's book: *The Rich Get Richer and the Poor Get Prison: Ideology, Class, and Criminal Justice*, 6th edition.

ACTIVITY

Watch some videos that display youth cultures and look for their language, values, symbols, etc. Have a look at *Rebel without a Cause* (1955); *Easy Rider* (1969); *Saturday Night Fever* (1977); *Heathers* (1988); and *Boyz N the Hood*, John Singleton's classic about surviving the pressures of family and street life in South-Central Los Angeles.

Social Change and Criminological Thinking

KEY ISSUES

▌ What is a late modern world and how is crime changing within it?

▌ What is the link between postmodernism and crime?

▌ What is the globalisation of crime?

▌ What is the impact of the 'risk society' on crime?

INTRODUCTION

The past few chapters have suggested a number of ways of thinking about crime that have been developed by criminologists over the past century and a half. Some of the ideas are now seen as outdated, but in general they have all provoked thought and can often be seen to persist – in new forms – to this day. We are still interested in ideas of the criminal person and of justice (Chapter 3). We still look at social explanations of crime and delinquency – such as the ideas established by the Chicago School (Chapter 4). And labelling, conflict theory and feminist theory are very much alive and well (Chapter 5). In this chapter, we will consider a few of the newer social trends as a background to the rest of the book. Once again, some of the ideas will be taken up in more detail later.

At the heart of this chapter is the idea that the world we live in is undergoing significant social change and that this is having an impact not only on the ways we think about crime but on the nature of crime itself. This chapter will suggest four general trends, each of which has specific implications for criminological thinking. These are:

- the movement to a late modern society;
- the drift towards postmodernist ideas;
- the speeding up of globalisation;
- the emergence of a risk society.

CRIME AND THE MOVEMENT TO LATE MODERNITY

Over the past decade or so, many sociologists have suggested increasingly that a somewhat different kind of society is in the making. In the past, a key perceived distinction that drove sociological work was that between traditional and modern society (Kivisto, 1998). For Marx, it was a move towards capitalism with growing conflict and exploitation; for Durkheim, it was a shift from mechanical society to organic solidarity (from a society based on similarity to one based on differences). And for Max Weber, it was a move towards bureaucracies (a process which George Ritzer has called McDonaldisation, whereby the principles of the fast food industry – efficiency, calculability, predictability and control – become increasingly applied to all of social life) (Ritzer, 2002).

But the modern world is increasingly seen as giving way to a late modern world, or to what the sociologist Beck calls a second modernity. (Box 6.1 suggests some of the key changes here; cf. Giddens, 1990, 1999.) As Ulrich Beck (2000) has powerfully put it:

> We live in an age in which the social order of the national state, class, ethnicity and the traditional family is in decline. The ethics of individual self-fulfilment and achievement is the most powerful current in modern society. The choosing, deciding, shaping human being who aspires to be the author of his or her own life, the creator of an individual identity, is the central character of our time. It is the fundamental cause behind changes in the family and the global gender revolution in relation to work and politics. Any attempt to create a new sense of social cohesion has to start from the recognition that individualism, diversity and scepticism are written into Western culture.
>
> (2000: 165)

BOX 6.1 THE COMING OF LATE MODERNITY

By 'the coming of late modernity' we mean to refer to a number of interlinked social, economic and cultural changes such as:

- Changes in capitalist production and exchange such as the emergence of mass consumerism, globalisation, the restructuring of the labour market, and the new insecurity of employment.
- Changes in families and households such as the movement of women into the paid labour force, the increased rate of divorce and the decreasing size of the family household; the tendency for more and more people to live on their own; the coming of the teenager as a separate and often unsupervised age grade; and the arrival of new patterns of intimacies (such as gay and lesbian partnerships).
- Changes in social ecology and demography such as the stretching of time and space brought about by cars, suburbs, commuting, information technology.

- The social impact of the electronic mass media such as the generalisation of expectations and fears; the reduced importance of localised, corporatist cultures; and changes in the conditions of political speech.
- The democratisation of social and cultural life such as the 'desubordination' of lower-class and minority groups, shifts in power ratios between men and women, the questioning of authority, and the rise of moral individualism.
- The reorganisation of class (and, in the United States, race) relations that occurred in the wake of late modernity's massive disruptions. This was made possible by the shifting economic interests of the skilled working class, the welfare state's self-destructive tendencies, and the economic recessions of the 1970s and 1980s. In the end, though, it was the political 'achievement' of leaders such as Margaret Thatcher and Ronald Reagan, with their reactionary mix of free-market economics, anti-welfare social policy and cultural conservatism (Garland and Sparks, 2000: 199).

Together, these dynamics have changed the collective experience of crime and welfare and the political meaning of both. Late modernity brought with it new freedoms, new levels of consumption and new possibilities for individual choice. But it also brought in its wake new disorders and dislocations – above all, new levels of crime and insecurity (Bauman, 1998). It is against the backdrop of such major changes that contemporary crime debates emerge (Garland and Sparks, 2000: 199; Young, 1999a; I. Taylor, 2000). We can summarise these changes briefly:

- As we enter a period of mass consumerism, so desires for commodities are increased. The need to have commodities grows, and there is an escalation in credit card use, with a potential increase in fraud.
- The restructuring of the labour market can lead to much more casual employment and work patterns, with more people entering the informal or underground economy. The new insecurity of employment can mean looking for alternative ways of survival, and crime may be one of these, especially in the informal economy.
- Changes in families and households have meant the growth of different kinds of household (from living alone to lone-parent households, from more and more people cohabiting to lesbian and gay partnerships) as well as growing numbers of women at work. These changes have led some critics to suggest that as the old traditional family declines, so the older controls on behaviour become weakened (Dennis, 1993; Morgan, 1978; Phillips, 2001). Others are projecting that as the population becomes older, so there will be a growth of both crimes among the elderly and the elderly as victims of crime (at present they figure relatively low on both counts) (Rothman *et al.*, 2000).
- As teenagers become a separate and often unsupervised age group, so their criminal activities and drug-using propensities increase.
- As girls become more equal, they may also become more prone to crime. The behaviour of teenage girls starts to change and become more aggressive and assertive.

- As we experience changes in social ecology, so all manner of new crimes connected to the environment come into being. Some writers have called these green crimes (they are discussed in Chapter 17).
- Shifts in demography and city life brought about by cars, suburbs, commuting – we now see the development of a 'night-time economy', and all manner of crimes that are facilitated by movement.
- The spread of new forms of information technology brings with it new patterns of crime – from cybercrimes to mobile phone theft.
- The social impact of the mass media such as film and television can produce images of crime through which people come to live their lives (see Chapter 18).

The exclusive society

An example of how crime is changing under conditions of late modernity can be found in the recent work of Jock Young in his book *The Exclusive Society* (1999a). In this he explores three kinds of division: economic (where people are excluded from the labour market), social (where people are excluded from civil society) and the expansion of a criminal justice system (which excludes more and more people from daily life). Young suggests that whereas there used to be a more consensual world of conformity – work and family were core values, the world was 'at one with itself' (Young, 1999a: 4) – from the 1960s onwards we see a world becoming torn more and more by crisis: 'from a society whose accent was on assimilation and incorporation to one that separates and excludes' (1999a: 7). Yet pluralism also grows – what he sees as a diversification of lifestyles, the immigration of people from other societies, and the proliferating glimpses of other societies. In this sense, everyone may now become a potential deviant. We have also seen the arrival of no-go zones, curfews and gated communities, while vast numbers of people start to experience penal exclusion – approaching 1.6 million are imprisoned in the United States, with 5.1 million under correctional supervision (1999a: 18). Young sees crime as the defining feature of modern societies – it is everywhere. True, there is a central core that is ordered and embedded, becoming an almost Disney-like 'squeaky-clean' world. But a cordon sanitaire encircles it, and we find whole groups subject to the new geographies of exclusion. He suggests that in all this,

> crime has moved from the rare, the abnormal, the offence of the marginal and the stranger, to a commonplace part of the texture of everyday life: it occupies the family, heartland of liberal democratic society as well as extending its anxiety into all areas of the city. It is revealed in the highest echelons of our economy and politics as well as in the urban impasses of the underclass.
>
> (1999a: 30)

Plate 6.1 Robocop – future image of crime control?

Source: © Rank Film Distributors, courtesy of the British Film Institute.

POSTMODERNISM AND CRIME

Closely allied to the above is the arrival of ideas and practices that have been called postmodern. **Postmodernism** is a much-contested field, but in general it suggests that a much less certain and more provisional view of the world is in the making. The grand or absolute truths that were being pursued in the modern world are now challenged and in their place we find partial and limited truths. Applied to criminology, it sees the whole criminology project of modernity as misguided. It still asks the same questions and still comes up with the same answers (though in more modern forms); and still the problem of crime remains. The whole criminology project has been misconceived, and it is time to recognise that.

Postmodernism tends to focus on contexts and meanings which differ from place to place rather than on grander abstractions. It sees a world made up of many shifting differences. And this brings with it a whole series of challenges to criminology – many of which were already there in some earlier versions of labelling theory (Cohen, 1997; Young, 1999a: 33). It is perhaps too early to see whether they are going to become prominent, for in effect they would lead to the disbandonment of criminology as a whole discipline as we know it now.

The basic arguments of postmodernism highlight that the search for a cause of the criminal, the search for general theories of crime, the look for generalities are indeed searches for grand meta-narratives that have now have had their day. *There is no one story to be told of crime.* Stories of crime now become fragmented, patchworked, pot-pourried. Indeed, postmodern criminology would probably not have problems with any of the ways of thinking of crime we have outlined above until they make grand claims for themselves – as being the 'truth' regarding crime. Our view is that postmodernism suggests *a more provisional world – one that is altogether less sure of itself*. Modernity brought many changes, and the criminological challenge of the twentieth century was to sift through these changes to 'solve' the crime problem. As was hinted at in Chapter 5 through the work of Foucault, criminology did not really work very well. Indeed, the more that people studied crime, the more crime seemed to grow! Although there has been much theorising about crime, many criminology books written and many courses taught, we seem to be no nearer to solving the problem of crime. Criminology as we once knew it may well have failed.

In the twenty-first century, this modern world is an accelerating one in which there is an increased sensitivity to diversities and differences. In this view, the world becomes less dominated by generalities and 'master narratives', and there is a turn towards 'local cultures' and their 'multiplicity of stories'. As Rob Stones suggests,

> Postmodernists argue . . . for respecting the existence of a plurality of perspectives, as against a notion that there is one single truth from a privileged perspective; local, contextual studies in place of grand narratives; an emphasis on disorder, flux and openness, as opposed to order, continuity and restraint.
>
> (1996: 22)

One study that claims to be a postmodern criminology is Stuart Henry and Dragan Milovanovic's *Constitutive Criminology: Beyond Postmodernism* (1996). It calls for 'an abandoning of the futile search for "the causes of crime"' and looks instead for 'the genealogies, drift, seductions, chaos, discourse, social constructions, structuration and structural coupling' (p. 153) as ways of thinking about crime. Constitutive criminology is based on the key assumption that human beings are responsible for actively constructing their social world primarily through language and symbolic representation, but at the same time are also shaped by the world they create. Constitutive criminologists argue that the basis of crime is the socially constructed and discursively constituted exercise of unequal power relations. For Henry and Milovanovic (1996: 116), crime is defined as 'the power to deny others their ability to make a difference'. For example, crime as 'harm' occurs when people have their property stolen from them or their dignity stripped from them, or when they are prevented from achieving a desired goal because of sexism, racism or ageism. Crime then becomes domination, whether by single individuals (e.g. robbers), collectives (e.g. organised criminals or corporations), or by state governments (as in genocide, for example). Furthermore, crime is the 'co-produced' outcome not only of humans and their environments, but also of human agents and the wider society through its excessive investment in crime – through crime prevention, criminal justice agencies, criminal lawyers, criminologists, crime news, crime shows, crime books, and so on. Indeed, criminal justice is seen as part of the problem, not the solution. In policy terms, constitutive criminologists emphasise the need to transform the prevailing social structures and institutional systems of oppression and to change the ways we think and talk about crime (e.g. through an activist engagement with the mass media – see Barak (1994) on 'newsmaking criminology'; see also Chapter 18).

Although some commentators have described constitutive criminology as one of the 'new criminologies' that warrants attention (Arrigo, 1997), others are more sceptical of constitutive theory's relatively unresearched state, the complexity of its arguments, its impact on revolutionising mainstream criminology, and its ability to offer practical strategies to reduce harm (Croall, 1996). Others worry that it still manages to assert the primacy of criminology.

A number of criminologists, for example, have more or less left the field of criminology for other priorities – priorities that no longer capture and keep them within the field of criminology. Carol Smart, for instance, in a now classic article sees no room for feminism within criminology – even though this was indeed her earliest claim (see Chapter 5). She now worries:

> It is a feature of post-modernism that questions posed within a modernist frame are turned about. So, for a long time, we have been asking 'what does feminism have to contribute to criminology [or sociology]?' Feminism has been knocking at the door of established disciplines hoping to be let in on equal terms. These established disciplines have largely looked down their nose (metaphorically speaking) and found feminism wanting. Feminism has been required to become more objective, more substantive, more scientific, more anything before a grudging entry could be granted. But now the established disciplines are themselves looking rather insecure and, as the door is opening, we must ask whether feminism really does want to enter?
>
> (1990: 83)

It is an irony of the times that some criminologists have decided to leave the field altogether for other (usually political) concerns at the very time when criminology has never been more popular among students.

COMPARATIVE CRIMINOLOGY, GLOBALISATION AND CRIME

A third trend in which contemporary criminology must be located has been the way the world has become increasingly connected. In Chapter 4 we showed how the sociologist Durkheim argued over one hundred years ago that crime was a feature of all societies. This is not to say that it is at the same level in all societies. To the contrary, there may be features of capitalism and late modern societies that bring with them the conditions for higher crime rates in some societies than in others. The rate of violent crime in the United States generally emerges as about five times greater than that of Western Europe; and the rate of property crime is twice as high. We are starting to enter here the field of criminology known as comparative or cross-cultural criminology: the branch of criminology that compares different societies and their patterns of crime and control. Nevertheless, the United Nations has conducted a number of crime surveys since 1972 and has suggested both that crime is on the increase in all parts of the world (but especially the West) and that there is an increased tendency to report crimes that occur. It commented in 1993:

The global picture is not an encouraging one. There has been an increase in the overall crime rate; and there is the difficult issue of the interrelationship between 'higher' and 'lower' crime rates in the context of socio-economic development. The future may be even more gloomy, as some projections seem to indicate.

(quoted in Findlay, 1999: 22)

Now crime has always existed across cultures – think of piracy, terrorism, espionage and arms dealing in the past, for example (Martin and Romero, 1992). What we are now seeing, however, is the multiple ways in which crime becomes not just a local phenomenon (as much of the previous discussion has depicted) but a world-linked one. Much crime flows across the globe. Hence an area of criminological thinking that is starting to develop is that of globalisation and crime.

BOX 6.2 WHAT DOES GLOBALISATION MEAN?

Globalisation is a very controversial topic and it has now entered criminology. What might it mean?

- 'Globalisation has something to do with the thesis that we all now live in one world' (Giddens, 1999).
- 'The process of increasing interconnectedness between societies such that events in one part of the world more and more have effects on peoples and societies far away' (Baylis and Smith, 1997: 7).
- 'Globalisation . . . refers both to the compression of the world and the intensification of consciousness of the world as a whole. . . . [It] does not simply refer to the objectiveness of increasing interconnectedness. It also refers to cultural and subjective matter namely, the scope and depth of consciousness of the world as a single place' (Robertson, 1992: 8).

Globalisation

Globalisation has become a popular term over the past decade, and is used to cover a wide array of concerns. Its meaning is far from clear. To start with, and simply, we can define it as *the increasing interconnectedness of societies*. **Globalisation of crime** may then be seen as *the increasing interconnectedness of crime across societies*.

Globalisation refers to the various processes by which the peoples of the world are incorporated into a single world society, global society (Albrow, 1990). It suggests that 'we all now live in one world' (Giddens, 1999a). More formally, David Held and his colleagues have argued that 'Globalisation is the widening, deepening and speeding up of world wide interconnectedness in all aspects of contemporary life, from the cultural to the criminal, the financial to the spiritual' (Held *et al.*, 1999).

We can get some quick idea of what is meant by globalisation when we think of the imagery of worldwide multicultural companies such as Coca-Cola, McDonald's,

Nike and Disneyland. These companies exist across the globe – and in a number of ways. They *produce* goods across many countries; they *market* goods across many countries; and they *present* their logos and images, which travel the globe ahead of them. Think of how McDonald's outlets can be found in many countries – even though the company had its origins in the United States. McDonald's are simultaneously loved by millions and hated by millions – as signs of convenience and the modern world, and as signs of corporation takeover and mass culture. Crime can be seen like this. It produces criminal goods, markets them and sends commodities – from arms and drugs to people and slaves – all over the globe.

But a linked concept is that of glocalisation, meaning that each community adapts and responds to the global flow. Coca-Cola is never quite the same in each country; there are modifications made. And this is true of global crime patterns too: although drug trafficking may involve globalisation – flows across the world – each culture has its distinct values and communities, which make its specific responses different.

The sociologist Manuel Castells (1998: ch. 3) has written about the 'global criminal economy' and, following the United Nations Conference on Transnational Crime in 1994, has identified at least six main forms it is taking across the world:

- *Arms and weapons trafficking.* This is a multi-billion-dollar industry whereby states or guerrilla groups are provided with weapons they should not have.
- *The trafficking in nuclear materials.* This entails the smuggling of nuclear weapon materials.
- *The smuggling of illegal immigrants.* There is now a widespread trade in people desperate to leave their home country to find security, work and a new way of life. Often this can be connected to international slavery, estimated to have involved around 27 million people (Bales, 1999). One recent account estimates that Chinese criminal gangs (Triads) make some $2.5 billion a year in trafficking migrants – often with disastrous consequences (Cohen and Kennedy, 2000: 154). For instance, in 2000 some fifty-eight Chinese people being smuggled into the United Kingdom were found dead on arrival; they had been packed into a lorry in unbearable conditions, with air vents closed. The driver was sent to prison for fourteen years.
- *The trafficking in women and children*, often linked to prostitution. Significant numbers of women and children may be moved from one country (usually the poor of Eastern Europe or the poor of Asia and Latin America) to richer countries where new sex markets are appearing (Kempadoo and Doezema, 1998).
- *The trafficking in body parts*, often called 'the new cannibalism'. Nancy Scheper-Hughes and Lois Wacquant say, 'we are now eyeing each other's bodies greedily as a potential source of detachable spare parts with which to extend our lives' (2002: 14). There is now a worldwide and thriving market in body organs from both live and dead donors. Sometimes these organs are taken from condemned or even executed prisoners (especially in China, where it is estimated that perhaps 2,000 organs are removed and sold each year (*New Internationalist*, April 1998: 15–17)). The flow is commonly one way: from the desperate poor to the needy rich (Scheper-Hughes and Wacquant, 2002).
- *Money laundering.*

Plate 6.2 Illegal immigrants from North African countries sit on the deck of the Guardia patrol boat as they arrive at Tarifa port after being intercepted on 9 September 2002. Spain has been battling to control a rapid rise in the influx of immigrants and had increased patrolling of the narrow and often treacherous Straits of Gibraltar that separate Morocco from mainland Spain.

Source: Anton Meres, Reuters 2002.

But this listing is far from complete. We can at least add to this 'green crimes' and cybercrimes, discussed elsewhere (see Chapter 18). Yet although these traffics in illegal commodities account for billions of pounds, there is one area which may well be the world's largest (perhaps after tourism) industry: the international trafficking in drugs.

BOX 6.3 INTERNATIONAL TRAFFICKING IN DRUGS

The illegal drug trade is found all over the world: cocaine in Colombia and the Andes, opium/heroin from the South-East Asian Golden Triangle, all along the Mexican border, Turkey and the Balkans, or Afghanistan and Central Asia (Castells, 1998: 169). In part, the proliferation of illegal drugs in the United States and Europe stems from 'demand': there is a very profitable market for cocaine and other drugs, as well as many young people willing to risk arrest or even violent death by engaging in the lucrative drug trade. But the 'supply' side of the issue also propels drug trafficking. In the South American nation of Colombia, at least 20 per cent of the people depend on cocaine production for their livelihood. Furthermore, not only is cocaine Colombia's most profitable export, but it outsells all other exports combined (including coffee). Clearly, then, understanding crimes such as drug dealing requires the analysing of social conditions both in the country of consumption and around the world. More and more, the comprehension of crime and deviance requires moving beyond the borders of one country to look at a host of international connections (see also Chapter 12).

BOX 6.4 THE GLOBALISATION OF SOCIAL CONTROL

In addition to crime taking on increasingly international dimensions, social control has also become linked to more and more international agencies. A good example of this is the Centre for International Crime Prevention, a United Nations organisation based in Vienna. Indeed, the UN has acknowledged the importance of crime prevention since 1948. At present it has three central programmes:

- The Global Programme against Corruption, which provides technical cooperation to a selection of developing and transitional countries, providing analyses of current problems and policies.
- The Global Programme against the Trafficking in Human Beings, which, as its name suggests, addresses trafficking in human beings, especially women and children. In a selection of countries, new structures are emerging for collaboration between police, immigration authorities, victim support groups and the judiciary, both within countries and internationally (linking countries of origin to destination countries).
- The programme for Assessing Transnational Organized Crime Groups: Dangerousness and Trends looks at organised crime groups across the world, focusing on forecasting future developments and strategies of such groups in order to facilitate the formulation of pre-emptive responses.

The rebirth of human rights theories

One of the consequences of global theories has been a major worldwide resurgence of interest in ideas concerning human rights, much of which is linked not just to rights but also to governmental mechanisms and crime. David Held and his colleagues refer to the 'human rights regime' that is spreading around the world, and cite an Argentinian human rights campaigner, Emilio Mignone, as saying 'The defense of human dignity knows no boundaries' (Held *et al.*, 1999: 65–70). There are over 200 human rights non-governmental organisations in the United States, a similar number in the United Kingdom and the rest of Europe, and it is growing all the time. Criminology's global concerns have aroused more and more interest in such rights issues (see Chapter 19).

THE RISK SOCIETY, ACTUARIAL JUSTICE AND CONTRADICTORY CRIMINOLOGIES

A fourth theme is that of 'risk'. 'Risk' is now a dominant theme in contemporary life, to the extent that virtually everything we do has some danger associated with it. There are two dominant explanations of our contemporary preoccupation with risk (Johnston, 2000: 23).

BOX 6.5 SOME MAJOR CHARTERS OF HUMAN RIGHTS

- United Nations Charter (1945)
- Charter of the World Health Organisation (1946)
- Universal Declaration of Human Rights (1948), which becomes the international Bill of Human Rights
- European Convention for the Protection of Human Rights and Fundamental Freedoms, and its eight protocols (1950)
- International Covenant on Economic, Social and Cultural Rights (1967)
- The UN Commission on Human Rights (UNCHR)
- The American Convention on Human Rights (1970)
- The African Charter on Human and People's Rights (1982)
- The Convention on the Rights of the Child
- Specific women's rights through the Fourth World Conference of Women Declaration and Platform for Action (1995)

See Ishay (1997).

One originates in the sociology of modernity and is primarily concerned with the emergence of an entirely new set of 'risky' social circumstances. Anthony Giddens (see Giddens, 1990) in his book *The Consequences of Modernity* (1999) argues that one of the defining features of late modernity is the development of a 'calculative attitude' in individuals and institutions to deal with the issues of risk, trust and security in these troubling times. He sees risk as being globalised (something that exists on a global scale rather than at a local level) yet also personalised, as it is built into people's subjective concerns about their identity.

Giddens's argument has much in common with Ulrich Beck's (1992) discussion of what he calls the 'risk society'. For Beck, the 'risk society' is a distinct stage of modernity that has replaced the 'class society' of the industrial era. He argues that politics in class society is concerned not with risk, but with the 'attainment and retention of social wealth' (Taylor, 1999: 207). In contrast, in the *world risk society*, new technologies are generating risks that are of a quite different order from those found throughout earlier human history. Of course, past societies were risky and dangerous places too – whole populations could be wiped out by major earthquakes, floods or plagues, for example. But Beck argues that new kinds of risks appear with the industrial world which are not 'in nature' but 'manufactured'.

These are associated with the many new technologies that generate new dangers to lives and the planet itself. These are humanly produced, may have massive unforeseen consequences, and may take many, many thousands of years to reverse. These 'manufactured risks' are taking us to the edge of catastrophe. The list of examples of new risks could be quite long: the changes in work and family patterns, fallout from the atomic bomb, the spread of networks of cars and planes throughout the planet, the arrival of AIDS as a major world pandemic, the development of genetically modified crops, the cloning of animals (and people), the deforestation of the planet, 'designer children' and 'surrogate mothering', the intensity of computer games and interaction; and so on and on. All have consequences that may be far-reaching and are at present unpredictable. Risk society, then, is a stage of development in which the pace of technological innovation generates global risks, such as nuclear war and environmental pollution. The risk society is a society of 'fate' as class divisions have been overridden by the similarity of destinies that we all share. For Beck, those of us who live in risk societies are no longer concerned with such matters as justice and equality. Instead, we try to prevent the worst, and consequently a 'risk society is one obsessed with security' (Johnston, 2000: 24). It is important to recognise that Giddens and Beck are concerned with the sociological preconditions of risk in late modernity, and neither explicitly addresses crime or punishment – although recent discussions of moral panics have found the thesis attractive (see Chapter 18 for further commentary on the reformulation of moral panic theory in light of these developments).

The second perspective has a rather different orientation, and has had more of an impact in criminology. This can be defined as a genealogy of risk. Broadly speaking, there are a set of authors who develop Michel Foucault's later work on governmentality (O'Malley, 1992; Garland, 1997; Rose, 1996; Smandych, 1999). In this work, risk is seen as a particular way of thinking born in the nineteenth century and is especially concerned with the historical development of the statistical and human sciences and their use of techniques to manage populations through health, welfare and social security reforms. According to this view, government during the twentieth century has become increasingly preoccupied with the management of risks through applying what are known as 'actuarial' techniques, which were developed in the insurance industries. What is important is that actuarial understandings of risk in insurance are associated with chance, probability and randomness as opposed to notions of danger and peril. It is important to keep this distinction in mind, for Beck and Giddens argue in contrast that in the risk society there has been an increase in the dangers arising from this latest phase in capitalism.

An especially influential statement of this second position is Malcolm Feeley and Jonathan Simon's (1992, 1994) discussion of what they term 'the new penology' in relation to a then largely unremarked set of transformations in criminal justice occurring in the United States. As they put it,

> the new penology is markedly less concerned with responsibility, fault, moral sensibility, diagnosis, or intervention and treatment of the individual offender. Rather it is concerned with techniques to identify, classify and manage groupings sorted by dangerousness. *The task is managerial, not transformative.*
>
> (1992: 452; emphasis added)

The new penology is based on **actuarialism**, probability calculations and statistical distributions to measure risk. Actuarialism underpins correctional policies. Feeley and Simon (1992) give the example of how at one extreme the prison provides maximum security at a high cost for those who pose the greatest risk, and at the other, probation provides low-cost surveillance for low-risk offenders. They coin the phrase 'actuarial justice' to express some of the internal tensions posed by the new penology. Jock

Young (1999: 67) develops these arguments further and explains that actuarialism is far from morally neutral as it involves the stripping of human relationships of their moral worth, 'rendering them "morally irrelevant"' (Bauman, 1995: 133, cited in Young, 1999a: 67).

The importance of Feeley and Simon's argument lies not simply in their view that the use of imprisonment, probation, parole and community punishments has in each case accelerated in recent times, but in that 'the new penology is in part the product of a societal accommodation to routinely high volumes of crime, as well as of the refinement of professional practices for monitoring, surveillance and aggregate management' (Sparks, 2000: 131). In other words, the causes of crime are no longer seen as important; instead, probabilities are central, for actuarial justice 'does not see a world free of crime but rather one where the best practices of damage limitation have been put in place' (Young, 1999b: 391).

It is clear that these authors have identified a new trend in crime control. However, one of the defining features of contemporary penal policy and practice is that they are governed by contradictory criminologies. In a series of influential publications, David Garland (1996, 2000, 2001b) signposts a set of developments associated with 'the culture of high crime societies' that are heralded in two types of contradictory criminology. One he describes as a *criminology of the self*, as it characterises offenders as rational consumers – just like us. The second is a *criminology of the other*, which defines the offender as a threatening stranger (Garland, 1996: 446). The criminology of the self gets its support from a wide range of recent theories, which include rational choice theory, routine activity theory and situational crime prevention theory, that combine to form a criminology of everyday life (see Felson, 1998). The defining feature of these theories is that they all start from the understanding that crime is a normal, common aspect of modern living. Crime has become a risk to be calculated, by offender and potential victim, rather than a deviation from civilised conduct caused by individual pathology or faulty socialisation – the hallmark of traditional criminology. Instead, the new criminologies of everyday life see crime as an outcome of normal social interaction.

What is also surprising about these new theories is the way in which policymakers have enthusiastically taken them up. The key significance of these theories is that their programmes for action are not addressed 'to state agencies such as the police, the courts and the prisons, but *beyond* the state' (Garland, 1996: 451; emphasis in original) to the organisations, institutions and individuals of civil society. The implication, then, is that the state has a limited capacity to effect change, and instead these theories look to the world of everyday life to reduce crime. So instead of relying on prisons to deter offenders, or the ability of the police to catch criminals, the sorts of programmes advocated include things like 'replacing cash with credit cards, building locks into the steering columns of cars', using CCTV in city centres, closing discos at different times, laying on extra late-night buses and using special routes to and from football matches. The central 'message of this approach is that the state alone is not, and cannot effectively be, responsible for preventing and controlling crime' (ibid.: 453). A central theme of neo-liberalism is being played out here, for what all these programmes are emphasising is that citizens themselves must take some of the responsibility for controlling crime – a strategy that merges with privatisation and welfare cuts that were characteristic of neo-liberal governments in the 1980s and 1990s.

However, it is also important to recognise that accompanying this administrative and largely technical, actuarial response to crime control, there has been an upsurge in the increasingly hysterical rhetoric and punitive language articulated by the political arm of the state. As Garland (1996: 460) argues, 'the punitive pronouncements of government ministers are barely considered attempts to express popular feelings of rage and frustration in the wake of particularly disturbing crimes', such as those surrounding the murders of young children that have been a deeply troubling aspect of recent times. These punitive responses are informed by a rather different criminology, which is of 'the other' and essentialises difference. As Garland (ibid.: 461) explains, it 'is a criminology of the alien other which represents criminals as dangerous members of distinct racial and social groups which bear little resemblance to "us"'. Consequently, offenders are defined as a different species of threatening, monstrous individuals for whom we should have no sympathy and for whom there is no effective help. The only practical and rational response is to have them taken out of circulation and incapacitated for the protection of the public, whether in long term imprisonment or, is becoming increasingly the case in the United States, by judicial killing.

So, to conclude, contemporary crime control is increasingly dualistic, polarised and ambivalent. As we have seen (p. 106) there is a *criminology of the self* that characterises offenders as rational consumers, just like us; and there is a *criminology of the other*, which invokes images of dangerous and outcast strangers. In the former, crime is seen as a matter of routine, and the intention is to promote preventive action, whereas the latter is concerned with demonising the criminal, while exciting popular fears and hostilities, and promoting support for state punishment. For Garland (1996: 459; emphasis in original) there is

> an emerging distinction between the *punishment* of crime, which remains the business of the state (and . . . becomes once again, a significant symbol of state power) and the *control* of crime, which is increasingly deemed to be 'beyond the state' in significant respects.

One sympathetic critic has argued that while Garland has grasped some of the ambivalence generated by the state in confronting its limits, his account 'achieves its effect by ignoring an array of other responses to crime which indicate quite diverse agendas and assessments of the fate of state-based crime control' (O'Malley, 1999: 181). John Braithwaite (2003: 13), however, argues that 'Garland makes a number of statements that are wrong at worst, misleading at best'. In other words, Garland is guilty of overlooking social responses to crimes of the powerful, which would reveal a rather different and more nuanced understanding of cultures of control.

SUMMARY

1   The contemporary world may be seen through the four key idea of late modernity, postmodernism, globalisation and a risk society.
2   Late modernity brought with it new freedoms, new consumption patterns and new possibilities for individual choice, alongside new levels of crime and insecurity.
3   Postmodernism suggests that there is no longer any chance of developing one general theory of crime, one dominant narrative. Instead, the world is seen as much more eclectic and provisional.
4   As globalisation speeds up and makes the world more and more 'one place', so there is also a globalisation of crime – with criminal activities ranging from money laundering to the trafficking of people – spreading across national borders.
5   'Risk' is now a dominant theme in contemporary life, and flags the ways in which the pace of technological innovation generates global risks, such as nuclear war and environmental pollution.
6   There is a criminology of the self in which offenders are seen as rational consumers and crime is seen as a matter of routine; and there is a criminology of 'the other', in which offenders are seen as dangerous and outcast strangers, exciting popular fears and hostilities, and promoting support for state punishment.

CRITICAL THINKING QUESTIONS

1   Does postmodernism mean the end of modern criminology as we know it? In what ways is criminology changing?
2   Is it fair to say that late modernity brings with it both an increasing crime rate and different patterns of crime?
3   Select any two areas of crime and consider how far they have become increasingly globalised.
4   What is the risk society? How far does this impact on crime?
5   Outline some of the major social changes that sociologists have suggested are taking place in the contemporary world. What implications do these have for (a) our understanding of crime; and (b) the nature and patterns of contemporary crime?

FURTHER STUDY

Altman, D. (2000) *Global Sex*, Chicago: University of Chicago Press. Deals with globalisation and sex, and has a considerable discussion on international prostitution.

Bauman, Z. (1998) *Globalisation*, Cambridge: Polity. A useful general guide to globalisation which does also suggest how the processes of globalisation may well be generating more social disorder and crime.

Cohen, R. and Kennedy, P. (2000) *Global Sociology*, Basingstoke: Macmillan. Excellent student text on globalisation, with a key chapter on crime (chapter 9).

Findlay, M. (1999) *The Globalisation of Crime*, Cambridge: Cambridge University Press. The first major study of crime and its global features.

Henry, S. and Milovanovic, D. (1996) *Constitutive Criminology: Beyond Postmodernism*, London: Sage. This is not an easy book, but it brings together a lot of ideas already discussed. Its claim is to build a new kind of constitutive or postmodern criminology that builds upon an array of different theories and that shuns any grand theory of crime.

MORE INFORMATION

The monthly magazine *New Internationalist* contains a wealth of global information.

See Steven Soderbergh's film *Traffic* for a vivid account of the international drug trade. The film won Oscars in 2001 and reveals drug trafficking on both sides of the law.

Centre for International Crime Prevention
United Nations Office for Drug Control and Crime Prevention
PO Box 500
A-1400 Vienna
Austria

United Nations Crime and Justice Information Network
http://www.uncjin.org
Provides links and information on the United Nations organisations combating crime on an international level including the following link:

United Nations Office on Drugs and Crime
http://www.odccp.org/crime_cicp_sitemap.html
The United Nations Office on Drugs and Crime (UNODC) is a global leader in the fight against illicit drugs and international crime.

United Nations Interregional Crime and Justice Research Institute: LMS bibliographic Database
http://www.unicri.it/bibliographic_database.htm
The Library Collection includes some 6,000 authors, as well as more than 300 series and 600 publishers. Documents are classified according to the LMS bibliographic field structure and subjects that are described according to the UNCRI Thesaurus:
http://www.unicri.it/unicri_thesaurus.htm

United Nations Interregional Crime and Justice Research Institute: World Directory of Criminal Resources

World Directory of Criminological Resources
www.unicri.it/html/world_directory_of_criminology.htm
This site contains more than 470 institutes covering some 70 countries. A number of countries, in particular developing ones, which do not have criminological institutes, have nevertheless requested that some of their bodies' services be included in the Directory.

PART 3 DOING CRIME

In this section, we introduce a range of topical areas in the study of crime. Different crimes raise different kinds of issues and this chapter attends to this. We do not look at all crimes but our chosen topics include property crimes, sexual offences, professional crime, drug use and what we also introduce as 'emotional crime'. We look, not just at the offenders, but also at the victims. Which is where we start . . .

Victims and Victimization

KEY ISSUES

▌ What are the different forms of victimization? How do they relate to power differentials in society?

▌ How does crime impact on individuals and the wider communities?

▌ What kinds of offences and their victims have been subject to most political and public attention, and which overlooked?

▌ What is the role of victims in the criminal justice process? What is their actual experience of the justice system?

INTRODUCTION

Crime is generally understood to be behaviour that is prohibited by criminal law. In other words, no act can be considered a crime, irrespective of how immoral or damaging it may be, unless it has been made criminal by state legislation. This conceptualisation appears straightforward enough. However, it tells us very little about the processes whereby certain harmful acts and victims routinely come to be identified and recognised as part of the crime problem while others remain hidden. A critical approach to the study of crime and its impact on individuals and society therefore requires us to reflect on questions such as: what is 'criminal'? How do legal conceptions of 'crime' and its victims come to be constructed?

Clearly, victims play a central role in initiating the criminal justice process. Without them, much of the work of the criminal justice process would come to a halt.

The numbers and types of cases entering the system and thereby eventually providing the workload for the courts, prison service and other conventional agencies, appear largely to be determined by the reporting behaviour of victims and witnesses, not action initiated by the police.

(Shapland, 1986: 210)

The fact that only a fraction of crime is reported to and recorded by the police, combined with low clear-up rates, means that only a small proportion of offences ever reach the court. (See Chapter 15 on the police and policing.) In all these cases, victim experiences can be prolonged and complex. An incident that occurred in perhaps a few minutes can become the subject of a series of inquiries that may last months or years after the event. Victims who come to court expecting that a trial will be an assertion of their wrongs can find that their probity is on trial as well.

So what do victims think of their experiences of the criminal justice system? Does the system fulfil their expectations of justice, or does the system further distress and disillusion them?

THE ROLE OF VICTIMS WITHIN THE CRIMINAL JUSTICE SYSTEM

In Britain, the role of victims within the criminal justice process is largely confined to reporting the crime and/or providing evidence. The significance of the victim's role in these areas is compounded by the fact that the vast majority of offences come to police attention through a victim's report rather than through patrolling activities. Furthermore, most crimes are solved through information obtained from the victim or another witness rather than through 'leads' developed independently by detectives (see Reiner, 2000; see also Greenwood *et al.*, 1977, on the United States).

Historically, however, the role of the victim was very different and much more extensive. Until the establishment of the New Police in 1829, local governance was based upon the fundamental principles of deterring and solving crime through individual and community self-regulation. Most crimes were considered to be a private matter between the offender and the victim (except, for example, in cases of treason or sedition). Private thief-takers established themselves to investigate offences for victims; many thief-takers also cashed in on the rewards offered by the government for the apprehension of offenders leading to conviction. The victim, or the victim's relatives or friends, would also make the decision whether or not to prosecute an offender, pay for a variety of legal documents and other expenses of prosecution and, more importantly, take on the role of prosecutor in court (Emsley, 1996a). This meant in effect some victims had greater access to justice (e.g. men of property) than others (women, especially in cases of sexual offences).

DEFINING CRIME AND VICTIMIZATION

Not all harmful activities are seen as criminal. As Steven Box (1983) has argued, power may itself determine that the crimes of the powerful have generally been excluded from public perceptions of the crime problem and, conversely, the victimization of the powerless may be understated. Criminal negligence leading to workplace injuries and deaths, environmental offences, the manufacture and sale of unsafe products, misconduct of corporations, politicians and the state, and so on are rarely perceived as 'real' crime (see Chapters 11, 17 and 19). These are also offences that do not have a direct, immediate and tangible victim. They go largely unreported and unprosecuted because of the problem of lack of victim awareness. Even when victims are prepared to take action, they and/or their families may have to embark on a long struggle to gain recognition of their victim status (for example, through the formation of a voluntary issue-based pressure group).

Conversely, there are no clear and unequivocal criteria to determine that acts defined as 'criminal' always cause harm to society. 'Victimless crimes' such as certain sexual acts between consenting adults, buying and selling of some illegal drugs and prostitution are often cited in this context (Schur, 1965). These are forms of behaviour that are illegal but consensual in nature. Because no criminal victimisation is occurring, the participants have no reason to complain to the police. The notion of 'victimless crime' has been used by some critics to condemn unjust laws and to further campaigns for legal reform, especially in offences against sexual morality (Jeffery-Poulter, 1991; Higgins, 1996; and see Chapter 9 of this book).

Whether or not the notion of 'victimless crime' is a valid one remains open to debate. For example, some feminists have argued that prostitution is not 'victimless'. Some women are coerced into it by individual men or criminal gangs. Others may choose to engage in prostitution and regard it as work, but prostitution is nonetheless a form of restricted and ultimately destructive choice, especially in countries that offer very limited options for women outside the commercial sex industry (McLeod, 1982; Miller, 1986; see also Chapter 9 of this book). Women run the risk of physical and sexual violence at the hands of clients or being harassed by the police on the streets. Society is also affected by the crime because prostitution objectifies women and reinforces stereotypical notions of women. From a law and order perspective, politicians and local residents who are in favour of clampdowns have also argued that street prostitution is not victimless as it may damage the reputation and quality of life in the neighbourhood. Similar arguments and counter-arguments have been raised in relation to illegal drug use in the context of the decriminalisation debate (see Chapter 12). In short, there are no clear, unequivocal definitions of 'consensus', 'harm', 'offender' and 'victim'. Such judgements are always informed by contestable, epistemological, moral and political assumptions (de Haan, 1990: 154).

THE HIERARCHY OF VICTIMIZATION

Clearly, some victims enjoy a higher status in the crime discourse, and their experiences of victimization are taken more seriously than others'. Many criminologists have highlighted the dangers of stigmatising the victims and of creating victim stereotypes. Nils Christie (1986: 18) defines the status of 'ideal victim' in the following way: 'By "ideal victim" I have . . . in mind a person or a category of individuals who – when hit by crime – most readily are given the complete and legitimate status of being a victim.' Put simply, the 'ideal' victim is typified by an elderly woman or child. Such people are considered weak, vulnerable, innocent and deserving of help, care and compassion. On the other hand, young men, homeless people, car owners who do not lock their cars, or a drunken victim of an assault are generally considered to be 'non-ideal victims' and less deserving of sympathy because of their characteristics, action (e.g. their risk-taking behaviour) or inaction (they should have protected themselves). As a great part of criminality is seen to be concentrated within certain groups and certain areas, both the stereotypical offender and the stereotypical victim may appear to be misfits inclined to unlawfulness, irresponsible, provocative and easily provoked.

The **hierarchy of victimization** (Box 7.1) and its impact on certain social groups may be best illustrated by the ambivalent position of women as victims of sexual and domestic violence (see Chapter 9). Historians have used a variety of sources, including court records, institutional records, newspapers and diaries, to show that in the past, only certain women and girls who presented themselves in certain ways were likely to succeed in bringing their case to public attention, or rarer still, to secure a conviction (Cox, 2003; Zedner, 1991). In the contemporary context, feminist criminologists have argued that focusing on the characteristics or behaviour of individual victims as precipitating factors in crime events has a tendency to reinforce gender stereotypes in explaining cases of rape and violence against women and in distinguishing between 'innocent' and 'blameworthy' victims. Indeed, the notion of victim precipitation can easily become shorthand for 'victim blaming', as the following excerpts illustrate:

> The chronically abused wife is one who permits her husband to beat her, refuses to take punitive action afterward, and remains in the same situation so that she may be beaten again. . . . A wife who has been beaten for the first time may be a victim. A wife who is beaten again is a co-conspirator.
>
> (clinical psychologist and marriage counsellor, quoted in Edwards, 1989: 165)

> Women who say no do not always mean no. It is not just a question of saying no, it is a question of how she says it, how she shows and makes it clear. If she doesn't want it she only has to keep her legs shut.
>
> (Judge Wild, 1982, quoted in Smart, 1989: 35)

> It is the height of imprudence for any girl to hitch-hike at night. This is plain, it isn't really worth stating. She is in the true sense asking for it.
>
> (Judge Bertrand Richards, 1982, quoted in Smart, 1989: 35)

As we see in what follows, such stereotyping has a serious impact on victims and the ways in which some social groups are dealt with by the criminal justice system. This in turn has led to unwillingness among some victims and witnesses to cooperate with the police and courts.

BOX 7.1 HIERARCHY OF VICTIMIZATION

The 'low-status, powerless groups' (Reiner, 2000: 93) whom the dominant majority in society see as troublesome or distasteful generally occupy the lower end of the hierarchy of victimization. Examples would be the homeless, the unemployed, those with alcohol and drug problems, prostitutes, youth adopting a deviant cultural style, football fans, and radical political organisations. The prime function of the police has always been to control and segregate such groups. And when members of such groups do report a crime to the police, they have to engage in a struggle to have their experiences taken seriously. This has often led to complaints from these social groups that they are being 'over-policed' as problem populations but 'under-policed' as victims. For example, the Lesbian and Gay Census 2001 found that although 1 in 4 respondents had been a victim of serious homophobic crime in the previous five years (including assault, blackmail, arson, rape, hate mail), 65 per cent of the victims did not report the crime to the police, mostly because they feared police harassment or had no confidence that the police would be sympathetic.

The hierarchy of victimization is also shaped by international politics. Not all those who died in a war have the same status as victims. For example, those from Allied countries who were killed during the Second World War were honoured as war heroes or remembered as civilian casualties while those associated with the Nazi regime (including innocent civilians who died in Japan as a result of the two atomic bombs) were seen as non-ideal victims. To a large extent, society's attitude to war victims is an encoded expression of wider political sentiment and relations.

DIFFERENT TYPES OF VICTIMOLOGY

While victimologists are highly critical of the traditional offender-oriented nature of criminology and share a common interest in developing victim-centred research, they differ in their assumptions and the focus of study. Various attempts have been made to classify the different strands of victimological thought. Karmen (1990) identifies three strands within **victimology**: the conservative, the liberal and the radical-critical. Each of these strands defines the scope of the discipline differently, reflects a particular understanding of the problem of crime, and connects with different positions within the victims' movement.

The *conservative* strand within victimology defines the discipline in four ways. First, it views crime as a distinct problem with particular focus on the highly visible forms of crime victimisation; second, it is concerned to render people accountable; third, it encourages self-reliance; and finally, it focuses on notions of retributive justice. This type of victimology generally aims to identify patterns of victimization and to examine the actions or patterns of 'lifestyle' of individual victims which may have contributed to the process of crime victimization. Indeed, many of the early victim studies within this tradition shared the assumption that victims are somehow 'different' from non-victims and that they are identifiable because they have particular, distinctive characteristics. For example, some writers set out to develop typologies of victims on the basis of psychological and social variables (von Hentig, 1948). Others, such as Mendelsohn (1956), have used the notion of culpability (from the 'completely innocent' to the 'most guilty victim') to understand the victimizing event though not without criticism (for examples of highly controversial studies, see Wolfgang's (1958) study of homicide and Amir's (1971) study of rape). In recent years, studies from this tradition have yielded some important information for policymakers and victims' movements and organisations. In particular, the development of national victim surveys has helped to place the issues of crime victimization and victimization prevention on the policy agenda (see the next section).

The *liberal* strand within victimology extends the conservative focus by including more hidden types of criminal victimization and abuses such as corporate or business crime in their analyses. Most victims of fraud are, by definition, unaware that they have been victimized at all, or unwilling to recognise that they have been conned (Box, 1983: 17). The intense media attention paid to high-profile business fraud cases and deceptions such as those involving Barings Bank, BCCI and the Maxwell pension fund has highlighted the plight of those who are their victims (including 800,000 depositors in 1.2 million bank accounts in over seventy countries in the case of the collapse of BCCI) and the devastating impact upon them (Levi and Pithouse, 1992; and see Chapter 11 of this book). The consequences of corporate crime may also extend to employees, tenants and consumers (Slapper and Tombs, 1999). This type of victimology is concerned with making 'the victim whole again' – for example, by considering the value of restitution, mediation and reconciliation as appropriate penal strategies.

The *radical-critical* strand within victimology sets out to extend the focus of the discipline even further. Its analysis extends to all forms of human suffering and is based on the recognition that poverty, malnutrition, inadequate health care and unemployment are all just as socially harmful as, if not more harmful than, most of the behaviours and incidents that currently make up the official 'crime problem'.

Furthermore, it considers the criminal justice system too to be a problem contributing to victimization. Thus, 'institutional wrong-doing that violates human rights' (Karmen, 1990: 12), police rule-breaking, wrongful arrest and false imprisonment, political corruption, and deviant or injurious actions of the state that may or may not be defined as 'crimes' are treated as legitimate areas for study (see Chapters 11, 15 and 19). By using broader social conceptions of victimization, this type of victimology promises to challenge dominant understandings of what constitutes the 'crime problem' and its impact on individuals and whole communities. In recent years, victimologists writing from this tradition have also turned to more structural explanations as a way of understanding the nature and process of victimization. For example, they have engaged in analysis of the wider economic and social context of victimization and structural powerlessness, and in political analysis of the rights of victims (see Mawby and Walklate, 1994).

CRIME VICTIMIZATION SURVEYS

A key aspect of victim-oriented research has been the development of crime victimization surveys. As Chapter 2 shows, the British Crime Survey (BCS) and other national victim surveys (e.g. in the United States, Canada, Australia, the Netherlands, Switzerland) have provided us with an alternative measure of crime and a more informed understanding of the impact of crime on victims, the social, economic and demographic characteristics of the victim population, and public attitudes to crime and the criminal justice system. Large-scale international victim surveys such as the International Crime Victim Survey (ICVS) have also been carried out so that some international comparisons can be made (see Newman, 1999). One of the key findings of the ICVS is that the experience of being criminally victimized has become a statistically normal feature of urban life around the world, though the type and extent of victimization vary. Local victim surveys with a narrower geographical focus have also made a significant contribution to our knowledge of crime. They have high-lighted the uneven distribution of risks of victimization, showing that certain age or social groups are more frequently subjected to crime than others.

Although crime victimization surveys have helped to redress an imbalance in early criminological works, provide insights into the hidden figures of crime and sensitise policymakers to the range and diversity of victim experiences with crime, they too have serious limitations. For one thing, they suffer from a general inability to tap certain forms of crime where there is no direct or clearly identifiable victim. Many crimes committed in the corporate boardroom, in the financial marketplace, on the Internet, or directed against the environment thus remain characterised by 'no knowledge, no statistics, no theory, no research, no control, no politics, and no panic' (Jupp *et al.*, 1999). Crime victimization surveys therefore carry with them very limited notions about what is crime and who are the victims. They have a tendency to focus the notion of criminality on the 'conventional' crimes while other equally harmful acts (and victims) remain hidden. Surveys that examine people's 'lifestyle' (cf. Hindelang *et al.*, 1978; Gottfredson, 1984) in order to assess how patterns of leisure activities and everyday behaviour affect the risks of victimization have also been criticised for ignoring the reality that lifestyles are often shaped by social forces and structural constraints.

There are also specific problems with using international victimization reports as a measure of crime. As we have seen in Chapter 2, international victimization surveys depend on the cultural perception of crime that may affect the respondents. Respondents in different countries may have different notions of thresholds concerning what they perceive as unacceptable and criminal behaviour. All this suggests that findings from victimization surveys must be interpreted very carefully, in the knowledge that any differences may reflect definitional variations as much as variations in prevalence or incidence.

SOCIAL VARIABLES IN CRIME VICTIMIZATION

Individuals are differentially placed in respect of crime – differentially vulnerable to crime, and differentially affected by crime. Indeed, there is evidence to suggest that the risk of crime victimization is unevenly distributed within and between different localities and various sections of the population. Existing victim surveys in Britain and elsewhere have highlighted social class, ethnicity, age and gender as key and intertwining variables in the patterns and rates of crime victimization.

Social class

Crime victimization surveys have consistently shown that the risk from property crime is unequally distributed among the population, with the poor generally bearing the greater burden of crime (see Chapter 8). Foster and Hope (1993) found in their analysis of BCS data that pockets of high unemployment in public housing estates also experienced very high rates of victimization. Indeed, many of the most deprived housing estates with drugs and/or high crime problems are found in areas evacuated by business and industry. Closure of local shops and other amenities reinforces a 'bad reputation' for the area and has adverse consequences for the availability of credit and insurance for residents (Pearson, 1987a). This has produced what the Rowntree Inquiry described as 'vicious cycles of decline in particular areas and on particular estates' (Rowntree Foundation, 1995).

The significance of class in crime victimization has been a key issue for one particularly influential perspective in British criminology since the mid-1980s. As Young (1986: 21) puts it, the central tenets of 'left realism' are to recognise that crime is 'a very real source of suffering for the poor and the vulnerable' and to 'take crime seriously'. John Lea and Jock Young in their pivotal work *What is To Be Done about Law and Order?* (1984) drew attention to the fact that most crime is intra-class and intra-racial, committed by relatively disadvantaged perpetrators on similarly relatively disadvantaged victims. Thus, working-class crime (street crime, burglary, personal violence) is seen as a problem of the first order. The task of the left, so they argue, is to accept this reality, try to understand it and do something about it, rather than deny or overdramatise it (for a critique of left realism, see Chapter 5).

Age

Contrary to popular imagination, children under the age of 1 are more at risk of being murdered than any other age group; many of the victims are killed by their parents or carers (Home Office, 1997). In general, the more socially vulnerable the victim and the more private or intimate the setting of the crime's commission, the less visible the crime. In recent years there have been a growing number of revelations about the extensive abuse of children who have been in the care of local authorities.

By the mid-1990s, allegations of sexual abuse by community home staff had surfaced in Leicestershire, Islington (London), Dumfries, Buckinghamshire, Northumbria and Cheshire. In 1997, a tribunal of inquiry into abuse in children's homes in North Wales heard evidence from some 300 survivors accusing 148 staff of systematic violence and exploitation (Muncie, 1999: 23). Another example is child sexual abuse by women. Social stereotypes of femininity and motherhood mean that the criminal justice and child protection systems generally fail to identify women as perpetrators of sexual abuse, and accounts of (male and female) child victims tend to be disbelieved or minimised (Turton, 2000). Even when cases of abuse *are* reported and recorded, they are often considered to be 'atypical', 'one-off scandals', and something distinct from the more familiar crises of law and order.

Elder abuse also remains largely hidden behind closed doors of private households or care homes. There are other problems with assessing the extent of elder victimization: elder abuse is not conceptualised in legal terms, is not a clearly defined offence, and has no satisfactory working definition. According to one case review of social services in England, some 5 per cent of pensioners regularly suffer victimization. This is almost certainly an underestimate. Non-reporting often results from concerns over domestic privacy, and few cases end up in official statistics, let alone in court (Brogden and Nijhar, 2000: 48–9). Another survey by Ogg and Munn-Giddings (1993) found that one in twenty older people reported some kind of abuse, with the highest prevalence for verbal abuse.

Specific questions about victimization of younger people under 16 were not included in the British Crime Survey until 1992. Since then, British Crime Surveys have repeatedly shown that young teenagers are at least as much at risk of victimization as adults, and for some types of crime, more at risk than adults and older teenagers irrespective of class, gender or place. Among the 12- to 15-year-olds, a third claimed they had been assaulted at least once, a fifth had had property stolen, a fifth had been harassed by people their own age, and a fifth harassed by an adult (Aye Maung, 1995). Young men aged 16 to 24 had the highest risk of being a victim of violent crime (Simmons and Dodd, 2003). Studies in Edinburgh (Anderson *et al.*, 1994), Glasgow (Hartless *et al.*, 1995) and Teesside (Brown, 1994) produced startlingly similar results indicating routine experience by children and teenagers of different forms of abuse in the home and on the street, harassment by adults and other young people, as well as other forms of serious crime (including physical assault and theft). Few of these experiences are reported to the police, however, and youth victimization (as opposed to youth offending) remains low on the priority lists of the police and politicians. This, combined with the experience for many young people of being 'moved on', or stopped and searched, contributed to the argument that young people are over-controlled (as delinquents) but under-protected (as victims) (Loader, 1996; Anderson *et al.*, 1994).

Gender

Chapter 2 explains that victim surveys and official statistics have consistently shown that men are more likely to be victims of violent attacks, particularly by strangers and by other men in public spaces. Many work-based injuries also take place, where assault and intimidation commonly occur between men – from either managers or colleagues, as a result of unsafe working practices (Stanko *et al.*, 1998), or in the course of providing services to the public (especially in occupations such as the police and health service workers, security guards, publicans and bar staff) (Budd, 1999).

Women on the other hand are more likely to be victimized at home (Mirrlees-Black, 1999; Simmons and Dodd, 2003). Women are the main victims of reported and unreported sexual violence. This gendered pattern of violence is notable around the world, especially in Latin America and Africa (Newman, 1999). Women are also more likely to have experienced persistent and unwanted attention (e.g. 'stalking') than men (Budd and Mattinson, 2000). Such experiences of victimization are often made invisible in conventional victim studies, however. Indeed, critics have argued that victim surveys that are based on measuring discrete events cannot fully comprehend the pervasive, underlying threat to security that characterises the experiences of many women. Women routinely learn to manage their lives structured and informed by their relationships with men they know. In these relationships, many women during their lifetime learn to deal with habitual violence, bullying or prolonged abuse, in what can be described as 'climates of unsafety' (Stanko, 1990). Feminists have also pointed to the continuities of the gendered nature of violence in both war (particularly mass rape) and peace ('femicide' and domestic violence) (Jamieson, 1998; Brownmiller, 1975).

Ethnicity

Crime victimization studies have found that in the United Kingdom, people belonging to ethnic minority groups are generally at greater risk of crime victimization than whites (Fitzgerald and Hale, 1996; Percy, 1998; Clancy *et al.*, 2001). However, there are important variations. Smaller-scale, local area studies have revealed even more complex patterns of risk of victimisation and variations within and between different groups (e.g. some studies found black women and elderly Asian men to be at more risk), localities and offences (Brown, 1984; Jones *et al.*, 1986; Crawford *et al.*, 1990; Jefferson and Walker, 1993; Webster, 1994). Ethnic minority groups are also routinely subject to racial violence and harassment (see Chapter 10). Indeed, some violent offences are best seen as a 'process', as the cumulative impact of threats, domestic assaults, name calling, racial insults, abuse, graffiti and punching cannot be captured by the mere counting of each individual incident (Bowling, 1998).

Perhaps more damagingly, minority ethnic groups have pointed to persistent police failure in protecting them from racist victimization. Such criticisms have gathered momentum in the wake of the Stephen Lawrence scandal of the late 1990s in which the Macpherson Report (1999) found 'institutional racism' to be pervasive within the Metropolitan Police (and by extension elsewhere) and that, as a result, ethnic minority groups are unjustly treated. The poor response to crime victimisation of particular sections of society has serious implications, especially against a background of conflicts between the police and black communities, serious problems long associated with police use of stop and search powers and a number of successful claims against the police for civil damages (see Chapter 15). Confidence in the police and cooperation with investigations have no doubt been harmed by tensions and negative encounters between the police and those belonging to ethnic minority communities. Indeed, victimization and attitudinal surveys have provided evidence to support this. Africans and Caribbeans have generally lower levels of satisfaction with the police than do white respondents, while results are more mixed among Asian respondents (see Bowling and Phillips, 2002: 135–8).

THE IMPACT OF CRIME

Not only are social groups and individuals differentially vulnerable to crime victimization, they are also differentially fearful about crime. Fear of crime has come to be regarded as 'a problem in its own right' (Hale, 1992), quite distinct from actual crime and victimization, and distinctive policies have been developed that aim to reduce levels of fear. British Crime Surveys now regularly investigate the levels and character of this fear, categorising and measuring the emotional reactions prompted by crime. The BCS shows that those who are most concerned about crime tend to be women, the poor, those in unskilled occupations and those living in the inner cities, council estate areas, or areas with high levels of disorder. The young are most concerned about car-related theft. Women (especially older women) are far more likely to feel unsafe at home or out alone after dark than men. People in partly skilled or unskilled occupations are found to be more fearful than those in skilled occupations, while those who consider themselves to be in poor health or with disability also have heightened levels of concern about crime (Simmons and Dodd, 2003). Black and Asian respondents are also found to be far more worried about all types of crime than white respondents. In another national survey of ethnic minorities, nearly one in four black and Asian respondents reported being worried about being racially harassed (Virdee, 1997). The meaning of such fears and anxieties is discussed in Chapter 10.

Victims of specific crimes may be affected by the crime itself (i.e. **primary victimization**) or the way in which others respond to them and the crimes (i.e. **secondary victimization**). A particular crime may have an effect on victims directly in a number of ways. They may be physically injured, incur financial loss or damage to property or lose time, as a result of the crime itself or of involvement in the criminal justice process. Most existing studies have concentrated on the impact of more serious personal or property crimes (as opposed to the majority of everyday crimes or other high-profile cases of business crime or criminal negligence). These studies have highlighted the acute stress, shock, sense of intrusion of privacy, and adverse physical, practical or financial effects suffered by many victims (Maguire and Corbett, 1987; Shapland et al., 1985; Brogden and Nijhar, 2000; Lurigio et al., 1990). In cases of violence, there is evidence from the British Crime Surveys to suggest that the most common emotional reaction is anger, followed by shock, fear, difficulty in sleeping,

Plate 7.1 Cartoon on home security system.

Source: © Cartoon Stock, London, www.CartoonStock. com.

"George, this new home security system you bought... how much did it cost?"

and crying. Victims of rape, sexual assault and abuse have been found to suffer persisting effects related to their physical and mental health – for example, emotional disturbance, sleeping or eating disorders, feelings of insecurity, or troubled relationships over a period of time (Maguire and Corbett, 1987; Kelly, 1988; Sales *et al.*, 1984; Smith, 1989).

Such negative impact may be exacerbated by the reaction of criminal justice agencies and other experts (e.g. medical services) to the victim. On the basis of a series of interviews with victims of interpersonal crimes, Shapland *et al.* (1985) found that many victims were poorly informed about the criminal justice process, including the possibility of state compensation. Perhaps more significantly, the study found that victims began with very positive views of the system's response to their problems, but became increasingly critical as their cases progressed. In the initial stages, much of the sense of secondary victimization felt by victims stems from their perceptions of the police as unsympathetic. Findings that the police are insensitive to victims are common to studies across a wide range of countries in which policing structures are very different (Newman, 1999). In the later stages, victims often perceive court appearances as threatening or bewildering.

The failings of the criminal justice system in the treatment of female victims have been well documented (Stanko, 1994; Dobash *et al.*, 1995). In particular, there has been public concern about the police's insensitive or even hostile treatment of female victims of sexual offences – for example, in acquaintance attacks or in cases where the woman's demeanour or dress code is seen to be 'provocative' (Edwards, 1989; Hanmer *et al.*, 1989; Gregory and Lees, 1999; see also Chapter 9 of this book). The problem of secondary victimization of some victims was dramatically highlighted in 1982 by an episode of Roger Graef's TV documentary on the Thames Valley Police which showed a very disturbing interrogation of a rape victim by two male officers. Indeed, the police response to men's violence against women is important not only for individual women's safety but also because of its social significance. The police define which types of attacks are to be taken seriously and proceeded with, and which types of attacks are to be condoned or dropped (i.e. 'no-crimed'). By making a distinction between 'innocent' and 'blameworthy' victims, the police are also making a distinction between attacks they deem to be justifiable in society and those that are not. This decision-making process demonstrates that the police do not offer unconditional protection to all victims against all forms of violence. Instead, moral judgements are constantly being made based on gendered assumptions (or stereotypical assumptions about race, age and sexuality), biases within the police occupational culture, and the associated definition of what counts as 'proper policing'. For example, calls to domestic disturbances have always been a significant part of the police workload. However, they tend to be dealt with by officers without recourse to criminal proceedings, even when evidence of assault is present. As Robert Reiner argues, '"Domestics" were seen as messy, unproductive and not "real" police work in traditional cop culture' (2000: 135). But to be fair, this problem has been recognised by the police, and much effort has been made to improve police responses to the problem of domestic violence in recent years with mixed results.

Finally, there has been an increased recognition of the pains of indirect victimization. For example, the families of murder victims may suffer the profound trauma of bereavement, compounded by the viciousness of the attack or the senselessness of the murder (Rock, 1998). Paul Iganski (2001: 628–31) has also drawn attention to the range of harms generated by certain crimes that extend well beyond the initially targeted victim. The 'waves of harm' (see Figure 7.1) generated by hate crimes spread beyond the individual to the victim's 'group' or community in the wider neighbourhood. As one respondent in his study explains, 'it tends to get people really anxious and excited and . . . we like to call them domestic terrorism' (Iganski, 2001: 630). Other persons who share the victim's characteristics – and come to hear of the victim's plight – may potentially be affected by a hate crime. They may respond as if they have been victimized themselves. In this sense, hate crimes constitute 'message crimes'. The wave of harm can also spread to other targeted or socially vulnerable groups within and beyond the victim's neighbourhood. Furthermore, hate crimes arguably strike at the core of societal values, offending the collective moral code (see Chapter 10).

TOWARDS A VICTIM-ORIENTED CRIMINAL JUSTICE PROCESS?

It has been increasingly recognised that the victim has a key role in the criminal justice process. After all, most crime would remain hidden and unpunished without the

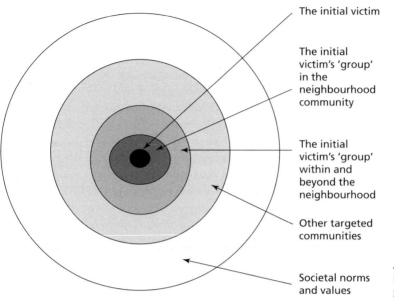

The initial victim

The initial victim's 'group' in the neighbourhood community

The initial victim's 'group' within and beyond the neighbourhood

Other targeted communities

Societal norms and values

Figure 7.1 Waves of harm generated by hate crimes.

cooperation of the victim in reporting the offence, providing evidence and acting as witness in court. The marginalisation and 'silencing' of many victims in the court process has been well documented (see Chapter 14), though more recent criminal justice developments in Britain and elsewhere may have gone some way to address that. There have been calls for increased victim participation in the criminal justice process, often in decisions as to bail, diversion from prosecution, levels of sentence and parole. A formal way of providing for victims' views to be taken into account is through what is known as a 'victim impact statement' (VIS) or 'victim statement' (VS). Such provisions are much more well developed in the United States than in the United Kingdom, and have received rather mixed receptions (Kelly, 1990; Justice, 1989). In the United Kingdom there is evidence to suggest that victim statements are supported by many decision-makers at the level of rhetoric (i.e. it is commonplace to endorse the idea of giving victims an opportunity to be 'heard') but not at the level of action (victim statements are sought and used only in a small minority of cases) (Morgan and Sanders, 1999). Critics have also argued that sentences should be a matter of public policy rather than dependent on the lottery of the forgiveness or anger of the victim, that the victim might feel even more frustrated and angry if the court appeared to ignore the VS/VIS, and that a more appropriate way forward might be to educate those working in the criminal justice agencies about the physical and psychological impact of victimisation on individuals and families (Ashworth, 1993; see also Miers, 1992).

So what are the limits and possibilities of developing a victim-oriented criminal justice system? In recent years, victim groups and voluntary or professional organisations have fought hard to raise victims' profile and to press for improved victim services and more sensitive treatment of victims by criminal justice agencies. In

BOX 7.2 VICTIM MOVEMENTS – SOME EXAMPLES AROUND THE WORLD

Victims, their families, voluntary or professional agencies and communities affected by crimes have mobilised themselves in different ways to force governments to take the problem of crime victimisation seriously.

In Brazil, where 300,000 people had been killed in the previous ten years, mainly as a result of the proliferation of guns in the country and urban violence (involving both criminal gangs and the state police), local communities and non-governmental organisations worked together in their attempt to find a solution to the problems of gun crime. On Mother's Day in 2001, the non-governmental organisation Viva Rio launched a campaign to bring together organisations and women from all sections of society (including mothers who had lost their children) to force the men of Brazil to give up their guns. Symbolically, a total of 100,000 weapons that had been seized by the police were heaped into a 400-square-metre pile and bulldozed in front of huge crowds in Rio de Janeiro. Community representatives also put pressure on the police not to involve children with guns, not to have guns in the open, and to put an end to police corruption.

In the United States a more conservative rights-based victim movement has been at the forefront of campaigns for extension of their role in judicial discretion (e.g. the right to make 'victim impact statements' to inform sentencing decisions) and often for a more punitive response to offenders. For example, the national community and victim's rights organisation Parents for Megan's Law was set up after a 7-year-old New Jersey girl was raped and murdered in 1994 by a paroled sex offender who had moved into her neighbourhood. The resulting legislative changes provide for stringent community notification requirements for convicted sex offenders if and when they get out of prison and, in some cases, for harsher sentences. Civil libertarians and other critics, however, have called the Megan's Law provisions a 'badge of infamy' that is attached to certain offenders for life. Other victim groups have also campaigned for indefinite confinement of sex offenders or for the retention or reintroduction of the death penalty for other offenders.

In Britain the central organ of the victim movement, Victim Support, has concentrated on lobbying for and providing services to individual victims (e.g. through the work of local volunteers), compensation, and provision for the victim in court. It has also been highly influential in shaping the government's 'Victim's Charter', which sets out the rights of victims, specifying how they are to be treated and the standards they can expect – for example, information about the progress of their case, about trial dates, and about bail and sentencing decisions. In addition, victim groups and concerned citizens have also been highly vocal in their demands for legislative changes or tougher sentencing in the aftermath of particular crimes (e.g. the murder of children, the Dunblane killings).

practice, expressions of victims' needs and interests are mediated by power differentials. Vocal, determined victim groups or those with most resources are generally better placed than the most vulnerable and least vocal victim groups to express their needs, lobby for change, or seek practical help or information. Furthermore, many critics have argued that the call for addressing victim needs and for orienting the criminal justice system away from the offender and towards the victim can easily become conflated with a populist 'law and order' approach to punishment. As Fattah (1986: 2–3) argues,

> Most victim advocates do not restrict their demands to a charter of victim rights or to a better lot for those who are victimized. These demands are usually coupled with, and in fact overshadowed by, calls for harsher penalties, stricter measures and more oppressive treatment of offenders. Getting-tough with offenders is often advanced as the central or, at least, as an essential component, of society's obligation to the victims of crime. . . . In this way, the noble cause of the victims of crime is used as a pretext to unleash suppressed vindictive impulses or as an excuse to act out the inhibited aggression against the offender.

While calls for 'justice' by victim groups can become overshadowed by or equated with a 'get tough' approach to crime and disorder, a victim-oriented criminal justice system also has the potential of paving the way for a more progressive approach to punishment. In recent years, there are signs of a growing interest around the world in communitarian ideas of reintegration and restorative justice whereby justice is primarily a process of reconciling conflicts and repairing harms or ruptures to social bonds resulting from crime (Braithwaite, 1989; Zehr, 1990). As Chapter 13 explains, the restorative justice model and the use of reintegrative shaming techniques, mediation and reparation aim to provide an alternative and more appropriate way of resolving disputes, confronting offenders with their wrongdoing and empowering the victims. However, one can argue that public demands for retribution as the organising principle of justice remain as strong as ever. For criminologists, the relationships between crime victims, offenders and the community will continue to be an important and highly contentious area of study.

SUMMARY

1 Victims play a central role in initiating the criminal justice process. In addition, there have been moves to increase victim participation at subsequent stages of the criminal justice process and to develop alternative means of resolving disputes, confronting offenders with their wrongdoing and empowering the victims.
2 Victimologists are highly critical of the traditional offender-oriented nature of criminology and share a common interest in developing victim-centred research. At the same time, they differ in their assumptions and the focus of study. There are at least three strands within victimology: the conservative, the liberal, and the radical-critical.

3   Some victims enjoy a higher status in the crime discourse, and their experiences of victimization are taken more seriously than others. In this sense, 'victim' is a social construct that reflects broader power differentials and stereotypes in society.

4   The risk of crime victimization is unevenly distributed within and between different localities and various sections of the population. Victim surveys and official statistics have consistently shown that men are more likely than women to be victims of violent attacks, particularly by strangers and by other men in public spaces. Women on the other hand are more likely to be victimized at home.

5   Victims may be affected by the crime itself or the way in which others respond to them and the crimes. There is also increasing recognition of the impact of indirect victimization on victims' families and communities.

CRITICAL THINKING QUESTIONS

1   Compile a list of ten stories about victims of different types of crime from any chosen newspaper. What do these stories tell you about the differential status of victims in media representations of crime? Is there a pattern to the types of victims who are portrayed as innocent and deserving of our help, and those who are seen as blameworthy?

2   Consider the advantages and disadvantages of increasing victim participation at different stages of the criminal justice process. What are the implications for procedural, substantive and negotiated justice (see Chapter 14)?

FURTHER STUDY

Davis, P., Francis, P. and Jupp, V. (2000) *Victimization: Theory, Research and Policy*, Basingstoke: Macmillan. A useful text examining the key theoretical and policy aspects of victimization studies.

Mawby, R. and Walklate, S. (1994) *Critical Victimology*, London: Sage. A critical and comparative analysis of victim services and other key issues facing crime victims within the criminal justice system.

Schur, E. M. (1965) *Crimes without Victims: Deviant Behavior and Public Policy*, Englewood Cliffs, NJ: Prentice Hall. A classic sociological text examining a range of 'victimless' crimes from the labelling perspective.

Wright, M. (1991) *Justice for Victims and Offenders*, Buckingham: Open University Press. A thought-provoking text on a restorative response to crime.

▌ MORE INFORMATION

Criminal Justice System Online: 'Victims Virtual Walkthrough'
http://www/cjsonline.org/virtual/victims.html
An interactive virtual tour that provides information about the criminal justice process as it relates to victims of crime.
The National Archive of Criminal Justice Data
http://www/icpsr.umich.edu/NACJD
Provides information on varous international crime victimization surveys

Crime and Property

CHAPTER 8

KEY ISSUES

▌ What can be identified as property crimes?

▌ How does the pattern of property crime vary across time and place?

▌ What are the characteristics of property crime offenders?

▌ How is the risk of victimization socially distributed?

INTRODUCTION

Official statistics around the world suggest that by far the most frequently reported crime is property crime (Newman, 1999). So what is property crime?

Broadly speaking, property crime involves stealing and dishonestly obtaining or damaging another's property, whether tangible goods or intangible property. All this may seem very straightforward. However, the distinction between what is unambiguously criminal and what is culturally tolerated behaviour is not always so clear-cut. For example, the dishonest acquisition of another's property is not always perceived as 'theft' by the offender or by the victim. Pickpocketing is seen as unacceptable and criminal, whereas hotel employees stealing food, wine or cash and hotel guests stealing linen, art or silverware from their rooms may be tolerated by the victim or justified as 'perks' or 'souvenirs' by the perpetrator. Similarly, we tend to associate 'fraud' with crime for gain or major financial scandals (see Chapter 11). Yet it is not always easy to draw a line between 'enterprise' and 'dishonesty', or between dishonest behaviour that is clearly 'illegal' and the hustles, scams and confidence tricks of 'con-merchants', false advertising of salespersons or pyramid schemes, and the behaviour of many others involved in everyday commercial exchanges.

In this chapter we look at the different forms and patterns of property crime, our attitudes towards its perpetrators, the characteristics of different types of property crime offenders, issues surrounding the risk of victimization and its distribution, and the impact of property crime on individual victims and communities. The aim is to challenge some of the popular assumptions about property crime and property crime offenders and to broaden our understanding of the crime problem and what is to be done about it.

PATTERNS OF PROPERTY CRIME

What we place into the category of 'property crime' makes a big difference to the range of behaviour we have to explain. Chapter 2 shows the problems of using crime and judicial statistics as a measure of actual levels of criminal activities in society. Nevertheless, crime statistics provide a useful starting point for understanding patterns of crime and the decisions of those responsible for controlling crime. From the 1830s onwards, crime has been classified into six main types: offences against the person; offences against property (with violence); offences against property (without violence); malicious offences against property; offences against the currency; and miscellaneous offences (Emsley, 2002). The pattern that can be drawn from the statistics shows a steady increase in crime, especially property crime, in the late eighteenth century, becoming much sharper from the first decade of the nineteenth century to the close of the 1840s, and then a general decline in crime until the end of the nineteenth century, except, most noticeably, for burglary (Emsley, 1996a: 32).

Many historians have explained the changing level of property crime by referring to the combined effects of key changes in British social and economic life during this period: population growth; urbanisation and the capitalisation of industry; and changing levels of unemployment and economic hardship. Historians who adopted a class conflict perception of society saw property crime as an element of the developing struggle between capital and labour. They argued that new work practices brought about by industrialisation, and changes in payment for labour and in notions of property ownership, meant that traditional rural popular culture and customs (e.g. gathering fallen wood for fuel, taking wild game, collecting scrap metal) were increasingly criminalised (Thompson, 1977). Seen in this light, the thefts of poor men might be understood as resistance to capitalism and new work discipline. Other historians, however, turn to social and court data that reveal a relationship between capital and labour far more complex than a simple class conflict model might suggest. They stressed the significance of changes in the administration of criminal justice (such as the establishment of the new police forces), the civilisation of the population, a diminishing fear about the dangerous classes, and a corresponding decline in the reporting and prosecuting of small-scale theft, especially in the second half of the mid-nineteenth century (see Emsley, 1996a). Court records show that most thefts involved everyday objects of relatively little value and that very many of the victims were relatively poor people. In the long run, the changes in the economy meant that people had more disposable income and more movable property, and shops had more goods for consumers, which in turn prompted changes in the opportunities for and style of theft.

The dominance of property offences continued into the twentieth century. Conventional and new forms of property crime were rampant during the Second World War even though it was commonly regarded as a golden age of community spirit and national pride. The war created massive opportunities for crime for everyone

– from organised gangs and professional criminals to 'ordinary' and 'respectable' people. Blackouts and bombed buildings made looting especially easy; because of rationing, many people took to fiddling and forging their food, petrol and clothes coupons; and profiteering and the black market boomed (Calder, 1991; Fraser, 1994). The steady increase of crime during the inter-war and post-war periods might arguably reflect the economic difficulties generated by the Depression as well as the temptations created by the first signs of the consumer society. For certain social classes and in certain areas of Britain, consumer booms (notably of the 1930s and 1950s) generated both more goods for those with disposable income and the desire for more goods, which very likely resulted in increased property crime. The consumer booms and technological revolution of the post-war decades put into circulation a mass of portable, high-value goods such as televisions, radios and stereos that presented attractive new targets and new opportunities for crime. For example, car crime rose sharply because there were many more valuable cars available on every city street at all times and often unattended than there were before the Second World War.

The range of property crime activities has also broadened significantly and, in some cases, developed into sophisticated transnational businesses generating high profits. For example, car theft is no longer simply a domestic problem or the province of teenagers engaged in random acts of theft. 'Thefts to order' (especially of luxury cars) are now well organised and sophisticated operations – from the theft itself, the forging of plates and documentation, through to the smuggling of the cars across the US–Mexican border or to 'far-flung destinations' such as Russia and China. Developments in computing and telecommunications technology have generated greater opportunities for theft and enabled new or existing forms of deviance to be carried out more extensively, more quickly, more efficiently and with greater ease of concealment (Grabosky and Smith, 1998; Thomas and Loader, 2000).

This argument can be extended to the emergence of 'new' everyday property crimes such as bank or credit card fraud. The expansion of automated banking and the increased use of 'plastic money' have posed a new set of risks to the banking industry and customers. The fraudulent use of stolen credit and bank cards was described as one of the fastest-growing, and most favoured, of financial crimes at local and street level in many societies in the late 1980s (Tremblay, 1986). The availability of cheap technology such as swipe machines, and simple techniques such as 'skimming', which involves reading and copying secret coded details on cards, has pushed up the costs of credit card fraud even further.

COMPARATIVE EXPERIENCES

With the notable exceptions of Japan and Switzerland, all the available evidence from industrialised countries points to a rapid and sustained increase in crime, especially property crime, in the post-war period. Such increases in crime have occurred not only in periods of economic downturn and depression but also during times of full employment and exceptional living standards. The 1960s were years of affluence, yet against all conventional wisdom, crime continued to rise in cities of the United States as well as in major centres of European countries.

Criminologists are divided as to the reasons behind such increase and, by implication, what should be done about it. For example, neo-conservatives such as James Q. Wilson have singled out the immediate post-war idea of a caring welfare state, the supposed permissiveness of the 1960s and the increases in crime as proof that social democratic theorising on the causes and solutions to crime was flawed (Wilson, 1975). The focus on the falling moral standards and weakening sources of social authority (especially in family standards) as major causes of crime had a significant influence on the law-and-order agendas on both sides of the Atlantic during the Bush, Reagan and Thatcher administrations. In contrast, writing from a left realist perspective, Jock Young has argued that even an absolute increase of prosperity at a national level tells us little about material inequality in society. According to the relative deprivation thesis, people have different expectations depending on what they feel they deserve. They may compare their economic situation with that of a reference group and feel relatively deprived when these expectations are not met. The argument is that faced with signs of evident wealth and possessions in neighbouring communities, unemployed youth could be motivated to commit street and property crimes because of emotional frustration, latent animosities and lack of opportunities (Young, 1986; Lea and Young, 1984; and see Chapter 5 of this book).

Following almost universal increases in property crime during the 1970s and 1980s, recorded property crimes in the United States, Britain and other European countries have since experienced a general decline. In the United States, recorded crime (comprising mainly property crimes such as shoplifting, vehicle thefts and burglaries) fell by 16 per cent over the period 1989–99. In England and Wales, property crime also generally fell during the latter part of the twentieth century (Barclay *et al.*, 2001). Criminologists are again divided as to the reasons behind such reductions in crime. While some American commentators have drawn attention to the

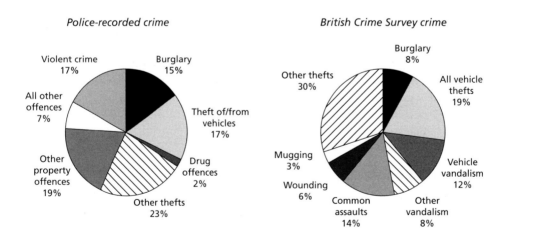

Figure 8.1 Police-recorded crime and British Crime Survey (BCS) crime by type of crime, 2002–3.

Source: Simmons and Dodd (2003).

Note: The BCS definition of common assault includes minor injuries. From 2002–3 the definition of recorded crime does not include minor injuries.

tougher criminal justice policies and substantial increase in imprisonment rates as possible explanations, the experience of other countries provides a counter to this. Canada's record on crime, for example, mirrors that of the United States, but without an equivalent increase in prison numbers. Variations in sentencing and imprisonment across Europe also challenge the idea that harsher punishment necessarily underlies the reduction in property crime (Newman, 1999).

THE HIDDEN FIGURE OF PROPERTY CRIME

In 2002–3, property offences accounted for around 80 per cent of all recorded crimes in England and Wales. They include burglary, theft and criminal damage (robbery offences are officially categorised as crime of violence). Of course, interpreting official statistics is fraught with difficulties. Official crime statistics do *not* provide an objective and incontrovertible measure of criminal behaviour. Instead, they often fluctuate according to the organisational constraints and priorities of the criminal justice system. For example, changes in police practices and priorities will have a significant effect on the official crime data. High-profile planned operations against a particular type of offence (such as burglary, drugs or street robberies) will inevitably bring about an increase in arrests and the discovery and recording of many new offences in the targeted areas. Conversely, numbers may fall owing to a withdrawal of police interest in a particular type of crime.

Globally, around two in three victims of burglaries report their victimization to the police. According to the International Crime Victim Survey (1989–96), the level of reporting is highest in New World nations (the United States, Canada, Australia, New Zealand) and Western Europe (over 80 per cent) but much lower in Latin America, Asia and Africa (between 40 and 60 per cent), mainly because the incident seems too 'trivial' or the victim feels nothing can be done about it (Mayhew and Van Dijk, 1997). In some countries, notably in Latin America, fear or dislike of the police is also a factor. The extent of insurance cover is another important factor. In most African and many Asian and Latin American countries, only between 10 and 20 per cent of the victim survey respondents (as opposed to at least 70 per cent in most industrialised countries) are insured against household burglary. All this suggests that a hidden figure of property crime exists around the world.

The dominance of property crime in the official crime data reflects not only the prevalence of certain types of property crime but also their high reporting rates. For instance, the British Crime Surveys (BCSs) have consistently shown that thefts of cars and burglaries in which something is stolen are almost always reported to the police, partly because of the seriousness of the offence, partly because victims who are insured need to report the crime in order to make an insurance claim. On the other hand, robbery, theft from the person, and attempted burglaries where nothing is stolen have traditionally resulted in much lower reporting and recording rates (Simmons and Dodd, 2003: 12–13).

Cross-national comparisons of victim survey data also suggest there are significant variations in the types of goods taken in burglaries and the motive behind the theft. In developing nations, stolen goods often include money, food and simple household objects such as cutlery or linen, most probably for personal use. One study in Central and Eastern Europe found that in many cases the burglars systematically stripped the home, even taking used clothes. 'In such cases the overall value of burglary might have been less, but the relative loss to the victim and the consequential impact of the crime might have been more pronounced' (quoted in Mawby, 2001: 41). In the more affluent countries, where most people keep their money and jewellery in the bank or in safes, burglars generally give preference to objects that are easily resold such as electrical appliances, VCRs, hi-fi equipment, furniture and art objects.

BOX 8.1 OPERATION BUMBLEBEE: A CASE STUDY OF A POLICE OPERATION AGAINST BURGLARY

Operation Bumblebee was launched across the Metropolitan Police area in 1993 as a high-profile campaign against burglary. There was huge publicity surrounding the operation through multi-agency partnerships, a poster and leaflet campaign, a 'stop and speak' campaign in crime 'hot spots' to create the impression of intensive police activity, and a 'Bumblebee property and crime prevention roadshow'. Significant police resources were directed towards preventing and solving burglary offences and raising public awareness of the problem. Dedicated burglary squads were set up to carry out intensive operations, targeting prolific local burglars or high-risk areas, backed up by surveillance teams and other services such as forensic science and local intelligence units.

Operation Bumblebee had a significant impact on the incidence of recorded burglary. In the seven months following its launch, recorded burglary offences fell by over 14,000, a decrease of 12.8 per cent. The police clear-up rate for burglary also increased from 10.9 per cent in 1992 to 15 per cent in 1993. There is no strong evidence to suggest that burglars had turned to other crimes or that there were widespread changes in police recording practices. However, research has highlighted several problems. Many of the offences were solved as a result of secondary detections, especially from post-sentence visits to offenders who then admitted other offences, not from primary detections. The 'stop and speak' campaign was seen to conflict with the style of local policing, and officers were apprehensive that such activity could be construed as harassment and would therefore lead to increased tension on the streets. Warning residents about burglaries using a public address system was also seen as counter-productive because of its contribution to fear of crime (Stockdale and Gresham, 1995).

PROFILE OF PROPERTY CRIME OFFENDERS

Throughout the eighteenth and nineteenth centuries, only a small number of property crimes involved large sums of money or very valuable objects, and very few cases involved violence. Perhaps unsurprisingly, most of the offenders brought before the courts for petty theft tended to be young, male, poorly educated (if educated at all) and poorly employed (if employed at all) in low-skilled, low-paid jobs such as labouring, domestic service and casual work. This pattern then continued into the late twentieth century, regardless of changes in the nature of low-skilled employment. All these factors informed the overall perception of criminality and reinforced conventional understandings of 'problem populations' in society.

It is undeniable that some people commit more serious property crimes than do others, and some people are more committed to a criminal lifestyle than others. Edwin Sutherland's (1937) classic formulation of professional thieves demonstrates their characteristics as a specialist occupational group defined by a level of commitment to illegal economic activities as a means of making a living. This insight paved the way for much subsequent criminological thinking and empirical work on the 'all-purpose criminal' who makes crime a career choice and a way of life: from the 'full-time miscreants' in British towns in the early 1960s (Mack, 1964), and short-term groups drawn together for specific 'project crimes' such as the Great Train Robbery (McIntosh, 1975), to the contemporary serious crime groups (Hobbs, 1995; and see Chapter 11 of this book).

A very broad distinction can be made between professional property crime and amateur property crime. These categories reflect the different motivations, levels of temptation, degree of skill, experience and planning, and illegitimate opportunity structures. For example, Maguire (1982) has identified three types of burglar:

"It's not 'just like taking towels from a hotel'. I think you should return it to the children's ward"

Plate 8.1 Cartoon of middle-class theft.

Source: © Cartoon Stock, London, www.CartoonStock.com.

low-level, middle-range and *high-level*. Low-level burglars are primarily juveniles and young adults. They lack a commitment to crime and do not usually think of themselves as 'thieves'. They tend to be opportunists whose involvement in crime is usually short-lived. Middle-range burglars usually begin their criminal careers at a young age and move into and out of crime. Generally, they are older, more skilful and experienced than low-level burglars and search out targets across a wider geographic area. They also tend to have access to external sources to assist them in the sale of their stolen property. High-level burglars are well connected with sources of information about goods to steal and with 'fences' who can dispose of large quantities of stolen goods. They carefully plan their crimes and possess skills and technical expertise to overcome complex security measures.

Of course, a wide variety of offences and characteristics of offenders can be found across a spectrum of property crime. To date, research on criminal careers has tended to concentrate on offenders involved in 'common' property crimes such as theft and vandalism (Farrington, 2002). Little research has been done on careers in other forms of property or financial crime such as consumer fraud, tax evasion, insider trading, embezzlement or money laundering. Some of these offences can be carried out only by those who hold office in a legitimate organisation or occupy an advanced position in the occupational hierarchy. Offenders may also move from one form of property crime (e.g. theft) to another (e.g. robbery), or from opportunistic offences (e.g. shoplifting) to more highly planned ones (e.g. stealing of museum pieces).

EVERYBODY DOES IT?

We should note that in between those deeply committed to a criminal lifestyle and those who occasionally steal or defraud lie a vast range of property criminals who are 'ordinary' or socially acceptable people. Almost two-thirds of adults interviewed in a recent study in England and Wales admitted to committing minor fraud (e.g. having paid cash in hand to evade taxes, having lied about an insurance claim, having claimed for refunds to which they are not entitled), but rarely think their behaviour is criminal. 'The worst offenders, and the chief victims, are the middle classes; typically young, employed high earners. . . . These are crimes that are committed at the kitchen table, or in supermarkets and restaurants' (*The Times*, 12 September 2003: 16). Similarly, studies in Canada suggest that shoplifting costs the retail trade over $1 million each day, and that between 1 in 12 and 1 in 20 customers admit to having stolen from shops (cited in Gabor, 1994: 73–4). Skyes and Matza's (1957) concept of neutralisation is useful to identify the techniques that many shoplifters use to deny or deflect blame for wrongdoing away from the perpetrator. For example, shoplifters may claim that shoplifting does not really hurt the store very much (denial of the injury caused) or that a particular store deserves to be ripped off because they exploit customers (denial of the victim). Such neutralisations allow individuals to redefine shoplifting as a more acceptable form of behaviour.

Theft by employees is also extremely widespread. In Britain the British Retail Consortium calculated that staff theft during 1997 cost shops a total of £374 million – that is, more than double the losses caused by burglaries and eight times greater than the cost of robberies (Park, 2001). The workplace has always been a key site of property crime. Indeed, Gerald Mars (1982: 1) wrote about the 'normal crimes of normal people in the normal circumstance of their work'. They include traders dealing in cash to evade VAT (Value Added Tax), taxi drivers who fiddle their takings, warehouse employees who overload and undercharge their friends, and shop assistants and cashiers in the retail trade 'voiding' a transaction or overcharging customers and pocketing the cash.

Occupational structure is a key variable in workplace crime. Mars contends that 'fiddles' are part of the elasticity of some occupations which emphasise individual entrepreneurship, flair, adaptability and professional autonomy, and in which group control of the workforce is low. For travelling sales representatives, journalists, lawyers, health professionals, academics and other relatively independent professionals, the conditions of work may create a criminogenic environment that opens opportunities and rationalisations for rule-bending and rule-breaking. For example, store managers can 'customise' their own 'shoplifting' by recategorising goods as old or damaged or altering stock records; journalists can fiddle their travelling expenses and slush money and rationalise these as 'perks' that come with the job. In contrast, in occupations that are highly structured and characterised by controlling rules, minimal autonomy and tight work-groups (e.g. in cargo-handling areas at airports, distribution centres and docks), fiddles often take place in the context of teamwork. Such practices are nothing new. Fiddling was common in the eighteenth century, when dockers often stole liquor, sugar or tea from cargoes as they unloaded them. Stolen items were then resold to grocers, publicans or ordinary people in the market (Emsley, 1996a).

THE SOCIAL DISTRIBUTION OF CRIME RISKS

Writing about the first BCS, Hough and Mayhew (1983: 15) cited the average household that could expect to be burgled 'once every 40 years'. Since the 1980s, the BCSs show that levels of risk have increased. Each year, 1 in 20 households are burgled or suffer an attempted burglary – equivalent to over 1.6 million burglaries in 1997. What these statistics fail to show is that burglary is unevenly distributed across time and space. For example, researchers have found that time patterns of burglars are often determined by the time patterns of their victims. Residential burglary occurs disproportionately during daytime when most households are unoccupied. On the other hand, commercial burglaries occur most often during the evening hours or at weekends when the business is closed. Studies in the United States also show that residents of large cities, renters and households headed by African-Americans, Hispanics or young people are more likely than others to be burgled (Shover, 1991).

In general, the risk of property crime victimization is unevenly distributed within and between different localities and various sections of the population.

Social class

Contrary to popular belief and anxieties about crime in rural and middle-class areas, researchers in Britain have consistently found that people living in run-down inner city areas and areas of council accommodation are particularly vulnerable to crime problems. Successive BCSs and police statistics have shown that, in general, poorer households with few home security measures in high-crime areas and areas of deprivation are most likely to experience residential burglary. In an evaluation of the incidence of crime in metropolitan inner-city areas compared with urban and suburban areas, Trickett *et al.* (1992) discovered that the prevalence of property offences was four times greater in the worst inner-city areas than in suburban areas and that the prevalence of offences against the person was eleven times as great. Similarly, Foster and Hope (1993) found in their analysis of BCS data that households in council estates with the highest levels of council tenure and poverty face a risk of burglary around five times greater than tenants who live in areas with less concentrated levels of council tenure and where tenants are better off. These households are also more likely to suffer a repeat burglary and are most affected by the crime(s).

Repeat victimization occurs when the same location, person, household, business or vehicle suffers more than one crime event over a specified period of time (Pease, 1998; Simmons and Dodd, 2003: 17–18). According to the National Board for Crime Prevention (1994), 4 per cent of victims experience 44 per cent of all crimes. For those who are subject to repeat victimization, it may become virtually impossible to differentiate the impact of discrete crimes from the generally poor quality of life. Those living in the inner city, council estates and areas of high physical disorder are also more likely than average to experience a second burglary within the year. In response, there is evidence to suggest that uninsured small businesses and young men living in deprived, high-crime areas are more likely to have purchased stolen goods as a means of minimising their losses (Sutton, 1998).

A similar pattern has emerged from local studies, indicating not only the problem of repeat victimization but also the 'lived reality' of people at risk. By focusing on particular localities these surveys (notably in Islington (London), Merseyside, Edinburgh and Rochdale) highlighted the higher levels of crime prevailing in socially deprived areas and the disproportionate victimization of women, of ethnic minority groups and of the poor (Crawford *et al.*, 1990; Kinsey, 1984; Mooney, 1993; Forrester *et al.*, 1988). Significantly, such high levels of social deprivation and crime victimization are also co-terminous with higher levels of poor health (see Chapter 12).

Ethnicity

According to the BCSs, ethnic minority groups (especially Pakistanis and Bangladeshis) are more at risk than whites of household crimes. It is of course extremely difficult to isolate ethnicity as a discrete variable in explaining patterns of victimization. Socio-economic factors and wider processes of racialisation may be at work here, if we take into account the fact that ethnic minority households are more likely than white households to experience poverty (that is, with incomes below half the national average) and to live in socially disadvantaged areas (Modood and Berthoud, 1997). Ethnic minority ethnic groups are also routinely subject to racial violence and harassment that range from murder, damage to property (including racist graffiti), to verbal and other forms of abuse of an isolated or persistent nature (see Chapter 10).

Age

Official statistics and self-report studies indicate the prevalence of property crime in young people's everyday life. Crime statistics have consistently found the 'typical offender' to be male (over 80 per cent of offenders known to the authorities) and young (almost half are under the age of 21). Similarly, according to a recent Youth Lifestyles Survey (Flood-Page *et al.*, 2000), almost 1 in 5 young people admitted committing at least one offence in the previous twelve months, and nearly three-quarters of all offences committed were property offences or fraud. However, any focus on young people as the perpetrators of crime should not be allowed to obscure or divert our attention away from the worryingly high levels of victimisation that young people suffer from their peers and adults. The BCSs have repeatedly shown that young people experience relatively more serious problems as victims of crime irrespective of class, gender or place (see Chapter 7). Few of these experiences are reported to the police, however, and youth victimization (as opposed to youth offending) remains low on the priority lists of the police and politicians.

Geography

Survey data has consistently highlighted the spatial concentration of the incidence of crime victimization – for example, in urban areas (as opposed to rural areas) and in the poorest 'striving areas' (as opposed to the wealthiest 'thriving areas').

It is not just the cities that have become synonymous with the 'crime problem'. Geographical research on crime and the use of computer-generated analyses of patterns of reported crime in different local police force areas (e.g. Crime Pattern Analysis) have pointed to particular concentrations of so-called 'hotspots' of crime. Research evidence in the United States and Britain suggests that even high-crime areas have their relatively safe micro-locations as well as their specific 'trouble-spot' areas (Sherman, 1995; Hope, 1985; Hirschfield *et al.*, 1995).

Writing from a different perspective, Ian Taylor (1997, 1999) highlights the shifting 'urban fortunes' behind the massive increase in crime in specific localities and regions from the late 1980s to early 1990s. For Taylor, the levels of crime in different localities are related to their varied capacities for responding to global economic competition, deindustrialisation and post-industrial restructuring. For example, industrial areas such as South Yorkshire which suffered the most recent loss of what was locally assumed to have been a secure labour market experienced the highest rates of increase in crime. On the other hand, Greater Manchester, 'the "youth capital" of the North of England with one of the largest post-Fordist labour markets in the

North', had the smallest increases in property crime and crime in general (I. Taylor, 1999: 134). Yet such 'new leisure zones' and their thriving alcohol-oriented night-time economy have other well-documented problems of violence and disorder (Hobbs et al., 2000; and see Chapter 12 of this book).

CONTROLLING PROPERTY CRIME

Our ideas about property crime (what form does it take?) and property crime offenders (who are they?) have also shaped our responses to the problem. 'Common' property offences such as petty theft, burglary and forgery were among the 200 or so offences punishable by death under the 'Bloody Code' in the eighteenth century. For example, the shoplifting of goods worth five shillings was a capital offence, as was stealing sheep or cattle. Transportation to penal colonies and prison were also used to punish a range of offenders. Indeed, prisons of different varieties have since emerged to occupy a central role in the criminal justice system even though their precise function and effectiveness are still subject to intense political and academic debate (see Chapter 16). Then as now, it was the 'quantity' rather than 'quality' of the offences that most concerned the public, legislators, the police and commentators on crime alike. The main exception was the periodic panic about violent street robberies (also known as 'garotting', or 'mugging' in the contemporary context) that prompted the revival of whipping for adults in the 1860s (Rawlings, 1999: 100, n. 1). Legislation and its enforcement were slow in keeping pace with the opportunities for large-scale theft, fraud and embezzlement provided by the expansion and development of the business and financial world during the nineteenth and early twentieth centuries (as they still are) (Robb, 1992; and see Chapter 11 of this book).

As Steven Box (1983) and others have indicated, there is considerable inconsistency in the way in which the criminal justice system perceives and treats 'the crimes of the powerless' as opposed to 'the crimes of the powerful' – business offenders. For example, if one measures the significance of property offences in terms of the value stolen, rather than the quantity of incidents, fraud has far greater importance than other categories. As Mike Levi (1993) points out, in April 1992 the Frauds Divisions of the Crown Prosecution Service were supervising cases involving nearly £4 billion. By contrast, the combined costs of the vast number of vehicle offences and burglaries for 1990 were estimated by the Association of British Insurers at under £1.3 billion.

The use of criminal justice response against low-level property crime offenders has particular consequences for those who are already economically and socially marginalised. Studies have shown that the rise in women's prosecutions from the 1980s onwards can be explained by a rise in specific areas, all related to continuing and worsening levels of female poverty (Carlen, 1988, 1998; Pantazis, 1999; and see Chapter 14 of this book). Similarly, the steep increases in the numbers of women received into prisons in the 1990s have been linked to the increased numbers of women in the categories of economic and social deprivation who have been traditionally more vulnerable to imprisonment (Carlen, 1998: 56).

BOX 8.2 KEY DEVELOPMENTS IN THE LAW AND PUNISHMENT OF PROPERTY CRIME IN BRITAIN

1808	Repeal of capital punishment for pickpockets
1820	Repeal of capital punishment for stealing in shops
1861 and 1916	Larceny Acts cover many types of stealing and provide for greater or lesser penalties depending on the nature of the property stolen, the place, the relationship between the thief and owner.
1968 and 1978	Theft Acts codify all offences against property and create a simplified definition of theft covering all types of stealing, embezzlement and fraud. The maximum sentence for theft is 10 years' imprisonment, 14 years for burglary and life imprisonment for robbery.
1971	Criminal Damage Act – maximum punishment for damage to property is 10 years' imprisonment, life imprisonment for arson.
1981	Forgery and Counterfeiting Act
1991	Criminal Justice Act reduces the maximum sentence for theft from 10 to 7 years' imprisonment.
1997	Crime (Sentences) Act increases prison sentences for certain categories of offenders, including a minimum of three years for a third offence of domestic burglary.

OTHER FORMS OF PROPERTY CRIME

So far we have concentrated on the more conventional forms of crime against property in everyday life. There are of course other forms of property crime with equally, if not more, harmful impact on individuals and communities alike.

Theft and illegal export of cultural property

The theft of cultural property is flourishing and now constitutes a major form of trans-national crime. Cultural property can be defined as movable or immovable property of great importance to the cultural heritage of every people. It can include monuments such as architectural works, sculptures, paintings, manuscripts, structures of an archaeological nature, cave dwellings, and sites that are significant from the historical, aesthetic, ethnological or anthropological points of view. Although looting of art treasures has long been a feature of warfare, illegal excavation and trade in stolen art and antiquities have been spurred by increasing pressure from the international art market. Crimes against cultural property have the potential for robbing entire cultures and nations of their cultural heritage (United Nations Educational, Scientific and Cultural Organisation 1997). In African countries such as Mali, the purchase for illegal export of cultural objects and looting of archaeological sites has increased rapidly since the 1970s. Objects tend to acquire higher prices the further they travel from 'home'. Art treasures, human remains, religious relics and sacred objects, furniture, and cultural objects in Nigeria, South Africa, Asia, Latin America, former Soviet-bloc countries and, to some extent, Western European countries such as Italy and Britain have been targeted in recent years (Box 8.3). Archaeological sites in the United States have also been looted and vandalised in the hunt for the best 'marketable' Native American artefacts.

The international trade in stolen, smuggled and looted art is estimated to be worth US$4.5–6 billion dollars per year (*New York Times*, 20 November 1995). Elaborate methods of distributing stolen art are often used to conceal the origin of the objects; as a result, it can take years to resolve disputes over the ownership of such art. For example, the Lydian Hoard, a collection of ancient treasures looted in Turkey, was purchased by New York's Metropolitan Museum of Art in the 1960s. It took the Turkish government almost twenty years to trace the whereabouts of the objects and another six years of legal action before the museum finally agreed to repatriate the objects. The illicit art market is populated by a mix of criminal organisations, individual thieves, 'fences' who act as the middle person, and unscrupulous collectors as well as legitimate traders such as antique dealers and institutions, including reputable auction houses (Conklin, 1994). This is yet another example of the symbiosis between legitimate and criminal activity, just like the cross-over activities in the entertainment and gambling industries, the arms trade and many other areas (see Chapter 11).

BOX 8.3 LOOTING AROUND THE WORLD

The British Parliamentary Report on Cultural Property: Return and Illicit Trade (2000) highlights the massive scale and impact of illicit excavations around the world. For example, the looting of the Early Bronze Age cemeteries of the Cycladic Islands in the Aegean may have resulted in the loss of 85 per cent of the relevant archaeological contents, and over 1,000 pieces of pottery worth about US$10 million are smuggled out of the Mayan region of Central America every month. Looting of sites in Italy is also a serious problem. A 1998 raid on a villa in Sicily seized some 30,000 Phoenician, Greek and Roman antiquities that were valued at US$20 million. The illegal trade, export and smuggling of Egyptian antiquities for sale abroad are known to cause substantial and irrevocable damage to Egypt's cultural heritage. The report suggests that England is one of the largest markets for illicitly traded property. Studies of antiquities from celebrated private collections in public exhibitions in Britain and North America during the 1990s, and the sale of antiquities in the London antiquities market suggest that an alarmingly high percentage of these objects had no provenance and history.

Theft of intellectual property

Theft of intangible property, such as copyright infringement, counterfeiting of trade-marks and making patented products, exists at different levels, from the individual computer owners who illegally copy video games or music at home (see Chapter 13) to the organised groups that engage in large-scale counterfeiting and smuggling.

Counterfeiting is a major activity for professional criminals in Britain, and has links globally, involving production of goods or currency and then distribution. Generally low risks and high profit margins make counterfeiting a very lucrative activity. Fake designer label clothing and other luxury items, counterfeit computer software and large-scale illegal reproduction of popular audio and video tapes are well-known examples. More everyday items such as soap powder, toys, shampoos, cleaning products and even tea bags have been subject to counterfeit and have resulted in injury (Croall, 1997). Currency counterfeiting faces the problem that daily use of money makes fake versions harder to pass, but this does not mean that such counterfeit circulation is uncommon. Indeed, the introduction of the euro across much of Europe in 2002 was predicted to be a boost to professional counterfeiters as this is a currency with which there is no history of familiarity and which is conceived and designed to be used in transactions across borders.

So who suffers and who benefits from the global trade in counterfeit goods? The answer is not always so clear-cut. Legitimate manufacturers and consumers (especially the poorer consumers who buy substandard or even dangerous counterfeit goods) are generally considered to be the main victims. In Nigeria, shortages of drugs and other technologies in the medical care system have led to the sale of 'counterfeit, substandard and otherwise dangerous substances', accounting for as much as 60–70 per cent of all drugs, and causing many instances of drug poisoning and death (Alubo, 1994: 97–8; and see Chapter 12 of this book). On the other hand, the counterfeiting industry arguably enables those who cannot afford the full prices to obtain similar consumer products and provides income for the unemployed, especially workers in developing nations.

Biopiracy

Finally, the question of 'who is the offender?' becomes even more contentious when applied to other non-conventional forms of property. For instance, patent law has been extended in recent years in such a way as to allow the ownership of DNA, cell lines and other biological materials. It has become possible for multinational corporations to 'own' DNA sequences and modified genes of animals and plants and to make significant profits through royalty charges for their use. Supporters of patent law point out that weak intellectual property regimes could foreclose opportunities for biotechnology research and product development. High research costs can drive up the price of the end products, many of which are important for public health needs. Critics, however, argue that the patenting of medicines, seeds, plants and – potentially – higher life forms by multinational corporations amounts to *biopiracy* and can have particularly serious consequences for the developing countries.

'Biopiracy' is a term that has been given to the practices of some companies that have asserted the right of ownership over genetic materials taken from living organisms (Manning, 2000). For example, the Africa Group in the World Trade Organisation has highlighted the serious implications that patents on seeds of staple food crops would have on the rights of indigenous communities to food security. It proposed in 1999, and again in 2001, that the mandated review of the Agreement on Trade-Related Aspects of Intellectual Property Rights should make clear that plants, animals and micro-organisms and their parts, and all living processes, *cannot* be patented. To some extent, these issues are related to the over-exploitation of the earth and its resources and have prompted some criminologists to reappraise more traditional notions of crimes and injurious behaviours and to examine the role that corporations and governments play in creating 'green crimes' (see Chapter 17).

NEW HORIZONS IN UNDERSTANDING PROPERTY CRIME

As Part 2 of this book shows, criminological explanations of why individuals commit property crime span a variety of perspectives from the dispositions of the individual offender to the social conditions associated with crime. For some offenders, survival and subsistence may well be the primary motivations for committing property crime. Other criminologists have argued that crimes such as shoplifting have to be understood in the broader context of the creation of needs, the structuring of consumption and the commodification of desire under late capitalism. Yet these societal processes alone cannot explain the meaning or the attractions of criminality.

Cultural criminologists (see Chapter 5) argue that criminology has traditionally underestimated the attractions in doing wrong or living 'on the edge'. The concept of 'edgework' was first put forward by the sociologist Stephen Lyng (1990; Lyng and Snow, 1986) in his analysis of voluntary risk-taking. He argues that 'edgework' can be understood as 'a type of experiential anarchy in which the individual moves beyond the realm of established social patterns to the very fringes of ordered reality' (Lyng, 1990: 882). Edgework activities that involve an observable threat to one's physical or mental well-being can be best illustrated by dangerous sports (such as skydiving, hang-gliding and rock-climbing) or by dangerous occupations (such as fire-fighting, combat soldiering, movie stunt work). More generally, edgework can also take the form of excessive drug use (which involves negotiating the boundary between sanity and insanity) or marathon running (which tests the limits of body). Lyng (1990: 863) argues that voluntary risk-taking provides 'a heightened sense of self and a feeling of omnipotence' for those who succeed in getting as close as possible to the edge without 'going over it'.

These ideas have been further developed by cultural criminologists such as Jeff Ferrell and Jack Katz. Katz (1988: 54) suggests that shoplifting can be understood as a version of a 'thrilling and sensually gratifying game'. It can be rewarding beyond the monetary gains – for example, providing the feelings of accomplishment when a theft is successful. Katz found that expressive motivations were highly prevalent in his interview data obtained from well-off college student shoplifters. Studies also found that burglars frequently cited excitement as part of their motivation, while others targeted occupied homes because such burglaries provide an 'illicit adventure' (cited in Mawby, 2001: 69).

Similarly, if we turn to the world of business, bank fraud, price-fixing or manipulating the stock market, all contain elements of the thrills and spills of risk-taking common to other aspects of social life. As Stan Cohen (1973b: 622) reminds us, 'some of our most cherished social values – individualism, masculinity, competitiveness – are the same ones that generate crime'. Indeed, it is the excitement and a sense of machismo in beating the competition in our 'enterprise' culture that arguably induces some managers and young city professionals to perform 'dirty deeds' in covert business activities – for example, to act as spies, phone-tappers, computer hackers, safe-breakers, forgers and saboteurs (Punch, 2000).

Property crime also has to be understood within the context of the expansion of the hidden economy and increased blurring of boundaries between employment and unemployment and between legal and illegal work. In an increasingly polarised society in which only 40 per cent of the population have secure employment, while the others are split between those in insecure employment (30 per cent) and a marginalised underclass of the unemployed (30 per cent) (Hutton, 1995), the gap between benefit entitlements and realistic standards of living in a consumer-oriented society is widening. Some commentators have argued that those young people who are without the protection of employment, family and welfare, or are trapped in the 'magic roundabout' of different training and enterprise schemes, are most likely to adopt one of the transient lifestyles or alternative 'careers' thrown up by local hidden economies, including 'fencing' stolen goods, 'hustling', unlicensed street trading, or acting as 'lookouts' or 'touts' (Carlen, 1996; Craine, 1997). Perhaps more significantly, many of these illegal activities are not considered as crime, just 'ordinary work' (Foster, 1990: 165; Taylor and Jamieson, 1997). All this points to the need to understand crime as a 'normal' rather than an 'exceptional' social phenomenon. Although property crime has been a constant focus of public and political attention, this chapter suggests that there is no singular 'crime problem' as such. Instead, there is a wide spectrum of illicit behaviour, misconduct, troubling and alarming events that are widespread and constantly occurring, and a variety of ways of conceiving of and thinking about everyday property crime.

SUMMARY

1   Official statistics and victim surveys indicate the prevalence of various types of property crime over time, among different social groups and across societies.

2   This is evident in the vast range of illegal activities committed by the general

public, the hidden and petty-criminal economies of everyday survival, the crimes committed by respectable people in the normal circumstances of their everyday jobs and by those who simply get a buzz out of leading life 'on the edge'.

3   While the risks of victimization and the impact of property crime remain highly differentiated and unevenly distributed, research studies have generally pointed to the higher levels of property crime prevailing in socially deprived areas and the disproportionate victimization of the poor, of young people and of minority ethnic groups.

4   Against a background of social change and technological advances, the range of property crime activities has broadened significantly or even developed into transnational businesses. New or existing forms of property crime can also be carried out more extensively, more quickly, more efficiently and with greater ease of concealment.

5   In addition to crimes that take place in the street or are directed at households, property crime also includes theft and illegal export of cultural property and theft of intellectual property. A critical study of these forms of crime requires reappraisal of more traditional notions of offending, harmful behaviour and property.

CRITICAL THINKING QUESTIONS

1   What evidence is there to suggest that many crimes against property are committed by socially acceptable people in their everyday life?
2   What are the limitations of the official picture of property crime?
3   How might criminological research advance our understanding of previously hidden forms of property crime around the world?

FURTHER STUDY

Emsley, C. (1996) *Crime and Society in England 1750–1900*, London: Longman. An accessible introduction to the history of the crime problem, perceptions of criminality and changes in the courts, the police and the system of punishment.

Mawby, R. (2001) *Burglary*, Cullompton, Devon: Willan. A useful overview of the key aspects of the problem of burglary and some of the recent developments and research studies in policy responses.

Newman, G. (ed.) (1999) *Global Report on Crime and Justice*, New York: Oxford University Press. A comprehensive text from the United Nations on crime, criminal justice and international crime victim surveys.

Shover, Neal (1996) *Great Pretenders: Pursuits and Games of Persistent Thieves*, Boulder, CO: Westview Press. A fascinating book on the criminal pathways and decision-making of offenders based on original studies and autobiographies of persistent thieves in the USA.

MORE INFORMATION

The Home Office: Research Development Statistics – Publications
http://www.homeoffice.gov.uk/rds/bcs.html
The National British Crime Survey provides up-to-date annual information on different types of crime, including property crime, which may or may not be reported to and recorded by the police. Full reports and summaries of BCS findings and many other research studies funded by the Home Office can be found here.

The International Crime Victim Surveys
http://www.unicri.it/icvs/
Information, publications and statistics on international crime victim surveys are available at this site.

CHAPTER 9

KEY ISSUES

▌ What are the major patterns of crimes linked to sex?

▌ How do they link to gender?

▌ Why do they provoke such hysteria?

▌ How are sex crimes changing?

▌ What can be done about them?

Crime and Sexuality

INTRODUCTION

In the grand sweep of crime, sex offences are officially not as common as many other offences. The Home Office recorded 36,690 for the year ending September 1998, 37,492 for the year ending 1999 (around 10 per cent of violent crime) – but they do seem to be on the increase, they are severely under-reported, and they do provoke a great deal of anxiety and concern. For reasons discussed in Chapter 2, being precise about criminal statistics is very difficult. There is always a large hidden figure, but in the case of sex offences such problems may be magnified because many victims do not wish to report the crimes at all – finding the glare of public recognition and scrutiny too traumatic. In some cases – often involving under-age offences – they may not even be aware that a crime has been committed. Further, even when a crime is reported, getting a conviction may be difficult: in 1989, 3,305 recorded cases of rape resulted in only 613 cautions or conviction (Sampson, 1994). Often, for instance, the women's accusations in a rape case may not be taken seriously. As the late Sue Lees (1996a: x–xi) argued, from her extensive analysis of the police, courts and victims in London:

> [I]t is simply inconceivable that the vast majority of women who report rape to the police are lying. Moreover, there is evidence that those women who do report are merely the tip of the iceberg, and yet this tip is further decimated as the criminal justice system runs its course.

BOX 9.1 TWO SOCIAL THEORIES OF SEXUALITY

Gagnon and Simon's *Sexual Conduct* (1973) is one of the landmark texts in the sociology of sexuality and is seen as the foundational text of what is now commonly known as the 'social constructionist' approach to sexuality. (A new edition is being planned.) Gagnon and Simon claim that there is no one, unified pattern of sexuality; instead, there are 'many ways to become, to be, to act, to feel sexual. There is no one human sexuality, but rather a wide variety of sexualities' (Gagnon, 1977, preface).

Three of their main themes which will help us think about sexuality and crime, are as follows:

- *Beware of the biological: it claims too much.* Sex crimes are rarely a matter of sex being a simple biological release. In contrast to classic ways of thinking about sexuality as biological, bodily and 'natural' – as *essentially* given – Gagnon and Simon aimed to show the ways in which human sexualities are always organised through economic, religious, political, familial and social conditions; any analysis that does not recognise this must be seriously flawed. Sexuality, for humans, is never just a free floating desire. It is always grounded in wider material and cultural forces.
- *Look for the symbols and meanings.* Human sexualities are always symbolic. With sex crimes we should always be looking out for motivations that are not simply or straightforwardly sexual. Sex may be performed out of rage, as aggression, as a hunt, as a hobby, because of a scarring experience, as a mode of transgression, as a form of violence.
- *Examine sexual scripts.* Human sexualities – including sex crimes – are probably best seen as evolving through scripts that suggest – the who? what? where? when? and why? of sexual conduct – as they guide our sexualities at personal, interactional and cultural-historical levels.

A second major contribution comes from the French historian of ideas Michel Foucault (introduced in Chapter 5). He argued that sexuality 'is the name given to a historical construct . . . a great surface network in which the stimulation of bodies, the intensification of pleasures, the incitement to discourse, the formation of knowledge, the strengthening of controls and resistances, are linked to one another, in accordance with a few major strategies of power' (Foucault, 1978: 106). Startlingly challenging conventional wisdom, he attacked the notion that sex had been repressed in the Victorian world, and claimed instead that sexuality in this period was a discursive fiction which had actually organised the social problems of the time. New species – like the homosexual, the pervert, the masturbating child, the Malthusian couple, the hysterical woman – had literally been invented and come into being as organising motifs for sexual problems and the spread of surveillance and regulation. The body had become a site for disciplinary practices and new technologies.

Table 9.1 Recorded sexual crime by number of offences 1991 and 1995 to 2002–3 and percentage change between 2001–2 and 2002–3, England and Wales (including adjustment for NCRS effect where available)

OFFENCE	1991	1995	1996	1997	1997–8	1998–9	1998–9	1999–2000	2000–1	2001–2	2002–3	Percentage change between 2001–2 and 2002–3
Buggery	1,127	818	728	645	657	567	566	437	401	356	287	–19
Indecent assault on a male	3,070	3,150	3,130	3,503	3,885	3,672	3,683	3,614	3,530	3,605	4,096	14
Gross indecency between males	965	727	553	520	483	353	354	286	167	164	198	21
Rape of a female	4,045	4,986	5,759	6,281	6,523	7,139	7,132	7,809	7,929	8,990	11,441	27
Rape of a male	—	150	231	347	375	502	504	600	664	730	852	17
Indecent assault on a female	15,792	16,876	17,643	18,674	18,979	19,463	19,524	20,664	20,301	21,790	24,811	14
Unlawful sexual intercourse with a girl under 13	315	178	171	148	156	153	153	181	155	169	187	11
Unlawful sexual intercourse with a girl under 16	1,949	1,260	1,261	1,112	1,084	1,133	1,135	1,270	1,237	1,331	1,514	14
Incest	389	185	157	183	189	139	139	121	80	94	99	5
Procuration	138	207	132	131	142	155	215	138	129	130	127	–2
Abduction	411	364	313	277	258	242	240	251	262	262	291	11

Bigamy	75	86	98	75	106	126	129	83	80	74	88	19
Soliciting or importuning by a man	—	—	—	—	—	1,107	973	1,028	1,655	2,107	27
Abuse of position of trust	—	—	—	—	—	—	—	12	416	676	63
Gross indecency with a child	1,147	1,287	1,215	1,269	1,314	1,271	1,293	1,365	1,336	1,661	1,880	13
TOTAL SEXUAL OFFENCES	29,423	30,274	31,391	33,165	34,151	34,915	36,174	37,792	37,311	41,427	48,654	17

Sexual offences are significantly under-reported to the authorities. Police and government action to support the victims of sexual assaults is likely to have increased the number of such incidents being brought to the attention of the police, and therefore recorded by them. The introduction of the NCRS has further increased the recording rate. Trends in the number of recorded sexual offences are therefore unlikely to reflect real experience of such crimes.

- Within the 2002–3 total of 48,654 offences, the police recorded 24,811 cases of indecent assault on a female, and 1,880 cases of gross indecency with a child.
- The number of recorded rapes was 12,293, 93 per cent of which were rapes of a female. There were also 4,096 recorded cases of indecent assault on a male.
- The number of recorded sexual offences was thought to be largely unchanged in 2002–3, after accounting for the effects of the NCRS (reliable estimates for this effect are not available, due to the relatively small number of occurrences).
- Sexual offences accounted for 5 per cent of police-recorded violence and 0.8 per cent of all police-recorded crime in 2002–3.

Source: Adapted from Table 3.04, p. 41 in *Crime in England and Wales, 2002–3*, Home Office

UNDERSTANDING SEX OFFENCES: SEX CRIMES, GENDER AND VIOLENCE

There are two major sets of explanations that have been used to understand an array of sex offenders. The first sets out psychological and psychiatric problems. With extreme cases of psychopathological sex killers, these probably have some major validity. But many sex crimes are much more common than this – indeed, their most conspicuous feature is that *they are overwhelmingly committed by men*. James Messerschmidt suggests that the history of many sex offences can be seen to originate with the violence of boys. He suggests that

> approximately 25 percent of adult male sex offenders report that their first sexual offence occurred during adolescence. Moreover a significant proportion of all male sexual offences are committed by persons under the age of eighteen – approximately 25 percent of rapes and 50 percent of cases of child sexual abuse can be attributed to adolescent male offenders.'
>
> (Messerschmidt, 2000: 3–4)

In many ways, sex crimes may be seen as a way of 'doing gender' and Messerschmidt has powerfully merged ideas of 'structured action' and 'doing gender' to see the ways in which men can draw upon social resources in the wider culture to give different meanings to their masculinities and to make sense of various criminal actions. Certain boys use sexual and assaultive violence as what might be called a 'masculine practice'.

Feminist perspectives

This also chimes with how feminists understand sexual violence, which is that most sex offences, far from being pathological, are intentional behaviour chosen by men as part of their attempt to construct their masculinity as dominant and powerful. Likewise, sexual abuse is understood as an expression of masculinity, of men's desire to be in control and dominant, and it is intimately connected to normal relations within society. However, there is considerable debate in feminist thought at the moment over whether it is appropriate to see all men as potential rapists and all women as victims.

Feminist theories often link crime to masculinities (see Chapter 5). Important here are the workings of *patriarchies*: systems of male dominance that serve the interests of men. Power plays a key role in understanding sex offending, ranging from sexual violence to prostitution and pornography. Some feminists such as Andrea Dworkin and Catherine MacKinnon have claimed that sexuality is organised by men for men and have denounced both 'heterosexuality' and heterosexual intercourse (Jackson and Scott, 1996).

The problem of violence against women includes several conceptually distinct yet overlapping concerns, which include rape, incest, battering, sexual harassment and pornography. English feminist sociologist Liz Kelly (1988) has argued that there is in fact a **'continuum of sexual violence'**, which ranges from the everyday abuse of women in pornographic images, sexist jokes, sexual harassment and women's engagement in compliant but unwanted marital sex, through to the 'non-routine' episodes of rape, incest, battery and sex murder. Kelly, with other feminists, suggests from research that most women have experienced some form of sexual violence. Sexual violence occurs in the context of men's power and women's resistance. Women are not passive victims. Feminist work is emphasising that they are 'survivors', with active agency, and that survival involves a rejection of self-blame, for once the abuse is made visible, it can be understood as precisely that, abuse.

Rape

Until the 1970s, the dominant way of understanding the crime of rape by society, the criminal justice system and criminology was that women were to blame for their assault. In the criminology literature at the time the concept of 'victim-precipitated' rape was in full currency. It was argued that rape is most likely to occur in situations where the victim's behaviour is seen as by the offender as signalling availability for sexual contact. Such situations were said to include those in which a woman agrees to sexual relations but changes her mind, fails to strongly resist sexual overtures, or accepts a drink from a stranger. Even wearing 'provocative clothing' could be taken as a sign of sexual availability. Such a way of thinking about rape was eventually seen to encourage an array of 'rape myths'. These myths are presumptions that women are tempting seductresses who invite sexual encounters, that women eventually relax and enjoy rape, that men have urgent and uncontrollable sexual needs, and that the typical rapist was a stranger or black man. In fact, the typical rapist is more likely to be a man acquainted or intimate with his victim, rather than a stranger or psychopath. These myths are also reproduced in the legal system, thereby making it very difficult for women to achieve justice and to hold men responsible for the harms they have perpetrated.

For example, there are contradictory societal expectations concerning rape. One view is that if a woman is raped, she should be too upset and ashamed to report it; the other is that she should be so upset that she will report it. Both these views exist, but it is the latter that is written into the law. Any delay in reporting is used against her. Furthermore, when she is in court she is expected to appear upset as a victim, but calm and controlled as a court witness. If in court she appears lucid as a witness, she is in danger of not coming across as a victim. If she appears too upset, she runs the risk of being seen as hysterical and therefore not believable (Lees, 1996). It would be fair to say that rape was the number one feminist issue of the 1970s, and the critique was directed toward dispelling these myths about the nature, the incidence, the perpetrators and the causes of rape.

During the 1970s, a number of key arguments were made by feminist writers. First, Susan Griffin argued in a path-breaking article that all women inhabit a mental world where they are constantly in fear of being raped:

> I have never been free of the fear of rape. From a very early age, I, like most women, have thought of rape as part of my natural environment – something to be feared

and prayed against like fire or lightning, I never asked why men raped; I simply thought of it as part of one of the many mysteries of human nature.

(1971: 26)

This 'fear of rape' suggests the second argument: that men have a 'trump card' to play in keeping women in their place. Thus, Reynolds suggests that rape is a prime mode of social control:

Rape is a punitive action directed towards females who usurp or appear to usurp the culturally defined prerogatives of the dominant role . . . [it] operates in our society to maintain the dominant position of males. It does this by restricting the mobility and freedom of movement of women by limiting their casual interaction with the opposite sex, and in particular by maintaining the male's prerogatives in the erotic sphere. When there was evidence that the victim was or gave the appearance of being out of place, she can be raped and the rapist will be supported by the cultural values, by the institutions that embody these values, and by the people shaped by these values – that is by the policy, courts, members of juries, and sometimes the victims themselves.

(1974: 62–8)

Stay in your homes; stay in suitable attire; stay loyal to your husbands; stay submissive in your manner – this is the message of rape to women. Working outwards, then, from the actual impact of rape on women, the third argument starts to suggest what is happening. Susan Brownmiller, in her highly influential book *Against Our Will*, put the thesis at its bluntest: 'From prehistoric times to the present, I believe, rape has played a critical function. It is nothing more or less than a conscious process of intimidation by which all *men* keep *all women* in a state of fear' (1975: 5; emphasis in original). Such a thesis has been taken up by many feminists, notably Dworkin (1981), and used as the basis for viewing male sexuality as the root of all women's oppression. Other commentators have been a little more cautious: Clark and Lewis, for example, state that they are not 'anti-male' but that they are opposed to 'any social system erected on the assumption of inequality between kinds of persons such that power and authority accrue only to a pre-elected subset' (1977: 166). Suggesting that marriage and rape laws have developed side by side, they argue that rape notions are linked to the idea that a woman is a man's property. A woman's sexuality thus becomes – in law – the property of her husband, and rape 'is simply theft of sexual property under the ownership of someone other than the rapist' (Clark and Lewis, 1977: 116). If a rape victim is a married woman and is therefore, according to Clark and Lewis, owned, then her husband must seek vengeance from the thief – the rapist – but if she is not so owned, she is at risk all the time for being so autonomous.

One of the most controversial points in the feminist literature on rape is on how it is legally defined. According to Section I of the Sexual Offences Act 1956, rape is defined as penetration of the vagina by the penis without the woman's consent. There are at least four ways in which this definition has been criticised.

First, it has contained, up until 1991, an unjustified major 'exclusion' clause. It was only in 1991 that the marital rape exclusion clause was abolished in England and

Wales, making rape within marriage illegal. This clause had been the subject of feminist campaigns for over twenty years. What it reflected was the law's view that a wife was her husband's property rather than an autonomous, self-determining person.

Second, it reflects a male fetish with one female orifice and one instrument for its violation. The focus only on vaginal penetration diverts attention away from the coercive and life-threatening experience of rape described by victims. It does not cover penetration of other parts of the body, nor the intrusion of other objects into the body, and nor does it cover other forms of sexual coercion such as forced oral sex, which many women report as just as humiliating. Furthermore, by viewing the penis as the primary rape weapon, the law reveals a male preoccupation with the risk of their respectable women getting pregnant rather than a concern for the physical and psychological injury during and after rape.

Third, its notion of consent places an unfair burden of proof on the victim, and because it is premised on the idea of a voluntary actor, it fails to include a consideration for coerced consent or submission other than under physical duress. In addition to wanting the concept of rape broadened to make it non-orifice- and non-instrument-specific, there are strong arguments for re-examining the concept of consent. One suggestion is that intent should be shifted from 'without the victim's consent' to 'coerced by the offender', because not only is consent legally difficult to establish, but it misses the fundamental point that it is the presence of coercion that distinguishes rape from other acts of sexual intercourse.

Fourth, it excludes other kinds of behaviour that are very similar in their effect to that which it includes. The legal definition of rape, and how the public view rape, as an aberrant act committed by sick individuals, misses one of the central arguments of feminist scholarship, which is that rape is an extension or exaggeration of conventional sexual relations and power differentials between women and men. Box (1983: 121) argues that one of the issues that we have to consider is how 'normal' sexual encounters can merge imperceptibly into sexual assaults of which rape is the most serious.

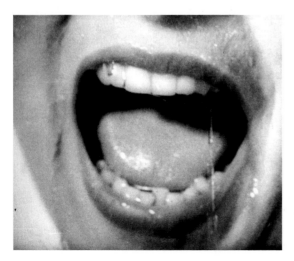

Plate 9.1 There is a long history of violence against women in films. Alfred Hitchcock's *Psycho* is considered to be a major depiction, and set into play a whole series of films in which women were brutally murdered (often in the bathroom!). This classic image features Janet Leigh in the famous scream shot.

Source: © Artificial Eye, courtesy of the British Film Institute.

Pornography

There is extensive debate within feminism on the issue of pornography, and currently opinion ranges from the belief that pornography is central to women's oppression and must be subject to state controls, through the understanding that it is against women's interests and must be campaigned against. Proponents of this view include Andrea Dworkin, Susan Griffin and Catherine MacKinnon, and they call for stricter laws, more intensive policing and (more severe) punishments for the creators, sellers and distributors of pornography.

The argument is that images of sexuality, heterosexuality and the connections between sex and violence reflect and reinforce masculinity, male power, and the depersonalisation, objectification and degradation of women. Their critique is not so much in terms of direct causal connections between media representations and behaviour as of sadomasochism and the celebration in much modern pornography of violence and death as well as sex. The kind of pornography that they allude to is of the highly extreme kind that involves rape, bestiality and children. Most people would wholly object to this kind of material.

However, it is not so easy to take this line on representations of women that are less obviously harmful, yet nevertheless contribute to a culturally sanctioned misogyny. One of the problems facing the feminist left is how far to take censorship while preserving democratic freedoms, since anti-pornography campaigns have attracted strong criticism from gay and lesbian groups because such legal regulation could be extended into other areas of sexual and social relations. There are also tensions between radical feminists and the perspectives of women who work as prostitutes or in the sex industry. For as Nicki Roberts, an ex-stripper, has argued,

> Feminist anti-porn campaigners or the Whitehouse brigade: it makes no difference to us. Both factions clamour for more repression and censorship at the hands of the state; both divert attention away from the real issue of women's poverty in this society; and both are responsible for the increased hounding and vilification of women who work in the sex industry.
>
> (1986, cited in Edwards, 1990: 151)

The issues raised by this confront real problems in contemporary feminism, which concern the complexity of responses to justice, the law, freedom and inequality. There is no easy answer to this, but one way is to understand that not all people are controlled or oppressed with the same tenacity, tyranny or consistency. Carol Smart's call for a postmodern feminism is one potential means of addressing and theorising this.

THE INSTRUMENTAL AND SYMBOLIC ROLE OF LAW IN SEX CRIMES

Laws may be seen as both instrumental and symbolic. The *instrumental* role is practical: it aims to bring about some specific desired effect such as to stop rape. The *symbolic* role is one of latent concern – acting for example as a litmus for many moral panics and discourses that tap into a wide range of social anxieties. For example, it is now well documented that while, instrumentally, campaigns against commercialised prostitution in the nineteenth century certainly had real consequences in shifting public health and strengthening women's lives, they also symbolised the controversies over purity, immigration, 'dirty women', 'the age of consent'. As a cultural symbol, prostituion touches on all the evils of the modern world and often is seen to create a contradictory tension between the exploitation of women and the lust of men. Thus, for example, the feminist values of nineteenth-century women led movements that were for moral reform, chastity, temperance. Many feminists of this era waged war over prostitution, the age of consent, contraception and the moral debauchery of men through drink. The evangelical moral reform society of the nineteenth century, with their enormous power to be co-opted by more conservative forces, organised many women both into criticism and into new ways of life that ignored the enemy of men. Indeed, the debates that we witnessed in the latter parts of the twentieth century around pornography and sexual violence were largely repeats of debates that were present at the turn of the century. In those days it was essentially a contest between the social purity movements and the sex reformers who were pitted against each other over such concerns as the age of consent, prostitution and pornography.

Another feminist commentator, Judith Walkowitz, comments:

> Begun as a libertarian sanction against the state sanction of male vice, the repeal campaign helped to spawn a hydra-headed assault against sexual deviation of all kinds. The struggle against state regulation evolved into a movement that used the instrument of the state for repressive purposes . . . they extended the meaning of sexuality. By ferreting out new areas of illicit sexual activity and defining them into existence, a new 'technology of power' was created that facilitated control over an ever-widening circle of human activity.
>
> (Walkowitz, 1984: 130–1)

As she comments, in the beginning women had some control; but as the movements grew, they lost this power, and the movements came to be used for wider ends.

Likewise, attacks on and anxieties concerning the so-called slum sex code and upon young men at taxi-dance halls in the early twentieth century were often a way of attacking lower-class men, and raised social class issues (White, 1993). 'Perverts' of all kinds seem to have stalked the nineteenth and twentieth centuries, symbolising an anarchic, non-reproductive, 'sick' kind of sex. Race often became an issue in battles over rape and lynching. Controversies over pre- and extra-marital sex reinforced patterns of the 'normal family'. In the late twentieth century, AIDS rapidly became the symbol not only of death, but of promiscuity, permissiveness and perversions: it marked out the good and the bad. And at the start of the twenty-first century, as we write this, a major concern over paedophile priests in the Catholic Church has energised controversies around religion, sexuality, homosexuality and child abuse (Loseke, 2003a).

Hence while, instrumentally, these campaigns try to stop a particular form of behaviour, symbolically they reassert existing moral orders. Over and over again, we find 'sexualities' being used in this way. Paraphrasing Mary Douglas's (1966) terms, we may say that sex often equals dirt and disorder, stuff out of place; and a society needs to purify itself of all this. Sexual problems emerge when there is a perceived threat to social values, be they religious, familial, feminist or medical. Behind every sexual problem there is almost certainly a perceived threat to aspects of the moral order and a group of crusaders struggling to define boundaries.

The panics around sex crimes

'Sex crimes' are a major social problem, with a history of generating anxiety and panic. Sometimes they enter public consciousness and reach levels of mass hysteria; sometimes we are hardly aware of them. And there are of course competing accounts of when and how they start to be noted and taken more seriously. Over half a century ago, the leading criminologist Edwin Sutherland summarised the passage of sex offence laws. His account still cannot be bettered:

> The diffusion of sexual psychopath laws has followed this course: a community is thrown into panic by a few serious sex crimes, which are given nation wide publicity; the community acts in an agitated manner; and all sorts of proposals are made; a committee is then appointed to study the facts and to make recommendations. The committee recommends a sexual psychopath law as the scientific procedure for the control of sex crime. The recommendation is consistent with the trend toward treatment policies in criminal justice in preference to policies of punishment.
>
> (1950: 142)

Sutherland was writing about the diffusion of such laws around 1937 in the United States. Today, much of his analysis is seen as one possible (and possibly even cyclical) response. Punitive and rehabilitative models come and go: there are periods of silence and periods when sex crime is a great issue.

The feminist writer Jane Caputi, for example, has argued that sex crime starts to appear as a phenomenon with the famous and widely cited Jack the Ripper case in the later nineteenth century. It not only generated huge moral anxiety in its day, but also signalled 'the age of sex crime', in which serial killers and mass murderers become more and more common – in reality and in the mythology of the times. (For instance, she suggests there were 644 serial sex killings in the United States in 1966 but 4,118 by 1982 (Caputi, 1988: 1–2).) She cites many examples: the 'Boston Strangler', 'Son of Sam', the 'Hillside Strangler', the 'Yorkshire Ripper', etc., as well as films that play to these fears: from the classics of *M* and *Psycho* to the more widespread teen slasher films such as the *Halloween* series. Her work outlines the creation of these fiends in the public minds, but at the same time shows how this is part of a wider issue of gender violence and aggression.

By contrast, the sociologist Philip Jenkins has traced the differential responses to a hundred years of sex crimes from the late nineteenth century to current times. He suggests (to summarise his argument) that

Originating in the Progressive era, the imagery of the malignant sex fiend reached new heights in the decade after World War II, only to be succeeded by a liberal model over the next quarter of a century. More recently, the pendulum has swung back to the predator model: sex offenders are now viewed as being little removed from the worst multiple killers and torturers. And in each era, the prevailing opinion was supported by what appeared at the time to be convincing research. One reality prevailed until it was succeeded by another.

(1998: 2)

He does not see these stages as evolutionary and necessarily objective: rather, they 'have ebbed and flowed – we forget as well as learn' (p. 3). 'The nature of sexual threats to children was perceived quite differently in 1915 than in 1930, and the child abuse issue was framed quite differently in 1984 than in 1994' (p. 215). At the heart of his analysis lie vigorous campaigning groups: child-savers, feminists, psychiatrists and therapists, religious and moralistic groups, and, of course, politicians.

Jenkins claims that children are at very low risk from homicide, making nonsense of the claims aired frequently in the 1980s that many thousands were killed each year by serial murders, pornographers or paedophile rings (p. 10) Looking at figures for the United States between 1980 and 1994, he concludes that despite the claims made, strangers killed about fifty-four children per year, and about five of these victims were involved as part of a sexual assault.

In summary, then, sexuality appears to be a major device used to tap into all sorts of social anxieties, to generate panic and to demarcate boundaries. Studies point to many different sources of these anxieties and boundary mapping, but they include anxieties over gender roles, heterosexuality, and the family; the importance of reproduction and pronatalism; concerns over the role of youth and childhood; race and racialised categories; the divisions between classes and 'class fears'; the nation-state itself; an overarching sense of moral progress and fears of decline; the very nature of ethical and religious systems; end of century/millennium fears; and even connections to the fear of death (for examples, see Bristow, 1977; Foldy, 1997; Hunt, 1998; McLaren, 1997; Showalter, 1990; Stein, 2001; Vass, 1986; Walkowitz, 1992; White, 1993).

BOX 9.2 SEX OFFENCES IN GLOBAL PERSPECTIVE

This chapter has largely focused upon UK sex offences, though there are many similarities with other Western cultures. Other societies have very different laws and hence different patterns of offence. We know that in some strongly religious Muslim societies (and Iran seems a central if changing case), the degree of surveillance over the lives of children and women on a day-to-day basis makes the possibility of any norm-violations (from masturbation to homosexuality) difficult indeed. Penalties are severe and executions are not uncommon for homosexuality. There are honour killings in some Islamic societies, whereby women may be punished by death (or raped) for actual (or even perceived) sexual (mis)conducts. In very many countries there is also little or no choice over who can be a sexual partner. In cultures torn by civil war, there also seems to be a widespread culture of war rape (it is estimated that some 40,000 women were raped in the Bosnian conflict), and in these desperate situations the whole culture is permeated by a violence that may also shape its sexualities (Allen, 1996).

Yet we are also now starting to sense the globalisation of sexualities, in which the world becomes smaller and more interconnected: a major reordering of time and space in sexual relations may be taking place. Talk about 'sexual problems' moves across the globe, and in the process often becomes transformed and modified by local cultures. Traditional sexual customs become subject to rapid social change. Media and digital-isation generate an information age haunted by the spectres of sexuality – from cybersex to cyber-rape. Postmodern values seem on the ascendant, giving priorities to ideas of sexual differences and sexual choices. Global capital turns local sex markets into international ones. World sexual cultures become more and more interconnected. With all this, it should not be surprising to find that long-standing patterns of sexualities becoming increasingly disturbed and disrupted (Altman, 2001).

THE CHANGING CHARACTER OF SEX CRIMES

Just what can be designated a 'sex crime' changes all the time, and it will interesting to examine a few illustrations briefly.

Homosexuality is an interesting case. For much of the nineteenth and twentieth centuries, it was against the law in most Western countries, Gradually it has become decriminalised over the past thirty years in those countries – though it does still remains illegal in some US states and in many parts of the world. Curiously, with the advance of a strong (and increasingly international) lesbian and gay movement, new issues have appeared such as universal lesbian and gay rights, including a universal age of consent and the inclusion of 'sexual orientation' in charters of human rights; and anti-discrimination laws, along with mandatory training in 'multi-culturalism' and 'gay affirmative action', have become common in many Western contexts. 'Registered partnerships' – and sometimes marriages – for lesbians and gays along with the right of lesbians and gays to adopt and have children have become key foci of a growing international lesbian, gay, bisexual and transgender movement (Adam *et al.*, 1999). New anti-gay crimes such as 'hate crimes' have been created and turned into social problems. A major reworking of the claims being made about homosexuality has been happening over the past thirty years; it can no longer be placed easily in a Western list of 'sex offences and crimes'.

Yet while all this is going on, there continues to be massive resistance to accep-tance of homosexuality in many countries. In most countries of Africa, Asia or Latin America, same-sex relations remain taboo: largely invisible, rarely discussed, officially non-existent, and embedded in religions, laws and beliefs that are deeply inimical to homosexuality. Even today, it is illegal in approximately seventy states in the world

Plate 9.2 In the summer of 2000 in the UK there was hysteria against sex offences and paedophilia. In Paulsgrove estate, Portsmouth, people organised into Residents Against Paedophilia and went on the march.

Source: Press Association.

as well as being subject to the death penalty in seven (an estimated 200 homosexuals are executed yearly in Iran: Baird, 2001: 13). Indeed, the partial acceptance of homosexuality in parts of the West is often used as a major example of the West's decadence (Baird, 2001: 12).

Prostitution, too, is an interesting case. It is often not against the law *per se*, but it is regulated because of concerns over health risks. In the United Kingdom, after the Wolfenden Report of 1957, living on immoral earnings, keeping a brothel, and soliciting by a 'common prostitute' became illegal: and subsequently in 1985, kerb crawling became an offence. Prostitution is not in itself illegal in England and Wales, but the selling of sexual services in a street or public place is, (under the Street

Offences Act 1959, section 1. In the United States, it is legal in some states, regulated in others, and outlawed in still others.

Likewise, pornography is a hotly contested issue, and although there have been many versions of obscenity law, in the main these days the issue of obscenity is most closely linked to the purchasing and ownership of child pornography (new laws were introduced in the 1980s that made not just the production and selling of such porn illegal but also its purchasing and ownership). And this has now been compounded by offences linked to the Internet.

Sex crimes on the Internet

Recently, we have started to see the emergence of a new area of sex offences as more and more people come to use the Internet to make sexual contacts, buy sexual wares and pursue all kinds of Websites that are saturated with every kind of sexual image you are ever likely to want (and not want) to see. All kinds of new potential criminal problems have emerged as a result: cyber-stalkers, cyber-rape, childhood security, paedophile abductions, camcorder sex, new forms of porn and ways of accessing it (alongside so-called cyborg sex and virtual sex). Such new forms are a largely uncharted area, and finding ways of regulating them through law and control agencies sees us with a new field of sex crimes just now in the making. In the United Kingdom, for instance, the government has set up groups such as the Task Force on Child Protection on the Internet and the Internet Watch Foundation to start tracking serious abuses on the Web.

BOX 9.3 CHILD PORNOGRAPHY, GLOBALISATION AND THE INTERNET

Another instance of globalisation at work is the relatively recent arrival of a complex network of worlds linked through the Internet that cater for interests in child pornography and paedophile abuse. By most accounts this is widespread, much condemned but quite hard to regulate, and it has generated extensive public talk about it as a problem in much of the Western media.

In his study of child pornography on the Internet, Philip Jenkins shows just how difficult it is to regulate a fragmented global network such as this. Although there are laws in many Western countries which make possession of pornographic pictures of anyone under 18 an imprisonable offence, other – often poorer – countries have much less stringent laws, and at times it seems that the use of young children for prostitution and pornography is almost condoned. Certainly, many of the images found on the Internet have originated in poorer 'bandit' countries (the former communist world, Asia and Latin America – and oddly, also Japan) where regulations are minimal. It may be hard to regulate in countries such as the United States or the United Kingdom, but it is almost impossible in other countries. And as Jenkins comments, 'Lacking a global moral consensus, there will always be areas of unevenness, fault lines in moral enforcement, and the child pornographers are likely to survive in these cracks' (2001: 203).

Changes in the law concerning sexual offences in the United Kingdom

During 1999 and 2000 the government instigated two wide-ranging reviews of sex offences and the workings of the Sex Offenders Act 1997, consulting a number of organisations ranging from lobby groups to children's charities. The review was set up with the following terms of reference:

- to provide coherent and clear offences which protect individuals, especially children and the more vulnerable from abuse and exploitation;
- to enable abusers to be properly punished;
- to be fair and non-discriminatory.

It was odd timing, for a few weeks after this announcement, widespread public concern was expressed about the dangers posed by sex offenders following the death of Sarah Payne. In response to this, a number of interim amendments, anticipating the work of the review, were introduced in autumn 2000 to strengthen the Sex Offenders Act.

The review team completed its work and published its recommendations in July 2000, and made a wide range of recommendations that have been considered carefully in light of over 700 responses received during a public consultation period.

The Sexual Offences Bill was introduced in the House of Lords on 28 January 2003 by Lord Falconer of Thoroton. It is generally seen as the most radical overhaul of sex offences legislation for fifty years, and details of its recommendations are contained in Box 9.4. One of its core concerns is that the law should be fair and non-discriminatory.

BOX 9.4 THE SEXUAL OFFENCES BILL 2003

The Bill details proposals to strengthen protection for children, vulnerable people and the public generally, and to strengthen the law in relation to sexual violence.

Children

- Children under 13 will not be capable in law of giving consent to any form of sexual activity. Any sexual intercourse with a child under 13 will be charged as rape.

continued

- There will be a range of new offences designed to tackle all inappropriate sexual activity with children, including a new offence of causing a child to engage in sexual activity – which will capture behaviour such as inappropriately persuading children to undress.
- There will be a new 'grooming' offence based on meeting a child with the intention of committing a sex offence, and civil order to apply both to Internet and offline grooming, which will enable restrictions to be placed on people displaying inappropriate sexual behaviour before an offence is committed.
- There will be new offences with severe penalties against those who sexually exploit children for their own gain. The new offences relating to sexual exploitation of a child will protect children up to the age of 18. The legislation will cover a range of activity, including buying the sexual services of a child, causing or encouraging children into sexual exploitation, facilitating the sexual exploitation of a child and controlling the activities of a child involved in prostitution or pornography.
- Maximum penalties for sexual offences against children and vulnerable people have been raised to reflect the severity of these crimes. Any offence involving penetration against a child under 13 or a person who lacks the capacity to consent will attract a life sentence.

Vulnerable people

- Three new categories of offences will give extra protection to those with a learning disability or mental disorder from sexual abuse, including 'breach of a relationship of care', to protect those who have the capacity to consent, but are vulnerable to exploitative behaviour.

The public

- A new order to make those known to have been convicted of sex offences overseas register as sex offenders when they travel to the United Kingdom, whether or not they have committed a crime in the United Kingdom.
- All those on the sex offenders' register will have to confirm their details in person annually.
- Offenders on the register will have to provide National Insurance details as a further safeguard against evasion.
- The period within which a sex offender must notify the police of a change of name or address is to be reduced from fourteen days to three.
- Sex Offender Orders and Sex Offender Restraining Orders are to be amalgamated into a Sexual Offences Prevention Order (SOPO) and made available for anyone convicted of a violent offence where there is evidence they present a risk of causing serious sexual harm.
- A new offence will be introduced to protect the public from unacceptable sexual acts in public, complementing existing public order offences.

- There will be a new offence to strengthen the law on indecent exposure.
- There will be a new offence of voyeurism, capturing those who observe others without their knowledge for sexual gratification.
- There will be new offences relating to the sexual exploitation of adults.
- There will be a new offence of trafficking in people for sexual exploitation.

Sexual violence

- The law on consent in regard to rape will be clarified.
- There will be a new offence of sexual assault by penetration.
- There will be a new offence of causing sexual acts without consent.
- The law on drug rape offences will be strengthened.
- Rape will be extended to include oral penetration.

The Sexual Offences Bill and the White Paper *Protecting the Public*, which was published on 19 November 2000, can be found on www.sexualoffencesbill.homeoffice.gov.uk.

SUMMARY

1   Sex crimes are not as common as many other offences, but they do seem to be on the increase.
2   Three theories are prominent in thinking about the sociological aspects of sexuality: scripting theory, discourse theory and feminist theories.
3   Sex crimes may best be understood as closely connected to the structuring of gender and the male use of power. Rape is a prime example of this.
4   Moral panics are often linked to sex crimes. At different periods in history, different kinds of sex crimes have been identified.
5   In 2003 a major overhaul of the sex offences legislation took place in the United Kingdom.
6   There is growing concern at the spread of paedophilia on the Internet.

CRITICAL THINKING QUESTIONS

1 Why are sex crimes seriously under-reported?
2 Discuss the factors that lead some men to commit rape and other acts of sexual violence.
3 Consider the processes by which sex crimes become identified as social problems.

4   Discuss the various policies for handling 'sex offenders' and consider which you think are most effective.
5   Why has there been so much interest in the problem of child sexual abuse and paedophilia in recent years?
6   Critically discuss the proposal of the new Sexual Offences Act in the UK.

FURTHER STUDY

Amnesty International (2001) *Crimes of Hate: Conspiracies of Silence*, London: Amnesty International. Useful review of the ways in which homosexuality remains a crime in many parts of the world.

Foucault, M. (1978) *The History of Sexuality*, Harmondsworth, Middlesex: Penguin. A highly influential study of the emergence of sexual categories and knowledge in modernity.

Jenkins, P. (1998) *Moral Panic: Changing Concepts of the Child Molester in Modern America*, New Haven, Yale University Press, and (2001) *Beyond Tolerance: Child Pornography on the Internet*, New York: New York University Press. Two books that deal with issues of paedophilia and child abuse.

Kelly, L. (1988) *Surviving Sexual Violence*, Cambridge: Polity. One of many influential feminist texts on sexual violence.

Loseke, D. (2003) *Thinking about Social Problems: An Introduction to Constructionist Perspectives*, New York: Aldine de Gruyter. (See also Loseke, D. (2003) 'Symposium on Paedophile Priests', *Sexualities*, 6 (1): 6–14. Useful in laying out the constructionist position on social problems – with lots of examples.

Silverman, J. and Wilson, D. (2002) *Innocence Betrayed: Paedophilia, the Media and Society*, Cambridge: Polity. Connects moral panic theory, media and sex crimes into a very readable discussion.

Thomas, T. (2000) *Sex Crime: Sex Offending and Society*, Cullompton, Devon: Willan Publishing. A straightforward introduction to the field.

MORE INFORMATION

The Home Office: The Sexual Offences Bill
http://www.homeoffice.gov.uk/justice/sentencing/sexualoffencesbill/index.html
Information on the Sexual Offences Bill and the White Paper *Protecting the Public*, which was published on 19 November 2000, can be found here.

The National Organisation for the Treatment of Abusers
www.nota.co.uk
NOTA is a growing group comprising practitioners, managers and policymakers for the public, private and voluntary sectors. As a result, NOTA brings a wide variety of perspectives to interventions with sexual aggressors.

The Child and Woman Abuse Unit
http://www.cwasu.org/
The Child and Woman Abuse Unit is based at London Metropolitan University and has a national and international reputation for its research, training and consultancy work. The unit exists to develop feminist research methodologies, theory and practice, especially in relation to connections between forms of sexualised violence.

Crime and Emotion

KEY ISSUES

▌ Can crime be 'fun'?

▌ What is the significance of self-esteem in the causation of violence?

▌ What part might 'respect' play in the criminal act?

▌ Could it be the case that sometimes offenders are unconsciously compelled to commit a crime?

INTRODUCTION

It might seem to be obvious that human emotions play a significant part in the commission of crime, in punishment and in social control. Indeed, the relationship between emotion and crime has fuelled the creative imagination. To take an intense emotion – passion, for instance – *la crime passionel* has inspired great works of literature, theatre, art, symphonies and the opera. It is perhaps the tragedy of crimes of passion that has inspired the artistic imagination; they are offences committed by wretched but ordinary people, not otherwise inclined to transgress. Fuelled by one or more of a myriad of emotions – the wounds of betrayal, the hurt of infidelity, broken hearts, wounded pride, spoiled virtue, jealousy, envy, and many more, they are criminalised by their acts. Passion comes to overrule reason – usually with dire consequences for the offender and the victim.

In Dante's *Inferno*, when Giovanni, Lord of Rimini, discovers his wife, Francesca, and his brother, Paolo the beautiful, in *flagrante*, he has them both killed. The tragedy inspired Tchaikovsky's symphonic poem *Francesca da Rimini*, and the opera of the same name by Riccardo Zandonai. In Shakespeare's tragic tale *Othello*, the enraged Othello 'the Moor' murders his wife, Desdemona, on account of her alleged adultery, and then kills himself in deep remorse when he realises he has been deceived into believing in her infidelity. In Bizet's *Carmen*, the smitten soldier Don José kills his love, the beautiful Gypsy Carmen, after she has a rapturous affair with the handsome toreador Escamillo. In 2002, the tragic tale was recast as a 'Hiphopera' by MTV and New Line Television, starring pop group Destiny's Child performer Byonce Knowles.

In the world of popular music, crimes of passion have been acted out in numerous songs. 'Delilah', the hit by Tom Jones, is a classic example of betrayal with fatal consequences (Figure 10.1).

REDISCOVERING EMOTION IN CRIME

Although crimes of passion have inspired great artistic works and enthralled audiences for centuries, the subject of emotion, it has recently been argued, has been only a peripheral interest within criminological inquiry and theory. De Haan and Loader, for instance, suggest that

> Many established and thriving modes of criminological reflection and research continue to proceed in ways that ignore entirely, or at best gesture towards, the impact of human emotions on their subject matter – if you doubt this, take a quick glance at almost any criminology textbook, whether of a conventional, radical or integrating bent.
>
> (2002: 243)

Delilah, Tom Jones 1968

I saw the light on the night that I passed by her window
I saw the flickering shadows of love on her blind
She was my woman
As she deceived me I watched and went out of my mind
My, my, my, Delilah
Why, why, why, Delilah
I could see that girl was no good for me
But I was lost like a slave that no man could free
At break of day when that man drove away, I was waiting
I cross the street to her house and she opened the door
She stood there laughing
I felt the knife in my hand and she laughed no more
My, my, my Delilah
Why, why, why Delilah
So before they come to break down the door
Forgive me Delilah I just couldn't take any more

Figure 10.1 *Delilah*, Tom Jones, 1968.

Source: *Delilah*, words and music by Les Read and Barry Mason © 1967. Reproduced by kind permission of Donna Music Ltd, London, WC2H 0QY.

However, while the impact of human emotion on crime appears to be in the process of rediscovery in theoretical criminology, it has hardly been neglected in the past by research on crime and deviance.

A provenance for the contemporary interest in crime and emotion can be traced back to Cohen's study (1955) of delinquent boys and the non-material motivations of delinquency, and to David Matza's book *Becoming Deviant* (1969), which focuses on the subjective motivations of deviant behaviour. Jack Katz's book *Seductions of*

Crime (1988) provided a path-breaking analysis of the interrelationship between crime and emotion, or what Katz calls 'the black box between background factors and subjective acts'. In the context of this intellectual provenance, some of the insights provided by the literature are illustrated in this chapter by focusing on some key human emotions that motivate crime.

'HATE CRIME'

Perhaps one of the most explicit connections drawn between crime and a specific emotion in recent years concerns the emergence of the concept of 'hate crime' in the United States. The United States Federal Bureau of Investigation (FBI) defines hate crimes as offences that are 'motivated in part or singularly by personal prejudice against others because of a diversity – race, sexual orientation, religion, ethnicity/ national origin, or disability'. While the term 'hate crime' is institutionalised in law in the United States – as in the Hate Crime Statistics Act 1990 – it has no legislative status in Britain. However, the term has been adopted by the Metropolitan Police Service (MPS) and other police services, and the media, and has become firmly established in popular discourse. It is contestable, however, whether 'hate crime' does in fact manifest hate.

For many people, the term 'hate crime' arguably conjures up an image of a violent crime committed by extremists, by neo-Nazis, racist skinheads and other committed

Plate 10.1 Metropolitan Police posters.

Source: © Metropolitan Police.

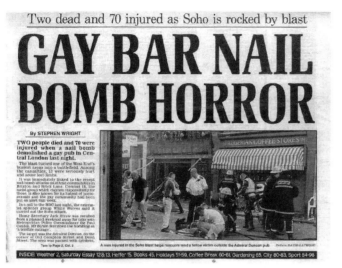

Two dead and 70 injured as Soho is rocked by blast

GAY BAR NAIL BOMB HORROR

By STEPHEN WRIGHT

TWO people died and 70 were injured when a nail bomb demolished a gay pub in Central London last night.

A man injured in the Soho blast helps rescuers tend a fellow victim outside the Admiral Duncan pub   *Picture: DAVID GAYWOOD*

INSIDE: Weather 2, Saturday Essay 12 & 13, Heffer 15, Books 45, Holidays 51-59, Coffee Break 60-61, Gardening 65, City 80-83, Sport 84-96

Plate 10.2 *Daily Mail* extract, 1 May 1999.

Source: extract © Atlantic Syndication; *photo*: David Gaywood.

bigots – in other words, hate-fuelled individuals who subscribe to racist, anti-semitic, homophobic and other bigoted ideologies. It is not surprising that many people think this way about hate crimes, because the media focus on the most extreme incidents – as is the case with crime reporting in general. The murder of Stephen Lawrence in south London in 1993, and the subsequent media coverage of the young men suspected of the murder, and the racist views they expressed, provide a prime example. Other extreme incidents in Britain that quite understandably gained notoriety include the bombing in May 1999 of the Admiral Duncan, a 'gay pub' in Soho, London (Plate 10.2), in which three died and scores were injured. The young man convicted, David Copeland, had a history of involvement with racist organisations. In the United States the brutality of the murder of James Byrd, an African-American – who was beaten unconscious, chained to the back of a pick-up truck and dragged for miles along rural roads outside the town of Jasper, Texas, in June 1998 – attracted widespread media coverage. The brutality of the murder and the fact that the two perpetrators were members of a white supremacist organisation evoked painful memories of lynching and historical racial violence in the United States. The callousness of the attack on the young gay man Matthew Shepard, who was pistol-whipped and left lashed to a fence in freezing conditions to die later in hospital in Wyoming in October 1998, generated considerable debate about homophobic bigotry. The incident itself and its repercussions have been portrayed in the play and film *The Laramie Project*.

Media coverage of extreme incidents of 'hate crime' perhaps leaves the impression that hate-fuelled bigots are behind many so-called hate crimes. This is hardly surprising, as the drama of extreme 'hate' is news, but only the most violent incidents make the headlines in the national press and on television. Anti-racist organisations such as Searchlight in Britain and the Southern Poverty Law Center in the United States – which do an incredibly valuable job of investigating and exposing the activities of racist extremists – might leave the impression too that attacks are mostly carried out by seriously bigoted thugs who are members of extremist organisations. But that is unlikely to be the case.

The small amount of research that there has been on hate crime offenders suggests that extremists are likely to be responsible for only a small proportion of incidents. Data on the characteristics of offenders supports this assertion. An analysis of the relationship between victim and suspect in homophobic incidents in January 2001, published by the MPS, showed that in just over one-fifth of incidents the recorded suspect was a neighbour. In over a quarter of incidents the suspects were other local people such as local youths. A similar analysis of racist incidents involving a snapshot of forty-nine incidents recorded by the Metropolitan Police Service on January 2001 showed very similar proportions of neighbours and other locals as suspects. Nearly 1 in 5 incidents were committed by schoolchildren. Such research, limited though it is, barely paints a picture of premeditated extremism at work behind incidents. Instead, the data suggest that many incidents occur as part and parcel of the victim's and the perpetrator's everyday lives.

'THRILL-SEEKING'

Given the paucity of research, there has been much speculation concerning the actions of 'hate crime' offenders, and numerous explanations have been offered, ranging from drunken pranks, social and economic crises, incitement by the media, and many others. Given the range of victims of hate crimes, the variety of offenders involved and the different social situations in which hate crimes occur, there can obviously be no single explanation, and in any one incident there may be a range of explanations. However, one thing does appear to stand out: many incidents seem to be committed *for the fun of it*, for the kicks, for the excitement, as well as for other reasons. According to scholars Jack Levin and Jack McDevitt from Northeastern University in Boston,

> Like young men getting together on a Saturday night to play a game of cards, certain hatemongers get together and decide to go out and destroy property or bash minorities. They want to have some fun and stir up a little excitement – at someone else's expense.

The payoff in such 'thrill-seeking hate crime', as Levin and McDevitt famously called it,

> is psychological as well as social: They enjoy the exhilaration and the thrill of making someone suffer. For those with a sadistic streak, inflicting pain and suffering is its own reward. In addition, the youthful perpetrators receive a stamp of approval from their friends who regard hatred and violence as 'hot' or 'cool'.
>
> (Levin and McDevitt, 2002: 67)

In a 'pick and mix' of bigotry, the victims of thrill-seeking hate crimes are often interchangeable. According to Levin and McDevitt again, 'When the first choice of victim to be attacked is unavailable, another will be substituted in their place' (1995: 7). An incident on a London street, a serious assault on an Orthodox Jewish teenager, reported in the *Jewish Chronicle* on 14 June 2002, shows how victims can be interchangeable. The Jewish victim first witnessed his assailants – two white youths – attacking an Asian man:

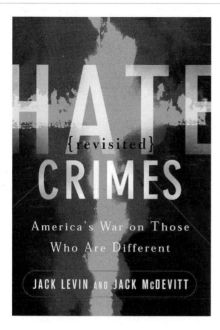

Jack Levin, Ph.D. is the Irving and Betty Brudnick Professor of Sociology and Criminology and director of the Brudnick Center on Conflict and Vioelnce at Northeastern University.

Jack McDevitt is the Associate Dean for Research and Graduate Studies and the Director of the Institute on Race and Justice at the Center for Criminal Justice Policy Research at Northeastern University's College of Criminal Justice.

'The culture of hate is important for singling out the victims of thrill hate attacks and justifying the violence perpetrated against them. Offenders target the members of certain groups because they regard them as inferior – perhaps even subhuman – and because they are convinced that their criminal behaviour will simply not engender the negative sanctions that crimes against more respectable groups might.'

Plate 10.3 *Hate Crimes Revisited* cover design.

Source: Cover design Rick Pracher, author biographies and photographs © Jack Levin and Jack McDevitt.

They were making monkey noises and slapping him on the head. . . . Then they saw me and said: 'Now here's a Yiddo.' Having just come back from Israel, I was on a high and told them: 'I'm Jewish and proud of it.' After that, they just went mad . . . they started pushing me and spinning me around. They smashed my glasses and punched me on the nose. I could feel blood on my face and it ran on to my jumper. Then they got me on the ground and kept on kicking me in the head and neck. I didn't pass out but felt detached. I could hear them shouting: 'You f***ing Jew; give me tuppence, Jew boy,' the usual things.

Commonly, a deep-seated and articulated bigotry arguably plays little role in the motivations of many of the perpetrators of such incidents. Where it does come into play, rather than acting out politically extremist ideas, offenders draw on 'everyday' bigotry to decide who is and who is not, an appropriate victim.

Attacks, then, might be seen as forms of recreation, carried out not as expressive acts of disaffection, alienation or marginalisation, but for the thrill, for the buzz. In the case of antisemitic incidents, Iganski and Kosmin (2003: 280) have observed that many reported incidents occur at the weekend, when Jews are perhaps most visible on the streets, and around communal buildings for religious observance. They argue that

> for many people – across all communities – the weekend is also the time to let off steam, wind down, let go and escape from the rationalization and regulation of the ordered weekday routines of work or school. A person's cultural and material capital influences the site and the form of their leisure. For some it's the golf club, the sports field, the cinema, the theatre, the concert hall. For others it's the pub and the streets. Some play with the children, watch television, go out for a meal, have a dance, listen to music. Others have a laugh, some take drugs, others get drunk, some have a fight, others engage in antisocial and delinquent behaviour . . . delinquency, antisocial behaviour, and violence, for some people are means of amusement that provide sensual rewards for the instigators.

Transgression can be seductive (see also Chapter 6 on cultural criminology). But this is not only because of the excitement it brings, the thrill, the escape from everyday routines. As Fenwick and Hayward argue,

> The seductiveness of crime is not only linked to the inherent excitement of the acts involved, but also to the more general feelings of self-realization and self-expression to which they give rise. It might be an unpalatable thought, but it is through such activities that individuals come alive.
>
> (2000: 49)

Keith Hayward further argues that the risk-taking involved in some offending involves a 'controlled loss of control'. In other words, in our reputedly insecure, unstable, but at the same time controlled, postmodern world, it is a way of self-actualisation:

> [N]ot only is it becoming more difficult to exert control and navigate a life pathway via the established (and crumbling) norms and codes of modernity but, at the same time, the individual is confronted by a reactive burgeoning culture of control, whether in the form of state-imposed criminal legislation and other modes of rationalization or private, decentralized forms of surveillance and other techniques. Given such circumstances, might it not be the case that many individuals will want to escape this conflicting situation by exerting a sense of control and self-actualization – to feel alive in an over-controlled yet at the same time highly unstable world? Moreover, might reflective risk calculation (such a prominent feature of our times) be the very instrumental device that enables that escape?
>
> (2002: 85)

SELF-ESTEEM

Excitement is not the only emotion involved in so-called hate crime. Levin and McDevitt argue that resentment – to one degree or another – can be found in the personality of most hate crime offenders, and it takes many forms. There are individuals who, perhaps because of some personal misfortune, feel rejected by, estranged from and wronged by society. They look for someone to target in venting their anger.

For others, their bitterness is fuelled by a perceived or real threat to their economic security, and some strike at those they think are to blame: newcomers, immigrants, asylum seekers. Larry Ray, David Smith, and Liz Wastell, drawing on interviews with sixty-five offenders in contact with the probation service in Greater Manchester, argue that much of the violence is related to the sense of shame and failure, resentment and hostility felt by young men who 'are disadvantaged and marginalised economically and culturally, and thus deprived of the material basis for enacting a traditional conception of working-class masculinity'. Such emotions, according to Ray and colleagues, 'readily lead to violence only in the case of young men (and occasionally for young women) for whom resorting to violence is a common approach to settling arguments and conflicts' (2003: 112).

The significance of self-esteem in the causation of violence has been explored by Thomas Scheff and colleagues. From their perspective, 'self-esteem concerns how we usually feel about ourselves. High self-esteem means that we usually feel justified pride in ourselves, low self-esteem that we often and easily feel ashamed of ourselves or try to avoid feelings of shame' (1989: 178). They propose that 'shame' is a primary emotion generated by the constant, incessant but commonly unacknowledged monitoring and negative evaluation of self in the eyes of others. Shame, however, is generally unacknowledged, and as an emotion it is seen to be socially unacceptable.

Self-esteem, in short, is a 'summary concept', representing how well a person overall manages shame. People with high self-esteem have had sufficient experience of pride to outweigh their experience of shame; they can manage shame. However, when a person has had an insufficient experience of pride, then shame becomes a calamity for them. When they experience some form of humiliation, real or imagined, rather than acknowledging it, it is masked with anger. The person is then caught in a 'shame–rage feeling trap'. According to Scheff and colleagues,

> In our theory, rage is used as a defense against threat to self, that is, feeling shame, a feeling of vulnerability of the whole self. Anger can be a protective measure to guard against shame, which is experienced as an attack on self. As humiliation increases, rage and hostility increase proportionally to defend against loss of self-esteem.

In short, violence is the consequence of trapped shame and anger.

RESPECT

Scheff and colleagues further argue that

> Pride and shame states almost always depend on the level of deference accorded a person: pride arises from deferential treatment by others ('respect'), and shame from lack of deference ('disrespect'). Gestures that imply respect or disrespect, together with the emotional response they generate, make up the deference/emotion system, which exerts a powerful influence on human behavior.
>
> (1989: 184–5)

The issue of 'respect' is a key theme presented by Elijah Anderson in his book *Code of the Streets* (1999). He argues that for many inner-city youths in his study, a street culture has evolved what he calls a code of the streets – a set of informal rules governing public behaviour and the use of violence. It can be traced to the sense of hopelessness and to the alienation that the youths feel from mainstream society and its institutions, due to the joblessness and the pervasive racism they experience.

'Respect' is 'at the heart of the code', according to Anderson. Respect is about 'being treated "right", or granted the deference one deserves'. But gaining and maintaining respect has to be a constant endeavour:

> In the street culture, especially among young people, respect is viewed as almost an external entity that is hard-won but easily lost, and so must constantly be guarded. The rules of the code in fact provide a framework for negotiating respect. The person whose very appearance – including his clothing, demeanor, and way of moving – deters transgressions feels that he possesses, and may be considered by others to possess, a measure of respect. With the right amount of respect, for instance, he can avoid "being bothered" in public. If he is bothered, not only may he be in physical danger but he has been disgraced or "dissed".
>
> (Anderson, 1994: 82)

One key aspect of a person's demeanour to convey and hold respect is 'having the juice': projecting an image, a willingness to resort to violence, having the nerve to throw the first punch, to pull the trigger, and, in the extreme, not being afraid to die, and not being afraid of taking another's life if needs be, if someone 'gets in their face', if disrespected. As Anderson suggests,

> one's bearing must send the unmistakable if sometimes subtle message to 'the next person' in public that one is capable of violence and mayhem when the situation requires it, that one can take care of oneself. The nature of this communication is largely determined by the demands of the circumstances but can include facial expressions, gait, and verbal expressions – all of which are geared mainly to deterring aggression. . . . Its proper display helps on the spot to check others who would violate one's person and also helps to build a reputation that works to prevent future challenges.
>
> (1994: 88, 92)

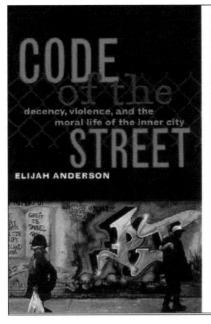

Elijah Anderson, Charles and William L. Day Distinguished Professor of the Social Sciences, and Professor of Sociology, at the University of Pennsylvania

'The hopelessness and alienation many young inner-city black men and women feel, largely as a result of endemic joblessness and persistent racism, fuels the violence they engage in. This violence serves to confirm the negative feelings many whites and some middle-class blacks harbor toward the ghetto poor, further legitimating the oppositional culture and the code of the streets in the eyes of many poor young blacks. Unless this cycle is broken, attitudes on both sides will become increasingly entrenched, and the violence, which claims victims black and white, poor and affluent, will only escalate.'

Plate 10.4 *Code of the Street* cover design and biography.

Source: © W. W. Norton and E. Anderson.

Respect is a scarce commodity. Deprived of achieving a sense of self-esteem through participation in the jobs market, and other institutions of mainstream society, 'everyone competes', according to Anderson,

> to get what affirmation he can of the little that is available. The craving for respect that results gives people thin skins. Shows of deference by others can be highly soothing, contributing to a sense of security, comfort, self-confidence, and self-respect. Transgressions by others which go unanswered diminish these feelings and are believed to encourage further transgressions. . . . Among young people, whose sense of self-esteem is particularly vulnerable, there is an especially heightened concern with being disrespected. Many inner-city young men in particular crave respect to such a degree that they will risk their lives to attain and maintain it.

(1994: 89)

Campaigning for respect holds its dangers in the face of transgression. As Anderson argues,

> since such a show of nerve is a forceful expression of disrespect toward the person on the receiving end, the victim may be greatly offended and seek to retaliate with equal or greater force. A display of nerve, therefore, can easily provoke a life-threatening response, and the background knowledge of that possibility has often been incorporated into the concept of nerve.

(1994: 92)

Cycles of violence and retaliation can ensue. 'Pay back', or revenge, is crucial to regain respect when disrespected.

REVENGE

To focus further on the emotion of 'revenge', but returning to the discussion of so-called 'hate crimes', experimental research with college students in the United States (Craig, 1999) indicates that 'hate crimes' might be more likely to generate a desire for revenge than crimes otherwise motivated. Especially, to quote Levin and McDevitt, 'When a group has suffered some degree of oppression, it becomes easier for its members to blame advantaged groups and justify criminal behaviour. In extreme cases, resentment may be translated into brutal acts of violence' (2002: 62). A brutal incident of black-on-white violence is graphically portrayed in the opening pages of Nathan McCall's best-selling autobiography *Makes Me Wanna Holler* (see Box 10.1). The vengeful anger and visceral resentment expressed by the attackers – generated by their experience of racism – reaches out to the reader from the text.

BOX 10.1 GET-BACK

The fellas and I were hanging out on our corner one afternoon when the strangest thing happened. A white boy, who appeared to be about eighteen or nineteen years old, came pedalling a bicycle casually through the neighbourhood. I don't know if he was lost or just confused, but he was definitely in the wrong place to be doing the tourist bit. Somebody spotted him and pointed him out to the rest of us. 'Look! What's that motherfucka doin' ridin' through here?! Is he *crraaaazy*?!'

It was automatic. We all took off after him. We caught him on Cavalier Boulevard and knocked him off the bike. He fell to the ground and it was all over. We were on him like white on rice. Ignoring the passing cars, we stomped him and kicked him. My stick partners kicked him in the head and face and watched the blood gush from his mouth. I kicked him in the stomach and nuts, where I knew it would hurt. Every time I drove my foot into his balls, I felt better; with each blow I delivered, I gritted my teeth as I remembered some recent racial slight:

> THIS is for all the times you followed me round in stores . . .
> And THIS is for the times you treated me like a nigger . . .
> And THIS is for G.P. – General Principle – just 'cause you white.

While we kicked, he lay there, curled up in the fetal position, trying to use his hands to cover his head. We bloodied him so badly that I got a little scared and backed off. The others, seeing how badly he was messed up, moved away too. But one dude kept stomping, like he'd gone berserk. He seemed crazy and consumed in the pleasure of kicking that white boy's ass. When he finished he reached down, and picked up the white dude's bike, lifted it as high as he could above his head, and slammed it down on him hard. The white guy didn't even flinch. He was out cold. I feared he might be dead until I saw him breathing.

We walked away, laughing, boasting, competing for bragging rights about who'd done the most damage. 'Man, did you see how red that cracker's face turned when I busted his lip? I almost broke my hand on that ugly motherfucka!'

Fucking up white boys like that made us feel good inside. I guess we must have been fourteen or fifteen by then, and it felt so good that we stumbled over each other sometimes trying to get in extra kicks and punches. When we bum-rushed white boys, it made me feel like we were beating all white people on behalf of all blacks. We called it 'getting' some get-back,' securing revenge for all the shit they'd heaped on blacks all these years. They were still heaping hell on us, and especially on our parents. The difference was, cats in my generation weren't taking it lying down.

Sometimes, when I sit back and think about the crazy things the fellas and I did and remember the hate and violence that we unleashed, it's hard to believe I was once part of all that – I feel so removed from it now that I've left the streets. Yet when I consider white America and the way it's treated blacks, our random rage in the old days makes perfect sense to me. Looking back, it's easy to understand how it all got started.

Source: © Nathan McCall, 1994 by kind permission of Random House.

There have been some occasions when racist incidents have provoked serious disorder in response. Rodney King was brutally beaten by four white Los Angeles police officers on 3 March 1991. The incident was caught on a home video camera, sent to a local news station and televised internationally. The police officers charged with the beating were acquitted on 29 April 1992. Serious rioting followed the announcement of the verdict. Fifty-four people died, and thousands were injured. In a shocking incident that was also captured on film and played back on the news, white truck driver Reginald Denny, who arrived at the wrong place at the wrong time, was dragged from his cab and beaten mercilessly. He was kicked in the head, beaten with bottles, and shot with a shotgun. Fortunately, some bystanders saved his life by bravely intervening.

Others are resentful and lash out when the safety and certainty of their world is threatened and challenged. Following the terrorist attack in 2001 against the World Trade Center in New York and against the Pentagon, attacks against Arab-Americans escalated. As Levin and McDevitt point out,

The attack on September 11, 2001, made a difficult situation even worse. While the economy had already begun a decline that was a recession in all but the formal definition, the attack on the World Trade Center and the Pentagon drove our economy deeper into decline. This time, however, there was someone to blame. The attack planned by Osama bin Laden and carried out by members of his Al Quaeda terrorist network deepened economic fears of the nation and created widespread anxiety about the possibility of further acts of terrorism being committed on our shores. It did not take very long for the purveyors of hate across the country to quickly blame the attack on Arabs and call for the deportation of all Arab-Americans. . . . What followed was an unprecedented increase in attacks on Arab-Americans and a broad-based scapegoating of Arabs for all economic and military problems.

(2002: 56–7)

THE TIMES WEDNESDAY SEPTEMBER 19 2001

3

AMERICA AT WAR: THE MUSLIM COMMUNITY

Racists seek revenge around the world

'My friend is paralysed. If this happens here, where can we go?'

Plate 10.5 *Times* extract, 19 September 2001.

Source: Text © News International Syndication; photo: Raoul Dixon, copyright North News and Pictures.

Notably, the FBI's hate crime statistics recorded a large increase in attacks against Muslims following '9/11'. There were 481 'anti-Islamic' incidents recorded for 2001, compared with 28 for 2000, and 32 in 1999. In Britain, in a poll of British Muslims by the BBC's radio news programme *Today* in the aftermath of the terrorist attack on the Pentagon and the destruction of the World Trade Center, 30 per cent of respondents reported perceived hostility or abuse towards them, or a member of their family, from non-Muslims as a result of the events on 11 September. However, it cannot be determined from the survey findings how much of the hostility was manifest as crime.

HUMILIATION AND RAGE

At the beginning of this chapter it was observed that crimes of passion have fuelled the artistic imagination. In closing the chapter, we return here to such crimes and draw from Jack Katz's analysis of the interrelationship of emotion and crime in his book *Seductions of Crime* (1988). In the book Katz covers a range of criminal and deviant behaviour – too extensive to cover in the brief introduction provided for his work here – but it is instructive to focus on cases of murder that Katz analyses using a variety of documentary sources. The incidents involving what Katz calls 'Righteous Slaughter' are impassioned acts committed in moments of rage – as is the case with many murders.

In the cases that Katz analyses, the victim-to-be inflicts a humiliation upon the killer-to-be: a wife caught by her husband *in flagrante* with another man; another tortured by her husband's infidelity; a man whose virility is challenged by his partner; a neighbour offended by another neighbour parking in front of their property. In each case, humiliation arises from the violation of a respected social role, such as husband, wife, virile male, property owner.

The would-be killer's reaction to the humiliation, according to Katz's analysis, is 'a last stand defence of respectability'. Their mortal act is not calculated in a premeditated sense to restore their self-worth. It is instead experienced as a compulsion, driven by rage arising from the killer's emotional comprehension of the humiliation they have suffered.

SUMMARY

1 Human emotions play a central role in the criminal act.
2 The study of the emotional dynamics of crime illuminates why particular crimes are committed by particular individuals under the circumstances in which they occur.
3 In some cases, unconscious seduction and compulsion is behind the motivation for the criminal act.

CRITICAL THINKING QUESTIONS

1 Is the term 'hate crime' inappropriate for the crimes so labelled?
2 How might crime be seductive?
3 Is the desire for revenge driven by other emotions?

FURTHER STUDY

Anderson, E. (1999) *Code of the Streets: Decency, Violence and the Moral Life of the Inner City*, New York: W. W. Norton. A highly illuminating ethnographic exploration of the social and cultural dynamics of interpersonal violence in the inner city.

Katz, J. (1988) *Seductions of Crime: Moral and Sensual Attractions of Doing Evil*, New York: Basic Books. An engaging analysis of the sensual and emotional dynamics of crime.

Levin, J. (2002) *The Violence of Hate*, Boston: Allyn and Bacon. A crafted explication of the relationship between bigotry and crime.

Levin, J. and McDevitt, J. (2002) *Hate Crimes Revisited: America's War on Those Who Are Different*, Boulder, CO: Westview. An influential and valuable evaluation of the social, cultural, motivational and policy context of hate and crime.

▌ MORE INFORMATION

American Psychological Association: 'Hate Crimes Today: An Age-Old Foe in Modern Dress'
http://www.apa.org/pubinfo/hate/homepage.html
A question-and-answer site shedding some clarification on the hate crime debate.

Hate Crime.org
http://www.hatecrime.org/
Information and links to related news articles concerning current events, political choices, and victims and further information.

National Gay and Lesbian Task Force: Information on hate crime laws
http://www.ngltf.org/issues/issue.cfm?issueID=12
NGLTF is the national progressive organisation working for the civil rights of gay, lesbian, bisexual and transgender people.

CHAPTER 11

KEY ISSUES

▌ How easy is it to define and understand different forms of crime concerned with the pursuit of power and profit?

▌ What kinds of activity have been engaged in by professional criminals in Britain?

▌ How new or old is financial crime?

▌ In what ways do the legitimate and illegitimate worlds of enterprise overlap?

Organisational and Professional Forms of Crime

INTRODUCTION

Various chapters of this book look at forms of crime where the emphasis is largely on the individual as criminal or victim (and sometimes both) and at locations of criminality and victimization, all of which are 'everyday' and generally occurring in the home or on the street.

This chapter is concerned with the following, divided into different areas or worlds of activity, motives and consequences (although it should become apparent that there is blurring and overlap between these categories):

- crime in the world of illegal enterprise – crime as an illegal profession;
- crime in the world of lawful professions – crime as abuse of legal professional status and resources;
- crime in the world of corporate-level business and commerce – crime as subversion or inversion of good corporate behaviour, producing negligence and/or illegality.

A final note before proceeding. As with so many other topics in this book, the range of possible issues and examples that could be covered here is enormous and all that can be provided is an indicative exploration.

Thinking about organisational and professional crime

In beginning to think about these rather different forms of crime, we are now talking about offending or deviance committed by or within organised structures, groups or associations. This is not to say we are concerned here only with 'criminal organisations', for clearly, individual employees or the self-employed commit crime at work or even engage in crime as their work. But what this chapter takes as the criteria for inclusion here are forms of crime that involve one or more of the following:

- a commitment to crime as a full-time activity – crime as a profession – working closely or loosely with others in criminal or legitimate networks;
- a benefit from and/or abuse of a professional and/or trusted position of some seniority or status – following from being an employee in an organisation and/or recognition of qualifications by professional or other bodies (e.g. providing validation of specialist competence);
- a temporary or long-standing criminal association or organisation for the pursuit of profit and/or power;
- a business or corporation that in part or whole 'goes wrong' and engages in crime or has actually been established as a legal organisational 'front' for criminal activity.

Note that the case of 'everyday crime' at work, such as pilferage and fiddles, sometimes referred to as 'hidden economy' or 'blue-collar crime', is discussed elsewhere (see Chapter 8).

Self-evidently, certain forms of crime depend on features of an organisation – for example, planning, coordination, concealment, group membership, and hierarchy. This applies to diverse examples of crime: for example, a 'project crime' (McIntosh, 1975) such as the diamond raid on the Millennium Dome in 2000 in which a gang used a JCB digger to break into the Dome, planning to steal £350 million worth of diamonds and then make an escape by speedboat on the Thames in a style said to have been inspired by the James Bond movie *The World is Not Enough*; or the coordinated concealment of financial mismanagement, misappropriation and fraud, as in the case of the international energy giant Enron and a subsequent wave of financial scandals, to be dealt with later in this chapter. Other crimes may seem to be tied to individual activity – for example, the fraudulent lawyer or doctor – but when examined can be seen to rely on factors such as the exploitation of systems, organisations and professional standing that all insulate the individual from suspicion or scrupulous investigation; abuse of trust and qualifications bestowed and supposedly guaranteed by professional associations; and victimization of clients and customers of services that are being offered. Numerous studies have highlighted characteristics common to both illegitimate and legitimate profit-oriented organisations. These include:

- entrepreneurialism;
- risk-taking;
- rule-breaking;
- specialist division of labour;

- investment strategies;
- managing evasion of unwelcome regulation;
- avoidance of harmful scrutiny or control;
- manipulation of financial systems and loopholes to avoid tax liabilities.

It can help to clarify what this chapter is focusing on if we briefly note what is excluded here. For example, youth crime may involve gangs and other more or less 'organised' groups (Hobbs, 1997; Newburn, 2002a; South, 1999a). However, the nature of organisation in such cases is, in Britain at least, generally of a short-lived, immature and non-elaborated form. Where more elaborated structures do emerge, these may provide socialisation into more established crime groups. For example, in Japan some youth gangs are associated with the Yakuza (Kersten, 1993), or in Los Angeles, there are gangs of young (and older) adults such as the Crips and the Bloods (Davis, 1992). These are readily seen as professional crime associations involved in control of territory for power and profit, and in illegal activity such as drug impor-tation and dealing. In cases such as these, at least some of the characteristics listed above will apply, and indeed the tradition of study of youth gangs from Thrasher (1927) onwards has been partly typified by the search for the forms of structure and value systems that sustain involvement of certain youth in gangs, delinquency and crime (see Chapter 4) leading to criminal careers (Foster, 1990: 165; South, 1999a).

On the other side of the criminal justice fence, the incidence of crime and deviance in organisational contexts such as the police and prisons is important to note here, but it has simply made sense to refer to such organisational crime in the chapters on these particular topics.

CRIME IN THE WORLD OF ILLEGAL ENTERPRISE

Professional crime was seen by Sutherland (1937: 197) as based upon a craft that had been learned, and it was this achievement that defined the 'professional' thief (or safecracker or forger or whatever) as someone who had learned their trade and, like 'physicians, lawyers or bricklayers' (ibid.), developed a variety of abilities and skills. (Here we can see elements of learning theory and Sutherland's idea of differ-ential association; see p. 78.) Of course, as many critics have pointed out, this is simply too neat and offers a rather romanticised notion of a career in crime, which in fact may provide little or no opportunity to learn skills and be more likely to result in a place in the crime economy as a 'mass labourer' than membership of what used to be called the 'aristocracy of labour' – the elite of the working class who possessed skills and craft knowledge that were always in demand and well rewarded (Lemert, 1958; Hobbs, 1994: 441; Ruggiero and South, 1995: 129–32). Nonetheless, the important point in Sutherland's work on 'the professional thief' was to draw attention to the idea of 'full-time crime'.

As Hobbs (1994: 444) notes, 'the practice of crime as a full time occupation can be traced to the decline of the feudal system in England, and to the need for those leaving the land to develop alternative forms of economic subsistence within the context of urbanization and the emergence of capitalism' (Roebuck and Windham,

1983). Full-time miscreants (Mack, 1964) were established in major metropolitan areas by the eighteenth century as the areas of the rich and the poor grew, and did so in ever-sharpening contrast. The business of the fence – a buyer and seller of stolen goods – was then, as now, a staple of the irregular and illegal economy of the city (Klockars, 1975; Sutton, 1998). Other forms of 'crime as business' were carried out by individualist criminal entrepreneurs or criminal 'firms' (Hobbs, 1988) – frauds, counterfeiting, robbery – but there are no signs in the history of British crime of large-scale organisation, and the comments by Low (1982: 195; Hobbs, 1994) concerning the underworld of Regency England are still largely applicable today: '[T]here were some big criminal entrepreneurs, but on the whole the criminal underworld was not organised, or even much influenced by its leading citizens: fortunately for the rest of society it remained essentially a community of small operators.'

In Britain today, criminal 'organisations' are probably more accurately described as semi-formal or informal associations of professional criminals (relatively small gangs, groups and networks) that remain small to medium-scale in the size and scope of their operations. They have been and remain subject to considerable flux and change in terms of membership and goals (Hobbs, 1995, 1997; Dorn *et al.*, 1992; Campbell, 1991). Nonetheless, it is, of course, the distinction of exhibiting some form of organisational capacity and modus operandi that means they are being discussed here.

Professional organised crime in Britain, 1930s–2000

The roots of modern professional organised crime in Britain lie in the 'hard man' gang culture of major cities such as Glasgow, Liverpool, Leeds, Birmingham and Newcastle (Freeman, 1996–7), the resilience of the illegal economies that prospered within but also assisted communities of poverty and marginality, and the enduring structure of the 'traditional neighbourhood family firm' (Hobbs, 2001; Samuel, 1981; Foster, 1990; Lea, 2002). In addition, social and population changes during and after the First World War were important: the dislocation of war in Europe brought refugees to Britain, some of whom settled into the criminal economies of survival and illegal opportunity; the old system of social class status, difference and deference was being eroded; and new opportunities for crime were emerging. Kohn (1992) explores these themes in relation to the emergence of subcultures of drugs and crime in the early twentieth century. However, as was the case with alcohol **Prohibition** in the United States from 1920 to 1933 and with the market for illegal drugs later in the century (see Chapter 12), where there is a prohibition of a commodity or service for which there is a demand, then an illegal supply, or the scope for corruption, will emerge (Nadelman, 1990). In Britain in the 1920s and 1930s, it was not the prohibition of alcohol sales but the illegality of street gambling and the high profits of the bookmakers who could legally take bets at racecourses that drew the attention of criminal groups (Campbell, 1994: 22). As Hobbs describes, 'These gangs operated several forms of protection racket. The gangs controlled the pitches, renting them at extortionate prices to the on-course bookmakers. . . . Fights were deliberately started if payment was slow and non-repayable loans were demanded. Profits were enormous' (Hobbs, 1994: 450).

The Second World War created the conditions for further social change but also reinforced the national experience and defining mentality of 'the British Isles' as something to be preserved against evil from elsewhere – a characteristic contributing to popular perceptions of organised crime (see p. 132). Specifically in relation to crime in this period, while community spirit and patriotism are seen as having helped Britain through 'the dark days of the Blitz' and the threat of invasion, a contrasting spirit of opportunism and profiteering was also evident, and what is commonly known as the 'black market' allowed minor fiddling of ration allowances as well as a significant trade in 'state-controlled goods or commodities that were in short supply' (Hobbs, 1994: 450). With the extension of rationing into the 1950s, 'competent criminals . . . found that the post-war market hardly differed from its wartime equivalent' (ibid.).

However, it was London in the late 1950s and the 1960s that became the location and period most associated with a high-profile 'gangland' in Britain, epitomised by the operations of the Kray brothers in the East End of London and the Richardson gang south of the river Thames (Pearson, 1973; Morton, 1992). The Krays cultivated celebrity and were photographed with show-business and sporting friends at charity events and at clubs in which they had an interest; the Richardsons had legitimate business dealings in scrap metal and illegitimate expertise in long-firm fraud (Levi, 1981), and were spreading their business interests beyond London before their arrest. But even so, at the end of the day, none of this was 'organised crime' on a grand scale.

Plate 11.1 The hearse containing the body of the infamous gangster Reggie Kray arrives at Chingford cemetery, having travelled some 12 miles through London's East End past crowds of well-wishers, 11 October 2000. Kray was buried alongside his brother Ronnie to bring to a close a final chapter in the history of the London hardmen who were both imprisoned for murder in 1968.

Source: © Reuters 2000; *photo*: Jonathan Evans.

In the 1960s and 1970s, affluence, consumerism, changing morality and new technologies expanded opportunities for criminal development and exploitation of various markets. Pornography, the counterfeiting of goods and VAT fraud were attractive and carried fewer risks than crimes such as armed robbery (Campbell, 1991). But the age of the criminal entrepreneur really arrived with the 1980s and the political promotion of a 'culture of enterprise' by the Conservative government of Margaret Thatcher (Hobbs, 1991). This is not to say that the market ideology of the new brand of conservatism 'caused' criminal enterprise, but many commentators agree that this was a period of significance in the reorientation of national values and the promotion of materialism. Suddenly, the wheeling and dealing culture of young men 'on the make' was a popular value system to aspire to, and markets – both legal and illegal – received a boost, domestically and internationally. Although women were also high achievers in this culture of aspiration, the impact in relation to crime was largely (though not exclusively – see the example below) a masculine matter (Newburn and Stanko, 1994; Messerschmidt, 1993; and see Chapter 12). While it was the so-called Big Bang of government-imposed deregulation in the financial operations of the City of London that changed the environment for business crime (see Carrabine *et al.*, 2002: 97; I. Taylor, 1999), the big bang that fuelled the new crime economy was undoubtedly the drugs 'explosion' of the 1980s (Dorn and South, 1987; and see Chapter 12). The central commodities here were heroin and cannabis, then later cocaine, ecstasy, LSD and amphetamines. In turn, the drugs economy has had its own influence on the global legal economy and its institutions (Castells, 1998; and see Chapter 6).

Writing at the end of the 1980s, the crime reporter Duncan Campbell (1991: 8) suggested that

> In a way, what has happened to British crime parallels what has happened to British industry. The old family firms . . . have been replaced by multinationals of uncertain ownership, branches throughout the world, profits dispersed through myriad outlets. . . . The 1990s [was] seen as a boom time for them, with the exploitation of a recreational western culture that wants its luxuries and its drugs. The legitimate businesses will run alongside the illegitimate ones.

Arguably this picture still holds. Some of the reminiscences of criminals such as safebreakers and thieves, recounted by Hobbs (1995), illustrate a world based on 'traditional' criminal crafts and skills that largely disappeared alongside the world of manufacturing, mining and steel and the one-time 'aristocracy of labour' mentioned earlier. The sharp contrast of the old with the new breed of criminal specialists is nicely relayed by the case of the 'female drug dealer who dresses smartly, uses a mobile phone and would not look out of place in a merchant bank or city finance house. Looking smart is part of her business method and she uses her gender to "fool" clients and police officers, who assume that as an attractive woman she is less competent' (Croall, 1998: 240; Hobbs, 1995: 25).

Ethnicity and the organisation of crime

The study of organised crime as a business for profit and power has been largely dominated by US work, and until as late as the 1980s this was greatly preoccupied with the operations and threat of the US Mafia or Sicilian Cosa Nostra and with themes such as the dangers of conspiracy and subversion from within US society but linked to external 'alien' roots. Prior to the fall of the Soviet Union, the twin threats of communism and organised crime obviously shared a high profile, although interestingly, throughout the period of the Cold War, J. Edgar Hoover, Director of the FBI, felt the former to be the greater threat. The classic, highly influential work on the Mafia as a highly organised and stratified empire of crime, spanning the United States from coast to coast, was Donald Cressey's (1969) *Theft of a Nation*. However, this portrayal has been seriously questioned, and the evidence upon which Cressey drew is now seen as discredited, as it relied heavily on the testimony of one key source whose reliability is doubted. This image of a Mafia empire dominated by the dons of major crime families was frequently depicted by the image (still used in newspaper graphics today) of an 'octopus of crime' with a controlling head and tentacles spreading out and embracing the nation (or the globe). In fact, much subsequent criminological research and law enforcement intelligence have demonstrated the mythical nature of this creature and instead emphasised the diversity of cooperating and competing criminal organisations – sometimes referred to as 'disorganised crime' (Reuter, 1984). This reconceptualisation does not suggest that such criminal groups do not exist or that they are incompetent or lacking in organisational skills or structures. Rather, it simply emphasises a more realistic picture of the mixed and fragmentary character of the criminal economy than is provided by images of monolithic and monopolistic criminal conspiracies.

Since the 1960s and accelerating since the 1980s, other criminal networks and associations have been identified as operating on their own home territory, in the United States and in various ways globally, including not only the US Mafia but also Colombian and Mexican cartels, Nigerian criminal networks, Japanese Yakuza, Chinese Triads, Russian Mafiyas, Jamaican Posses, and so on (Castells, 1998, ch. 3; Southwell, 2002).

Importantly, whatever form it takes, 'organised crime' is therefore easily seen as a threat from beyond national borders, and reactions can be strongly fuelled by national anxieties and prejudices. For Britain this point is worth further consideration. Historically, although some crime groups such as the Sabini family were successful in the racetrack and then the greyhound, drinking and gambling businesses during the years from 1910 to the Second World War (Hobbs, 1994: 450), in general there has been little sign of 'alien threat'. Maltese gangsters attracted some police and newspaper notoriety in the 1950s, and attempts by figures with American Mafia connections to move into the legalised gambling industry in Britain in the 1960s were effectively stamped on by the police and Home Office. Indeed, part of the celebrity of the Krays and the Great Train Robbers of 1963 was that in the 'swinging sixties', when English culture was seen as exciting and breaking the mould, here were distinctive examples of a 'home-grown' 'underworld' taking on 'the establishment' on their own terms. All this struck a popular chord (Campbell, 1994: 134; Carrabine *et al.*, 2002: 87–8).

Since the 1970s and 1980s, however, multi-ethnic Britain has produced criminal groups based on its own diverse ethnic communities, although as Ruggiero (2000) and others have shown, 'contrary to alien conspiracy theories the "outsiders" do not change the society. Rather the society and its existing structures provide the opportunities for crime and deviance, as well as the accompanying motivations and rationalizations' (Carrabine *et al.*, 2002: 90).

However, the extent to which ties into ethnic communities translate into international criminal operations or conspiracies is complex and debatable. On the one hand, Stelfox (1998: 400), a detective superintendent in the Greater Manchester Police, notes:

> Evidence given to the Home Affairs Committee on Organized Crime (1994) suggests that locally based criminals in the UK are unlikely to be members of any international organized crime group. At most some gangs from ethnic communities will belong to local variations of traditional crime groups from their country of origin. . . . They may acquire the name of a traditional crime group through a process of labelling by the community, the media or the police, or they may adopt it themselves as a way of enhancing their status in the community. But the use of a name such as Triad, does not necessarily imply an operational connection with an organized crime group.

And in relation to one of the most notorious but probably most misused labels for black criminal groups – the Yardies – Stelfox (1998: 400) remarks that this term

> is often used as though it was the name of an organized crime group such as the Mafia or the Cosa Nostra. However it originated as the name given to criminals in Jamaica. Latterly it has come to be used as a description for any Afro-Caribbean criminal involved in drugs distribution but does not refer to any single group which could be considered as an organized crime group.

As noted in the first quotation from Stelfox, it may serve the interests of a criminal group to be identified as a dangerous force, but of course this can also serve the interests of resource-hungry law enforcement agencies keen to draw attention to the seriousness of the challenges they face.

On the other hand, as Hobbs (1998) indicates, it is increasingly the case that even the most localised crime group can connect to the global stage (whether dealing in commodities from elsewhere or seeking to move profits out of the country), while 'current research indicates that even the classic "international" criminal organisations function as interdependent *local* units' (ibid.: 419; emphasis added). Hence, today we must consider at least some, though not all, forms of organised crime activity in terms of both local dimensions (e.g. 'doing the job', distributing 'the goods') and international connections and resources (e.g. overseas demand for stolen works of art, for drugs such as ecstasy produced in the UK, for wildlife items – rare animals, birds, eggs; or overseas banks, lawyers, accountants and others that can help to launder profits or disguise the provenance of stolen goods). While a 'local' criminal project such as a raid on a warehouse or a lorry hijacking can still be seen as a familiar kind of venture, we also begin to see the complexity of the late modern criminal economy. We can give some sense of this 'big picture' in the following way.

Following the organised terrorism attack on the World Trade Center in 2001, President Bush announced (on 24 September 2001) the intention of the United States to 'choke off' the sources of funding for terrorist groups by seizing or freezing their assets. This was a strong and easy political soundbite to make. However, if such a strategy is to be effective beyond the governmental borders of the United States, then it has to involve the banking systems of other countries because these are twenty-four-hour, globally interlocking and mutually interdependent structures. This point may seem to take us into the territory of political crime and the financial criminals who help hide funds and indeed it does. But it is also a further reminder of the significance of the idea of 'glocalisation' – put simply, that the local matters to the global and vice versa – because if we leave aside the specific nature of terrorist groups (we could talk instead of the assets of illegal arms traders, pornography distributors, drug traffickers, etc.), then once we recognise the enormous scale of the movement of murky money at the global level, the next obvious question is, where do these criminal profits come from? The following passage from a report on money laundering prepared for the United Nations comprehensively illustrates the kinds of links and chains that transform illicit cash from the street into digital transactions on the legal electronic financial markets and conveys this message about the interlocking global complexity and 'glocalised' nature of late modern criminal economies:

> Sweatshops in big cities in the industrialized countries hire illegal aliens who are brought in by smuggling groups that may also deal in banned or restricted commodities, are financed by loan sharks who may be recycling drug money and make cartel agreements with trucking companies run by organized crime families, all in order to sell their goods cheaply to prestigious and eminently respectable retail outlets that serve the general public. The masses of street peddlers in the big urban centres of developing countries sell goods that might be smuggled, produced in underground factories using fake brand-name labels or stolen from legitimate enterprises, thereby violating customs, intellectual property and larceny laws. They pay no sales or income taxes but make protection payments to drug gangs that control the streets where they operate. The drug gangs might then use the protection money as operating capital to finance whole-scale purchases of drugs or arms.
>
> (Blum *et al.*, 1998)

CRIME IN THE WORLD OF LAWFUL PROFESSIONS

The American criminologist Edwin Sutherland was notable not only for his work on the idea of the professional criminal but even more so for his elaboration of the idea of 'white-collar crime'. Sutherland first drew attention to the significance of this concept in his address to the American Sociological Society in 1939 and its publication the following year (Weisburd *et al.*, 2001: 1–26). It is widely acknowledged that this was a significant insight both conceptually and politically, and indeed it was once even suggested that were a Nobel Prize awarded for criminology, Sutherland would have been a worthy recipient for this contribution (Nelken, 1994: 361). However, dispute around definitions arose almost straight away. For a start, Tappan (1947) criticised Sutherland for attaching the term 'crime' to a variety of activities that did not necessarily break any criminal laws. To some extent this was, of course, Sutherland's point: the criminal law focuses downward on the poor and marginal, not upward on the affluent and mainstream. Yet the respectable middle and upper classes can engage in business and professional activities that can be far more financially or physically injurious to others, and with wider repercussions, than the offences for which working-class criminals are prosecuted and convicted. Furthermore, a factor of even greater significance for Sutherland (1949: 13) was that the crimes of respectable professionals violate the trust that society places in them: 'The financial loss from white collar crime, great as it is, is less important than the damage to social relations. White collar crimes violate trust and therefore create distrust: this lowers morale and produces social disorganization.' The application of the term 'crime' is a signal about what may indeed not be legally 'criminal' but arguably should be, given its far-reaching seriousness. This is a tradition that has continued in the critical areas of criminology and does not mean that writers are ignorant of the law when they refer to, for example, the 'crimes' of the powerful (see Chapter 5) but rather that they are drawing attention to biases in the law-making and criminal justice systems (Reiman, 2001).

A further definitional problem arises in relation to what Sutherland was actually including in his idea of 'white-collar crime'. As Nelken (1994: 362) has pointed out, Sutherland's original concept

> is built on the *overlap* of (at least) three different types of misbehaviour (crimes). The first refers to any crime committed by a person of high status (whether or not in the course of their occupation); the second to crimes committed on behalf of organizations (by people of any status); and the third to crimes committed against organizations (whether or not these are carried out by people working in the same organization, another organization, or no organization at all). Sutherland focuses on that *area of overlap in which people of high status use organizations to commit crimes for their organizations* – against workers, consumers, or other organizations including competitors and the government. [emphasis added]

In general, we find this area of 'overlap' (italicised in the preceding quotation) useful in guiding discussion in this and the next section, but here we also focus on crimes committed by 'high-status' criminals on their own behalf. It is clearly wise to bear in mind the difficulty criminologists have had in providing hard-and-fast distinctions between white-collar and corporate criminality. It is also not entirely clear where all these definitional problems place those working within the offices of national and local government, whether as civil servants or politicians. Here too, qualified professional specialists in law, finance, medicine, accountancy, and so on work with autonomy and discretion, and with similar opportunities to their commercial-sector counterparts to connive at corrupt practices and benefit from fraud, bribery, theft and malpractice. Furthermore, in the world of 'politics as a profession', Cohen (1996: 11) reminds us that the one thing as old as political power is political corruption:

> [T]he post-Watergate era has seen a quite unprecedented and uninterrupted series of public scandals about corrupt government in Western democracries. . . . In some cases, criminal activities (bribery, corruption, embezzlement, theft) were used for personal greed, in others for party political gain, in yet others to subvert basic and constitutional rules.

One Secretary-General of Interpol, Cohen notes, has remarked that 'it is becoming difficult to draw a clear line between what he called "normal" political business corruption and hard core, organized crime activity' (ibid.).

Of course, the mere fact that the criminological debate about the concept of white-collar crime is generally dated back to Sutherland's work does not mean that such crime was previously unknown! The business boom of Victorian England produced early versions of the banking frauds and stock swindles that became familiar in the 1980s (Robb, 1992). Further, from the nineteenth century onwards, the growth of commerce, of bureaucratic methods of organisation and administration, of offices and their practices and technologies of accounting and filing, and of divisions of labour, all produced the infrastructure and conditions for the successful running of capitalism but also for the increasing diversity of criminal opportunity.

Crime and the professions

We expect to be able to trust professionals, and this is the basis on which we 'entrust' them with our finances, our health, our security and personal information, or give permission to them to act upon our behalf in all manner of intimate ways and relationships. As mentioned, Sutherland noted the damaging consequences of the abuse of trust as a key feature of white-collar crime, and it is worth considering how these and other effects follow from examples of such crime.

The following discussion of some areas of professional practice illustrates both common themes within, and specific examples of, the criminality of trusted professionals. We can do no more than be indicative here, and readers should remember two important points about what follows. First, we are not saying that crime in the professions is so prolific that 'you can't trust anybody these days' (although this is a fairly common saying!). Second, however, we do emphasise that we are not just talking about 'a few bad apples', and the cases cited here should not be assumed to be extreme scenarios. As with the long history of police misconduct and corruption, we are talking about crimes and deviance that are largely hidden but quite widespread and deeply damaging.

Bankers as criminals

As Rawlinson (1998: 356) puts it,

> when money becomes a commodity in itself, subject to the vagaries of the market, banks find themselves caught up in the same competitive battles as other enterprises. Attracting customers becomes crucial, provoking banks into a less discerning concern over the quality of clients during straitened times.

The classic case of an outwardly legitimate and successful large-scale enterprise that actually harboured a wide range of illicit activity is that of the international but partly London-based Bank of Credit and Commerce International (BCCI) (Passas, 1995; Croall, 1998: 282–3; Punch, 1996). To operate as a criminal organisation required the knowing involvement of many banking personnel, and the Governor of the Bank of England subsequently described BCCI as dominated by a 'criminal culture', although, as Spalek (2001) points out, the victims of the conspiracy also included numerous employees. Those who were part of the conspiracy reaped high profits, with the losers being ordinary savers and some commercial and public body investors who lost the funds of shareholders and taxpayers. As Croall (1998: 282) notes,

> at his trial, one of the participants, Abbas Ghokal, was said to have run up a £795 million debt to the bank and to have been involved with a series of swindles, false documents, and a sham financial structure which funded his lavish lifestyle.

But BCCI is perhaps only the most prominent example of banking crime, and notable of course because its activities were exposed. Other banks and financial institutions, in particular those operating in tax havens such as the Channel Islands, the Cayman Islands, Lichtenstein and elsewhere, have also been involved in similar activities: money laundering, bribery to facilitate contracts or avoid regulations, false accounting, theft of clients' money, evasion of foreign exchange regulations, and so on.

The case of Nick Leeson is probably at the other end of the scale of criminal ambition, for it was not Leeson's intention to criminally bankrupt Barings Bank, but this is what he managed to do by his uncontrolled dealing on the Singapore stock market. Leeson's criminality lay in his concealment of enormous mounting losses and, as with a gambler believing their luck will change, his continued use of yet more of the bank's money in attempts to recoup his losses (Punch, 1999). But if Leeson was criminal in his actions, it could also be said that his managers back in London were guilty of incompetent oversight and rule-breaking themselves, 'sending sums of money to Leeson in Singapore for amounts that in some instances exceeded both the bank's assets as well as limits set by the Bank of England' (Gobert and Punch, 2003: 19).

Health professionals as criminals

Medical practitioners have expertise and autonomy and can engage in the frauds and fiddles of white-collar criminality. In the United States a huge number of fraudulent claims are made to insurance companies for treatment that has not actually been carried out and, on a smaller scale, there have been a number of cases in the United Kingdom in recent years in which doctors and dentists have claimed payments from the National Health Service for visits to patients or for treatments that have not occurred. The same insulation from close scrutiny and the deep trust that society places in doctors can also be abused in the most extreme way, as was demonstrated in the case of Harold Shipman, a GP in Todmorden, then later in Hyde in Greater Manchester. Over the course of twenty-three years, Shipman is believed to have murdered at least 215 of his patients. He had previously been convicted in 1976 of obtaining pethidine (a strong opiate-type drug) by forgery and deception, and later that year, in the name of a dying patient, he obtained enough morphine to kill 360 people. Nonetheless, he was simply given a stiff warning from the General Medical Council and allowed to continue to practise as a GP. Shipman was convicted in January 2000 and given fifteen life sentences but committed suicide in 2004. Since this case, it has been proposed that all NHS trusts and the police should have investigation teams to check on doctors and nurses suspected of abuse and mal-practice. The inclusion of nurses partly follows from the case of Beverley Allitt. Allitt was a nurse who received thirteen life sentences in May 1993 on being convicted of murdering four children and attacking nine others while working on a children's ward between February and April 1991. The subsequent Clothier Inquiry report noted that vital clues about what was happening were missed during the time she was employed at the hospital.

Health and pharmacy professionals deal on a daily basis with medicines that are themselves very valuable commodities and targets for theft. Historically and today, some professionals abuse their positions and divert medicines for personal use (usually stimulant or sedative drugs for recreation or for an addiction). Of course, such drugs are also stolen in small-scale burglaries and larger-scale warehouse raids or lorry hijackings. Medicines may be stolen or diverted because they have great value in the illegal trade in drugs of recreation and addiction, or may be profitably sold for their original medical use in Third World regions where they are scarce. The latter practice might actually occur because a Western government has declared a product unsafe for domestic consumption but then supports the sale of the same product to other parts of the world (Dowie, 1979). Braithwaite's (1984) and Abraham's (1995) studies of the pharmaceutical industry illustrate how the promotion of a benign image masks price-fixing, improper influence on regulatory systems, industrial espionage, knowing distribution of unsafe drugs, and the 'dumping' of drugs that are not approved by Western countries in developing states desperate for medicines and with laxer regulations.

Lawyers as criminals

Like health professionals, lawyers are generally 'safe hands' and trustworthy, but occupy a position in which it is easy to act in unscrupulous fashion and abuse trust. Lawyers can be employed by criminal organisations or themselves operate corruptly by, for example, inflating fees, forgery, pocketing money that should be passed on to clients, and engaging or colluding in frauds or even blackmail. The specialist expertise of lawyers and the high regard in which they are usually held leave many opportunities for abuse of this position. For example, immigrant asylum seekers seeking advice and support concerning residence should use only services licensed by the Office of the Immigration Services Commissioner (OISC, established in 1999 under the Immigration and Asylum Act). However, as the National Criminal Intelligence Service reported in its 2003 Threat Assessment of Serious and Organised Crime, 'a small number of corrupt solicitors and immigration advisors support the facilitation process by fraudulently completing asylum or work-permit applications for clients'. The OISC also noted that 'many are also involved in illegal activities such as document forgery and people trafficking' (McVeigh, 2003).

Again, the theme of connections between the local and the global is made by some of these examples. However, the examples of BCCI and the pharmaceutical industry also indicate and confirm the difficulty of precisely defining white-collar and corporate crime. BCCI was a case involving corrupt individuals within a corrupt organisation that nonetheless somehow managed to operate as a legal, respectable and apparently competent institution for many years. Pharmaceutical companies have been the subject of various criminological studies and journalistic investigations exposing corporate criminality, but the question of the responsibility that the decision-makers within a company actually bear has proved to be far less straightforward than we might think (see Box 11.1, p. 202).

CRIME IN THE WORLD OF CORPORATE-LEVEL BUSINESS AND COMMERCE

The crimes of the powerful

Pearce's book *Crimes of the Powerful* (1976) was a Marxist critique of the bias of law, capitalism and control systems in favour of a ruling class and at the expense of the working class (see also Chapter 5). He used case studies from the United States to show how corporate interests had at times struck alliances with and made use of organised crime to suppress the labour unions and how the law had been used to control the powerless through the criminalisation of troublesome activity. In the same critical tradition within criminology, probably the most sustained and continually updated catalogue of examples of crimes of the powerful is the US overview by Jeffrey Reiman, nicely (and accurately) called *The Rich Get Richer and the Poor Get Prison* (2001; also discussed in Chapter 5). In a supplementary essay to the book, Reiman and Leighton (2003) focus on what they call 'the big crime story of 2002', which, for a change, was not 'the usual tale of murder and mayhem among the poor' but 'a long and complicated saga of corporate financial shenanigans that caused a significant drop in stock market prices'. The energy stocks corporation Enron, along with its compliant auditors Arthur Andersen (and here we could add accountants to our list of professionals who can be criminals; see also Cohen, 2003), were at the heart of scandalous revelations about unscrupulous and illegal business practices, but the case was soon followed by similar exposures at major companies such as Tyco, Xerox, AOL-TimeWarner, and by problems at some major US banks such as Citigroup.

While Enron boasted a remarkable record of growth and was symbolised by an impressive headquarters with a statue of the Enron symbol proudly displayed outside, in fact the enterprise was something of a house of cards and on 2 December 2001 was declared bankrupt – one of the largest bankruptcies ever, with debts over \$31 billion. As Reiman and Leighton (2003) explain,

> Enron was subsequently accused of having perpetrated a massive 'disinformation' campaign, hiding the degree of its indebtedness from investors by treating loans as revenue, hiding company losses by creating new firms with company capital and then attributing losses to them and not to Enron, and encouraging company employees to buy and hold Enron stock while its executives apparently knew of its shaky condition and were busy selling off their own shares.

Plate 11.2 Night view of the Enron sign at the company headquarters in Houston. Enron employees leave the building in downtown Houston, Texas, late on 7 February 2002. Under harsh questioning before Congress, former Enron corporation Chief Executive Jeffrey Skilling shouldered no blame for the bankrupt energy trader's collapse and said he had no reason to believe it was in financial trouble when he left in August 2001.

Source: © Reuters; *photo*: STR.

So the new century began as the old one had ended. Table 11.1 shows just a sample of the corporate crime cases that came to light in the United Kingdom during the 1990s.

While fraud and financial malpractice are one key area of corporate criminality, they are not necessarily the most injurious. Corporate negligence and management failing have also been held to be responsible for a variety of events in which great loss of life has occurred. Key cases from the late 1980s to today include the sinking of the *Herald of Free Enterprise* ferry; the King's Cross fire; and rail crashes at Clapham, Paddington, Southall, Ladbroke Grove, Hatfield and Potters Bar. Although public inquiries and academic studies can point to failings within the actions or inaction of organisations and individuals, the law does not at present allow for the prosecution of a crime of corporate killing or corporate manslaughter. After much promising and then stalling by the Labour government, legislation in this area may be pending (see Box 11.1).

Table 11.1 Corporate crime cases in the United Kingdom in the 1990s

COMPANY NAME	DATE BEGINNING THE INVESTIGATION	OUTLINE OF CASE	AMOUNT DEFRAUDED	THOSE AFFECTED	OUTCOME	SOURCE
County Natwest and Blue Arrow	1989	Concerning rights issue of shares	£837 million	Shareholders	Suspended sentences for some, others acquitted	Serious Fraud Office Annual Report 1991–2
The Blackspur Group plc (Leasing company of print machinery)	1990	Conspiracy to defraud individual financial institutions and one offence of fraudulent trading	The company collapsed with debts of £60 million	Banks and other financial institutions and hence their savers and investors	Two company directors sentenced to 3 years each – released after 9 months and disqualified from acting as company directors for 8 years	Serious Fraud Office Annual Report 1994–5
Maxwell Group	1991	Missing pension funds attributed to Robert Maxwell	£500 million	Pensioners of the company	Robert Maxwell disappeared, presumed committed suicide. Maxwell's sons subsequently acquitted	Serious Fraud Office Annual Report 1995–6
BCCI and Gulf group (Bank of Credit and Commerce International)	1991	Fraudulent activities between Gulf Group (Abbas Ghokal) and BCCI – £335 million stolen from account of the ruler of Abu Dhabi by BCCI. Junior employees became directors of phoney companies. All eventually led to collapse of bank	£800 million (though estimates vary)	Local authorities, local tax payers including individuals with savings in bank	Abbas Ghokal sentenced to 14 years and asked to pay £2.94 million by way of confiscation order with a further 3 years imprisonment. A number of others also implicated, tried and sentenced	Serious Fraud Office Annual Report 1996–7
Butte Mining plc	1992	Conspiracy to defraud in relation to a gold, silver, lead	£60 million	Mining consultancy firm Robertsons Reserves in	Three British directors found guilty and received	Serious Fraud Office Annual Report 1998–9

Company	Year	Description	Amount	Victims	Outcome	Source
and zinc mining business – paper trail started in Jersey, then Hong Kong, New Zealand, Monaco, France, Switzerland, and Canada as well as Butte, Montana				Llandudno and shareholders	sentences ranging from 18 months to 3 years	Serious Fraud Office Annual Report 1996–7
MTM plc (chemicals manufacturer)	1993	Falsifying accounts and making false statements	£250 million	Individual investors, pension funds and City institutions	Sentence of 2 years' imprisonment	Serious Fraud Office Annual Report 2000–1
Facia Group and Banking officials from London branch of United Mizrahi Bank	1996	Fraud and corruption. Company sought to obtain loans to finance corporate expansion by side-stepping proper bank procedures	£13 million	The bank, and, indirectly, the employees of the companies the Facia group bought – these included Salisburys, Sock Shop, Red or Dead, Torq Ltd, Saxone, Trueform, Freeman Hardy Willis	A lengthy trial started on 31 May 2000 and concluded 25 January 2001. Defendants found guilty and sentences imposed on different individuals of 5 years, 2 years, and 30 months. One participant disqualified in 2001 from acting as company director for 12 years	
Muirpace Ltd (commodities firm) sold to Thompson International	1998	The fraudulent sale of grain warrants	£32 million	Thompson International, others in the Thompson Group and company's own clients	Sentence of 3 years 9 months – disqualification from acting as company director for 7 years	Serious Fraud Office Annual Report 2000–1
Wickes plc	1999	Fraudulent trading and making false statements of company's profits between 1994 and 1996	£18.3 million	Shareholders	All five executives sent to trial were acquitted	Serious Fraud Office Annual Report 2002–3

BOX 11.1 PROSPECTS FOR LAW ON CORPORATE CRIMINAL MANSLAUGHTER/NEGLIGENCE

- Under the Conservative government, in 1996 the Law Commission produced a report, *Legislating the Criminal Code: Involuntary Manslaughter* that highlighted the ineffectiveness of the law in this area and published a draft bill that recommended the creation of an offence of 'corporate killing'.
- In 1997 the Labour Party manifesto promised to legislate on corporate manslaughter.
- After Labour's 1997 election victory the then Home Secretary, Jack Straw, said that 'the new government believed those whose criminal negligence caused the deaths of innocent people should not escape punishment' (Bright, 2002: 6).
- The Confederation of British Industry has vigorously opposed plans for new legislation, arguing that it would be unworkable (Hodge, 2003: 3).
- But under current legislation, the Crown Prosecution Service is reluctant to bring corporate manslaughter cases because they are notoriously difficult to prove and win. 'There have only ever been five successful prosecutions and these have all been against small companies' (King, 2003: 10).
- Labour failed to follow up its manifesto commitment to legislate, but in 2000 did commence a wide consultation exercise about the proposed new offence. Not all those in the business world oppose action, and Ruth Lea of the Institute of Directors said in 2002, 'For business to look as if it is getting away with murder is extraordinary. It's common justice that if someone is killed through gross negligence that someone should be held responsible' (Bright, 2002: 6).
- In May 2003 the Home Secretary, David Blunkett, announced the intention to publish a draft bill on reform of the law, but critics say this will concentrate 'virtually all the punishment on companies, rather than their managers and directors'.
- The history of demands for laws on corporate killing go back to at least 1965 when the bridge that Glanville Evans was working on collapsed and he fell into the River Wye. A prosecution failed, and since then, 'more than 31,000 people have been killed at work or through commercially related disasters such as train crashes. Safety reports have shown that management failures are responsible in most cases' (Hodge, 2003: 3).

Transnational corporate crimes

With regard to business crime in a transnational context, Michalowski and Kramer (1987: 34) suggest that

> The increasing global reach of modern transnational corporations [TNCs] aggravates the difficulties of arriving at a satisfactory conception of corporate crime. TNCs at times engage in practices which, while they would be illegal in their home nations, are legal in a number of host nations.

Whether originating from legal or illegal sources, such crimes may have consequences related to social, health and economic as well as law enforcement issues in Britain or other countries.

The relocation by Western TNCs of high-pollution industries in less developed countries is notable here (Michalowski and Kramer, 1987: 37), resulting in the costs of crimes and offences against the environment and wildlife, and related damage to human health now and for future generations (South, 1998a, b; Croall, 1998: 280; and see Chapter 17).

Another example would be the enormous international catalogue of health and safety offences and breaches of regulations that have led to deaths and injuries as a result of what some have termed 'corporate violence' (Croall, 1992; Wells, 1993; Slapper and Tombs, 1999) and the crimes of toxic capitalism (Pearce and Tombs, 1998). This latter idea is worth briefly expanding upon but it also raises an important question about the context of crimes of large-scale organisations, for despite the phrase coined by these authors, capitalism does not have a monopoly on such offending. The common characteristics of cost-cutting, negligence and under-investment in health and safety have featured as readily – in the past and today – within the bureaucratic cultures of enterprises of communist and totalitarian states as they have in capitalist ones. In this respect, and in conclusion, when looking at large-scale, 'corporate' organisational crime, we can bring together the themes of:

- businesses operating to subvert or invert good corporate practice (see Gobert and Punch, 2003);
- the significance of transnationalisation and globalisation in respect of where crimes are committed and in terms of their effects;
- and the idea of the risk society (see Chapter 6).

Beck (1992) has drawn attention to the irony of a world much improved by advances in science, industry and technology yet which now also suffers the multiple, unintended (though not always unforeseen) consequences, generating a constant awareness of the dangers of life in a 'risk society'. In the 1990s it was obviously not *intended* that the poor design and inadequate safety precautions at the Chernobyl nuclear plant in Ukraine should lead to an explosion that killed workers, irradiated a huge area and left a legacy of radiation-related diseases for a regional population and the spread of a radiation 'cloud' that reached Cumbria in the United Kingdom – but that is what happened. And, as Pearce and Tombs (1998: ix) note, 'If the chemical industry has provided enormous material benefits, equally the costs have been enormous, even catastrophic', yet 'the destructive nature of the industry – the death, injury, ill-health, and environmental devastation which it causes – remains particularly poorly recognised and challenged.'

SUMMARY

1 Professional crime is changing, and while robbery and burglary will always be with us, new generations of career criminals seek to keep themselves at the cutting edge of developments in the commercial, electronic and financial sectors. They seek profitable loopholes and niches to exploit while at the same time generating enormous business through illicit provision of pornography, drugs and now smuggled humanity – to be used as labour or in the sex industry.

2 Law enforcement and criminal intelligence can respond only if they too keep at this cutting edge.

3 Criminologists actually know relatively little about the workings of white-collar and corporate crime, and this has changed little since the early 1990s when Nelken (1994a: 367) noted that 'far more is needed on the modus operandi – the "how" of white collar crime (motivation, meaning, actions, decisions, alliances, escape routes, "techniques of neutralisation" etc)'.

4 It remains as plain as ever that there is enormous disparity in the way that different crimes are treated and that a fair justice system would seek to rectify this through more effective investigation and prosecution of the crimes of the powerful.

5 Transnational crime is now a major challenge (Jameson et al., 1998; Gros, 2003). As Cohen (1996: 12) remarks, 'there is a worldwide movement of capital and goods uncontrolled and uncontrollable by sovereign states. Its criminal strands are obvious: after oil, the second largest international commodity traded in the world is drugs. In the ex-Soviet Union, illegal arms trading and direct involvement in the black economy have led to a "criminalized military". The concept of "gangster capitalism" is now routine.'

6 A new conception of policing and countering crime needs to be similarly transnational and global (Gros, 2003).

CRITICAL THINKING QUESTIONS

1 Professional criminals and organised crime groups are among the most popular subjects of novels, television programmes and films. Review a small sample and identify the key characteristics of the criminal careers and/or organisations featured.

2 Is 'greed' the explanation for both professional and corporate crime? If not, what else do we have to consider?

3 Draw or describe a hypothetical 'chain' that could link a crime (you choose) committed in Edinburgh to a contact in Rotterdam and an air ticket to the Cayman Islands.

4 If we accept the benefits of a more globalised society, do we have to accept the accompanying risks of globalised crime?

5 Check news reports and the Websites of professional associations such as the British Medical Association or Solicitors Complaints Bureau for evidence about the misconduct or criminality of professionals.

FURTHER STUDY

Croall, H. (2001) *Understanding White Collar Crime*, Buckingham: Open University Press. A key text reviewing studies and theories concerning white-collar and corporate crime.

Friman, H. R. and Andreas, P. (1999) *The Illicit Global Economy and State Power*, Oxford: Rowman and Littlefield. Contributors cover crime networks, links with states, the trades in drugs and in hazardous waste, and the wider global context.

Hobbs, D., Hadfield, P., Lister, S. and Winlow, S. (2003) *Bouncers: Violence and Governance in the Night-time Economy*, Oxford: Oxford University Press. Ethnography and analysis of licit and illicit aspects of the growing night-time economy, also discussing regeneration schemes, use of private security, and drug and alcohol problems in pub- and club-land.

Weisburd, D., Waring, E. and Chayel, E. (2001) *White Collar Crime and Criminal Careers*, Cambridge: Cambridge University Press. Longitudinal, quantitative study of the backgrounds and criminal careers of white-collar criminals, challenging some taken-for-granted assumptions.

Winlow, S. (2001) *Badfellas: Crime, Tradition and New Masculinities*, Oxford: Berg. A study of crime, culture, masculinity and community based on insightful ethnography and fieldwork.

MORE INFORMATION

The Web of Justice site provides numerous links to other Websites concerned with crime, corruption and power:
http://www.co.pinellas.fl.us/bcc/juscoord/eorganized.htm

The United Nations site on organised crime provides a source about global developments in crime and control and links to national sites:
http://www.unodc.org/unodc/organized_crime.html

The Nathanson Centre Website provides a searchable bibliographic data base to help locate other relevant studies:
http://www.yorku.ca/nathanson/search.htm

The Criminal Justice Resources Website provides links to other sites both official – such as the FBI and Royal Canadian Mounted Police – and unofficial such as journalist and community sites concerned with various forms of crime:
http://www.lib.msu.edu/harris23/crimjust/orgcrime.htm

CHAPTER 12

Drugs, Alcohol, Health and Crime

KEY ISSUES

▌ How do drugs and alcohol contribute to crime?

▌ What can history tell us about the legal and cultural status of drugs and alcohol?

▌ Is drug use becoming more of a 'normalised' feature of everyday life?

▌ How can we illustrate important connections between crime and health issues?

INTRODUCTION

The 'drugs problem' is one of the main headline crime stories of our times. As such, it can often seem a relatively simple issue of drug supply, user demand and associated crime. In fact, it is a highly complex subject in which problems of international politics, the legacy of history and the subcultures of use, as well as the economics of drug markets, law enforcement and provision of treatment services all interact. By contrast, alcohol and its association with crime is relatively neglected, although in fact it is probably of more real significance as a cause or factor in crimes of violence and crimes on the road.

Importantly, drugs and alcohol are also health issues yet criminology largely overlooks the significance of the dimension of health (see Box 12.1). This chapter therefore adopts an innovative approach to these subjects and takes a holistic approach to the study of illegal and legal drugs in society.

CONTROLLING ILLICIT DRUGS AND ALCOHOL

Drugs and alcohol have been the subjects of varying forms of control. Their histories diverge from the early twentieth century, with alcohol remaining legal while drugs such as cannabis and opium became illegal.

BOX 12.1 THINKING ABOUT LINKS BETWEEN ILLEGAL DRUGS, ALCOHOL, CRIME AND HEALTH

Consider, for example:

- the link between intravenous drug use and AIDS/HIV or hepatitis C;
- the contribution of alcohol to crimes of violence – a problem not just for the police but also, in the United Kingdom, for the National Health Service;
- the fact that manslaughter deaths on the road caused by intoxication are recorded not just in the crime statistics but also in the mortality statistics;
- that offenders with mental health problems face additional difficulties and the courts and services face additional considerations in dealing with them;
- that alcohol may be a legal 'drug' but supplying alcohol to minors is illegal, and over-indulgence by young people can lead to health hazards and hospitalisation;
- that medicine and, in particular, psychiatry are powerful systems of social regulation or social control.

In the eighteenth and nineteenth centuries it was largely the 'demon drink' that was seen as a problem for society, a threat to the health and morals of the individual and his or her family, and subversive of the good habits and social order of a civilised society. Concerns about respectability and restraint were paramount for the new middle class; an emerging medical profession was keen to flex its developing muscle as a source of influential expert opinion; and the women's movement, religious groups and elements of working-class socialism all embraced a commitment to **temperance**. The agenda for *control* of intoxication had emerged. New scientific specialists produced theories of 'disease' to explain a variety of conditions such as alcoholism and addiction but also, for example, homosexuality, insanity and criminality (see Chapter 3). New clinical terms such as 'narcomania' and 'morphinism' (see Berridge, 1999) reflected new approaches to knowledge, power, control of the body and the triumph of rationality over unreasonable desire (Turner, 1996). So we see medical treatment directed at the moral and mental health of individuals; the popularisation of images of the drunkard or opium smoker as a broken body, degraded and enslaved; and the celebration of the moral values of abstinence and hard work.

In the early twentieth century, the agenda for drug control was partly shaped by a continuing commitment to controls by the law and the police (Lee and South, 2003). Some of the laws that came into force were the result of domestic concerns (Kohn, 1992), but around 1912 to the 1920s the drug issue also became internationalised, with treaties and agreements being produced to define and categorise drugs and establish what was prohibited and what was permissible in legal trade for medical and research purposes (McAllister, 2000). Effectively, this is an early example of 'globalisation' – a theme referred to in several chapters. In Britain – but not, for example, the United States – a different form of control was also exercised through the medical profession. Following the Rolleston Committee report of 1926, doctors had won the right to prescribe drugs such as heroin and morphine to dependent users or 'addicts' and thereby 'maintain' them in a way that was aimed at enabling them to live as a useful citizen and keeping them from the criminal market for drugs. While on the one hand this was an early example of the medicalisation of a social problem (Zola, 1972; Conrad and Schneider, 1992), it was also an important early precedent for the practice that in the 1980s became known as harm reduction.

The late 1960s and early 1970s saw increasing criminalisation of drug dealers and drug users caught by the police in possession of prohibited drugs. At the same time, users seeking or directed to treatment services (the new Drug Dependency Units established from 1967) faced a tougher and more abstinence-oriented regime. This further medicalisation of the problem developed under the direction of psychiatrists, emphasising how drugs have become associated with mental health. This link is returned to later.

In the 1980s and into the twenty-first century, in the face of increased use of heroin and then the public health alarm around the appearance of AIDS/HIV (Dorn and South, 1987; Strang and Stimson, 1991), practice-based responses reflecting harm reduction became accepted and mirrored in some official policy (O'Hare *et al.*, 1992). Yet at the same time, law enforcement agendas were strengthened, particularly focusing on national and international large-scale traffickers (Dorn *et al.*, 1992). Links between drug trafficking and professional organised crime groups (see p. 367 and Chapter 11) have become a major target for police, Customs and international cooperation between enforcement agencies. Money-laundering of drugs profits is a large-scale and complex business in itself, and since 11 September 2001 has become an even higher enforcement priority, owing to concerns of intelligence agencies that drugs profits help to fund terrorist groups.

Prohibition and control remain the dominant message, yet today there is perhaps far more debate than ever before about the best way to 'deal' with 'the drugs problem'. For some, it is not self-evident that prohibition of drugs is necessary, and far from evident that it is a successful policy. So various positions compete: proposals for legalisation or decriminalisation (see Box 12.2), **harm reduction**, stepping up the eradication of drug crop cultivation and anti-smuggling efforts, zero tolerance approaches to use and so on. Thus, in the early twenty-first century we can see increased *contestation* about drugs.

BOX 12.2 LEGALISATION/DECRIMINALISATION: PROS AND CONS

The debate about the 'decriminalisation' or 'legalisation' of drugs is both old and new. It is old in the sense that drugs that were once legally available have come to be controlled, but at the beginning of the twentieth century there were debates about whether this was best done by the methods of policing or those of medicine (Lee and South, 2003; Berridge, 1984). In the United States, after the 1914 Harrison Act, law enforcement became the dominant approach, while in the United Kingdom, after acceptance of the Rolleston Committee report published in 1926, medical management was allowed but within the framework of legal control.

In terms of the recent debate (Inciardi, 1999), the supporting argument for the legalisation option is that presently illegal drugs cause less harm than legal drugs: it is their illegality that is responsible for related harm (e.g. through adulteration; through the committing of crime to obtain drugs; and because of the profitability of illegal supply, hence the growth of major crime groups and the incentive to commit violence or murder to protect profits). A counter-argument is that legal drugs are widely available, illegal drugs are not: the health, social and crime-related consequences of the widespread legal availability of drugs are therefore unknown. The decriminalisation/legalisation arguments are unlikely to gain government support in the foreseeable future because of the powerful influence of international prohibitionist agreements and assumptions that this would be politically unpopular with the voting public. However, recent research and independent inquiries (Runciman, 2000) have suggested that in fact there is room for greater flexibility in the interpretation of these treaties than governments have generally acknowledged, and so a careful yet more imaginative 'middle way' may be possible.

The anomaly of alcohol

Among the concerns of social reformers in the nineteenth century, the abuse of alcohol loomed large. It is therefore intriguing that the control of alcohol went in the opposite direction to that of other drugs. During the First World War, regulations under the Defence of the Realm Act introduced both the first legal controls over cocaine and opium and also the alcohol licensing laws, which restricted the opening times of public houses and considerably tightened up the regulations relating to the sale, purchase and consumption of alcohol. However, thereafter drugs became subject to ever-increasing and widening controls but alcohol availability was liberalised. War-time restrictions were barely enforced, and while the Licensing Act 1921 signalled that alcohol was an intoxicant that needed some regulation, throughout the twentieth century it became, as the Royal College of Psychiatrists (1986) put it, 'our favourite drug'. Outlets multiplied, from beyond the pub to the corner shop and now the supermarket and cross-Channel hypermarkets, and drinking patterns changed, with women significantly increasing their consumption since the 1980s. For all this, the legal status of alcohol does not mean it has no connections with crime. Entirely to the contrary: for example, because there is value in avoiding the higher taxation on alcohol imposed in Britain, smuggling from across the Channel is profitable; and alcohol is a serious intoxicant associated with crime in various ways. This is returned to below.

However, it is drugs that have had the higher profile in relation to crime and social problems. Therefore, the following questions arise:

- Where do drugs come from? Is this a local, national or global matter?
- How much of a problem do drugs pose? How many people take drugs and who says it's 'a problem' at all?
- What are the connections between drugs and crime?

DRUGS AS A GLOBAL ISSUE

The opium trade in the nineteenth century

The original international opium traffickers were the great colonial traders such as Britain and the Netherlands (McAllister, 2000: 9–39). In the nineteenth century, Britain invested heavily in the export of opium from India to China, and although opium became a profitable commodity for China itself (Berridge, 1999: xxvi), originally the country was a victim of market exploitation by the British Empire. Britain wanted certain luxury goods that China produced but needed to balance the trade and did so via the export of opium. When China sought to close its ports to this importation, Britain went to war against China on two occasions (1839–42 and 1856–8) to secure the future of its profits. This history partly explains why domestic control over opiate use in Britain was so limited at this time.

The drugs trade in the late twentieth century

Since the end of the 1970s and the early 1980s, changes relating to the geopolitics of opium production and to international trafficking routes have been significant. The British opiate market of the 1960s was primarily fed by a combination of leakage of pharmaceutically produced drugs from the legal prescribing system and then by 'street heroin' produced and distributed from the Golden Triangle region of South-East Asia (Ruggiero and South, 1995). However, by around 1980 what became known as the Golden Crescent area (including Afghanistan and Pakistan) was producing most of the heroin reaching Britain. Global trafficking origins, routes and destinations today are shown in Figure 12.1.

Alongside increasing availability, the fact that heroin produced from these sources could be smoked and did not need to be prepared for injection was a very influential factor in the widespread upsurge in heroin use in Britain in the 1980s (Pearson, 1987b; Dorn and South, 1987). This form of heroin could be heated and the smoke snorted or sniffed (a practice known as 'chasing the dragon'; Auld et al., 1986), and these methods overcame common fears of needles and injecting. This way of using heroin took on a comfortable familiarity, like smoking a cigarette or pipe.

In retrospect, the 1980s was a watershed decade. The explosion of the international heroin trade was quickly followed by the growth of the cocaine market, with Colombian crime groups initially aiming production at demand in the United States but by the end of the 1980s also targeting Europe (Lewis, 1989; Ruggiero and South, 1995; see also Chapter 6). Money-laundering, corruption of police and customs officials, the stimulation of local drugs micro-economies based on drug supply and

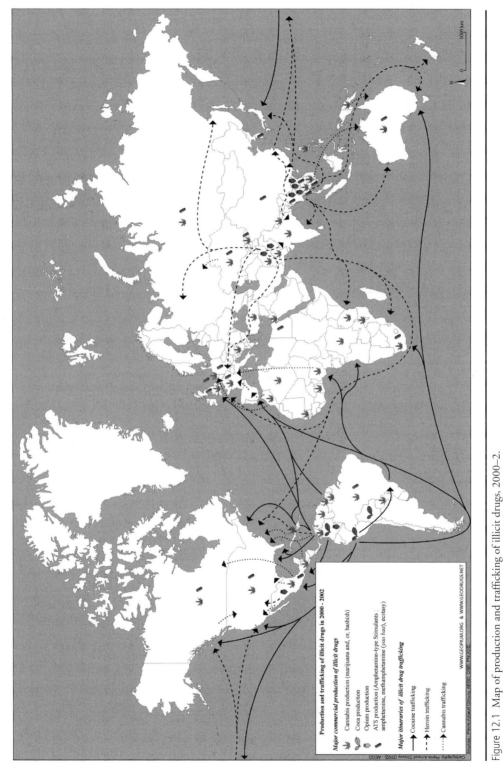

Figure 12.1 Map of production and trafficking of illicit drugs, 2000–2.

Source: Pierre-Arnaud Chouvy, AEGD, OGD, PNUCID. Published in *Geopolitical Drug Newsletter*, 11 September 2002: 4–5.

Production and trafficking of illicit drugs in 2000 – 2002

Major commercial production of illicit drugs

- Cannabis production (marijuana and, or, hashish)
- Coca production
- Opium production
- ATS production (Amphetamine-type Stimulants : amphetamine, methamphetamine (*yaa baa*), ecstasy)

Major itineraries of illicit drug trafficking

→ Cocaine trafficking

--→ Heroin trafficking

····→ Cannabis trafficking

WWW.GEOPIUM.ORG & WWW.GEODRUGS.NET

Cartography : Pierre-Arnaud Chouvy, AEGD, OGD, PNUCID.

1000 km

N

demand and the profits from acquisitive crime generated to pay for drugs all followed (Lee and South, 2003). And in mid-2003, heroin was making a comeback. Opium production in Afghanistan had been curbed by the fundamentalist Taliban regime, but Western intervention to remove the Taliban because of their association with Osama bin Laden and the Al-Qaida terrorist organisation had the ironic effect of removing one 'threat' but thereby rekindling another. Contrary to Western assumptions, post-Taliban Afghanistan has not seen the reduction in opium production that was supposed to follow, but rather a massive increase. In 2002, 3,400 tonnes was produced, up 700 tonnes on 2001 (*Observer*, 6 July 2003: 6). The result is that 'only £5 will buy enough to keep a smoker in a state of euphoria for hours. Puffing the heated white powder – "chasing the dragon" – is the delivery method for the new heroin takers who see syringes as dirty and dangerous' (ibid.). It is a sign of the resilience of the international drugs trade that twenty years after the first wave of heroin smoking, this news story suggests that a pattern is repeating itself – and even the price of the drug has proved inflation resistant.

ARE DRUGS 'A PROBLEM'?

Certainly governments, the media and the public see drugs as a major threat to society. Even the strongest supporters of liberalisation or legalisation would acknowledge that drugs cause harm to individuals, families and the wider community, although their argument is that these harms and problems follow from the criminalisation of drugs and drug users, and the inadequacy of support services

Of course, the 'problem' status of drugs can also be seen in terms of the labelling or social constructionist position (see Chapter 5) that this is a result of the application of labels and processes of stigmatisation representing the agenda of moral entrepreneurs and agents of control rather than a rational policy. The effect of stigmatisation may also, of course, be to enable drug users to affirm their identities as deviant, rebellious and members of subcultures differing from 'straight' society (Young, 1971). On the other hand, there are arguments that the moral and cultural landscape has changed and that drugs have come out of the subcultures and on to the dance-floor. In fact, we are probably taking about two different landscapes. For the homeless heroin user, stigmatisation and their distance from mainstream society remain highly significant. For today's recreational drug users, official definitions and prohibitions seem to be increasingly ignored or subverted, and new scripts and meanings about the place of drugs in everyday life are being created, incorporating cannabis, Ecstasy, amphetamine and cocaine (South, 1999b).

A 2003 Department of Health report, *Statistics on Smoking, Drinking and Drug Use among Young People in 2002*, 'reveals that while general levels of drug usage amongst young people have levelled-off, there has been a sharp increase in the use of cocaine and ecstasy amongst 16–24 year olds' (Druglink, 2003: 2). Thus, the argument goes that for many young people, use of at least some kinds of drugs has become *normalised* (Parker et al., 1998; Hammersley et al., 2003).

So has drug use now become a 'normal' part of everyday life for young people? One argument is that although 'normalisation' does not mean that everyone is now a drug user, nonetheless, it is now non-acquaintance with drugs or drug users that has become 'the deviation from the norm'. Others argue that drug use has not become a 'normal' activity for the majority of young people: prohibitions, peer-group resistance, parental attachment and preference for alternative expressive activities remain central to their lives. Both arguments (Parker *et al.*, 1998; Shiner and Newburn, 1999; South, 1999b) would seem to have some validity across late modern societies, and MacDonald and Marsh (2002) usefully suggest that a process of 'differentiated normalisation' may be occurring, with some young people remaining anti-drug abstainers, some being frequent recreational users, and some serious, problematic drug users.

While some studies suggest that drug use has been in decline or has stabilised, others suggest that at least some forms of drug use are increasing. One major survey of school-aged children (Balding, 2000) suggests an overall fall in use of drugs among this group, from prevalence among 14- and 15-year-olds of 32 per cent in 1996 to 21 per cent in 1999. This is interesting, because throughout the 1990s, the British Crime Survey indicated increasing numbers of people who have 'ever used' a drug (Table 12.1).

Apart from surveys, we can also look at law enforcement statistics about drugs and crime but must also recognise that these are limited in what they can tell us. Realistically, such statistics can reflect only known detections, seizures and convictions; drugs offences are, of course, not reported in the same way that robberies or burglaries are (see Chapters 7 and 8). Statistics suggesting large volume seizures may be seen as an indicator of enforcement success. Alternatively, though, they could be viewed as a reflection of trafficking success, because it takes only a few large seizures to inflate law-enforcement 'performance indicator' year-end figures, yet a drop in seizure statistics does not necessarily reflect a drop in importation and dealing. In most countries, police and Customs agencies generally feel unable to realistically claim much more than a 10–15 per cent interception rate. In Britain, seizures of heroin, cocaine and cannabis have fallen in recent years even though intelligence indicates increasing global production and trafficking. Just indicatively, in 2000, up to 30 tonnes of heroin and 40 tonnes of cocaine were estimated by police to have reached the UK market but only 2 tonnes of heroin and 3 tonnes of cocaine had been seized (Druglink, 2001: 6).

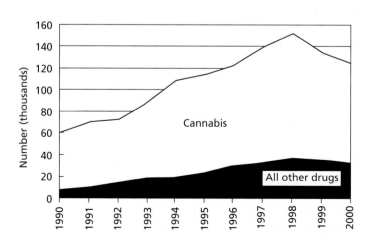

Figure 12.2 Drug seizures in the United Kingdom, 1990–2000.

Source: *Drug Seizure and Offender Statistics 4/02*, 17 May 2002, John M. Corkery.

Table 12.1 'Ever used a drug?'; British Crime Survey data

Drugs are used by many different people and in many situations. Here is what the national and local surveys found:

In general

- Drug use has increased significantly in recent years. This includes increases in use of medicines and an increase in cigarette smoking, alcohol consumption and illegal and other socially unacceptable drugs, especially among young people.
- Illegal drug use is only an occasional activity for most people.
- Most illegal drug use is experimental or on a relatively controlled, recreational basis.
- Most people who use drugs – be it legal or illegal substances – do not come to serious harm.
- Recent trends mean that soon the majority of parents of school-aged children in many areas will have tried illegal drugs when they were young.

Age of use

- Use of drugs (other than medicines) tends to become significant by the age of 14 for many young people, and both numbers using and quantities consumed increase throughout the remaining teenage years.
- Most young people moderate their use of, or completely stop using, illegal drugs and moderate their alcohol use by their mid- to late twenties when they 'settle down' and take on adult responsibilities.
- A small, but significant, number of people continue to use illegal drugs, and particularly cannabis, into their thirties. Many of these people are parents.

The British Crime Survey found the following results for drug use among a cross section of the population in 1998.

Proportion of young adults who have used drugs in their lifetime, in the last year or in the last month

	16–19 yrs	20–24 yrs	25–29 yrs	30–39 yrs	40–59 yrs
Ever used	49%	55%	45%	35%	17%
Last year	31%	28%	19%	9%	3%
Last month	22%	17%	11%	4%	2%

Source: Home Office, British Crime Survey 1998, as published on the DrugScope Website at www.drugscope.org.uk

For a full report on prevalence, see the DrugScope Annual Report on the UK Drug Situation.

DRUGS AND CRIME

The most evident examples of drugs and crime activity can be distinguished at two levels:

- street-level drugs offenders, including the activities of users sufficiently dependent that they become involved in crime to generate funds, or those already engaged in criminality who are then initiated into drug use;
- the activities of professional crime groups involved in organising drugs distribution.

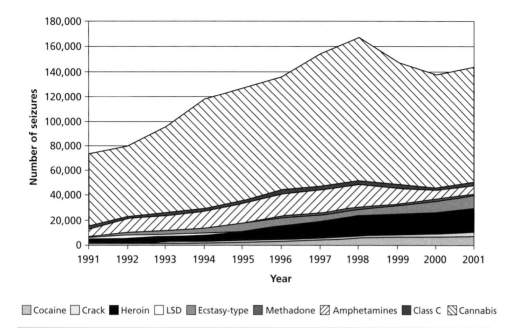

Figure 12.3 Number of seizures by main drug type, United Kingdom, 1991–2001.

Source: *Findings 202*, John M. Corkery and Jennifer Airs.

Drugs offenders

In July 2003, television news reports on Home Office crime statistics shared two themes. The first was the fact that adjustments to the recording of offences and then to the counting rules made it difficult to understand whether crime had risen or fallen! (The problems with criminal statistics are discussed in Chapter 2.) The second issue central to reports was the connection between drugs and crime. Here the proposition was that whether crime overall had increased or not, a significant underlying trend in relation to a range of offences – burglary, shoplifting, violence, gun crime – was their connection to offenders' dependence on drugs, and to violence and 'turf wars' associated with drug dealing. Such connections are real, though they should not be overblown, and furthermore there is no obvious pattern that represents or explains drug offending.

There is an enormous amount of research on the 'drugs–crime' connection and, perhaps unsurprisingly, there is no single conclusion about such a relationship. There is no dispute that there is an association between drugs and crime, but this is not straightforward. It is straightforward that the very illegality of drugs will make their possession and supply an offence. Thereafter things are more complicated: does drug use lead to crime or does involvement in a criminal lifestyle lead to use of drugs? Heroin and crack users with a serious addiction may be committing a considerable amount of acquisitive crime to fund their habit (Bennett *et al.*, 2001), but at the same time, as Seddon (2002) argues, a link between drugs and crime is in fact only found among a minority of drug users – the 3% or so of illicit drug users who are termed 'problem' users. Within this group, the association is primarily between use of heroin and/or crack cocaine and commission of certain economic/property offences (especially drug selling, shoplifting, burglary and other theft).

For others, the route to drug use may be through involvement in an array of routes into delinquent and criminal lifestyles (Auld *et al.*, 1986; Hammersley *et al.*, 1989; Pudney, 2002), and drugs are just one commodity bought and sold in the pleasure markets of the late modern illicit economy (Ruggiero and South, 1997; Hobbs *et al.*, 2003).

Criminal groups and the drug market

Hobbs (1998: 415) has summarised findings from the extensive literature on British professional crime groups (see Chapter 11; and see also Dorn and South, 1990; I. Taylor, 1999) regarding the way the drugs market attracted increased involvement from professional criminals from the 1980s onwards:

> The flexibility that is apparent within the contemporary serious crime 'community' assures . . . considerable scope for innovative engagement with the market. These engagements create disintegrated criminal firms . . . operating within multiple, interwoven networks of legitimate and illegitimate opportunity. . . . Within the drug market . . . trade is carried out between networks of these small flexible firms, for disorganized crime mirrors disorganized capitalism.

In other words, the drugs market provides opportunities for entrepreneurial criminals to trade in a highly profitable commodity. In many ways, such illegal enterprise will have characteristics not dissimilar to those of legal businesses, albeit that while disagreements and contract disputes in the legal market may be resolved via the courts, increasingly the illegal drugs market uses violence and even murder as a form of dispute resolution and contractual enforcement.

When Hobbs refers to such business as 'disorganised', he does not mean those involved are incompetent; rather, he is pointing to the fragmented and fluid nature of the market (Reuter *et al.*, 1990; Bean, 2002: 97–119). This understanding of the entrepreneurial mix in the market is important and has replaced the formerly prevalent and more limited notion of a simple 'pyramid' model of the market, once central to police assumptions (Broome Report, 1985). This model assumed the dominance of drugs trafficking organisations by a 'Mr Big' or several such hidden hands and was shaped less by evidence of market structure and more by an expectation that the hierarchical organisation of police detective work reflected a hierarchy of criminal organisation. In other words, at divisional level, local police countered local dealers and related crime; force-wide drug squads were more intelligence led and pursued middle-level dealers; while regional crime squads and their 'drugs wings' targeted drug crime operating nationally and internationally (Bean, 2002: 123). The idea of the mixed, fluid and relatively open market is more useful, and even where significant cartels can be pointed to – such as that led by Pablo Escobar in Colombia in the 1980s – these are operating in competitive markets, accompanied by significant levels of corruption and violence. Indeed, some recent research suggests that the fragmentary, flexible, temporary and *ad hoc* nature of some forms of transnational crime, such as heroin trafficking and smuggling of humans, means that 'traditional' crime organisations such as Triads and La Cosa Nostra are of declining significance (Zhang and Chin, 2003).

CONTROLLING DRUGS

Efforts to exercise control have been reflected in a long series of legislative Acts (see Box 12.3); in increasingly specialised forms of law enforcement, from local drugs squads (Collison, 1995) to national agencies (see p. 208 and Chapter 15; and Lee and South, 2003); and in secondary ways through an emphasis on drugs as a problem for everybody: a community issue requiring action from within the school curriculum, from housing associations and local government housing departments, and from health services (Lupton *et al.*, 2002). This agenda was a key element of the Crime and Disorder Act 1998, which established local partnerships led by police and local councils to develop integrated strategies for the reduction of drug misuse and dealing.

BOX 12.3 TIMELINE: UK LEGISLATION AND INFLUENCES ON THE CONTROL OF DRUGS

1908 The Poisons and Pharmacy Act regulates sale of cocaine

1912 The Hague Convention (International Opium Convention) requires signatory nations to limit opiate use, manufacture and trade to medical purposes; close opium dens; and implement laws against unauthorised possession and/or sale.

1916 The Defence of the Realm Act, Regulation 40B controls the possession of cocaine.

1920 The Dangerous Drugs Act implements the Hague Convention; this is mainly concerned with opium but also introduces some controls on cannabis.

1925 The Dangerous Drugs Act amends the 1920 Act and restricts the import and export of coca leaf and cannabis.

1926 The Rolleston Committee Report (Interdepartmental Committee on Morphine and Heroin Addiction) recommends that the prescribing of morphine and heroin be allowed where it is part of a therapeutic programme of maintenance for the incurably addicted or of gradual withdrawal.

1951 The Dangerous Drugs Act consolidates previous Acts.

1961 The First Brain Committee Report (Interdepartmental Committee on Drug Addiction) fails to detect signs of change and feels that new controls on heroin and cocaine are unnecessary.

continued

1965	The Second Brain Committee Report discusses a significant increase in drug use and recommends that doctors 'notify' the Home Office about addicts in treatment, and restrictions on the availability of heroin and cocaine prescriptions.
1967	The Dangerous Drugs Act implements the Brain recommendations and introduces police powers to stop and search individuals and vehicles for drugs.
1968	The Medicines Act regulates the production and distribution of medicines, e.g. whether they are available only on prescription, or without a prescription but only from a pharmacist, or generally available from any shop.
1971	The Misuse of Drugs Act – still the main legislation (with subsequent amendments) covering controlled drugs, divided into three classes: Class A, e.g. heroin, cocaine, LSD, opium; Class B, e.g. amphetamines, barbiturates and, previously, cannabis, which has (from 2004) moved to; Class C, also including, for example, steroids, various tranquillisers and stimulants.
1979	The Customs and Excise Management Act – which complements the 1971 Act, penalising trafficking in controlled drugs.
1986	The Drug Trafficking Offences Act introduces provisions for seizure of the assets of traffickers unless they can be proved to have no connection with the profits of drug crime (importantly, the burden of proof was moved from the prosecution to the defendant); it also made the sale or supply of certain drugs paraphernalia illegal (e.g. cannabis pipes).
1988	The Road Traffic Act makes it an offence to drive if unfit owing to drink or drugs. The police can stop those they suspect of being under such influence and request saliva, urine or blood samples to test.
1994	The Drug Trafficking Act updates the 1986 Act.
1997	The Crime (Sentences) Act introduces minimum sentences of seven years for those convicted of a Class A drug trafficking offence for the third time.
1998	The Crime and Disorder Act introduces a new Drug Treatment and Testing Order (DTTO).
2000	The Criminal Justice and Courts Act introduces a new sentence of Drug Abstinence Order.

Source: adapted from the Runciman Report (2000), J. Cohen (2002).

ALCOHOL AND CRIME

According to Cesare Lombroso (see also Chapter 3),

> Alcohol . . . is a cause of crime, first because many commit crime in order to obtain drinks; further, because men sometimes seek in drink the courage necessary to commit crime, or an excuse for their misdeeds; again, because it is by the aid of

drink that young men are drawn into crime; and because the drink shop is the place for meeting of accomplices, where they not only plan their crimes but squander their gains . . . it appears that alcoholism occurred oftenest in the case of those charged with assaults, sexual offences, and insurrections. Next came assassinations and homicide; and in the last rank those imprisoned for arson and theft, that is to say, crime against property.

(Lombroso, 1911/1968: 95–6)

However, it is not as clear as Lombroso implies that alcohol 'causes' crime; rather, it appears to have an effect in relation to crime (Alcohol Concern, 2001; All Party Group on Alcohol Misuse, 1995; *The Lancet*, 1999; Man *et al.*, 2002; McMurran and Hollin, 1989: 386; Raistrick *et al.*, 1999):

- Data from the British Crime Surveys and other sources consistently show that heavy drinking and drunkenness are linked with aggression and violence.
- Facial injuries and wounds to the victim are associated with heavy drinking by the assailant (although the victim may also have been drinking).
- Drinking and driving is the leading cause of death among young people aged 15–24.
- The British Medical Association suggests that the offender or victim had been drinking in 65 per cent of murders, 75 per cent of stabbings, 70 per cent of beatings and 50 per cent of fights or domestic assaults.
- One-third of people are intoxicated when they are arrested.
- Heavier users of alcohol are more likely to have criminal records and to admit to criminal acts than those who are moderate drinkers or non-drinkers.
- Even when alcohol and committing crime can be shown to be related it is difficult to point to a causal direction, i.e. which came first – the drinking or the crime?

Alcohol consumption obviously has an effect on the drinker, but it is easily understood that social contexts and psychological factors influence how these effects are experienced and manifested. Similarly, understanding the role of alcohol (or indeed other drugs) in relation to the committing of crimes needs sensitivity not just to the interaction between pharmacology and physiology, but also to immediate social context and wider cultural norms. As with the idea that users 'learn' how to interpret and 'enjoy' drug effects (Becker, 1963), so it is the case that belief about how alcohol is 'supposed' to affect behaviour, alongside the influences of context and culture, is as important in shaping behaviour as the amount of alcohol consumed (Borrill and Stevens, 1993; Pearson, 1992; Deehan, 1999).

Images of alcohol use on television, in films and in advertising promote an association with desirable lifestyles, fun, sex and success, with obvious connections to the culture of the carnivalesque and seductions of crime (Katz, 1988) that have been discussed in relation to youth offending, hedonism and susbstance use (Collison, 1996). Such advertising is designed to appeal to both young men and young women. Use by the latter has been increasing steadily since the 1980s. Nonetheless, it is particularly in relation to masculinity that the association between alcohol consumption and offending, including violence, has been seen as a serious problem (Tomsen, 1997; Graham and Wells, 2003).

Plate 12.1 Young people drinking in Newcastle city centre – part of a thriving night-time economy.

Source: © North News and Pictures.

The economic boom of the night-time economy (Hobbs *et al.*, 2003) has assisted the regeneration of some inner-city areas and has created opportunities for employment and leisure in the 24/7 city but has also led to developments of criminological interest: a new arena for masculine play and power, to be enjoyed but also fought over; the proliferation of venues legally selling alcohol and where drugs are illegally easily available; development of protection rackets and turf wars between criminal entrepreneurs; increases in alcohol-related injuries requiring medical attention; and in relation to control, the growth of the use of bouncers and private security as the feudal forms of regulation of the night-time life of the city (see also Chapter 15).

Raistrick *et al.* (1999: 55) summarise the findings of a wide body of research and note several other connections between alcohol and crime:

- Intoxication may tip the balance between contemplating crime and committing it.
- Public disorder is commonly linked to drinking by young people on the street and in public places.
- Alcohol use may be a financial motive for crime.
- Alcohol problems can produce a home environment in which antisocial and abusive behaviour occurs, such as domestic violence, child abuse and cruelty towards animals.

Whether alcohol use is related to disorder and violence in the community or in the home, there are many avenues to explore for explanations of links. The complexity of this task is indicated by the intertwining of alcohol dependence, offending and imprisonment, and indications of mental illness and social exclusion (see Box 12.4).

■ BOX 12.4 OFFENDERS, ALCOHOL AND MENTAL HEALTH

- One study revealed that 63 per cent of men and 39 per cent of women serving prison sentences had been hazardous or harmful drinkers in the year prior to incarceration (Singleton *et al.*, 1997)
- As many as 90 per cent of prisoners have a mental illness and/or substance misuse (including alcohol) problem (Department of Health, 2001).
- People who are dependent on alcohol are more likely to be homeless on release from prison than those who are not (Revolving Doors Agency, 2002).

Source: Alcohol Concern Website.

DRUGS, ALCOHOL, CRIME AND COMMUNITY: A PUBLIC HEALTH ISSUE

Following the election of the Labour government in 1997, 'crime and community' became the focus of considerable attention in social inclusion interventions (Matthews and Pitts, 2001). Focusing on youth in the community, a report from the National Association for the Care and Resettlement of Offenders (NACRO, 2001: 15) suggested that 'background research into the relationship between health and youth crime is far from extensive', but 'That which exists . . . suggests a high correlation between substance misuse, adverse mental health and a range of other health-related problems on the one hand, and offending by children and young people on the other.'

In a broader sense, while the impact of crime on the psychological and social health of the victim has been acknowledged (see Chapter 7), it has probably not been well understood. Research by the Public Health Alliance (McCabe and Raine, 1997) found that

> The effects of the fear of crime, rather than crime itself, on the health of individuals and communities has been largely underestimated. In particular, the impact of 'incivilities' on well being is not well recognised . . . both victims of crime and non-victims identified a deterioration in their quality of life and adopted a range of coping mechanisms likely to be detrimental to health, in particular increased use of alcohol, smoking and use of both licit and illicit drugs.

Connecting crime and health issues

Contemporary criminology has largely overlooked health as a variable of relevance but, at the same time, public health has also tended to neglect violence and assault as relevant. As Shepherd and Farrington (1993: 89–90) observe, 'Until recently, assault has not been treated as a public health problem, despite the fact that it is a major threat to health and a major cause of disparities in health between richer and poorer segments of the community.' Shepherd and Lisles (1998: 355) found that overall, and consistent with the findings of the British Crime Survey, 'about four times more incidents [involving violence and assault] come to the attention of [Accident and Emergency Departments] than are recorded by the police'. Such data are a potentially important source of information about violent crime (Hobbs *et al.*, 2002: 354) that goes unreported in criminal justice statistics.

In a valuable review of the literature, Robinson *et al.* (1998) have identified several categories of connections between health and crime, including:

- the impacts of crime and fear of crime on physical and psychological health;
- the health needs of victims;
- costs to the health services.

Crime-related injury and victimization lead to health problems and the need for services. However, costs to the health services (and hence wider society) do not solely result from care of the injured. In recent years, violence against health service staff in Britain has increased significantly, and so worrying is this trend that the National Health Service (NHS) has made a key policy commitment to reduce violence against its employees. Further, as is familiar to any viewers of prime-time hospital and police drama series, the emergency services are repeatedly exposed to events such as major accidents or to physical and emotional damage to victims, which in turn contribute to mental ill health and post-traumatic stress for emergency service staff (Brayley, 2001). Hence, the costs of crime and violence to society are felt directly and indirectly in personnel and financial costs to health and related services.

Crime, public health and social inequalities

With reference to violent crime and health inequalities, a study by Shepherd (1990: 293–4) shows that the assault rate was higher the greater the ranking of the area of residence in terms of social and material deprivation. More recently, Hope (2001) has investigated the positive correlation between social deprivation and crime victimization. On a national scale, data from the British Crime Survey for 2000 reflect higher 'concern' about crime among deprived groups – the poor, those in unskilled occupations, residents in inner-city and council estate areas – and also reports that those who considered themselves to be in poor health or who had a limiting illness or disability had heightened levels of concern about crime (Kershaw et al., 2000: 47–9, table A7.9).

The importance of public health and its relevance for crime and victimization issues was given serious emphasis by the Acheson Report (1998: 53) on health inequalities. This report observed that both fear of crime and violence and victimization can have damaging consequences for health. It noted the simple but significant (yet frequently neglected) point that increased risk of ill health *and* of crime victimization are highest among those already most disadvantaged. Furthermore:

> Although the evidence is incomplete, the link between income inequality, social cohesion and crime has important policy implications. It suggests that crime prevention strategies which only target the perpetrators and victims of crime and the high crime areas in which both groups live, will not achieve a significant reduction in crime unless they are accompanied by measures to reduce income inequality and promote social cohesion.
>
> (Acheson, 1998: 54)

Hence, public health is sometimes described as 'social medicine', and its aims can be seen to coincide with much work in criminology concerned with the effects of social exclusion – for example, strategies for health improvement that require reductions of inequalities and of poverty, of pollution, of sources of ill health and transmittable disease in the community, and of crime and victimization.

Public health as social policing

Public health can be seen as a benign system of inspection, information gathering, regulation and intervention but also, precisely because of these characteristics, can be understood in the sense developed by Foucault (1975) as part of the dispersal of disciplinary power throughout the major institutions of modern society. Public health therefore has a role in the 'policing' of our health and of services and businesses that have an impact on our health, deploying various professionals such as health visitors, nutritionists and environmental health officers (who focus on pollution, food purity, hygiene in food stores and so forth; on 'food crimes', see Carrabine *et al.*, 2002, ch. 4; Croall, 1998: 280). Public health is also about preventing disease and illness and promoting reduction of harm. So, to return to drug misuse and AIDS/ HIV, the public health approach adopted in the United Kingdom has been far more effective than the US emphasis on a response by the criminal justice system. It is also important to see that in the contemporary context of public policy, multi-agency strategies and initiatives have come to occupy a central place. As noted earlier, following the Crime and Disorder Act 1998, health authorities have been required participants in the development of crime and community safety partnerships and strategies, while the Drug Treatment and Testing Orders, introduced under the same Act, require the court, probation and statutory and voluntary sector drugs agencies to work together.

The idea of recognising physical and mental health as relevant to understanding crime is receiving interest in various ways. But of course this is not a new development. As earlier chapters indicate, it can be 'functional' to society to identify, blame and stigmatise those who are 'tainted' or ' misfits': the vagrant, the imbecile, the pariah marked by disease, from the leper of the Middle Ages to the AIDS victim today. Religious, moral and medical judgements have long created categories of risk and danger and techniques for redemption, rehabilitation or treatment (Cohen, 1985). Since the nineteenth century, the medical profession – in particular, psychiatry – has come to be the secular successor to religion as the arbitrator of status as 'healthy' or 'sick', and has acquired the power to exercise forms of authority that can be hard to challenge. Some writers, both sociologists of health and medicine (Zola, 1972; Conrad and Schneider, 1992) and criminologists (Cohen, 1985; Sim, 1990), have drawn attention to the power of medicine as a form of social control.

MEDICINE AS A FORM OF SOCIAL CONTROL

Medical and psychiatric interventions as social control

Antidepressant drugs such as tranquillisers have been seen by some as a pharmaceutical tool that society uses to pacify women discontented with the drudgery and limitations of domestic life. The medicalisation of female deviance, the drive to normalise women's behaviour according to particular ideals of femininity and the tendency of medical professionals to over-prescribe mood-altering drugs for women are common practices (Ettore, 1992). In the United States, significantly more women than men receive prescriptions for antidepressants, tranquillisers and sedatives. Within prisons (see p. 224), the use of psychotropic drugs on male inmates is often justified with reference to 'problems of institutional control', while female inmates tend to be drugged in the name of 'treatment' in an attempt to correct their deviant behaviour in a psychological–social–physiological manner. Such drugs in prison have been described as a 'liquid cosh', their use being a soft technique of control and prison management (Sim, 1990).

The British government's proposals in the White Paper *Reforming the Mental Health Act* (2000) included some welcome proposals to 'modernise' mental health legislation but also contained a disturbing provision 'to incarcerate people according to the opinions of others regarding the likelihood that they would behave dangerously at some point in the future' (Farnham and James, 2001: 1926). There is an important debate here. Society rightly expects government to act to minimise harm to citizens and provide protection from dangerous people. In this case, the proposals from government addressed the unwillingness of psychiatrists to perform a professional function as agents of control and engage in controversial clinical adjudication about the risks and dangers posed by some mentally ill people with a history of offending. The government therefore proposed new procedures and a new category of risk individuals. The problem is that the intention to increase the social safety of the majority has attracted criticism about the inadequacy of the means by which such predictions about risk might be made and about the civil liberties and human rights implications for the mentally ill. Some may therefore see such proposals as a 'conscious deception', employing a diagnostic category called 'dangerous severe personality disorder', with virtually no credibility, as the basis for a policy driven by a government-inspired 'public-protection agenda . . . pushed through in the guise of a health-care intervention' (ibid). Others – politicians, members of the general public, pressure groups representing victims of violent, disordered offenders – might argue that public safety is the first priority.

The medicalisation of control in prisons

The use of psychotropic drugs to control inmates in institutions is far from new. In the nineteenth and early twentieth centuries, those committed to prisons or asylums might be given 'sleeping draughts' to 'modify' their behaviour. Following the Second World War, the emergence of the multinational drug industry produced large-scale manufacture and availability of powerful new drugs with sedative or other behaviour-modification properties (McAllister, 2000). Particularly from the 1970s, as prisons experienced crises of disorder and protest, the demand for enhanced security meant that medical management of prisoners took on new significance. In the United States there is similar evidence of use of psychotropic drugs in prisons since at least the 1970s. These offer a 'quick, cheap and effective' aid to the warehousing of increasing numbers of inmates in cramped conditions.

Diagnosis and medication may vary in relation to gender and ethnicity, and in one UK study, Genders and Player (1987) found that large doses of antidepressants, sedatives and tranquillisers were prescribed to women in prison, who received proportionately five times more medication as men. Around ten years later, a 1998 parliamentary debate gave rise to concerns that strong tranquillising drugs are routinely prescribed to young women prisoners who mutilate themselves, and are also used as pacifiers and substitutes for illegal drugs despite the side effects of their own addictive potential (Hansard, 22 October 1998: col. 1400).

Critics also argue that psychiatric medicine and the criminal justice system operate with ethnocentric assumptions or racist stereotypes that are introduced into medical or legal judgements. Hence, African and Caribbean psychiatric in-patients are more likely than whites to be defined as 'aggressive', placed in secure units and subjected to invasive forms of treatment such as intramuscular medication and electro-convulsive therapy. During the 1980s a number of cases involving black prisoners in Britain raised concerns about the nature of their psychiatric assessments, the inappropriate and/or inadequate medical treatment they received, the question of force-feeding, the use of drugs as a technique for control, and their certification as mentally ill, leading to transfer to a mental hospital, thereby influencing the criteria for eligibility for release.

However, yet again there are two sides to the issue, for one very important criticism of the prison system is that far too many people with mental health problems and other illnesses are held in totally inappropriate prison conditions when they should be in hospital settings.

Medicine and the criminal justice system

The medical and allied health professions have come to play an increasingly central role in the criminal justice system:

- Medical experts are called to give evidence at criminal trials, though not without controversy: psychiatric diagnoses once credible may now be criticised, for example the idea of homosexuality as a dangerous perversion. Since 2003, medical evidence about the statistical improbability of more than one infant death occurring in a family has been seriously questioned, leading to several convictions for murder being overturned, prosecution cases failing, and in 2004, official steps being taken to re-open many previous cases.
- The courts may receive psychiatric reports on offenders to help determine their fitness to stand trial and their comprehension of their actions and the consequences.
- Secure hospitals run as psychiatric and therapeutic institutions are the 'prisons' for those who cannot, for various reasons, be sent to traditional jails, but these institutions also perform valuable therapeutic functions.
- The police employ 'police surgeons' – that is, medically qualified staff (usually contracted local GPs) – to provide health assessments and care for those held in custody.
- Prisons have medical wings with their own health care staff (although the system is now being incorporated into the NHS).

- Psychiatric nurses in secure institutions need to employ therapeutic techniques but also are effectively jailers and may need to use techniques of restraint and coercion. The majority will work to high standards, but, as with prison officers there are cases of serious abuse of power and patients.

- In relation to drug offenders, as already indicated, the criminal justice and health systems are increasingly linked, with the latter seen as offering those willing to take the opportunity, a diversionary route away from crime and from punishment by the criminal justice system.

The report from NACRO (2001) referred to earlier suggested that 'current developments in social policy present real opportunities for broadening the debate and incorporating the results into a humane and constructive approach to reducing youth crime', and made the case for 'joined-up' thinking and for multi-agency approaches to community problems that cross crime prevention and public health. As others have suggested, in some cases this might usefully and sensibly involve redefining some crime matters as public health matters. The policing and regulation of drug misusers is an obvious candidate, as proposed by Maher and Dixon (1999) and, rather notably, in 2002 by the Drugs Subcommittee of the Association of Chief Police Officers (NACRO, 2002: 14).

Alcohol services have frequently and justifiably complained that when compared to the priority and funding attached to dealing with illegal drug problems, they have been the neglected Cinderella services. Yet as we have seen, alcohol is as relevant to a strategy for reducing crime and victimization as illegal drugs. Of particular note here is the increasing significance of the night-time economy, fuelled by the economics of the successful leisure industry and welcomed by local and national government as a contributor to urban regeneration. This high-profit industry also produces high profits for the Treasury as highly taxed alcohol sales boom. Yet there is a clear tension between this development and certain concerns on the crime reduction and policing agendas, as late-night 'binge' drinking is associated with public disorder and violence; local residents' fear of crime and victimization is increased, and the new leisure landscape is increasingly 'policed' not by public police but by private security and bouncers (Hobbs *et al.*, 2003).

SUMMARY

1   In this chapter we have described the history of controls and policy concerning alcohol and illegal drugs. We have discussed the complex relationships between alcohol, drugs and crime, and also examined the widening availability of drugs and alcohol.

2   The idea that drug use is becoming 'normalised' can be seen as an important but debatable proposition. Certainly, though, for some intoxicant consumers, a mix of alcohol and illegal drugs has become a regular menu of choice. This has important implications for education about 'drugs' but also for health.

3   The chapter has adopted a holistic approach and addressed not only crime and control matters but also the health implications of rising alcohol and drug use,

broadening out to also consider other dimensions of the link between health and crime, such as mental health problems and social deprivation.

4 The introduction of health issues into criminological consideration is overdue and also draws attention to the role of health professionals as gatekeepers and controllers. The specialism of public health can be seen as social medicine but also as a form of surveillance and control. This function is explored in relation to debates about the role of psychiatrists.

5 Health services and therapeutic/control interventions also extend into the prison system and are part of new forms of diversion into treatment for drug-using offenders appearing before the courts.

CRITICAL THINKING QUESTIONS

1 Consider the debates about decriminalisation versus the prohibition of drugs. What is the evidence on both sides?

2 Can you provide examples of how 'good intentions' in the criminal justice and health systems have produced 'bad outcomes'?

3 Consider the growth of the night-time economy and its implications for crime and disorder.

4 Read this chapter alongside Chapter 11 and review the links between drugs and major crime from the local to the global.

FURTHER STUDY

Bean, P. (2002) *Drugs and Crime*, Cullompton, Devon: Willan. A review of the literature on drugs and crime with particular focus on criminal justice responses.

Berridge, V. (1999) *Opium and the People*, rev. edn, London: Free Association Books. The 'classic' social history of the place of opium in English life in the nineteenth century, its' legality and the development of moves toward control.

Roberts, M. (2003) *Drugs and Crime: From Warfare to Welfare*, London: NACRO. A thorough and lively overview of the criminological and policy literature concerning drugs, criminal justice, treatment and prospects for policy change.

South, N. (ed.) (1995) *Drugs, Crime and Criminal Justice*, 2 vols, Aldershot: Dartmouth.

South, N. (2002) 'Drugs, Alcohol and Crime', M. Maguire, R. Morgan and R. Reiner (eds) *The Oxford Handbook of Criminology*, Oxford: Oxford University Press. These volumes reprint various classic and more recent studies covering drug use, cultures, crime and criminal justice.

MORE INFORMATION

Drugscope
http://www.drugscope.org.uk/
An invaluable site with access to an online encyclopaedia about drugs and to Drugscope's library.

Alcohol Concern
http://www.alcoholconcern.org.uk/
This site provides links to many other useful sites.

Russell Webster: Consultant in Substance Misuse and Crime
http://www.russellwebster.com/
The main purpose of this Website is to signpost UK resources on substance misues and crime on the Internet.

PART 4 CONTROLLING CRIME

In this section, we look at the workings of the social control process – at the philosophies behind it, and how it may be changing shape in the twenty-first century. We focus on the police, the courts, prisons and their alternatives.

Thinking about Punishment

INTRODUCTION

This chapter provides an overview of criminological thinking on punishment, which can be simply defined as 'a legally approved method designed to facilitate the task of crime control' (Garland, 1990: 18). However, the fact that punishment causes pain, suffering and harm raises important ethical dilemmas. Consequently, the punishment of offenders requires moral justification, for as Nicola Lacey (1988: 14) points out, the power to punish derives from the legal authority of the state to do things that would otherwise be *prima facie* morally wrongful'. Moral philosophy is the contemporary branch of thinking that concerns itself with distinguishing between the age-old questions of identifying what is 'right' and 'wrong' and establishing 'good' and 'evil' through defining what ought to be the proper goals of punishment. Such questions are explicitly normative in that they ask what aims and values a system of punishment must fulfil if it is to be morally acceptable.

A second distinctive perspective can be regarded as a sociology of control, for while it does attend to the uses of punishment, it does so through considering the wider aspects of social control to reveal the 'deeper structures' of penal systems (Cohen, 1984). Although there is a tendency to evade complex normative issues, this approach nevertheless does 'raise basic questions about the ways in which society organizes and deploys its power to punish' (Duff and Garland, 1994: 22). The difference can be put simply through using Barbara Hudson's (1996: 10/2003: 10) distinction, which maintains that the philosophy of punishment deliberates on how things *ought* to be, whereas the sociology of control tells it like it really *is* through explaining why particular societies adopt specific modes of punishment.

Although the principles of each philosophical justification will be emphasised, it is important to recognise that the different rationalities coexist in uneasy hybrid combinations; as Nigel Walker (1991: 8) puts it, 'in practice Anglo-American sentencers tend to be eclectic, reasoning sometimes as utilitarians but sometimes, when they are outraged by a crime, as retributivists'. Similarly, while there are competing forms of sociological explanation, which often fundamentally differ over how the same issues should be interpreted, the overall argument is that punishment, as a social institution, is an inherently complex business that needs to be approached from a range of theoretical perspectives, as no single interpretation will grasp the diverse meanings generated by punishment.

PHILOSOPHICAL JUSTIFICATIONS

Every time a court imposes a sentence, it emphatically declares, in both a physical and a symbolic sense, the sovereignty of the political power to which it owes judicial authority. Most criminologists would argue that as a consequence of this

> close proximity between the power to punish and the wider power to *rule*, it has become an axiom of political theory that the act of judicial sentencing requires to be justified by reference to some greater moral or ethical principle than merely the will of either the sentencer or the *de facto* law-giver.
>
> (Brownlee, 1998: 34; emphasis in original)

As we will see, the various competing justifications rooted in opposing ideas over what the purpose of punishment should be tend to fall into one of two distinctive groups. Those that see the aim of punishment as the prevention of future crimes are generally referred to as **reductivist**, and those that look to the past to punish crimes already committed are typically known as **retributivist**. In practice, however, most criminal justice systems fashion quite contradictory justifications, so that the different rationalities often coexist in uneasy hybrid combinations.

Reductivist principles

Reductivism justifies punishment on the grounds of its alleged future consequences. These arguments are supported by the form of moral reasoning known as utilitarianism. This moral theory was most famously advanced by Jeremy Bentham (1748–1832), as he argued that moral actions are those that produce 'the greatest happiness of the greatest number' of people. For punishment to reduce future crimes, the pain and unhappiness caused to the offender must be 'outweighed by the avoidance of unpleasantness to other people in the future – thus making punishment morally right from a utilitarian point of view' (Cavadino and Dignan, 2002: 34). By pointing to a future or greater 'good', reductivist principles focus on the instrumental 'ends' of punishment. The avoidance of further crime can be achieved through a number of strategies, such as:

- deterring potential criminals;
- reforming actual criminals; or
- keeping actual or potential offenders out of circulation.

Deterrence

Deterrence is based on the idea that crime can be discouraged through the public's fear of the punishment they may receive if they break the law. For Bentham and contemporary thinkers, a distinction is drawn between *individual* and *general* deterrence. Individual deterrence is said to occur when someone finds the experience of punishment so unpleasant that they never wish to repeat the infraction for fear of the consequences.

There is a long history of governments introducing severe punishments through claims that harsher penalties will produce special deterrence effects. The results, however, are modest at best. For instance, the introduction of 'short, sharp shock' regimes into detention centres for young offenders in England and Wales by the Conservative government in the early 1980s 'proved to have no better post-release reconviction scores than centres operating the normal regime', and likewise, the popular American 'boot camps' of the 1990s, based on the aggressive training regimes of US marines, 'have not been shown to be at all effective in discouraging reoffending' (Dunbar and Langdon, 1998: 10).

In addition to these empirical doubts over the effectiveness of such strategies, there are also more general moral objections raised against individual deterrence, as it:

- can be used to justify punishing the innocent, as what matters is the communication of the penalty (Duff, 1996: 3);
- can allow for punishment in excess of that deserved by the offence; and
- is primarily concerned with offences that might be committed in the future, rather than the offences that have actually been committed (Hudson, 1996: 27/2003: 25).

Individual deterrence, then, is of little value as a moral justification for penal policy. On the other hand, general deterrence seems to offer a more plausible justification. This is the idea that offenders are punished not to deter the offenders themselves, but to discourage other potential offenders. There can be little doubt that the existence of a system of punishment has some general deterrent, but it is important to recognise that the effects are easily overestimated. In recognition of these difficulties, reductivists can also justify punishment on the basis of reform or rehabilitation.

Reform and rehabilitation

The term 'reform' is generally used to refer to the nineteenth-century development of prison regimes that sought to change the offender through a combination of hard labour and religious instruction, whereas 'rehabilitation' describes the more individualised treatment programmes introduced in the twentieth century in conjunction with the emergence of the welfare state (Garland, 1985). Both are based on the idea that punishment can reduce crime if it takes a form that will improve the individual's character so that they are less likely to reoffend in the future.

When the 'rehabilitative ideal' was at its height in the 1950s and 1960s, it was strongly informed by positivist criminology, which viewed criminal behaviour not as freely willed action but as a symptom of some kind of mental illness that should be 'treated', just as an illness is treated. From around the mid-1970s it became widely assumed that whatever reform measures were chosen, the research showed that 'nothing works' (Martinson, 1974). This message became accepted less because of its validity than because it suited the mood of the times, in which there was a general move to the political right on both sides of the Atlantic and a widespread backlash against any form of welfarist solutions to social problems.

However, there are indications that rehabilitation is undergoing something of a revival, as there have been recent attempts to find 'what works' (McGuire, 1995, Hollin, 1999; Crow, 2001). Few now maintain the appropriateness of 'medical' models of punishment, or claim that science can provide a cure for all criminality. Rehabilitation programmes are now seen as measures that might 'facilitate change' rather than 'coerce a cure' (Cavadino and Dignan, 2002: 38). Aside from the question mark over the effectiveness of rehabilitation programmes, there are important moral objections raised by the very assumption that criminals need reform – a view criticised in Aldous Huxley's *Brave New World* (1994) and Anthony Burgess's *Clockwork Orange* (1962) – and, as is seen later in this chapter, by the criminologist Stan Cohen (1985), who offers a dystopian vision of an oppressive control net that intrudes into practically every aspect of our lives (see also Box 13.2).

Incapacitation

The idea that an offender's ability to commit further crimes should be removed, either physically or geographically (through locking them up, removing offending limbs or killing them), is generally referred to as incapacitation. In contrast to other justifications of punishment, the logic of incapacitation appeals to neither changing the offender's behaviour nor searching for the causes of the offending. Instead, it advocates the protection of potential victims as the essence of punishment, as opposed to the rights of offenders. Many contemporary criminal justice strategies currently subscribe to the doctrine of incapacitation. In part, this is because it fills the void created by the collapse of rehabilitation and the associated argument that 'nothing works' in the 1970s, but also because it claims to offer a means of social defence through removing offenders from society and thereby eliminating their capacity to commit further crimes.

Examples of current criminal justice sentencing policy that are informed by the logic of incapacitation include the 'three strikes and you're out' penalty and selective incapacitation, both of which usually involve long periods of incarceration. More generally, incapacitation has become the main philosophical justification for imprisonment in countries that subscribe to the notion that 'prison works', as it takes many persistent and serious offenders off the streets and thereby, it is claimed, reduces the crime rate (Murray, 1997).

The model for this approach is what is known as the US 'prison experiment'. There has been a dramatic growth in the prison population over the past thirty years (Mauer, 2001). For instance, in 1970 there were 196,000 prisoners in state and federal prisons in the United States, but by the turn of the new century the figure exceeded 2 million, and it has been estimated that if current US trends continue, '30 per cent of all black males born today will spend some of their lives in prison' (Garland, 2001a: 6). Critics argue that the 'experiment' of increasing the prison population in this way has been funded by the diversion of public expenditure from welfare to the prison, while the level of violence, particularly among the young and disadvantaged, continues to severely affect life in many North American cities (Currie, 1996), while others point to the alarming racial dimension to this strategy of containment (Wacquant, 2001).

Retributivist principles

In its simplest form, retributivism is the view that wrongdoers should be punished because they deserve it, irrespective of any future beneficial consequences. This principle dates from antiquity. For instance, the Code of Hammurabi is among the first written legal codes and enshrined the phrase 'an eye for an eye' in 1750 BC in Babylon. The code is thus based on the concept of *lex talionis* – 'the law of retaliation'. This principle was developed by the Enlightenment philosopher Immanuel Kant (1724–1804) into a highly influential critique of utilitarian justifications of punishment, which use offenders 'merely as means' rather than fully recognising their humanity so that the innocent can be deliberately punished if it is expedient to do so. For Kant, the duty to punish was a **categorical imperative** that restored the moral equilibrium – a view that led him to declare, famously, that even on the dissolution of society 'the last murderer remaining in prison must first be executed' (quoted in Walker, 1991: 77). Nevertheless, the increasing attraction of utilitarian justifications in the nineteenth and twentieth centuries led to retributivism falling from favour as it appealed to archaic and reactionary feelings of revenge. Yet one of the more striking developments of the past thirty years has been the revival of retributivist ideas under the guise of 'just deserts'.

Just deserts

During the 1950s and 1960s, the penal system was generally understood to be an important element in the welfare state's programme of social engineering. It would prevent crime through deterring potential offenders and incapacitating actual offenders, and it was hoped that treatment programmes would rehabilitate offenders. As we have seen, by the mid-1970s the institutions of the welfare state were under serious attack from all shades of the political spectrum, not simply because of their perceived failure but also because of their moral costs. In addition to neo-conservative critics (Wilson, 1975), liberal thinkers also began to reassert the importance of justice over utility and of individual rights against the claims of the state (Rawls, 1972; Dworkin, 1978). One important 'manifestation of this moral shift was that theorists began to focus on the rights of the guilty as well as those of the innocent' (Duff and

Garland, 1994: 10). This gave birth to a prisoners' rights movement that chimed with broader conceptions of civil rights, so that the need to protect prisoners and others from the arbitrary and discretionary powers of state bureaucracies became paramount (Fogel, 1975).

It is in this context that the 'new retributivist' arguments emerged, and formulated the principle of '**just deserts**', which insists that offenders should be punished only as severely as they deserve, in reaction against the unfair excesses of rehabilitation and the 'get tough' incapacitative drive from conservatives. The leading advocate of this movement, Andrew von Hirsch (1976), proposed that greater consistency and certainty should lie at the centre of the criminal justice system, with punishment fitting the crime rather than the person. Key elements here are *proportionality* – the offender should be sentenced according to what the act deserves; and *denunciation* – condemnation of the offence through restoring the moral equilibrium while expressing social disapproval.

These principles, in certain important respects, recall the arguments of the classical criminologist Cesare Beccaria (1738–94) for due process in the criminal justice system and are based on a similar understanding of the social contract, which is supposed to apply equally and fairly to everyone. Retributive punishment is thereby regarded as ensuring that offenders do not profit from their wrongdoing. Yet as critics have argued, the fundamental flaw in this line of thinking is that it is applicable only if social relations are just and equal, otherwise there is no equilibrium to restore. In reality, offenders tend to be already socially disadvantaged, so that punishment actually increases inequality rather reducing it (Cavadino and Dignan, 2002: 42).

Hybrid compromises

So far we have been setting out the fundamental philosophical justifications and discussing their respective limitations, yet it is important to emphasise that in practice most criminal justice systems combine these differing rationales in uneasy combinations. For instance, it is generally acknowledged that the 'just deserts' approach to criminal justice proposed by liberals critical of rehabilitation in the 1970s had by the 1980s become co-opted by the political right (Hudson, 1987). The clearest indication of this is the strategy pursued by the Conservative government which culminated in the Criminal Justice Act 1991. This piece of legislation repeatedly emphasised the principle of 'just deserts' as the aim of criminal justice, with a greater stress on proportionality in sentencing, yet at the same time the Act designated community penalties (discussed in more detail below) as 'punishment in the community' in an effort to reinforce the tough 'law and order' image of the government.

Shortly after the legislation was introduced, the Conservatives appeared to abandon 'just deserts' in an effort to further strengthen their punitive credentials in favour of another hybrid combination of incapacitation and deterrence – famously declared by the Home Secretary of the time, Michael Howard, in his insistence that 'prison works'. For some critics, the 'populist punitiveness' of John Major's Conservative government has continued under New Labour (Carrabine *et al.*, 2000: 194–6). One indication of this is the insistence that imprisonment should not be reserved only for serious offenders but is also suitable for persistent petty offenders.

This directly contradicts the principle that punishment should fit the crime, and it has been reported that when Jack Straw was Home Secretary, he explicitly stated that he wanted to end the 'just deserts' philosophy through arguing that 'it is time to make the sentence fit the offender rather than the offence' (Cavadino and Dignan, 2002: 53). Clearly, the fundamental justifications can exist in different combinations, but to explain why these uneasy compromises might be more than simply passing fashions it is to sociological forms of explanation that we now turn.

BOX 13.1 RESTORATIVE JUSTICE: A NEW JUSTIFICATION FOR PUNISHMENT?

Some criminologists are now arguing that restorative justice brings fresh and more just relationships between offenders and victims. The arguments are based partly on the principle of reparation: that those who offend should do something to repair the wrong they have done, and in so doing acknowledge the harm they have caused. Although reparation can take many forms and has a long history, such as paying a fine (through the courts) to compensate a victim or carrying out unpaid work that will benefit the community, there is an important sense in which there is a recognition of the rights of victims to have redress for the harm they have suffered. It is partly as a result of these developments that restorative justice has gained momentum as an alternative to modern Western systems of punishment.

Over the past ten years the principles of restorative justice have moved from the margins of criminology to the centre of lively debates not only in the discipline but also in criminal justice policy. The origins of restorative justice are diverse, yet all arise from disillusionment with modern systems of criminal justice. Its supporters include penal abolitionists, social theologians, post-colonial critics and the victims' movement, who are united in their efforts to redefine justice as a process of shoring up rifts in communities through helping the victim and offender overcome their trauma through forms of 'reintegrative shaming' (Braithwaite, 1989). Scandinavian penal abolitionists (Christie, 1977) have been arguing since the 1970s that state punishment is oppressively authoritarian and ought to be based on an alternative conceptualisation of 'redress' that disperses decision-making among a much more heterogeneous community (de Haan, 1990). Another important set of developments have been the 'rediscovery' of distinctive indigenous systems of justice. For instance, 'family group conferences' arose through Maori criticism of the dominant Western juvenile justice system that had stripped the community of responsibility for dealing with its young, and 'sentencing circles' , which were revived in the Yukon Territory, Canada, are 'an updated version of the traditional sanctioning and healing practices of Canadian Aboriginal peoples' (Bazemore and Taylor-Griffiths, 2003: 78).

Although there have been scattered mediation schemes in England and Wales since the 1970s, the Crime and Disorder Act 1998 and the Youth Justice and Criminal Evidence

continued

Act 1999 have formally introduced elements of restorative justice as a mainstream response to youth offending in a number of different ways, including family group conferences based on the New Zealand model, reparation orders for offenders aged 10 and older, and consultation with victims before any reparative intervention is organised (Gelsthorpe and Morris, 2002: 246). Restorative justice is not without its critics, who point out that there are few safeguards to protect the most vulnerable groups from the pious moralising of reintegrative shaming. This absence of account-ability compounds the lack of protection for the offender in terms of appeals to legal process and due rights (Ashworth, 2003); while a former supporter has become highly sceptical of the claims made by the more evangelical advocates (Daly, 2002). Fundamental issues remain over whether restorative justice challenges social control or casts the net of social control deeper into the community.

SOCIOLOGICAL EXPLANATIONS

Instead of asking questions concerning punishment's effectiveness or justification, sociologists 'attend to the ways in which penal policy is determined by political forces and the struggle of contending interests, rather than by normative argument or relevant empirical evidence' (Duff and Garland, 1994: 32). In exploring the deeper role that punishment plays in society, a number of competing perspectives can be identified. Each is informed by a social theory that can be traced back to the 'founding fathers' of sociology, as authors tend to adopt a Durkheimian approach or a Marxist position and then critically disregard other ways of thinking. What the chapter will now do is set out the main sociological explanations of punishment that are derived from the work of Durkheim, Marx and Foucault before discussing feminist critiques of these 'malestream' perspectives.

Although these diverse approaches cannot simply be bolted together to form the definitive sociological statement on punishment, as there are fundamental differences of interpretation, there is an important sense in which sociology reveals the complex and multi-faceted dimensions of punishment as a social institution that otherwise remain hidden. Nevertheless, the overall argument follows David Garland's (1990: 2) insistence that criminologists must develop 'a more pluralistic approach' to capture the 'richness of meaning' generated by punishment.

Durkheim and social solidarity

The distinctive contribution of Émile Durkheim (1858–1917) lies in the way that he examined the relationships between crime, law and punishment to reveal the mechanisms that create and sustain **social solidarity**. This sociological approach is often referred to as functionalism, as he argued that whatever aspect of social life is being studied, it must be approached from the perspective of discovering what role it performs in preserving social stability and promoting moral consensus. Although his ideas have been dismissed for their inherent conservatism, there is an important sense in which he draws attention to the functions that punishment plays in maintaining social order in the face of rapid economic change and political upheaval.

Durkheim's theory of punishment is initially advanced in his most famous book, *The Division of Labor in Modern Society* (1893/1960), and is then extended in the article 'Two Laws of Penal Evolution' (1901/1984) to give a more nuanced understanding of historical change. In *The Division of Labor* he develops his classic theory on the emergence of specialised work in modern societies through distinguishing between simple, pre-industrial societies in which there is little division of labour and more advanced societies in which people perform complex, specialised tasks.

At the core of his work is a concern with social solidarity, by which he means the shared conventions, meanings and moralities that hold societies together. In each type of society, he saw punishment as playing an important role in the creation of solidarity, and he goes so far as to say that 'passion is the soul of punishment', as punishment arouses furious moral indignation and a ritualised expression of social values against those who had violated the sacred moral order. Even though modern 'penal systems may try to achieve utilitarian objectives, and to conduct themselves rationally and unemotively', the strength of Durkheim's account is how it reveals that 'at an underlying level there is still a vengeful, motivating passion which guides punishment and supplies its force' (Garland, 1990: 31).

Punitive passions and degradation rituals

There is an important sense in which Durkheim draws attention to the expressive qualities of punishment: how 'all healthy consciences' come together to reaffirm shared beliefs through dutiful outrage that constructs a 'public wrath' (cited in Giddens, 1972: 127). In the controversial work of the German philosopher Friedrich Nietzsche (1844–1900), an altogether more sinister account of punitive sentiments is offered in his *Genealogy of Morals*, where he argues that punishment gratifies sadistic and cruel tendencies in the human condition. He explains that 'to witness suffering does one good, to inflict it even more so – that is a harsh proposition, but a fundamental one, an old, powerful, human all-too-human proposition . . . in punishment there is so much that is *festive!*' (Nietzsche, 1887/1996: 50; emphasis in original). In his history of ethics, Nietzsche (ibid.: 46–7) sought to expose the Judaeo-Christian and liberal traditions of compassion, equality and justice as products of brutal and cruel processes – how they 'have long been steeped in blood' and 'not even with old Kant: the categorical imperative gives off a whiff of cruelty'. Of course, modern penal systems deny any association with cruelty, humiliation, malice and sadism, but Nietzsche insists that these passions continue to exist, even though we are now in what the psychoanalyst Sigmund Freud (1856–1939) would call denial, as 'the pleasure in cruelty' barely troubles 'even the most delicate hypocritical conscience' (Nietzsche, ibid.: 49).

A less disturbing account of punitive passions is outlined by the Chicagoan social psychologist George Herbert Mead (1863–1931). Mead followed Durkheim by maintaining that there was a close relationship between punishment and social solidarity, but his account differs in that he argued that the collective hostility toward a criminal had the effect of 'uniting members of the community in the emotional solidarity of aggression' (Mead, 1918: 591). Mead did not regard this intense emotion as healthy but promoted a number of harmful consequences. As Claire Vallier (2002a: 31) puts it, 'the spirals of rage emanating outwards from a heinous crime were traumatising rather than healing'.

The Durkheimian tradition has continued to provide insightful analyses of how penal rituals provoke symbolic and emotive effects. For instance, the Danish sociologist Svend Ranulf argued that criminal law developed as a consequence of middle-class moral indignation (Barbalet, 2002), while Harold Garfinkel (1956a: 420–4) argued that the rituals of the courtroom should be understood as a 'degradation ceremony', as 'moral indignation serves to effect the ritual destruction of the person denounced' by defining the accused as an enemy of all that is good and decent in society – a view subsequently developed by Pat Carlen (1976) in her analysis of magistrates' justice (see also Chapter 14).

The legacy of the Durkheimian tradition has been summarised by drawing attention to the fact that in modern penal systems there is a crucial division

> between the *declaration* of punishment, which continues to take the form of a public ritual and which is continually the focus of public and media attention, and the *delivery* of punishment that now characteristically occurs behind closed doors and has a much lower level of visibility.
>
> (Garland, 1991: 125; emphasis in original)

Plate 13.1 (a) Two women shout abuse at a police van carrying Maxine Carr from Peterborough on 18 September 2002. Carr was arrested and charged with attempting to pervert the course of justice over a police investigation into the murder of two young girls in Soham, Cambridgeshire.

Source: © Reuters; *photo*: Ian Waldie.

(b) A boy stands next to a banner as he awaits the departure of Ian Huntley from Peterborough Magistrates' Court on 10 September 2002. Police mounted a heavy security operation outside the court after hundreds of protestors turned up the previous month when Maxine Carr, Huntley's girlfriend, was charged with perverting the course of justice.

Source: © Reuters; *photo*: Darren Staples.

So while Durkheim and his contemporaries identify the *function* of modern punishment in reassuring public sentiment, they have rather less to say about the *form* it takes – issues that are addressed in the following perspectives.

Marx and political economy

Marxist analyses of punishment not only address a whole range of themes ignored by Durkheim, but also reinterpret many of those that Durkheim does deal with. The legacy to sociology of Karl Marx (1818–83) was to insist that societies must be understood in terms of how economic structures condition social practices. Consequently, Marxists tend to consider punishment in relation to economic structures and examine the class interests served by penal practices. In marked contrast to Durkheim, they argue that punishing offenders for breaking laws maintains and reinforces the position of the ruling class, rather than benefiting society as a whole, and that punishment as a social institution plays an important political role as a repressive state apparatus.

One of the earliest Marxist analyses of punishment was carried out by the German Marxist scholar Georg Rusche. It was later written up with the assistance of Otto Kirchheimer and published in 1939 through the exiled Frankfurt School of Social Research in New York, as *Punishment and Social Structure*. It is a work that charts the changing deployment of penal methods from the Middle Ages up to the early decades of the twentieth century. Rusche and Kirchheimer's analysis highlights the relationships between the form that punishments take and the economic requirements of particular modes of production. They argue in a much-quoted passage that

> Every system of production tends to discover punishments which correspond to its productive relationships . . . it is self-evident that enslavement as a form of punishment is impossible without a slave economy; that prison labour is impossible without manufacture or industry, that monetary fines for all classes of society are impossible without a monetary economy.
>
> (1939/1968: 5–6)

These arguments have subsequently been criticised on the grounds of what is known as economic determinism, as they excessively (and eventually incoherently) rely on the concept of 'labour market' to explain forms of punishment.

Nevertheless, Rusche and Kirchheimer emphasise what other commentators have called the principle of **less eligibility** as vital to the management of inequality in capitalist societies, by which they mean that 'the standard of living within prisons (as well as for those dependent on the welfare apparatuses) must be lower than that of the lowest stratum of the working class' (Rusche and Kirchheimer, 1939: 108). Their basic thesis has been developed by Dario Melossi and Massimo Pavarini (1981), who argue that the prison has developed as *the* response to crime in capitalist societies because of the development of wage labour, which crucially has put a price on time, an important consequence of which is that it now seems natural that criminals should pay for their crimes by doing time, since workers are rewarded for their labour by the hour. Although this argument does rightly emphasise the importance of economic relations on penal practices, it does so in a way that minimises the significance of other crucial factors.

Punishment, ideology and class control

In contrast, other Marxists have stressed the role of punishment in ideological class struggles and the maintenance of state power. The elements of such an interpretation are present in the work of the Russian legal theorist E. B. Pashukanis (1924/1978), as he argues that the penal sanctions of capitalist societies articulate bourgeois mentalities and ideological conceptions relating to the commodity form: an exchange transaction in which the offender pays a debt and concludes the contractual obligation through serving a prison sentence (a clear influence on Melossi and Pavarini, 1981). In this manner, the ideological content of capitalist societies and bourgeois values (such as fair trading and liberty) is reaffirmed in spite of the harsh realities that exist in such societies (such as inequality and impoverishment).

As Garland (1990: 118) argues, this account is developed by the social historian Douglas Hay (1975) in his analysis of eighteenth-century criminal law, drawing attention to its dual functions of ideological legitimation and class coercion. In particular, he regards the expansion of capital punishment as a 'rule of terror' on the part of the landed aristocracy over thousands of landless poor, with the exercise of clemency (where the lord of the manor speaks to fellow gentry on behalf of a tenant at risk of severe punishment) being regarded by Hay as a central factor contributing to the culture of deference still in evidence today among rural peasantry. Writing from within a humanistic tradition of Marxism, E. P. Thompson contends that the law can function ideologically to legitimate the existing order, but that

> people are not as stupid as some structural philosophers suppose them to be. They will not be mystified by the first man who puts on a wig. . . . If the law is evidently partial and unjust, then it will mask nothing, legitimize nothing, contribute nothing to any class's hegemony.
>
> (1977: 262–3)

The clear implication is that the law is an 'arena for class struggle' rather than the exclusive possession of a ruling class (ibid.: 288). However, critics of this form of Marxist analysis point out that the criminal law and penal sanctions command a wide degree of support from the subordinate classes (the very population said to be controlled and regulated by such mechanisms of class rule) and that such practices afford a degree of protection previously unrealised (Fine, 1985). Nevertheless, one of the strengths of Marxist analysis is that it invites us to think of punishment not as a simple response to crime but as an important element in 'managing the rabble' (Irwin, 1990: 2) – matters that are now considered in the work of Michel Foucault, who, for some, marks a decisive break with Marxism.

Foucault and disciplinary power

Over the past thirty years or so, the French philosopher Michel Foucault (1926–84) has cast an enormous influence over criminology – even though he was rather scathing of the discipline. His work can be located in a tradition begun by Nietzsche, who was highly sceptical of Western rationality, and continues in the disenchanted sociology of Max Weber (1864–1920), who wrote pessimistically of an 'iron cage' of rationality and bureaucracy that will ultimately imprison us all. Foucault's (1977) *Discipline and Punish* is not simply a detailed analysis of the emergence of the prison in the nineteenth century (see Chapter 16), but also an account of how power operates in the modern era. The book opens with a striking juxtaposition of two entirely different styles of punishment that illustrate the fundamental transformations that had taken place in penal practices, namely the disappearance of the public spectacle of violence and the installation of a different form of punishment by the early nineteenth century, which is captured in a bland listing of the rules from an institutional timetable used in a Paris reformatory.

On a broader scale, these developments are illustrative of how power operates in modern society, and Foucault sets himself the ambitious task of 'writing the history of the present' (1977: 31). One influential commentator has summarised Foucault's argument in the following way:

> [T]he 'Great Incarcerations' of the nineteenth century – thieves into prisons, lunatics into asylums, conscripts into barracks, workers into factories, children into school – are to be seen as part of a grand design. Property had to be protected, production had to be standardised by regulations, the young segregated and inculcated with the ideology of thrift and success, the deviant subjected to discipline and surveillance.
>
> (Cohen, 1985: 25)

The new disciplinary mode of power which the prison was to represent belonged to an economy of power quite different from that of the direct, arbitrary and violent rule of the sovereign. Power in capitalist society had to be exercised at the lowest possible cost, both economically and politically, while its effects had to be intensified and extended throughout the social apparatus.

Although Foucault's work continues to be influential, as we will see in the next section, it has been criticised for:

- its 'appalling' historical inaccuracies (Braithwaite, 2003: 8);
- its 'impoverished' understating of subjectivity (McNay, 1994: 22);
- its preference for 'ascetic description' over normative analysis (Habermas, 1987: 275);
- not being able to tell the difference between prison and life outside.

The punitive city and surveillance society

It is more than a little ironic that at the very moment when Foucault's (1977) analysis of the 'Great Incarcerations' was published, many Western societies seemed to be radically reversing the institutional response to deviance through processes of **decarceration** and the use of alternative sanctions in the community. Community corrections came to be regarded as a more humane and less stigmatising means of responding to offenders, while treating mental illness in the community was generally seen as preferable to the asylum. However, a number of authors were sceptical and argued that treatment in the community amounted to malign neglect, with the mentally ill being left to fend for themselves in uncaring environments (Scull, 1977). In criminology, Stan Cohen (1979, 1985) has maintained that the development of community corrections marks both a continuation and an intensification of the social control patterns identified by Foucault (1977). This 'dispersal of discipline' thesis insists that there is now a blurring of where the prison ends and the community begins (see Box 13.2), with an accompanying increase in the total number of offenders brought into the system.

BOX 13.2 A VISION OF SOCIAL CONTROL

Stan Cohen wrote this nearly twenty years ago – does it still sound like the future?

Mr and Mrs Citizen, their son Joe and daughter Linda, leave their suburban home after breakfast, saying goodbye to Ron, a 15-year-old pre-delinquent who is living with them under the LAK (Look After A Kid) scheme. Ron will later take a bus downtown to the Community Correctional Centre, where he is to be given two hours of Vocational Guidance and later tested on the Interpersonal Maturity Level scale. Mr C. drops Joe off at the School Problems Evaluation Centre from where Joe will walk to school. In his class are five children who are bussed from a local Community Home, four from a Pre-Release Facility and three who, like Ron, live with families in the neighbourhood. Linda gets off next – at the GUIDE Centre (Girls Unit for Intensive Daytime Education) where she works as a Behavioural Contract Mediator. They drive past a Threequarter-way House, a Rape-Crisis Centre and then a Drug-Addict Cottage, where Mrs C. waves to a group of boys working in the garden. She knows them from some work she does in RODEO (Reduction of Delinquency Through Expansion of Opportunities). She gets off at a building which houses the Special Parole Unit, where she is in charge of a 5-year evaluation research project on the use of the HIM (Hill Interaction Matrix) in matching group treatment to client. Mr C. finally arrives at work, but will spend his lunch hour driving around the car again as this is his duty week on patrol with TIPS (Turn In a Pusher). On the way he picks up some camping equipment for the ACTION weekend hike (Accepting Challenge Through Interaction with Others and Nature) on which he is going with Ron, Linda and five other PINS (Persons In Need of Supervision).

(Cohen, 1985: 224–5)

While Cohen (1985) chronicled the recruitment of friends, relatives and neighbours into the web of surveillance through curfews, tracking and tagging that now pervades 'the punitive city' (Cohen, 1979), a debate ensued over the applicability of Foucault's ideas to contemporary patterns of punishment (Bottoms, 1983; Nelken, 1989; I. Taylor, 1999). Other developments since the 1990s include the rapid expansion of electronic, information and visual technologies, all of which greatly enhance the surveillance capacities of the state (see Chapter 18). Today, surveillance operates in so many spheres of daily life that it is impossible to avoid – a situation well described in the following passage:

> Most of our social encounters and almost all our economic transactions are subject to electronic recording, checking and authorization. From the Electronic Funds Transfer at Point of Sale (EFTPOS) machine for paying the supermarket bill or the request to show a barcoded driver's license, to the cellphone call or the Internet search, numerous everyday tasks trigger some surveillance device.
>
> (Lyon, 2001: 146)

Likewise, urban fortress living has quickly moved from being a dystopian vision (Cohen, 1985) to become a reality in Los Angeles (Davis, 1992, 1999), so that contemporary surveillance is both inclusionary for some – offering a sense of safety, security and order for some city dwellers – and exclusionary for others – prohibiting certain teenagers from entering panoptic shopping centres while planners develop sadistic street environments to displace homeless people from particular localities. John Fiske (1998) has further analysed the video surveillance of the American city to reveal how it is a rapidly developing control strategy focused on the young black male and is a disturbing instance of the totalitarian undercurrents in late modern democracies. Whereas Ray Coleman and Joe Sim (2000: 636) have argued that the deployment of closed-circuit television (CCTV) in city centres is not simply a crime prevention technology, but a troubling response to 'gaps left by a series of legitimation deficits around policing and in urban governance generally' (see also Haggerty and Ericson, 2000; Hobbs *et al.*, 2000 for further commentary on surveillance and the governance of 'urban frontiers' in these times of 'post-privacy').

Plate 13.2 A barrel-shaped bus bench that offers a minimal surface for uncomfortable sitting while making sleeping impossible, Hill Street, Downtown, Los Angeles.

Source: © Second Council District, Los Angeles City, *photo*: Melkon Melkonian, Field Rep.

Feminist challenges

It will be clear that these main philosophical and sociological traditions have largely ignored the punishment of women, and it is only in the past thirty years or so that studies of the control of women have appeared. Nevertheless, it is important to emphasise that the study of gender continues to be marginalised, and, as Ngaire Naffine (1997: 5) has argued, criminology remains a male-dominated discipline consisting largely of academic men studying criminal men. Naffine maintains that the 'costs to criminology of its failure to deal with feminist scholarship are perhaps more severe than they would be in any other discipline'. A clear instance of this is the widespread finding that when women are punished, this is as much about upholding conventional gender stereotypes as penalising criminality (Carlen, 1983; Edwards, 1984; Howe, 1994).

Moreover, the control of women indicates processes of **transcarceration**, which is defined as the movement of offenders between different institutional sites (Lowman *et al.*, 1987). Feminist studies have shown how there is a continuum of regulation in women's lives that encompasses the penal system, mental health and social welfare systems through to informal social (and antisocial) controls (Cain, 1989; Smart, 1995). The overall picture that emerges from this work is a more nuanced understanding of disciplinary control once the variable application to women and men is considered. For instance, it is clear that women are much more likely to be controlled by psychiatry and social work, while men are more readily incarcerated. It would seem that gender divisions are as fundamental to structuring punishment as are those of class and race.

Feminist jurisprudence

In recent years, there have been a growing number of proposals for a 'feminist jurisprudence' (Carlen, 1990; Daly, 1989; Naffine, 1990) based on two main premises. The first is that legal categories that are supposedly gender-neutral are in fact male; the second, and much more controversial among feminists, is that there is a kind of reasoning, characteristic to women, that is excluded from criminal justice decision-making (Hudson, 2003: 180). While feminist scholars continue to emphasise the need to bring women's experiences and voices into criminological and legal theorising, there is widespread dispute over whether there is a universal 'female voice'.

The idea that women have a distinctive form of moral reasoning and are more concerned with finding solutions to specific and concrete problems than men, who are more concerned with the application of general abstract rules, is primarily associated with the work of Carol Gilligan (1982) in her book *In a Different Voice*. She termed the female moral style 'the ethic of care', in contrast to the male 'logic of justice', and argued that both voices should have equal weight in moral reasoning; in practice, 'women's voices were misheard or judged as morally inferior to men's' (Daly, 2002: 65). Consequently, feminist criminologists have called for legal processes to admit expert witnesses with specific feminist viewpoints to qualify masculine constructions of crime and punishment (O'Donovan, 1993; Valverde, 1996).

This concept of feminist moral reasoning is controversial. Carol Smart (1989) has argued that it advances a view of men and masculinity as beyond culture and history, which serves to distort women's experiences. At the same time, the work appears to want to replace one unitary view of the world, the male view, with another unitary, and ultimately distorting, female view. Sandra Walklate (2001: 167) further explains that this 'desire to replace one world view with another fails to remove feminism from the traps of both essentialism (men and women are naturally and fundamentally different) and determinism (people, men nor women, have no choice)'. Overall, Smart's work is sceptical as to whether it is possible or even desirable to strive for a way of thinking through the law that represents all women's (or even all men's) experiences. Nevertheless, these debates effectively demonstrate that criminologists need to examine crime and punishment from a gendered perspective.

We have looked at the nature and key debates surrounding the different dimensions of crime in Part 3. In Part 4, we move from an examination of the competing ideas about crime and criminality (i.e. What is crime? Who is a criminal?) to a discussion of the principles and practices in criminal justice and punishment (i.e. What is to be done about it?).

SUMMARY

1   The power to punish derives from the legal authority of the state to do things that would otherwise be *prima facie* morally wrongful. Consequently, the pain, suffering and cruelty caused by punishment require some form of moral justification.

2   This chapter has reviewed a number of competing philosophical positions that seek to legitimate the harm (e.g. deterrence, retribution, rehabilitation etc.) through forms of moral reasoning that define what ought to be the proper goals of punishment.

3   In contrast sociological approaches to punishment have tended to consider the wider aspects of social control so that the deeper structures of penal systems are revealed to indicate the ways in which penal policy is determined by political forces rather than by abstract philosophical argument or relevant empirical evidence.

4   The chapter has also described how the punishment of women challenges conventional thinking and reviewed the arguments surrounding feminist moral reasoning.

CRITICAL THINKING QUESTIONS

1   Compare the differences between reductivists and retributivists over how punishment should be justified and how much punishment ought to be inflicted.

2　In what ways, if any, is the current US prison 'experiment' 'a totalitarian solution without a totalitarian state' (Bauman, 1995: 206)?

3　Why might punishment provoke solidarity and hostility among the public?

4　How does the principle of 'less eligibility' continue to inform contemporary practices of punishment?

5　In a pamphlet for a prisoners' rights campaign, Michel Foucault (quoted in Eribon, 1992) once remarked that '[T]hey tell us that the prisons are over-crowded, but what if the entire population is over imprisoned?' What do you take to be the implications of this assertion?

6　Can you make a case for feminist jurisprudence?

FURTHER STUDY

Cavadino, M. and Dignan, J. (2002) *The Penal System: An Introduction*, 3rd edn, London: Sage. An indispensable guide, which provides an accessible overview.

Garland, D. (1990) *Punishment and Modern Society: A Study in Social Theory*, Oxford: Clarendon Press. This is an authoritative discussion of sociological explanation.

Hudson, B. (2003) *Understanding Justice*, 2nd edn, London: Sage. Another wide ranging and accessible guide.

Lacey, N. (1988) *State Punishment: Political Principles and Community Values*, London: Routledge. This text offers thorough accounts of philosophical justifi-cations for punishment.

Smart, C. (1995) *Law, Crime and Sexuality: Essays in Feminism*, London: Sage. This book gives insight into feminist analysis in this area.

Walker, N. (1991) *Why Punish?*, Oxford: Oxford University Press. A lively introduction to pholosophical positions.

MORE INFORMATION

The Home Office: Publications: A Guide to the Criminal Justice System in England and Wales

http://www.homeoffice.gov.uk/rds/cjspub1.html

Publication available online, on the criminal justice process in England and Wales.

Criminal Justice System

http://www.cjsonline.org/home.html

This is another site that has useful information on the criminal justice process in England and Wales.

Crown Office and Procurator Fiscal Service
http://www.crownoffice.gov.uk/
This site has information on the Scottish criminal justice system plus a selection of other links for reference.

Criminal Justice System Northern Ireland
http://www.cjsni.gov.uk/
A site on the criminal justice process in Northern Ireland.

The Proceedings of the Old Bailey
http://www.oldbaileyonline.org/
A fully searchable online edition of the largest body of texts detailing the lives of non-elite people ever published, containing accounts of over 100,000 criminal trials held at London's central criminal court.

The Criminal Justice Process

KEY ISSUES

▌ What are the key stages of the criminal justice process?

▌ What happens when the process goes wrong?

▌ What do we mean by 'justice'?

▌ How do different social groups experience the criminal justice process?

INTRODUCTION

Questions of crime and questions of the control of crime are not easily separated. Patterns of recorded crime are, after all, to a very large extent determined by efforts made by various kinds of gatekeepers to report, detect, judge and punish criminal activities. This chapter provides an overview of the key stages of the criminal justice process and the key institutions involved: the police, the Crown Prosecution Service, the Probation Service and the judiciary. It looks at some of the main gatekeeping decisions that underpin the working of each area, the principles and realities of justice, and the main sociological approaches to the everyday activities of the courts.

THE HISTORICAL CONTEXT

Historians and sociologists have looked at how and why criminal justice processes and allied forms of and ideas about deviancy control underwent significant changes at particular points in time (see, for example, Hay *et al.*, 1975; Ignatieff, 1978; Rothman, 1971; Foucault, 1977; and Chapter 16 of this book). In his book *Visions of Social Control*, Stan Cohen (1985: 13–14) wrote of the transformations in the master patterns and strategies for controlling crime, delinquency and other types of socially problematic behaviour from the pre-modern to the modern period in Western industrial societies. As Chapter 13 shows, many of these key transformations are reflected in the changing principles and practices of punishment. There have been other major shifts: for example, the increasing involvement of the state, the development of a centralised, rationalised and bureaucratic apparatus in deviancy control, and the increasing professionalisation and expansion of accredited experts. These were evident in the developments of criminal justice in Britain in the nineteenth century, notably the central elements of the adversarial trial (e.g. legal representation, and the ability to call and examine your own witnesses, to cross-examine the prosecution witnesses, to address the jury) and the emergence of a full-time, trained police force and other professionals such as lawyers and medical experts (Emsley, 1996b; Rawlings, 1995). Gradually, policing, prosecution and other activities within the courtroom came to be seen as skilled work and the preserve of specialised formal agencies and professional agents.

Another key aspect of the modern criminal justice process is that criminal cases are no longer regarded as a private affair between the victim and the perpetrator of crime. In general, once a crime has been reported to the police, most victims are unaware of the processes involved in detection and in deciding whether or not to prosecute. Instead, decisions on how to deal with crimes are regarded as the concern of the state, its prerogative and duty, and trials become a contest between the state (as prosecutor) and the offender (as defendant). As Nils Christie (1977, 2000) has argued, the growth of the modern 'crime control industry' means that crime or 'conflicts' have become the official 'property' of the state. As we shall see, the organisational framework of the courts underlines this point. The opposing parties, the judge, the structural position of the experts, the construction of a case and conduct of trial based on formal criminal procedures and rules of legal relevance – all this underlines that the court system is a social organisation for the handling of conflicts. Both victims and offenders become marginalised in this situation. They face the problem of entering the courts as non-professional outsiders and passive spectators where they lack knowledge of the courtroom as a process (for more recent debates about victim participation in the criminal justice process, see Chapter 7).

OVERVIEW OF CRIMINAL JUSTICE INSTITUTIONS

Elements of the formal legal-correctional apparatus for the control of crime and delinquency such as the police, courts and prisons are found in virtually all countries, albeit with different names and involving different criminal justice procedures. There are also significant variations in the legal system within the United Kingdom. For example, the age of criminal responsibility is 8 in Scotland and 10 in England and Wales, and Northern Ireland. Young offenders are generally dealt with in specialist forums, notably the Scottish Children's Hearings System, in which lay panel members consider and make decisions on the supervision and welfare needs of the child. The public prosecution services also have different roles and responsibilities. Unlike its counterpart in England and Wales (see the subsection on the Crown Prosecution Service on p. 255), the Procurator Fiscal Service in Scotland has a wider responsibility for directing the investigation and prosecution of crime and diverting offenders from court by issuing a warning. Once the case comes to court, the 'not proven' verdict is a unique feature of the Scottish legal system. Finally, criminal justice institutions are sometimes subject to intense political scrutiny. In Northern Ireland the Criminal Justice Review Group was set up in 1998 under the Good Friday Agreement to undertake a wide-ranging review of criminal justice, and made 294 recommendations for change in areas as diverse as the prosecution service, courts, the judiciary, youth conferencing, community safety, victims and witnesses, law reform and international cooperation.

In England and Wales the criminal justice institutions cost around £13 billion per year to run and constitute the fourth largest component of total public expenditure (after social security, health and personal social services, and education). The Home Office, the Attorney General's Office and the Department of Constitutional Affairs are the three main government departments with overall responsibility for the key criminal justice institutions in England and Wales, providing the policy framework, objectives and targets, funding development and support functions (Home Office, 2000a: ch. 1).

- The Home Office deals with matters relating to criminal law, the police, prisons and probation. The Home Secretary also has general responsibility for internal security.
- The Department of Constitutional Affairs, set up in 2003 to replace the Lord Chancellor's Department, oversees developments in constitutional issues, freedom of information and matters relating to the judiciary.
- The Attorney General's Office supervises the Crown Prosecution Service (CPS), which is responsible for the independent prosecution of nearly all criminal cases instituted by the police. It is headed by the Director of Public Prosecutions.

Two overarching aims and associated objectives have been set by the current Labour government to provide a strategic direction for the criminal justice institutions (Home Office, 2000a: ch. 1).

Aim A: To reduce crime and the fear of crime and their social and economic costs.

Objectives:
- to reduce the level of actual crime and disorder;
- to reduce the adverse impact of crime and disorder on people's lives;
- to reduce the economic costs of crime.

Aim B: To dispense justice fairly and efficiently and to promote confidence in the rule of law.

Objectives:
- to ensure just processes and just and effective outcomes;
- to deal with cases throughout the criminal justice process with appropriate speed;
- to meet the needs of victims, witnesses and jurors within the system;
- to respect the rights of defendants and to treat them fairly;
- to promote confidence in the criminal justice system.

While politicians tend to suggest that these goals are all equally achievable, the reality is that choices have to be made over which are to be prioritised. As we see throughout this chapter and others, the criminal justice process involves many conflicting values, aims and interests, such as convicting the guilty versus protecting the innocent from wrongful conviction; ensuring just processes versus achieving just outcomes; protecting the rights of defendants versus meeting the needs of victims (see Chapter 7); enforcing the law versus maintaining order (see Chapter 15); and delivering punishment (see Chapter 13) without imposing disproportionate cost, with consequent harm to other public services.

BOX 14.1 ADVERSARIAL VERSUS INQUISITORIAL APPROACHES TO CRIMINAL JUSTICE

The system of justice in England and Wales is sometimes referred to as an 'adversarial system' of justice. This is different from an 'inquisitorial' system of justice, as found in some other countries. In the adversarial system the magistrate(s) or jury decide on a verdict, having heard two opposing presentations of the case. The prosecution and defence parties present their case as they see fit and tactically cross-examine witnesses. Not guilty pleas result in a contest (hence the term 'adversarial') between the two parties arguing over the facts of a case. This might be contrasted to the inquisitorial approach adopted in many continental European countries, where there is a continuing judicial supervision of the process from the beginning of the investigation to the decisions in sentencing. In an inquisitorial system a judge is involved in the preparation of evidence by the police and in how the various parties are to present their case at the trial. The judge questions witnesses while prosecution and defence parties can ask supplementary questions. The influence of the judge in the trial process tends to reduce the level of contest between the two parties. In contrast, the English judge will usually have little knowledge about the case before the trial; he or she will not have been engaged in supervising any investigation, taking statements from witnesses or the accused, or making bail decisions. Nor, except in rare circumstances, would he or she be consulted over decisions to release from prison (Home Office 2000a: ch. 4; Uglow, 2002).

KEY STAGES OF THE CRIMINAL JUSTICE PROCESS

Chapter 2 explains that official statistics on reported and recorded crime indicate not 'real' amounts of crime but how events are defined and processed by social control agents. Official offenders are not representative of all those who break the criminal law; instead, they should be seen as those who have survived the **process of attrition**. Others are, in effect, 'filtered out' of the criminal justice process between the commission of a deviant act, its discovery by the victim, its reporting to and recording by the police, then during charge, prosecution, conviction and at the point of sentence. These are the key stages of the criminal justice process (Figure 14.1). A proportion of convicted offenders who reoffend may subsequently re-enter the criminal justice process and go through the key stages again. According to official statistics, the proportion of convicted males who were convicted of a further offence within five years varied between 1 in 2 and 4 in 5, while the proportion of convicted females who were convicted of a further offence varied between 1 in 2 and 1 in 4 (Prime *et al.*, 2001).

So how do decisions taken at each stage affect the wider processes of assessing, managing and punishing offenders? We can identify a number of institutions and decision-makers involved in the key stages within the criminal justice process in England and Wales.

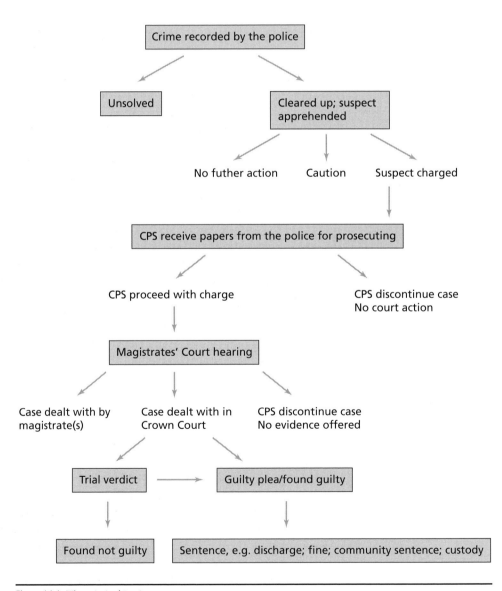

Figure 14.1 The criminal justice process.

The police

The police are by far the most researched group in the criminal justice system (Brown, 1996). They are also, perhaps, the most significant, because of their gatekeeping function in the system. The police operate as an important initial filter on public reports. Although the police have a statutory responsibility to record crimes, they retain much discretion about whether and how to deal with possible offences that come to their attention. Reports from the public may be disbelieved, or considered trivial, or deemed not to concern a criminal offence (Bottomley and Coleman, 1981; Coleman and Moynihan, 1996). According to latest British Crime Survey (BCS) figures, 43 per cent of all offences are reported to the police and 68 per cent of reported offences are recorded by the police. 'Put another way, this means that only a third of crimes against private individuals and their households end up in the recorded crime count' (Simmons and Dodd, 2003: 11). The number of offences 'discovered' by the police themselves are also subject to changes in law-enforcement activities. High-profile planned operations against a particular type of offence (e.g., drugs or burglary) will inevitably bring about an increase in arrests and the discovery and recording of many new offences in the targeted areas. Conversely, numbers may fall if there is a withdrawal of police interest in a particular type of area.

Even if a suspect is detected and charged (around 1 in 4 offences recorded by the police), police still retain significant discretion over the processing of cases. Police arrest does not always lead to prosecution. Around 1 in 4 suspects are released from pre-charge detention with no further action (NFA), and many suspects (especially young people) are dealt with outside the court system through the use of police cautioning. Although there are national standards that set out the formal criteria for prosecution and caution (e.g. evidential sufficiency or public interest), research studies have pointed to the overriding influence of police working rules in shaping police discretion and case outcomes (Gelsthorpe and Giller, 1990; Lee, 1998; McConville et al., 1991; Sanders, 1988; and see Chapter 15 of this book). The influence of the initial decisions taken and the way in which information is gathered, sifted through and put together to become a case by the police also endures through later decisions, such as bail, mode of trial, and plea.

The Crown Prosecution Service

Once the police have begun proceedings, the case is passed to the Crown Prosecution Service (CPS). Created under the Prosecution of Offenders Act 1985 as part of wider criminal justice reform in England and Wales, the CPS consists of salaried lawyers whose task is to review cases to decide whether prosecution commenced by the police should continue, to consider the appropriateness of charges, and to conduct prosecutions in courts. As well as the CPS, other bodies such as Customs and Excise, the Inland Revenue, the Serious Fraud Office and the Department of Trade and Industry also bring prosecutions.

In principle, the CPS as a public prosecution service exists to provide effective scrutiny of cases, to secure consistency in decision-making, and to filter out weak prosecution cases from the criminal justice process. The police are seen as too close to the case and inclined to proceed even when there is insufficient evidence against the suspect or to ignore vital clues considered irrelevant to the case for prosecution. The independence of Crown prosecutors is to be the key to effective control of police discretion. In practice, typically fewer than 1 in 10 cases sent to the CPS are discontinued (Home Office, 2002a: table 6.2). The low discontinuance rate could be due to the strength of the cases. But as Doreen McBarnet (1981: 100) argues in the Scottish context, cases for prosecution and convictions in court are socially constructed in nature:

> [S]trong and weak cases do not miraculously appear after an incident ready formed like tablets of stone on Mount Sinai. They are the product of a process of construction in which both the technical skills of lawyers and the structural opportunities and limitations offered by the legal system play their part in shaping what facts get into the courts and just how strong or weak a case can be *independent* of the incident in question. [emphasis in original]

In the process of case construction, the 'independence' of the CPS is limited because of its reliance on the police for information (Crown prosecutors cannot realistically go through all paperwork or listen to all taped interviews), its organisational position (they are on the same side of the adversarial system) and its operational philosophy (to ensure that the prosecution policy is carried out efficiently) (McConville *et al.*, 1991; Sanders, 1988).

The judiciary

In a liberal democracy, the doctrine of the separation of powers dictates that there has to be a degree of separation of functions between the three essential bodies of the state: the legislature, the executive and the judiciary. For example, the judiciary, which adjudicates upon conflicts between state institutions, between state and individual, and between individuals, is independent of political influence in its members' interpretation of the law and their judgments in a particular case. In practice, the separation of powers has never been absolute, and the imprecision of the doctrine has sometimes led to different interpretations of the meaning of, or even acrimonious debates about, 'judicial independence' (e.g. over sentencing policies and practices).

Three sets of decision-makers have evolved in the judiciary through the past ten centuries in England and Wales: magistrates, judges and jury. Criminal cases are dealt with in either the magistrates' court or the Crown Court (usually involving the more serious cases or when the defendant elects for a Crown Court trial). When defendants are aged under 18, their cases are generally dealt with in the specialist youth court.

There are about 30,000 lay magistrates and about 100 district judges (formerly known as stipendiary magistrates). In contrast to district judges, who are full-time legally trained professionals and normally sit alone in larger urban courts, lay magistrates (also known as Justices of the Peace) are chosen from a cross-section of the community. They are unpaid, sit part-time on local benches, and represent an important lay element in the process whereby the public play a part in the administration of justice and sentencing. In practice, the composition of the lay magistracy is unbalanced, less in terms of gender than of age, race and class (Morgan and Russell, 2000). How this affects the quality of justice is subject to debate, but there is evidence to suggest that some defendants (especially those from an African or Caribbean background) consider magistrates' courts to be biased towards the prosecution, are more likely to opt for trial by jury, and believe that the Crown Court offers a fairer and fuller hearing with a higher chance of acquittal (Hedderman and Moxon, 1992; Fitzgerald, 1993).

The vast majority (over 90 per cent) of criminal cases are dealt with in magistrates' courts. The remaining cases are heard before a judge (who decides on the sentence) and jury (who decide on guilt). The Crown Court, which usually deals with more serious and complex cases is presided over by a full-time judge. It also hears appeals against conviction in a magistrates' court, or decides on sentences in the more serious cases referred from magistrates' courts. The jury system has been hailed as a symbol of participatory democracy. The involvement of the public in the criminal justice process arguably gives people confidence in its fairness, ensures that unpopular or unjust laws cannot be enforced, and operates as a defence against the oppressive use of state power (for example, in 1985 the jury refused to convict Clive Ponting, a civil servant, under the Official Secrets Act 1911 despite a clear ruling by the judge as to the illegality of his conduct). The right to be tried by twelve of one's peers is also described by many as a fundamental right (Darbyshire, 1991), even though it is hard to draw any meaningful conclusions about the democratic credentials of a country by the presence or absence of a jury system. For example, Germany and the Netherlands do not have a jury system in criminal cases, while Belgium and France use it only in serious cases. Critics of the jury system suggest that jury trials are costly and time-consuming. In 1997 the average costs of court proceedings at magistrates' court were £550 for a 'guilty' plea and £1,700 for a 'not guilty' plea, while the average costs of proceedings at the Crown Court were around £17,500 for a 'not guilty' plea and £2,600 for an uncontested case (Harries, 1999). There are many trials in which juries fail to prevent wrongful convictions – from the high-profile cases of miscarriage of justice (see p. 260) to the more routine successful appeals against convictions. Critics also argue that juries may not be representative of society, and that trials for some crimes (such as major frauds) may be too complex for juries to follow (see Findlay and Duff, 1988).

The Probation Service

The national Probation Service plays a key role in the criminal justice process at the sentencing stage. It assists magistrates and judges in their sentencing decisions through the provision of pre-sentence reports and bail information reports. In the area of youth justice, the Crime and Disorder Act 1998 established Youth Offending Teams (involving, for example, the police, social services, education, probation and health services) to assess young offenders, to reduce youth offending within a context of wider problems (from poor parental supervision and domestic violence or abuse, to truancy, school exclusion, substance misuse or mental health problems), and to enforce community sentences for young offenders.

Probation, or the practice of releasing offenders from court with some kind of condition that they behave themselves in future, has of course been central to the history of community sentences (Raynor and Vanstone, 2002; May, 1991). Originally set up as a community response to offending in the nineteenth century (as 'police court missionaries'), the Probation Service became a formalised agency of full-time professionals under the Probation Offenders Act 1907. Against a background of emerging psychological and environmental explanations of crime and human behaviour (see Chapter 3), the original role of probation practitioners was to 'advise, assist and befriend' the offender (e.g. through one-to-one supervision and practical help). However, as the rehabilitative ideals increasingly came under attack and the debate over 'toughened-up' community-based penalties (e.g. intensive probation, inclusion of more demanding conditions, curfew) intensified in the latter half of the twentieth century, the role of the Probation Service in enforcing punishment and surveillance in the community remains highly contentious.

Taken together, these institutions have the main responsibility of administering justice and managing and controlling the official criminal population up to the point of sentencing. Their decisions and activities at any one point in the criminal justice process have a cumulative effect at a later stage of the process. Of course, crime and

Plate 14.1 The Birmingham Six with Chris Mullen, MP, outside the Old Bailey in London after their convictions were quashed, 14 March 1991. Left to right: John Walker, Paddy Hill, Hugh Callaghan, Chris Mullen, MP, Richard McIlkenny, Gerry Hunter, William Power.

Source: © PA Photos 2003; *photo*: Sean Dempsey.

its control have never been the concern of criminal justice professionals alone. Statutory organisations working in the areas of public health, education and housing at central and local government level have developed their services and multi-agency partnerships around particular notions of 'antisocial behaviour', crime prevention and community safety (Newburn, 2002b; McLaughlin and Muncie, 2000). Penal establishments have been built with private money and run by the private sector (Matthews, 1989). Charities and voluntary groups have also been very much involved with crime- and treatment-related work since at least the nineteenth century. Prostitutes, abused children, child abusers, vagrants, drug and alcohol users, mentally disordered offenders, battered women, ex-prisoners and many other groups have all been the subject of specific charitable campaigns by organisations ranging from the Female Mission to the Fallen to Women's Aid, from the Temperance Movement to Alcoholics Anonymous, from the Howard League for Penal Reform to the National Association for the Care and Resettlement of Offenders (NACRO). All this suggests that different elements of civil society, broadly defined, play a major part in the definition, detection, and reform of criminals.

THE NATURE OF CRIMINAL JUSTICE

So what kind of justice does the British criminal process deliver? There are at least three approaches to understanding the nature of criminal justice: by examining respectively the procedural safeguards (i.e. **procedural justice**), the substantive outcomes (i.e. **substantive justice**), and the negotiations and social interactions involved in the routine production of justice (i.e. **negotiated justice**).

Procedural justice

The criminal justice process is the most explicit coercive apparatus of the state. It is therefore crucial in a liberal democracy that police and courts can interfere with the liberties of citizens only within the constraints of law, not by the arbitrary exercise of power. This in essence is the rule of law – that is, the sovereignty or supremacy of law above every individual. For those caught up within the criminal justice process, principles of legality and equality before the law demand that a person's legal rights are protected, that there are checks and balances upon judicial power, and that justice is administered according to standards that are publicly known, fair and seen to be just. Formal independence of the courts from the state is an essential check on the power of executive government. Independence from the other criminal justice agencies also makes the courts a neutral forum, which is a key part of due process. The concept has been brought to bear in a number of stages of the criminal justice process. For example, arrested persons must be informed as to what the charges are and be given the opportunity to defend themselves. Evidence gathered by the police should be reliable and acquired by lawful means. Proceedings should normally be conducted in open court so that justice is seen to be done. There should be clear standards of proof and strict rules and formal procedures of evidence to ensure that evidence admitted into court is of an admissible nature and fairly presented (see Ashworth, 1998; Sanders and Young, 2000).

When legal rules and procedures are ignored or not impartially applied, injustice in the form of abuse of power or wrongful conviction can occur. Wrongful convictions can result through police malpractice, because the prosecution withholds evidence, because the trial judge is biased or from faulty forensic evidence (Greer, 1994). The cases of the Birmingham Six, the Guildford Four and the Maguire Seven are among the most publicised examples of miscarriages of justice. In each of these cases, the defendants were wrongfully convicted and served long prison sentences for alleged Irish Republican Army (IRA) terrorist acts. Their convictions were eventually quashed by the Court of Appeal following years of campaigning by relatives, friends and public figures for a review of their cases (Rozenberg, 1993). Andrew Ashworth (1998: 14) sums up the abuse of power by the police and other deficiencies within the criminal justice process that were exposed by these cases: the concoction or falsification of evidence by police officers; oppressive questioning and violence by the police; non-disclosure of vital evidence by forensic scientists and/or by the prosecution to the defence; slow and cumbersome appeal procedures; and a general reluctance to accept that the police had not told the truth.

BOX 14.2 MISCARRIAGES OF JUSTICE

The most high-profile 'miscarriages of justice' in Britain concerned alleged Irish Republican Army (IRA) terrorist suspects who were imprisoned for up to sixteen years on false confessions and dubious evidence in the early 1970s before being released. The wrongful convictions focused on the cases of the 'Birmingham Six' (for two explosions in Birmingham which resulted in 21 deaths); the 'Guildford Four' (for explosions in Guildford and Woolwich); and Judith Ward (for several explosions, including one on the army bus). After years of campaigning, all their cases went to successful appeals, and ten of the eleven people concerned in these cases were released in 1991–2 and given compensation (the eleventh had already died in prison). It was subsequently revealed that the suspects had been assaulted by the police, intimidated with further threats of severe violence, deprived of sleep, and relentlessly questioned. Some 'confessed' or signed confessions that were fabricated by the investigating officers. The police were also found to have withheld vital information from the courts.

Another notorious case is that of the 'Cardiff Three', convicted in 1990 of the murder of a Cardiff prostitute. Their convictions were also overturned by the Court of Appeal (in 1992) on the grounds that the interrogations amounted to bullying and oppression by the police and a 'travesty', and that the interviews should have been excluded from evidence. This case is particularly significant because it occurred some years after the implementation of the Police and Criminal Evidence Act 1984 (PACE), which put in place regulation of pre-trial investigation and routine tape-recording of police interviews. This perhaps suggests that the officers did not think that their approach was unacceptable. (For information concerning PACE, see Box 15.4, p. 281.)

By the early 1990s, public confidence in the police and the justice system had eroded to such an extent that a royal commission was appointed (Royal Commission on Criminal Justice, 1993). Attempts have since been made to introduce stronger legal safeguards for defendants, and the Criminal Cases Review Commission was created under the Criminal Appeal Act 1995 to investigate miscarriages of justice and to refer cases back to the Court of Appeal. The Human Rights Act 1998 also incorporates rights protected under the European Convention on Human Rights into domestic law and has since been used to mount a number of challenges to the criminal justice system (concerning, for example, the right not to incriminate oneself, and the rights of prisoners). Critics, however, have pointed to other recent legislative developments that give extensive powers to the state (e.g. on detention and disclosure of information under the Anti-terrorism, Crime and Security Act 2001) in the aftermath of the terrorist attacks on the United States on 11 September 2001. The point remains that criminal justice professionals work in a social context with built-in assumptions about how cases are constructed and how critical questions that may embarrass other actors in the system are to be filtered out. As Maurice Punch points out in relation to the systemic failures of criminal justice,

> What raised the miscarriages of justice to the system level was the *collusion* of other actors in the system – supervisory officers who did not intervene when violence occurred, senior officers who signed 'dodgy' statements, forensic specialists who went to work uncritically (and even unprofessionally), prosecutors who did not probe sensitive areas in the material given to them, judges who turned a blind eye to discrepancies in evidence and the Home Office which forestalled an appeal for so long.
>
> (2003: 188; emphasis in original)

So far, we have concentrated on unsafe convictions and miscarriages of justice where the innocent are imprisoned as clear examples of where the criminal justice process 'goes wrong'. Critics would argue that the process also fails to deliver justice where it fails to prosecute and/or convict many who should be prosecuted and convicted. For example, the extremely low convictions for rape, as a percentage of recorded complaints (falling from around 25 per cent in 1985 to 7 per cent in 2000), have been identified as a major problem by many feminists and criminal reform groups. Victims may feel let down or angry as a result; however, there is evidence to suggest that their treatment by criminal justice agencies and the court experience itself can also produce a sense of unfairness, bewilderment or pain (see Chapter 7).

BOX 14.3 CONFIDENCE IN THE CRIMINAL JUSTICE SYSTEM

The 2000 British Crime Survey measured overall public confidence in different aspects of the system and found that although a majority are confident that the criminal justice system respects the rights of people accused of committing crimes and treats them

continued

fairly (69 per cent were very/fairly confident), less than half believe it is effective in bringing people who commit crimes to justice (46 per cent very/fairly confident), and only a third that it deals with cases promptly and efficiently (34 per cent very/fairly confident). Just a quarter are confident that the criminal justice system meets the needs of victims of crime (26 per cent very/fairly confident). Furthermore, the young and the over 60s tend to have more confidence in the criminal justice system than those aged 30–59.

Source: Chivite-Matthews and Maggs (2002).

Substantive justice

'Unjust' or ineffective outcomes may arise even when legal rules are formally adhered to and supposedly 'neutral' criteria in criminal justice decision-making (for example, in cautioning, bail decisions, sentencing) are applied. A classic example is the differential impact of a fine on offenders with and without financial means. Furthermore, concerns have been raised, both from within criminology and from within social movements (such as the feminist movement and anti-racist activist groups), that existing criminal justice policies and procedures may have the effect of punishing a higher proportion of one social group than another.

Gender

The question of whether male and female offenders are treated differently in the criminal justice system has been subject to much criminological debate. The so-called chivalry hypothesis – that is, that the police, courts and other agencies extend greater leniency towards all women – has been disputed by most empirical studies (Eaton, 1986; Carlen, 1983; Daly and Bordt, 1995; Player, 1989; and see Chapter 9 of this book). Instead, there is evidence to suggest that the opposite is true: that some female offenders and delinquents may be 'doubly punished' for transgressing their gender roles and are more likely to be disciplined in a penal–welfare complex (Gelsthorpe, 1989; Cain, 1989; Allen, 1987; but see Hedderman and Hough, 1994).

Other feminists have also argued that equality of treatment in effect means treating women 'the same as men' and questioned whether this is always appropriate to the circumstances surrounding women's offending and the resources and treatment they may need to help them reintegrate into society or avoid reoffending (Hudson, 1993; Naffine, 1995). As Mary Eaton (1986: 97) concludes in her research study,

Hillbury Court treats men and women equally, i.e. they receive similar sentences when they appear in similar circumstances. However, men and women rarely appear in similar circumstances – the differences in their recorded criminal involvements are as marked as the differences between the sexes in other areas of life. Formal equality within the strictly defined area of the court does not affect the substantial inequality of women and men who appear before the court.

Indeed, structural inequalities meant that as a group, women had, historically, always been poorer than men (occupying more menial jobs, combining periods of paid employment with periods of unpaid childcare, earning less during their working lives therefore having fewer savings and reduced pensions, and so on). More recent studies have suggested that the recent rise in women's prosecutions and imprisonment rates can be explained by a rise in specific crimes, almost all related to continuing and worsening levels of female poverty: benefit fraud, television licence evasion, prostitution and drug-related offences (Carlen, 1988, 1998; Pantazis, 1999; Taylor, 1993). Some men and women – for example, young black men, minority ethnic women, gays and lesbians, and those belonging to minority faith groups – are also more likely to experience multiple forms of marginalisation than others. Adopting legal safeguards and giving equal treatment to the few men and women who appear before the court in similar circumstances may satisfy the court's procedural criteria of justice, but this does not in itself achieve 'just' and effective outcomes.

Ethnicity

The majority of studies have consistently shown that black people (especially young black males) are over-represented throughout the criminal justice process, with proportionately more being stopped and searched (Norris *et al.*, 1992; Home Office, 2000b; Jefferson and Walker, 1992; Clancy *et al.*, 2001), arrested by the police (Bucke, 1997; Home Office, 2000c), being prosecuted in court (Home Office, 2000c; Phillips and Brown, 1998) and being sentenced to prison once in crown courts (Hood, 1992). Whether these variations are due to any direct discrimination against minority groups in the criminal justice process (as Hood's sentencing study has shown) or a combination of other factors (e.g. patterns of offending, suspects entering not guilty pleas, not showing appropriate signs of 'remorse') has been subject to intense debates. Quantitative research methods are typically used to assess whether race has a separate or independent effect on decision-making over and above any other factors such as age, class or area of residence (see, for example, Hudson's (1989) survey of sentencing decisions and finding of 'residual discrimination' against African and Caribbean males in more mundane offences). There are, however, particular problems in attempting to isolate the variable of 'race' and measure the possible extent of racial discrimination at particular stages of the criminal justice process (see Reiner, 1993).

While adopting legal safeguards and ensuring procedural justice may have some impact on the worst excesses of 'institutionalised racism' within the criminal justice system (Macpherson, 1999; and see Chapter 15 of this book), this does not address the underlying racist constructions of criminality or other 'antisocial' behaviour, the patterned social and economic inequalities, and the associated exclusionary and monitoring processes of ethnic minorities as a social group (Bowling and Phillips, 2002).

Negotiated justice

The third approach to understanding the nature of criminal justice is to consider the negotiations and social interaction involved in the routine production of justice. In principle, the trial is the focal point of the ideology of democratic justice. The trial is generally portrayed as rational decision-making within the overall values of the rule of law. It is where the process of legal battle is not only carried out but put on public display. But we should be cautious in accepting trial outcomes in these terms – there are elements in the management of the courts and trials that directly contradict and undermine this. As Uglow (2002) has argued,

> Offenders are processed and disposed of as efficiently as possible in terms of time and resources. Key performance indicators relate to such issues as cost per case, the time taken between first appearance in magistrates' court and committal or between committal and trial or the backlog of cases for a particular court. . . . This leads to pressure to speed up cases and to the negotiation of outcome. The defendant's role can be reduced to passivity especially where there are on-going professional relationships between the defence and prosecution lawyers, the police, probation services, court administrators and judges. Thus there is a divergence between the official and articulated ideals of the courtroom and the organisational reality that exists behind them.

In practice, the vast majority of cases processed through the criminal justice system are routinely resolved through a guilty plea. In the magistrates' courts, over 90 per cent of defendants on summary trial plead guilty. Most of these cases involve relatively minor matters that almost always end in a fine. A contested trial in a magistrates' court is therefore very rare. It is not surprising that the nature of most courtroom appearances has been described as routine, boring, ritual, unproblematic processing of cases (Carlen, 1976). Even in the crown court, the rate of guilty pleas is currently around 60 per cent (Home Office, 2000a).

A number of key sociological studies in the 1960s and 1970s in Britain and the United States have examined the interactional, informal and bureaucratic aspects of the routine production of a guilty plea (Bottoms and McClean, 1976; Skolnick, 1966; Baldwin and McConville, 1977; Carlen, 1976). A particularly contentious issue is the use of plea bargaining between prosecution and defence. In the US context, the widespread use of explicit negotiations over charge and sentence is seen to facilitate smooth functioning of the justice system; it is seen as beneficial, as there is no risk of complete loss at trial for either side in the courtroom drama. However, such bargaining has been criticised for the pressure it places on innocents to plead guilty and the fact that it penalises those who exercise their constitutional right to trial. From a different perspective, some critics have also argued that plea bargaining allows offenders to escape appropriate punishment for their crimes. Although explicit plea bargaining over sentence with the judge is not permitted in England and Wales, some form of 'sentencing discount' does exist, and plea sometimes determines not just the length but also the type of sentence (see Sanders and Young, 2000: ch. 7). In the context of negotiated justice, it is perhaps inevitable that some innocent people plead guilty. According to a research study commissioned by the Royal Commission on Criminal Justice, over 10 per cent of those who plead guilty in the Crown Court claim to be innocent (Zander and Henderson, 1993).

Even when a case goes to trial, we might also think about the trial as storytelling. Often it is the side that puts together the most credible narrative that wins. Studies conducted from a micro-sociological perspective have highlighted how justice is negotiated and judicial order is maintained through control of the formal rules and symbolic boundaries of courtroom interaction. The use of a high level of ritual in the formal procedures, and complex legal language and gestures by court professionals to 'cool out' defendants and to systematically deny them a speaking part, has been well documented (Cicourel, 1968; Parker *et al.*, 1989; Dell, 1971). For example, Pat Carlen (1976) has shown how control in court is achieved through 'situational rules'. The court team – magistrates, judge, clerk of court, police, lawyers, probation officers – manages to make the defendant a 'dummy player' by ruling any challenge he or she poses to the ritual, administration or legitimacy of the law as being 'out of place, out of time, out of mind, or out of order'. All this reflects the imbalance between the power and resources available to the prosecutor/state as opposed to the individual accused. The geography of the court carries this on: the elevated bench, private access to judge's chambers, the judge's throne-like chair, the defendant in the dock, the public at the back of the court so that we are allowed to observe but not to participate. Carlen suggests that the organisation of space is such as to impede communication, especially for those who are not part of the routine cast (including both the victim and the accused). Distances are much greater than one would normally use for disclosure of private or traumatic incidents, or indeed for effective intervention. Communication is conducted and carefully managed through the lawyers. Indeed, the mode of discourse in the courtroom involves either interrogation or monologue, both of which are extraordinary or even resented when they occur in day-to-day conversation.

Of course, sociologists have long been interested in the actual 'drama of inter-action' and the use and avoidance of the rules of interaction. Erving Goffman (1959) wrote of 'the presentation of self' and an individual's efforts to create specific impressions in the minds of others, especially through the use of distinctive elements such as 'performances' (props, costume, rituals). In the courtroom setting, the dramatic elements of the spatial, presentational and linguistic conventions all help to create the court as a sharp rite of transition. The high level of ritual contributes to the sense of the authority of the court and towards establishing the authoritative version of the events and interpreting and explaining those events not merely in the courtroom but also for the outside world.

The ceremonial stripping of an individual of their dignity as a prelude to judicial punishment has also been thoroughly explicated and analysed by Harold Garfinkel (1956). He wrote of the 'degradation ceremonies' through which an entire com-munity formally stigmatises an individual and destroys their total identity: 'Any communicative work between persons, whereby the public identity of an actor is transformed into something looked on as lower in the local scheme of social types, will be called a "status degradation ceremony".' The ceremonial order of the court proceedings represents one particular form of 'status degradation ceremony' in the modern context. There are various conditions of a successful degradation ceremony:

- the denunciation must be public.
- The denouncer must be invested with the right to speak in the name of wider ultimate values of the community.
- The denounced person and event must be defined as instances of a uniformity, not as unique, an accident or a coincidence.
- The characteristics of the typed person and event should be contrasted with a counter-conception (e.g. the features and habits of a mass murderer versus the features and habits of a peaceful citizen).
- The denounced person must be ritually separated from a place in the legitimate order (i.e. made to stand out/made 'strange').

As Garfinkel (1956) has suggested, the trial is a process of recasting the defendant away from their own identity and into a stereotyped social role (mugger, hooligan, drunk, vagrant). The trial becomes a degradation ceremony that reduces the defendant to a lower status. Through this process, broader patterns of social authority and of social power are once again demonstrated.

CRIMINAL JUSTICE IN CRISIS?

Critics have argued that by the end of the twentieth century, it is the criminal justice system itself that has been put on trial. Although the criminal justice agencies enjoyed an unprecedented period of growth in overall resources and powers, the official crime rate escalated to unparalleled levels.

> The sheer number of individuals entering and re-entering the system was threatening to paralyse the functioning of the courts. . . . Spiralling rates of re-offending were increasing levels of victimization and the public's fear of crime and growing intolerance generated demands for more police officers, tougher policing strategies and harsher sentences, which in turn thrust even more people into the system. . . . To cap it all, a series of high profile miscarriages of justice undermined public confidence in the ability of the criminal justice system to identify the guilty and protect the rights of the innocent.
>
> (McLaughlin and Muncie, 2000: 170)

Against this background of 'failure to deliver', some Home Office statements have even conceded, in classic Durkheimian fashion, that a certain level of crime is normal and inevitable and that it is unrealistic to expect any set of policies to drastically reduce the crime rate (Young, 1992: 104). There is no doubt that the contradictions and tensions in the criminal justice system in terms of values, interests, stated aims and actual practices will continue to exist.

SUMMARY

1   Official statistics on crime do not indicate 'real' amounts of crime but how events are defined and processed by social control agents. The key stages of the criminal justice process include discovery of the offence by the victim, reporting to and recording by the police, charge, prosecution, conviction and sentence.

2   A number of institutions and decision-makers are involved in the key stages within the criminal justice process up to the point of sentencing in England and Wales: the police, the Crown Prosecution Service, the judiciary and the Probation Service. Their decisions and activities at any one point in the criminal justice process have a cumulative effect at a later stage of the process

3   Unsafe convictions and miscarriages of justice whereby the innocent are imprisoned are clear examples of cases in which the criminal justice process has gone wrong. Victims may also feel let down by the criminal justice process when it fails to prosecute and/or convict many who should be prosecuted and convicted.

4   There are at least three approaches to understanding the nature of criminal justice: by examining the procedural safeguards (procedural justice), the substantive outcomes (substantive justice), and the negotiations and social interactions involved in the routine production of justice (negotiated justice).

CRITICAL THINKING QUESTIONS

1   Consider the key stages of the criminal justice process and identify the factors that could affect whether a case proceeds to the next stage or is filtered out of the criminal justice process. How can we ensure that the decisions taken are always fair and just?

2   Look at 'The Proceedings of the Old Bailey' Website (see under 'More information'). In what ways would the props, rituals and status degradation ceremonies in twenty-first-century courtrooms differ from those in the eighteenth century?

3   Find out about the gender, age and ethnic composition of the lay magistracy in your local area (the Magistrates' Association Website is a useful starting point). How does it compare with the national picture? And do you think that a more balanced lay magistracy would necessarily deliver better justice?

FURTHER STUDY

Davies, M., Croall, H. and Tyrer, J. (1998) *An Introduction to the Criminal Justice System in England and Wales*, 2nd edn, Harlow: Longman. A very useful introductory text on the key components, policy and practice issues in the criminal justice system in England and Wales.

Duff, P. and Hutton, N. (eds) (1999) *Criminal Justice in Scotland*, Aldershot: Ashgate. A socio-legal account of the Scottish criminal justice process and its constituent institutions.

McBarnet, D. (1981) *Conviction: Law, the State and the Construction of Justice*, London: Macmillan. A pioneering socio-legal study of the routine construction of justice in court.

McConville, M. and Wilson, G. (2002) *The Handbook of the Criminal Justice Process*, Oxford: Oxford University Press.

Sanders, A. and Young, R. (2000) *Criminal Justice*, London: Butterworths. Two accessible and very useful texts which synthesize and review the key concepts, debates and controversies in criminal justice.

MORE INFORMATION

The Home Office: Publications: A Guide to the Criminal Justice System in England and Wales
http://www.homeoffice.gov.uk/rds/chspub1.html

Publication available online, on the criminal justice process in England and Wales.
Criminal Justice System
http://www.cjsonline.org/home.html
This is another site that has useful information on the criminal justice process in England and Wales.

Crown Office and Procurator Fiscal Service
http://www.crownoffice.gov.uk/
This site has information on the Scottish criminal justice system plus a selection of other links for reference.

Criminal Justice System Northern Ireland
http://www.cjsni.gov.uk/
A site on the criminal justice process in Northern Ireland.

The Proceedings of the Old Bailey
http://www.oldbaileyonline.org/
A fully searchable online edition of the largest body of texts detailing the lives on non-elite people ever published, containing accounts of over 100,000 criminal trials held at London's central criminal court.

On the criminal justice process in Scotland: see the Crown Office and Procurator Fiscal Service web site, www.crownoffice.gov.uk

CHAPTER 15

Police and Policing

▌ INTRODUCTION

In a book entitled *The Future of Policing*, the authors Rod Morgan and Tim Newburn (1997: 10) argue: 'We must establish what the fundamental role and function of the police are to be. But we must also decide how and by whom these responsibilities are to be defined.' Clearly, these authors are talking about how police work may change in the future. But given that the modern English police were established in 1829, it might seem strange that it is still necessary to be asking questions about 'what the **police** do' and 'to whom are they accountable'. Yet these remain important questions now and for the future.

In this chapter we address these questions, outline the history of the police, review some of the key debates surrounding the police institution, police powers and accountability, and consider the diversity of **policing**. As Robert Reiner (2000: 1–2) has argued, '"police" refers to a particular kind of social institution, while "policing" implies a set of processes with specific social functions. . . . A state-organized specialist "police" organization of the modern kind is only one example of policing.' Given that police work is about the exercise of authority and the regulation of conflicts in society, it is inherently controversial and inevitably contested. The police must be seen in terms of 'what they do' and 'how they do it' but also be discussed critically, so we also look at 'what they do but shouldn't do'.

HISTORICAL ORIGINS AND CONTINUITIES

Originally, the idea of 'police' had its roots in the idea of the good order or administration of the city-state (Emsley, 1996b). In modern democracies, police rely upon consensus, legitimacy and legal authority, although there are also many examples from the twentieth century and today of states that are more authoritarian and employ police in explicitly political ways to support their regime. The police states of Nazi Germany and the Soviet Union were extreme examples.

In Britain, the full-time, professional police we are familiar with today developed from a patchwork of policing of a highly variable pattern. Towns and country parishes generally relied on community-based systems of the 'watch', local constables and private 'thief-takers', but there was little uniformity and, according to many historians, considerable inefficiency (Emsley, 1996b; Rawlings, 2002). In cases of riot and disorder, a military solution was an option, employing local militia or the army. Nonetheless, even in the late eighteenth and early nineteenth centuries, the national mood was suspicious of a 'standing police force', not least because of fears of Continental systems of police spies. Influential political objections and the reluctance of the wealthy classes to support an initiative likely to lead to an increase in taxation defeated several attempts to introduce a Police Bill, and parliamentary committees considered and rejected the idea of a police force for the capital five times! However, the Home Secretary in Wellington's government, Sir Robert Peel, was a committed advocate of the benefits of a public force and persisted with the idea, eventually gaining the support of Parliament for the 1829 Metropolitan Police Act. This covered Greater London but not the City of London (an anomaly that continues, with the latter still having its own small police force). The new police and their commissioner were made responsible to the Home Secretary. Under the Municipal Corporations Act of 1835, major boroughs throughout England were obliged to establish forces answerable to the local watch committee, with the process being completed for other areas of the country from 1856.

Importantly, some of the issues facing the new police of the nineteenth century are still raising questions today. First, the police personify the coercive power of the state, and from the start played a pivotal role in regulating people's everyday activities through their patrol practices. The principal arguments put forward in Parliament for the creation of the Metropolitan Police were that it would be valuable in helping to prevent crime. But with increased anxieties about fast-growing cities and slums full of poor, anonymous and potentially 'dangerous classes', there was a gradual extension of the powers of the new police to regulate city life (Emsley, 1983; Petrow, 1994).

Not every section of society was affected in the same way. The police were often called upon to enforce a law that favoured one social group over another – for example, evicting tenants, enforcing the masters' terms of employment, and maintaining order at workers' demonstration. A variety of new legislative powers, by-laws and regulations designed mainly to cope with the problems generated by industrialisation and urbanisation tended to direct police attention to particular social groups such as the homeless, loitering youths, beggars, Gypsies, travelling hawkers and prostitutes (Emsley, 1996a). In effect, enforcing the new statutes (e.g. over vagrancy or street trading) meant that police work increasingly impinged upon the lives of what Vic Gatrell *et al.* (1980: 335) described as 'the 30 per cent or more at the base of the social pyramid'.

The new police also performed the important symbolic and legitimating function of representing and enforcing the values of dominant authority. They were (and still are) often represented as 'the thin blue line' that divides order from chaos. The introduction of street patrolling led to an increase in the number of arrests for misdemeanours, especially drunkenness and disorderly behaviour by men. Again, it was in those poor working-class districts that men were to be found indulging in the boisterous customs, recreations and pastimes such as Sunday drinking, cock-fighting and street gambling which offended Victorian perceptions of public morality and which the new police were directed to control as 'domestic missionaries' (Storch, 1976).

Second, the new police did not receive an easy welcome from the public and had to gain acceptance over time. The relationship between the police and the policed was particularly fraught in some communities. According to some historians, working-class hostility to the police continued well into the second half of the nineteenth century, as evidenced in the numbers of assaults on the police (Storch, 1975; Weinberger, 1981). Other accounts of policing in some working-class neighbour-hoods related to the feud-like relationship between the police and young people in the inter-war years (Cohen, 1979; Pearson, 1983).

The post-war period was the high point of public support for, and belief in, public policing. The cosy image of the helpful and admired British bobby, with its hey-day in the 1950s and early 1960s, was exemplified in the BBC television series *Dixon of Dock Green* from this period. Nevertheless, distrust of the police, allegations of abuse of discretionary police powers and the over-policing of particular social groups at the neighbourhood or street level remain. Indeed, police use of force, mass 'stop and search' operations, excessive surveillance and unnecessary armed raids, especially in the centres of African, Caribbean and Asian communities, have continued to be controversial (see Bowling and Phillips, 2002; Keith, 1993; Cashmore and McLaughlin, 1991). Take police use of 'stop and search' powers as an example. Overall, black people were recorded as being 8 times more likely to be stopped and searched than white people (Home Office, 2002c: 5; see also Box 15.5 on p. 282). Indeed, insensitive policing was seen to have played a pivotal role in triggering the urban riots that occurred in Britain in the early and mid-1980s (Scarman, 1981). The over-policing of particular sections of society has serious implications, especially against a background of the continuing revelations about police misconduct and miscarriages of justice (see p. 260).

Third, in the nineteenth century, police clashed with protestors and rioters in conflicts over strikes, rights, poverty, and in opposition to the police themselves (Emsley, 1996a). Given that protestors and rioters often appealed to 'the common good' (e.g. defending communities or challenging unjust laws), the policing of public order was – and still is – morally ambiguous. In the United States too, the early 1960s saw major political concern and debate about civil rights and law and order. As Waddington (1996: 116) has argued,

Few would now suggest that those who rioted periodically throughout the nineteenth century in pursuit of the franchise or trade union rights were morally wrong, although illegal violence was certainly used in doing so. Those who opposed Moseley's Fascists in the 1930s are rarely considered in hindsight to have been a riotous mob, but are credited as defending higher political ideals. . . . Black civil rights activists who systematically defied racist laws are sanctified and their leader – Martin Luther King – has acquired the status of a secular saint. . . . The verdict of history is that the 'bad guys' in these, and many other confrontations, between states and their respective citizens are the forces of repression – principally the police.

Plate 15.1 (a) Seattle police block the street during a protest march against the World Trade Organization (WTO), in front of the Washington State Convention Centre in downtown Seattle, 3 December 1999.

Source: © Reuters 1999; *photo*: STR.

(b) A demonstration by hunger marchers is broken up by mounted London police, 13 November 1932.

Source: © Mary Evans Picture Library; *photo*: Achille Beltrame in *La Domenica del Corriere*.

In the late twentieth century and into the new century, police have been involved in confrontations with trade union and social movements concerned with national strikes (the miner pickets), protests against the building of new motorways (New Age travellers) and export of live animals, and one-day global demonstrations against multinational capitalism and world poverty (the 2000 Seattle World Trade Organisation protests and 2001 demonstrations at the G8 summit in Genoa, Italy). Indeed, there are many examples of police in both authoritarian states and democracies using tear gas, pepper sprays, water cannon, plastic bullets and baton charges to disperse illegal assemblies and riotous crowds, with a view to restoring a particular form of 'order'. All this highlights the important fact that public order policing is 'irreducibly political'; it is 'a highly visible representation of the relationship between state and citizen' (Waddington, 1996: 129), and raises the question of *whose order* police have to maintain (see also Jefferson, 1990).

BOX 15.1 TIMELINE: KEY DEVELOPMENTS IN BRITISH POLICING

1829	Metropolitan Police Act
1835	Municipal Corporations Act
1839	Rural Constabulary Act
1856	Police Act
1916	Police Act – women undertake police duties such as patrols
1960–2	Royal Commission on the Police
1964	Police Act – transformed the structure of British policing: 117 police forces are amalgamated into 43 in 1966; new arrangements for oversight of the police shared between chief constables, police authorities and Home Secretary
1981	The Brixton (London) disorders (10–12 April); the Scarman Report that followed criticises the methods used by the Metropolitan Police
1984	Police and Criminal Evidence Act (PACE) – consolidates police powers but introduces new safeguards for suspects
1984	Police Complaints Authority (PCA) established
1984–5	Miners' strike – in response, government use of the police on a national scale, coordinated and controlled centrally
1986	Crown Prosecution Service (CPS) established, taking over previous roles of the police in the prosecution process
1993	Royal Commission on Criminal Justice (Runciman Report)
1994	Police and Magistrates' Courts Act reduces the power of police authorities, giving greater control to the Home Office
1995	First woman chief constable appointed
1997	Police Act – new National Crime Squad established; police received enhanced powers for surveillance operations

1998	Crime and Disorder Act places emphasis on cooperation between the police, local authorities and other agencies; introduces various 'orders' available to the police and courts to curb anti-social behaviour
1999	The Macpherson Report follows an inquiry into the murder of Stephen Lawrence and concludes that the police investigation was incompetent, marred by institutional racism and failure of leadership from senior officers
2002	Police Reform Act

Source: Revised from chapter by South in Budge *et al.* (2001)

POLICE ROLES AND FUNCTIONS

Most Western, continental European countries have several police organisations, whereas the United Kingdom has only one (albeit with different jurisdictions in Scotland and Northern Ireland). For example, in France the military-style police *Gendarmerie* operate alongside a patchwork of local forces; similarly, in Belgium the national police force, the *Rijkswacht*, operates alongside some 589 municipal police forces (Mawby, 1999).

The primary forms of police in England and Wales are the forty-three statutory metropolitan and regional forces. The police are distinguished from other public services by their specific capacity to exercise *legitimate coercive force* (Bittner, 1974). Indeed, the authority that the police exercise in compelling the compliance of other citizens is underwritten by the fact that police officers are 'monopolists of force in civil society' (ibid.). There are also a number of 'specialist' forces operating with the authority of the state but within particular 'private' spaces, for example the British Transport Police, the Ministry of Defence Police, the Royal Parks Police and the UK Atomic Energy Authority Police.

Historically and in the contemporary context, the image of public police has been predominantly one of crime fighter. On this view, the primary police roles involve:

- the prevention of crime;
- the detection of criminals;
- the preservation of order.

The question of whether police actually have an effect on crime is a central one – though not easily answered. First, there are major problems of interpreting the rise and fall of recorded crime rates (see Chapter 2). Second, there is little evidence to suggest that any police strategy alone can reduce crime (Audit Commission, 1993; Eck and Maguire, 2000). Increasing police patrols is a measure that would seem to be popular with the public, but unless this increase were to a level of saturation that many might begin to find uncomfortable – more of an intrusion than a guarantee of security – then the chances of the police being 'in the right place at the right time' would be somewhat slim. Indeed, one study estimated that a patrolling officer in London was likely to pass within 100 yards of a burglary in progress once every eight years, and even then might not know that the offence was taking place or be able to catch the perpetrator (Clarke and Hough, 1984: 6–7).

An alternative strategy is 'hot-spot' policing whereby patrolling officers focus on a single problem (e.g. drug dealing) in a single location. Although there is evidence that this may reduce crime in the area, there is lingering concern that such intensive police efforts may merely work to displace crime to other locales. For example, targeted police operations appear to have limited long-term impact on drug dealing activities and drug availability, and some local drugs economies continue to flourish (Lupton *et al.*, 2002; Edmunds *et al.*, 1996; Jacobson, 1999). In addition, such concentrated police efforts cannot occur in all locations at all times, so their use will necessarily be limited. The most prominent example of intensive 'hot-spot' policing in action is the so-called zero tolerance strategy in New York City from the mid-1990s (Box 15.2). The strategy is based on the principle that by clamping down on minor street offences and incivilities, more serious offences will be curtailed. This often translates into more intensive policing or specific operations against under-age smoking or drinking, obstruction by street traders, public urination, graffiti writing, and the arrest or moving on of beggars, prostitutes, pickpockets, fare dodgers, 'squeegee merchants', abusive drunks, litter louts, and so on (Burke, 1998; Silverman, 1999). Many politicians and senior police officers have argued that the approach is a success, reducing rates of robbery and murder. Critics, however, question the precise reasons for any decline in crime rates and the efficacy of the zero tolerance strategy overall. Indeed, there are question marks over the social costs involved and whether it is ever possible to disentangle the effect of good police work from broader changes in the economic and social context (Bowling, 1999).

BOX 15.2 ZERO TOLERANCE POLICING IN NEW YORK

Tens of thousands of New Yorkers arrested for minor offences could receive compensation for being illegally strip searched under Mayor Rudolph Giuliani's policy of 'zero tolerance' policing. Under the proposed $50 million (£33.6 million) settlement, New York City would pay compensation ranging from $250 to $22,500 to as many as 50,000 people who were illegally subjected to routine strip-searches after being arrested for 'quality of life' offences. Many of them were first-time offenders arrested for such misdemeanours as loitering or fare-jumping on the subway system. The class-action suit cited examples of men and women who were ordered to undress for visual inspection, and to squat and cough to empty their body cavities.

Mr. Giuliani's 'zero tolerance' policing has sharply reduced crime in New York during his past seven years in office. But civil rights activists have argued – particularly after the police shooting of several innocent men – that his offensive on crime has come at too great a price.

(*The Times*, 11 January 2001)

The detection or 'clear-up' rate (i.e. the proportion of cases in which a suspect was identified and charged) has been used by many as the standard indicator of police effectiveness in crime-fighting. In Britain, detection rates have been generally falling across almost all crime types, albeit at different rates, at a time of unprecedentedly increased resources. Only a small proportion of cases (about 1 in 4 recorded cases) are ever 'cleared up' by the police. Police efficiency also varies significantly according to the types of offences. Those types of offence where there is a high likelihood of the victim being able to identify the offender (e.g. violence against the person), or because knowledge of the offence directly identifies the offender (e.g. possession of drugs), will inevitably have a higher detection rate than others (e.g. burglary). In 2002–3 the detection rates varied from 12 per cent for burglaries, 16 per cent for theft and handling stolen goods, 50 per cent for violent crimes, to 93 per cent for drug offences (Simmons and Dodd, 2003).

In practice, a great deal of police work is mundane and not directly crime related. Research studies have consistently shown that a high proportion of police time is actually spent carrying out tasks that do not involve crime control – for example, calming disturbances, negotiating conflicts and responding to a wide range of emergencies (see Audit Commission, 1993; Shapland and Hobbs, 1989). Indeed, many classic studies of the police role in the 1960s and 1970s in the United States (Bittner, 1967; Cumming *et al.*, 1965) and in Britain (Banton, 1964; Cain, 1973) point to the service elements in police work and the role of the police as a twenty-four-hour 'social service' (Punch and Naylor, 1973).

In the contemporary context, the balance between the crime-fighting and the service roles of the police remains a 'highly contentious issue' and subject to intense policy debate. The important point is that the police officer is not, and never has been, simply a law enforcement officer. As the first major study of police in Britain, that by Michael Banton (1964), suggests, the police often resolve problems or disputes by forms of 'peacekeeping' intervention that do not rely on law enforcement: 'the most striking thing about patrol work is the high proportion of cases in which policemen [*sic*] do not enforce the law' (1964: 127).

In recent years the police have increasingly been expected to achieve performance indicator targets and to reorientate the culture of policing around an explicit mission of service delivery and ethos of consumerism. For some criminologists, this is an indication of the way police work has become part of a managerialist approach to crime control (see below). Others have emphasised that we now live in a society concerned with the calculation and removal of risk (Feeley and Simon, 1994), and that the police have become a key element in the risk-reduction matrix of control. In the Canadian context, Ericson and Haggerty (1997) argue that the police have now become 'knowledge workers' in a risk society. One of the main functions of the police is to act as the processors of information for a range of commercial and government agencies or community organisations (health, insurance, public welfare, financial matter, education) and their risk-management needs, rather than for criminal prosecution and punishment.

POLICE CULTURE

Police organisations are known to be characterised by features of the police occupational culture. As Robert Reiner suggests,

> An understanding of how police officers see the social world and their role in it – 'cop culture' – is crucial to an analysis of what they do, and their broad political function. This is not to suggest a one-to-one correspondence between attitudes and behaviour . . . many observational studies of police work have shown that officers regularly fail to enact in practice the attitudes they have articulated in the canteen or in interviews. . . . An important distinction can indeed be made between 'cop culture' – the orientations implied and expressed by officers in the course of their work – and 'canteen culture' – the values and beliefs exhibited in off-duty socializing.

> (2000: 85)

It should be emphasised that the police culture is neither monolithic nor unchanging. It varies according to the views of police elites, department styles, the power structure of a community, different patterns and problems of the policing environments, and specific situations. Some elements of the police occupational culture are shared by front-line officers and managers alike, although there is evidence that points to the internal differences and tensions between 'street cops' (with their sense of professionalism based on experience and grounded knowledge) and 'management cops' (with a more bureaucratic and education-based notion of police professionalism) (Ianni and Ianni, 1983; Holdaway, 1983).

Nevertheless, there are some general characteristics of the occupational culture that are common to police forces in modern liberal democracies. In summarising existing knowledge of police culture, Reiner (2000: 89–101) wrote that police culture emphasises the following core features:

- a sense of mission;
- action orientation;
- cynicism;
- suspicion;
- isolation and solidarity;
- conservatism;
- racial prejudice;
- machismo;
- pragmatism.

Taken together, these core features of police culture reflect a fundamental police worldview of 'them and us'/'insider versus outsider'. They are also linked to the perception of the police officer as a 'craftsman' whose skills are essentially honed through practice at the 'sharp end' out on the streets (see Manning (1979) on the need to become a 'good practical copper'). These values, norms and craft rules are important because they shape the **working rules** that police officers internalise, which in turn become the effective principles that guide their decision-making and use of discretion (Policy Studies Institute, 1983; McConville et al., 1991).

Police discretion is inevitable and sometimes desirable, given the nature and circumstances of everyday police work: the need to make choices at every level about priorities, the need to interpret general legal rules in specific enforcement situations, and the low visibility of street-level policing from the point of view of managerial scrutiny. The problem is that police discretion is often exercised in discriminatory ways. The social functions and focus of police work remain remarkably stable over time, as some social groups were and still are more likely to be subject to police attention than others (for a discussion of 'police property', see Lee, 1981; see also Chapter 7 for a discussion of 'hierarchy of victimization'). A series of biases involving not only the stereotypes used by the occupational culture but also elements of the law, organisational deployment and police practices, cumulatively produce patterns of bias on lines of class, gender and ethnicity (Brogden *et al.*, 1988: 146–50). Critics argue that the stereotypes used by the occupational culture have also resulted in discrimination against black police officers (Holdaway, 1996; Holdaway and Barron, 1997), female officers (Halford, 1993; Anderson *et al.*, 1993; Martin, 1996) and gay or lesbian officers (Burke, 1993). The extent to which police culture and practices can be altered is debatable, as attempts at reform have led to some successes (Foster, 1989 in the United Kingdom; Skolnick and Bayley, 1986 in the United States) and failures (Chan, 1997 in Australia).

BOX 15.3 THE STEPHEN LAWRENCE MURDER AND THE MACPHERSON INQUIRY

On 22 April 1993, Stephen Lawrence, a young black teenager, was murdered in an unprovoked attack carried out by white assailants. The police investigation into his death was grossly inadequate and the racist nature of the attack given little attention. A long campaign by Stephen's family and supporters called for an official inquiry into the police handling of the case, failure to follow up important information available at the start of the investigation, and lack of success in providing evidence that could lead to the prosecution of identified suspects. The call for an inquiry was resisted by the Metropolitan Police and rejected by Conservative Home Secretaries. In 1998 the new Home Secretary, Jack Straw, asked Sir William Macpherson, a former High Court judge, to chair an official inquiry into the case. Sir William examined three specific allegations against the police: that they were incompetent, racist and corrupt. Macpherson (1999) did not find evidence of corruption but firmly concluded that the police investigation had been 'marred by a combination of professional incompetence, institutional racism, and a failure of leadership by senior officers'. Individuals had failed, but so had the system; and the micro-processes of conduct in the Lawrence case exposed the institutionalised shortcomings of the Metropolitan Police.

Naturally, comparison was made with the report prepared by Lord Scarman into the riots in 1981, which had found evidence of racism within the police and made important recommendations concerning police–community relations and the need for racism awareness training for the police. Macpherson's reminder of the intervening

continued

lack of progress in improving police recruitment of minorities and changing police culture has been disturbing. Perhaps more significantly, he went further than Scarman and argued that racism was a problem that could be viewed as pervasive throughout the Metropolitan Police (and, by implication, throughout the police service nationally). The report referred to the idea of institutional racism to describe this state of affairs, defining it in the following way:

> The collective failure of an organisation to provide an appropriate and professional service to people because of their colour, culture or ethnic origin. It can be seen or detected in processes, attitudes and behaviour which amount to discrimination through unwitting prejudice, ignorance, thoughtlessness and racist stereotyping which disadvantage minority ethnic people.
>
> (Macpherson Report, 1999: para. 6.34)

POLICE ACCOUNTABILITY

So what can we do to ensure that the police do the job required of them? This in essence is the meaning of **police accountability**. To whom are the police accountable, and do mechanisms set up to control police actions actually work? There are three models of rendering police accountable for their actions: legal accountability, political accountability and managerial accountability.

Legal accountability

Under the model of legal accountability of police work, the law provides control over police actions by laying down particular limits to police powers and how they can be exercised. For example, the Police and Criminal Evidence Act 1984 (PACE) gave new powers to the police but at the same time incorporated more controls over their use. These include requirements to tell suspects why they are being arrested or stopped and searched, and to record the incident (see Box 15.4). However, critics argue that such rules require police to offer legally acceptable justifications for their decisions and operations *after* they have been undertaken, and that this form of retrospective accountability is indirect and limited (Lustgarten, 1986; Brogden *et al.*, 1988; McLaughlin, 1994; Macpherson, 1999; Scarman, 1981). Indeed, the continuing police misconduct (see p. 260) and the miscarriages of justice that took place since the implementation of PACE (see Chapter 14) provide a clear reminder of the limited effectiveness of legal control of police actions.

BOX 15.4 THE 1984 POLICE AND CRIMINAL EVIDENCE ACT (PACE)

The 1984 Police and Criminal Evidence Act (PACE) sets out the powers of the police and the procedures they must follow in relation to investigation of offences, arrest and detention.

- It aims to regulate police practices by balancing police powers with safeguards for suspects.
- It originates in the report of the 1981 Royal Commission on Criminal Procedure, which formalised various existing powers as a general power 'to stop and search people or vehicles' where an officer has reasonable grounds for suspecting possession of stolen or prohibited items.
- It introduces new safeguards regarding the questioning of suspects: the require-ment to tape-record the interview and to have a complete account of the entire interview.
- It allows the suspect the right to have a solicitor present and to say nothing to the police. This measure helps protect against self-incrimination and, coupled with audio (and possibly in the future video) recording, safeguards against the police seeking false confessions.

Political accountability

Given the selective nature of police work (i.e. responding to a near-infinite amount of crime with finite resources), critics argue that police choices about which laws to uphold, against whom, and by what means are inevitably *political* decisions (Brogden *et al.*, 1988: 161). Under the model of political accountability, control over police operations is to be taken by political institutions in a democracy 'on behalf of the people'. The Police Act 1964 established a 'tripartite' structure of control in England and Wales (with the exception of London, where the Metropolitan Police Authority was not established until 1999), comprising the chief constable, the Home Office and the Police Authority (made up of locally elected councillors, magistrates and, under the Police and Magistrates' Courts Act 1994, 'independent' members). The precise relationship between police authority, chief constable and the Home Office has been subject to considerable debate (Jefferson and Grimshaw, 1984; Reiner and Spencer, 1993; Jones and Newburn, 1996). Local police authorities had a responsibility to secure and maintain an adequate and efficient force for the area, had the powers to appoint chief constables and could require their retirement on efficiency grounds, and shared police costs with central government. In practice, most police authorities were less than equal partners with their chief constables and were unable to exert effective control over policing policies, actions and priorities, though a small number of police authorities were very active and high-profile opponents of their local chief constables and police policies in the 1980s, notably in Merseyside and Manchester (see McLaughlin, 1994).

Managerial accountability

Finally, the Home Office has been at the forefront in pressing for a fundamental shake-up of the managerial structures and processes, personnel policies, and working practices of the police organisation in order to promote sound management and cost-effectiveness. More specifically, these changes have involved the Home Office setting national policing objectives and quantifiable performance indicators covering key operational functions to facilitate inter-force comparisons, as well as standardising recruitment, equipment and training (Savage *et al.*, 2000: 26–30; McLaughlin and Muncie, 2000). Such changes have to be understood against wider managerialist reforms introduced by successive governments from the 1980s to extract administrative efficiency, effectiveness and 'value for money' from their substantial financial investment in criminal justice agencies. The police have been subject to focused inspections by a revamped HM Inspectorate of Constabulary (HMIC) and to periodic reviews by the Audit Commission (Audit Commission, 1996). The police are now compelled to think about their activities and to provide detailed information

---

BOX 15.5 THE POLICE AND THE PUBLIC: FINDINGS FROM THE 2000 BRITISH CRIME SURVEY

So what do the public think about the police? The 2000 British Crime Survey interviewed a nationally representative sample of people aged 16 and over living in private households in England and Wales and asked a range of questions about experiences of crime, victimization, their contacts with their local police and their assessment of the performance of the police.

A total of 78 per cent of respondents said their local police did a 'very' or 'fairly good job'. According to the survey, levels of confidence in the police remained virtually unchanged through the 1990s. However, ethnic minority groups have lower levels of confidence: 71 per cent of Asian and 74 per cent of black respondents said the police did a 'very' or 'fairly good job'. Around a quarter of respondents had been contacted by the police and 35 per cent had contacted the police themselves. Victims of crime interviewed in 2000 were less satisfied with the police response than victims included in the 1994 survey – 57 per cent, down from 67 per cent. One in five respondents said they could remember being 'really annoyed' by the behaviour of a police officer during the past five years, and a fifth of these made a formal complaint. Of continuing topicality is the issue of whether police are biased in their use of stop and search powers and discriminate against ethnic minorities: the proportion of respondents stopped by the police while driving (12 per cent) or on foot (3 per cent) remained relatively stable through the 1990s. Young black and Asian males aged 16 to 29 were particularly likely to be stopped.

Source: Sims and Myhill (2001)

about the costs, resource use and evidence of police effectiveness. Although performance targets, league tables and charters for 'consumers' of police services may be crude (and easily manipulated) indicators of police performance, they have placed police work under the spotlight as never before. Indeed, local police forces and police authorities may be compelled to account publicly for differences in effectiveness in detection, efficiency, resourcing, and people's levels of satisfaction with the police.

Taken together, these formal mechanisms are designed to ensure that the police do the job required of them. There are also punitive mechanisms set up to deal with police abuse of power, such as the complaints and discipline procedure. An independent element of oversight is held to lie in the Police Complaints Authority (PCA), which can investigate complaints made by the public. However, this has been seen by many complainants as a weak and compromised body, given that it is senior police officers who are appointed to investigate complaints of wrongdoing or mistakes (see Maguire and Corbett, 1991). Under the Police Reform Act 2002, the PCA is likely to be replaced by a new agency employing its own civilian investigators to pursue inquiries about serious allegations – for example, where a death is alleged to have occurred as a result of police action or inaction. Nevertheless, as Sanders and Young (2002: 1065) have argued, many victims are deterred from complaining and instead prosecute or sue the police. In particular, civil claims increased in number throughout the 1980s and 1990s, involving the awarding of significant punitive damages against the police in some cases.

POLICE DEVIANCE AND CRIMINALITY

There is a long history of police deviance and malpractice in Britain and elsewhere (Mollen Commission, 1994; Sherman, 1974; Punch, 1985). As Maurice Punch (2003: 171–2) argues, many of the cases that have been exposed impinge on fundamental abuses of the rule of law, due process and human rights:

> In Spain there was a secret unit (GAL) that carried out the murders of ETA members (i.e., Basque separatists) associated with terrorism. The former Minister of the Interior and a number of police officers have been jailed in relation to this clandestine policy. . . . In South Africa testimony before the 'Truth Commission' revealed close cooperation between the police and the underworld in attacks on ANC (African National Congress) members during the period of the apartheid regime (Truth and Reconciliation Committee 1999). . . . In New York the Mollen Commission (1994) revealed that corruption and violence seemed to go together. Suspects were 'tuned up' (severely beaten) by officers. Some police officers were closely involved with drug dealers, had themselves become drug users and were prepared to do dirty work for the dealers (including 'riding shotgun' for them and even committing murders).

In Britain, in recent years the problem of police misconduct and rule-bending has attracted a great deal of public and official attention. Indeed, research and official inquiries have found evidence of a range of corrupt activities in police work, including: opportunistic theft; acceptance of bribes to lie on oath; providing tip-offs to criminal associates; destroying evidence; planting of drugs or stolen property on individuals; illegal searches; involvement in violence; participation by police officers in drug dealing; and protection of major drug operations (see Newburn, 1999). Most officers facing criminal or disciplinary procedures are from the lower ranks but there have also been cases involving some senior officers (Her Majesty's Inspector of Constabulary, 1999).

In 1998 the then Commissioner of the London Metropolitan Police, Sir Paul Condon, acknowledged that there may have been up to 250 corrupt police officers serving in his force at this time, which suggests that the pursuit of an unknown number of criminal investigations may have been seriously compromised. In response, a special squad of anti-corruption investigators, including accountants and private surveillance experts, was established to target officers believed to be implicated not only in accepting bribes but also in offences that included planning and carrying out armed robberies, large-scale drug dealing, and violence against the public. Such a high-profile response to police corruption is reminiscent of the campaign of Sir Robert Mark, the reforming chief of the Metropolitan Police in the 1970s, who was charged by government with rooting out corruption, especially in specialised units such as the Obscene Publications Squad and the Drugs Squad.

Why does police misconduct matter? Police deviance often arouses in the public a sense of disillusionment and betrayal. After all, citizens expect public officials to be impartial, trustworthy and dependable. This is particularly true of the police, who enforce many of the laws at their discretion, who have the power to deprive some-one of their freedom and to use legitimate force, and who can carry out or refrain from an investigation into the conduct of individuals or groups that could lead to severe sanctioning. Police deviance is therefore generally assumed to undermine public confidence in the police. In some cases, police misconduct has also led to the imprisonment of innocent people while the guilty remain unpunished. Indeed, public confidence in the police has been damaged by continuing revelations about their involvement in the suppression of evidence, leading to wrongful convictions and gross miscarriages of justice, as well as involvement of some officers – occasionally on a very wide scale – in routine rule-bending in order to secure convictions. For example, in the 1980s, the now-disbanded entire Regional Crime Squad of the West Midlands Police was found to have fabricated evidence, physically and psychologically abused suspects, and written false criminal confessions (Walker and Starmer, 1999; and see Chapter 14).

The suspicion that a large number of convictions may be unsafe has not abated, and the Home Office has even had to establish a special Criminal Appeals Unit to examine a long history of cases in which confidence about the actions of the police and/or reliability of the evidence can be seen as in doubt. Part of the problem is that association with lawbreakers (e.g. informants) and contact with sources of temptation (such as large sums of money, especially in drug cases) are in fact intrinsic to the job of policing. Indeed, police rule-bending and rule-breaking can be seen not only as a problem of the deviant cop slipping into bad ways (i.e. the 'rotten apple' metaphor), but as an indication of systemic failures (the alternative metaphor of 'rotten orchards')

(Punch, 2003). Such failures are inextricably related to the nature of police organisations (e.g. the low visibility of police work), the character of occupational culture (internal solidarity, 'cutting corners'), and the particular opportunities and pressure for results presented by the environment that is policed.

PRIVATISATION AND PLURALISATION IN POLICING

The history of policing demonstrates the recent nature of the idea that the 'public police' are the natural and only holders of certain powers and responsibilities relating to crime. In fact, the notion of a 'public monopoly' over policing is and always has been a fiction (Garland, 1996; Jones and Newburn, 2002: 133). The public 'police' should not be assumed to be the providers of everything that might be described as 'policing'. Certainly, since the 1960s and 1970s there has been a growing division of policing labour in society owing much to the expansion of the private security sector (South, 1988). The history of private provision is, of course, much longer, going back to private associations and patrols in the nineteenth century, and continuing through the establishment of private guard companies before the Second World War. According to Jones and Newburn (2002: 134), 'in Britain, the 1951 census of population estimates about 66,000 private security employees compared with approximately 85,000 police officers', indicating that the plurality of policing was well established if not well recognised even then. One reason for the relative invisibility of this sizeable number would have been that many such employees would have been 'in-house' watchmen and guards. In more recent decades, business models have encouraged the use of the service sector and the 'downsizing' of non-essential staff, which would mean the replacement of such in-house staff by contracted security.

The contract sector has also been able to provide services that replace those previously provided by state bodies, on the grounds either that public service resources are then 'freed up' or that they are a cheaper but also more efficient provider. So, patrols of public space, and use of security companies to escort and guard prisoners, replace jobs previously undertaken by police or prison officers. The patrol of public but privately owned space – the 'mass private property' of shopping malls (Shearing and Stenning, 1987) – has arguably changed the street-level face of policing, although it is easy to overestimate the significance of this, and it remains the public police who will be involved in major incidents and public order problems. The role in prisoner supervision also reflects the fact that private companies now run some prisons. All this has become a transnational industry of significance. As Button (2002: 25) notes,

> there is now a large global security market containing some very sizeable companies that operate on an international basis (for example Group 4 Falck, Securitas, Securicor, and Wackenhut). Group 4 Falck, for instance, operates in 50 countries, has a £1.6 million turnover, employs 125,000 staff worldwide and provides services from guarding and the management of prisons to the provision of ambulance and fire-fighting services.

It is obviously important to understand contemporary policing in terms of this plurality. Loader (2000; and see Button, 2002: 15) has offered a classification of policing organisations along the following lines:

- policing *by* government – Home Office police forces and agencies such as the National Crime Squad;
- policing *through* government – services supplied by contractors (private security) but on behalf of government;
- policing *above* government – international developments at levels of cooperation, intelligence-sharing, strategy, etc., such as Europol and Interpol;
- policing *below* government – officially endorsed activities such as Neighbourhood Watch, as well as officially discouraged vigilantes and other extra-legal 'popular justice' groups.

To some critics, the proliferation of policing institutions and processes indicates that security itself has become increasingly commodified and Spitzer (1987) argues that nowadays, security is bought and sold in the marketplace like any other commodity. But the problem is that the consumption of that commodity (e.g. in the form of bolts, alarms, electronic surveillance, street patrols) may not produce a corresponding feeling of security. Instead, the opposite may happen: 'the more we enter into relationships to obtain the security commodity, the more insecure we feel' (Spitzer, 1987: 50). Furthermore, there is the problem of a highly inequitable system of policing in which the rich can buy protection from private police and retreat behind 'gated' enclaves (see Davis, 1992 on Los Angeles), coupled with 'a poor police policing the poor' (Bayley, 1994: 144). However the futures for policing in the twenty-first century map out, the issue of police powers, the impact of policing, and the control of public police and alternative forms of policing will remain high on the criminological agenda.

SUMMARY

1 The police are distinguished from other public services by their specific capacity to exercise legitimate coercive force. Notwithstanding the popular image of the police as crime fighters and their role in preventing crime, detecting criminals and maintaining order, a great deal of everyday police work is not crime related.

2 Historically and in the contemporary context, a series of biases involving the social functions of police, elements of the law, police occupational culture and organisational deployment have produced patterns of bias in police work on lines of class, gender and ethnicity.

3 Police accountability matters, because police work is about the exercise of authority and the regulation of conflicts in society, which is highly controversial and contested. There are three models of rendering police accountable for their actions: legal accountability, political accountability and managerial accountability.

4 Police rule-bending and rule-breaking can be seen not only as a problem of individual deviance but also as an indication of systemic failures. Systemic failures

are related to the nature of police organisations, the character of occupational culture, and the particular opportunities and pressure presented by the environment that is policed.

5 Contemporary policing is also carried out by a variety of individuals, groups and techniques.

CRITICAL THINKING QUESTIONS

1 The 'Robocop' scenario of 'the future of law enforcement' is of privatised, heavily armed police officers. Debate what policing in Britain might look like in twenty years' time.

2 According to the ideas of Max Weber, organisations like the police should enjoy considerable support and be able to exert authority: 'dominant groups are able to issue commands and orders that the subordinate actors accept as the basis for their own behaviour. . . . Domination takes this form of authority when it is based on a claim to the *legitimacy* of the commands' (Scott, 1996: 23). Do the police today actually have this kind of authority and legitimacy?

3 'Bad apples' or 'rotten barrels'? Discuss in relation to police deviance.

FURTHER STUDY

Banton, M. (1964) *The Policeman in the Community*, London: Tavistock. A pioneering sociological study of the police based on an analysis of field diaries of a sample of Scottish police officers, observation, and interviews (both in Britain and in the USA).

Cashmore, E. and McLaughlin, E. (1991) *Out of Order? Policing Black People*, London: Routledge. A text that critically examines the problem of policing and race issues and the research literature.

Emsley, C. (1996) *The English Police: A Political and Social History*, 2nd edn, Harlow: Longman. An accessible introduction to the history of the 'new police' and the changing social and political contexts in England from the 19th to mid-20th centuries.

Johnston, L. (2000) *Policing Britain: Risk, Security and Governance*, Harlow: Longman. A useful overview of the key issues in the study of police, public and commercial policing and risk management in the UK.

Mawby, R. (ed.) (1999) *Policing across the World: Issues for the Twenty-first Century*, London: UCL Press. A useful text that looks at the police systems in selected countries and issues in policing from an international perspective.

Newburn, T. (ed.) (2003) *Handbook of Policing*, Cullompton, Devon: Willan. A comprehensive and up to date collection of readings that examine the issues, debates and recent transformations in many key areas of the police and policing.

Reiner, R. (2000) *The Politics of the Police*, 3rd edn, Oxford: Oxford University Press. An excellent text covering the history of the police, the sociology of policing, and the law and politics of the police in the UK.

MORE INFORMATION

A Web of History: The Peel Web
http://dspace.dial.pipex.com/town/terrace/adw03/peel/laworder/police.htm
An introduction to the formation of the police service.

The Home Office: Police
http://www.homeoffice.gov.uk/crimpol/police/index.html
Provides an insight into the working of the police force.

The Police Complaints Authority
http://www.pca.gov.uk
The PCA is an independent body set up by the government to oversee public complaints against police officers in England and Wales, plus the National Crime Squad, National Criminal Intelligence Service, British Transport, Ministry of Defence, Port of Liverpool, Port of Tilbury, Royal Parks and UKAEA police.

The UK Police Service Portal
http://www.police.uk/
This site provides links to official police forces – both regional and non-regional – and related organisations.

Association of Police Authorities
http://www.apa.police.uk/apa_home.htm
The national voice for police authorities in England, Wales and Northern Ireland. Includes publications and links to other useful sites.

CHAPTER 16

KEY ISSUES

▌ What are the international differences in imprisonment?

▌ Why has incarceration become the dominant response to crime?

▌ How is the prison system in crisis?

▌ What are the causes of prison unrest?

Prisons and Imprisonment

INTRODUCTION

Imprisonment provokes profound questions of justice, to the extent that the use of penal institutions provides a stark barometer of the condition of democracy in any society. This point has long been recognised, for de Tocqueville observed in the 1830s that while 'the United States gives the example of the most extended liberty, the prisons of that same country offer the spectacle of the most complete despotism' (Garland, 1990: 11). Prisons continue to be the most controversial institutions in modern penal systems and occupy a central place in popular sentiment and political rhetoric on punishment, even though in no jurisdiction are the majority of convicted offenders actually sent to prison (Sparks, 2002: 202). The task of this chapter is to examine imprisonment as a social practice that generates deep-seated disputes while introducing the key themes that define contemporary prisons in Western societies, not least since there is considerable consensus that the penal system in England and Wales has been in a state of ever-deepening crisis since the 1960s.

While few informed commentators would deny that the penal system has serious, if not irreversible, problems, perhaps the key question is, how is it able to maintain a semblance of order for most of the time in the face of grave and often intractable difficulties? Moreover, the term 'crisis' implies a critical point in time, usually short-lived, when either a situation ends in catastrophe or the danger is averted. Yet the penal system has not yet totally collapsed (though it came close to it in April 1990), nor has it or various governments of the day begun genuinely to address the structural properties that give rise to the periodic symptoms of malaise (such as overcrowding, brutality, riots, strikes, and so forth) to anything like the extent necessary to proclaim a dramatic improvement in the condition of the system. Instead, it makes more sense to view the penal 'crisis' as an enduring feature of the past few decades, one that is composed of several interweaving components that not only compromise the ability of the state to maintain order but also challenge moral sensibilities on what the purposes of imprisonment might, or ought to, be. In other words, the severe problems in prisons that are the subject of this chapter are as much moral and philosophical matters as practical and material ones.

COMPARING PENAL SYSTEMS

The penal crisis, at a very basic level, can be regarded as simply too many offenders and too few prison places, a situation that has given rise to overcrowding, under-staffing, decrepit conditions and poor security, and a prison sentence continues to be the harshest penalty available to the courts of England and Wales. Currently, around 110,000 offenders are each year committed to the 137 institutions that make up the prison estate, which provides employment for over 43,000 staff to keep them there (Prison Service, 2001). All this stands in stark contrast to the situation just over fifty years ago, for in 1946 there were about forty prisons, approximately 15,000 prisoners, and around 2,000 staff (Morgan, 2002: 1117).

The reasons for this striking increase are complex, and even though conclusions drawn from international comparisons should always be treated with caution, it is clear that England and Wales consistently use imprisonment to a greater extent than practically every other country in Western Europe. For instance, in 2002, 139 persons were incarcerated per 100,000 population in England and Wales, compared to 96 in Germany, 95 in Italy, 93 in the Netherlands, and 68 in Sweden (Walmsley, 2003: 5). Such crude comparisons also indicate that England and Wales lie some way behind the global leaders in imprisonment – Russia, the United States, China and South Africa – as well as most of the countries in Eastern Europe (see South and Weiss, 1998 for further comparative analysis of penal systems). In this chapter we will be primarily

Number of prisoners

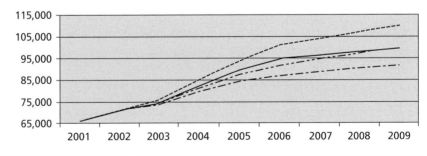

Figure 16.1 Alternative scenarios for prison population projections, England and Wales, 2001–9.

Source: John Simes, *Projections of Long-Term Trends in the Prison Population to 2009*, Home Office Research Studies 14/02.

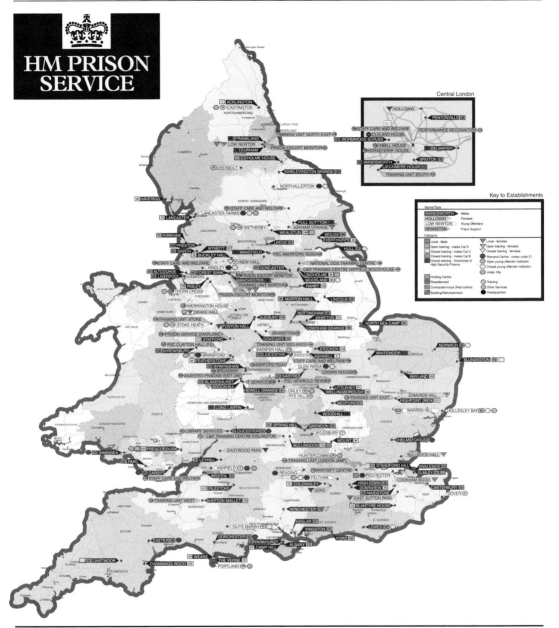

Figure 16.2 Map of HM Prison Service locations.

Source: HM Prison Service, Internal Communications Department.

concerned with documenting the problems to be found in the English and Welsh prison system. While Scotland has a separate system, much of what we discuss extends beyond national boundaries. Nevertheless, in order to appreciate the problems of the present, it is vital that the concerns of the past are first outlined, as these issues continue to shape contemporary penal systems.

THE ORIGINS OF IMPRISONMENT

Before the eighteenth century, imprisonment was only one, and by no means the most important, element in systems of punishment. Throughout pre-industrial Europe, courts drew upon a much wider range of sentences than is possible today. The range of penal measures included aggravated forms of the death penalty, such as breaking on the wheel (with bodies left to rot on the device as warnings to the living), through to minor sanctions such as warnings not to repeat the offence. In between lay a diverse variety of more and less serious forms of corporal punishment (such as mutilation, branding and whipping), forms of public shaming (such as the pillory), forms of bondage (such as galley servitude, transportation and the workhouse), banishment, fines, and a host of other minor prohibitions (Spierenburg, 1998).

The historian Ralph Pugh (1968) has described how in medieval England imprisonment came to serve three main uses:

- custodial (detaining those awaiting trial or sentence);
- coercive (forcing fine defaulters and debtors into making good their misfortune);
- punitive (as punishment in its own right).

These legal distinctions continue to be significant, yet it is important to recognise that the main purposes of the medieval prison were custodial and coercive, with the sentences likely to have been corporal or capital, and it was not uncommon 'for a person to be sentenced and hanged or flogged on the same day' (McConville, 1998: 118).

However, as feudal systems of existence began to break down with the advent of mercantile capitalism, large numbers of people migrated from rural areas to burgeoning towns and cities. This new population was viewed as being composed of vagrants, beggars, robbers and the unemployed, so that during the sixteenth and seventeenth centuries across Europe there began to emerge a range of secular institutions (the precursors of modern imprisonment) that sought to confine the growing numbers of poor, homeless and dispossessed citizens. From the sixteenth century, bridewells, workhouses and transportation to colonies came to complement conventional forms of corporal and capital punishment, as a means of distinguishing the 'deserving' from the 'undeserving' poor and fuelling colonial expansion (see the timeline in Box 16.1 for historical details of the developments discussed in this chapter).

Nevertheless, it was eighteenth-century Enlightenment critics that promoted the prison as the generalised response to crime, as opposed to the public spectacles of suffering that were losing their legitimacy in England as well as other parts of Europe (Spierenburg, 1984). While there are competing explanations as to why the prison came to be the dominant response to crime from the end of the eighteenth century, which are discussed below, it is important to emphasise that for much of the eighteenth century the bridewells, workhouses and local gaols were characterised by disorder and neglect. It was this widespread squalor, disease and corruption that a number of penal reformers, including John Howard and Elizabeth Fry, campaigned to end. They were opposed to the indiscriminate mixing of men and women, the lack of segregation between the tried and the untried, the open sale of alcohol, the gambling and the generally filthy conditions, with diseases such as typhus being rife. Many of the institutions were also run as private enterprises for profit; there is evidence that many bridewells had become lucrative brothels (Zedner, 1995).

BOX 16.1 TIMELINE: KEY DEVELOPMENTS THAT CREATED THE MODERN PENAL SYSTEM

1166 The Assize of Clarendon, legislation by Henry II that seeks to establish a gaol in every English county, a task completed by the thirteenth century.

1556 The first bridewell is converted from a little-used royal palace in London (known as Saint Bridget's well), becoming the earliest recorded 'house of correction'.

1717 The Transportation Act provides for the considerable expansion of transportation to the colonies (which had begun over a century earlier).

1779 Hulks introduced, which were broken-down transportation ships (also referred to as 'floating hells') moored on river banks that acted as penal warehouses after the loss of the American War of Independence.

1779 The Penitentiary Act includes proposals for improved diet, paid labour in prisons and the building of two 'ideal penitentiary houses'.

1823 The Gaol Act imposes a new classification system involving the separation of men and women.

1838 A separate juvenile prison is established at Parkhurst.

1852 Transportation is abandoned and government introduces the Australian 'ticket of leave' scheme, the precursor of parole.

1865 The Prison Act formally amalgamates the gaol and house of correction.

1868 Public ceremonies of execution end.

1877 The Prison Act brings control of local prisons under central government, and a Prison Commission is established under the charge of the Home Secretary.

1895 The Gladstone Committee on Prison reports and recommends rehabilitation and treatment as priorities for the prison system rather than simply punishing offenders.

Influenced by religious piety and Enlightenment reason, the reformers advocated the benefits of classification, isolation and sanitation. Howard's widely publicised description of the abuses and distress encountered in these institutions and his comprehensive proposals for change, combined with the effects of the American War of Independence of 1776, which left the government with nowhere to send those sentenced to transportation, lay behind the Penitentiary Act 1779. These two developments led central government to build new prisons known as 'penitentiaries' in an effort to reform the convicted and deter any others (Harding *et al.*, 1985). The Act promoted a new vision of imprisonment that would unite the punitive and reformative through hard labour and religious instruction in a system in which prisoners were classified into groups, while profits from their labour paid prison staff.

During the nineteenth century it was increasingly assumed that only the state could be entrusted with preventing neglect and creating reformatory systems of prison discipline through solitary confinement, surveillance and the daily grind of the treadmill. This assumption led to the Penal Servitude Act 1863 and the Prison Act 1865 (which abolished the distinction between gaols and houses of correction to create a 'new' institution known as 'prison') and culminated in the nationalisation of the prison system in 1877, which brought prisons under centralised state control.

WHY PRISON?

The question that needs to be answered is why the prison became the dominant response to crime across Europe and North America from the end of the eighteenth century. Until the 1970s, the explanation would have been that imprisonment represents an enlightened, humanitarian, progressive response to the barbarism of earlier epochs. This Whig view of history emphasised how early forms of punishment, based on vengeance, irrationality and cruelty, had been replaced by informed, professional and expert intervention and would celebrate the zeal of benevolent reformers in explaining why contemporary penal systems exist. However, this interpretation has been widely challenged by a range of 'revisionist' histories of the 'Great Incarcerations' (Cohen, 1985).

The earliest work that looked behind the rhetoric of reformers and asked why particular punishments gain prominence during certain historical periods is provided by George Rusche and Otto Kirchheimer (1939/1968). As Chapter 13 shows, their argument is informed by a Marxist understanding of social relations and highlights the relationships between the form of punishment and the economic requirements of particular modes of production. For instance, they argue that the prison emerged with the advent of industrial capitalism as a means of creating a submissive and regulated workforce.

Their account has been criticised for the way in which it provides a one-dimensional explanation of penal relations that prioritises the significance of the labour market at the expense of other factors. A more sophisticated account is Michael Ignatieff's (1978) analysis of the birth of imprisonment. He rejects economic functionalism and argues that incarceration was a response to the crisis in class relations wrought by the Industrial Revolution as it served to establish the legitimacy of the law and was understood as an element of a larger vision of securing popular consent in an increasingly unequal, class-divided society.

However, the most influential 'revisionist' history of imprisonment is Michel Foucault's *Discipline and Punish* (1977), which argues that the emergence of the prison does not mark a more humanitarian form of punishment. Instead, it represents an attempt to punish more efficiently and extensively in order to create a disciplined society, through the techniques of surveillance, classification and examination perfected in the new institutional spaces (e.g. Bentham's Panopticon). The originality of Foucault's argument lies in the importance he attaches to the relationship between power and forms of knowledge. The emergence of the prison is just one instance of the dispersal of new forms of knowledge, and his project is to examine how domination is achieved and how individual subjectivity is socially constructed. The prison has always been a failure, as it does not reduce crime, yet the reason why it persists is that it stands at one end of a continuum in which surveillance and regulation have become normalised throughout society. Foucault coins the phrase 'carceral archipelago' to describe the chain of institutions that stretch out from the prison, to imply that Western liberal democracies are intimately bound up with forms of oppression.

Although 'revisionist' histories continue to be influential, a number of critics have found fault with the way in which:

- all social relations have been described in the language of domination;
- complex processes are oversimplified;
- the instrumental aspects of punishment are exaggerated;
- the wide social support for punishment is ignored (Garland, 1990).

Moreover, there is a failure to consider the punishment of women, which problematises thinking on the role and development of incarceration. For instance, the fact that women are more likely to be treated as 'mad' rather than 'bad' poses questions that conventional and revisionist historians are unable to answer.

In addition, feminist historians and criminologists have demonstrated how the ideological practice of institutional confinement began much earlier for women than for men. Mary Bosworth's (2000) analysis of the Hôpital de la Salpêtrière – the main hospital–prison complex for women in Paris from 1656 up to 1916 – indicates that many of the practices commonly held to originate in nineteenth-century penitentiaries in fact emerged far earlier, in the seventeenth and eighteenth centuries. Likewise, Sherrill Cohen (1992) emphasises how the existence of separate institutions for women across Europe from the sixteenth century onward for women, such as Magdalene houses for 'repentant' prostitutes, combined penitence, religious instruction and reformative labour in ways that anticipate developments in the nineteenth century.

It was also the case that women made up a considerable percentage of the population of bridewells. It has even been estimated that for much of the seventeenth and eighteenth centuries in London, the number of women confined in bridewells was often greater than the number of men (Matthews, 1999: 14), while Victorian responses frequently 'drew attention to "crimes of morality" committed by women, such as prostitution or public drunkenness' (Zedner, 1991a: 309). Clearly, the lessons to be learned from 'herstory' are not only that the confinement of women in the early modern period challenges conventional and revisionist chronologies, but also that women were central to the burgeoning practices of institutional exclusion, segregation and control. As Bosworth (2000: 277) puts it, 'considering the gendered nature of the history of imprisonment broadens the focus and understanding of the criminologist about the meaning of confinement'.

THE MODERN PRISON ESTATE

Imprisonment in England and Wales continues to be dominated by this Victorian legacy. Nevertheless, it is important to recognise that there are now a range of institutions, which can be grouped under two main types. First, there are local prisons and remand centres whose primary task is to receive and deliver prisoners to the courts, and to allocate those serving sufficiently long sentences to the second set of institutions. These are Young Offender Institutions and adult training prisons, which are further subdivided into closed and open institutions for men and women. This subdivision reflects a prisoner security classification and the level of security that institutions provide. All prisoners are classified A, B, C or D according to a scheme devised in 1966 by Lord Mountbatten (Home Office, 1966) following a series of notorious prison escapes that pushed the issue of security to the top of the political agenda.

Mountbatten's recommendations have done much to shape the penal system of today. Category A prisoners are those 'whose escape would be highly dangerous to the public or police or to the security of the state', and while Mountbatten thought that such prisoners would probably number no more than 120, a recent estimate puts the current figure at some 700 (Morgan, 2002: 1143). Category D prisoners are those 'who could be trusted under open conditions' (Home Office, 1966). Category B and C prisoners are those held in closed conditions providing more or less security. Trial and remand prisoners are, with the exceptions of those provisionally categorised as A, all assumed to be Category B.

The allocation of sentenced Category A prisoners has been the subject of a long-running controversy. Mountbatten called for the concentration of all Category A prisoners into one single-purpose maximum security fortress that would ensure not only that high-risk prisoners were to be kept in secure surroundings but that security could be relaxed in other regimes. This proposal was quickly rejected on the basis that concentrating all high-risk prisoners within a single fortress would mean that maintaining order and providing a constructive regime would be near impossible in a prison composed of 'no-hopers'. Instead, a policy of 'dispersal' was adopted, whereby maximum security prisoners were spread around among a few high-security prisons. There are currently five 'dispersal' prisons plus a further five that have high-security arrangements, and it is becoming increasingly common for institutions to have multiple functions.

It is fair to say that while the **dispersal policy** might have solved the problem of perimeter security, it has intensified the problems of internal control. For within the prison system, the presence of a small number of maximum security prisoners affects the vast majority of other prisoners, who are subjected to much more custodial regimes. It is also important to recognise that the system of classification maintains a sharp differentiation between dispersal prisons, training prisons and local prisons, to the extent that the latter have come to bear the brunt of the chronic overcrowding, squalid conditions and understaffing that characterise some of the dimensions of the prison crisis, while the dispersal and training prisons have to a large extent been protected. The crisis is composed of the following sets of interrelated issues:

- an expanding prison population;
- overcrowded and decrepit conditions;
- authority and legitimacy deficits;
- severe social consequences.

CONTEMPORARY CRISES

The expanding prison population

In order to make sense of the increases in the prison population, it is instructive to consider longer-term trends. It is clear that since the 1950s, the growth in the prison population has consistently kept ahead of available space in penal institutions. This is in marked contrast to the inter-war era, when prisons were routinely half full. For instance, in 1928 there were only just over 11,000 prisoners in a system that could offer 20,000 cells. By 1938 the number of prisoners remained around the 11,000 mark, but many prisons had been closed on the grounds that they were no longer required (Stern, 1993: 24).

During the post-war era, however, there was a fivefold increase in recorded crime (from 280,000 in 1938 to 1,334,000 in 1965). During this period the courts' proportionate use of imprisonment actually decreased (with the fine replacing probation as the main form of sentence), yet the prison population tripled – from 11,100 in 1938 to 32,500 in 1968 (Bottoms, 1987: 181). Even though the prison population rose modestly during the 1980s, and reached a peak at around 50,000 in 1988–9, it then declined in the early 1990s to around 45,000. Between 1993 and 1998 it increased rapidly by some 47 per cent to reach 65,300 and then declined slightly, only to increase from January 2001 to reach a new peak of 71,220 in June 2002 (Home Office, 2002b).

Nevertheless, it is important to recall that there has been a policy of **bifurcation** operating across criminal justice policy since at least the mid-1970s (Bottoms, 1977), which enables governments to pursue both 'soft' and 'tough' sentencing options simultaneously. For instance, in mid-1980, 22 per cent of prisoners were serving sentences of over four years; by mid-2000 this figure stood at 46 per cent of adult male prisoners (Home Office, 2001: 76). These changes are partly explained by the intro-duction of parole in 1967 and subsequent developments in its use (see Morgan, 2002: 1130–2), but the important point to note is that long-term prisoners dominate life in most training prisons and consequently preoccupy prison administrators, with important consequences for the remaining prisoners.

Overcrowding and conditions

Prison overcrowding is predominantly a post-war phenomenon, and even though there have been episodic attempts to expand the prison estate, for the most part these efforts have been insufficient to stave off serious overcrowding in the system. The problem is partly explained by the inflexibility of prison space, but there have been, and remain, clear policy preferences to concentrate overcrowding in local prisons and remand centres so that resources can be used to optimise the regime in training prisons and make best use of the facilities available there. The rationale behind this policy is the assumption that for prisoners serving short sentences there is too little time to achieve results; for example, at the end of the last century 'roughly 80 per cent of local prisons and around one-third of all prisons were overcrowded by more than 20 per cent (with the worst handful being of the order of 70 per cent overcrowded)' (Sparks, 2001: 213–14).

The effects of overcrowding contribute to a sense of crisis in many ways. Most obviously, the problem of numbers has a deleterious impact on conditions, and it is beyond doubt that prisoners who begin their carceral career, as most do, in a local prison will typically find themselves in the midst of the worst conditions that the penal system can inflict, where overcrowding has been a daily feature of life within many of these institutions for over three decades. The problem of numbers has to be located in the context of dilapidated physical conditions in which prisoners are contained, combined with poor sanitation, scarcely edible food, decaying, cramped cells, clothing shortages and brief, inadequate family visits.

Compounding this wretchedness is the severely restricted and oppressive regimes that are imposed, since there are neither the space, facilities nor resources to provide prisoners with a range of training, work and educational opportunities when there are too many prisoners to cope with. Such abject conditions have been condemned by the European Committee for the Prevention of Torture, who concluded that the overcrowding, insanitary facilities and impoverished regimes found at three Victorian local prisons (Brixton, Wandsworth and Leeds) amounted to inhuman and degrading treatment (Committee for the Prevention of Torture, 1991).

Authority and managerialism

The crisis of authority (Cavadino and Dignan, 2002: 200–5) refers not only to the long and bitter industrial relations between prison staff and management but also to major changes in the philosophy and organisational form of prison administration. In the post-war era there has been a shift in the source of authority in prisons from a highly personalised form of charismatic power to systems based on bureaucratic rules and procedures, while further organisational changes have meant that the Prison Service, formerly a Department of State within the Home Office, became a semi-autonomous executive agency in 1993, and privatisation (the contracting out of public services to the private sector) is now an important and controversial feature of the penal landscape.

It is highly debatable whether these organisational changes have been able to tackle the continuing crisis of authority, as there are clearly deep and long-standing legitimacy problems in the Prison Service, caused in some respects by the demise of rehabilitation in the 1970s as the guiding purpose of penal practice. The subsequent turn to managerialist issues in the 1980s and 1990s only served to undermine a sense of mission within the service, save for meeting narrow management objectives and performance indicators. It is also highly significant that the definitive statement on the causes of prison riots in the English context emphasised the importance of

legitimacy in securing the acquiescence of the confined (Woolf and Tumim, 1991). In particular, the implication is that there are variable conditions that render it more or less likely that prisoners will accept, however conditionally, the authority of their custodians.

SOCIAL CONSEQUENCES

Youth custody

It is no coincidence that the modern youth justice system emerged at the middle of the nineteenth century, at the same time as 'adolescence' and 'juvenile delinquency' was 'discovered'. The deep ambivalence of the Victorians towards children was played out in the various discourses surrounding childhood – children were simultaneously idealised, worshipped and protected as well as being feared, exploited and regulated (Hendrick, 1990). During this period, many social reformers and philanthropists directed their energies towards 'saving' and 'protecting', demanding that young people should be removed from the 'adult' prison population and placed in separate institutions. The Youthful Offenders Act 1854 provided the basis of the reformatories for the 'dangerous classes', and legislation three years later established 'industrial schools' for the 'perishing classes' (Hebdige, 1988: 21).

The Children Act 1908 was a major piece of legislation that created juvenile courts, barred under-14s from prison and created 'borstals' to cater for 16- to 21-year olds (a 'juvenile adult' category) based on welfare principles. The Children and Young Persons Act 1933 further underlined the move towards welfare through prohibiting capital punishment for those under 18, and reorganised the reformatory and industrial schools into 'approved schools' that provided young offenders with education and training, while remand homes kept juveniles apart from adults. In the post-war period, the dramatic rise in crime and prison overcrowding contributed to continuing changes in penal policy as legislation introduced the detention centre in the 1950s. Detention centres were intended to provide a brief, unpleasant custodial experience, but while their development was slow, they would return under the guise of a 'short, sharp shock' in the 1980s.

The Children and Young Persons Act 1969 proved to be a high-water mark in the welfare era and introduced the principle of diversion. The general aim was to keep young offenders out of the youth justice system or, where it was absolutely necessary, to send them to juvenile court for 'care', and to 'treat' young offenders rather than punish them. These developments have provoked considerable debate among criminologists over their 'net-widening' effects and intensification of disciplinary power (Cohen, 1985). The Act also abolished the system of approved schools and remand homes and replaced them with 'community homes', and it was intended that detention centres and borstals should be phased out and replaced by 'intermediate treatment'.

However, in 1970 a Conservative government replaced a Labour administration that refused to fully implement the Act as responses to rising juvenile crime rates increasingly switched from a 'welfare' approach to one of 'justice'. As the 1970s

BOX 16.2 ALTERNATIVES TO PRISON

Some alternatives to prison have quite considerable histories, while others have been introduced only relatively recently. Anne Worrall (1997) identifies three distinctive groupings. 'Self-regulatory' penalties involve some form of public shaming that is assumed to be sufficient to deter offenders from further lawbreaking. 'Financial' penalties generally tend to be paid to the central administration of a criminal justice system, though it is possible, and some would argue desirable, for some form of compensation to be paid to the victim. 'Supervisory' sentences have increased in number since the 1970s and involve elements of rehabilitation (through education and welfare programmes), reparation (through unpaid work in the community) and incapacitation (through curfews and electronic tagging).

The use of alternatives to prison gathered force as part of a **decarceration** movement (see also Chapter 13) in the 1970s when various non-custodial sentences came to be regarded as a more humane and less stigmatising means of treating offenders. Equally importantly, many governments were keen to find less expensive, but equally demanding, alternatives to imprisonment in the face of growing economic problems facing welfare states. Many proponents have since argued for displacing the use of specific parts of the prison system (e.g. juvenile detention), while others have concentrated on advocating alternative community-based sanctions. The overall pattern has been one of expansion, with such penalties accompanying rather than being an alternative to an increasing prison population.

progressed, it became obvious that a process of bifurcation, or a 'twin-track approach' (Bottoms, 1977), was occurring, in that custodial sentences increased for serious juvenile offenders while the use of cautions was adopted for less serious offenders.

The election of a Conservative government in 1979 that took a pledge to 'stand firm against crime' saw the return of traditional criminal justice values in the Criminal Justice Act 1982, but also saw borstals and indeterminate sentences replaced by 'youth custody' – with the institutions becoming known as youth custody institutions. As Lorraine Gelsthorpe and Allison Morris (2002: 240) argue, the 1980s witnessed 'a period of "law and order" and "crime control", with policies which were designed to reassert the virtue and necessity of authority, order and discipline'. Widespread concern over increases in juvenile crime in the 1990s, fuelled by joyriding in deprived council estates, widespread publicity over persistent young offenders, and the murder of James Bulger by two 10-year-old boys, forced the main political parties into rethinking their positions on crime and punishment into what has become known as 'populist punitiveness' (Bottoms, 1995).

One of the consequences was that a fierce controversy over whether the principle of *doli incapax* should be upheld ensued. This refers to the age of criminal responsibility. In England and Wales it is 10 years, and children under that age cannot be found guilty of a criminal offence. Children between 10 and 13 were presumed to be *doli incapax* (incapable of criminal intent), and despite vehement opposition from the Home Secretary, the principle was 'upheld on the grounds that there is wisdom in protecting young children against the full rigour of the criminal law' (Gelsthorpe and Morris, 2002: 241). Nevertheless, the age of criminal responsibility is unusually low in comparison with most of the rest of Western Europe, where offenders under the age of 14 are dealt with by civil proceedings.

There is considerable debate over whether the New Labour government elected in 1997 has ushered in a 'new youth justice' (Goldson, 2000). Certainly the Crime and Disorder Act 1998 and the Youth Justice and Criminal Evidence Act 1999 brought many new proposals and activities. There are too numerous to detail here (see Newburn, 2002a for an overview), but do significantly include the setting up of the Youth Justice Board, the creation of Youth Offending Teams, and the restructuring of the non-custodial penalties available to the youth court (including elements of restorative justice – see Chapter 13).

Critics of New Labour's youth justice policy are especially concerned with the government's continuing reliance on custodial sentences for young offenders, with campaigners arguing 'that the Government's "obsession" with teenagers on street corners had contributed to the sharp rise in the number of young people in prison'. In particular, there has been 'a ninefold rise in the number of children under 15 being sentenced to custody' (Bright, 2003: 9).

BOX 16.3 TIMELINE: KEY DATES IN YOUTH CUSTODY

1838	The first separate juvenile prison established at Parkhurst.
1901	A penal reformatory to house young offenders opens at Borstal, Kent, a name that in time would come to be applied to all institutions for young offenders
1908	The Children's Act creates a separate system of juvenile justice.
1948	The Criminal Justice Act promotes wider use of borstals, though more punitive detention centres would come to prominence in the 1950s.
1969	The Children and Young Persons Act 1969 introduces the principle of diversion based on the ethics of 'care' and 'treatment'.
1982	Borstal training is replaced by youth custody and the ideological reintroduction of the 'short, sharp shock' in detention centres.
1999	The Youth Justice and Criminal Evidence Act is a key element in New Labour's restructuring of juvenile justice.

Gendered prisons

It has been estimated that women, on average, make up about 4 per cent of the total prison population (Walklate, 2001: 169). Since imprisonment is largely experienced by young adult men, most criminologists argue that the organisation and culture of the prison system reflect this dominance, to the extent that there are very different regimes for male and female prisoners. For instance, the tendency has been to define women prisoners as mad or sad rather than bad, and the regimes have reinforced traditional stereotypes of motherhood and domesticity (Carlen, 1983; Bosworth, 1999).

The fact that there are far fewer women in prison has serious consequences, as there are only a dozen or so geographically disparate institutions, which both makes it extremely difficult for female prisoners to sustain relationships with friends and family and compounds the marginalisation of women in the system. However, this marginalisation has begun to change, as the drastic increases in the female prison population over the past decade and a series of scandals have pushed the issue of women's imprisonment to the forefront of policy debates.

For instance, between 1990 and 1998 the female prison population doubled, and reached 3,350 in 2000, the highest level since 1901 (Home Office, 2001). The sense of crisis in women's prisons extends far beyond numbers. Since the mid-1990s, the media have widely reported on the shocking practices of manacling mothers in labour, and degrading methods of drug testing; Holloway Prison, the largest prison for women, was deemed too filthy to inspect by the Chief Prisons Inspector; and in 2002 more women killed themselves in prison than ever before.

Some of these issues are highlighted in Box 16.4, which graphically illustrates the point that prisons, 'even the most reformed ones, produce damage and diseases, in varied forms and intensity they produce damaged and ill people' (Gallo and Ruggiero, 1991: 278). Nevertheless, there are some signs that the government is sufficiently concerned about the increase in women prisoners to have announced a Strategy for Women Offenders, with a view to reducing the number of women in prison (NACRO, 2001–2: 27–8).

BOX 16.4 THE PAINS OF IMPRISONMENT

A young woman hanged herself in prison last Wednesday morning. She was 29, awaiting trial for petty theft – that is, she had not been found guilty of any crime – and had been in jail for less than 26 days.

Her death has not yet been announced and her name will remain a secret until later this week, when her family has been informed. Once it is made public, however, the Government will be forced to make another stark admission: that her death has made 2002 the year more women killed themselves in prison than ever before.

Britain's prison population is soaring. Last week the Government admitted that the number of prisoners would increase by almost 40 per cent over the next decade, taking it to more than 100,000 for the first time.

The figures conceal a more desperate story: that of a female prison population out of control and increasing at three times the rate of its male counterpart. It is a population in which over 90 per cent of its members have severe mental health problems, 63 per cent attempt suicide and almost 95 per cent harm themselves in some way during their sentence.

Stephanie Langley, sentenced at the age of 25 to 14 years for drug smuggling, reduced to 11 years on appeal, believes prisons have become a dumping ground for mentally unstable women. 'I saw people come in to prison totally sane and normal and, six months later, be zooming about the exercise yard in a totally mad way pretending to be an aeroplane,' she said. 'I watched people scar themselves with glass, razors, scouring pads, cleaning equipment, burn themselves and dig holes in themselves. It wasn't attention seeking – it was pure desperation. My best friend committed suicide because she, like almost every other woman there, had had a very traumatic life and just couldn't cope with prison,' she added.

Britain imprisons a greater percentage of its female population than any other country in the European Union, except Portugal and Spain, and the number continues to soar; around 11,000 women have been imprisoned so far this year – about 20 per cent of whom are on remand.

In the past year alone, there has been a 23 per cent increase in the size of the female population and a 180 per cent rise in the past decade . . .

Langley made around seven serious attempts to commit suicide during her sentence. She also regularly cut her wrists and ankles with razors, hoarded sedatives to take them all at once and developed a range of eating disorders and psychological problems.

'I had been a deeply troubled girl before I went to jail, but this was slowly killing me. There was no one to help me, no one I trusted. In a man's prison, there's a solidarity, but in a woman's prison there's nothing but madness, aggression and pain.'

Langley was raped when she was a teenager and exposed to a range of sexual abuse during her childhood. Yet in Durham Prison she was forced to work alongside Rosemary West.

Source: Hill 2002: © *The Observer*.

Ethnicity, nationality and racism

The picture presented by the statistics is that prisoners in England and Wales are disproportionately young, poor and belonging to ethnic minorities, with few occupational skills or academic qualifications. Moreover, they are likely to be suffering from psychiatric distress (Sparks, 2001: 215–16). Recent figures indicate that 19 per cent of male prisoners and 25 per cent of female prisoners are members of ethnic minorities; two-thirds of them are African or Caribbean (Morgan, 2002: 1133). There are a number of reasons for this over-representation. One key factor is nationality, and it has been noted that 9 per cent of the prison population comprises foreign nationals (a growing trend observed across Europe), while another is the relative youthfulness of the various ethnic minority groups compared to the white population, which means that over-representation is all the more likely to occur (Morgan, 2002: 1134).

Elaine Genders and Elaine Player (1989) have provided substantial evidence of racial discrimination within prisons. For example, they found that the best jobs were regularly allocated to white prisoners, as prison officers believed that Afro-Caribbean prisoners were arrogant, lazy and anti-authority. More recently, the official inquiry into the racist murder of Zahid Murabek in March 2000 by his fellow cellmate in Feltham Young Offender's Institution found that institutional racism pervaded Feltham, which led to the Prison Service inviting the Commission for Racial Equality to carry out a formal inquiry into racism in prisons. The first part of the report identified twenty 'systemic failures' by the Prison Service to prevent the murder (Commission for Racial Equality, 2003).

A second part of the report, to be published later in 2003, will comment more generally on racial discrimination. It has also been argued that the brutal deaths of ethnic minorities while in prison custody is similar to the deaths of Africans and Caribbeans in police custody, as there is 'a tendency for prison staff to overreact to disruptive behaviour by African/Caribbean prisoners, whereby the stereotype of "Big, Black and Dangerous" seems to predominate in determining their response' (Bowling and Phillips, 2002: 208). It is beyond doubt that racism and racial discrimination continue to be a shameful reality in English prisons.

PRISON SOCIOLOGY

Prisoner subcultures and 'mind games'

Much of the classic literature in sociology (e.g. Clemmer, 1958; Sykes, 1958; Goffman, 1962; Mathiessen, 1965; Cohen and Taylor, 1972/1981) arises from monograph research on life in prisons. These studies have illuminated the day-to-day routines and struggles within institutions. Although this early work was preoccupied with prisoner subcultures and how they mitigated against the pains of imprisonment, especially in US penitentiaries, more recent British sociological writing tends to emphasise the complexity of responses to confinement. These vary a great deal according to the category of prison, the quality of its regime, and the shifting patterns of stratification.

For example, Richard Sparks, Anthony Bottoms and Will Hay (1996: 176–81) have indicated in their study of two long-term dispersal prisons (where one might expect the presence of well-developed subcultures) that simple analogies based on class structures, with 'gangsters' portrayed as the 'ruling class' and 'nonces' as a 'lumpenproletariat', are seriously misleading. Instead, a rather more fluid pattern of competing groups (based on ethnic or regional affinities as much as on 'business' interests) was in evidence as compared with the rigid separation of roles and group solidarity that was a defining characteristic of the classic subculture research.

As Rock (1996: 40) puts it, with reference to a women's prison, there is not one prisoner world 'but many'. This point is developed by Carrabine (2004) in his discussion of the culture of a local prison, whose captive membership is constantly in flux as new prisoners arrive to be allocated elsewhere, others are returning from dispersal prisons under 'transfers', yet more will be seeing out short-term sentences, and always there will be those deemed 'unsuitable' for training prisons – the 'old lags' who have been imprisoned on many previous occasions. His argument is not only that antagonisms, friendships and influence constantly have to be renegotiated amid the frantic pace of daily change and upheaval on the wings and landings of local prisons but that it is the staff occupational culture that plays a pivotal role in shaping institutional interactions, not least because prison officers spend a far greater proportion of their working lives in the same place than either the prisoners or their managers.

Another illustration of sociological analysis is provided in Kathleen McDermott and Roy King's (1988) discussion of the 'mind games' played on the wings and landings of five English prisons. These authors provide a number of game metaphors to illustrate the various degrees of conflict between prisoners and staff. One of the most basic prison rituals is going to the lavatory, and this is one of the many routine degradation rituals faced in prisons, as the toilet was then a bucket in the cell (the practice of 'slopping out' was said to have officially ended in April 1996, although there continues to be evidence that prisoners do not have adequate access to toilets).

Consequently, one way of making do is through what McDermott and King (1988: 360) call *pass the parcel*. This refers to the ways in which excrement is wrapped up in parcels and thrown out of a window, which is partly functional as it relieves prisoners from spending time with the stench. Yet it is also a gesture of anger, as the parcel, has to be cleared up by someone else, and using prison clothing as the wrapper brings the issue back to the authorities, where it belongs. However, the game is not played by the staff, as they do not clear up the mess: they organise prisoners to do this, and ultimately the prisoners suffer through clothing shortages.

Survival games continue when prisoners are permitted outside their cells, as their encounters with staff, prisoners and arbitrary rules that govern their lives increase. For staff to survive, they have to develop skills both to avoid an assault in the heat of the moment, and, in the longer term, to avoid reprisals in a future riot. Prison staff are often in a situation where they have to bear the brunt of prisoners' frustrations but are powerless to relieve them, and they tend to play the *sloping shoulders game*: this is where an officer passes on prisoners' requests to another officer, invariably away from the first officer's landing, so that the officer on the landing is not immediately turning down the request. Meanwhile, prisoners are involved in *charades*. This is usually played by sex offenders who are anxious to avoid the label 'nonce'. For example, one prisoner was called this by another prisoner in their study, and though the sex offender knew he would lose, he challenged the prisoner to a fight, which earned him respect and an avoidance of the more severe beating he would have later received from a group of prisoners in his cell or in the recess.

Prison riots and the problem of order

Few would deny that prisons are dangerous places, and while violence is often described in terms of the characteristics of individual prisoners, such an understanding leaves much unexplained (Edgar *et al.*, 2003). The level of violent incidents in prisons indicates that intimidation, assaults and abuse form part of the everyday routine, whereas riots and disturbances are much rarer and pose a '*special problem* of the occasional complete or near-complete breakdown of order' (Sparks *et al.*, 1996: 2; emphasis in original).

Riots and disturbances can be further distinguished in the sense that a riot involves the authorities losing 'control of a significant number of prisoners, in a significant area of the prison, for a significant amount of time' (Useem and Kimball, 1989: 4), whereas a disturbance is a step down from a riot as there are fewer prisoners involved and the administrators do not lose control of any part of the institution. It can still involve collective protest over conditions, through refusing to eat or stopping work, for example. While these definitions can be criticised for their vagueness, they do have the advantage of highlighting the ways in which the problem of order is a daily feature of institutional life, for even though major riots are rare events, they do not occur abruptly in an otherwise tranquil vacuum, and have multi-faceted causes.

Moreover, the term 'riot' is a pejorative one, summoning images of frenzied mob violence, and historians have indicated how the label has been used by ruling elites to discredit the revolutionary crowd in European history (Rudé, 1964). Prison riots are disturbing, complex and diverse events that raise profound questions over human action, social structure, historical context and political reasoning. In Bert Useem and Peter Kimball's (1989) examination of nine prison riots in the United States, they provide a fresh understanding of prison disorder as it introduces the issue of legitimacy as crucial to structuring institutional stability. Their argument is that well-managed prisons instigate conformity, whereas breakdowns in administrative control render imprisonment illegitimate in the eyes of the confined.

This study anticipates Lord Woolf's conclusion that the twenty-five-day occupation of Strangeways Prison in Manchester during April 1990 was due to widely shared feelings of injustice, and the explicit argument is that there are variable conditions under which the confined accept or reject custodial authority (Woolf and Tumim, 1991). It is difficult to overestimate the significance of Woolf's report, as it not only marks a decisive break with previous government understandings of prison unrest but is universally regarded as the most important examination of the prison system in the past hundred years, while the recipe of reform he advocated is widely understood as one that will take the prison system out of the nineteenth century and into the twenty-first.

The concept of legitimacy locates the study of prison riots in the broader problem of order familiar to social and political theorists. By doing so, it establishes that there are no simple answers to the question of why prisoners rebel in the ways that they do (Carrabine, 2004). In fact, it raises the pressing issue of how such matters as age, class, gender, race, religion and sexuality challenge a universalising notion such as legitimacy. Perhaps the unsettling conclusion to be drawn from this case study on prison riots is that they ought to happen more often. Explaining why they do not involves recognising that prisons typically generate diverse forms of social order in spite of the frequently illegitimate distributions of institutional power and severe crises outlined earlier in this chapter.

SUMMARY

1 Prisons are the most controversial institutions in modern penal systems and occupy a central place in popular sentiment and political rhetoric on punishment.
2 The chapter has reviewed a number of competing explanations of the historical reasons why the prison became the dominant response to crime across Europe and North America from the end of the eighteenth century.
3 The account of the modern prison estate that followed demonstrated how there are a range of interrelated issues that contribute to a sense of crisis in the system, with grave social consequences.
4 The chapter has also included illustrations of sociological analyses of prison life in relation to 'mind games' and the problem of order.

CRITICAL THINKING QUESTIONS

1 In what ways does gender challenge historical and contemporary accounts of imprisonment?
2 What are the key components of the prison crisis?
3 Why does youth custody involve elements of rescue, rehabilitation and repression?
4 Can you explain why the prison system is orderly most of the time?

FURTHER STUDY

Cavadino, M. and Dignan, J. (2002) *The Penal System: An Introduction*, 3rd edn, London: Sage. The best criminological introduction to imprisonment, which covers the central issues in a broad and lively fashion.
Matthews, R. (1999) *Doing Time: An Introduction to the Sociology of Imprisonment*, Basingstoke: Macmillan. This is a more detailed sociological account of imprisonment.
Stern, V. (1993) *Bricks of Shame*, London: Penguin. This is a compassionate and thought-provoking examination of the institution.

MORE INFORMATION

The Home Office
http://www.homeoffice.gov.uk
Provides access to a wide range of information on the CJS generally.

The Home Office: Publications
http://www.homeoffice.gov.uk/rds/pubsintro1.html
Provides access to a wide range of publications.

HM Prison Service
http://www.hmprisonservice.gov.uk/
Contains news, reports, statistics and prison rules for prisons in England and Wales.

The Scottish Prison Service
http://www.sps.gov.uk
Contains news, reports, statistics and prison rules for prisons in Scotland.

The Prison and Probation Ombudsman
http://www.ppo.gov.uk/
The Prisons and Probation Ombudsman provides access to annual reports and publications.

Report of Her Majesty's Chief Inspector of Prisons
http://www.homeoffice.gov.uk/justice/prisons/index.html
A link to a report by the Inspector of Prisons can be found here along with further information on the Inspectorate.

The Howard League for Penal Reform
http://www.howardleague.org/
Information, links and publications on penal reform.

National Association for the Care and Rehabilitation of the Offender (NACRO)
http://www.nacro.org.uk/
This site has information on penal reform and lists relevant publication.

Prison Reform Trust
http://www.prisonreformtrust.org.uk/
Information on the Prison Reform Trust, which aims at creating a just, humane and effective penal system.

Youth Justice Board for England and Wales
www.youth-justice-board.gov.uk.
Contains information on policies, news, press releases and details of youth offending teams.

The Guardian: Prisons
http://www.guardian.co.uk/prisons
The *Guardian*'s coverage of prison issues is an excellent resource.

The Observer: Special Reports
http://www.observer.guardian.co.uk/crimedebate
This offers further critical commentary on prison issues.

PART 5 GLOBALISING CRIME

In this section, we examine some of the newer issues that are fast getting on the agenda for crminologists. These new topics include such matters as 'Green Crimes', the importance of the media, human rights and globalisation. A concluding chapter looks at the future of crime and control in the twenty-first century.

The Greening of Criminology

In early May 2000 a US Coast Guard cutter, the *Sherman*, chased a Russian-crewed, Korean-owned, Honduran-registered ship, the *Arctic Wind*, across the Alaskan seas. The *Arctic Wind* had been spotted fishing for salmon. A few years earlier, nobody would have taken much notice but now it was breaking the agreement of a 1991 UN General assembly resolution banning such fishing. The captain of the *Sherman* ordered his crew to prepare to open fire at the *Arctic* and in the face of this, the ship was boarded for inspection. 'In addition to finding a ton of salmon already in the vessel's hold, the inspectors watched as some 14 kilometres of nets were pulled up that had collectively ensnared 700 salmon, 6 shark, 50 puffins, 12 albatross and a porpoise' (French and Mastny, 2001: 166).

This is a very simple example of a 'green crime'. The plundering of the earth's resources has not until recently been thought of as a crime. Yet as is now well known, the earth and its resources are being wasted and overexploited. Through this, numerous crimes, violations, deviations and irregularities are perpetrated against the environment. These *green crimes*, then, may initially simply be defined as *crimes against the environment* (South, 1998a, b).

GLOBALISATION AND THE RISK SOCIETY

Environmental degradation is nothing new, but it was really only in the latter years of the twentieth century – as pollution accelerated – that global awareness of the problems grew. It is now apparent that any understanding of the natural environment and its problems must also be global in scope. Regardless of divisions into nation-states, the planet constitutes a single *ecosystem*, defined as *the system composed of the interaction of all living organisms and their natural environment*. This must mean that responses to this global problem cannot be the task of one country alone; the problem is part of the process of globalisation that we have discussed throughout this book (see especially Chapter 6).

We may also see this problem as part of what the German sociologist Ulrich Beck (1992) has called 'the risk society', whereby *modern industrial societies create many new risks – largely manufactured through modern technologies – that were unknown in earlier days*. The new technologies are generating risks that are of a quite different order from those found throughout earlier human history. Of course, past societies were risky and dangerous places too: whole populations could be wiped out by major earthquakes, floods or plagues, for example. But Beck argues that new kinds of risks appear with the industrial world that are not 'in nature' but 'manufactured'. These are associated with the many new technologies which generate new dangers to lives and to the planet itself. These dangers are humanly produced, may have massively unforeseen consequences, and may take many, many thousands of years to reverse. These 'manufactured risks' are taking us to the edge of catastrophe: to 'threats to all forms of life on this planet', to 'the exponential growth of risks and the impossibility of escaping them'.

Risk is associated with a society that tries to break away from tradition and the past, and where change and the future become more valued. All these changes – from the railway to the computer, from genetic engineering to nuclear weapons – have consequences that we cannot easily predict. The emergence of 'green crimes' is part of these new risks, bringing new patterns of crime which could not have been easily foretold a century or so ago.

BOX 17.1 A BRIEF HISTORY OF ENVIRONMENTAL DEGRADATION

Pre-1500	Global extinctions of whole species – up to 90 per cent were lost at the end of the Permian and Cretaceous periods; many large mammals lost; some species through overhunting. Microbe movements leading to epidemics; long-term natural climate changes.
1500–1760	European ecological expansion and capitalist growth starts to lead to rising resource shortage and land degradation; demographic movements and ecological transformation of the Americas.
Modern: 1760–1945	Capitalist industrialisation, urbanisation, concentration, ecological expansion and colonialisation . . . local resource exhaustion, urban air, soil and water pollution, change in rural environments and forest loss, some global extinction of species and some contribution to global warning

Contemporary	Global warming, marine depletion, water in short supply, deforestation, desertification, soil exhaustion, overspills, hazardous waste, acid deposition, nuclear risks, decline of the global ecosystem comes with Western growth and consumption. Socialist industrialisation, industrialisation of the South, new risks from technology and warfare.

Sources: Harrison and Pearce (2000);
Held *et al.* (1999: 391)

TWO OPENING EXAMPLES

The explosion at the Union Carbide chemical plant at Bhopal in India in December 1984 (Plate 17.1), may serve as a good opening example of a green crime – for it is commonly agreed to be the world's worst environmental accident so far (although Chernobyl is a clear 'rival' for this claim). This accident followed from corporate negligence and mismanagement (Pearce and Tombs, 1993). The plant used highly toxic chemicals in its production process; when water somehow mixed with these, the resulting explosion was catastrophic. Estimates of fatalities and of those seriously affected in the immediate aftermath and subsequently have varied, with official, academic and media reports suggesting around 6,000 or more fatalities, plus 60,000 people seriously affected by the toxic gases and over 20,000 permanently injured as a result of exposure. Of key importance here is the argument that far fewer people would have died, been injured or affected had the plant not been located so close to the shanty towns of the poor. The ultimate impact of the event on the local natural environment and wildlife – twenty years on – is still not clear.

To take another example: consider the effects of our use of chlorofluorocarbons (CFCs) as a propellant in aerosol spray cans and as a gas in refrigerators, freezers and air conditioners. CFCs may have improved our lives in various ways; but as they were released into the atmosphere, they reacted with sunlight to form chlorine atoms, which, in turn, depleted ozone. The ozone layer in the atmosphere serves to limit the amount of harmful ultraviolet radiation reaching the earth from the sun. Thus, the 'hole' in the ozone layer in the atmosphere over Antarctica, and its thinning in the northern hemisphere, may produce a rise in human skin cancers and have countless other effects on plants and animals. While an international agreement has been reached to phase out the use of CFCs, many unscrupulous people prefer to maximise their short-term convenience by continuing to use them. By 1997 the black market global trade in CFCs rivalled the trade in narcotics. Moreover, in spite of global efforts to cut other emissions, some soft drink companies are seeking to market a new self-cooling can that will chill warm drinks in two minutes when opened – and release nearly as much pollution as the cars we drive today.

Plate 17.1 Union Carbide Plant. Thousands of animals perished in the disaster caused by a poisonous gas leak from the Union Carbide pesticide factory in Bhopal, India, on 4 December 1984. Chemicals leaked from the plant during the night, killing more than 2,000 people and affecting 200,000 others.

Source: Associated Press; *photo*: Thiang.

TYPES OF GREEN CRIMES

Green criminology suggests that we reappraise more traditional notions of crimes, offences and injurious behaviours and start to examine the role that societies (including corporations and governments) play in generating environmental degradation. Criminology, then, is starting to recognise the finite nature of the earth's resources and how this generates new problems of damage and harm. In a very simple fashion, we can initially identify two main clusters of crimes. First are those crimes that result directly from the destruction and degradation of the earth's resources, and second are those crimes that are symbiotic with or dependent upon such process. We will consider each briefly in turn.

Primary green crimes

There are four main primary categories of green crimes in which the environment becomes degraded through human actions – all of which have become the subject of legislative efforts in recent years. These new categories are crimes of air pollution, crimes of deforestation, crimes of species decline and against animal rights, and crimes of water pollution.

Crimes of air pollution

The burning of fossil fuels releases about 6 billion tons of carbon into the air each year, adding about 3 billion tons annually to the 170 billion tons that have settled since the Industrial Revolution. The rate of growth in carbon emissions is around 2 per cent per year. New crimes and causes here may involve those who pollute the air through cars and planes, the burning of corporate waste and wars. A recent concern has been over the atmospheric environmental impact of the Gulf War and the output of oil wells that were set ablaze, as well as the deleterious effect on combatants (Gulf War Syndrome), believed to be a consequence of the use of anti-chemical warfare agents.

Here potential criminals are governments and big business, as well as consumers.

Crimes of deforestation

The world is losing 7 million hectares of fertile land a year owing to soil degradation, and about 10 million hectares of forest land a year (about the size of South Korea). While there is less land, more food is needed. The world has lost half of its forests over the past eight thousand years, and between 1960 and 1990 about 20 per cent of the world's tropical forest was lost. Between 70 and 95 per cent of the earth's species live in the world's disappearing tropical forest. The world's population is becoming increasingly urbanised: 37 per cent urban in 1970, the figure is projected to be 61 per cent by 2030. New crimes and criminals here would include those who deal in the destruction of rainforests and valuable lands; those who exploit natural resources for their own ends; and 'black markets' that develop around the sale of many of these valuable commodities.

An example of a new kind of environmental crime may be the use of herbicidal chemical sprays against certain plant crops, the source of illicit cocaine and cannabis, in various Central and Latin American countries, which has damaged more than just the original targets: coca bushes and marijuana plantations. These anti-drug crop sprays have, of course, also affected other crops, introduced contamination into the food chain and water-table, and been linked to a variety of health problems, birth defects, stillbirths, and so on (Del Olmo, 1987). In this instance, the war against drugs may actually generate new green crimes.

Crimes of species decline and animal rights

We are losing fifty species a day. Forty-six per cent of mammal and 11 per cent of birds species are said to be at risk. By 2020, 10 million species are likely to have become extinct. And yet there are major traffics in both animals and animal parts across the world (not to mention also the serious trafficking in human body parts; Scheper-Hughes and Wacquant, 2002).

Criminology should be taking seriously old crimes and new violations that arise in relation to land animal and aquatic life. Examples include the resurgence of dog fights, badger-baiting and other 'animal spectacles' for entertainment purposes, reported by official agencies and the media in both the United Kingdom and United States; or the 'fishing wars' on the Atlantic coast and in the North Sea, which involve conflicts over resource management, physical clashes, matters of international law, and new forms of regulation.

Crimes of water pollution

At present, some 500 million people lack any drinking water; and this figure may reach 2.5 billion by 2025. Freshwater ecosystems are in decline everywhere. Some 25 million people die every year from drinking water contaminated with pollutants. Some 58 per cent of the world's reefs and 34 per cent of all fish may be at risk. And yet again, others pollute the waters, overfish the sea, and spill oil into it. For instance, 'since the notorious *Exxon Valdez* incident in Alaska's Prince William Sound in 1989, at least 1.1 million tons of oil have spilled worldwide – equivalent to some 30 *Valdez* accidents' (Brown *et al.*, 2001: 179). See Harrison and Pearce (2000); World Reosurces Institute Website; *New Internationalist*, nos. 269, 278, 287, 289; and Brown *et al.*, (2004).

Secondary or symbiotic green crimes

What we call symbiotic green crime is crime that grows out of the flouting of rules that seek to regulate environmental disasters. There are, for instance, numerous minor and major examples of governments breaking their own regulations and contributing to environmental harms (Day, 1991).

State violence against oppositional groups

State's condemn 'terrorism' but, of course, have always been perfectly capable of resorting to terrorist-type methods when in conflict with oppositional groups. A notorious example is the 1985 sinking of the Greenpeace flagship *Rainbow Warrior* in Auckland harbour, New Zealand (Plate 17.2). This was a crime of terrorist violence carried out by commandos from the French secret service. In this operation, sanctioned at cabinet level within the French government, 22 kilos of explosive was used to blow up the Greenpeace ship as an expression of French anger over its use in protest activities against French nuclear tests in the Pacific. Miraculously, of the thirteen crew on board, only one was killed in the blast (Day, 1991: 281–4).

In his book *The Eco-wars*, Day (1991) charts a variety of similar state-sponsored acts of violence and intimidation against environmental activists or groups. His comments on these and the *Rainbow Warrior* affair are highly relevant to the idea of a criminology that takes environmental issues and politics seriously:

> The most unusual aspect of the Rainbow Warrior affair was that, to some degree at least, the murder mystery was solved. Although justice was not done, the truth came out. There have been many other acts of state terrorism linked with the anti-

nuclear war but it is seldom possible to prove that they are linked directly to government officials. Indeed, if the agents had not been caught red-handed, there is no doubt that Greenpeace activists would have been scoffed at for pointing the finger at the French government. Their accusation would have been dismissed as just one more lunatic fringe conspiracy theory. Why, after all, would the French government worry about the activities of a small-scale anti-nuclear protest group? Surely only a total paranoid would believe that violent action was necessary to stop such a group. The answer is that when it comes to nuclear issues the French – and the governments of *all* nuclear powers – *are* paranoid. In every case where a government has committed itself to nuclear weapons or nuclear power, all those who oppose this policy are treated in some degree as enemies of the State.

(Day, 1991)

Plate 17.2 The *Rainbow Warrior* lying in Auckland harbour, New Zealand on 10 July 1985, after being sunk by French agents just before it was due to sail to Mururoa Atoll in the South Pacific to protest against French nuclear testing in the area.

Source: © Associated Press; *photo*: *New Zealand Herald*.

Hazardous waste and organised crime

The limited regulation over waste dumping, especially in advanced Western industrial nations, has created a highly profitable domestic and international trade in illegal disposal and dumping of hazardous toxic waste. This has manifested itself in new forms of corporate organised crime, sometimes – perhaps even frequently – with tacit state acknowledgement (Szasz, 1986; Scarpitti and Block, 1987; Van Duyne, 1993; Ruggiero, 1996),

Toxic and general waste-dumping is an increasingly significant crime. Ruggiero (1996: 139–40) cites cases involving criminal groups from Germany transporting hazardous waste into France, and an entrepreneur in northern England who ran a legal waste-disposal firm and alongside this a service providing illegal dumping of 'hard to dispose of' waste. According to Ruggiero (ibid.), Italy has offered some particularly striking examples of this new area of criminal entrepreneuriality:

> In Italy, traditional organized crime based in the south has often offered waste-disposal services to entrepreneurs operating in the north. Among the firms serviced in 1990 was ACNA, which produced dioxane and operates in Lombardy. In describing this activity of organized crime in Naples, the Commissione Antimafia . . . commented: 'The seawater of large parts of Naples province is polluted mainly because of illegal waste dumping, authorized dumping constitutes only 10% of the total waste actually disposed of in the bay of Naples.'

Ruggiero (ibid.) also notes that

> The illegal disposal of hazardous waste has been thoroughly studied in the USA, where in some cases the involvement of organized crime reaches all aspects of the business, from the control of which companies are officially licensed to dispose of waste to those which earn contracts with public or private organizations and to the payment of bribes to dump-site owners, or the possession of such sites. . . . Paradoxically, the development of this illegal service runs parallel with an increase in environmental awareness, the latter forcing governments to raise costs for industrial dumping, which indirectly encourages industrialists to opt for cheaper solutions.

BOX 17.2 THE CRIMINALISATION OF ENVIRONMENTAL OFFENCES

There are many legal and policy issues raised by green crimes. Various populations may be exposed to hazardous waste and emissions, but cases attempting to establish liability and responsibility for this have often proved unresolvable in courts of law.

Consider how we should respond to green crimes.

The use of criminal and civil law, and of effective enforcement strategies, leads to a debate about *criminalisation* as an effective tool for regulation. Although there are now many international laws in place, the case against this approach alone is that (i) there are frequently legal problems in getting to the stage of bringing a prosecution, and (ii) if this does happen, pollution cases are notoriously difficult to prove in terms of culpability and 'knowing intent'; (iii) even if a prosecution is brought and is successful, penalties are usually modest relative to the damage done: if the corporation is fined, it will absorb such costs and/or simply pass them on to consumers. Attempts to identify and sanction key responsible individuals have had only rare success (Geis and Di Mento, 1995; Ridley and Dunford, 1994).

Potentially more effective is Braithwaite's (1989) notion of 'shaming'. Adapted for present purposes, this is an argument based on the proposition that corporate image is a more vulnerable target for censure and sanctions than corporate assets. Bad publicity and the projection of a negative image about offending businesses can hurt public relations, profits and share prices. The argument would be that being a bad corporate citizen is bad news for a company; it hurts community relations and finds disfavour with government, and with other businesses in the same sector that desire a clean image. In some respects this view carries a degree of realism and sophistication in its strategy that are lacking in the 'get tough' enforcement, and 'let's cooperate' compliance models. However, this is also an argument with its own limitations, not least in that it may be naïve about the extent to which corporate business really cares about 'image', or conversely it may well underestimate how hard business will fight to undermine critics (Rowell, 1996). It is also a view that may overestimate the extent to which the general public actually care about what corporations do, especially if their offences are committed in another country, and particularly if this is in the developing world.

THE MAKING OF GREEN CRIMES: CRIMINALISING ENVIRONMENTAL ISSUES

A major part of criminology is concerned with the study of law-making – criminalisation. Although environmental crimes highlight a new field of criminalisation in the making, its roots lie in the recent past. In most industrialised countries, health statutes and criminal laws usually date from the late nineteenth and early twentieth centuries.

Early legislation

Think of Western Europe in the 1940s and 1950s. Each nation was committed to a programme of reconstruction and reindustrialisation. The aim was to build a better post-war world, and indicators of economic growth suggested that this was a possibility, not a dream. However, in major cities across Europe, centres of growing populations, expanding transport systems and new enterprises, as well as in regions of high industrial concentration, a new social problem was being produced. In itself, of course, this 'new' problem – pollution – was hardly unfamiliar to these cities and regions. The industries of the nineteenth century – mining, smelting, refining, and so on – all changed the landscape and affected air quality, with health consequences for local populations. It was the scale and severity of pollution that were new. For example, in London in 1952 the number of deaths caused by the 'killer smog' (which sounds like a science-fiction fantasy but was actually dense atmospheric pollution) caused public alarm and calls for action, leading to the Clean Air Act 1956. In parts of Eastern Europe, such problems were, we now realise, even greater (Carter and Turnock, 1993).

The growth of environmental legislation

Legislation in various forms has gained pace internationally since the mid-twentieth century, and the 1972 United Nations Conference on the Human Environment is generally credited with giving rise to further enhanced awareness of the need for environmental regulations. It led to a Declaration and an Action Plan with 109 recommendations in six broad areas (including human settlements, natural resource management, pollution, educational and social aspects of the environment, development, and international organisations) and to a programme to manage the 'global commons', and established a UN environmity programme. Subsequent world conferences include the Earth Summit held at Rio in 1992 and Earth Summit 2 in New York in 1997. Box 17.3 suggests a few of the key agreements which now await detailed study by criminologists.

BOX 17.3 A SMALL SAMPLE OF SELECTED INTERNATIONAL AGREEMENTS ON THE ENVIRONMENT

1972 London Convention on the Prevention of Marine Pollution by Dumping of Wastes and Other Matter (78 parties): bans dumping at sea of radioactive and highly toxic wastes, as well as incineration and dumping at sea of all forms of industrial waste.

1973 Washington Convention on International Trade in Endangered Species of Wild Fauna and Flora (CITES) (152 parties): restricts trade in species that are either threatened with extinction or that may become endangered if their trade is unregulated. See www.cites.org.

1973 (updated 1978) International Convention for the Prevention of Pollution from Ships (MARPOL) (112 parties). Restricts discharges of oil, sewage, garbage, noxious liquids at sea.

1987 Montreal Protocol on Substances that Deplete the Ozone Layer (175 parties): requires the gradual phasing out of chlorofluorocarbons, halons and other synthetic chemicals that damage the atmosphere.

1988 Basel Convention on the Control of Transboundary Movements of Hazardous Wastes and Their Disposal (141 parties): restricts international export of hazardous waste from industrial to developing countries, unless the importing country agrees to accept them. Amendment of 1994 completely bans all exports, but is still not in force.

1997 Kyoto Protocol to the 1992 UN Framework Convention on Climate Change (30 parties, not yet in force): requires industrial countries to reduce emissions of carbon dioxide by 6–8 per cent by 2008–12.

Source: French and Mastny (2001: 169–70 and footnote 7)

GREEN CRIMES, SOCIAL COSTS AND SOCIAL EXCLUSION

An important aspect of green crimes – as with so many crimes – is their link to inequalities. Indeed, we can speak of *environmental racism* as the pattern by which environmental hazards are perceived to be greatest in proximity to poor people, and especially those belonging to minorities. For example, while many homes in rich countries can consume more than 2,000 litres of good-quality water every day, some 500 million people around the globe suffer from an almost total lack of drinking water. The World Health Organisation suggests a basic requirement of 150 litres per day per household. This basic, and quite low, standard could well be achieved for the whole world if so much water were not squandered by the West (*New Internationalist*, 2001, no. 23).

Historically, factories that spew pollutants have been built in and near districts inhabited by the poor, who often work there. As a result of their low incomes, many could afford housing only in undesirable localities, sometimes in the very shadow of the plants and mills. Although workers in many manufacturing industries have organised in opposition to environmental hazards, they have done so with limited success, largely because the people facing the most serious environmental threats have the least social power to begin with. As with many crimes, then, there are identifiable victims, who are often from less advantaged groups. We can see this as happening both locally and globally.

Developing nations as 'dump sites'

Since the mid-1970s, most Western countries have toughened up anti-dumping and pollution laws (on the recent UK experience, see Lowe *et al.*, 1996; Weale, 1996). It would be naïve, however, to suppose that such problems have been mitigated, let alone eradicated, by tougher laws. What the regulations in advanced Western nations have done is to create an international trade in dumping. Toxic waste defined as unsuitable for landfill burial in the West may be shipped to developing countries that do not have similar regulatory laws, or lack enforcement resources, or that welcome such waste because its disposal yields profit, paid for in needed foreign currency. This whole combination of factors is conducive to corruption. In many cases, the export of such waste would not normally be granted export licences by North American or West European regulatory agencies, and the proper procedure should be for such waste to be reprocessed to reduce its toxicity before disposal. This is, however, potentially very expensive, and hence the waste may be moved illegally. Toxic waste does not seem to be a problem so long as we can find somewhere else to dump it other than our *own* back yard.

One example of such evasion of regulations and re-routing of waste is described by Block (1993). In this case, toxic waste was moved from the United States to Northern Europe under false bills of lading and was then trans-shipped to the impoverished West African nation of Benin. There the government's soldiers unloaded the waste and drove it north, dumping it near Benin's border with the state of Niger (ibid.: 104).

Local communities as dump sites

Environmental discrimination is a fact of life for many poor communities. Restrictions on housing opportunities (often through discriminatory practices) have led to all manner of environmental hazards. Thus, black communities often find their housing situated right next to 'garbage dumps, hazardous-waste landfills, incinerators, smelter operations, paper mills, chemical plants, and a host of other polluting industries' (Bullard, 1990: xiv); 'industries often follow the simplest opportunities and dump their stuff in economically poor and politically powerless black communities.'

Recent developments in southern California – what has been called the Toxic Rim – present a picture of an unfolding ecological nightmare in which victims simply do not count. As Davis (1994: 19) reported 'choking on its own wastes, with its landfills overflowing and its coastal waters polluted, Los Angeles is preparing to export its garbage and hazardous land-uses to the eastern Mojave and to Baja California. Instead of reducing its production of dangerous wastes, the city is simply planning to 'regionalise' their disposal. In sum, the formation of this waste-belt will accelerate the environmental degradation of the entire American West (and part of Mexico). Today, a third of the trees in southern California's mountains have already been suffocated by smog, and animal species are rapidly dying off throughout the polluted Mojave Desert. Tomorrow, Los Angeles' radioactive and carcinogenic wastes may be killing life as far away as Utah or Sonora. The Toxic Rim will be a zone of extinction' (see also Davis, 1993 on the legacy of military and nuclear arms testing). In this scenario, US domestic pollution problems are displaced to a toxic rim inhabited only by those who 'don't count'.

Moreover, as already stated, the disposal of waste generally, and toxic waste in particular, as well as the siting of controversial high-pollution industries, are also displaced or 'regionalised' in another way: by exporting them to the developing world. Here the environmental victims may still remain largely hidden or forgotten, at least until catastrophe occurs.

In response, environmental activism has emerged in the affected (often black) communities, and is often linked to national groups. The call for social and environmental justice has now been taken up within a wide network of activists engaged in 'toxic struggles' (Hofrichter, 1993), who employ strategies similar to those of the the civil rights, anti-war and anti-nuclear movements. As Hofrichter (ibid.: 4) defines the idea, environmental justice

> is about social transformation directed toward meeting human need and enhancing quality of life – economic equality, health care, shelter, human rights, species preservation and democracy – using resources sustainably. . . . Environmental problems . . . remain inseparable from other social injustices such as poverty, racism, sexism, unemployment, urban deterioration, and the diminishing quality of life resulting from corporate activity.

This emergent and strengthening environmental justice movement has provided the 'conceptual starting point' for the exploration of ideas such as environmental racism and victimization, and the need for an environmental victimology (Williams, 1996).

BOX 17.4 GREEN CRIMES AFFECTING LOCAL COMMUNITIES

Love Canal is an area near Niagara Falls, USA. In 1978 and over the next two years, the story of past dumping of hazardous toxic waste in the area emerged. This was a very serious story because of what had been built on the land after the dumping. In the 1940s, Love Canal was an abandoned navigation channel, and for years a company called Hooker Chemical had simply disposed of thousands of drums of toxic chemical waste directly into the canal (Szasz, 1994: 42).

In 1952 the canal was covered up. A year later, the Hooker company sold the land to the Niagara Falls Board of Education. A school was built. Developers built homes and 'unsuspecting families' moved in. In the 1970s, after heavy rains, chemical wastes began to seep to the surface, both on the school grounds and into people's yards and basements. Federal and state officials confirmed the presence of eighty-eight chemicals, some in concentrations 250 to 5,000 times higher than acceptable safety levels. Eleven of these chemicals were suspected or known carcinogens; others were said to cause liver and kidney ailments (ibid.).

The Love Canal case received massive media attention and for a while highlighted the fact that damaging the environment with no regard for future generations was not illegal or a crime. New US laws had already been drafted, though, and in 1979 stricter federal regulations were introduced (though many were then reversed by the Reagan administration; see Snyder, 1991: 226–7; Vogel, 1986). At the time, the US Environmental Protection Agency estimated that 80 per cent of waste was being disposed of 'improperly, inadequately or illegally' (Szasz, 1994: 44).

FIGHTING BACK: GREEN MOVEMENTS OF RESISTANCE AND CHANGE

Globally, there are numerous political and pressure groups working around environmental issues, albeit in both positive and negative ways. Pro-environment groups range from the extreme (those that embrace terrorism), and the controversial (a philosophy that puts animal life before human life, e.g. various animal rights campaigns), to the more local forms of NIMBYism (Not In My Back Yard!) through the 'new social movements' of New Age travellers and ecofeminism, to middle-range versions of the political left, centre and right (Paehlke, 1995), as well as local, specific-interest groups ('save our wildlife' or NIMBY protesters; Szasz (1994)).

However, broader political critiques of the state and capitalism have also been directed toward environmental crimes which may symbolically be held to stand for much more. One of the most famous examples in Europe, described by Day (1991: 219–20) as being the 'first ecologically motivated assassination', was the 1980 murder of Enrico Paoletti by the far-left group Front Line. Paoletti was industrial director of a subsidiary of the Swiss Hoffman La Roche corporation, which operated a chemical plant in Seveso, northern Italy. In 1976, an explosion at the plant resulted in the release of a dioxin cloud that killed virtually all the town's domestic animals and caused severe skin disease problems for many adults and children. The explosion was shown to be the result of negligence, and Paoletti and several other executives were arrested. However, defence lawyers produced various legal obstructions, causing delay, and all were released on bail. Paoletti's subsequent 'execution' was justified by Front Line as the exercise of punishment that the formal system of prosecution was unable to deliver.

The importance of the feminist critique of masculine violence against the environment (Collard with Contrucci, 1988), and, in the United States, the emergence of networks of black activists working against environmental damage to their communities (Bullard, 1990), are expressions of protest that a forward-looking criminology should take note of.

We should also note the incorporation of green issues into mainstream political party agendas, into the work of the important bureaucracies charged with overseeing environmental issues, and into popular, (largely, but not exclusively) middle-class, eco-conscious frameworks: for example, in Britain, as membership of trade unions has declined, membership of green and animal welfare organisations has risen dramatically.

In this respect, according to one reading of the future (at least on the European stage), the politics of environmental issues have some significant popular appeal, and are not necessarily as closed as pessimists might assume.

A GREEN BACKLASH?

The 'backlash' against green concerns should certainly not be underestimated. Rowell (1996) identifies the main source of such a movement as arising from corporate and political power in the United States. While we must acknowledge that such power is globalised, nonetheless it would be foolish to underestimate the specificities of European political and policy processes. Pressure groups and politicians concerned about pollution, the rights of communities, evasions of environmental law, and so on already work very successfully within the world of European Union (EU) lobbying and legislation at Brussels, and in other parts of Europe (e.g. Herrnkind, 1993). Furthermore, in his study of the construction of European environmental policy, Ruzza (1996: 216) encouragingly observes that

> Because of their international background, [EU] bureaucrats are very sensitive to the climate of opinion in several countries, and far less isolated than some of their critics would argue. They are very aware of the Weberian metaphor of the iron cage and its shortcomings, and together with a strong pro-European ideology, often display apprehension on the way the [European] dream is actualised.

The implication of this analysis is that the ground on which to build policy-oriented criminological work is fertile rather than barren – not least because the environment is treated as a pan-national responsibility, a 'public good' for which the EU may be more concerned than the individual member governments, which will often prioritise domestic interests (although they too must recognise that it is not in national interests to have a population suffering the consequences of a deteriorating environment). Hence, despite the complicity of the state in some cases of environmental damage and the power of corporate offenders, there is no desire here to present a 'conspiratorial' view or to assert or imply that 'nothing can be done'. The development of public health improvements, the massive proliferation of environmental legislation, and the resources put into regulation, inspection and prosecution all affirm social commitment to environmental protection. From the local activism of community groups through issue-prioritising bureaucracies to the breadth of international law, there are powerful presures at work, and tools available, for environmental action. How long this may be the case is, however, a different question.

A criminology concerned about social justice on an equitable planet should take advantage of such current opportunities, for there are also less promising assessments of how environmental issues will fare in the future. Rowell (1996: 372) considers the future of the global backlash against environmental concern and suggests that this will start to get worse. We are already aware of such things as the 'fish wars', but as conflicts over resources intensify in the coming decades, so we may well have overt conflicts around 'water, wood, whales, metals, minerals, energy, cars and even consumerism'. Rowell has documented how state and corporate power has been mobilised against such new 'enemies':

> [W]ith the collapse of communism, environmentalists are now increasingly being identified as a global scapegoat for threatening the vested interest of power: the triple engines of unrestricted corporate capitalism, right-wing political ideology and the nation state's protection of the *status quo*. . . . The green backlash, born out of both the success of the environmental movement and its failure, is still to run its course. Many more activists will be intimidated, beaten up, vilified and killed for working on ecological issues.
>
> (ibid.: 372)

In his book *Green Political Thought* (1990: 158), Dobson argues that in many respects, green strategies for change 'respond to post-modern celebrations of difference, diversity, unfoundedness and humility'. To pursue this view, it might be argued that modernity celebrates economic development and that its cost–benefit calculations regarding the environment rest largely on whether environmental resources can reproduce themselves or more can be found. Only when this modus operandi is endangered does conservation become an issue for the corporate and political agendas.

On the other hand, a *post*modern view of global resources would celebrate their diversity, the amazing fecundity of the natural world, and the opportunities for experiential and aesthetic pleasure that are offered. Hence, conservation *per se* might not be a postmodern virtue, but the need to ensure the continuation of diversity is a postmodern necessity. This proposition raises the challenge of what a postmodern form of 'regulation' might involve.

WAYS AHEAD IN A RISK SOCIETY

Why is there so little effective protest about environmental damage? Why is it so difficult to engage mass support for environmental concerns? (Beck, 1995). These questions find one answer in the perspective put forward by Beck in his celebrated book *The Risk Society* (1992). For Beck, the limited project outlined here – to suggest some foundations for a green criminology – would be just one aspect of the need to reformulate scientific and social thought generally in the direction of 'thinking green'. Beck argues that how pollution and other threats are interpreted is frequently limited and constrained by a hegemonic clutch of narrow ideas and viewpoints: environmental issues are 'generally viewed as matters of nature and technology, or of economics and medicine' (ibid.: 25):

> [W]hat is astonishing . . . is that the industrial pollution of the environment and the destruction of nature, with their multifarious effects on the health and social life of people, which only arise in highly developed societies, are characterised by a *loss of social thinking*. This loss becomes caricature – this absence seems to strike no one, not even sociologists themselves. [emphasis in original]

The argument here is that criminology similarly needs to be reminded of this absence of 'social thinking about the environment'. To add a green perspective to criminology is neither a threat nor an irrelevance; rather, it offers another possibility for enrichment of the field, as well as reflecting an awareness about vital twenty-first-century issues.

From the policing of motorway protests, through international Customs efforts to curb trade in endangered species and toxic waste, to future crimes that are on the horizon – for example, trafficking in the products of genetic engineering of animal, plant and human life – a whole new future for criminological research is opening up. Far more than many subjects of traditional criminological concern, green issues connect with changes in the world we live in now and, perhaps even more importantly, the world the next generation will inherit.

SUMMARY

1   As part of the many ways in which criminology is developing, diversifying and maturing in the twenty-first century, there has recently been the growth of a green criminology that focuses upon crimes against the environment.

2   These crimes may come about simply because of the violation of international agreements and laws about the environment; or they may come about through various forms of exploitation, corruption and associated state or corporate crimes which find ways of avoiding or abusing such legislation.

3   Green crimes are a feature of a global risk society and need to be located in such a framework.

4   At this early stage in its development, a green criminology has four main tasks:
    (a) to document the existence of green crimes in all their forms and to evolve basic

typologies and distinctions such as that between primary and secondary green crimes;

(b) to chart the ways in which the laws have been developed around this area, and to assess the complications and political issues generated;

(c) to connect green crimes to social inequalities;

(d) to assess the role of green social movements (and their counter-movements involved in a backlash) in bringing about such change.

CRITICAL THINKING QUESTIONS

1   Do we really need a 'green criminology'? Is it just another field of study that is really part of white-collar and organisational crime – another instance of the crimes of the powerful that does not really need its own special 'field' of study?

2   Look up green social movements, such as Greenpeace, on the Web, and explore some of the latest campaigns and issues. (See the 'More Information section' at the end of the chapter.) In the light of what you have read in this chapter, can you see where there is a potential for both primary and secondary green crimes?

3   What do you understand by the 'risk society'? How might criminology use such an idea?

FURTHER STUDY

Adam, B., Beck, U. and Van Loon, J. (eds) (2000) *The Risk Society and Beyond*, London: Sage.

Beck, U. (1992) *Risk Society*, London: Sage. The now classic and key statement of the emergence of a risk society, though it is far from being an 'easy read'.

Beck, U. (2000) *World Risk Society*, Cambridge: Polity Press.

Brown, Lester R. *et al.* (2004) *State of the World: 2004. A Worldwatch Institute Report on Progress toward a Sustainable Society*, London: Earthscan. Published annually, this collection of essays focuses on a range of environmental dangers in global perspective. Chapter 9 of this edition discussed 'Controlling international environmental crime'.

Carson, R. (1962) *Silent Spring*, Boston: Houghton Mifflin. This book about the dangers of chemical pollution helped launch the environmental movement in the United States and elsewhere.

Edwards, S., Edwards, T. and Fields, C. (eds) (1996) *Environmental Crime and Criminality: Theoretical and Practical Issues*, New York: Garland. A very welcome collection of essays on the subject of 'environmental crime and criminality'.

Garner, R. (2001) *Environmental Politics*, 2nd edn, London: Prentice Hall. Provides a succinct summary of the main issues, splits and groupings around 'environmentalism'.

The journal *Social Justice* brought out a special issue, 'Environmental Victims', and the editor, Christopher Williams, proposes the development of an 'environmental victimology' (Williams, 1996: 6).

MORE INFORMATION

One of many mappings of the environmental crisis can be found in the *AAAS Atlas of Population and Environment* (Berkeley: University of California Press, 2000) edited by Paul Harrison and Fred Pearce. Probably the prime resource for up-to-date information and discussion on ecosystems and the environment is the World Resources Institute. It produces a major annual volume (e.g. *World Resources 2000–1, People and Ecosystems – The Fraying Web of Life.* Elsevier Science), and its Website is http://www.wri.org/wri/

The online environmental community
http://www.envirolink.org/
A major resource for Websites connected to the environment.

Europe and Environmental Crime
http://europa.eu.int.comm/environment/crime/
The pages of the European online site that deals with the environment and crime.

Earthscan
http://www.earthscan.co.uk/
Provides resources and books giving information about the state of the environment.

Friends of the Earth
http://www.foe.org/
Greenpeace
http://www.greenpeace.org/international_en/
The two major activist Websites.

CHAPTER 18

KEY ISSUES

▌ Do the media cause violence?

▌ Have moral panics outlived their criminological usefulness?

▌ Why do we fear crime while consuming accounts of it so avidly?

▌ What are the main forms of crime on the Internet?

Crime and the Media

INTRODUCTION

The relationships between crime and the media have long been the subject of intense debate. In particular, a preoccupation with the supposed harmful effects of popular culture on public morality has been a recurring theme in social commentary since at least the sixteenth century – when it was argued that popular songs were especially dangerous as they all too often presented criminals as heroes (Barker and Petley, 1997: 7). For instance, in 1751 the famous author and then magistrate Henry Fielding wrote, in response to a widely reported crime wave, his *Enquiry into the Causes of the Late Increase in Robbers*, in which he commented that the 'too frequent and expensive Diversions among the lower kinds of People . . . hath almost totally changed the Manners, Customs and Habits of the People, more especially of the lower sort' (cited in Pearson, 1983: 186–7). As Hal Gladfelder (2001: 163) explains, the problem for Fielding was that the 'reckless and levelling pursuit of pleasure is dangerous not just because it leads the poor into robbery and theft when they run out of money; rather, pleasure for the "lower Orders" is already criminal itself'. Fielding is clearly characterising the urban poor as a dangerous class apart from respectable society – an alien and disruptive race resisting 'the hierarchical authority embodied in the law' (Gladfelder, 2001: 14). As we will see, debates over the harmful effects of the media continue to be driven by this same powerful combination of class antagonism, generational fear, social change, symbolic decline and technological development.

Yet at the same time, the media, and popular culture more generally, are fascinated with crime, whether this be as diverse forms of 'entertainment' in such staples as cop shows, crime novels, comics and films or as 'news' in television documentaries, newspaper articles and broadcast bulletins, to the extent that maintaining a distinction between 'fact' and 'fiction' is becoming increasingly difficult. This is partly a consequence of the rapid growth in 'reality' TV that blurs the 'boundaries between fact, fiction, and entertainment' (Carrabine *et al.*, 2002: 129) in such programmes as *Crimewatch, Police Camera Action* and *Car Wars*. In addition, the live broadcasting of spectacular events on rolling news programmes has recently become common, such as the O. J. Simpson car chase and subsequent trial, while the momentousness of the destruction of the World Trade Center on 11 September 2001 ('9/11') owed much to the fact that the graphic images were televised around the world, so that initial reactions were formed 'within established media interpretative frames (including the plots and images of countless Hollywood movies)' (Stevenson, 2003: 1).

BLURRING BOUNDARIES

Nevertheless, it is important to emphasise that the popular fascination with crime has a long history and that the boundaries between fact and fiction have always been fairly fluid. For instance, much of the recent scholarship on crime writing in the seventeenth and eighteenth centuries (Davis, 1983; Gatrell, 1994; Rawlings, 1992) examines how the flourishing commercial trade in crime and execution reports (in such genres as criminal biographies, gallows speeches and trial reports) vicariously mapped for readers a transgressive underworld, with their popularity owing as much to the development of new printing technologies and improved means of book distribution as a lens 'that brought into focus much of what was most disturbing, and most exciting, about contemporary experience' (Gladfelder, 2001: 5). It is this complex dynamic between the popular fascination with and fear of crime that we are especially concerned with in this chapter.

The transformations in media technology wrought by print, telegraph and wireless communication that gave birth to the electronic age from the mid-twentieth century have led some commentators to describe **mediatisation** as a powerful force that has eroded the divisions between 'fact and fiction, nature and culture, global and local, science and art, technology and humanity', to the extent that 'the media in the twenty-first century have so undermined the ability to construct an *apparent* distinction between reality and representation that the modernist episteme has begun to seem somewhat shaky' (Brown, 2003: 22, emphasis in original). In other words, the advent of postmodernity has meant that it is becoming increasingly impossible to distinguish between media image and social reality (Osborne, 1995: 28). These are provocative arguments that have profound consequences for how criminologists should understand the relationships between crime and the media.

In criminology, three distinctive approaches can be identified. The first assesses whether the media, 'through depictions of crime, violence, death and aggression', can be said to 'cause' criminal conduct (Kidd-Hewitt, 1995: 1), in what has been called the 'ill effects' debate (Barker and Petley, 1997). The second examines how crime news unjustly stereotypes groups (Cohen, 1972) in the orchestration of moral panics (Hall *et al.*, 1978) and thereby heightens public fear of crime. The third and more recent development attends to a broader consideration of how crime and punishment have been consumed (Carrabine *et al.*, 2002), imagined (Young, 1996) and represented (Sparks, 1992) in popular culture, which begins on the basis that there are a diverse range of media forms to excavate, as opposed to the singular pre-occupation with news content found in earlier critical media studies (Cohen and Young, 1973). This chapter begins by reviewing these three approaches and concludes with a discussion of crime in cyberspace, which provides an especially challenging site for criminologists to investigate, as the Internet is 'frequently depicted as a dark virtual domain inhabited by a mixture of dissenting computer hackers, organized criminals, extremist political groups and purveyors of pornographic images' (Thomas and Loader, 2000: 1).

MEDIA EFFECTS, POPULAR ANXIETIES AND VIOLENT REPRESENTATIONS

The question of whether media representations of violence have damaging effects upon audiences is one of the most researched issues in the social sciences, and despite the amount of time and money spent on the topic, no clear evidence for or against such behavioural claims has yet been produced (Livingstone, 1996). Given that several thousand studies have failed to reach convincing conclusions, it is reasonable to suppose not only that 'the wrong question is being asked' (Brown, 2003: 108), but that the agnostic verdicts expose the limits of 'empirical social science' (Reiner, 2002: 396).

Most of the **'effects' studies** are based on banal and outmoded understandings of science, whereby a group of subjects typically undergo various forms of exposure to a media stimulus (such as a film, programme or video extract) in an approximation of laboratory conditions, and some aspect of their behaviour is measured in relation to attitudes before and after the experiment. Critics argue that:

- the artificiality of such experiments fatally compromises them (Surrette, 1998: 122–3);
- they fail to 'place "effects" in their social contexts' (Murdock, 1997: 69);
- there is a spurious 'psycho-logic' in the studies, as they rely on 'mechanistic fairy-tales about how audiences process messages' (Vine, 1997: 125).

None of these critics denies that the media have 'effects', as the point of the media is to communicate, but they say that the problem is assuming that the relationship is simple and straightforward while misunderstanding the ways in which media socially construct reality.

Nevertheless, in public opinion the overwhelming view is that there is a direct causal link between media violence and real violence, and it is this common-sense assumption that drives the dominant research tradition, rather than that tradition challenging the question itself. In making such a challenge, it is important to recognise that the 'effects' debate is as old as popular culture, with the most recent controversies surrounding 'video nasties', computer games and the Internet. As Sheila Brown (2003: 27) argues, 'the debate gathered force through high profile cases exemplified in the UK by the murder of Liverpool toddler James Bulger (Smith, 1994) by two young boys who were famously alleged to have viewed 'video nasties'. In trying to explain the appalling murder, police speculated that the boys had copied scenes from *Child's Play 3* (1991), a film rented by the father of one of the boys a month before the murder. The judge thought that 'violent video films may in part be an explanation' (cited in Schubart, 1995: 222), and the *Sun* launched a campaign to burn all copies of the film – even though it was never actually proved that either child had ever seen the video. Clearly, it is the appeal of such simple and convenient mythologies that demands explanation.

One way of approaching the issue is to consider who is supposed to be at risk from the supposed harmful effects of the media. As Martin Barker and Julian Petley (1997: 5) argue, it is not 'the "educated" and "cultured" middle classes, who either don't watch such rubbish, or else are fully able to deal with it if they do so', who are assumed to be most susceptible; instead, 'those who are most "affected" are the young, especially the working-class young'. They go on to explain how in the nineteenth century the music hall and lurid stories in 'penny dreadfuls' were blamed for inciting hooliganism, while almost since its inception the cinema has been accused of encouraging 'copycat' crime. From the 1930s, when Hollywood was blamed for the growth of 'motor bandits', up to *Natural Born Killers* in the 1990s, there has been a constant claim that violence in the media is imitated by young viewers. Likewise, Graham Murdock (1997: 68) points out that

> the simple image of direct effects draws its power from a deep reservoir of social fear and dogma which first formed in the mid-nineteenth century as commentators begin to link the social costs of modernity with the proliferation of new forms of popular entertainment.

These arguments correspond with Pearson's (1983) 'history of respectable fears', which demonstrates how popular anxieties in the present often rely on idealised images of the past and are driven as much by generational fear as class antagonism in the creation of moral panics over social problems.

We return to the scapegoating function of moral panics in the next section, for it is important to emphasise that in refusing to ask different questions, the complex issues of how the media represent violence have yet to be adequately addressed in criminology, and it is on such matters that future research should be directed. For instance, one question might be how 'the eroticisation of violence and the spread of pornography as an industry' have altered 'the newsworthiness of sex crimes' and redefined 'acceptable behaviour' (Osborne, 1995: 43), while the press coverage of rape trials continues to distort and demean victims (Lees, 1996b; Meyers, 1997). As Brown (2003: 114–15) suggests, criminologists need to appreciate 'the many faceted ways in which violence is inscribed within media representations'. A focus on the diverse meanings generated by violence might also explain 'why the audience of a splatter movie react with laughter instead of fear when faced with violence, blood, mutilations and killings' (Schubart, 1995: 218).

Zygmunt Bauman's (1995) argument that the global reach of media technology has brought a new barbarism into the fabric of our everyday lives is especially important in developing a more nuanced understanding of mediated violence. Global news stories involving war, terrorism, hatred, killing and starvation have meant that now ordinary interactions take place amid this backcloth of cruelty. Bauman claims that the sheer volume of these images has a desensitising effect on viewers and produces a mass indifference to the spectacle of cruelty. It has been estimated that only a seventh of the world's population live in relatively secure democratic zones of peace, while the rest live in zones where warlords, random acts of violence, and civil and international wars are commonplace (Keane, 1996).

Michael Ignatieff's (1994) political journalism in *Blood and Belonging* has also described this descent into barbarism. For instance, Ignatieff explained that large parts of the former Yugoslavia were now ruled by figures that had not been seen in Europe since late medieval times: warlords. He described the warlords of Serbia and Croatia as 'bandits', 'criminals' and 'serial killers', wandering around a feudal landscape with their postmodern apparatus of mobile phones, faxes and state-of-the-art weaponry. Away from the roadblocks, banditry and visible warfare of the Balkans, similar processes are at work in Ignatieff's account. Germany, for example, is struggling to contain ethnic nationalism in its modern Western European form: the white racist youth gang. For Stan Cohen (1996), the atrocities that have become a daily part of life in so many parts of the world are a consequence of the collapse of distinctions between political dispute and criminal violence.

Nick Stevenson (1999: 132) has suggested that this spectacle of cruelty underlines the stark contrast 'between viewers whose main experience of violence is mediated and those who are living within the orbit of the constant threat of its eruption'. He further develops this point through a discussion of the study by Phillip Schlesinger and his colleagues (1992) of women viewers of violent films, which revealed that even 'the most sympathetic portrayal of women who were subject to violence was viewed by women who had had similar experiences with extreme forms of ambivalence' (Stevenson, 1999: 132). The overall concern, especially with regard to acts of sexual violence, even if they were negatively represented, was that they could be watched in a pleasurable way and thus legitimate violence against women in real life.

DRAMATISING CRIME, MANUFACTURING CONSENT AND NEWS PRODUCTION

Investigating the ways in which the press and broadcast news report crime is now an established field in criminology and owes much to the pioneering work of critical scholars in the 1960s and 1970s who sought to unmask the ideological role of the media. The central issue is not whether the media cause troubling 'copycat' behaviour by young people, but rather how the media promote damaging stereotypes of social groups, especially the young, to uphold the status quo. As Chapter 5 shows, Stan Cohen's (1972) formulation of moral panic has proved to be highly influential, as the argument is that the demonising of deviants serves to reinforce boundaries of normality and order. In fact, there is evidence to suggest that he initially intended the term to be 'a modest and descriptive one' (Sparks, 1992: 65), as he subsequently cautioned against being 'obsessed with debunking' (Cohen, 1985: 156), and in his more recent work he is concerned with explaining the apparent public indifference to media images of distant suffering through forms of 'denial' (Cohen, 2001). Nevertheless, it is important to recognise that in his and Jock Young's (1971) early studies there was a strong Durkheimian emphasis on how societies are able to cohere through uniting in moral indignation against deviant groups.

In this regard, both Cohen and Young saw that the media's need to maintain circulation in competitive markets through the 'ethos of "give the public what it wants" involves a constant play on the normative worries of large segments of the population; it utilizes outgroups as living Rorschach blots on to which collective fears and doubts are projected' (Young, 1973: 316). Moreover, this process was possible only through 'exaggerating grossly the seriousness of events' (Cohen, 1973a: 228). As Young then explained, 'newspapers select events which are *atypical*, present them in a *stereotypical* fashion and contrast them against a backcloth of normality which is *overtypical*' (1974: 241; emphasis in original).

The emphasis on how the media distort reality was subsequently developed through a neo-Marxist understanding of ideology by Stuart Hall and his colleagues at the Birmingham Centre for Contemporary Cultural Studies in their *Policing the Crisis: Mugging, the State, and Law and Order* (1978). In this book the somewhat vague Durkheimian notion of social control is replaced by a more rigorous concern with state power. Hall *et al.* (ibid.) introduced Gramsci's (1971) concept of hegemony to help us understand the timing of the moral panic that emerged in the early 1970s around mugging as an important element in securing consent at a time of political crisis. These have proved to be controversial arguments, and their analysis has been criticised for claiming that the criminality crisis over mugging was contrived by ruling elites to deflect attention away from the economic crisis facing the British state, while the authors have also been accused of ignoring the impact of crime on the working class (Young, 1987).

Nevertheless, the overall legacy of this approach is that it is a sustained attempt to analyse the 'social production of news' to reveal the ways that the media 'inculcate and defend the economic, social, and political agenda of privileged groups' (Herman and Chomsky, 1988: 302). More recent studies have qualified the conspiratorial determinism of these earlier accounts, but crucially, they do not reject the view that political forces and economic constraints 'limit access to the production, distribution and consumption of information' (Schlesinger and Tumber, 1994: 8). Robert Reiner (2002: 404–6) defines this work as 'cultural conflict', as it highlights the struggles that take place on newsroom floors between journalists, editors, owners and sources.

Yet while these accounts might portray a more fluid and contingent picture of news production, they do not fundamentally change the role of crime news. It has been argued that in the final instance the 'news media are as much an agency of *policing* as the law-enforcement agencies whose activities and classifications are reported on' (Ericson *et al.*, 1991: 74; emphasis in original). In other words, they 'reproduce order in the process of representing it' (Reiner, 2002: 406). In addition, journalists are 'better seen as bureaucrats than as buccaneers, [and] begin their work from a stock of plausible, well-defined, and largely unconscious assumptions' (Curran and Seaton, 1994: 265). These more recent studies continue to argue that the organisational requirements of news production reinforce a tendency towards the standardised and ideological nature of news content so that the state is able to secure consent for its actions.

However, some have come to argue that in today's news environment of digital, satellite and cable technologies, with news coming in many different forms, including 'serious', 'soft', 'hard' and 'popular', delivered online as well as via traditional print and global broadcasting, with increasing concentration of media ownership, new approaches to 'the complex and more differentiated field of news production' (Cottle, 2003: 16) will need to be developed. One example is the growth in 'alternative media' exemplified in the network of Independent Media Centres or Indymedia (http://www.indymedia.org) that came to prominence during the demonstrations in Seattle against the World Trade Organisation summit meeting there on 30 November 1999 to provide an outlet for the anti-capitalist movement. It has since expanded into 'the most thorough working-out on the Internet of the conditions and processes of alternative media projects' (Atton, 2003: 53).

Other critics have become wary of using the notion of moral panic, as it is often used indiscriminately and 'applied to anything from single mothers to working mothers, from guns to Ecstacy, and from pornography on the Internet to the dangers of state censorship' (Miller and Kitzinger, 1998: 221), and have insisted that the concept is 'deeply in need of revisiting and revamping' (McRobbie, 1994: 198). For instance, it has been suggested that the 1990s witnessed a 'total panic' around young people from alcopops through to the film *Trainspotting*, via riots on peripheral council estates to children murdering children (Brown, 1998: 46–52).

In order to 'revamp' moral panic theory, a number of authors (Critcher, 2003; Jewkes, 1999; Reiner *et al.*, 2001; Thompson, 1998; Ungar, 2001) have recently turned to the concept of 'risk society', as formulated by the theorist Ulrich Beck (1992), to try to understand contemporary anxieties and insecurities. For instance, it has been argued that the increased frequency of dramatic moral narratives in the mass media in the 1990s is partly a response to the increased pressures of market competition, but is also a key means by which

> the at-risk character of modern society is magnified and is particularly inclined to take the form of moral panics in modern Britain due to factors such as the loss of authority of traditional elites, anxieties about national identity in the face of increasing external influences and internal diversity.
>
> (Thompson, 1998: 141)

Chas Critcher (2003: 164), one of the co-authors of *Policing the Crisis* (Hall *et al.*, 1978), has conceded that it may well 'be useful to rethink moral panics as discourses about risk' in his recent overview of the topic.

Nevertheless, one of the main problems with the classic formulations and the recent attempts to refine the concept of moral panics is captured in Richard Sparks's (2001: 199) telling criticism that these authors remain committed to

> a style of analysis which treats the detailing of media "contents" or "mythologies" (depending on methodological preference) as a largely self-sufficient activity, and which tends to enter grand and mostly unsustainable generalizations about their hold on public opinion or their ideological predominance.

Of course, this is not to suggest that investigating media representation is un-important, but to caution against assuming a straightforward relationship between state power, media content and public opinion. It is also important to emphasise that the news is only one source of information about crime and that there is 'a complex intertextuality of media forms' (Brown, 2003: 24) that include film, drama, documentary, radio, fiction, 'true crime' and 'reality TV' and that media audiences commute between in their daily lives. It is to this diversity that we now turn.

IMAGINING TRANSGRESSION, REPRESENTING DETECTION AND CONSUMING CRIME

There is a sense in which stories of transgression are central to every culture's imagining of its origins, while the process of discovery is often said to be a universal function of all narrative fiction. For instance, detective 'fiction has been compared with the myth of original sin, the first loss of innocence in the Garden of Eden, and the myth of Oedipus, whose discovery of his origins is also a discovery of his crimes' (McCracken, 1998: 51). In Gladfelder's discussion of literary scholarship on the rise of the novel from the mid-seventeenth century, he explains how commentators were

> unsettled from the outset by the genre's concentration on the experience of a range of socially disruptive figures familiar from the network of criminal narrative: socially climbing servants (as in *Pamela*), illegitimate and outcast children (as in *Tom Jones*), runaway and fortune-hunting adventurers (as in *Robinson Crusoe*).
>
> (2001: 7)

Yet it is the pleasures and dangers posed by transgression and Otherness that make such narratives so seductive for readers. We will return to the ambiguity provoked by criminal texts later in the chapter, for it is important to begin by offering a glimpse of the diversity of crime narratives that can be encountered through television viewing, cinema-going and reading popular fiction.

To take popular fiction, the detective story is one of the most studied **genres**, as its origins are usually traced from Edgar Allen Poe's 1841 short story 'The Murders in the Rue Morgue', which organises the narrative around the intellectual genius of a detective hero, Auguste Dupin, who reconstructs the scene of a crime and catches the guilty party through the clues and traces left behind. It was this innovation that Conan Doyle was to translate into a commercially successful formula in his Sherlock Holmes stories, the first of which appeared in 1887 (Bennett, 1990: 212). However, in accounting for the development of detective fiction we need to recognise its rich social meanings, rather than simply celebrate the individual genius of a particular author. In exploring these developments, Carrabine, *et al.* (2002: 120–31) draw on the work of the literary critic Walter Benjamin (1892–1940) to examine how the 'private eye' of detective fiction complements the 'panoptic eye' of disciplinary power, through rendering social relations totally legible to the gaze of power, as it has been argued that the classical detective story embodies the totalitarian aspiration of a

Plate 18.1 The hitman as existential hero in the 1990s: John Travolta and Samuel L. Jackson on the job in *Pulp Fiction*, 1994.

Source: Courtesy of the British Film Institute. © Pulp Fiction, A Bond Apart/Jersey Films/Miramax Films.

transparent society rendered visible through the exercise of power and the registration of knowledge (Moretti, 1990: 240).

Yet one of the central themes that begins to emerge in the early twentieth century and continues up to contemporary representations of crime on television, at the cinema and in literature concerns the 'ambivalent but central place of the city in modern sensibility and the place of the individual moral agent in the face of social organizations too extensive to direct or comprehend' (Sparks, 1992: 36). In other words, a far more ambiguous and complex set of relationships obtain between the city, crime and detection. A sense of the range of narratives is given in Table 18.1, which is taken from Reiner's (2002) discussion of media representations of policing and will allow the reader to compare and contrast the ways in which class, power and place structure the various stories.

In his discussion of the concepts of narrative and **genre**, Nick Lacey (2000: 229) argues that 'the TV cop programme is one of the most interesting genres broadcast on television', as it 'is a genre that is continually being "reinvented" as new variations are tried in an attempt to replace tiring cornerstones of the schedules'. Moreover, there is an important sense in which 'detective fictions might be considered to be phenomena which bear the imprint of their times' (Sparks, 1993: 99). This position is developed by Charlotte Brundson (1998: 225) when she argues that the genre 'in its many variants, works over and worries at the anxieties and exclusions of being

Table 18.1 Law enforcement stories

TYPE	HERO	CRIME	VILLAIN	VICTIM	SETTING	POLICE ORGANISATION	PLOT STRUCTURE
Classic sleuth	Grey-celled wizard (usually amateur)	Murder by person(s)/method unknown	Personal motive – outwardly respectable	Exceptionally murderable	Respectable upper-class, often rural	Honest, well-meaning, rule-bound plods	Order – crime – red herrings – deduction – order restored
Private eye	Self-employed. Motive: honour. Skill: dedication, moral intuition	Greed and/or passion murder. Mystery not crucial	Apparently respectable and/or professionals. Several cross-plotting	Not always clear. Client (i.e. apparent victim) often morally dubious	Respectable upper-class façade masking corruption, and underworld links	Brutal, corrupt, but may be tough and efficient	Moral disorder – private eye hired – blows, brawls, bullets, broads and booze – use of moral sense – 'solution' – moral disorder continues normally
Police procedural	Routine cops, using footwear, fingerprints and forensic labs	Murder, usually for gain. Whodunnit less important than how apprehended	Usually professional and not sympathetic	Ordinary, respectable folk. Weak, guileless innocents	Cross-section of urban life, including cops' home	Team of dedicated professionals. Hierarchical but organic division of labour	Order – crime(s) – one damn thing after another – use of police procedures – order restored
Vigilante	Lone-wolf cop or amateur	Bestial behaviour by habitual, not necessarily economic, criminal	Psychopathic. Unsympathetic even if 'analysed'	Tortured innocents, though gullible	Urban jungle, ruled by naive, incompetent elite	Rule-bound bureaucrats v. wise street cops	Rampage in urban jungle – ruthless chase – elites try to restrain vigilante – defiance – 'normal' jungle life restored
Civil rights	Professional, dedicated, legalistic cop	Mystery to allow hero to exhibit professionalism	Usually personal motive, with modicum of sympathy to justify concern for rights	Respectable/ influential: strong pressure for 'results'	Unequal society. Money and status 'talk'	Servants of power	Unfair order – crime – innocent accused – professionalism – solution – fairer order

Undercover cop	Skill is courage + symbiosis with underworld: ability to 'pass'	Organised racket	Professional organised structure. Leader unknown (or proof required)	Ordinary citizens	Underworld	Team of professionals to give hero back-up	Order – crime – infiltration – hero's rise in racket – solution – combat – order
Police deviance	Honest 'loner' cop	Police brutality or corruption	Other law-breaking cops	Suspects or ordinary citizens	Police station + underworld	Rotten basket, or bad apples	Police deviance – investigation – control of deviance or of investigator
Deviant police	Rogue cop or Freudian fuzz	Police protagonist's brutality or corruption	Professional crooks who 'invite' his brutality or corruption	Suspects, processed by protagonist, or general public	Police station + underworld	Generally honest but bad apple(s)	Temptation – fall of protagonist – chance of redemption – redemption/death
Let 'em have it	Elite gangbusters	Organised racket	Known gang (maybe unknown leader)	Ordinary folk	Underworld v. overworld	Tough combat unit	Order – rackets – battle – victory – order
Fort Apache	Team of routine cops	'Raids', skirmishes with ethnic minority enemy	Ghetto toughs, and renegade or foolish whites	Ordinary folk	Police outpost in hostile enemy territory	Beleaguered minority. Camaraderie broken by discipline and deviants	Cold war – incident – threat of all-out war – troublemakers neutralised – cold war
Police community	Routine patrol cops: very human	Many petty misdemeanours. Tempt cop to cynicism	No specific person. Real villain is despairing cynicism	Ordinary citizens. Many are unsavoury 'assholes'	Police station/car, contrasted with city jungle and domestic tensions	Brotherhood, 'family' of disparate types	Picaresque. Will cop save or lose his soul?
Community police	Routine patrol bobby: very human	Petty, if any	Prodigal son, if any	Ordinary folk. Salt-of-the-earth types	Organic integrated community	Microcosm of larger community. Non-divisive hierarchy and specialisation	Order – everyday human problem – police use moral wisdom + social bonds – order restored

Source: Reiner *The Politics of the Police,* 3rd edn. Oxford: Oxford University Press. (2000: 150–2)

British and living here, now'. An indication of her style of analysis is given in Box 18.1, where she discusses the popular detective series *Inspector Morse* in the context of a broader discussion of 'heritage television' that offers 'a certain image of England, partly through its dominant structure of feeling, an elegiac nostalgia, and partly through its production values and export destiny, which offer the (tasteful) pleasures of money on the screen' (Brundson, 1998: 230).

BOX 18.1 *INSPECTOR MORSE*

Inspector Morse (Zenith for Central Television, 1987–93, with subsequent single films) was the most popular television crime series of the late 1980s, regularly attracting audiences of around fifteen million. Set in contemporary Oxford, the twenty-eight broadcast films were based on the novels of Colin Dexter, with additional scripts by, among others, Juliet Mitchell, Alma Cullen, Daniel Boyle and Peter Buckman, and starred John Thaw (Inspector Morse) and Kevin Whately (Sergeant Lewis). . . . For our purposes, the other interesting quality of *Inspector Morse* is the way in which, although it is clearly and firmly located in a present in which there are heroin addicts ('The Dead of Jericho', 1987), American tourists ('The Wolvercote Tongue', 1988), female pathologists (third season, 1989) and too much fizzy beer, it also seems to be set in the past. On the one hand, the high production values and the focus on the single investigator (with sidekick) link the series with other 'retro-crime' series such as *The Adventures of Sherlock Holmes* (Granada TV, 1984–5), *Agatha Christie's Poirot* (LWT-Carnival Films, 1989–), *Campion* (BBC1, 1989) and *Miss Marple* (BBC1/AandE/Network 7, 1984–92), many of which were also extremely successful, particularly in terms of overseas sales. This is the terrain of the private investigator and the English country-house murder. *Morse* is the only one of these series set in the present, but it shares some of the iconographic elements of an England of village greens, country pubs and yokel locals. However – and this contributes a pleasing tension to the series – the casting of John Thaw as Morse repeatedly returns us to the history of the police series on television, for Thaw's previous success as Inspector Regan of *The Sweeney* (1975–8) underlies his stardom as Morse, providing, for the viewer familiar with this history, a *frisson* at every burst of bad temper and the memory of another type of crime story. Indeed, the very first *Morse*, 'The Dead of Jericho', appears to offer a self-conscious recognition of John Thaw's generic history, opening and closing with Morse's maroon classic Jaguar smashed up in two different, unavoidable (and successful) bids to stop escape attempts by villains. It is as if we are being forcibly reminded that in the 1970s we watched a different kind of police series. Regan would not have given a second thought to the crashing of his car; Morse's pain is palpable, but the uncomfortable integrity of the two men is very similar. Jack Regan, dismissing the attractions of promotion in 1975, observed that there was 'nothing up there except ulcers and disappointment' ('Jackpot', tx 9

January 1975). Morse too is shown not to get promotion. The inference in each case is that it is their responsibility toward a higher morality rather than to their superiors, which prevents their elevation. While *The Sweeney* was aggressively contemporary in a way which contrasts strongly with *Morse*, the two share the invocation of what is presented as an old-fashioned integrity. The morality in both series suggests that individuals are responsible for their wrong-doing, even if only Jack Regan and Morse have the unerring gaze with which to detect this responsibility.

(Brundson: 228–9)

So far we have been primarily concerned with the representation of crime, but it is important to emphasise that particular cultural technologies, such as cinema, television, fiction and news publishing, each have distinct properties and histories that regulate not only the conditions of their production but also the manner of their consumption. For instance, television viewing takes place typically in a private domestic context and has a characteristically conversational mode of address, whereas cinema-going is primarily a *public* event and its typical mode of presentation is the single, complete performance (see Abercrombie, 1996: 10–12, who identifies at least seven key differences). In other words, while film and television might appear to be ostensibly similar media, as they combine sound and image, are used primarily for entertainment and information, and use the conventions of narrative fiction, we need to be alert to the distinctiveness of cultural technologies and be aware that readers and viewers deploy specific interpretative frameworks in positioning themselves between the world and the **text** (the word 'text' here refers to meaning generated through images and sounds as well as the written word).

An example of this is the distinction between 'quality' newspaper titles – the 'un-popular press' as they are dubbed by some 'lowbrow' editors (Allan, 1999: 112) – and the 'tabloid' news. Regarding the former, John Fiske (1992: 49) argues that a 'believing subject' is constructed who generally accepts the claims made as true, for 'the social reality it produces is the habitat of the masculine, educated middle class, the habitat that is congenial to the various alliances formed by the power-bloc in white patriarchal capitalist societies'. In contrast, he argues that

The last thing that tabloid journalism produces is a believing subject. One of its most characteristic tones of voice is that of sceptical laughter which offers the pleasures of disbelief, the pleasures of not being taken in. The popular pleasure of 'seeing through' them . . . is the historical result of centuries of subordination which the people have not allowed to develop into subjection.

(Fiske, 1992: 49)

While Fiske (1992) can be criticised for romantically privileging resistance, many readers will have experienced there own 'sceptical laughter' at some tabloid stories, and his emphasis on the pleasure of the text is one that has a considerable legacy in cultural and literary theory (Barthes, 1975). As Carrabine *et al.* (2002: 131–4) have argued, there are a range of psychoanalytical and sociological approaches to media audiences that criminologists need to engage with in order to understand the pleasures of crime.

One approach is to draw on Sigmund Freud's (1958) essay 'The Uncanny' – a term covering the unfamiliar, weird, creepy and dismal experiences provoked by reading horror stories. It has been argued that an important 'feature of the uncanny is the ambiguity of the known/unknown which makes our reaction ambivalent; we are curious and repelled, we feel both pleasure and fear when facing the uncanny in fiction' (Schubart, 1995: 227). This feeling of ambivalence is central, and arises 'not when we face the unknown, but when we face the previously known and now forgotten' (Schubart, 1995: 226). Horror is at its most effective when it is left to the readers' imagination to conjure up the monstrous. As Scott McCracken (1998: 50) argues in relation to detective fiction, 'we read for the uncertainties provoked by the mystery rather than the security given by the solution'. As has been recognised in the debate concerning fear of crime, the psychoanalytical preoccupation with subjectivity can open up new avenues for criminologists to travel (Hollway and Jefferson, 2000), while others have begun to unravel the ways in which anxieties around crime are intimately bound up with feelings towards place and changing fortunes in the face of globalisation and free market processes (Taylor, 1997; Girling *et al.*, 2000).

CRIME IN CYBERSPACE

We now turn to a key media technology that has so far been discussed only briefly, as the Internet is part of an information revolution that has crucial implications for representations of crime as well as offering opportunities for committing and being a victim of crime. The Internet is a global network of interconnected computers, and while rumours that

> it started life as a sinister US military experiment may be somewhat exaggerated . . . a computer network called ARPANET run by the US Defense Department from 1969 was a primary component of the super-network which would eventually become the internet, and the US Government was definitely interested in a network that could withstand nuclear attack.
>
> (Gauntlett, 2000: 4)

For some commentators, 'the criminal reality of the Internet is not the all engulfing "cyber-tsunami", but, like the terrestrial world, a large range of frequently occurring small-impact crimes' (Wall, 2001: xi). The types of activity that might be regarded as criminal include:

- accessing, creating and distributing child pornography;
- Websites espousing misogynist, homophobic or racist hate;
- copyright violations of intellectual property rights through 'digital piracy';
- electronic harassment (including spamming, stalking and extortion);
- hacking (encompassing simple mischief through to political protest).

[handwritten margin note: Misogynist – hatred of women.]

However, Douglas Thomas and Brian Loader (2000: 2) have encouraged us to regard cybercrime as 'a significantly new phenomenon', as the processes of economic globalisation, which are being facilitated by the Internet and Web-based information and communication technologies (ICTs), not only provide the conditions for the lucrative expansion of international information markets, but also raise, as Manuel Castells (1996, 1998) argues, the prospect of globally organised criminal networks.

The new ICTs not only make it much easier for criminals to bypass national boundaries, but also offer 'more sophisticated techniques to support and develop networks for drugs trafficking, money laundering, illegal arms trafficking, smuggling and the like' (Thomas and Loader, 2000: 3). Yvonne Jewkes (2003: 20–1) suggests that cybercrimes can be classified into two categories: 'new crimes using new tools'. These are crimes like hacking and sabotage through viruses, and 'conventional crimes' using ICTs, which include fraud, stalking and identity theft. She acknowledges that there are a number of additional activities that are not strictly illegal but would be considered harmful to some users, including certain forms of pornography and unsolicited email in the form of 'spam'. Her discussion provides a useful character-isation of some of the most serious crimes and harms posed by ICTs, which we now briefly outline.

Most public concern over the Internet centres on *child pornography* and the dual problems of illegal pornography of minors, and children accessing sites with pornographic content (Chatterjee, 2001). However, it has been argued that, iron-ically, it was online pornography that fuelled the rapid growth of the Internet and illustrated its commercial promise (Di Filipo, 2000; Wall, 2001), while demands for tougher sanctions have provoked fierce debate about censorship and, it is argued, reveal 'much about the fear of technological advancement and about authorities' inclination to police *people* under the guise of policing crime' (Jewkes, 2003: 22; emphasis in original).

The use of the Internet to perpetuate *hate crime*, especially from groups on the political far right – including neo-Nazi, White Aryan Resistance, Ku Klux Klan and anti-gay groups – remains largely unregulated, with several thousands of sites preaching violence and intolerance. As Brown (2003: 164) suggests, this 'immediately deflates the claims of those who see in the cyber a global community, for the "community", as in the real world, is itself the focus of political and pathological hatred'.

A major consequence of the information and communications revolutions is that they have significantly undermined *intellectual property rights*. The best-known case is that of Napster, the free music download service that was forced to suspend operating in 2001 when the Record Industry Association of America took it to court for copyright infringement. The numerous peer-to-peer file-swapping services that have since emerged suggest that 'digital piracy' will continue to undermine record company profits. It has even been recently estimated that 'something like 4 million people are online at any moment down-loading and sharing music tracks from which the companies derive no royalties whatsoever' (McNaughton, 2003: 6).

There are a number of forms of *electronic harassment*, which range from 'spamming' (sending unsolicited commercial email) to online personal defamation, stalking, extortion and identity theft. It has been 'estimated that up to 750, 000 US citizens will have their identities stolen in 2002 for the purposes of accessing credit card accounts, securing loans and cashing cheques' (Jewkes, 2003: 26). *Hacking* is an activity that involves breaking into computer systems and networks to 'embrace so many different virtual acts of sabotage, intrusion, infiltration, and "theft", or "fraud" that a unifying definition is not immediately apparent' (Brown, 2003: 157–8). In working towards a definition, it is important to recognise that the more criminally oriented 'are normally defined as "crackers"' (Cere, 2003: 152), while Paul Taylor's (1999, 2000, 2003) work rejects the dominant, contrasting images of hackers as either rebellious cyberpunks or microserf geeks trying to bring down governments and intelligence agencies, and instead repositions them in a male-dominated world acting out psycho-sexual fantasies.

Rinella Cere (2003) has examined the role of 'hacktivism' in circulating information and gathering support for radical politics and the anti-capitalist movement. She considers the uprising of the indigenous people, the Zapatistas, against occupation by a tyrannical government in Chiapas, Mexico, which began on 1 January 1994 to be the first political struggle to become a 'cyberwar' and contends that

> despite the difficulties of access and attempts at sabotage by the Mexican state, the Internet has succeeded in the promotion of passionate discussion not just about the struggle in Chiapas, but more widely about the failures of global capitalism and market-driven neoliberalism around the world.
>
> (Cere, 2003: 155)

Meanwhile, the issue of *state surveillance* of citizens has been a rather under-reported aspect of the new ICTs, but one that was brought into sharp focus by the events of 11 September 2001 and, in particular, use of the 'Echelon network', a US intelligence search system that is, it is claimed,

> used to monitor communications traffic (especially Internet and mobile phone communications) of European citizens, politicians and military personnel; a sophisticated 'eavesdropping' device that is justified on grounds of terrorism and crime, but has been found routinely to intercept valuable private commercial data (Hamelink, 2000). In addition, listening devices called 'carnivores' have been installed at several ISPs [Internet Service Providers] to monitor email traffic.
>
> (Jewkes, 2003: 30–1)

The implications of these monitoring activities have been understood as 'one element of the creeping normalisation of surveillance that embraces CCTV cameras, electronic databases, "smart" identity cards, digital fingerprinting and all manner of other innovations presented in the name of technological progress' (Jewkes, 2003: 34). For instance, the *commercial surveillance* of consumers on the Internet is an additional and rapidly growing phenomenon, ranging from so-called cookies (client-side persistent information), which give extensive tracking capacities to companies eager to exploit data on individuals, to the data-processing company Internet Profiles (I/PRO), which provides information on how well and by whom sites are used. I/PRO's clients are said to include Yahoo!, Compuserve and Netscape among others (Lyon, 2001: 102).

David Lyon's (2003) recent work assesses the consequences of increased surveillance in the aftermath of '9/11' – where consumer data have merged with those collected by policing and security forces. As with other developments, 9/11 did not prompt the introduction of communications interceptions, as it is one of the oldest methods of surveillance used by military intelligence agencies, but 'not long after 9/11 it became clear that forms of business analysis were being retooled for anti-terrorist purposes' (Lyon, 2003: 119). Taken together, these activities strongly suggest that criminologists need to be at the forefront of debates questioning what constitutes cybercrime and recommending suitable responses to the harm generated in cyber-space.

SUMMARY

1   The popular fascination with crime has a long history and the supposed harmful effects of the media on morality have been a recurring theme in social commentary.
2   This chapter has assessed whether the media cause violence through representations of violence and concluded that such arguments rest on idealised images of the past and are driven by a combination of generational fear and class antagonism.
3   In addition we have outlined the extent to which the news media produce negative stereotypes of social groups and discussed the arguments around the concept of moral panic.
4   Much criminological attention has focused on the news media. In this chapter we have also examined a broader range of narratives about criminality found in popular culture and considered how stories of transgression are central to story telling.
5   The chapter has also addressed the diverse forms of criminal conduct found on the Internet and concluded with a discussion of the recent merging of state and commercial surveillance activity.

CRITICAL THINKING QUESTIONS

1   What do you understand by the term 'mediatization'?
2   Why do present-day anxieties rely on idealised images of the past?
3   Do you think that the concept of moral panic has outlived its usefulness?
4   Are you a 'believing subject' of broadsheet newspapers?
5   In what ways, if any, does cybercrime challenge conventional thinking about crime?

FURTHER STUDY

Brown, S. (2003) *Crime and Law in Media Culture*, Buckingham: Open University Press. This text offers a wide-ranging account of crime and popular culture.

Jewkes, Y. (2003) *Dot.cons: Crime, Deviance and Identity on the Internet*, Cullompton, Devon: Willan. This is an edited collection of essays that provide important starting points for the criminological analysis of crime and deviance in cyber space.

Sparks, R. (1992) *Television and the Drama of Crime: Moral Tales and the Place of Crime in Public Life*, Milton Keynes: Open University Press. An influential examination of 'cop shows' that draws on social theory, media studies and criminology.

MORE INFORMATION

Independent Media Centre
www.indymedia.org
Daily articles produced by a collective of independent media organisations and journalists.

Media Studies.Com
http://www.newmediastudies.com/
A Website for the study of new media, with articles, reviews, guides and other resources.

Human Rights and Crimes of the State

INTRODUCTION

It is a now well-worn dictum that the concern with human rights has become a 'secular religion'. In the early 1990s, Stanley Cohen argued that 'with the so-called death of the old meta-narratives of Marxism, liberalism and the Cold War, human rights will become the normative political language of the future' (1993/1996: 491). This has materialised as the discourse of human rights became the dominant paradigm in the late twentieth century – and now the early twenty-first century – through which international and domestic conflicts are viewed.

In recent years, the atrocity of the attacks of 11 September 2001 on the World Trade Center and the Pentagon and the so-called war against terrorism that has followed, the war in Afghanistan and the subsequent treatment of Al-Qaeida suspects, and the legalities and ethics of the war in Iraq have all dominated the headlines. Unfortunately, persistent and long-standing abuses of human rights in countries such as China, Chechnya, the United States, Cuba, Iran, Israel, Syria and numerous other nations do not make the news. Human rights violations in practice are committed by individuals, whether or not they are acting on behalf of, or as agents of, 'the state'. However, the issue of human rights inherently involves 'the state' either as a guarantor – or protector – of the rights of its own citizens, or alternatively as the violator of the rights of its citizens, or the citizens of other countries. As Stanley Cohen also argued, in many countries around the world, state agents are the normal violators of legally protected rights for citizens (1993). It might seem self-evident, then, that human rights violations and state crimes are by definition congruent. Few criminologists, though, have explored the relationship between human rights and state crimes, and few textbooks explore the connections. This chapter seeks to discuss the links that have been made, and suggest some additional directions.

THE EMERGENCE AND INSTITUTIONALISATION OF THE HUMAN RIGHTS PARADIGM

The human rights story has been eloquently told by Geoffrey Robertson in his book *Crimes against Humanity* (1999). But it is instructive to rehearse it in outline here to set the context for the discussion that follows of criminology and human rights. There are perhaps two key periods in history that marked the emergence of the notion that individuals, irrespective of the state in which they are citizens, have some fundamental and inviolable rights. The first was literally a revolutionary period in the latter half of the eighteenth century involving the American struggle for independence from Britain and the overthrow of despotism in France. The principle of liberty of the individual as a precondition for, and a restriction on, the power of the state was a key political principle for which the revolutions were fought. They laid down a legacy of 'rights' that were the precursors of contemporary human rights as institutionalised in human rights legislation. The Declaration of the Rights of Man and the Citizen following the 1789 French Revolution, for instance, set down an influential legacy for rights in European history. Similarly, the incorporation of the 1791 Bill of Rights into the US Constitution left an immense legacy for rights in the United States.

The second significant period in history for the creation of a universal system of human rights lay in the ashes of the Second World War and the Holocaust. The United Nations Universal Declaration of Human Rights in 1948 was framed in response to the horror of Nazi genocidal policy (and also the terror of the Japanese military occupation of Asia), the inhumanity of the concentration camps, and the abomination of the gas chambers and other extermination projects of the Nazis that have come to be called the Holocaust (Robertson, 1999). The trials at Nuremberg of individual Nazis for their crimes, following the end of the war, laid down a legal legacy that led to the Declaration. Charges were called, for the first time, 'crimes against humanity'. The logic of the charge was that future state agents who authorised torture or genocide against their own populations were criminally responsible in international law, and might be punished in any court capable of capturing them. For the first time, it could be said that individuals had a right to be treated with a minimum of civility by their own governments.

With the Universal Declaration, the idea of human rights triumphed in principle, but in practice they were subsequently honoured more in the breach than in the observance in the latter half of the twentieth century. The Charter's pledges on human rights were severely restricted, in that the duty was to *promote* human rights, not to guarantee them as a matter of law for all citizens. Over the next half-century the UN Declaration would be flouted again and again with gross violations of human rights.

CRIMINOLOGY, HUMAN RIGHTS AND CRIMES OF THE STATE

In an influential essay written under the emerging movement of 'critical criminology' in the late 1960s and early 1970s, Herman and Julia Schwendinger (1970/1975) argued that criminologists should not confine their attention to crime as defined by the criminal law enacted by nation-states. Instead, they should apply a humanistic alternative to traditional legalistic notions of crime: fundamentally, they should become the defenders of human rights rather than guardians of social control imposed by the criminal law. Criminology was to become a political activity as well as an academic enterprise.

Herman and Julia Schwendinger's argument served as a critique of the neglect of human rights by academic criminology. Part of the explanation for the omission arguably lies in what David Matza suggested was the success of positivist criminology. In his book *Becoming Deviant* (1969), Matza argued that 'among their most notable achievements, the criminological positivists succeeded in what would seem impossible. They separated the study of crime from the workings and theory of the state.' In short, criminology had separated crime from politics. Matza's target was not simply the biological positivism of Lombroso but also the sociological positivism of the Chicago School and the later subcultural theory.

The radical criminology of the early 1970s began to shift the focus of academic criminology in part to crimes of the powerful. The excesses of the Vietnam War provided a momentum for an analysis of state crimes, particularly by criminologists in the United States. In his presidential address to the American Society of Criminology in 1989, William J. Chambliss hoped that his analysis of what he termed 'state-organized crime' would serve at the very least 'as a reminder that crime is a political phenomenon and must be analysed accordingly' (Chambliss, 1989/1994: 183). Chambliss defined 'state-organized crime' as crime carried out by officials as a matter of policy. In the words of Chambliss, by his definition it 'does not include criminal acts that benefit only individual officeholders, such as the acceptance of bribes or the illegal use of violence by the police against individuals, unless such acts violate existing criminal law and are official policy' (ibid.: 184). In his description of state-organised crime, Chambliss included state-supported piracy, narcotics smuggling, money-laundering, arms smuggling, and state-organised assassinations and murders. He did not, however, frame his discussion in the language of human rights, or even refer to human rights. Accordingly, Stanley Cohen (1993) argued that although 'questions about state crimes and human rights were placed on the criminological agenda by radicals . . . the human rights connection became lost' (1993/1996: 490).

By the late 1980s, though, the subject re-emerged from two directions. One context was external to the discipline, and lay in the growth of the international human rights movement. In Cohen's words,

> this is one way – from the outside – that criminologists as citizens who read the news, must have become aware of the subject of human rights violations and crimes of the state. Not that you know about this awareness if you just read criminological texts.

(1993/1996: 491)

The other direction from which human rights re-emerged in criminology as a discipline was, in Cohen's view, through the growth of victimology, in which there are many echoes of human rights in feminist debates about female survivors of male violence, debates about children's rights, and the concerns about the victims of corporate crime.

While human rights issues have not completely been ignored by criminology as a discipline, the connections between state crime, politics and human rights have been explicitly drawn by criminologists only since the early 1990s, although drawing such connections does remain a minority pursuit. Recently, some major directions have been taken, however. Eugene McLaughlin (2001) examines the issue of violent political crime committed by and against the state. He cites Max Weber's defining characterisation of the state (1958/1970: 77) as 'a human community that successfully claims the monopoly of the legitimate use of physical force within a given territory'. The state's monopoly on the legitimate use of force is problematic in a number of ways:

- State agencies such as the military or police can legitimately use force where it is defined as being in the public interest and is sanctioned by the state. This covers wars, anti-terrorist campaigns and public order situations. State officials can legitimately kill, injure, intimidate and torture people.
- The definition of what is legitimate violence is highly contested and ideologically constructed. This can be seen in the distinctions drawn in the media and by governments to describe politically motivated violence. For instance, terms such as 'terrorists', 'guerrillas' and 'freedom fighters' are in fact judgements on the legitimacy of the groups involved, even though they are by and large committing very similar acts. For instance, those condemned as 'terrorists' by some are honoured as 'freedom fighters' by others.
- While the actions of terrorists are condemned because they use terror for political ends and target innocent civilians, similar terror targets are used by governments, particularly in war. In fact, a major feature of warfare in the twentieth century was the targeting and terrorising of civilians as a legitimate military strategy, especially with the development of air warfare and saturation bombing. This happened during the Second World War with the destruction of Dresden and the dropping of atomic bombs on Hiroshima and Nagasaki. Of course, one moral defence of those actions is that they brought about the end of a war that had seen the Nazis and Japanese commit the most appalling crimes against humanity.

Another important direction in the incorporation of human rights concerns and crimes of the state taken in criminology as a discipline has involved the criminology of war. In 1998, Ruth Jamieson argued that war is an area which conventional criminology has consistently ignored, but there are at least three reasons why it should become a central area of concern:

- As an empirical area of study, war offers a dramatic example of mass violence and victimization in the extreme.

- Acts and violations in war are carried out through state action which in many instances should be more properly understood as state crime.
- War and states of emergency usher in massive increases in social regulation, punishment, new surveillance techniques and a corresponding derogation of civil rights.

Some notable studies have been undertaken in the field of what might be called the criminology of war. Kelman and Hamilton in their book *Crimes of Obedience* (1989) examined the My Lai massacre during the Vietnam War in May 1968 when a platoon of US soldiers massacred some 400 civilians. From this case and other sanctioned massacres they identify some conditions that enable crimes of obedience to occur. Zygmunt Bauman in his book *Modernity and the Holocaust* (1989) proposed that the genocidal extermination of the Holocaust was a logical extension of modern social organisation: a product of modernity, not a return to some form of pre-Enlightenment barbarism. The conditions for the Holocaust are precisely those that have helped to create industrial society, and include such things as the division of labour, modern bureaucracy, rationality, science, and so forth. The central part of his explanation of the Holocaust is the social production of moral indifference in modern societies. This indifference was created by the routinisation and dehuman-isation of the victims by ideological definition. Bureaucratisation was essential in this process, as the elimination of unwanted people was considered to be an administrative task. Stanley Cohen's recent book *States of Denial* (2001) provides an analysis of personal and political ways in which troubling realities are evaded, and how organised atrocities, genocide, torture and political crimes are denied by perpetrators and bystanders.

CASE STUDIES OF DEBATES ON CRIME AND HUMAN RIGHTS

As discussed above, the connections between human rights and state crimes became lost in the focus of critical criminology on state criminality. The connections were, though, pursued in scholarship on the sociology of law, social control and punishment (Cohen, 1993). From this endeavour, two case studies are provided below involving legal, ethical and moral questions about the state's use of violence involving, first, the use of torture, and second, capital punishment.

Is torture ever justified?

Writing in the latter half of the eighteenth century, Cesare Beccaria noted that

> The torture of a criminal while his trial is being put together is a cruelty accepted by most nations, whether to compel him to confess a crime, to exploit the contradictions he runs into, to uncover his accomplices, to carry out some mysterious and incomprehensible metaphysical purging of his infamy, (or, lastly, to expose other crimes of which he is guilty but with which he has not been charged).
>
> (Bellamy, 1995: 39)

In the twentieth century, the overt use of torture was universally condemned. Article 5 of the Universal Declaration of Human Rights states that 'No one shall be subjected to torture or to cruel, inhuman or degrading treatment or punishment.' The condemnation of torture is echoed also in Article 7 of the International Covenant on Civil and Political Rights.

Despite the universal condemnation of torture, however, it was notoriously used in the latter half of the twentieth century as an instrument of state terror to intimidate and silence political opposition in Chile, Uruguay, Argentina, and a number of other countries. (The chapter 'Torture' by Darren J. O'Byrne in his book *Human Rights: An Introduction* (2003) provides a disturbing catalogue of such use of torture.) In the twenty-first century, torture continues to be inflicted upon victims around the world.

Perhaps because it is such an abhorrent subject, few criminologists have engaged with some fundamental conceptual and ethical questions about torture. However, such questions are not simply a matter for internal academic debate, as they shed light on real dilemmas for contemporary criminal justice practice. Torture, to use the words of R.G. Frey, is 'the deliberate infliction of violence, and, through violence, severe mental and/or physical suffering upon individuals' (1992: 1252). However, a fundamental conceptual question to consider about this definition – and one that Frey raises – is precisely what counts as torture? Does it always have to include physical suffering? Can torture involve mental suffering alone? If it can solely be mental suffering, then where is the line to be drawn between mental distress that counts as torture and distress that doesn't? The 'good cop, bad cop' routine is well known from fictional representations of interrogation scenes on television: it is a form of mental intimidation, so would it qualify as torture too?

An important ethical question about torture is whether there are ever any circumstances in which the moral evil of torture might be inflicted so that good may come. An absolutist position on this question would be that torture can never, ever be justified: the pain inflicted makes it wrong in any circumstances. But a utilitarian consequentialist approach to the question would not rule out the use of torture altogether. Let's take a recent example. A case in Germany that came to trial in 2003 generated considerable public debate. In September 2002 police in Frankfurt arrested the kidnapper of an 11-year-old boy when he went to collect the ransom he had demanded. After hours of questioning, however, the kidnapper failed to reveal the whereabouts of the boy, who, unbeknown to the police, had been murdered by the kidnapper before his arrest. Fearing that the victim was in imminent mortal danger if he were not found, the deputy police chief of Frankfurt ordered police officers to threaten to torture the kidnapper to attain the necessary information. Upon so being threatened, he told police the whereabouts of the boy, who was subsequently found dead.

With media coverage ahead of the trial, the case aroused intense debate about whether the threat to resort to torture was justified, even though it is unlawful according to the German criminal code and the German Constitution, and contravenes international human rights provisions. Some commentators believed that the threat of torture was understandable given the circumstances. (See also Chapter 13 on punishment and Chapter 14 on policing.)

Capital punishment

According to Amnesty International, in 2003 the death penalty was still retained by eighty-three countries. China accounts for the vast majority of executions. Although records for the country are limited, Amnesty International estimates that in China in 2002 at least 1,060 people were executed. That same year, there were at least 113 executions carried out in Iran, and 71 in the United States.

Moral objection to capital punishment rests on the seemingly incontrovertible proposition that the death penalty violates the basic and universal right to life, and, in the words of Amnesty International, is 'the ultimate cruel, inhuman and degrading punishment'. But is an offender's right to life forfeited when they unlawfully take a life themselves, and hence is capital punishment justified? Some moral arguments suggest that it is.

One major argument is that the death penalty served on convicted murderers serves as a deterrent against potential acts of murder. This argument is concerned with utilitarian, or consequentialist, justice: in other words, the example made of the few will serve the greater good by deterring potential offenders who might be inclined to commit murder. There are, however, a number of arguments that severely weaken the deterrence argument;

- To serve as a real deterrent, the threat of punishment must be real. In some countries that retain the death penalty, however, the odds of a convicted murderer serving life imprisonment instead of losing their life are strongly in the offender's favour.
- The principle of deterrence works on the assumption that the potential for committing murder involves a means–end calculation, with potential offenders rationally weighing the odds of escaping detection against the possibility of being caught and a death sentence imposed. The offender makes a 'risk assessment', if you like: the greater the penalty, the greater the risk, the stronger the potential deterrent – in theory. However, O'Byrne (2003: 218) points out that most killings are crimes of passion. Others are committed when the offender is under the influence of alcohol or another drug, and others are suffering from a mental illness when they commit their crime. None of these circumstances involves a careful calculation of the risk involved.
- Other penalties, such as life imprisonment, may conceivably serve as a greater deterrent than the death penalty. Beccaria, for instance, argued that 'It is not the intensity, but the extent of a punishment which makes the greatest impression on the human soul. For our sensibility is more easily and lastingly moved by minute but repeated impressions than by a sharp but fleeting shock' (Bellamy, 1995: 67). Illuminating an inherent paradox in the deterrent effect of capital punishment, Beccaria further argued that 'if it is important that men often see the power of the law, executions ought not to be too infrequent: they therefore require there to be frequent crimes; so that, if this punishment is to be effective, it is necessary that it not make the impression that it should make. That is, it must be both useful and useless at the same time' (Bellamy, 1995: 68–9).

These arguments against the deterrent effect of capital punishment are essentially empirical ones that can be settled by comparing the murder rate in countries that retain the death penalty with the murder rate in those that have abolished capital punishment. O'Byrne (2003: 219) presents such a calculation, citing evidence that some studies have shown a decline in homicide after the abolition of the death penalty, and some an increase in the murder rate after the introduction of capital punishment. The deterrent effect, therefore, is not invariably borne out in practice.

There is perhaps a stronger moral argument for the use of the death penalty rooted in retributive justice (Reiman, 1988). By deliberately causing the death of another, the murderer incurs a moral debt: the loss of his or her own life is earned as a just desert. By taking another person's life, the offender has treated their victim as having lesser worth than they afford to themself, as presumably they would not willingly accept the same act to be inflicted against themself. Capital punishment for those who commit murder restores an equilibrium. The wrongdoer experiences suffering to the same extent that they inflicted upon another. The 'golden rule' of 'doing unto others what one would want others to do unto one' is restored, as the punishment impresses upon the offender that their worth is equal to that of their victim. It also has a symbolic value by reaffirming publicly the moral commitment to the 'golden rule' as a societal value. On these grounds, Geoffrey Reiman (1988) defends capital punishment in principle. He opposes it in practice, however, as in the United States, imposition of the death penalty is discriminatory. To take just one example: the odds of a black person being sentenced to death for the murder of a white victim are far higher than the corresponding odds when a white person murders a black victim.

THE STATE, CRIME AND CONFLICTS BETWEEN FUNDAMENTAL HUMAN RIGHTS: CASE STUDIES

At the beginning of this chapter it is noted that the issue of human rights inherently involves the state either as a guarantor or protector of the rights of its own citizens, or alternatively as the violator of the rights of its citizens, or the citizens of other countries. In some instances, though, where the criminal law is concerned, fundamental rights are thrown into competition. To illustrate this, two case studies are provided below, focusing first on the exemplary punishment of so-called hate crime offenders, and second, the criminalisation of Holocaust denial. In both cases there are claims that the criminal law overrides the fundamental human right to freedom of expression.

Punishing 'hate crime'

In the United States, most states have laws that impose extra punishment for so-called hate crimes – crimes that are motivated by hate or prejudice – in excess of the usual punishment for the same crimes when motivated by other reasons. (In Britain, offenders in racially aggravated and religiously aggravated crimes are given additional punishment too.) Such laws have been subject to a fiercely contested debate about whether they infringe the fundamental human right to freedom of expression – and, by association, the freedom of thought and conscience that lies behind expression – because things the offender says are usually used as the main indicator of the motives behind the crime. The right to freedom of expression is a fundamental right enshrined in article 19 of the Universal Declaration of Human Rights, and in the United Kingdom recently in article 10 of the Human Rights Act 1998 (Box 19.1). Fundamentally, therefore, the punishment of hate crime offenders is essentially a human rights issue.

BOX 19.1 HUMAN RIGHTS ACT 1998

Article 10: Freedom of expression

1 Everyone has the right to freedom of expression. This right shall include freedom to hold opinions and to receive and impart information and ideas without interference by public authority and regardless of frontiers. This Article shall not prevent States from requiring the licensing of broadcasting, television or cinema enterprises.
2 The exercise of these freedoms, since it carries with it duties and responsibilities, may be subject to such formalities, conditions, restrictions or penalties as are prescribed by law and are necessary in a democratic society, in the interests of national security, territorial integrity or public safety, for the prevention of disorder or crime, for the protection of health or morals, for the protection of the reputation or rights of others, for preventing the disclosure of information received in confidence, or for maintaining the authority and impartiality of the judiciary.

Critics of hate crime laws argue that the additional punishment of hate crimes over and above the underlying crimes amounts to the punishment of ideas (Gey, 1997), 'bad character' (Hurd, 2001) or 'certain attitudes of mind' (Phillips, 2002). In their influential book *Hate Crimes, Criminal Law and Identity Politics*, James Jacobs and Kimberly Potter argue that the laws provide 'extra punishment for values, thoughts, and opinions which the government deems abhorrent' (Jacobs and Potter, 1998: 10). In other words, the laws amount to the enforcement of a public morality by the state.

In this vein, one British newspaper columnist, Melanie Phillips, has suggested that hate crime laws are 'an Orwellian response to prejudice' (2002). A columnist on the *Boston Globe* newspaper, Jeff Jacoby, has argued that hate crime laws amount to an assault on freedom of speech and belief, and ought to have no part in the criminal justice system of a liberal democracy (2002).

Supporters of hate crime laws in the United States argue that the laws do not punish opinion – the thought behind crimes – or the motivation. Instead, additional punishment is meted out for the additional harm caused by hate crimes over and above the underlying crimes (Weinstein, 1992; Lawrence, 1999; Levin, 1999). Hate crimes allegedly victimize many individuals beyond the persons immediately at the receiving end (Iganski, 2001).

The contest between the two sides in the hate crime debate might be resolved by empirically demonstrating whether or not crimes motivated by 'hate' do indeed hurt more than when they are otherwise motivated. If they do, exactly what is the nature of the harms inflicted? Do they amount to something other than offence against the offender's motivating values, or in other words, the ideas in their head? These are the important sociological questions.

But the whole debate about the merits of hate crime laws may even be fundamentally flawed. Kahan (2001) argues that opponents of hate crime laws cannot claim that the laws are illegitimate because they take the offender's values into account in determining punishment when the criminal law generally does not, because the criminal law commonly does use an offender's motivating values to determine the seriousness of the offence and the appropriate punishment. In Kahan's own words:

> Conceptually and practically speaking it is impossible to draw a distinction between the harms that violent criminals inflict and the values that motivate them to act. Hate crime laws do punish offenders for their aberrant values in this sense. But so do the rest of the provisions that make up the criminal law. It's impossible to imagine things otherwise.
>
> (ibid.: 193)

To apply Kahan's reasoning, self-defence, for instance, is seen as a mitigating factor in terms of culpability for a crime even though the consequences of the crime might be identical to those of the same offence committed out of malice. Through the criminal law, states reward 'good' – or normatively desirable – values and punish 'bad' values. What do you think? Do 'hate crime' laws punish offenders for undesirable thoughts in their heads, or do 'hateful' motives matter in judging the seriousness of crimes?

Outlawing Holocaust denial

It was observed that although the human rights provisions enshrined in the 1948 United Nations Universal Declaration of Human Rights had a long political and philosophical provenance, they were framed in response to the horror of Nazi genocidal policy. In an insidious distortion of history, however, some people deny that the atrocities of the Holocaust actually occurred on the scale that they did. The modern human rights movement is therefore undermined by a questioning of the events that served as its instigator. It provides a particularly ironic test case for the conflict over rights because a number of countries – including Austria, Belgium, France, Germany, Spain and Switzerland – have made Holocaust denial a criminal offence. Offenders, however, claim the right to free speech.

Table 19.1 Estimated number of Jews killed by the Nazis[1]

COUNTRY	JEWISH POPULATION SEPTEMBER 1939	NUMBER OF JEWS MURDERED	PERCENTAGE OF JEWS MURDERED
Poland	3,300,000	2,800,000	85.0
USSR, occupied territories	2,100,000	1,500,000	71.4
Rumania	850,000	425,000	50.0
Hungary	404,000	200,000	49.5
Czechoslovakia	315,000	260,000	82.5
France	300,000	90,000	30.0
Germany	210,000	170,000	81.0
Lithuania	150,000	135,000	90.0
Holland	150,000	90,000	60.0
Latvia	95,000	85,000	89.5
Belgium	90,000	40,000	44.4
Greece	75,000	60,000	80.0
Yugoslavia	75,000	55,000	73.3
Austria	60,000	40,000	66.6
Italy	57,000	15,000	26.3
Bulgaria	50,000	7,000	14.0
Others (Danzig, Denmark, Estonia, Luxemburg, Norway)	20,000	6,000	30.0
Total	8,301,000	5,978,000	72.0

[1] With few exceptions there are no exact statistics of Jews killed. Thus all statistics are estimates.

Source: Adapted from Leon Poliakov and Josef Wulf (eds), *Das Dritte Reich und die Juden: Dokumente und Aufsaetze* (Berlin: Arani-Verlag, GmbH, 1955: 229 as reprinted by Paul R. Mendes-Flohr and Jehuda Reinharz (eds) (1980) *The Jews in the Modern World: a Documentary History*, (New York: Oxford University Press: 520).

In Western Europe, before the defeat of the Third Reich, denial of atrocities committed was heard well before the genocide had reached its full conclusion. In the years immediately following the Second World War, in the early 1950s, neo-Nazis in Germany claimed that 'the fairy tale of the 6 million' had been invented by the Allies to divert attention away from the atrocities they themselves had committed. The view was also propagated that the atrocities against Jews and others were carried out secretly by fanatics. Hitler, it was claimed, was unaware of their activities. Doubts were cast on the number of Jews murdered. Variants of all of these claims have been subsequently reproduced, and in the late 1960s and the 1970s a number of publications were distributed which have since become celebrated works of Holocaust denial among those who subscribe to the ideas. Today, a number of them can be read on the Internet by following links from the Websites of extreme-right groups. The publications are often presented in a scholarly format, but they are characterised by distortion and falsification of the sources used. In his publication *Die Auschwitz Luge*, Thies Christophersen claimed that Auschwitz was just a gigantic armaments factory. Richard Harwood, in his publication *Did Six Million Really Die?*, claimed that the 'myth' that 'no less than six million Jews were exterminated' was designed to 'arouse sympathy' for the State of Israel and to extract financial reparation from Germany. In France, Robert Faurisson even challenged the authenticity of Anne Frank's diary, claiming that it is a literary hoax. American execution technologist Fred Leuchter, following a visit to the relics of concentration camps in Germany, famously concluded that he could find 'no evidence that any of the facilities normally alleged to be execution gas chambers were ever used as such'. His report – the 'Leuchter Report' – has become another celebrated work among Holocaust deniers. Leuchter's activities have been documented in the film *Mr Death* (1999), directed by Errol Morris.

In Britain in the late 1990s the problem of Holocaust denial attracted worldwide media attention. Professor Deborah Lipstadt, Director of Judaic Studies at Emory University, Atlanta, was sued for libel over an allegation in her book *Denial of the Holocaust* that historian David Irving 'is one of the most dangerous spokespersons for Holocaust denial' (Lipstadt, 1994: 181). (For details of the case, see Guttenplan 2000.)

Just as a dominant argument for giving exemplary punishment to 'hate crime' offenders rests on the alleged harms they inflict, the rationale for outlawing Holocaust denial rests upon the hurt that it inflicts too. Distortion and misrepresentation of the historical facts of the Holocaust are both insulting and offensive to the memory of those who perished, those who survived, and their descendants.

In 1995 the European Parliament's Kahn Commission proposed that all member states should establish specific offences of Holocaust denial and the trivialisation of other crimes against humanity.

IS INEQUALITY A CRIME?

In concluding this discussion of crime and human rights, it is instructive to return to the arguments made by Herman and Julia Schwendinger (1970/1975), as they provided a major influence on some of the directions taken in criminology discussed in this chapter. One of their key arguments was that egalitarian ideals serve as human rights. There is a long historic commitment to egalitarian goals as of right. The *Declaration of the Rights of Man* following the 1789 French Revolution demanded that all 'persons are equally eligible to all honours, places and employments, according to their different abilities, without any other distinction than that created by their virtues and talents' (quoted in Tom Paine, 1791–2/1984: 111). This appears to invoke the principle of equality of opportunity, and such a principle – which some call 'formal equality of opportunity' – provides the moral framework for legal protection against discrimination in liberal democratic states, such as the Race Relations Act, Sex Discrimination Act and Disability Discrimination Act in Britain.

However, the provision of equality of opportunity can paradoxically comfortably coexist with considerable inequalities of outcome, and in fact it does! Philosopher Anthony Flew has argued that what has usually been meant by 'equality of opportunity' would be better described as open competition for scarce resources. The equality here lies in the sameness of the treatment of all the competitors in an open competition, and the only opportunity which is equal is precisely the opportunity to compete on these terms.

(1981: 45)

In short, equality of opportunity legitimises inequality. It is a conservative doctrine, as it preserves the status quo in terms of the social class structure. Accordingly, Herman and Julia Schwendinger argued that

If the traditional egalitarian principle that all human beings are to be provided the opportunity for the free development of their potentialities is to be achieved in modern industrial societies, then persons must be regarded as more than objects who are to be 'treated equally' by institutions of social control. All persons must be guaranteed the fundamental prerequisites for well-being, including food, shelter, clothing, medical services, challenging work and recreational experiences, as well as security from predatory individuals or repressive imperialistic social élites. These material requirements, basic services and enjoyable relationships are not to be regarded as rewards or privileges. They are rights!

(1970/1975: 133–4)

If individuals are not guaranteed by the states in which they live 'the fundamental prerequisites for well-being', to use the Schwendingers' words, are they being denied their fundamental human rights? And are they therefore the victims of state crime? These are questions that the criminology of human rights and state crime has not yet adequately explored.

SUMMARY

1   The issue of human rights inherently involves 'the state' either as a guarantor, or protector, of the rights of its own citizens, or alternatively as the violator of the rights of its citizens, or the citizens of other countries.
2   A focus on state crime reminds us that crime can be a political phenomenon.
3   The study of human rights and crime has been a marginal topic in academic criminology.
4   Much of the study of state crime has not been framed in the language of human rights.
5   When states attempt to guarantee the rights of their citizens, conflicting rights may collide.

CRITICAL THINKING QUESTIONS

1 Can torture be proscribed absolutely?
2 Are all violations of human rights state crimes?
3 Are there any state crimes that do not involve violations of human rights?
4 Are there any circumstances in which you think capital punishment is justified? Can you support it in principle but perhaps not in practice? Should 'hate' be punished as crime?
5 Should 'hate' be punished as a crime?
6 Should Holocaust denial be a crime?

FURTHER STUDY

Lawrence, Frederick M. (1999) *Punishing Hate: Bias Crimes under American Law*, Cambridge, Mass.: Harvard University Press. A comprehensive analysis of the case for hate crime laws.

O'Byrne, Darren J. (2003) *Human Rights: An Introduction*, Harlow: Longman. An excellent introduction to human rights issues and debates.

Robertson, Geoffrey (1999) *Crimes against Humanity*, Harmondsworth: Penguin. A highly readable introduction to the history and philosophy of human rights and their incorporation into international law.

Shermer, Michael and Grobman, Alex (2000) *Denying History*, Berkeley, Calif.: University of California Press. An accessible critical analysis of Holocaust denial and its proponents.

MORE INFORMATION

Amnesty International
http://www.amnesty.org/
A Website on the worldwide movement campaigning for internationally recognised human rights.

Death Penalty Information Centre
http://www.deathpenaltyinfo.org
This Website has information on issues concerning capital punishment.

Futures of Crime, Control and Criminology

CHAPTER 20

KEY ISSUES

▌ This chapter poses
questions about the
futures of crime, control
and criminology.

▌ It reviews links between
past, present and future.

▌ The expansion of the
criminological horizon is
discussed.

▌ Criminology is an exciting,
ongoing but continually
'unfinished' project.

INTRODUCTION

Criminology addresses a wide range of problems, issues and challenges to society. It investigates, and theorises about, crime and control developments that threaten and protect the social, moral and economic orders of life that we take for granted. Most of these challenges are familiar and long-standing, but the various media (factual and fictional) and their audiences are most interested in sensational or new developments – hence the fascination with serial murderers and the success of numerous recent films depicting futuristic scenarios of crime and control. In drawing this book to a close, what can we say about the current and future state of crime, control and criminology?

VISIONS OF THE FUTURE?

One starting question is whether we can identify different views about the 'futures' of crime and control, as distinct from views about the 'futures' of criminology. In some respects, for example, we might reasonably predict that whatever the future nature of crime and control, different but already existing varieties and areas of criminology will be applied and developed further in research and theory. So, one 'future' of criminology could simply be 'more of the same' but with interesting and important diversifications.

On the other hand, a more dramatic vision might assume that some of the 'big changes' in crime, control and criminology referred to in earlier chapters will see further amplification, eventually resulting in 'paradigm changes' (Kuhn, 1962) in the field of study, or, at the very least, profound changes and innovations in the types and characteristics of different criminological perspectives. In some ways this may be the vision of the future we want to hear about, because we expect the future to be dramatically different. But the future arrives only slowly, and even dramatic events are heralded by signs that should prepare us for them (though whether we always take appropriate notice is a different matter).

In fact, the vision of a radically different future in criminology may be harder to justify as an assumption than one might think. This is because if we look back over the twentieth century, for all the different changes in crime (and, equally importantly, in perceptions of crime), developments in understanding have – by and large – been the products of new variations on existing criminological themes and traditions. The fact that this history is full of references to 'breaks' and 'breakthroughs', new insights and new criminologies, and so on, partly reflects criminology's amnesia (Young, 1979) about the past, as old ideas and perspectives are recycled, combined, reinvented and renamed. To be sure, much that was overlooked or required serious and overdue attention has been attended to – the development of the feminist perspective being a notable example. But on the other hand, as several commentators have queried, what do we find that is really 'new' when we look at the 'new' postmodernist ideas within criminology? In fact, we find ideas strongly rooted in symbolic interactionism, labelling perspectives and media theories. In short, the criminological kaleidoscope (Downes, 1988) remains a recognisable mechanism within which existing patterns of problems, methods and theories receive an occasional 'shake-up' to produce variations on the familiar and, every now and then, the strikingly 'new' criminological image that shapes the view of new possibilities for a new generation (see, for example, the concluding section to this chapter).

On this basis, looking to the futures of crime, control and criminology could be a modest project that extrapolates from some current trends and considers how they may develop. This is nonetheless an important exercise, and we follow up the idea in this chapter, although readers of this book should by now feel quite well positioned to do some of this 'futurology' themselves. Our discussions of crime, control and criminology have indicated relevant dominant characteristics and trends, and so, with a little use of the criminological imagination, readers can assess for themselves whether certain kinds of crime or theory are in ascendance or decline.

This chapter is therefore organised as a kind of ongoing 'debate' between arguments that might suggest that 'the future will be much like today but different' (i.e. the criminological imagination of the future will continue to invent and reinvent theory based on theory from the past) and an argument that 'the future will bring momentous changes but its shape is unknowable' (i.e. features of crime and control will alter so radically that the criminological imagination will necessarily be stretched in entirely new ways). Whichever vision is correct, it is possible to argue that the project of criminology is continually 'unfinished' and ever-changing.

THE PERSISTENCE OF THE PAST

As in any speculative exercise, it is worth remembering that the future is not just about 'the new' but also about the persistence of 'the old'. 'The poor are always with us', goes the saying, but so are the rich, so there are certainly persuasive reasons (based on existing evidence and theory) to assume that some current patterns of crime will simply continue as they are. At the same time, some currently insignificant areas of crime may become important in ways that we *cannot easily predict*, while others that are currently neglected will attract more attention because of social and demographic changes that we *can predict*.

For example, on the one hand, in the United Kingdom (though not in the United States) early-twentieth-century concerns about links between drugs and crime had largely evaporated by the end of the 1920s (Parssinen, 1983; Lee and South, 2003), and thereafter for the following decades, right into the late 1950s, there was little evidence that could have provided the basis for a prediction about the worldwide scale of the drugs and crime industry that emerged from the 1970s and 1980s. On the other hand, there are a host of previously neglected issues that have come to greater prominence in recent years as social attitudes and tolerance have changed, media and professional attention has increased and the law has begun to catch up – issues such as child abuse, domestic violence, animal cruelty, and abuse of older people. Taking the latter, in terms of predictions it is easy to see that the growth of an ageing population in a society in which traditional family obligations of care have been eroded and demand for state and private care resources makes them increasingly rare and expensive, there exist the conditions that can produce abuse of older people. Hence, we could 'predict' that we will see more abuse of the elderly, but also, because more people are living longer, perhaps in need of 'extra' income and resources, as any savings are depleted and pensions lose value, we could also 'predict' an increase in the criminality of older people.

It is also worth looking back at the past to remind ourselves that our contemporary picture of crime is also shaped by how it has been responded to via social, administrative and statistical changes in previous decades. The ways in which statistics are altered – for example, to rationalise procedures or as a result of different ways of pursuing certain offences (see Chapter 2) – have a significance that can even distort our understanding of the social history of the past. For example, H. Taylor (1999) notes that the explanation from the Home Office for a dramatic fall in prosecutions for non-indictable offences between the First World War and 1930 assumed that 'society had suddenly civilized to the extent that wife-beating, assaults, truancy, drunkenness, immorality, begging, child cruelty, vandalism and other similar "minor" offences had really fallen by two-thirds'. Taylor argues that this seems unbelievable and that, instead, 'many of these offences must have continued to be committed but were probably dealt with by agencies or departments of government other than the police'. As we have seen in earlier chapters, changes in the recording of crime, the diversification and extension of forms of social control, the pluralisation of policing, and the growth of multi-agency responses to crime and social problems all mean that in the future, as in the past, it may not be as easy as we tend to assume to obtain a 'true' picture of the nature and extent of crime in society. For criminology, a general lack of appreciation of history (Carrabine *et al.*, 2002: 25–50) means that this is a point for future reflection.

THE EXTENSION OF CURRENT TRENDS

Generally, the extension of current trends into the near future might run as follows (South, 1997; Carrabine *et al.*, 2002). Left, liberal and right political perspectives might find consensus about some future trajectories of crime even if they differ strongly about the causes and remedies – although, even then, there has been serious convergence, and this itself is a trend worth watching. Agreement might suggest that the increasing growth of socially excluded, marginal groups in society will lead to more property crime, burglary, shoplifting, theft from the person, and similar crimes. A consumer culture, fuelled by diversity of choice, advertising and aspiration, aims to create, meet and stimulate the needs and desires of all, but it is only those with the necessary income (legal or illegal) who can be full consumers. We are surrounded by the signs and symbols of consumerism; the obsessions of materialism; the fetishism of designer-label fashion; the globalisation of commercialism; and the processes of McDonaldisation. A culture of narcissism (Lasch, 1979) values appearances, experiences, hedonism and disposable possessions yet still leaves people feeling unfulfilled, empty, in search of more. The mountain of aspirations for people to climb just gets bigger and higher. Writers from different perspectives within criminology, from Merton's theory of adaptation to the left realists and those interested in the 'seductions of crime' and a cultural criminology, have been interested in this kind of scenario. Those who can easily climb some or all of this mountain are the 'included' – the employed, settled, householding individuals and families, who also benefit from the peaks in the economic cycle and are sufficiently cushioned to survive and ride out the troughs. But for the 'excluded' – the poor and disadvantaged (see the discussions in Chapters 7, 8 and 12) – such a situation may be aspired to but out of reach. The coincidence of low attainment, poverty, poor housing and poor health, and disproportionate levels of petty and minor property crime can be common outcomes.

As Sutherland (1949) suggested so many years ago, the focus of the criminal justice agencies will be upon these offenders rather than those in positions of advantage who are committing crimes of more economic or social seriousness (see Chapter 11). Unless the future brings radical or revolutionary social change (see Lea, 2002), this is unlikely to look much different. The crimes of the middle and managerial classes are likely to follow, at least in the West, current trends – with respectable employees, professionals and employers being both victims and perpetrators of crime. As we saw in Chapter 11 (and see also Carrabine *et al.*, 2002), the pressures of domestic and global competition, the continued erosion of the bases and virtues of trust, and the inability of late modern market capitalism to regulate corporate activity, are all factors contributing to such trends.

Drug-related crime shows little sign of abeyance, although (as discussed in Chapter 12), at least at the levels of users and small dealers, it is likely to remain unclear whether involvement in drug cultures leads to criminality or involvement in crime cultures leads to drug use and dealing. This is important for a 'future' in which both the illicit economy and the drugs trade are among the major growth industries for the two will increasingly fuel each other. Regardless of this particular debate, the profits of drug distribution will continue to stimulate significant developments in criminal organisation, further diversification into legitimate commerce, and intrusion into political processes via corruption and economic influence (Castells, 1996). The local as well as the global dimensions of drug trafficking are complex and enormously resistant to legal controls, quasi-military interventions or development aid efforts. Criminal and legitimate enterprises blur with increasing significance (Ruggiero, 1996; Punch, 1996); global politics and financial swings can affect patterns of both legal and illegal trade and migration (Jamieson *et al.*, 1998). The breakdown of borders is encouraging more transnational crimes such as fraud, terrorism and extortion, directed against governments and corporations.

Armed conflicts in the Middle East, in Eastern Europe, in Africa and Asia remind us that crimes of war and violations of human rights are affecting hundreds of thousands of people on a daily basis (Chapter 19; and see Cohen, 2001). Similarly, crimes against the environment such as pollution and environmental exploitation, and resulting problems such as damage to public health and victimization of local populations, are now matters for international crime and control agendas to take seriously (Chapter 17; and see South, 1998a, b).

In this representation of trends, we clearly seem to have moved from a world of the past where crime was generally seen as a local problem to a new landscape requiring understanding of the global contours of crime. However, we must not romanticise or produce a cosy caricature of the past. Some forms of crime have always relied on cross-border markets. There is nothing new to the international dimension of crimes of war; the cross-continental slave and then drugs trades, while legal in earlier centuries, were forerunners of today's major international crimes; the development of international travel and means of communication has a long history, always facilitating crime along the way.

We tend to assume that the past rested on more solid foundations, where the differences and continuities between localities and the nation-state were well established, and tradition was a serious social force. Yet across the West, wars and occupations, conflicts between labour and capital, the rise and decline of empires, and so on, have all meant that the securities and certainties of the past may have been more insecure and elusive than we sometimes think. The path from the past to the future may simply be one of 'continuity of change'. Nonetheless, today, globalisation and glocalisation, 'McDonaldisation' and 'postmodernisation', 'wars in the name of peace' and 'terrorism in the name of religion', may all mean that the world around us is experiencing such change at a faster pace. Does all this create new contexts and conditions for crime?

THE PRESENT INTO THE FUTURE

Some politicians, journalists and academics have referred to the implications of globalisation in terms of a 'new world order', although, according to critics, the subtext is that the United States represents the 'new world' and will dominate the 'new order'. Even before 11 September 2001, and certainly since, it is probably more appropriate to see globalisation as accompanied by fragmentations, risk, corrupting influences and the proliferation of small-scale wars of violence and gross violations of human rights – in short, a new world 'dis-order' of expanding criminogenic situations and influences. Yet still, even on this new global stage, we can return to the evident persistence of global crimes of the past, changing but continuing as crimes of the present and the future. Drug trafficking and pornography distribution are obvious examples transformed by global transport and communications systems (for the latter, particularly the World Wide Web), while the human slave trade is an echo of a shameful past that has become newly profitable in recent years as a consequence of global inequalities that encourage the poor to pay high prices to be smuggled across borders. A further example of the past revived as a crime of today and the future is piracy. The concerns of the world of electronic communications about forms of e-piracy (see Chapter 8) seem to chime with our times, and it is assumed that piracy as robbery on the high seas is long gone. However, as Raja (2003) points out, modern piracy is in fact a 'booming, vicious business, netting billions of dollars. The gangs use speedboats to pounce on cargo ships, board them using grappling hooks, ropes or poles, and then flee with the loot'. Here, new gangs and technology simply update the old. In some ways, the 'futures' of crime, control and criminology can be mapped by looking at how old crimes mutate into new ones.

CRIMINOLOGICAL THINKING – PRESENT AND FUTURE?

Most commentators would agree that the past thirty years have seen major transformations in the nature of crime control as a result of a remarkable increase in post-war crime rates. The substantial escalation in crime has had at least three consequences for 'thinking about crime' (Carrabine, 2004).

First, it has given rise to intense debate on the left between neo-Marxist 'idealists' and social democratic 'realists', and, on the right, the return to biological positivism and folk demonism. Somewhere in between, according to current 'criminological classifications', comes the development, by officials associated with the Home Office and various academics focusing on the crime prevention agenda, of an 'administrative criminology' that has come to regard crime as a normal, if regrettable, outcome of everyday life. From a certain vantage point, all of this mix, dispute and competition makes sense in terms of how a 'postmodern' vision of the future of criminology might develop (South, 1997). The old-fashioned grand theoretical overviews that promised certainty of explanation (such as Marxism and functionalism) have been replaced by the fragmentation of narratives and a story of the collapse of deference, the embrace of difference and the disguising of difficulty.

Second, crime both in the popular imagination and in personal experience has become a central feature of public concern and cultural consumption. Moreover, certain kinds of 'hidden' crime, such as domestic violence, child sex abuse and rape, have become more visible, while forms of corporate, white-collar and state crime have periodically attracted sustained attention in ways that would have been unimaginable thirty years ago. Yet it remains the case that crimes of the powerful and those committed in the home are under-represented in recorded crime figures, and, as feminist research has consistently demonstrated, violence against women is widespread and exists throughout the class structure.

The third consequence of the increase in crime is the ways in which 'law and order' has become politicised from the mid-1960s. This was to prove a telling factor in the Conservative victory at the 1979 election and is now central to party politics. Through the 1980s it became clear that no political party could afford to remain silent on 'law and order' and it took Labour a substantial period of time to convince the electorate that it too could be 'tough on crime' while also being 'tough on the causes of crime'. From the 1970s, forms of government based on welfare state models of economic management and responses to social problems came under attack and were replaced by, first, New Right administrations, for example in Australia, Britain, New Zealand and the United States, and then by otherwise traditionally left-liberal governments that combined their revised philosophies with free market principles and traditional conservative values. In all this history of political realignment, the overt politicisation of crime and control was, and is likely to remain, fundamentally key to vote-winner strategies and social policies. For the future, the subject of crime and its control can only become even more a matter of political significance.

Returning to the theme of globalisation, all this is occurring in ways that mean what was once political rhetoric – 'declaring war on crime and drugs' – has come to be literally true. Broad support might follow the idea that, under the flag of international peacekeeping, military forces might be sent to intervene in cases of state genocide, but the question is whether the same support should follow use of armed forces by states (the United States, the United Kingdom and others) in anti-terrorist or anti-drugs activities on the soil of other countries? The debates raised by the invasion of Iraq and blurring of lines between military and criminal issues here (for example, one set of justifications for the action against Iraq in 2003 is that this was a non-accountable regime guilty of murder, kidnapping and torture) is an indication of complexities to come.

CRIMINOLOGICAL FUTURES?

Overall, these developments may imply that new ways of thinking about crime and control are now necessary – although bear in mind our earlier cautions about the legacy and power of the past. How these new 'ways of thinking' might develop is harder to know. An optimistic view might take the emergence of national and global promotion of the human rights agenda as a key starting point, albeit with realistic acknowledgement of the barriers facing this project (Cohen, 2001). Nonetheless, the gains of movements and success of some proliferating legislation concerned with human rights, civil liberties and acknowledgement of the victimization of minorities, women and children might be achievements we can project into 'one' future of responses to crime and violations. On the other hand, these developments based on rights and universalism are already matched by many other trends in the politics, practice and criminology of risk control that emphasise a need for future technologies and techniques that are arguably less liberal in their implications. To take one relevant future vision along these lines, we can move briefly into the world of fiction.

In Philip Kerr's (1992) dark detective thriller *A Philosophical Investigation*, he describes a future of techno-control of criminals, of sadistic murders by serial killers, and of life amplified by virtual reality. Kerr's novel has a nice joke about the search for the power of predictive techniques as found at the heart of positivist criminology (see Chapter 3), and in the novel, the Metropolitan Police Information Department runs the 'LOMBROSO' programme embracing: the 'philosophical' justification for acceptance of the principles of biological determinism; a computer analysis of a 'national survey of all British males' ongoing from 2010; and a clinical procedure to determine whether certain brains lack the inhibitors that prevent male aggressive behaviour. This is LOMBROSO itself – Localisation of Medullar Brain Resonations Obliging Social Orthopraxy. All marvellously impressive nonsense and yet . . . In September 2002, at a conference called 'Psychiatry and the Problem of Evil', Professor Adrian Raine of the University of California presented research arguing that 'violent and anti-social behaviour is most likely to have a neurological basis . . . triggered only when early brain impairment is combined with social factors such as breakdown in parent–child relationships'. The research identifies 'a distinctive pattern of damage to the pre-frontal cortex in murderers, suggesting the mechanisms inhibiting aggression were impaired' (Hinsliff, 2003). Elsewhere, 'computer forecasts that predict where and when crimes will happen by analysing past patterns' go beyond the already common police 'crime maps' that identify likely crime spots (Singer, 2003).

In Box 20.1, we provide several other examples of new and future developments taken from the leading science news magazine *New Scientist* and other sources. These developments again illustrate the importance of understanding the past and present to get a sense of future possibilities, for both science fiction and science fact can only take existing problems, issues and trends as their starting points and working material for new ideas, solutions and visions. Importantly, though, these genres can cross-fertilise, and one famous example is the origin of electronic tagging as an idea in a Spiderman comic.

BOX 20.1 EXAMPLES OF NEW AND FUTURE DEVELOPMENTS

'Pentagon creates a Big Brother so Uncle Sam can keep his eye on us'

The motto of the Information Awareness Office in Washington DC reads 'Knowledge is Power' and just a few months into its life, it's clear that the newly founded Pentagon offshoot aims to become very powerful indeed . . . the IAO has begun work on a global computer surveillance network which will allow unfettered access to personal details currently held in government and commercial databases around the world. . . . The system would also use video technology to identify people at a distance [and has been termed] 'Total Information Awareness'.

(*Observer*, 17 November 2002: 25)

'Surgical tags plan for sex offenders'

Britain is considering a controversial scheme to implant electronic tags surgically in convicted paedophiles amid fears that the extent of child abuse has been massively underestimated . . . the government could track the paedophiles by satellite, with a system similar to that used to locate stolen cars.

(*Observer*, 17 November 2002: 1)

'There's no pill for curing a hellish upbringing'

What makes some maltreated kids triumph over their early problems while others turn antisocial or violent? A supportive school, caring friends, perhaps the right social worker or a loving relative – any or all of these may ride to the rescue in particular cases. But if you're looking for a more reliable factor, try a brain enzyme called monoamine oxidase . . . research suggests that people with an abundance of the enzyme are more likely to tough-out an unhappy or abusive childhood and lead a normal life than those born with lacklustre levels . . . theologians and ethicists [have raised] concerns about [the] implications [of this research] for our understanding of free will and moral responsibility. . . . Many critics will look at the study and think it proves that science is still in thrall to its eugenics past, determined to put genetic makeup at the centre of complex social issues where it has no place. . . . Yet being true doesn't make a scientific explanation useful in practical terms. . . . These boys [the study was of male victims] are not victims of a toxic brain chemistry. They are victims of a toxic childhood. Take away the latter and you don't have a problem.

(*New Scientist*, 10 August 2002: 25)

'How radioactive fallout from the 1950s is fingering today's illegal drug dealers'

The fallout from cold war nuclear tests may prove the undoing of drug barons. Forensic scientists are using the rate at which the leftover radioactivity is taken up by living things to pinpoint precisely when plant-derived drugs were grown. Impurities such as pollen in a drug batch can be used to work out *where* a shipment was cultivated but knowing *when* the drugs were grown is also extremely useful evidence.

(*New Scientist*, 18 January 2003: 16)

'Moscow drama spurs hunt for "non-lethals"'

The world looked on in horror when Russian special forces stormed a Moscow theatre to try and free more than 800 people held hostage for three days in

continued

October [2002]. About 130 of them were killed by a 'calmative gas' pumped into the theatre to prevent terrorists blowing up the building. The incident brought into sharp focus the role that so-called non-lethal weapons will play in future conflicts and the very real risks they pose. . . . 'Non-lethal' weapons don't have to kill to cause concern. . . . The Veiling Glare Laser, for example, . . . is intended to temporarily blind its targets by zapping them with ultra-violet light that is supposed to make eye lenses fluoresce. Even more sci-fi is the Pulsed Energy Projectile, a laser that would vaporise whatever it hits. If that happens to be clothes – or skin – the resulting ball of hot plasma would knock people off their feet. Both these devices could leave victims blind for life which might make them illegal under a 1995 amendment to the UN Convention on Certain Conventional Weapons.

(*New Scientist*, 21/28 December 2002: 23)

RISK AND RISKY POPULATIONS AS THE FUTURE FOCUS OF CONTROL?

Kerr's LOMBROSO and the other developments described are concerned with a project that is at once both desirable and frightening. We want to prevent crime, but do we want to be able to do so by the use of a science of criminology that can predict from an early age who will, and who will not, be a good or bad citizen?

A common feature in much recent development in theories of crime, control and criminal justice is the prioritisation and pursuit of earlier prediction of risk in order to enhance response. The idea of 'the present' as one of increasing precariousness and risk is worth further examination if we assume it will remain influential into the future. This is not only because of its current wide influence but also because it is now attracting some serious criticism.

The importance of the risk analysis arguments, originally associated with the idea of actuarial justice (see Chapter 6) or a 'new penology', is that this is 'in part the product of a societal accommodation to routinely high volumes of crime, as well as of the refinement of professional practices for monitoring, surveillance and aggregate management' (Sparks, 2000: 131). In other words, the causes of crime are no longer seen as important. Instead, probabilities are central for a form of actuarial justice that 'does not see a world free of crime but rather one where the best practices of damage limitation have been put in place' (Young, 1999b: 391).

It is clear that writers on risk have identified a new trend in crime control. Crime has become a risk to be calculated, by offender and potential victim, rather than a deviation from civilised conduct caused by individual pathology or faulty socialisation – the hallmarks of traditional criminology. Instead, the new criminologies of everyday life see crime as an outcome of normal social interaction (Garland, 2001). What is surprising about these new theories is the way in which policymakers have enthusiastically taken them up and hence how the dystopian vision of Kerr's LOMBROSO programme might in truth seem enormously attractive to those in charge of the risk prevention agenda (for another fictional vision with a similar theme, see Cordy, 1999; for critiques of the Garland argument, see Matthews, 2002; Young, 2003).

RISK PREVENTION, THE FUTURE AND THE PAST

For Rose (2000: 7), a writer interested in Foucauldian (see Chapters 5 and 13) under-standings of discipline, surveillance and control, a recent resurgence of biological explanations of crime and deviance has coincided with 'a renewed emphasis upon the moral culpability of all offenders', all 'linked with some rather general shifts in the government of conduct in "advanced" liberal societies'. Rose argues that 'these new biological conceptions of the origins of pathological conduct focus on individuals, and are bound up with a new "public health" conception of crime control' (ibid.).

However, as Rose has to acknowledge, not all those who have investigated the idea of a future of control based on biological science and prediction see much to be greatly concerned about. Zimring (1996: 106), who has served on the US National Academy of Science Panel on the Understanding and Control of Violent Behavior, clearly doubts

> that genetics will ever play a major role in violence prevention in the United States. . . . The prediction of violence even in previously violent adults is an error-prone exercise. The selection of children at high risk for serious violence as adults is pure science fiction.

This kind of debate will continue, and is as much about politics as it is about science. What some may see as the excesses and extremes of social control, others may see as sensible and innovative new interventions. For example, Rose refers to 'biological criminology' as an 'element in the more general rise of public health strategies of crime control focussing on the identification of, and preventive inter-vention upon, aggressive, risky or monstrous anti-citizens' (2000: 24). For Rose, this is evidently worrying and represents the gathering momentum of new alliances, networks and techniques of control. Others might read the use and usefulness of biomedical, psychiatric and public health sciences and services rather differently, for example as ethically grounded and evidence-based sources of treatment, rehabilitation and intervention.

Whether 'monstrous anti-citizens' deserve to be identified and intervened against takes us back to some of the fundamental debates in criminology discussed earlier: the issues of labelling and the defining of crime and deviance. But at the same time, there are few positions that would argue against the idea that the 'monstrousness' of some crimes – child murder for example – requires deeper understanding and serious response.

So what are we to make of all of this debate and research? First, there is much to do. Criminology has many problems, but none is so great that it requires us to abandon the subject (Smart, 1990). Rather, renewal is one of the strengths of the field (South, 1997). The study of criminology is exciting and challenging. As Muncie *et al.* (1996: xxiv) have argued, there is and always will be an inherent tension in criminology between those who seek continually to challenge and expand the tradi-tional boundaries of criminological discourse and those who remain content to operate within criminology's self-imposed constraints. Ultimately, the tensions and internal debates within criminology may be seen as its greatest strength rather than a signal of criminology's demise. 'Criminology will always appear to be in a process of "becoming". Its work will never seem to be complete' (ibid.).

SUMMARY

1   This chapter has emphasised that the future for crime, control and criminology may be dramatically different but is likely to see more modest change.

2   Thinking about continuity between the past, present and future is a way of helping to think about how current crimes may mutate into crimes of the future.

3   New dimensions of crime, control and criminology have emerged around themes such as human rights and the control of risk, and there may be considerable tension between these two directions for the future.

4   Science fiction is frequently less far from science fact than we may assume.

5   Criminology is evidently a lively and 'living' subject – growing and revitalising, with both old questions to ponder and new ones to explore.

CRITICAL THINKING QUESTIONS

The 'big question' is – what do you think the future of

• crime;
• control;
• criminology;

will look like?

FURTHER STUDY

Barak, G. (2001) 'Crime and Crime Control in an Age of Globalization: A Theoretical Dissection', *Critical Criminology*, 10(10): 57–72. Examines the impact of globalization on both crime and crime control at the national and global levels and draws upon a 15-nation survey of crime and crime control in developed, developing and post-traditional nation-states.

Nelken, D. (ed.) (1994) *The Futures of Criminology*, London: Sage. Although getting a little dated as a book about 'futures' still a very useful collection covering various directions and debates, including postmodernist and comparative approaches.

Nellis, M. (2003) 'News Media, Popular Culture and the Electronic Monitoring of Offenders in England and Wales', *Howard Journal of Criminal Justice*, 42(1): 1–31. An article connecting a number of themes reflecting current practice in criminal justice, links to fiction and media, and to scenarios of the future.

Newburn, T. (2003) 'The future of policing', in T. Newburn (ed.) *The Handbook of Policing*, Cullompton, Devon: Willan. Examines the likely influences on the future of policing, e.g. demography, politics, pluralisation and outlines what possible developments may occur.

GLOSSARY

actuarialism   Probability calculations and statistical distributions to measure risk and which underpin correctional policies.

alcohol prohibition   In the United States, the 'Volstead' Act (1919) prohibited the sale and production of alcohol, leading to the 'bootlegger business', i.e. the illegal production and distribution of alcohol for consumption in secret venues, providing a highly profitable boost to the activity of organised criminal groups. Prohibition was repealed in 1933.

anomie   A condition where norms are confused or break down. There is a lack of normative regulation, which could lead to deviant behaviour. Merton produced a typology of responses to anomie.

bifurcation   Refers to the dual-edged approach to crime control whereby tougher measures are used for more serious offenders while less severe measures are used for ordinary offences.

biopiracy   A term given to the practices of some companies that have asserted the right of ownership over genetic materials taken from living organisms.

categorical imperative   A principle of moral philosophy derived from the Enlightenment thinker Immanuel Kant, who insisted that certain duties are absolute and unconditional.

classicism   The Enlightenment view of crime that stresses free will and rationality and the corresponding rationality of the justice system.

concentric zone theory (or **zonal theory**)   Holds that city centres are business districts bordered by a ring of factories, followed by residential rings with housing that becomes more expensive the further it stands from the noise and pollution of the city's centre.

constitutional theories   Theories such as Lombroso's that locate the origins of criminality in a person's biological or psychological make-up.

constitutive criminology   A postmodernist theoretical perspective on crime in contrast to a modernist one.

continuum of sexual violence   Ranges from the everyday abuse of women in pornographic images, sexist jokes, sexual harassment and women's engagement in compliant but unwanted marital sex, through to the 'non-routine' episodes of rape, incest, battery and sex murder. (Note: this is not meant to be a continuum that simply moves along lines of severity of the act.)

control theory   Holds that delinquent acts result when an individual's bond to society is weak or broken. There are four bonds: attachment, involvement, commitment and belief.

cross-cultural (or comparative) criminology   The branch of criminology that compares different societies and their patterns of crime and control.

cultural property   Movable or immovable property of great importance to the cultural heritage of every people.

decarceration   The process that refers to the deliberate move away from imprisonment as the central penal sanction towards the use of alternative sanctions, usually in the community.

determinism According to the positivist school, people become criminals through factors largely out of their control – be they biological, psychological or social.

deterrence Based on the idea that crime can be discouraged through the public's fear of the punishment they may receive if they break the law.

differential association Crime is basically learned in the same ways as everything else. Edwin Sutherland's theory came ultimately to be presented as nine propositions (given in the text of Chapter 4).

discourses Bodies of ideas and language, often backed up by institutions.

dispersal policy Introduced in the wake of a series of prison escapes in Britain in the 1960s, so that maximum security prisoners are spread around a few high-security prisons.

ecosystem The system composed of the interaction of all living organisms and their natural environment.

'effects studies' Studies that seek to establish whether the media cause crime through representations of violence.

emotion A mental state involving how a person feels rather than thinks.

Enlightenment thinking Thought that emerged during the eighteenth century in the West and that championed rationality, science and progress, alongside the importance of the individual and the tolerance of different beliefs.

epistemological Relating to the theory of knowledge.

ethnography A research approach in which the researcher participates – overtly or covertly – for a lengthy period of time in the daily lives of those being studied and listens, observes, asks questions, and collects whatever data are available.

feminist criminology A criminology that puts women at the centre of the analysis.

free will According to the classical school, people possess reason. This means that they can calculate the course of action that is in their self-interest. This in turn gives them a degree of freedom.

functionalist perspective A theory that looks at the ways in which societies become integrated as their various parts perform various functions.

gender-aware criminology A criminology that puts gender at the centre of the analysis.

genres One of the ways in which differences between narratives can be defined through identifying the conventions that other texts in the same grouping share.

globalisation of crime The increasing interconnectedness of crime across societies.

green crimes Crimes against the environment.

green criminology A reappraisal of more traditional notions of crimes, offences and injurious behaviours and an examination of the role that societies (including corporations and governments) play in generating environmental degradation.

harm reduction As an alternative to insistence on abstaining from drug use, this is an approach to working with users to minimise the possibility of serious harms such as AIDS or overdose.

hierarchy of victimization A concept that captures the unequal status that victims experience in the crime discourse and in the treatment by criminal justice agencies. Those at the top are regarded as innocent and deserving of help and sympathy, those at the bottom less so.

human rights Rights that belong to all people.

humiliation The experience of a loss of respect or self-esteem.

instrumental laws Laws whose aim is practical: to bring about some specific desired effect such as the stopping of rape.

just deserts A justification for punishment which insists that offenders should be punished only as severely as they deserve. It was a reaction against the unfair excesses of rehabilitation and the 'get tough' drive from conservatives during the 1970s.

labelling theory Highlights social reaction and suggests that crime may be heightened by criminal sanctions.

late modernity One of many concepts used to characterise a new emerging social order after modernity and capitalism.

legitimacy In the context of prisons, the process whereby institutional power gains a moral grounding through prisoners consenting to the authority of staff and regimes.

less eligibility A penal doctrine which maintains that offenders should endure harsher institutional regimes than the poorest free citizens.

McDonaldisation The principles of the fast food industry become increasingly applied to all of social life.

marginalisation A state in which people live on the edge of society and outside the mainstream with little stake in society overall.

mediatisation Refers to the process whereby the rapid expansion of the media has undermined distinctions between image and reality.

Megan's law Named after Megan Kanka, a 7-year-old girl from New Jersey who was sexually assaulted and killed by a convicted sex offender living in the same street.

moral panic The heightened awareness of certain problems relating to crime at key moments.

negotiated justice The construction of cases, negotiations (e.g. between the defence and prosecution) and social interaction involved in the routine production of justice.

neutralisation, techniques of A series of strategies through which the individual's 'bond' to society is weakened, hence making that individual more likely to commit crime.

'normalisation' Although not everyone is now a drug user, nevertheless (the argument runs) it is now non-acquaintance with drugs or drug users that has become the deviation from the norm. The drugs in question are usually those associated with leisure cultures, such as cannabis, Ecstasy, amphetamines or cocaine. Others reject the idea: particularly for the majority of young people, persisting prohibitions, peer-group resistance, parental attachment and preference for alternative activities remain central to their lives. Both arguments appear to have some validity.

occupational culture The values, norms, perspectives and informal rules that can inform the conduct of those engaged in a particular occupation (in the context of this book, the police). It has many variations and can change according to particular situations and the interactional processes of each encounter.

paradigm A general view of how the world works.

partisan One-sided; adhering to a particular cause.

patriarchies Systems of male dominance that serve the interests of men.

police A state-organised institution with specific powers and a mandate to prevent and investigate crime or disorder.

police accountability The institutional arrangements made to ensure that the police do the job required of them.

policing A set of activities aimed at maintaining security and the social order through surveillance and the threat of sanctioning. It can be carried out by a variety of people and techniques.

positivism In criminology, 'positivism' highlights (a) scientific methods in the study of crime; (b) the importance of criminal types; and (c) theories of cause or aetiology.

postmodernism Grand or absolute truths are challenged, and in their place we find partial and limited truths: a much less certain and more provisional view of the world is in the making.

primary and secondary deviance The distinction between original and effective causes of deviance: primary deviation arises from many sources and is minor and insignificant; secondary deviation is pivotal because stigma and punishment make it so.

primary and secondary victimization Primary victimization refers to the direct impact of crime on the victims while secondary victimization refers to additional negative impact resulting from the way others (especially criminal justice agencies) respond to them and the crime.

primary green crimes Crimes that degrade the environment, as for example actions that pollute the air or water, or result in a decline in the number of species – biodiversity.

procedural justice Formal adherence to legal rules and safeguards throughout the criminal justice process and the impartial application of neutral criteria in criminal justice decision-making.

process of attrition The process of filtering of cases at different stages of the criminal justice process.

Prohibition See **alcohol prohibition.**

property crime Stealing and dishonestly obtaining or damaging another's property, which includes both tangible goods and intangible property.

reductivist Refers to justifications of punishment that regard the prevention of future crimes as the moral basis on which to base systems of punishment.

rehabilitation Based on the idea that punishment can reduce crime if it takes a form that will improve the individual's character so that they are less likely to reoffend in the future. It tends to view criminal behaviour not as freely willed action but as a symptom of some kind of causal factor, whether this be economic, social or personal.

relative deprivation A perceived disadvantage arising from a specific comparison.

repeat victimization Occurs when the same location, person, household, business or vehicle suffers more than one crime event over a specified period of time.

respect Deference, esteem and regard.

retributivist Justifications of punishment that insist that only the crimes of the past should be punished.

rights Claims supported by some justification.

risk society Beck's idea that modern industrial societies create many new risks – on a global scale and largely manufactured through modern technologies – that were unknown in earlier days. Examples include nuclear war and environmental pollution.

secondary deviance *See* **primary and secondary deviance**

secondary victimization *See* **primary and secondary victimisation**

self-esteem A positive opinion about oneself.

sexual script Sexuality is seen as not simply biological, but also connected to social meanings. Scripts help define the who, what, where, when and why of sexual conduct.

shame A painful emotion arising from an awareness of inadequacy, guilt or dishonour.

social solidarity A key element of Durkheim's sociology, it refers to the sources of integration that preserve social stability and promote moral consensus in the face of rapid economic change and political upheaval.

substantive justice Just and effective outcomes of criminal justice decision-making that take into account social inequalities and their impact on different social groups.

survey Systematic data collection about the same variables or characteristics from a number of respondents or cases.

symbiotic or secondary green crimes Ways in which existing criminal networks exploit degradations of the environment still further (e.g. through the trading of the products of organised green crimes, say in animals, products, or through the illegal dumping of waste products).

symbolic laws Laws that act to highlight (symbolise) key issues. They may serve as a litmus test for many moral panics and discourses that tap into a wide range of social anxieties.

temperance The commitment to abstinence from alcoholic drink, associated in particular with early-twentieth-century social and religious movements.

text Implies not simply a novel or the written word in general but that all cultural objects generate meaning, which can equally be through images or sounds as well as the written word.

transcarceration The movement of offenders between different institutional sites, state agencies and correctional programmes, so that the network of social control is expanded rather than reduced.

transgression The act of overstepping boundaries or limits established by rules, laws, principles, custom, convention or tradition.

victimology An area of study that is concerned with the victim of crime. Often described as a subdiscipline of criminology.

working rules Rules that those following a particular occupation – in this case, that of police officer – internalise so that they become the effective principles that guide their decisions and actions.

BIBLIOGRAPHY

Abercrombie, N. (1996) *Television and Society*, Cambridge: Polity.

Abraham, J. (1995) *Science, Politics and the Pharmaceutical Industry: Controversy and Bias in Drug Regulation*, New York: UCL/St Martin's Press.

Acheson, D. (1998) *Health Inequalities*, London: Department of Health.

Adam, B., Beck, U. and Van Loon, J. (eds) (2000) *The Risk Society and Beyond*, London: Sage.

Adams, R. (1992) *Prison Riots in Britain and the USA*, Basingstoke: Macmillan.

Adler, P. A. and Adler, P. (1998) 'Forward: Moving Backward', in J. Ferrell and M. Hamm (eds) *Ethnography at the Edge: Crime, Deviance and Field Research*, Boston: Northeastern University Press.

Albrow, M. (1990) *The Global Age*, Cambridge: Polity.

Alcohol Concern (2001) www.alcoholconcern.org.uk/

All Party Group on Alcohol Misuse (1995) *Alcohol and Crime: Breaking the Link*, London, Alcohol Concern.

Allan, S. (1999) *News Culture*, Buckingham: Open University Press.

Allen, B. (1996) *Rape Warfare: The Hidden Genocide in Bosnia-Herzegovina and Croatia*, Minneapolis: University of Minnesota Press.

Allen, H. (1987) *Justice Unbalanced*, Milton Keynes: Open University Press.

Altman, D. (2001) *Global Sex*, Chicago: University of Chicago Press.

Alubo, S. O. (1994) 'Death for Sale: A Case Study of Drug Poisoning and Deaths in Nigeria', *Social Science and Medicine*, 38 (1): 97–103.

Amir, M. (1971) *Patterns of Forcible Rape*, Chicago: University of Chicago Press.

Amnesty International (2001) *Crimes of Hate: Conspiracies of Silence*, London: Amnesty International.

Anderson, E. (1994) 'The Code of Streets', *Atlantic Monthly*, 5: 80–94.

Anderson, E. (1999) *Code of the Streets: Decency, Violence and the Moral Life of the Inner City*, New York: W. W. Norton.

Anderson, N. (1923) *The Hobo: The Sociology of the Homeless Man*, Chicago: University of Chicago Press.

Anderson, R., Brown, J. and Campbell, E. (1993) *Aspects of Sex Discrimination within the Police Service in England and Wales*, London: Home Office Police Research Group.

Anderson, S., Kinsey, R., Loader, I. and Smith, C. (1994) *Cautionary Tales: Young People, Crime and Policing in Edinburgh*, Aldershot: Avebury.

Arrigo, B. (1997) Review of Stuart Henry and Dragan Milovanovic's *Constitutive Criminology*, *Theoretical Criminology*, 3: 392–6.

Ashworth, A. (1986) 'Punishment and Compensation: Victims, Offenders and the State', *Oxford Journal of Legal Studies*, 6: 86–122.

Ashworth, A. (1993) 'Victim Impact Statements and Sentencing', *Criminal Law Review*, 498–509.

Ashworth, A. (1998) *The Criminal Process*, 2nd edn, Oxford: Oxford University Press.

Ashworth, A. (2003) 'Is Restorative Justice the Way Forward for Criminal Justice?', in E., McLaughlin, R. Fergusson, G. Hughes and L. Westmarland (eds) *Restorative Justice: Critical Issues*, London: Sage.

Atton, C. (2003) 'Organization and Production in Alternative Media', in S. Cottle (ed.) *Media Organization and Production*, London: Sage.

Audit Commission (1993) *Helping with Enquiries: Tackling Crime Effectively*, London: HMSO.

Audit Commission (1996) *Streetwise: Effective Police Patrol*, London: HMSO.

Auld, J., Dorn, N. and South, N. (1986) 'Irregular Work, Irregular Pleasures: Heroin in the 1980s', in R. Matthews and J. Young (eds) *Confronting Crime*, London: Sage.

Baird, V. (2001) *The No-Nonsense Guide to Sexual Diversity*, London: New Internationalist/Verso.

Bakhtin, M. (1984) *Rabelais and His World*, Bloomington: Indiana University Press.

Balding, J. (2000) *Young People and Illegal Drugs into 2000*, Exeter: Schools Health Education Unit.

Baldwin, J. and McConville, M. (1977) *Negotiated Justice*, London: Martin Robertson.

Bales, K. (1999) *Disposable People: New Slavery in the Global Economy*, Berkeley: University of California Press.

Banton, M. (1964) *The Policeman in the Community*, London: Tavistock.

Barak, G. (ed.) (1994) *Media, Process, and the Social Construction of Crime: Studies in Newsmaking Criminology*, New York: Garland.

Barak, G. (2001) 'Crime and Crime Control in an Age of Globalization: A Theoretical Dissection', *Critical Criminology*, 10 (10): 57–72.

Barbalet, J. (2002) 'Moral Indignation, Class Inequality and Justice: An Exploration and Revision of Ranulf', *Theoretical Criminology*, 6 (3): 279–97.

Barclay, G., Tavares, C. and Siddique, A. (2001) *International Comparisons of Criminal Justice Statistics 1999*, Home Office Statistics Bulletin, Issue 6/01, May, London: Home Office.

Barker, M. and Petley, J. (eds) (1997) *Ill Effects: The Media/Violence Debate*, London: Routledge.

Barthes, R. (1975) *The Pleasure of the Text*, New York: Hill and Wang.

Barton, B. F. and Barton, M. S. (1993) 'Modes of Power in Technical and Professional Visuals', *Journal of Business and Technical Communication*, 7 (1): 138–62.

Bauman, Z. (1989) *Modernity and the Holocaust*, Cambridge: Polity.

Bauman, Z. (1992) *Intimations of Postmodernity*, London: Routledge.

Bauman, Z. (1995) *Life in Fragments: Essays in Postmodern Morality*, Oxford: Blackwell.

Bauman, Z. (1998) *Globalization: The Human Consequences*, Cambridge: Polity.

Bayley, D. H. (1994) *Police for the Future*, New York: Oxford University Press.

Baylis, J. and Smith, S. (eds) (1997) *The Globalization of World Politics*, Oxford: Oxford University Press.

Bazemore, G. and Taylor-Griffiths C. (2003) 'Conferences, Circles, Boards, and Mediations: The "New Wave" of Community Justice Decisionmaking', in E. McLaughlin, R. Fergusson, G. Hughes and L. Westmarland (eds) *Restorative Justice: Critical Issues*, London: Sage.

Bean, P. (2002) *Drugs and Crime*, Cullompton, Devon: Willan.

Beck, U. (1992) *Risk Society: Towards a New Modernity*, London: Sage.

Beck, U. (1995) *Ecological Politics in an Age of Risk*, Cambridge: Polity.

Beck, U. (2000) *World Risk Society*, Cambridge: Polity.

Becker, H. S. (1963) *Outsiders: Studies in the Sociology of Deviance*, New York: Free Press.

Becker, H. (1967) 'Whose Side Are We On?', *Social Problems*, 14: 239–47.

Beirne, P. (1993) *Inventing Criminology: Essays on the Rise of 'Homo Criminalis'*, Albany: State University of New York Press.

Bellamy, R. (ed.) (1995) *Beccaria: On Crimes and Punishments and Other Writings*, Cambridge: Cambridge University Press.

Bennett, T. (1990) 'Knowledge, Power, Ideology: Detective Fiction', in T. Bennett (ed.) *Popular Fiction: Technology, Ideology, Production, Reading*, London: Routledge.

Bennett, T., Holloway, K. and Williams, T. (2001) *Drug Use and Offending*, Findings 148, London: Home Office.

Bentham, J. (1789/1970) *An Introduction to the Principles of Morals and Legislation*, ed. J. H. Burns and H. L. A. Hart, London: Athlone.

Benton, T. (1984) *The Rise and Fall of Structural Marxism: Althusser and His Influence*, Basingstoke: Macmillan.

Berridge, V. (1984) 'Drugs and Social Policy: The Establishment of Drug Control in Britain, 1900–1930', *British Journal of Addiction*, 79: 1.

Berridge, V. (1999) *Opium and the People*, rev. ed., London: Free Association Books.

Best, J. (1990) *Threatened Children: Rhetoric and Concern about Child Victims*, Chicago: University of Chicago Press.

Best, J. (2001) *Damned Lies and Statistics*, Berkeley, CA: University of California Press.

Biegel, S. (2001) *Beyond Our Control? Confronting the Limits of Our Legal System in the Age of Cyberspace*, Cambridge, MA: MIT Press.

Biggs, S., Phillipson, C. and Kingston, P. (1995) *Elder Abuse in Perspective*, Buckingham: Open University Press.

Blum, J., Levi, M., Naylor, R. and Williams, P. (1998) *Financial Havens, Banking Secrecy and Money Laundering*, New York: United Nations Office for Drug Control and Crime Prevention.

Bishop, R. and Robinson, L. (1998) *Night Market: Sexual Cultures and the Thai Economic Miracle*, London: Routledge.

Bittner, E. (1967) 'The Police on Skid Row: A Study in Peacekeeping', *American Sociological Review*, 32: 699–715.

Bittner, E. (1974) 'Florence Nightingale in Pursuit of Willie Sutton: A Theory of the Police', in H. Jacob (ed.) *The Potential for Reform of Criminal Justice*, Beverly Hills, CA: Sage.

Block, A. (1993) 'Defending the Mountaintop: A Campaign against Environmental Crime', in F. Pearce and M. Woodiwiss (eds) *Global Crime Connections*, Basingstoke: Macmillan.

Borrill, J. and Stevens, D. (1993) 'Understanding Human Violence: The Implications of Social Structure, Gender, Social Perception and Alcohol', *Criminal Behaviour and Mental Health*, 3: 129–41.

Bosworth, M. (1999) *Engendering Resistance: Agency and Power in Women's Prisons*, Aldershot: Dartmouth.

Bosworth, M. (2000) 'Confining Femininity: A History of Gender, Power and Imprisonment', *Theoretical Criminology*, 4 (3): 265–84.

Bottomley, K. and Coleman, C. (1981) *Understanding Crime Rates*, Farnborough: Saxon House.

Bottoms, A. (1977) 'Reflections on the Renaissance of Dangerousness', *Howard Journal of Criminal Justice*, 16: 70–96.

Bottoms, A. (1980) 'An Introduction to "The Coming Crisis"', in A. Bottoms and R. Preston (eds) *The Coming Penal Crisis*, Edinburgh: Scottish Academic Press.

Bottoms, A. (1983) 'Neglected Features of Contemporary Penal Systems', in D. Garland and P. Young (eds) *The Power to Punish*, London: Heinemann.

Bottoms, A. (1987) 'Limiting Prison Use: Experience in England and Wales', *Howard Journal of Criminal Justice*, 26: 177–202.

Bottoms, A. (1995) 'The Philosophy and Politics of Punishment and Sentencing', in C. Clarkson and R. Morgan (eds) *The Politics of Sentencing Reform*, Oxford: Clarendon Press.

Bottoms, A. E. and McClean, J. D. (1976) *Defendants in the Criminal Process*, London: Routledge and Kegan Paul.

Bottoms, A. E. and Wiles, P. (2003) 'Environmental Criminology', in M. Maguire, R. Morgan and R. Reiner (eds) *The Oxford Handbook of Criminology*, 3rd edn, Oxford: Oxford University Press.

Bowling, B. (1998) *Violent Racism: Victimization, Policing and Social Context*, Oxford: Clarendon Press.

Bowling, B. (1999) 'The Rise and Fall of New York Murder', *British Journal of Criminology*, 39 (4): 531–54.

Bowling, B. and Phillips, C. (2002) *Racism, Crime and Justice*, Harlow: Longman.

Box, S. (1983) *Power, Crime and Mystification*, London: Routledge.

Boyle, K., Hadden, T. and Hillyard, P. (1975) *Law and State: The Case of Northern Ireland*, London: Martin Robertson.

Bozovic, M. (ed.) (1995) *The Panopticon Writings of Jeremy Bentham*, London Verso.

Brajuha, M. and Hallowell, L. (1986) 'Legal Intrusion and the Politics of Fieldwork: The Impact of the Brajuha Case', *Urban Life*, 14: 454–78.

Braithwaite, J. (1984) *Corporate Crime in the Pharmaceutical Industry*, London: Routledge.

Braithwaite, J. (1989) *Crime, Shame and Reintegration*, Cambridge: Cambridge University Press.

Braithwaite, J. (2003) 'What's Wrong with the Sociology of Punishment', *Theoretical Criminology*, 7 (1): 5–28.

Brayley, N. (2001) 'Coping with the Effects of Traumatic Stress', *PCW Review*, 4: 24–5.

Bright, M. (2002) 'Fury over Delay to "Corporate Killing" Law', *Observer*, 21 July: 6.

Bright, M. (2003) 'Youth Hit Hardest by Wave of New Laws', *Observer*, 13 April: 9.

Bristow, E. J. (1977) *Vice and Vigilance: Purity Movements in Britain since 1750*, Totowa, NJ: Rowman and Littlefield.

Brogden, M. and Nijhar, P. (2000) *Crime, Abuse and the Elderly*, Cullompton, Devon: Willan.

Brogden, M., Jefferson, T. and Walklate, S. (1988) *Introducing Policework*, London: Unwin Hyman.

Broome Report (1985) *Working Party on Drugs Related Crime*, London: Association of Chief Police Officers.

Brown, C. (1984) *Black and White in Britain*, The Third PSI Survey, London: Policy Studies Institute.

Brown, J. (1996) 'Police Research: Some Critical Issues', in F. Leishman, B. Loveday and S. Savage (eds) *Core Issues in Policing*, Harlow: Longman.

Brown, L. R. *et al.* (2001) *State of the World: 2001. A Worldwatch Institute Report on Progress toward a Sustainable Society*, London: Earthscan.

Brown, L. R. *et al.* (eds) (2004) *The State of the World: 2004. A Worldwatch Institute Report on Progress toward a Sustainable Society*, London: Earthscan.

Brown, S. (1994) *Whose Challenge? Youth, Crime and Everyday Life in Middlesbrough*, published report to Middlesbrough City Challenge Partnership, Middlesbrough: Middlesbrough City Challenge.

Brown, S. (1998) *Understanding Youth and Crime: Listening to Youth?* Buckingham: Open University Press.

Brown, S. (2003) *Crime and Law in Media Culture*, Buckingham: Open University Press.

Brownlee, I. (1998) *Community Punishment: A Critical Introduction*, Harlow: Longman.

Brownmiller, S. (1975) *Against Our Will: Men, Women and Rape*, New York: Simon and Schuster.

Brundson, C. (1998) 'Structure of Anxiety: Recent British Television Crime Fiction', *Screen*, 39 (3): 223–43.

Bucke, T. (1997) *Ethnicity and Contacts with the Police: Latest Findings from the British Crime Survey*, Home Office Research Findings 59, London: Home Office.

Budd, T. (1999) *Violence at Work: Findings from the British Crime Survey*, London: Home Office.

Budd, T. and Mattinson, J. (2000) *The Extent and Nature of Stalking: Findings from the 1998 British Crime Survey*, Home Office Research Study 210, London: Home Office.

Bullard, R. (1990) *Dumping in Dixie: Race, Class and Environmental Quality*, Boulder, CO: Westview Press.

Bulmer, M. (1984) *The Chicago School of Sociology: Institutionalization, Diversity, and the Rise of Sociological Research*, Chicago: University of Chicago Press.

Burgess, A. (1962) *A Clockwork Orange*, London: Heinemann.

Burke, M. E. (1993) *Coming Out of the Blue*, London: Cassell.

Burke, R. H. (ed.) (1998) *Zero Tolerance Policing*, Leicester: Perpetuity Press.

Burke, R. H. (2001) *An Introduction to Criminological Theory*, Cullompton, Devon: Willan.

Button, M. (2002) *Private Policing*, Cullompton, Devon: Willan.

Cain, M. (1973) *Society and the Policeman's Role*, London: Routledge and Kegan Paul.

Cain, M. (ed.) (1989) *Growing Up Good: Policing the Behaviour of Girls in Europe*, London: Sage.

Calder, A. (1991) *The Myth of the Blitz*, London: Cape.

Campbell, A. (1984) *The Girls in the Gang: A Report from New York City*, Oxford: Basil Blackwell.

Campbell, D. (1991) *That Was Business, This Is Personal*, London: Mandarin.

Campbell, D. (1994) *The Underworld*, London: BBC Books.

Caputi, J. (1988) *The Age of Sex Crime*, London: Women's Press.

Carlen, P. (1976) *Magistrates' Justice*, London: Martin Robertson.

Carlen, P. (1983) *Women's Imprisonment: A Study in Social Control*, London: Routledge and Kegan Paul.

Carlen, P. (1988) *Women, Crime and Poverty*, Buckingham: Open University Press.

Carlen, P. (1990) *Alternatives to Women's Imprisonment*, Buckingham: Open University Press.

Carlen, P. (1996) *Jigsaw: A Political Criminology of Youth Homelessness*, Buckingham: Open University Press.

Carlen, P. (1998) *Sledgehammer: Women's Imprisonment at the Millennium*, Basingstoke: Macmillan.

Carter, F. and Turnock, D. (1993) *Environmental Problems in Eastern Europe*, London: Routledge.

Carrabine, E. (2004) *Power, Discourse and Resistance: A Genealogy of the Strangeways Prison Riot*, Aldershot: Dartmouth.

Carrabine, E., Lee, M. and South, N. (2000) 'Social Wrongs and Human Rights in Late Modern Britain: Social Exclusion, Crime Control and Prospects for a Public Criminology', *Social Justice*, 27 (2): 193–211.

Carrabine, E., Cox, P., Lee, M. and South, N. (2002) *Crime in Modern Britain*, Oxford: Oxford University Press.

Carson, R. (1962) *Silent Spring*, Boston: Houghton Mifflin.

Cashmore, E. and McLaughlin, E. (1991) *Out of Order? Policing Black People*, London: Routledge.

Castells, M. (1996) *The Rise of Network Society*, Oxford: Blackwell.

Castells, M. (1998) *End of Millennium*, Oxford: Blackwell.

Cavadino, M. and Dignan, J. (2002) *The Penal System: An Introduction*, 3rd edn, London: Sage.

Centre for Contemporary Cultural Studies (1980) *Women Take Issue*, London: Hutchinson.

Centre for Contemporary Cultural Studies (1982) *The Empire Strikes Back*, London: Hutchinson.

Cere, R. (2003) 'Digital Counter-cultures and the Nature of Electronic Social and Political Movements', in Y. Jewkes (ed.) *Dot.cons: Crime, Deviance and Identity on the Internet*, Cullompton, Devon: Willan.

Chambliss, W. J. (1989/1994) 'State Organized Crime', in N. Passas (ed.) *Organized Crime*, London: Dartmouth.

Champion, J. D. (2000) *Research Methods for Criminal Justice and Criminology*, Upper Saddle River, NJ: Prentice Hall.

Chan, J. (1997) *Changing Police Culture: Policing in a Multicultural Society*, Cambridge: Cambridge University Press.

Chatterjee, B. (2001) 'Last of the Rainmacs: Thinking about Pornography in Cyberspace', in D. Wall (ed.) *Crime and the Internet*, London: Routledge.

Chivite-Matthews, N. and Maggs, P. (2002) *Crime, Policing and Justice: The Experience of Older People*, Home Office Statistical Bulletin 8/02, London: Home Office.

Christie, N. (1977) 'Conflicts as Property', *British Journal of Criminology*, 17 (1): 1–15.

Christie, N. (1986) 'The Ideal Victim', in E. A. Fattah (ed.) *From Crime Policy to Victim Policy*, Basingstoke: Macmillan.

Christie, N. (2000) *Crime Control as Industry*, 2nd edn, London: Routledge.

Cicourel, A. (1968) *The Social Organization of Juvenile Justice*, New York: John Wiley.

Clancy, A., Hough, M., Aust, R. and Kershaw, C. (2001) *Crime, Policing and Justice: The Experience of Ethnic Minorities*, Findings from the 2000 British Crime Survey, Home Office Research Study 223, London: Home Office.

Clark, L. and Lewis, D. (1977) *Rape: The Price of Coercive Sexuality*, Toronto: Women's Press.

Clarke, J., Hall, S., Jefferson, T. and B. Roberts (1976) 'Subcultures, Cultures and Class', in S. Hall and T. Jefferson (eds) *Resistance through Rituals: Youth Subcultures in Post-war Britain*, London: Routledge.

Clarke, R. and Hough, M. (1984) *Crime and Police Effectiveness*, London: Home Office.

Clemmer, D. (1958) *The Prison Community*. New York: Rinehart.

Cloward, R. and Ohlin, E. L. (1960) *Delinquency and Opportunity: A Theory of Delinquent Gangs*, New York: Free Press.

Cohen, J. (2002) *Understanding Drugs and the Law*, London: Drugscope.

Cohen, N. (2003) 'The Numbers Game', *Observer*, 29 June: 29.

Cohen, P. (1972) 'Subcultural Conflict and Working Class Community', *Working Papers in Cultural Studies*, 2: 5–52.

Cohen, P. (1979) 'Policing the Working Class City', in B. Fine, R. Kinsey, J. Lea, S. Picciotto and J. Young (eds) *Capitalism and the Rule of Law*, London: Hutchinson.

Cohen, R. and Kennedy, P. (2000) *Global Sociology*, Basingstoke: Macmillan.

Cohen, S. (1955) *Delinquent Boys: The Culture of the Gang*, Glencoe, IL: Free Press.

Cohen, S. (1971) *Images of Deviance*, Harmondsworth: Penguin.

Cohen, S. (1972) *Folk Devils and Moral Panics: The Creation of the Mods and Rockers*, London: MacGibbon and Kee.

Cohen, S. (1973a) 'Mods and Rockers: The Inventory as Manufactured News', in S. Cohen and J. Young (eds) *The Manufacture of News*, London: Constable.

Cohen, S. (1973b) 'The Failures of Criminology', *The Listener*, 8 November: 622–5.

Cohen, S. (1979) 'The Punitive City: Notes on the Dispersal of Social Control', *Contemporary Crises*, 3 (4): 341–63.

Cohen, S. (1980) 'Symbols of Trouble: Introduction to the New Edition', in *Folk Devils and Moral Panics*, 2nd edn, London: MacGibbon and Kee.

Cohen, S. (1984) 'The Deeper Structures of the Law, or "Beware the Rulers Bearing Justice"', *Contemporary Crises*, 8: 83–93.

Cohen, S. (1985) *Visions of Social Control: Crime, Punishment and Classification*, Cambridge: Polity.

Cohen, S. (1992) *The Evolution of Women's Asylums since 1500: From Refuges for Ex-prostitutes to Shelters for Battered Women*, Oxford: Oxford University Press.

Cohen, S. (1993) 'Human Rights and Crimes of the State: The Culture of Denial', *Australian and New Zealand Journal of Criminology*, 26 (1): 87–115.

Cohen, S. (1996) 'Crime and Politics: Spot the Difference', *British Journal of Sociology*, 47 (1): 1–21.

Cohen, S. (1997) 'Intellectual Scepticsm and Political Commitment', in P. Walton and J. Young (eds) *The New Criminology Revisted*, Basingstoke: Macmillan.

Cohen, S. (2001) *States of Denial: Knowing about Atrocities and Suffering*, Cambridge: Polity.

Cohen, S. and Taylor, L. (1972/1981) *Psychological Survival: The Experience of Long-Term Imprisonment*, Harmondsworth: Penguin.

Cohen, S. and Young, J. (eds) (1973) *The Manufacture of News*, London: Constable.

Coleman, C. and Moynihan, J. (1996) *Understanding Crime Data: Haunted by the Dark Figure*, Buckingham: Open University Press.

Coleman, R. and Sim, J. (2000) '"You'll Never Walk Alone": CCTV Surveillance, Order and Neo-liberal Rule in Liverpool City Centre', *British Journal of Sociology*, 51 (4): 623–39.

Collard, A. with Contrucci, J. (1988) *Rape of the Wild: Man's Violence against Animals and the Earth*, London: Women's Press.

Collier, R. (1998) *Masculinities, Crime and Criminology*, London: Sage.

Collison, M. (1995) *Police, Drugs and Community*, London: Free Association Books.

Collison, M. (1996) 'In Search of the High Life: Drugs, Crime, Masculinity and Consumption', *British Journal of Criminology*, 36 (3): 428–44.

Colvin, M. (1992) *The Penitentiary in Crisis: From Accommodation to Riot in New Mexico*, Albany: State University of New York Press.

Commission for Racial Equality (2003) *The Murder of Zahid Mubarek: A Formal Investigation by the Commission for Racial Equality into HM Prison Service of England and Wales, Part 1*, London: CRE.

Committee for the Prevention of Torture (1991) *Report to the United Kingdom Government on the Visit to the United Kingdom Carried Out by the CPT from 29 July 1990 to 10 August 1990*, Strasbourg: Council of Europe.

Conklin, J. (1994) *Art Crime*, London: Praeger.

Conrad, P. and Schneider, W. (1992) *Deviance and Medicalization*, St Louis: Mosby.

Cordy, M. (1999) *Crime Zero*, London: Bantam.

Cornish, D. and Clarke, R. (eds) (1986) *The Reasoning Criminal*, New York: Springer-Verlag.

Cottle, S. (ed.) (2003) *Media Organization and Production*, London: Sage.

Cox, P. (2003) *Gender, Justice and Welfare: Bad Girls in Britain, 1900–1950*, Basingstoke: Palgrave Macmillan.

Craig, K. M. (1999) 'Retaliation, Fear, or Rage: An Investigation of African American and White Reactions to Racist Hate Crimes', *Journal of Interpersonal Violence*, 14 (2): 138–51.

Craine, S. (1997) 'The "Black Magic Roundabout": Cyclical Transitions, Social Exclusion and Alternative Careers', in R. MacDonald (ed.) *Youth, the 'Underclass' and Social Exclusion*, London: Routledge.

Crawford, A., Jones, T., Woodhouse, T. and Young, J. (1990) *Second Islington Crime Survey*, London: Middlesex Polytechnic.

Cressey, D. R. (1969) *Theft of the Nation*, New York: Harper and Row.

Cressey, P. G. (1932) *The Taxi-Dance Hall*, Chicago: University of Chicago Press.

Critchley, C. (2003) *Moral Panics and the Media*, Buckingham: Open University Press.

Croall, H. (1992) *White Collar Crime*, Buckingham: Open University Press.

Croall, H. (1996) 'Crime: Understanding More and Condemning Less?', *Reviewing Sociology*, 10 (3).

Croall, H. (1997) 'Business, Crime and the Community', *International Journal of Risk, Security and Crime Prevention*.

Croall, H. (1998) *Crime and Society in Britain*, London: Longman.

Croall, H. (2001) *Understanding White Collar Crime*, Buckingham: Open University Press.

Cromwell, P. F. (ed.) (1996) *In Their Own Words: Criminals on Crime*, Los Angeles: Roxbury.

Crow, I. (2001) *The Treatment and Rehabilitation of Offenders*, London: Sage.

Cullen, F. T. and Agnew, R. (2003) *Criminological Theory: Past to Present (Essential Readings)*, 2nd edn, Los Angeles: Roxbury.

Cumming, E., Cumming, I. and Edell, L. (1965) 'The Policeman as Philosopher, Guide and Friend', *Social Problems*, 12: 276–86.

Curran, J. and Seaton, J. (1994) *Power without Responsibility: The Press and Broadcasting in Britain*, London: Routledge.

Currie, E. (1996) *Is America Really Winning the War on Crime and Should Britain Follow Its Example?*, London: NACRO.

Daly, K. (1989) 'Criminal Justice Ideologies and Practices in Different Voices: Some Feminist Questions about Justice', *International Journal of the Sociology of Law*, 17: 1–18.

Daly, K. (1997) 'Different Ways of Conceptualizing Sex/Gender in Feminist Theory and Their Implications for Criminology', *Theoretical Criminology*, 1 (1): 25–51.

Daly, K. (2002) 'Restorative Justice: The Real Story', *Punishment and Society*, 4 (1): 55–79.

Daly, K. and Bordt, R. L. (1995) 'Sex Effects and Sentencing: An Analysis of the Statistical Literature', *Justice Quarterly*, 12 (1): 141–75.

Daly, K. and Chesney-Lind, M. (1988) 'Feminism and Criminology', *Justice Quarterly*, 5 (4): 498–538.

Darbyshire, P. (1991) 'The Lamp That Shows That Freedom Lives: Is It Worth the Candle?', *Criminal Law Review*, 740.

Davies, M., Croall, H. and Tyrer, J. (1998) *An Introduction to the Criminal Justice System in England and Wales*, 2nd edn, Harlow: Longman.

Davis, L. (1983) *Factual Fictions: The Origins of the English Novel*, New York: Columbia University Press.

Davis, M. (1992) *City of Quartz: Excavating the Future in Los Angeles*, London: Verso.

Davis, M. (1993) 'Dead West: Ecocide in Marlboro Country', *New Left Review*, 200: 49–73.

Davis, M. (1994) *Beyond Blade Runner: Urban Control – The Ecology of Fear*, Open Magazine Pamphlet series, New York: New Press.

Davis, M. (1999) *Ecology of Fear: Los Angeles and the Imagination of Disaster*, New York: Metropolitan Books.

Davis, P., Francis, P. and Jupp, V. (2000) *Victimization: Theory, Research and Policy*, Basingstoke: London: Macmillan.

Day, D. (1991) *The Eco-wars*, London: Paladin.

de Haan, W. (1990) *The Politics of Redress: Crime, Punishment and Penal Abolition*, London: Sage.

de Haan, W. and Loader, I. (2002) 'On the Emotions of Crime, Punishment and Social Control', *Theoretical Criminology*, 6 (3): 243–53.

Deehan, A. (1999) *Alcohol and Crime: Taking Stock*, Policing and Crime Reduction Unit, London: Home Office.

Del Olmo, R. (1987) 'Aerobiology and the War on Drugs: A Transnational Crime', *Crime and Social Justice*, 30: 28–44.

Delgado, R. and Stefancic, J. (1997) *Must We Defend Nazis?* New York: New York University Press.

Dell, S. (1971) *Silence in Court*, Occasional Papers on Social Administration 42, London: Bell.

Dennis, N. (1993) *Rising Crime and the Dismembered Family*, Choice in Welfare Series 13, London: IEA.

Department of Health (2000) *Reforming the Mental Health Act*, London: DoH.

Department of Health (2001) *Changing the Outlook: A Strategy for Developing and Modernising Mental Health Services in Prisons*, London: DoH.

Department of Health (2003) *Statistics on Smoking, Drinking and Drug Use among Young People in 2002*, London: The Stationery Office.

Di Filipo, J. (2000) 'Pornography on the Web', in D. Gauntlett (ed.) *Web.studies: Rewiring Media Studies for the Digital Age*, London: Arnold.

Ditton, J. (1977) *Part-Time Crime: An Ethnography of Fiddling and Pilferage*, Basingstoke: Macmillan.

Dobash, R. E. and Dobash, R. P. (1992) *Women, Violence and Social Change*, London: Routledge.

Dobash, R., Dobash, R. and Noaks, L. (eds) (1995) *Gender and Crime*, Cardiff: University of Wales Press.

Dobson, A. (1990) *Green Political Thought*, London: Unwin Hyman.

Dorn, N. and South, N. (eds) (1987) *A Land Fit for Heroin?* Basingstoke: Macmillan.

Dorn, N. and South, N. (1990) 'Drug markets and law enforcement', *British Journal of Criminology*, 30 (2): 171–88.

Dorn, N., Murji, K. and South, N. (1992) *Traffickers: Drug Markets and Law Enforcement*, London: Routledge.

Douglas, J. and Rasmussen, P. (1977) *The Nude Beach*, Beverly Hills, CA: Sage.

Douglas, M. (1966) *Purity and Danger*, Harmondsworth: Penguin.

Dowie, M. (1979) 'The Corporate Crime of the Century', *Mother Jones*, November.

Downes, D. (1988) 'The Sociology of Crime and Social Control in Britain, 1960–1987', in P. Rock (ed.) special issue, *British Journal of Criminology*, 28 (2): 175–87.

Downes, D. and Rock, P. (1979) *Deviant Interpretations: Problems in Criminology*, Oxford: Clarendon Press.

Downes, D. and Rock, P. (1998) *Understanding Deviance: A Guide to the Sociology of Crime and Rule Breaking*, 3rd edn, Oxford: Oxford University Press.

Druglink (2003) 'Cocaine Gains Popularity Among Teenagers', *Druglink*, 18 (5): 2.

Duff, R. (1996) 'Penal Communications: Recent Work in the Philosophy of Punishment', in M. Tonry (ed.) *Crime and Justice: A Review of Research*, 20: 1–97.

Duff, R. (2001) *Punishment, Communication and Community*, Oxford: Oxford University Press.

Duff, P. and Hutton, N. (eds) (1999) *Criminal Justice in Scotland*, Aldershot: Ashgate.

Duff, R. and Garland, D. (1994) 'Introduction: Thinking about Punishment', in R. Duff and D. Garland (eds) *A Reader on Punishment*, Oxford: Oxford University Press.

Dunbar, I. and Langdon, A. (1998) *Tough Justice: Sentencing and Penal Policies in the 1990s*, London: Blackstone.

Dunhill, C. (1989) 'Women, Racist Attacks and the Response from Anti-racist Groups', in C. Dunhill (ed.) *The Boys in Blue: Women's Challenge to the Police*, London: Virago.

Durkheim, É. (1893/1960) *The Division of Labor in Modern Society*, Glencoe, Ill.: Free Press.

Durkheim, É. (1895/1988) *The Rules of Sociological Method*, London: Routledge.

Durkheim, É. (1901/1984) 'Two Laws of Penal Evolution', in S. Lukes and A. Scull (eds) *Durkheim and the Law*, Oxford: Basil Blackwell.

Dworkin, A. (1981) *Pornography: Men Possessing Women*, London: Women's Press.

Dworkin, A. (1987) *Intercourse*, London: Arrow Books.

Dworkin, R. (1978) *Taking Rights Seriously*, London: Duckworth.

Eaglestone, R. (2001) *Postmodernism and Holocaust Denial*, Cambridge: Icon Books.

Eaton, M. (1986) *Justice for Women?* Buckingham: Open University Press.

Eck, J. and Maguire, E. (2000) 'Have Changes in Policing Reduced Violent Crime? An Assessment of the Evidence', in A. Blumstein and J. Wallman (eds) *The Crime Drop in America*, Cambridge: Cambridge University Press.

Edgar, K., O'Donnell, I. and Martin, C. (2003) *Prison Violence: The Dynamics of Conflict, Fear and Power*, Cullompton, Devon: Willan.

Edmunds, M., Hough, M. and Urquia, M. (1996) *Tackling Local Drug Markets*, Crime Detection and Prevention Series Paper 80, London: Home Office.

Edwards, S. (1984) *Women on Trial*, Manchester: Manchester University Press.

Edwards, S. (1989) *Policing Domestic Violence*, London: Sage.

Edwards, S. (1990) 'Violence against Women, Feminism and the Law', in L. Gelsthorpe and A. Morris (eds) *Femionist Perspectives in Criminology*, Milton Keynes: Open University Press.

Edwards, S., Edwards, T. and Fields, C. (eds) (1996) *Environmental Crime and Criminality: Theoretical and Practical Issues*, New York: Garland.

Emsley, C. (1983) *Policing and Its Context 1750–1870*, Basingstoke: Macmillan.

Emsley, C. (1996a) *Crime and Society in England 1750–1900*, 2nd edn, Harlow: Longman.

Emsley, C. (1996b) *The English Police: A Political and Social History*, 2nd edn, Harlow: Longman.

Emsley, C. (2002) 'The History of Crime and Crime Control Institutions', in M. Maguire, R. Morgan and R. Reiner (eds) *The Oxford Handbook of Criminology*, 3rd edn, Oxford: Oxford University Press.

Engels, F. (1845/1958) *The Condition of the Working Class in England*, Oxford: Basil Blackwell.

Eribon, D. (1992) *Michel Foucault*, London: Faber and Faber.

Ericson, R. and Haggerty, K. (1997) *Policing the Risk Society*, Oxford: Clarendon Press.

Ericson, R., Baranek, P. and Chan, J. (1991) *Representing Order*, Milton Keynes: Open University Press.

Ettore, E. (1992) *Women and Substance Use*, Basingstoke: Macmillan.

Evans, P. (1980) *Prison Crisis*, London: George Allen and Unwin.

Farnham, F. and James, D. (2001) '"Dangerousness" and Dangerous Law', *The Lancet*, 358: 1926.

Farrington, D. P. (1997) 'Human Developments and Criminal Careers', in M. Maguire, R. Morgan and R. Reiner (eds) *The Oxford Handbook of Criminology*, 2nd edn, Oxford: Oxford University Press.

Farrington, D. (2002) 'Developmental Criminology and Risk-Focused Prevention', in M. Maguire, R. Morgan and R. Reiner (eds) *The Oxford Handbook of Criminology*, 3rd edn, Oxford: Oxford University Press.

Farrington, D. and Morris, A. (1983) 'Sex, Sentencing and Reconviction', *British Journal of Criminology*, 23 (3): 229–48.

Fattah, E. A. (1986) 'On Some Visible and Hidden Dangers of Victim Movements', in E. A. Fattah (ed.) *From Crime Policy to Victim Policy*, Basingstoke: Macmillan.

Feeley, M. and Simon, J. (1992) 'The New Penology: Notes on the Emerging Strategy of Corrections and Its Implications', *Criminology*, 30 (4): 449–74.

Feeley, M. and Simon, J. (1994) 'Actuarial Justice: The Emerging New Criminal Law', in D. Nelken (ed.) *The Futures of Criminology*, London: Sage.

Felson, M. (1998) *Crime and Everyday Life*, Thousand Oaks, Calif.: Pine Forge.

Fenwick, M. and Hayward, K. J. (2000) 'Youth Crime Excitement and Consumer Culture: The Reconstruction of Aetiology in Contemporary Criminology', in J. Pickford (ed.) *Youth Justice: Theory and Practice*, London: Cavendish.

Ferrell, J. (1998) 'Criminological Verstehen: Inside the Immediacy of Crime', in J. Ferrell and M. Hamm (eds) *Ethnography at the Edge: Crime, Deviance and Field Research*, Boston: Northeastern University Press.

Ferrell, J. and Hamm, M. (eds) (1998) *Ethnography at the Edge: Crime, Deviance and Field Research*, Boston: Northeastern University Press.

Ferrell, J. and Saunders, C. R. (1995) *Cultural Criminology*, Boston: Northeastern University Press.

Findlay, M. (1999) *The Globalisation of Crime*, Cambridge: Cambridge University Press.

Findlay, M. and Duff, P. (eds) (1988) *The Jury under Attack*, London: Butterworths.

Fine, R. (1985) *Democracy and the Rule of Law*, London: Pluto.

Fishbein, D. (1990) 'Biological Perspectives in Criminology', *Criminology*, 28 (3): 27–71.

Fishbein, D. (2000) *Biological Perspectives on Criminology*, Belmont, CA: Wadsworth.

Fiske, J. (1992) 'Popularity and the Politics of Information', in P. Dahlgren and C. Sparks (eds) *Journalism and Popular Culture*, London: Sage.

Fiske, J. (1998) 'Surveilling the City: Whiteness, the Black Man and Democratic Totalitarianism', *Theory, Culture and Society*, 15 (2): 67–88.

Fitzgerald, M. (1977) *Prisoners in Revolt*, Harmondsworth: Penguin.

Fitzgerald, M. (1993) *Ethnic Minorities and the Criminal Justice System*, Royal Commission on Criminal Justice, Research Study 20, London: HMSO.

Fitzgerald, M. and Hale, C. (1996) *Ethnic Minorities, Victimization and Racial Harassment: Findings from the 1988 and 1992 British Crime Surveys*, London: Home Office.

Fitzgerald, M. and Sim, J. (1979) *British Prisons*, Oxford: Basil Blackwell.

Fitzgerald, M. and Sim, J. (1982) *British Prisons*, 2nd edn, Oxford: Basil Blackwell.

Flew, A. (1981) *The Politics of Procrustes*, London: Temple Smith.

Flood-Page, G., Campbell, S., Harrington, V. and Miller, J. (2000) *Youth Crime: Findings from the 1998/99 Youth Lifestyles Survey*, Home Office Research Study 209, London: Home Office.

Fogel, D. (1975) *We Are the Living Proof: The Justice Model for Corrections*, Cincinnati, Ohio: Anderson.

Foldy, M. S. (1997) *The Trials of Oscar Wilde: Deviance, Morality and Late Victorian Society*, New Haven, Conn.: Yale University Press.

Forrester, D., Chatterton, M. and Pease, K. (1988) *The Kirkholt Burglary Prevention Project, Rochdale*, Crime Prevention Unit Paper 13, London: Home Office.

Foster, J. (1989) 'Two Stations: An Ethnographic Study of Policing in the Inner City', in D. Downes (ed.) *Crime and the City*, Basingstoke: Macmillan.

Foster, J. (1990) *Villains: Crime and Community in the Inner City*, London: Routledge.

Foster, J. and Hope, T. (1993) *Housing, Community and Crime: The Impact of the Priority Estates Project*, Home Office Research Study 131, London: HMSO.

Foucault, M. (1977) *Discipline and Punish: The Birth of the Prison*, Harmondsworth: Penguin.

Foucault, M. (1978) *The History of Sexuality*, vol. 1, trans. R. Hurley London: Allen Lane.

Foucault, M. (1975/1980) 'Prison Talk', in *Power/Knowledge: Selected Interviews and Other Writings*, Brighton: Harvester Press.

Fox, V. (1973) *Violence behind Bars: An Explosive Report on Prison Riots in the United States*, Westport, Conn.: Greenwood Press.

Fraser, F. (1994) *Mad Frank*, London: Little, Brown.

Freeman, N. (1996–7) 'That Was Business – This Is Personal: Professions of Violence in English Cinema from Brighton Rock to the Krays', *Close-Up: The Electronic Journal of British Cinema*, 1, Winter, www.shu.ac.uk/services/lc/closeup

French, H. and Mastny, L. (2001) 'Controlling International Environmental Crime', in L. R. Brown (ed.) *State of the World*, London: Earthscan.

Freud, S. (1958) 'The Uncanny', in *On Creativity and the Unconscious: Papers on the Psychology of Art, Literature, Love, Religion*, New York: Harper and Row.

Frey, R. G. (1992) 'Torture', in L. C. Becker and C. B. Becker (eds) *Encyclopedia of Ethics*, Chicago: St James Press.

Friedman, A. (1996) '"The Habitats of the Sex Crazed Perverts": Campaigns against Burlesque in the Depression Era in NYC', *Journal of the History of Sexuality*, 7 (2): 203–37.

Friman, H. R. and Andreas, P. (1999) *The Illicit Global Economy and State Power*, Oxford: Rowman and Littlefield.

Gabbidon, S., Greene, H. T. and Young, V. D. (eds) (2001) *African American Classics in Criminology and Criminal Justice*, Thousand Oaks, CA: Sage.

Gabor, T. (1994) *Everybody Does It*, Toronto: University of Toronto Press.

Gagnon, J. (1977) *Human Sexualities*, New York: Scott Foresman.

Gagnon, J. and Simon, W. (1973) *Sexual Conduct: The Social Sources of Sexuality*, Chicago: Aldine.

Galliher, J. F. (1995) 'Chicago's Two Worlds of Deviance Research: Whose Side Are They On?', in G. A. Fine (ed.) *A Second Chicago School? The Development of a Postwar American Sociology*, Chicago: University of Chicago Press.

Gallo, E. and Ruggiero, V. (1991) 'The "Immaterial" Prison: Custody as the Manufacture of Handicaps', *International Journal of the Sociology of Law*, 19 (3): 273–91.

Gamson, J. (1990) 'Rubber Wars: Struggles over the Condoms', *Journal of the History of Sexuality*, 1 (2): 262–82.

Garfinkel, H. (1956a) 'Conditions of Successful Degradation Ceremonies', *American Journal of Sociology*, 61: 420–4.

Garfinkel, H. (1956b) 'The Trial as a Degradation Ceremony', *American Journal of Sociology*, 66:

Garland, D. (1985) *Punishment and Welfare*, Aldershot: Gower.

Garland, D. (1990) *Punishment and Modern Society: A Study in Social Theory*, Oxford: Clarendon Press.

Garland, D. (1991) 'Sociological Perspectives on Punishment', in M. Tonry (ed.) *Crime and Justice: A Review of Research*, 14: 115–65.

Garland, D. (1996) 'The Limits of the Sovereign State: Strategies of Crime Control in Contemporary Society', *British Journal of Criminology*, 36 (4): 445–71.

Garland, D. (1997) '"Governmentality" and the Problem of Crime', *Theoretical Criminology*, 1 (2): 173–214.

Garland, D. (2000) 'The Culture of High Crime Societies: Some Preconditions of Recent "Law and Order" Policies', *British Journal of Criminology*, 40 (3): 445–71.

Garland, D. (2001a) 'Introduction: The Meaning of Mass Imprisonment', *Punishment and Society*, 3 (2): 5–7.

Garland, D. (2001b) *The Culture of Control: Crime and Social Order in Contemporary Society*, Oxford: Clarendon Press.

Garland, D. (2003) 'Of Crime and Criminals: The Development of Criminology in Britain', in M. Maguire, R. Morgan and R. Reiner (eds) *The Oxford Handbook of Criminology*, 3rd edn, Oxford: Oxford University Press.

Garland, D. and Sparks, R. (2000) 'Criminology, Social Theory and the Challenge of Our Times', *British Journal of Criminology*, 40 (2): 189–204.

Garland, D. and Young, P. (eds) (1983) *The Power to Punish: Contemporary Penality and Social Analysis*, London: Heinemann.

Garner, R. (2001) *Environmental Politics*, 2nd edn, London: Prentice Hall.

Gatrell, V. A. C., Lenman, B. and Parker, G. (eds) (1980) *Crime and the Law: The Social History of Crime in Western Europe since 1500*, London: Europa.

Gatrell, V. (1994) *The Hanging Tree: Execution and the English People, 1770–1868*, Oxford: Oxford University Press.

Gauntlett, D. (2000) *Web.Studies: Rewiring Media Studies for the Digital Age*, London: Arnold.

Gay, P. (1970) *The Enlightenment: An Interpretation*, London: Wildwood House.

Geis, G. and Dimento, J. (1995) 'Should We Prosecute Corporations and/or Individuals?', in F. Pearce and L. Snider (eds) *Corporate Crime*, Toronto: University of Toronto Press.

Gelsthorpe, L. (1989) *Sexism and the Female Offender*, Aldershot: Gower.

Gelsthorpe, L. and Giller, H. (1990) 'More Justice for Juveniles: Does More Mean Better?', *Criminal Law Review*, March: 153–64.

Gelsthorpe, L. and Morris, A. (2002) 'Restorative Justice: The Last Vestiges of Welfare', in J. Muncie, G. Hughes and E. McLaughlin (eds) *Youth Justice: Critical Readings*, London: Sage.

Genders, E. and Player, E. (1987) 'Women in Prison: The Treatment, the Control and the Experience', in P. Carlen and A. Worrall (eds) *Gender, Crime and Justice*, Milton Keynes: Open University Press.

Genders, E. and Player, E. (1989) *Race Relations in Prison*, Oxford: Clarendon Press.

Gey, S. G. (1997) 'What if Wisconsin v Mitchell Had Involved Martin Luther King Jnr? The Constitutional Flaws of Hate Crime Enhancement Statutes', *George Washington Law Review*, 65: 1014–70.

Giddens, A. (1972) *Émile Durkheim: Selected Writings*, Cambridge: Cambridge University Press.

Giddens, A. (1990) *The Consequences of Modernity*, Cambridge: Polity.

Giddens, A. (1999) *Runaway World: How Globalisation Is Reshaping Our Lives*, London. Profile Books.

Giddons, D. (1994) *Talking about Crime and Criminals: Problems and Issues in Theory Development in Criminology*, Englewood Cliffs, NJ: Prentice Hall.

Gilligan, C. (1982) *In a Different Voice*, Cambridge, Mass.: Harvard University Press.

Girling, E., Loader, I. and Sparks, R. (2000) *Crime and Social Change in Middle England: Questions of Order in an English Town*, London: Routledge.

Gladfelder, H. (2001) *Criminality and Narrative in Eighteenth-Century England: Beyond the Law*, Baltimore: Johns Hopkins University Press.

Gobert, J. and Punch, M. (2003) *Rethinking Corporate Crime*, London: Butterworths.

Goffman, E. (1959) *The Presentation of Self in Everyday Life*, Garden City, NY: Doubleday.

Goffman, E. (1962) *Asylums: Essays on the Social Situation of Mental Patients and Other Inmates*, Harmondsworth: Penguin.

Goldson, B. (2000) *The New Youth Justice*, Lyme Regis: Russell House.

Goode, E. (1990) 'Crime Can Be Fun: The Deviant Experience', *Contemporary Sociology*, 19 (1): 5–12.

Gordon, P. (1990) *Racial Violence and Harassment*, 2nd edn, London: Runnymede Trust.

Goring, C. (1913/1972) *The English Convict: A Statistical Study*, London: HMSO.

Gottfredson, M. (1984) *Victims of Crime: The Dimensions of Risk*, Home Office Research Study 81, London: HMSO.

Gottfredson, M. R. and Hirschi, T. (1990) *A General Theory of Crime*, Stanford, CA: Stanford University Press.

Gould, S. J. (1999) *The Mismeasure of Man*, New York: Norton.

Gouldner, A. (1973) *For Sociology: Renewal and Critique in Sociology Today*, London: Allen Lane.

Grabosky, P. and Smith, R. (1998) *Crime in the Digital Age: Controlling Telecommunications and Cyberspace Illegalities*, New Brunswick, NJ: Federation Press.

Graham, K. and Wells, S. (2003) '"Somebody's Gonna Get Their Head Kicked In Tonight!": Aggression among Young Males in Bars – a Question of Values?', *British Journal of Criminology*, 43 (3): 546–66.

Gramsci, A. (1971) *Selections from Prison Notebooks*, London: Lawrence and Wishart.

Greenwood, P., Chaiken, J. and Petersilia, J. (1977) *The Criminal Investigation Process*, Lexington, MA: D. C. Heath.

Greer, S. (1994) 'Miscarriages of Justice Reconsidered', *Modern Law Review*, 57: 58.

Gregory, J. and Lees, S. (1999) *Policing Sexual Assault*, London: Routledge.

Griffin, S. (1971) 'Rape: The All American Crime', *Ramparts*, September: 26–35.

Gros, J.-G. (2003) 'Trouble in Paradise: Crime and Collapsed States in the Age of Globalisation', *British Journal of Criminology*, 43 (1): 63–80.

Gusfield, J. (1981) *The Culture of Public Problems: Drinking–Driving and the Symbolic Order*, Chicago: University of Chicago Press.

Guttenplan, D. D. (2000) 'The Holocaust on Trial', *Atlantic Monthly*, 285 (2): 45–66.

Habermas, J. (1987) *The Philosophical Discourse of Modernity*, Cambridge: Polity.

Haggerty, K. and Ericson, R. (2000) 'The Surveillant Assemblage', *British Journal of Sociology*, 51 (4): 605–22.

Hale, C. (1992) *Fear of Crime: A Review of the Literature*, Canterbury: University of Kent.

Halford, A. (1993) *No Way up the Greasy Pole*, London: Constable.

Hall, S. (1980) 'Cultural Studies: Two Paradigms', *Media, Culture and Society*, 2: 57–72.

Hall, S. and Jefferson, T. (eds) (1976) *Resistance through Rituals: Youth Subcultures in Post-war Britain*, London: Routledge.

Hall, S., Critcher, C., Jefferson, T., Clarke J. and Roberts, B. (1978) *Policing the Crisis: Mugging, the State and Law and Order*, London: Macmillan.

Hamelink, C. (2000) *The Ethics of Cyberspace*, London: Sage.

Hammersley, M. (2001) 'Which Side Was Becker On? Questioning Political and Epistemological Radicalism', *Qualitative Research*, 1 (1): 91–110.

Hammersley, R., Forsyth, A., Morrison, V. and Davis, J. (1989) 'The Relationship between Crime and Opioid Use', *British Journal of Criminology*, 84: 1029–44.

Hammersley, R., Marsland, L. and Reid, M. (2003) *Substance Use by Young Offenders: The Impact of Normalisation of Drug Use in the Early Years of the 21st Century*, Research Study 261, London: Home Office.

Hamilton, P. (1996) 'The Enlightenment and the Birth of Social Science', in S. Hall, D. Held, D. Hubert and K. Thompson (eds) *Modernity: An Introduction to Modern Societies*, Oxford: Blackwell.

Hanmer, J. and Saunders, S. (1984) *Well Founded Fear*, London: Hutchinson.

Hanmer, J., Radford, J. and Stanko, E. (1989) *Women, Policing and Male Violence: International Perspectives*, London: Routledge.

Harding, C., Hines, B., Ireland, B. and Rawlings, P. (1985) *Imprisonment in England and Wales: A Concise History*, London: Croom Helm.

Harries, R. (1999) *The Cost of Criminal Justice*, Home Office Research Findings 103, London: Home Office.

Harrison, P. and Pearce, F. (2000) *AAAS Atlas of Population and Environment*, Berkeley: University of California Press.

Hartless, J., Ditton, J., Nair, G. and Phillips, S. (1995) 'More Sinned against Than Sinning: A Study of Young Teenagers' Experience of Crime', *British Journal of Criminology*, 35 (1): 114–33.

Harvey, D. (1989) *The Condition of Postmodernity*, Oxford: Basil Blackwell.

Hay, D. (1975) 'Property, Authority, and the Criminal Law' in D. Hay, P. Linebaugh and E. P. Thompson (eds) *Albion's Fatal Tree: Crime and Society in Eighteenth-Century England*, Harmondsworth: Penguin.

Hay, D., Linebaugh, P. and Thompson, E. P. (eds) (1975) *Albion's Fatal Tree: Crime and Society in Eighteenth-Century England*, Harmondsworth: Penguin.

Hayward, K. (2002) 'The Vilification and Pleasures of Youthful Transgression', in J. Muncie (ed.) *Youth Justice: Critical Readings*, Buckingham: Open University Press.

Hebdige, D. (1988) *Hiding in the Light*, London: Comedia.

Hedderman, C. and Hough, M. (1994) *Does the Criminal Justice System Treat Men and Women Differently?* Home Office Research Findings 10, London: Home Office.

Hedderman, C. and Moxon, D. (1992) *Magistrates' Court or Crown Court? Mode of Trial Decisions and Sentencing*, Home Office Research Study 125, London: HMSO.

Heidensohn, F. (1987) 'Women and Crime: Questions of Criminology', in P. Carlen and A. Worrall (eds) *Gender, Crime and Justice*, Buckingham: Open University Press.

Held, D., McGrew, A. G., Goldblatt, D. and Perraton, J. (1999) *Global Transformations: Politics, Economics and Culture*, Cambridge: Polity.

Hendrick, H. (1990) 'Constructions and Reconstructions of British Childhood: An Interpretative Survey 1800 to the Present', in A. James and A. Prout (eds) *Constructing and Reconstructing Childhood*, London: Falmer.

Henman, A., Lewis, R. and Malyon, T. (eds) (1985) *Big Deal: The Politics of the Illicit Drug Business*, London: Pluto.

Henry, S. and Milovanovic, D. (1996) *Constitutive Criminology: Beyond Postmodernism*, London: Sage.

Her Majesty's Inspectorate of Constabulary (1999) *Police Integrity: Securing and Maintaining Public Confidence*, London: Home Office.

Herman, E. and Chomsky, N. (1988) *Manufacturing Consent: The Political Economy of the Mass Media*, New York: Pantheon.

Hermes, J. (2000) 'Of Irritation, Texts and Men: Feminist Audience Studies and Cultural Citizenship', *International Journal of Cultural Studies*, 3 (3): 351–67.

Herrnkind, M. (1993) 'Grüne Kriminalpolitik im Schweizer Kanton Zug', *Burgerrechte und Polizei*, 45 (2): 72–5.

Higgins, P. (1996) *Heterosexual Dictatorship: Male Homosexuality in Postwar Britain*, London: Fourth Estate.

Hill, A. (2002) '"No One Leaves This Place with Her Sanity Intact"', *Observer*, 1st December: 10–11.

Hindelang, M. J., Gottfredson, M. R. and Garofalo, J. (1978) *Victims of Personal Crime: An Empirical Foundation for a Theory of Personal Victimization*, Cambridge, MA: Ballinger.

Hinsliff, G. (2003) 'Diet of Fish "Can Prevent" Teen Violence', *Observer*, 14th September.

Hirschfield, A., Brown, P. and Todd, P. (1995) 'GIS and the Analysis of Spatially Referenced Crime Data: Experiences in Merseyside UK', *International Journal of Geographical Information Systems*, 9 (2): 191–210.

Hirschi, T. (1969) *Causes of Delinquency*, Berkeley: University of California Press.

Hobbs, D. (1988) *Doing the Business: Entrepreneurship, the Working Class and Detectives in the East End of London*, Oxford: Clarendon Press.

Hobbs, D.(1994) 'Professional and Organized Crime in Britain', in M. Maguire, R. Morgan and R. Reiner (eds) *The Oxford Handbook of Criminology*, Oxford: Oxford University Press.

Hobbs, D. (1995) *Bad Business: Professional Crime in Modern Britain*, Oxford: Oxford University Press.

Hobbs, D. (1997) 'Criminal Collaboration: Youth Gangs, Subcultures, Professional Criminals and Organized Crime', in M. Maguire, R. Morgan and R. Reiner (eds) *The Oxford Handbook of Criminology*, end edn, Oxford: Oxford University Press.

Hobbs, D. (1998) 'Going Down the Glocal: The Local Context of Organised Crime', *Howard Journal of Criminal Justice*, 37 (4): 407–22.

Hobbs, D. (2001) 'The Firm: Organizational Logic and Criminal Culture on a Shifting Terrain', *British Journal of Criminology*, 41 (4): 549–60.

Hobbs, D., Lister, S., Hadfield, P., Winlow, S. and Hall S. (2000) 'Receiving Shadows: Governance and Liminality in the Night-time Economy', *British Journal of Sociology*, 51 (4): 701–17.

Hobbs, D., Hadfield, P., Lister, S. and Winlow, S. (2002) '"Door Lore": The Art and Economics of Intimidation', *British Journal of Criminology*, 42: 352–70.

Hobbs, D., Hadfield, P., Lister, S. and Winlow, S. (2003) *Bouncers: Violence and Governance in the Night-time Economy*, Oxford: Oxford University Press.

Hodge, N. (2003) 'Manslaughter Business Placed on Hold', *Tribune*, 10 January, 67 (1): 3.

Hofrichter, R. (1993) *Toxic Struggles: The Theory and Practice of Environmental Justice*, Philadelphia: New Society.

Holdaway, S. (1983) *Inside the British Police*, Oxford: Basil Blackwell.

Holdaway, S. (1996) *The Racialisation of British Policing*, Basingstoke: Macmillan.

Holdaway, S. and Barron, A. M. (1997) *Resigners: The Experience of Black and Asian Police Officers*, Basingstoke: Macmillan.

Hollin, C. (1999) 'Treatment Programmes for Offenders: Meta-analysis, "What Works", and Beyond', *International Journal of Psychiatry and Law*, 22: 361–72.

Hollway, W. and Jefferson, T. (2000) 'The Role of Anxiety in Fear of Crime', in T. Hope and R. Sparks (eds) *Crime, Risk and Insecurity*, London: Routledge.

Home Office (1966) *Committee of an Enquiry into Prison Escapes and Security* (Mountbatten Report), Cmnd 3175, London: HMSO.

Home Office (1997) *Criminal Statistics for England and Wales 1996*, Cm 3764, London: Home Office.

Home Office (1998) *Crime and Disorder Act 1998. Racially Aggravated Offences*, http://www.homeoffice.gov.uk/cdact/racagoff.htm

Home Office (2000a) *A Guide to the Criminal Justice System in England and Wales*, London: Home Office, www.homeoffice.gov.uk

Home Office (2000b) *Statistics on Race and the Criminal Justice System*, Research, Development and Statistics Directorate, London: Home Office.

Home Office (2001) *Prison Statistics England and Wales 2000*, Cmnd. 5250, London: HMSO.

Home Office (2002a) *Criminal Statistics England and Wales 2001*, Cm 5696, London: Home Office, www.archive.official-documents.co.uk

Home Office (2002b) *Prison Population Brief, England and Wales: June 2002*, London: HMSO.

Home Office (2002c) *Statistics on Race and the Criminal Justice System: A Home Office Publication under Section 95 of the Criminal Justice Act 1991*, London: Home Office.

Hood, R. (1992) *Race and Sentencing*, Oxford: Oxford University Press.

Hope, T. (1985) *Implementing Crime Prevention Measures*, Home Office Research Study 86, London: HMSO.

Hope, T. (2001) 'Crime Victimisation and Inequality in Risk Society' in R. Matthews and J. Pitts (eds) *Crime, Disorder and Community Safety*, London: Routledge.

Hough, M. and Mayhew, P. (1983) *The British Crime Survey*, Home Office Research Study 76, London: HMSO.

Howe, A. (1994) *Punish and Critique: Towards a Feminist Analysis of Penality*, London: Routledge.

Hudson, B. (1987) *Justice through Punishment*, Basingstoke: Macmillan.

Hudson, B. (1989) 'Discrimination and Disparity: The Influence of Race on Sentencing', *New Community*, 16 (1): 23–34.

Hudson, B. (1993) *Penal Policy and Social Justice*, Basingstoke: Macmillan.

Hudson, B. (1996) *Understanding Justice*, London: Sage.

Hudson, B. (2003) *Understanding Justice*, 2nd edn, London: Sage.

Hunt, A. (1998) 'The Great Masturbation Panic and the Discourse of Moral Regulation in Nineteenth and Early Twentieth Century Britain', *Journal of the History of Sexuality*, 8 (4): 575–615.

Hunt, D. M. (1999) *O. J. Simpson: Facts and Fiction*, Cambridge: Cambridge University Press.

Hurd, H. (2001) 'Why Liberals Should Hate "Hate Crime Legislation"', *Law and Philosophy*, 20: 215–32.

Hutton, W. (1995) *The State We're In*, London: Jonathan Cape.

Huxley, A. (1994) *Brave New World*, London: Flamingo.

Ianni, E. R. and Ianni, R. (1983) 'Street Cops and Management Cops: The Two Cultures of Policing', in M. Punch (ed.) *Control in the Police Organization*, Cambridge, Mass.: MIT Press.

Iganski, P. (1999) 'Why Make Hate a Crime?', *Critical Social Policy*, 19 (3): 386–95.

Iganski, P. (2000) 'Should Holocaust Denial Be Punished as Hate Speech?', *Runnymede Bulletin*, September: 17–18.

Iganski P. (2001) 'Hate Crimes Hurt More', *American Behavioral Scientist*, 45 (4): 626–38.

Iganski, P. and Kosmin, B. (2003) 'Globalized Judeophobia and Its Ramifications for British Society', in P. Iganski and B. Kosmin (eds) *A New Antisemitism? Debating Judeophobia in 21st Century Britain*, London: Profile.

Ignatieff, M. (1978) *A Just Measure of Pain: The Penitentiary in the Industrial Revolution 1750–1850*, London: Macmillan.

Ignatieff, M. (1994) *Blood and Belonging: Journeys into the New Nationalism*, London: Vintage.

Inciardi, J. (1977) 'In Search of the Class Cannon: A Field Study of Professional Pickpockets', in R. S. Weppner (ed.) *Street Ethnography: Selected Studies of Crime and Drug Use in Natural Settings*, Beverly Hills, CA: Sage.

Inciardi, J. (1999) *The Drug Legalization Debate*, 2nd edn, Thousand Oaks, CA: Sage.

Institute for Jewish Policy Research (2000) *Combating Holocaust Denial through Law in the United Kingdom*, London: Institute for Jewish Policy Research.

Irwin, J. (1990) *The Jail: Managing the Underclass in American Society*, Berkeley: University of California Press.

Ishay, M. (ed.) (1997) *The Human Rights Reader*, London: Routledge.

Jackson, S. and Scott, S. (1996) *Feminism and Sexuality: A Reader*, Edinburgh: Edinburgh University Press.

Jacobs, J. and Potter, K. (1998) *Hate Crimes. Criminal Law and Identity Politics*, New York: Oxford University Press.

Jacobson, J. (1999) *Policing Drug Hot-Spots*, Home Office Police Research Series 109, London: Home Office.

Jacoby, J. (2002) 'Punish Crime, Not Thought Crime', in P. Iganski (ed.) *The Hate Debate*, London: Profile.

Jamieson, R. (1998) 'Towards a Criminology of War in Europe', in V. Ruggiero, N. South and I. Taylor (eds) *The New European Criminology: Crime and Social Order in Europe*, London: Routledge.

Jamieson, R., South, N. and Taylor, I. (1998) 'Economic Liberalization and Cross-border Crime: The North American Free Trade Area and Canada's Border with the USA', *International Journal of the Sociology of Law*, 26 (2): 245–72 and 26 (3): 285–319.

Janowitz, M. (ed.) (1996) *W. I. Thomas on Social Organization and Social Personality*, Chicago: University of Chicago Press.

Jefferson, T. (1990) *The Case against Paramilitary Policing*, Milton Keynes: Open University Press.

Jefferson, T. (2002) 'Masculinities and Crime', in M. Maguire, R. Morgan and R. Reiner (eds) *The Oxford Handbook of Criminology*, 3rd edn, Oxford: Oxford University Press.

Jefferson, T. and Grimshaw, R. (1984) *Controlling the Constable: Police Accountability in England and Wales*, London: Muller/Cobden Trust.

Jefferson, T. and Walker, M. (1992) 'Ethnic Minorities in the Criminal Justice System', *Criminal Law Review*, 81: 83–95.

Jefferson, T. and Walker, M. (1993) 'Attitudes to the Police of Ethnic Minorities in a Provincial City', *British Journal of Criminology*, 33 (2): 251–66.

Jeffery-Poulter, S. (1991) *Peers, Queers, and Commons: The Struggle for Gay Law Reform from 1950 to the Present*, London: Routledge.

Jenkins, P. (1996) *Paedophiles and Priests: Anatomy of a Contemporary Crisis*, Oxford: Oxford University Press.

Jenkins, P. (1998) *Moral Panic: Changing Concepts of the Child Molester in Modern America*, New Haven, Conn.: Yale University Press.

Jenkins, P. (2001) *Beyond Tolerance: Child Pornography on the Internet*, New York: New York University Press.

Jewkes, Y. (1999) *Moral Panics in a Risk Society: A Critical Evaluation*, Crime, Order and Policing Occasional Paper Series 15, Scarman Centre, Leicester: University of Leicester.

Jewkes, Y. (2003) 'Policing the Net: Crime, Regulation and Surveillance in Cyberspace', in Y. Jewkes (ed.) *Dot.cons: Crime, Deviance and Identity on the Internet*, Cullompton, Devon: Willan.

Johnston, L (1996) 'Policing Diversity: The Impact of the Public–Private Complex in Policing', in F. Leishman, B. Loveday and S. Savage (eds) *Core Issues in Policing*, Harlow: Longman.

Johnston, L. (2000) *Policing Britain: Risk, Security and Governance*, Harlow: Longman.

Jones, T. and Newburn, T. (1996) *Policing and Disaffected Communities: A Review of the Literature*, London: Policy Studies Institute.

Jones, T and Newburn, T (2002) 'The Transformation of Policing', *British Journal of Criminology*, 42 (1): 129–46.

Jones, T., Maclean, B. and Young, J. (1986) *The Islington Crime Survey*, Aldershot: Gower.

Justice (1989) *Justice, Sentencing: A Way Ahead*, London: Justice.

Jupp, V. (1989) *Methods of Criminological Investigation*, London: Allen and Unwin.

Jupp, V., Davies, P. and Francis, P. (1999) 'The Features of Invisible Crimes', in P. Davies, P. Francis and V. Jupp (eds) *Invisible Crimes: Their Victims and Their Regulation*, Basingstoke: Macmillan.

Jupp, V., Davies, P. and Francis, P. (eds) (2000) *Doing Criminological Research*, London: Sage.

Kahan, D. M. (2001) 'Two Liberal Fallacies in the Hate Crimes Debate', *Law and Philosophy*, 20: 175–93.

Kamir, O. (2001) *Every Breath You Take: Stalking Narratives and the Law*, Ann Arbor: University of Michigan Press.

Karmen, A. (1990) *Crime Victims: An Introduction to Victimology*, Pacific Grove, CA: Brooks Cole.

Katz, J. (1988) *Seductions of Crime: Moral and Sensual Attractions of Doing Evil*, New York: Basic Books.

Keane, J. (1996) *Reflections on Violence*, London: Verso.

Keith, M. (1993) *Race, Riots and Policing: Law and Disorder in a Multi-racist Society*, London: UCL Press.

Kelly, D. (1990) 'Victim Participation in the Criminal Justice System', in A. J. Lurigio, W. G. Skoken and R. C. Davis (eds) *Victims of Crime: Problems, Policies and Programs*, Newbury Park, Calif.: Sage.

Kelly, L. (1988) *Surviving Sexual Violence*, Cambridge: Polity Press.

Kelman, H. C. and Hamilton, V. L. (1989) *Crimes of Obedience*, New Haven, CT: Yale University Press.

Kempadoo, K. and Doezema, J. (1998) *Global Sex Workers: Rights, Resistance and Redefinition*, London: Routledge.

Kerr, P. (1992) *A Philosophical Investigation*, London, Arrow.

Kershaw, C., Budd, T., Kinshott, G., Mattinson, J., Mayhew, P. and Myhill, A. (2000) *The 2000 British Crime Survey*, London: Home Office.

Kersten, J. (1993) 'Street Youths, *Bosozoku and Yakuza*: Subculture Formation and Social Reactions in Japan', *Crime and Delinquency*, 39 (3): 277–95.

Kidd-Hewitt, D. (1995) 'Crime and the Media: A Criminological Perspective', in D. Kidd-Hewitt and R. Osborne (eds) *Crime and the Media: The Post-modern Spectacle*, London: Pluto.

King, C. (2003) 'A Case to Answer?', *Care and Health*, 42, 13–26 August: 10–11.

King, R. D. and Wincup, E. (eds) (2000) *Doing Research on Crime and Justice*, Oxford: Oxford University Press.

Kinsey, R. (1984) *Merseyside Crime Survey*, Edinburgh: Centre for Criminology, University of Edinburgh.

Kivisto, P. (1998) *Key Ideas in Sociology*, London: Sage/Pine Forge Press.

Klockars, C. (1975) *The Professional Fence*, London: Tavistock.

Kohn, M. (1992) *Dope Girls*, London: Lawrence and Wishart.

Kuhn, T. S. (1962) *The Structure of Scientific Revolutions*, Chicago: University of Chicago Press.

Lacey, N. (1988) *State Punishment: Political Principles and Community Values*, London: Routledge.

Lacey, N. (2000) *Narrative and Genre: Key Concepts in Media Studies*, Basingstoke: Macmillan.

Lancet, The (1999) 'Alcohol and Violence', *The Lancet*, 336, 17 November: 1223–4.

Landesco, J. (1929) *Organized Crime in Chicago*, Chicago: Illinois Association for Criminal Justice.

Lasch, C. (1979) *The Culture of Narcissism*, New York: Norton.

Lawrence, F. M. (1999) *Punishing Hate: Bias Crimes under American Law*, Cambridge, MA: Harvard University Press.

Lea, J. (2000) 'The Macpherson Report and the Question of Institutional Racism', *Howard Journal of Criminal Justice*, 39 (2): 219–37.

Lea, J. (2002) *Crime and Modernity*, London: Sage.

Lea, J. and Young, J. (1984) *What Is To Be Done about Law and Order?* London: Pluto.

Lee, J. A. (1981) 'Some Structural Aspects of Police Deviance in Relations with Minority Groups', in C. Shearing (ed.) *Organizational Police Deviance*, Toronto: Butterworths.

Lee, M. (1998) *Youth, Crime and Police Work*, Basingstoke: Macmillan.

Lee, M. and South, N. (2003) 'Policing and Drugs', in T. Newburn (ed.) *The Handbook of Policing*, Cullompton, Devon: Willan.

Lees, S. (1996a) 'Unreasonable Doubt: The Outcomes of Rape Trials', in M. Hester, L. Kelly and J. Radford (eds) *Women, Violence and Male Power*, Buckingham: Open University Press.

Lees, S. (1996b) *Carnal Knowledge: Rape on Trial*, London: Penguin.

Lemert, E. (1951) *Social Pathology*, New York: McGraw-Hill.

Lemert, E. (1958) 'The behavior of the systematic check forger', Social Problems, 6: 141–9.

Lemert, E. (1967) *Human Deviance, Social Problems and Social Control*, Englewood Cliffs, NJ: Prentice Hall.

Leo, R. A. (1995) 'Trial and Tribulation: Courts, Ethnography, and the Need for Evidentiary Privilege for Academic Researchers', *American Sociologist*, 26: 113–34.

Leonard, E. B. (1982) *Women, Crime and Society*, New York: Longman.

Levi, M. (1981) *The Phantom Capitalists*, Aldershot: Gower.

Levi, M. (1993) *The Investigation, Prosecution and Trial of Serious Fraud*, Research Paper Report 14, London: Royal Commission on Criminal Justice.

Levi, M. and Pithouse, A. (1992) 'The Victims of Fraud', in D. Downes (ed.) *Unravelling Criminal Justice*, Basingstoke: Macmillan.

Levin, B. (1999) 'Hate Crimes: Worse by Definition', *Journal of Contemporary Criminal Justice*, 15 (1): 6–21.

Levin, J. (2002) *The Violence of Hate*, Boston: Allyn and Bacon.

Levin, J.and McDevitt, J. (1993) *Hate Crimes: The Rising Tide of Bigotry and Bloodshed*, New York: Plenum.

Levin, J. and McDevitt, J. (1995) 'Landmark Study Reveals Hate Crimes Vary Significantly by Offender Motivation', *Klanwatch Intelligence Report*, Southern Poverty Law Center, August.

Levin, J. and McDevitt, J. (2002) *Hate Crimes Revisited: America's War on Those Who Are Different*, Boulder, CO: Westview Press.

Lévi-Strauss, C. (1966) *The Savage Mind*, London: Weidenfeld and Nicolson.

Lewis, R. (1989) 'European Markets in Cocaine', *Contemporary Crises*, 13: 35–52.

Lipstadt, D. (1994) *Denying the Holocaust: The Growing Assault on Truth and Memory*, New York: Plume.

Livingstone, S. (1996) 'On the Continuing Problem of Media Effects', in J. Curran and M. Gurevitch (eds) *Mass Media and Society*, London: Arnold.

Loader, I. (1996) *Youth, Policing and Democracy*, Basingstoke: Macmillan.

Loader, I (2000) 'Plural Policing and Democratic Governance', *Social and Legal Studies*, 9: 323–45.

Loffreda, B. (2000) *Losing Matt Shepard: Life and Politics in the Aftermath of Anti-gay Murder*, New York: Columbia University Press.

Lofland, J. (1966) *Doomsday Cult*, Englewood Cliffs, NJ: Prentice Hall.

Lombroso, C. (1876) *L'uomo delinquente*, Turin: Fratelli Bocca.

Lombroso, C. (1911/1968) *Crime: Its Causes and Remedies*, Montclair, NJ: Patterson Smith.

Lombroso-Ferrero, G. (1911) *Criminal Man: According to the Classification of Cesare Lombroso*, New York: Putnam; repr. Montclair, NJ: Paterson Smith, 1972.

Loseke, D. (2003a) 'We Hold These Truths to Be Self Evident: Problems in Pondering the Pedophile Priest Problem: Symposium on Pedophile Priests', *Sexualities*, 6, February: 6–14.

Loseke, D. (2003b) *Thinking about Social Problems: An Introduction to Constructionist Perspectives*, 2nd edn, New York: Aldine de Gruyter.

Low, D. (1982) *Thieves' Kitchen: The Regency Underworld*, London: Dent.

Lowe, P., Ward, N., Seymour, S. and Clark, J. (1996) 'Farm Pollution as Environmental Crime', *Science as Culture*, 5 (4): 588–612.

Lowman, J., Menzies, R. and Palys, T. (eds) (1987) *Transcarceration: Essays in the Sociology of Social Control*, Aldershot: Gower.

Lupton, R., Wilson, A., May, T., Warburton, H. and Turnbull, P. (2002) *A Rock and a Hard Place: Drug Markets in Deprived Neighbourhoods*, Home Office Research Study 240, London: Home Office.

Lurigio, A. J., Skogan, W. G. and Davis, R. C. (eds) (1990) *Victims of Crime: Problems, Policies and Programs*, Newbury Park, Calif.: Sage.

Lustgarten, L. (1986) *The Governance of Police*, London: Sweet and Maxwell.

Lyng, S. (1990) 'Edgework: A Social Psychological Analysis of Voluntary Risk Taking', *American Journal of Sociology*, 95 (4): 851–86.

Lyng, S. and Snow, D. (1986) 'Vocabularies of Motive and High Risk Behavior: The Case of Skydiving', in E. J. Lawler (ed.) *Advances in Group Processes*, Greenwich, CT: JAI.

Lyon, D. (2001) *Surveillance Society: Monitoring Everyday Life*, Buckingham: Open University Press.

Lyon, D. (2003) *Surveillance after September 11*, Cambridge: Polity.

Mac an Ghaill, M. (1994) *The Making of Men*, Buckingham: Open University Press.

McAllister, W. (2000) *Drug Diplomacy in the Twentieth Century*, London: Routledge.

McBarnet, D. (1981) *Conviction: Law, the State and the Construction of Justice*, London: Macmillan.

McCabe, A. and Raine, J. (1997) *Framing the Debate: The Impact of Crime on Public Health*, Birmingham: Public Health Alliance.

McCall, N. (1994) *'Makes Me Wanna Holler': A Young Black Man in America*, New York: Vintage.

McConville, M. and Wilson, G. (2002) *The Handbook of the Criminal Justice Process*, Oxford: Oxford University Press.

McConville, M., Sanders, A. and Leng, R. (1991) *The Case for the Prosecution*, London: Routledge.

McConville, S. (1998) 'The Victorian Prison: England, 1865–1965', in N. Morris and D. Rothman (eds) *The Oxford History of the Prison: The Practice of Punishment in Western Society*, Oxford: Oxford University Press.

McCracken, S. (1998) *Pulp: Reading Popular Fiction*, Manchester: Manchester University Press.

McDermott, K. and King, R. (1988) 'Mind Games: Where the Action Is in Prisons', *British Journal of Criminology*, 28 (3): 357–77.

McDevitt, J., Balboni, J. M., Bennett, S., Weiss, J. C., Orchowsky, S. and Walbolt, L. (2000) *Improving the Quality and Accuracy of Bias Crime Statistics Nationally: An Assessment of the First Ten Years of Bias Crime Data Collection*, Boston: Center for Criminal Justice Policy Research, Northeastern University, and Justice Research and Statistics Association.

MacDonald, R. and Marsh, J. (2002) 'Crossing the Rubicon: Youth Transitions, Poverty, Drugs and Social Exclusion', *International Journal of Drug Policy*, 13: 27–38.

McGuire, J. (ed.) (1995) *What Works: Reducing Re-offending*, Chichester: Wiley.

McGuire, M., Morgan, R. and Reiner, R. (2002) *The Oxford Handbook of Criminology*, 3rd edn, Oxford: Clarendon Press.

McIntosh, M. (1975) *The Organisation of Crime*, London: Macmillan.

McIntosh, M. (1978) 'Who Needs Prostitutes?', in C. Smart (ed.) *Women, Sexuality and Social Control*, London: Routledge.

Mack, J. (1964) 'Full-Time Miscreants, Delinquent Neighbourhoods and Criminal Networks', *British Journal of Sociology*, 15: 38–53.

McLaren, A. (1997) *The Trials of Masculinity*, Chicago: University of Chicago Press.

McLaughlin, E. (1994) *Community, Policing and Accountability*, Aldershot: Avebury.

McLaughlin, E. (2001) 'Political Violence, Terrorism and States of Fear', in J. Muncie and E. McLaughlin (eds) *The Problem of Crime*, 2nd edn, London: Sage/Open University.

McLaughlin, E. and Muncie, J. (2000) 'The Criminal Justice System: New Labour's New Partnerships', in J. Clarke, S. Gewirtz and E. McLaughlin (eds) *New Managerialism, New Welfare?*, London: Sage.

McLaughlin, E. and Murji, K. (1997) 'The Future Lasts a Long Time: Public Policework and the Managerialist Paradox', in P. Francis, P. Davies and V. Jupp (eds) *Policing Futures: The Police, Law Enforcement and the Twentieth-First Century*, Basingstoke: Macmillan.

McLeod, E. (1982) *Women Working: Prostitution Now*, London: Croom Helm.

McMurran, M. and Hollin, C. (1989), 'Drinking and Delinquency', *British Journal of Criminology*, 29 (4): 386–93.

McNaughton, J. (2003) 'Maddening Thing Is That Record Firms Could Have Done It', *Observer*, Business Section, 4th May: 6.

McNay, L. (1994) *Foucault: A Critical Introduction*, Cambridge: Polity.

Macpherson, Sir W. (1999) *The Stephen Lawrence Inquiry: Report of an Inquiry by Sir William Macpherson of Cluny*, Cm 4262, London: The Stationery Office.

McRobbie, A. (1994) *Postmodernism and Popular Culture*, London: Routledge.

McRobbie, A. and Thornton, S. (1995) 'Rethinking Moral Panics for Multi-mediated Social Worlds', *British Journal of Sociology* 46 (4): 559–74.

McVeigh, D. (2003) 'Rogue Advisors Profit from Asylum Misery', *Tribune*, 67 (3)2: 5.

Maguire, M. (1982) *Burglary in a Dwelling*, London: Heinemann.

Maguire, M. (1997) 'Crime Statistics, Patterns, and Trends: Changing Perceptions and their Implications', in M. Maguire, R. Morgan and R. Reiner (eds) *The Oxford Handbook of Criminology*, 2nd edn, Oxford: Clarendon Press.

Maguire, M. and Corbett, C. (1987) *The Effects of Crime and the Work of Victim Support Schemes*, Aldershot: Gower.

Maguire, M. and Corbett, C. (1991) *A Study of the Police Complaints System*, London: Home Office.

Maguire, M., Morgan, R. and Reiner, R. (2002) *The Oxford Handbook of Criminology*, 3rd edn, Oxford: Oxford University Press

Maher, L. and Dixon, D. (1999) 'Policing and Public Health', *British Journal of Criminology*, 39, 4: 488–512.

Man, L.-H., Best, D., Marshall, J., Godfrey, C. and Budd, T. (2002) *Dealing with Alcohol Related Detainees in the Custody Suite*, Home Office Findings 178, London: Home Office.

Manning, P. (1979) 'The Social Control of Police Work', in S. Holdaway (ed.) *The British Police*, London: Edward Arnold.

Manning, P. K. (2000) 'Policing New Social Spaces', in J. Sheptycki (ed.) *Issues in Transnational Policing*, London: Routledge.

Mars, G. (1982) *Cheats at Work: An Anthropology of Workplace Crime*, London: George Allen and Unwin.

Martin, C. (1996) 'The Impact of Equal Opportunities Policies on the Day-to-Day Experiences of Women Police Constables', *British Journal of Criminology*, 36 (4): 510–28.

Martin, T. and Romero, A. (1992) *Multinational Crime*, London: Sage.

Martinson, R. (1974) 'What Works? Questions and Answers about Prison Reform', *The Public Interest*, 35: 22–54.

Marx, K. and Engels, F. (1845/1975) *Collected Works*, vol. 4: 248–9, Moscow: Progress Publishers; London: Lawrence and Wishart.

Mathiesen, T. (1965) *The Defences of the Weak*, London: Tavistock.

Mathiesen, T. (1974) *The Politics of Abolition*, London: Martin Robertson.

Matthews, M. (2002) 'Crime Control in Late Modernity: A Review Essay', *Theoretical Criminology*, 6 (2): 217–27.

Matthews, R. (1989) *Privatizing Criminal Justice*, London: Sage.

Matthews, R. (1999) *Doing Time: An Introduction to the Sociology of Imprisonment*, Basingstoke: Macmillan.

Matthews, R. and Pitts, J. (2001) 'Beyond Criminology?', in R. Matthews and J. Pitts (eds) *Crime, Disorder and Community Safety*, London: Routledge.

Matza, D. (1964) *Delinquency and Drift*, New York: Wiley.

Matza, D. (1969) *Becoming Deviant*, Englewood Cliffs, NJ: Prentice Hall.

Mauer, M. (2001) 'The Causes and Consequences of Prison Growth in the United States', *Punishment and Society*, 3 (2): 9–20.

Maung, N. A. (1995) *Young People, Victimisation and the Police*, Home Office Research Study 140, London: Home Office.

Mawby, R. (ed.) (1999) *Policing across the World: Issues for the Twenty-first Century*, London: UCL Press.

Mawby, R. (2001) *Burglary*, Cullompton, Devon: Willan.

Mawby, R. and Walklate, S. (1994) *Critical Victimology*, London: Sage.

Maxfield, M. G. and Babbie, E. (1995) *Research Methods for Criminal Justice and Criminology*, Belmont, CA: Wadsworth.

May, T. (1991) *Probation: Politics, Policy and Practice*, Milton Keynes: Open University Press.

Mayhew, P. and Van Dijk, J. J. M. (1997) *Criminal Victimisation in Eleven Industrialised Countries: Key Findings from the 1996 International Crime Victims Survey*, The Hague: Ministry of Justice, WODC.

Mead, G. (1918) 'The Psychology of Punitive Justice', *American Journal of Sociology*, 23: 577–602.

Mead, G. H. (1934) *Mind, Self and Society*, Chicago: University of Chicago Press.

Melossi, D. and Pavarini, M. (1981) *The Prison and the Factory: The Origins of the Penitentiary System*, Basingstoke: Macmillan.

Mendelsohn, B. (1956) 'Une nouvelle branche de la science bio-psycho-sociale: victimologie', *Revue Internationale de Criminologie et de Police Technique*, pp. 10–31.

Merton, R. K. (1938) 'Social Structure and Anomie', *American Sociological Review*, 3: 672–82.

Messerschmidt, J. (1993) *Masculinities and Crime: Critique and Reconceptualization of Theory*, Lanham, Md: Rowman and Littlefield.

Messerschmidt, J. W. (1997) *Crime as Structured Action*, London: Sage.

Messerschmidt, J. W. (2000) *Nine Lives: Adolescence Masculinities, the Body and Violence*, Boulder, Col.: Westview.

Meyers, M. (1997) *News Coverage of Violence against Women: Engendering Blame*, London: Sage.

Michalowski, R. and Kramer, R. (1987) 'The Space between Laws: The Problem of Corporate Crime in a Transnational Context', *Social Problems*, 34 (1): 34–53.

Miers, D. (1992) 'The Responsibilities and the Rights of Victims of Crime', *Modern Law Review*, 55: 482.

Miller, A. (1962) 'The Bored and the Violent', *Harper's*, 25, November, reprinted in P. O'Malley and S. Mugford (1994) 'Crime, Excitement, and Modernity', in G. Barak (ed.) *Varieties of Criminology: Readings from a Dynamic Discipline*, Westport, CT: Praeger.

Miller, D. and Kitzinger, J. (1998) 'AIDS, the Policy Process and Moral Panics', in D. Miller, J. Kitzinger, K. Williams and P. Beharrell (eds) *The Circuit of Mass Communication*, London: Sage.

Miller, E. (1986) *Street Women*, Philadelphia: Temple.

Mirrlees-Black, C. (1999) *Domestic Violence: Findings from a New British Crime Survey Self-Completion Questionnaire*, Home Office Research Study 191, London: Home Office.

Mirrlees-Black, C. and Ross, A. (1995) *Crimes against Retail and Manufacturing Premises: Findings from the 1994 Commercial Victimization Survey*, Home Office Research Study 146, London: Home Office.

Mirrlees-Black, C., Budd, T., Partridge, S. and Mayhew, P. (1998) *The 1998 British Crime Survey*, Home Office Statistical Bulletin 19/96, London: Home Office.

Modood, T. and Berthoud, R. (1997) *Ethnic Minorities in Britain: Diversity and Disadvantage*, London: Policy Studies Institute.

Mollen Commission (1994) *Report of the Commission to Investigate Allegations of Police Corruption and the Anti-corruption Procedures of the Police Department*, New York: Mollen Commission.

Mooney, J. (1993) *The North London Domestic Violence Survey*, London: Middlesex University.

Moretti, F. (1990) 'Clues', in T. Bennett (ed.) *Popular Fiction: Technology, Ideology, Production, Reading*, London: Routledge.

Morgan, P. (1978) *Delinquent Fantasies*, London: Temple Smith.

Morgan, R. (2002) 'Imprisonment: A Brief History, The Contemporary Scene, and Likely Prospects', in M. Maguire, R. Morgan and R. Reiner (eds) *The Oxford Handbook of Criminology*, Oxford: Oxford University Press.

Morgan, R. and Newburn, T. (1997) *The Future of Policing*, Oxford: Clarendon Press.

Morgan, R. and Russell, N. (2000) *The Judiciary in the Magistrates' Courts*, Home Office RDS Occasional Paper 66, London: Home Office.

Morgan, R. and Sanders, A. (1999) *The Uses of Victim Statements*, Home Office RDS Occasional Paper, London: Home Office.

Morton, J. (1992) *Gangland*, London: Little, Brown.

Muncie, J. (1999) *Youth and Crime: A Critical Introduction*, London: Sage.

Muncie, J. (2001) 'The Construction and Deconstruction of Crime', in J. Muncie and E. McLaughlin (eds) *The Problem of Crime*, 2nd edn, London: Sage/Open University.

Muncie, J., McLaughlin, E. and Langan, M. (eds) (1996) *Criminological Perspectives: A Reader*, London: Sage/Open University.

Muncie, J., McLaughlin, E. and Langan, M. (eds) (2003) *Criminological Perspectives: A Reader*, 2nd edn, London: Sage/Open University.

Murdock, G. (1997) 'Reservoirs of Dogma: An Archaeology of Popular Anxieties', in M. Barker and J. Petley (eds) *Ill Effects: The Media/Violence Debate*, London: Routledge.

Murray, C. (1997) *Does Prison Work?* London: Institute for Economic Affairs.

NACRO (2001) 'Children, Health and Crime', *Impact: International Journal of Health Equality*, 1: 13–15.

NACRO (2001–2) 'Women Offenders', *Safer Society*, 11: 27–8.

NACRO (2002) 'Drug Misuse Is a Health Issue, Say Police Chiefs', *Safer Society*, 13: 14.

Nadelman, E. (1990) 'Global Prohibition Regimes: The Evolution of Norms in International Society', *International Organization*, 44 (4): 479–526.

Naffine, N. (1990) *Law and the Sexes*, London: Allen and Unwin.

Naffine, N. (1995) *Gender, Crime and Feminism*, Aldershot: Dartmouth.

Naffine, N. (1997) *Feminism and Criminology*, Cambridge: Polity.

National Board for Crime Prevention (1994) *Wise after the Event: Tackling Repeat Victimisation*, London: Home Office.

Nelken, D. (1989) 'Discipline and Punish: Some Notes on the Margin', *The Howard Journal*, 28 (4): 245–54.

Nelken, D. (1994a) 'White Collar Crime', in M. Maguire, R. Morgan and R. Reiner (eds) *The Oxford Handbook of Criminology*, Oxford: Oxford University Press.

Nelken, D. (ed.) (1994b) *The Futures of Criminology*, London: Sage.

Nellis, M. (2003) 'News Media, Popular Culture and the Electronic Monitoring of Offenders in England and Wales', *Howard Journal of Criminal Justice*, 42 (1): 1–31.

Newburn, T. (1999) *Understanding and Preventing Police Corruption: Lessons from the Literature*, Home Office Police Research Studies 110, London: Home Office.

Newburn, T. (2002a) 'Young People, Crime, and Youth Justice', in M. Maguire, R. Morgan and R. Reiner (eds) *The Oxford Handbook of Criminology*, 3rd edn, Oxford: Oxford University Press.

Newburn, T. (2002b) 'Community Safety and Policing: Some Implications of the Crime and Disorder Act 1998', in G. Hughes, E. McLaughlin and J. Muncie (eds) *Crime Prevention and Community Safety: New Directions*, London: Sage.

Newburn, T. (ed.) (2003) *Handbook of Policing*, Cullompton, Devon: Willan.

Newburn, T. and Stanko, B. (eds) (1994) *Just Boys Doing Business*, London: Routledge.

Newman, G. (ed.) (1999) *Global Report on Crime and Justice*, New York: Oxford University Press.

Nicole, H. R. (1997) *Creating Born Criminals*, Chicago: University of Illinois Press.

Nietzsche, F. (1887/1996) *On the Genealogy of Morals*, Oxford: Oxford University Press.

Norris, C., Fielding, N., Kemp, C. and Fielding, J. (1992) 'Black and Blue: An Analysis of the Influence of Race on Being Stopped by the Police', *British Journal of Sociology*, 43: 207–24.

Nussbaum, M. (1999) *Sex and Social Justice*, New York: Oxford University Press.

O'Byrne, D. J. (2003) *Human Rights: An Introduction*, Harlow: Pearson.

O'Donovan, K. (1993) 'Law's Knowledge: The Judge, the Expert, the Battered Woman, and Her Syndrome', *Journal of Law and Society*, 20 (4): 427–37.

Ogg, J. and Munn-Giddings, C. (1993) 'Researching Elder Abuse', *Ageing and Society*, 13: 389–413.

O'Hare, P., Newcombe, R., Matthews, A., Buning, E. and Drucker, E. (1992) *The Reduction of Drug Related Harm*, London: Routledge.

O'Malley, P. (1992) 'Risk, Power and Crime Prevention', *Economy and Society*, 21 (3): 242–75.

O'Malley, P. (1999) 'Volatile and Contradictory Punishment', *Theoretical Criminology*, 3 (2): 175–96.

Osborne, R. (1995) 'Crime and the Media: From Media Studies to Post-modernism', in D. Kidd-Hewitt and R. Osborne (eds) *Crime and the Media: The Post-modern Spectacle*, London: Pluto.

Paehlke, R. (1995) 'Environmental Harm and Corporate Crime', in F. Pearce and L. Snyder (eds) *Corporate Crime: Contemporary Debates*, Toronto: University of Toronto Press.

Paine, T. (1791–2/1984) *Rights of Man*, with an introduction by E. Foner, Harmondsworth: Penguin.

Painter, K. and Farrington, D. (1998) 'Marital Violence in Great Britain and Its Relationship to Marital and Non-marital Rape', *International Review of Victimology*, 5: 257–76.

Pantazis, C. (1999) 'The Criminalization of Female Poverty', in S. Watson and L. Doyal (eds) *Engendering Social Policy*, Buckingham: Open University Press.

Park, C. (2001) 'The Three Faces of Retail Theft', *New Zealand Security*, February/March (available online: www.ecoliving.co.nz/nzsecurity/mag. Accessed 20 December 2001)

Park, E., Burgess, E. W. and McKenzie, R. D. (1925) *The City*, Chicago: University of Chicago Press.

Parker, H., Sumner, M. and Jarvis, G. (1989) *Unmasking the Magistrates: The 'Custody or Not' Decision in Sentencing Young Offenders*, Milton Keynes: Open University Press.

Parker, H., Aldridge, J. and Measham, F. (1998) *Illegal Leisure: The Normalization of Adolescent Recreational Drug Use*, London: Routledge.

Parker, H. J. (1974) *View from the Boy: A Sociology of Down-Town Adolescents*, Newton Abbot: David and Charles.

Parsons, T. (1960) *Structure and Process in Modern Society*, New York: Free Press.

Parssinen, T. (1983) *Secret Passions, Secret Remedies: Narcotic Drugs in British Society, 1820–1930*, Manchester: Manchester University Press.

Pashukanis, E. B. (1924/1978) *Law and Marxism: A General Theory*, London: Ink Links.

Passas, N. (1995) '"I Cheat, Therefore I Exist?" The BCCI Scandal in Context', in N. Passas (ed.) *Organized Crime*, Aldershot: Dartmouth.

Patrick, J. (1973) *A Glasgow Gang Observed*, London: Eyre Methuen.

Pearce, F. (1976) *Crimes of the Powerful*, London: Pluto.

Pearce, F. and Tombs, S. (1993) 'US Capital versus the Third World: Union Carbide and Bhopal', in F. Pearce and M. Woodiwiss (eds) *Global Crime Connections*, Basingstoke: Macmillan.

Pearce, F. and Tombs, S. (1998) *Toxic Capitalism: Corporate Crime and the Chemical Industry*, Aldershot: Ashgate.

Pearson, G. (1983) *Hooligan: A History of Respectable Fears*, Basingstoke: Macmillan.

Pearson, G. (1987a) 'Social Deprivation, Unemployment and Patterns of Heroin Use', in N. Dorn and N. South (eds) *A Land Fit for Heroin? Drug Policies, Prevention and Practice*, Basingstoke: Macmillan.

Pearson, G. (1987b) *The New Heroin Users*, Oxford: Blackwell.

Pearson, G. (1992) 'The Role of Culture in the Drug Question', in G. Edwards, M. Lader and C. Drummond (eds), *The Nature of Alcohol and Drug Related Problems*, Oxford: Oxford University Press.

Pearson, J. (1973) *The Profession of Violence*, London: Panther.

Pease, K. (1998) *Repeat Victimisation: Taking Stock*, Crime Detection and Prevention Paper 90, London: Home Office.

Pepinsky, H. and Quinney, R. (eds) (1991) *Criminology as Peacemaking*, Bloomington: Indiana University Press.

Percy, A. (1998) *Ethnicity and Victimization: Findings from the 1996 British Crime Survey*, Home Office Statistical Bulletin 6/98, London: Home Office.

Petchesky, R. P. (2000) 'Sexual Rights: Inventing a concept, Mapping an International Practice', in R. Parker, R. M. Barbosa and P. Aggleton (eds) *Framing the Sexual Subject: The Politics of Gender, Sexuality and Power*, Berkeley: University of California Press.

Petrow, S. (1994) *Policing Morals: The Metropolitan Police and the Home Office 1870–1994*, Oxford: Clarendon Press.

Phillips, C. and Brown, D. (1998) *Entry into the Criminal Justice System: A Survey of Police Arrests and Their Outcomes*, Home Office Research Study 185, London: Home Office.

Phillips, M. (2001) *America's Social Revolution*, London: Civitas.

Phillips, M. (2002) 'Hate Crime: The Orwellian Response to Prejudice', in P. Iganski (ed.) *The Hate Debate*, London: Profile.

Player, E. (1989) 'Women and Crime in the Inner City', in D. Downes (ed.) *Crime in the City*, Basingstoke: Macmillan.

Plummer, K. (1979) 'Misunderstanding Labelling Perspectives', in D. Downes and P. Rock (eds) *Deviant Interpretations*, London: Martin Robertson.

Plummer, K. (1995) *Telling Sexual Stories: Power, Change and Social Worlds*, London: Routledge.

Plummer, K. (2003) *Intimate Citizenship: Private Decisions and Public Dialogues*, Seattle: University of Washington Press.

Policy Studies Institute (1983) *Police and People in London*, 4 vols, London: Policy Studies Institute.

Polsky, N. (1967) *Hustlers, Beats and Others*, Chicago: Aldine.

Presdee, M. (1994) 'Young People, Culture, and the Construction of Crime: Doing Wrong versus Doing Crime', in G. Barak (ed.) *Varieties of Criminology: Readings from a Dynamic Discipline*, Westport, Conn.: Praeger.

Prime, J., White, S., Liriano, S. and Patel, K. (2001) *Criminal Careers of Those Born between 1953 and 1978, England and Wales*, Home Office Statistical Bulletin 4/01, London: Home Office.

Presdee, M. (2000) *Cultural Criminology and the Carnival of Crime*, London: Routledge.

Prison Service (2001) *Prison Service: Annual Report and Accounts, April 2000 to March 2001*, HC 29, London: Prison Service.

Pudney, S. (2002) *The Road to Ruin? Sequences of Initiation into Drug Use and Offending by Young People in Britain*, Home Office Research Studies 253, London: Home Office.

Pugh, R. (1968) *Imprisonment in Medieval England*, Cambridge: Cambridge University Press.

Punch, M. (1985) *Conduct Unbecoming*, London: Tavistock.

Punch, M. (1996) *Dirty Business: Exploring Corporate Misconduct*, London: Sage.

Punch, M. (1999) 'Tackling business crime within companies', *Security Journal*, 12 (2): 39–52.

Punch, M. (2000) 'Suite Violence: Why Managers Murder and Corporations Kill', *Crime, Law and Social Change*, 33: 243–80.

Punch, M. (2003) 'Rotten Orchards: "Pestilence", Police Misconduct and System Failure', *Policing and Society*, 13 (2): 171–96.

Punch, M. and Naylor, T. (1973) 'The Police: A Social Service', *New Society*, 24: 358–61.

Radford, J. (1987) 'Policing Male Violence – Policing Women', in J. Hanmer and M. Maynard (eds) *Women, Violence and Social Control*, Basingstoke: Macmillan.

Rafter, N. H. (1997) *Creating Born Criminals*, Chicago: University of Illinois Press.

Raistrick, D., Hodgson, R. and Ritson, B. (eds) (1999) *Tackling Alcohol Together*, London: Free Association Books.

Raja, M. (2003) 'The Pirates Who Still Rule the Waves', *The Week*, 13 September: 14, quoting Asia Online, Hong Kong.

Rawlings, P. (1992) *Drunks, Whores and Idle Apprentices: Criminal Biographies of the Eighteenth Century*, London: Routledge.

Rawlings, P. (1995) 'The Idea of Policing: A History', *Policing and Society*, 5: 129–49.

Rawlings, P. (1999) *Crime and Power: A History of Criminal Justice, 1688–1998*, Harlow: Longman.

Rawlings, P. (2002) *Policing: A Short History*, Cullompton, Devon: Willan.

Rawlinson, P. (1998) 'Russian Organised Crime: Moving Beyond Ideology', in V. Ruggiero, N. South and I. Taylor (eds) *The New European Criminology*, London: Routledge.

Rawls, J. (1972) *A Theory of Justice*, Oxford: Oxford University Press.

Ray, L., Smith, D. and Wastell, L. (2003) 'Understanding Racist Violence', in E. A. Stanko (ed.) *The Meanings of Violence*, London: Routledge.

Raynor, P. and Vanstone, M. (2002) *Understanding Community Penalties*, Buckingham: Open University Press.

Reiman, J. (1979) *The Rich Get Richer and the Poor Get Prison: Ideology, Class and Criminal Justice*, New York: Wiley.

Reiman, J. (1988) 'The Justice of the Death Penalty in an Unjust World', in K. Haas and J. A. Inciardi (eds) *Challenging Capital Punishment: Legal and Social Science Approaches*, Newbury Park, CA: Sage.

Reiman, J. (2001) *The Rich Get Richer and the Poor Get Prison*, 6th edn, Boston: Allyn and Bacon.

Reiman, J. and Leighton, P. (2003) *Getting Tough on Corporate Crime? Enron and a Year of Corporate Financial Scandals* (supplement to Reiman, 2001).

Reiner, R. (1985) *The Politics of the Police*, Hemel Hempstead: Harvester Wheatsheaf.

Reiner, R. (1992a) *The Politics of the Police*, 2nd edn, Hemel Hempstead: Harvester Wheatsheaf.

Reiner, R (1992b) 'Police Research in the United Kingdom: A Critical Review', in N. Morris and M. Tonry (eds) *Modern Policing*, Chicago: University of Chicago Press.

Reiner, R. (1993) 'Race, Crime and Justice: Models of Interpretation', in L. Gelsthorpe (ed.) *Minority Ethnic Groups in the Criminal Justice System*, Cambridge: Institute of Criminology, University of Cambridge.

Reiner, R. (2000) *The Politics of the Police*, 3rd edn, Oxford: Oxford University Press.

Reiner, R. (2002) 'Media Made Criminality: The Representation of Crime in the Mass Media', in M. Maguire, R. Morgan and R. Reiner (eds) *The Oxford Handbook of Criminology*, 3rd edn, Oxford: Oxford University Press.

Reiner, R. and Spencer, S. (eds) (1993) *Accountable Policing: Effectiveness, Empowerment and Equity*, London: Institute for Public Policy Research.

Reiner, R., Livingstone, S. and Allen, J. (2001) 'Casino Culture: Media and Crime in a Winner–Loser Society', in K. Stenson and R. Sullivan (eds) *Crime, Risk and Justice: The Politics of Crime Control in Liberal Democracies*, Cullompton, Devon: Willan.

Reuter, P. (1984) *Disorganised Crime*, Cambridge, MA: MIT Press.

Reuter, P., MacCoun, R. J. and Murphy, P. (1990) *Money from Crime: A Study of the Economics of Drug Dealing in Washington, DC*, Santa Monica, CA: Rand.

Revolving Doors Agency (2002) *Where Do They Go? Housing, Mental Health and Criminal Justice*, London: Revolving Doors.

Reynolds, L. (1974) 'Rape as Social Control', *Catalyst*, 8: 62–88.

Ridley, A. and Dunford, L. (1994) 'Corporate Liability for Manslaughter: Reform and the Art of the Possible', *International Journal of the Sociology of Law*, 22: 309–28.

Ritzer, G. (2002) *The McDonaldization Reader*, London: Sage.

Robb, G. (1992) *White Collar Crime in Modern England: Financial Fraud and Business Morality 1845–1929*, Cambridge: Cambridge University Press.

Robert, K. M. (1938) 'Social Structure and Anomie', *American Sociological Review*, 3: 672–82.

Roberts, M. (2003) *Drugs and Crime: From Warfare to Welfare*, London: NACRO.

Robertson, G. (1993) *Freedom, the Individual and the Law*, London: Penguin.

Robertson, R. (1992) *Globalization*, London: Sage.

Robertson, G. (1999) *Crimes against Humanity*, London: Penguin.

Robinson, F., Keithley, J., Robinson, S. and Childs, S. (1998) *Exploring the Impacts of Crime on Health and Health Services: A Feasibility Study*, Durham: Sociology and Social Policy, University of Durham.

Rock, P. (1996) *Reconstructing a Woman's Prison: The Holloway Redevelopment Project*, Oxford: Clarendon Press.

Rock, P. (1998) *After Homicide*, Oxford: Clarendon Press.

Rock, P. (2002) Sociological Theories of Crime', in M. Maguire, R. Morgan and R. Reiner (eds) *The Oxford Handbook of Criminology*, 3rd edn, Oxford: Oxford University Press.

Roebuck, J. and Windham, G. (1983) 'Professional theft', in G. P. Waldo (ed.) *Criminal Careers*, Beverly Hills CA: Sage.

Rojek, C. (2003) *Stuart Hall*, Cambridge: Polity.

Rose, N. (1996) 'The Death of the Social? Re-figuring the Territory of Territory', *Economy and Society*, 25 (3): 327–56.

Rose, N. (2000) 'The Biology of Culpability: Pathological Identity and Crime Control in a Biological Culture', *Theoretical Criminology*, 4 (1): 5–34.

Rothman, D. (1971) *The Discovery of the Asylum*, Boston: Little, Brown.

Rothman, D. (1980) *Conscience and Convenience: The Asylum and Its Alternatives in Progressive America*, Boston: Little, Brown.

Rothman, M., Entzel, P. and Dunlop, B. (eds) (2000) *Elders, Crime and the Criminal Justice System*, New York: Springer-Verlag.

Rowell, A. (1996) *Green Backlash: Global Subversion of the Environment Movement*, London: Routledge.

Rowntree Foundation (1995) *Income and Wealth: Report of the Joseph Rowntree Foundation Inquiry Group*, York: Joseph Rowntree Foundation.

Royal College of Psychiatrists (1986) *Alcohol: Our Favourite Drug*, London: Tavistock.

Royal Commission on Criminal Justice (RRCJ) (1993) Report, Cm 2263, London: HMSO.

Rozenberg, J. (1993) 'Miscarriages of Justice', in E. Stockdale and S. Casale (eds) *Criminal Justice under Stress*, London: Blackstone.

Rubin, G. (1984) 'Thinking Sex', in C. S. Vance (ed.) *Pleasure and Danger*, London. Routledge.

Rudé, G. (1964) *The Crowd in History*, New York, Wiley.

Ruggiero, V. (1996) *Organized and Corporate Crime in Europe: Offers That Can't Be Refused*, Aldershot: Dartmouth.

Ruggiero, V. (2000) 'Transnational Crime: Official and Alternative Fears', *International Journal of the Sociology of Law*, 28: 187–99.

Ruggiero, V. and South, N. (1995) *Eurodrugs: Drug Use, Markets and Trafficking in Europe*, London: UCL Press.

Ruggiero, V. and South, N. (1997) 'The Late-Modern City as a Bazaar', *British Journal of Sociology*, 48 (1): 55–71.

Runciman Report (2000) *Report of the Independent Inquiry into the Misuse of Drugs Act 1971*, London: Police Foundation.

Rusche, G. and Kirchheimer, O. (1939/1968) *Punishment and Social Structure*, New York: Russell and Russell.

Ruzza, C. (1996) 'Inter-organizational Negotiations in Political Decision Making: Brussels' ECB Bureaucrats and the Environment', in C. Samson and N. South (eds) *The Social Construction of Social Policy*, Basingstoke: Macmillan.

Sales, E., Baum, M. and Shore, B. (1984) 'Victim Readjustment following Assault', *Journal of Social Issues*, 40 (1): 117–36.

Sampson, A. (1994) *Acts of Abuse: Sex Offenders and the Criminal Justice System*, London: Routledge.

Samuel, R. (1981) *East End Underworld: Chapters in the Life of Arthur Harding*, London: Routledge.

Sanders, A. (1988) 'The Limits to Diversion from Prosecution', *British Journal of Criminology*, 28: 513–32.

Sanders, A. and Young, R. (2000) *Criminal Justice*, 2nd edn, London: Butterworths.

Sanders, A. and Young, R. (2002) 'From Suspect to Trial', in M. Maguire, R. Morgan and R. Reiner (eds) *The Oxford Handbook of Criminology*, 3rd edn, Oxford: Oxford University Press.

Sapsford, R. (1996) *Researching Crime and Criminal Justice*, Milton Keynes: Open University Press.

Savage, S., Charman, S. and Cope, S. (2000) *Policing and the Power of Persuasion: The Changing Role of the Association of Chief Police Officers*, London: Blackstone.

Scarce, R. (1994) '(No) Trial (But) Tribulations: When Courts and Ethnography Conflict', *Journal of Contemporary Ethnography*, 23: 123–49.

Scarce, R. (1995) 'Scholarly Ethics and Courtroom Antics: Where Researchers Stand in the Eyes of the Law', *American Sociologist*, 26: 87–112.

Scarman, Lord (1981) *The Scarman Report: Report of an Inquiry*, London: HMSO.

Scarpitti, A. and Block, A. (1987) 'America's Toxic Waste Racket', in T. S. Bynum (ed.) *Organized Crime in America: Concepts and Controversies*, New York: Criminal Justice Publishers.

Scheff, T. J. (1966) *Being Mentally Ill*, London: Weidenfeld and Nicolson.

Scheff, T. J., Retzinger, S. M. and Ryan, M. T. (1989) 'Crime, Violence, and Self-Esteem: Review and Proposals', in A. Mecca, N. J. Smelser and J. Vasconcellos (eds) *The Social Importance of Self-Esteem*, Berkeley: University of California Press.

Scheper-Hughes, N. and Wacquant, L. (eds) (2002) *Commodifying Bodies*, London: Sage.

Schlesinger, P., Dobash, R., Dobash, R. and Weaver, K. (1992) *Women Watching Violence*, London: British Film Institute.

Schlesinger, P. and Tumber, H. (1994) *Reporting Crime: The Media Politics of Criminal Justice*, Oxford: Clarendon Press.

Schubart, R. (1995) 'From Desire to Deconstruction: Horror Films and Audience Reactions', in D. Kidd-Hewitt and R. Osborne (eds) *Crime and the Media: The Post-modern Spectacle*, London: Pluto.

Schur, E. (1963) *Crimes without Victims: Deviant Behavior and Public Policy*, Englewood Cliffs, NJ: Prentice Hall.

Schwendinger, H. J. and Schwendinger, J. (1970/1975) 'Guardians of Order or Defenders of Human Rights?', in I. Taylor, P. Walton and J. Young (eds) *Critical Criminology*, London: Routledge and Kegan Paul.

Scott, J. (1996) *Stratification and Power: Structures of Class, Status and Command*, Cambridge: Polity.

Scott, M. (1968) *The Racing Game*, Chicago: Aldine.

Scott, W. R. (2001) *Institutions and Organizations*, 2nd edn, London: Sage.

Scraton, P. (1999) 'Policing with Contempt: The Degrading of Truth and Denial of Justice in the Aftermath of the Hillsborough Disaster', *Journal of Law and Society*, 26 (3): 273–97.

Scull, A. (1977) *Decarceration: Community Treatment and the Deviant – A Radical View*, Englewood Cliffs, NJ: Prentice Hall.

Seddon, T. (2002) 'Five Myths about Drugs and Crime', *Safer Society*, 14, Autumn.

Shapland, J. (1986) 'Victim Assistance and the Criminal Justice System', in E. A. Fattah (ed.) *From Crime Policy to Victim Policy*, Basingstoke: Macmillan.

Shapland, J. and Hobbs, D. (1989) 'Policing on the Ground' in R. Morgan and D. Smith (eds) *Coming to Terms with Policing*, London: Routledge.

Shapland, J., Willmore, J. and Duff, P. (1985) *Victims in the Criminal Justice System*, Aldershot: Gower.

Shaw, C. (1930) *The Jack Roller*, Chicago: University of Chicago Press.

Shearing, C. and Stenning, P. (1987) '"Say Cheese!" The Disney Order That Is Not So Mickey Mouse', in C. Shearing and P. Stenning (eds) *Private Policing*, Newbury Park, CA: Sage.

Shepherd, J. (1990) 'Violent Crime in Bristol: An Accident and Emergency Department Perspective', *British Journal of Criminology*, 30: 289–305.

Shepherd, J. and Farrington, D. (1993) 'Assault as a Public Health Problem', *Journal of the Royal Society of Medicine*, 86: 89–92.

Shepherd, J. and Lisles, C. (1998) 'Towards Multi-agency Violence Prevention and Victim Support', *British Journal of Criminology*, 3: 351–70.

Sherman, L. (1974) *Police Corruption*, New York: Anchor.

Sherman, L. W. (1995) 'Hot Spots of Crime and Criminal Careers of Places', in J. Eck and D. Weisburd (eds) *Crime and Place*, New York: Criminal Justice Press.

Shermer, M. and Grobman, A. (2000) *Denying History: Who Says the Holocaust Never Happened and Why Do They Say It?*, Berkeley: University of California Press.

Shiner, M. and Newburn, T. (1999). 'Taking Tea with Noel: The Place and Meaning of Drug Use in Everyday Life' in N. South (ed.) *Drugs, Cultures, Controls and Everyday Life*, London: Sage.

Shover, N. (1991) 'Burglary', in M. Tonry (ed.) *Crime and Justice: A Review of Research*, vol. 14, Chicago: University of Chicago Press.

Shover, N. (1996) *Great Pretenders: Pursuits and Games of Persistent Thieves*, Boulder, CO: Westview Press.

Showalter, E. (1991) *Sexual Anarchy: Gender and Culture at the Fin de Siècle*, London. Bloomsbury.

Silverman, E. (1999) *NYPD Battles Crime: Innovative Strategies in Policing*, Boston: Northeastern University Press.

Silverman, J. and Wilson, D. (2002) *Innocence Betrayed: Paedophilia, the Media and Society*, Cambridge: Polity.

Simmons, J. and Dodd, T. (2003) *Crime in England and Wales 2002/2003*, London: Home Office.

Sim, J. (1990) *Medical Power in Prisons*, Buckingham: Open University Press.

Sim, J., Scraton, P. and Gordon, P. (1987) 'Introduction: Crime, the State and Critical Analysis', in P. Scraton (ed.) *Law, Order and the Authoritarian State*, Milton Keynes: Open University Press.

Sims, L. and Myhill, A. (2001) *Policing and the Public: Findings from the 2000 British Crime Survey*, Home Office Research Findings 136, London: Home Office.

Singer, E (2003) '"And Here Is the Local Crime Forecast [.]"', *New Scientist*, 16 August, 179 (2408): 13.

Singleton, N., Meltzer, H., Gatward, R., Coid, J. and Deasy, D. (1997) *Psychiatric Morbidity among Prisoners*, London: Office for National Statistics.

Skolnick, J. (1966) *Justice without Trial*, London: Wiley.

Skolnick, J. and Bayley, D. (1986) *The New Blue Line*, New York: Free Press.

Skrobankek, S., Boonpakdee N. and Jatateero, C. (1997) *The Traffic in Women: Human Realities of the International Sex Trade*, London: Zed Books.

Skyes, G. M. and Matza, D. (1957) 'Techniques of Neutralization: A Theory of Delinquency', *American Sociological Review*, 22: 664–70.

Slapper, G. and Tombs, S. (1999) *Corporate Crime*, Harlow: Longman.

Smandych, R. (1999) *Governable Places: Readings on Governmentality and Crime Control*, Aldershot: Ashgate.

Smart, C. (1989) *Feminism and the Power of the Law*, London: Routledge.

Smart, C. (1990) 'Feminist Approaches to Criminology, or Postmodern Woman Meets Atavistic Man', in L. Gelsthorpe and A. Morris (eds) *Feminist Perspectives in Criminology*, Buckingham: Open University Press.

Smart, C. (1995) *Law, Crime and Sexuality: Essays in Feminism*, London: Sage.

Smart, C. (1997) *Women, Crime and Criminology: A Feminist Critique*, London: Routledge.

Smelser, N. (1962) *Theory of Collective Behavior*, New York: Free Press.

Smith, D. (1994) *The Sleep of Reason: The James Bulger Case*, London: Century.

Smith, L. (1989) *Concerns about Rape*, Home Office Research Study 106, London: HMSO.

Smith, R. and Windes, R. R. (2000) *Progay/Antigay: The Rhetorical War over Sexuality*, Thousand Oaks, Calif.: Sage.

Snodgrass, J. (1982) *The Jack-Roller at Seventy*, Lexington, MA: D. C. Heath.

Snyder, L. (1991) 'The Regulatory Dance: Understanding Reform Processes in Corporate Crime', *International Journal of the Sociology of Law*, 19: 209–36.

Soloway, I. and Walters, J. (1977) 'Workin' the Corner: The Ethics and Legality of Ethnographic Fieldwork among Active Heroin Addicts', in R. S. Weppner (ed.) *Street Ethnography: Selected Studies of Crime and Drug Use in Natural Settings*, Beverly Hills, CA: Sage.

South, N. (1988) *Policing for Profit*, London: Sage.

South, N. (ed.) (1995) *Drugs, Crime and Criminal Justice*, 2 vols, Aldershot: Dartmouth.

South, N. (1997) 'Late-Modern Criminology: "Late" as in "Dead" or "Modern" as in "New"?', in D. Owen (ed.) *Sociology after Postmodernism*, London and Thousand Oaks, CA: Sage.

South, N. (1998a) 'Corporate and State Crimes against the Environment: Foundations for a Green Perspective in European Criminology', in V. Ruggiero, N. South and I. Taylor (eds) *The New European Criminology*, London and New York: Routledge.

South, N. (1998b) 'A Green Field for Criminology? A Proposal for a Perspective', *Theoretical Criminology*, 2 (2): 211–34.

South, N. (ed.) (1999a) *Youth Crime, Deviance and Delinquency*, 2 vols, Aldershot: Dartmouth.

South, N. (ed.) (1999b) *Drugs: Cultures, Controls and Everyday Life*, London: Sage.

South, N. (2002) 'Drugs, Alcohol and Crime', in M. Maguire, R. Morgan and R. Reiner (eds) *The Oxford Handbook of Criminology*, 3rd edn, Oxford: Oxford University Press.

South, N. and Weiss, R. (eds) (1998) *Comparing Prison Systems: Toward a Comparative and International Penology*, Reading: Gordon and Breach.

Southwell, D. (2002) *Dirty Cash: Organised Crime in the 21st Century*, London: Virgin.

Spalek, B. (2001) 'Regulation, White Collar Crime and the Bank of Credit and Commerce International', *Howard Journal of Criminal Justice*, 40 (2): 166–79.

Sparks, R. (1992) *Television and the Drama of Crime: Moral Tales and the Place of Crime in Public Life*, Milton Keynes: Open University Press.

Sparks, R. (1993) 'Inspector Morse: "The Last Enemy"', in G. Brandt (ed.) *British Television Drama in the 1980s*, Cambridge: Cambridge University Press.

Sparks, R. (2000) 'Perspectives on Risk and Penal Politics', in T. Hope and R. Sparks (eds) *Crime, Risk and Insecurity*, London: Routledge.

Sparks, R. (2001) 'Prisons, Punishment and Penality', in E. McLaughlin and J. Muncie (eds) *Controlling Crime*, London: Sage.

Sparks, R. (2002) 'Prisons, Punishment and Penality', in E. McLaughlin and J. Muncie (eds) *Controlling Crime*, 2nd edn, London: Sage.

Sparks, R. Bottoms, A. and Hay, W. (1996) *Prisons and the Problem of Order*, Oxford: Clarendon Press.

Spierenburg, P. (1984) *The Spectacle of Suffering: Executions and the Evolution of Repression*, Cambridge: Cambridge University Press.

Spierenburg, P. (1998) 'The Body and the State: Early Modern Europe', in N. Morris and D. Rothman (eds) *The Oxford History of the Prison: The Practice of Punishment in Western Society*, Oxford: Oxford University Press.

Spitzer, S. (1987) 'Security and Control in Capitalist Societies: The Fetishism of Security and the Secret Thereof', in J. Lowman, R. J. Menzies and T. S. Palys (eds) *Transcarceration: Essays in the Sociology of Social Control*, Aldershot: Gower.

Stanko, E. (1990) *Everyday Violence*, London: Pandora.

Stanko, E. (1994) *Perspectives on Violence*, London: Quartet.

Stanko, E., Marian, L., Crisp, D., Manning, R., Smith, J. and Cowan, S. (1998) *Taking Stock*, Uxbridge, Middlesex: Brunel University.

Stanko, E. A., Kielinger, V., Paterson, S., Richards, L., Crisp, D. and Marsland, L. (2003) *Grounded Crime Prevention: Responding to and Understanding Hate Crime*, Mainz: Weisser-Ring.

Stein, A. (2001) *Strangers in Our Midst*, Boston: Beacon.

Stelfox, P. (1998) 'Policing Lower Levels of Organised Crime in England and Wales', *Howard Journal of Criminal Justice*, 37 (4): 393–406.

Stern, V. (1993) *Bricks of Shame*, London: Penguin.

Stevenson, D. (2003) *Cities and Urban Culture*, Buckingham: Open University Press.

Stevenson, N. (1999) *The Transformation of the Media: Globalisation, Morality and Ethics*, Harlow: Longman.

Stockdale, J. and Gresham, P. (1995) *Combating Burglary: An Evaluation of Three Strategies*, Crime Detention and Prevention Series Paper 59, London: Home Office.

Stones, R. (1996) *Sociological Reasoning*, Basingstoke: Macmillan.

Storch, R. (1975) 'The Plague of Blue Locusts: Police Reform and Popular Resistance in Northern England 1840–57', *International Review of Social History*, 20: 61–90.

Storch, R. (1976) 'The Policeman as Domestic Missionary', *Journal of Social History*, 9 (4): 481–509.

Strang, J. and Stimson, G. (eds) (1991) *AIDS and Drug Misuse*, London: Routledge.

Sumner, C. (1976) 'Marxism and Deviancy Theory', in P. Wiles (ed.) *Sociology of Crime and Delinquency in Britain*, vol. 2, London: Martin Robertson.

Surette, R. (1998) *Media, Crime and Criminal Justice: Images and Realities*, Belmont, CA: Wadsworth.

Sutherland, E. (1937) *The Professional Thief*, Chicago: University of Chicago Press.

Sutherland, E. (1950) 'The Diffusion of Sexual Psychopath Laws', *American Journal of Sociology*, 56: 142–8.

Sutherland, E. (1956) *The Sutherland Papers*, ed. A. K. Cohen, A. R. Lindesmith and K. Schlussler, Bloomington: Indiana University Press. Republished as Sutherland, E. (1973) *On Analyzing Crime*, ed. K. Schlussler, Chicago: University of Chicago Press.

Sutherland, E. H. (1949) *White Collar Crime*, New York: Holt, Rinehart and Winston.

Sutherland, E. with Locke, H. J. (1936) *Twenty Thousand Homeless Men*, Philadelphia: J. B. Lippincott.

Sutton, M. (1998) *Handling Stolen Goods and Theft*, Home Office Research Study 178, London: Home Office.

Sykes, G. (1958) *The Society of Captives*, Princeton, NJ: Princeton University Press.

Szasz, A. (1986) 'Corporations, Organised Crime and the Disposal of Hazardous Waste: An Examination of the Making of a Criminogenic Regulatory Structure', *Criminology*, 24 (1): 1–27.

Szasz, A. (1994) *EcoPopulism: Toxic Waste and the Movement for Environmental Justice*, Minneapolis: University of Minnesota Press.

Tannenbaum, F. (1938) *Crime and the Community*, New York: McGraw-Hill.

Tatchell, P. (2002) 'Some People Are More Equal Than Others', in P. Iganski (ed.) *The Hate Debate*, London: Profile.

Tappan, P. (1947) 'Who Is the Criminal?', *American Sociological Review*, 12: 96–102.

Taylor, A. (1993) *Women Drug Users: An Ethnography of a Female Injecting Community*, Oxford: Clarendon Press.

Taylor, H. (1999) 'Forging the Job: A Crisis of "Modernisation" or Redundancy for the Police in England and Wales, 1900–1939', *British Journal of Criminology*, 39 (1): 113–35.

Taylor, I. (1997) 'Crime, Anxiety, and Locality: Responding to the Condition of England at the End of the Century', *Theoretical Criminology*, 1 (1): 53–76.

Taylor, I. (1999) *Crime in Context: A Critical Criminology of Market Societies*, Cambridge: Polity.

Taylor, I. (2002) 'The Political Economy of Crime', in M. Maguire, R. Morgan and R. Reiner (eds) *The Oxford Handbook of Criminology*, 3rd edn, Oxford: Oxford University Press.

Taylor, I. and Jamieson, R. (1997) '"Proper Little Mesters": Nostalgia and Protest in De-industrialised Sheffield', in S. Westwood and J. Williams (eds) *Imagining Cities: Scripts, Signs, Memory*, London: Routledge.

Taylor, I. and Taylor, L. (eds) (1973) *Politics and Deviance*, Harmondsworth: Penguin.

Taylor, I., Walton, P. and Young, J. (1973) *The New Criminology: For a Social Theory of Deviance*, London: Routledge and Kegan Paul.

Taylor, P. (1999) *Hackers: Crime in the Digital Sublime*, London: Routledge.

Taylor, P. (2000) 'Hackers – Cyberpunks or Microserfs?' in D. Thomas, and B. D. Loader (eds) *Cybercrime: Law Enforcement, Security and Surveillance in the Information Age*, London: Routledge.

Taylor, P. (2003) 'Maestros or Misogynists? Gender and the Social Construction of Hacking', in Y. Jewkes (ed.) *Dot.cons: Crime, Deviance and Identity on the Internet*, Cullompton, Devon: Willan.

Thomas, D. and Loader, B. D. (eds) (2000) *Cybercrime: Law Enforcement, Security and Surveillance in the Information Age*, London: Routledge.

Thomas, T. (2000) *Sex Crime: Sex Offending and Society*, Cullompton, Devon: Willan.

Thompson, E. P. (1963) *The Making of the English Working Class*, Harmondsworth: Penguin.

Thompson, E. P. (1977) *Whigs and Hunters: The Origin of the Black Act*, Harmondsworth: Penguin.

Thompson, J. (1995) *The Media and Modernity*, Cambridge: Polity.

Thompson, K. (1998) *Moral Panics*, London: Routledge.

Thrasher, F. (1927) *The Gang*, Chicago: University of Chicago Press.

Tomsen, S. (1997), 'A Top Night: Social Protest, Masculinity and the Culture of Drinking Violence', *British Journal of Criminology*, 37 (1): 90–102.

Tithecott, R. (1997) *Of Men and Monsters: Jeffrey Dahmer and the Construction of the Serial Killer*, Madison: University of Wisconsin Press.

Tremblay, M. (1986) 'Designing Crime: The Short Life Expectancy and the Workings of a Recent Wave of Credit Card Bank Frauds', *British Journal of Criminology*, 26: 234–53.

Trickett, A., Osborn, D., Seymour, J. and Pease, K. (1992) 'What Is Different about High Crime Areas?', *British Journal of Criminology*, 32: 81–9.

Turner, B. (1996) *The Body and Society*, 2nd edn, London: Sage.

Turton, J. (2000) 'Maternal Sexual Abuse and Its Victims', *Childright*, 165: 17–18.

Uglow, S. (2002) *Criminal Justice*, London: Sweet and Maxwell.

Ungar, S. (2001) 'Moral Panic versus the Risk Society: The Implications of the Changing Sites of Social Anxiety', *British Journal of Sociology*, 52 (2): 271–91.

United Nations Educational, Scientific and Cultural Organisation (UNESCO) (1997) *Preventing the Illicit Traffic in Cultural Property. A Resource Handbook for the Implementation of the 1970 UNESCO Convention*, Paris: UNESCO.

US Federal Bureau of Investigation (1999) *Hate Crime Data Collection Guidelines*, Washington, DC: Federal Bureau of Investigation, US Department of Justice.

Useem, B. and Kimball, P. (1989) *States of Siege: U.S. Prison Riots, 1971–1986*, Oxford: Oxford University Press.

Vallier, C. (2002a) *Theories of Crime and Punishment*, Harlow: Pearson.

Vallier, C. (2002b) 'Punishment, Border Crossings and the Powers of Horror', *Theoretical Criminology*, 6 (3): 319–37.

Valverde, M. (1996) 'Social Facicity and the Law: A Social Expert's Eyewitness Account of the Law', *Social and Legal Studies*, 5 (2): 201–18.

Van Dijk, J. J. M. (1985) 'Regaining a Sense of Community and Order', in European Committee on Crime Problems, *Research on Crime Victims*, Strasbourg: Council of Europe, 145–64.

Van Dijk, J. J. M., Mayhew, P. and Killias, M. (1990) *Experiences of Crime across the World: Key Findings of the 1989 International Crime Survey*, Deventer, The Netherlands: Kluwer.

Van Duyne, P. (1993) 'Organised Crime and Business Crime Enterprises in the Netherlands', *Crime, Law and Social Change*, 19: 103–42.

Vass, A. (1986) *AIDS: A Plague in Us*, Cambridge: Venus Academica.

Vine, I. (1997) 'The Dangerous Psycho-logic of Media "Effects"', in M. Barker and J. Petley (eds) *Ill Effects: The Media/Violence Debate*, London: Routledge.

Virdee, S. (1997) 'Racial Harassment', in T. Modood and R. Berthoud (eds) *Ethnic Minorities in Britain*, London: Policy Studies Institute.

Vogel, D. (1986) *National Styles of Regulation: Environmental Policy in Great Britain and the United States*, Ithaca, NY: Cornell University Press.

Vold, G. B. (1958) *Theoretical Criminology*, Oxford: Oxford University Press.

von Hentig, H. (1948) *The Criminal and His Victim*, New Haven, Conn.: Yale University Press.

von Hirsch, A. (1976) *Doing Justice: The Choice of Punishments*, New York: Hill and Wang.

von Hirsch, A. (1985) *Past or Future Crimes: Deservedness and Dangerousness in the Sentencing of Criminals*, Manchester: Manchester University Press.

Wacquant, L. (2001) 'Deadly Symbiosis: When Prison and Ghetto Meet and Merge', *Punishment and Society*, 3 (1): 95–134.

Waddington, P. A. J. (1996) 'Public Order Policing: Citizenship and Moral Ambiguity', in F. Leishman, B. Loveday and S. Savage (eds) *Core Issues in Policing*, Harlow: Longman.

Walker, C. and Starmer, K. (1999) *Miscarriages of Justice: A Review of Justice in Error*, London: Blackstone.

Walker, N. (1991) *Why Punish?*, Oxford: Oxford University Press.

Walklate, S. (1995) *Gender and Crime: An Introduction*, London: Prentice Hall.

Walklate, S. (2001) *Gender, Crime and Criminal Justice*, Cullompton, Devon: Willan.

Walkowitz, J. (1980) *Prostitution and Victorian Society: Women, Class and the State*, Cambridge: Cambridge University Press.

Walkowitz, J. (1984) 'Male Vice and Female Virtue: Feminism and the Politics of Prostitution in Nineteenth Century Britain', in A. Snitow, C. Stansell and S. Thompson (eds) *Power and Desire: The Politics of Sexuality*, London: Virago.

Walkowitz, J. R. (1992) *City of Dreadful Delight: Narratives of Sexual Danger in Late Victorian London*, London: Virago.

Wall, D. (2001) 'Cybercrimes on the Internet', in D. Wall (ed.) *Crime and the Internet*, London: Routledge.

Walmsley, R. (2003) *World Prison Population List*, 4th edn, London: The Stationery Office.

Walton, P. and Young, J. (1997) *The New Criminology Revisited*, Basingstoke: Macmillan.

Walzer, M. (1986) 'The Politics of Michel Foucault', in D. Couzens Hoy (ed.) *Foucault: A Critical Reader*, Oxford: Basil Blackwell.

Watney, S. (1997) *Policing Desire: Pornography, AIDS and the Media*, 3rd edn, London: Cassell.

Weale, A. (1996) 'Grinding Slow and Grinding Sure? The Making of the Environment Agency', *Environmental Management and Health*, 7 (2): 40–3.

Weber, M. (1958/1970) *From Max Weber: Essays in Sociology*, trans. and ed. H. J. H. Gerth and C. W. Mills, London: Routledge and Kegan Paul.

Webster, C. (1994) *The Keighley Crime Survey*, Bradford and Ilkley Community College.

Weeks, J. (1989) *Sex, Politics and Society: The Regulation of Sexuality since 1800*, 2nd edn, Harlow: Longman.

Weinberger, B. (1981) 'The Police and the Public in Mid 19th Century Warwickshire', in V. Bailey (ed.) *Policing and Punishment in 19th Century Britain*, London: Croom Helm.

Weinstein, J. (1992) 'First Amendment Challenges to Hate Crime Legislation: Where's the Speech?', *Criminal Justice Ethics*, 11 (2): 6–20.

Weisburd, D., Waring, E. and Chayel, E. (2001) *White Collar Crime and Criminal Careers*, Cambridge: Cambridge University Press.

Wells, C. (1993) *Corporations and Criminal Responsibility*, Oxford: Clarendon Press.

White, K. (1993) *The First Sexual Revolution*, New York: New York Press.

Whittle, S. (2002) *Transgender laws*, London: Routledge.

Wilkins, L. T. (1967) *Social Policy, Action and Research*, London: Tavistock.

Williams, C. (1996) 'Environmental Victims: An Introduction', in C. Williams (ed.) *Environmental Victims*, special issue of *Social Justice*, 23 (4): 1–6.

Williams, R. (1983) *Keywords: A Vocabulary of Culture and Society*, 2nd edn, London, Fontana,

Willis, P. (1977) *Learning to Labour: How Working Class Kids Get Working Class Jobs*, London: Saxon House.

Wilson, J. Q. (1975) *Thinking about Crime*, New York: Basic Books.

Winlow, S. (2001) *Badfellas: Crime, Tradition and New Masculinities*, Oxford: Berg.

Wiseman, J. P. (1970) *Stations of the Lost*, Englewood Cliffs, NJ: Prentice Hall.

Witte, R. (1996) *Racist Violence and the State*, Harlow: Longman.

Wolfgang, M. (1958) *Patterns in Criminal Homicide*, Philadelphia: University of Pennsylvania Press.

Wolfgang, M. (1960) 'Cesare Lombroso', in M. Hermann (ed.) *Pioneers in Criminology*, London: Stevens.

Woolf, H. and Tumim, S. (1991) *Prison Disturbances April 1990*, Cm 1456, London: HMSO.

Worrall, A. (1997) *Punishment in the Community: The Future of Criminal Justice*, Harlow: Addison Wesley Longman.

Wright, M. (1991) *Justice for Victims and Offenders*, Buckingham: Open University Press.

Yablonsky, L. (1965) 'Experiences with the Criminal Community', in A. Gouldner and S. M. Miller (eds) *Applied Sociology*, New York: Free Press.

Young, A. (1996) *Imagining Crime: Textual Outlaws and Criminal Conversations*, London: Sage.

Young, J. (1971) *The Drugtakers*, London: Paladin.

Young, J. (1973) 'The Myth of the Drug Taker in the Mass Media', in S. Cohen and J. Young (eds) *The Manufacture of News*, London: Constable.

Young, J. (1974) 'Mass Media, Drugs and Deviance', in P. Rock and M. Mackintosh (eds) *Deviance and Social Control*, London: Tavistock.

Young, J. (1975) 'Working Class Criminology', in I. Taylor, P. Walton and J. Young (eds) *Critical Criminology*, London: Routledge.

Young, J. (1979) 'Left Idealism, Reformism and beyond: from New Criminology to Marxism' in B. Fine, R. Kinsey, J. Lea, S. Picciotto and J. Young (eds) *Capitalism and the Rule of Law*, London: Hutchinson.

Young, J. (1986) 'The Failure of Criminology: The Need for a Radical Realism', in J. Young and R. Matthews (eds) *Confronting Crime*, London: Sage.

Young, J. (1987) 'The Tasks Facing a Realist Criminology', *Contemporary Crises*, 11: 337–56.

Young, J. (1992) 'The Rising Demand for Law and Order and Our Maginot Lines of Defence against Crime', in N. Abercrombie and A. Warde (eds) *Social Change in Contemporary Britain*, Cambridge: Polity.

Young, J. (1997) 'Left Realist Criminology: Radical in Its Analysis, Realist in Its Policy', in M. Maguire, R. Morgan and R. Reiner (eds) *The Oxford Handbook of Criminology*, 2nd edn, Oxford: Clarendon Press.

Young, J. (1999a) *The Exclusive Society*, London: Sage.

Young, J. (1999b) 'Cannibalism and Bulimia: Patterns of Social Control in Late Modernity', *Theoretical Criminology*, 3 (4): 387–407.

Young, J. (2003) 'Searching for a New Criminology of Everyday Life: Review of D. Garland *The Culture of Control*', *British Journal of Criminology*, 42: 445–61.

Zander, M. and Henderson, P. (1993) Crown Court Study, Royal Commission on Criminal Justice Research Study 19, London: HMSO.

Zedner, L. (1991a) 'Women, Crime, and Penal Responses: A Historical Account', in M. Tonry (ed.) *Crime and Justice: A Review of Research*, 14: 307–62.

Zedner, L. (1991b) *Women, Crime and Custody in Victorian England*, Oxford: Clarendon.

Zedner, L. (1995) 'Wayward Sisters: The Prison for Women', in N. Morris and D. Rothman (eds) *The Oxford History of the Prison*, Oxford: Oxford University Press.

Zehr, H. (1990) *Changing Lenses*, Scottdale, PA: Herald Press.

Zhang, S. and Chin, K.-L. (2003) 'The Declining Significance of Triad Societies in Transnational Illegal Activities', *British Journal of Criminology*, 43 (3): 469–88.

Zimring, F. (1996) 'Genetics of Crime: A Skeptic's Vision of the Future', *Politics and the Life Sciences*, 15 (1): 105–6.

Zimring, F. and Hawkins, E. (1995) *Incapacitation: Penal Confinement and the Restraint of Crime*, Oxford: Oxford University Press.

Zola, I. (1972) 'Medicine as an Institution of Social Control', *Sociological Review*, 20: 487–504.

Zurcher, L. A., Jr and Kirkpatrick, R.G. (1976) *Citizens for Decency: Antipornography Crusades as Status Defense*, Austin: University of Texas Press.

WEBLIOGRAPHY

METHODOLOGY AND MEASUREMENT IN CRIMINOLOGY (CHAPTER 2)

Statistics Canada
http://www.statcan.ca/start.html
Produces national statistics on the population, resources, economy, society and culture of Canada.

Federal Bureau of Investigation
http://www.fbi.gov/homepage.htm
The FBI is the principal investigative arm of the United States Department of Justice.

FBI: Hate Crime Data Collection Guidelines
http://www.fbi.gov/ucr/hatecrime.pdf
FBI: National Incident-Based Reporting System on Hate Crimes.

Australian Bureau of Statistics
http://www.abs.gov.au/
The Australian Bureau of Statistics is Australia's official statistical organisation.

The Home Office
http://www.homeoffice.gov.uk/
The Home Office is the government department responsible for internal affairs in England and Wales.

The Scottish Executive
http://www.scotland.gov.uk/
The Scottish Executive is the devolved government for Scotland. It is responsible for most of the issues of day-to-day concern to the people of Scotland, including health, education, justice, rural affairs and transport.

UK Data Archive at the University of Essex:
http://www.data-archive.ac.uk/
The UKDA provides resource discovery and support for secondary use of quantitative and qualitative data in research.

The Question Bank
http://qb.soc.surrey.ac.uk/
Questions from the British Crime Survey can be read online at the Question Bank, University of Surrey.

THE ENLIGHTENMENT AND EARLY TRADITIONS (CHAPTER 3)

Crimetheory.Com
www.crimetheory.com
A Website that provides brief introduction to a number of theories and theorists relevant to Part 2 of the book ('Thinking about crime') in general.

EARLY SOCIOLOGICAL THINKING ABOUT CRIME (CHAPTER 4)

The Émile Durkheim Archive
http://durkheim.itgo.com/anomie.html
A comprehensive Website on Durkheim's life and works.

The University of Chicago: Department of Sociology
http://sociology.uchicago.edu/overview/history.html
Gives a brief history of the original Chicago School theorists.

The Chicago School of Pragmatism
http://www.pragmatism.org/genealogy/Chicago.htm
Provides a brief history of the foundation of the Chicago School of Pragmatism and its members.

The Society for Human Ecology (SHE)
http://www.societyforhumanecology.org/
This is an international interdisciplinary professional society that promotes the use of an ecological perspective in both research and application.

RADICALISING TRADITIONS: LABELLING, NEW CRIMINOLOGIES AND THE GENDER ISSUE (CHAPTER 5)

Howard S. Becker homepage
http://home.earthlink.net/~hsbecker/.
A comprehensive site with a selection of published papers and links.

Allyn & Bacon Publishers
http://www.ablongman.com/signup/
Jeffrey Reiman's book: *The Rich Get Richer and the Poor Get Prison: Ideology, Class, and Criminal Justice*, 6th edition.

SOCIAL CHANGE AND CRIMINOLOGICAL THINKING (CHAPTER 6)

United Nations Crime and Justice Information Network
http://www.uncjin.org
Provides links and information on the United Nations organisations combating crime
on an international level including the following link:

United Nations Office on Drugs and Crime
http://www.odccp.org/crime_cicp_sitemap.html
The United Nations Office on Drugs and Crime (UNODC) is a global leader in the
fight against illicit drugs and international crime.

United Nations Interregional Crime and Justice Research Institute: LMS
bibliographic Database
http://www.unicri.it/bibliographic_database.htm
The Library Collection includes some 6,000 authors, as well as more than 300 series
and 600 publishers. Documents are classified according to the LMS Bibliographic
field structure and subjects that are described according to the UNCRI Thesaurus:
http://www.unicri.it/unicri_thesaurus.htm

United Nations Interregional Crime and Justice Research Institute: World Dictionary
of Criminal Resources

World Directory of Criminological Resources
www.unicri.it/html/world_directory_of_criminology.htm
This site contains more than 470 institutes covering some 70 countries. A number
of countries, in particular developing ones, which do not have criminological
institutes, have nevertheless requested that some of their bodies' services be included
in the Directory.

VICTIMS AND VICTIMIZATION (CHAPTER 7)

Criminal Justice System Online: 'Victims Virtual Walkthrough'
http://www.cjsonline.org/virtual/victims.html
An Interactive virtual tour that provides information about the criminal justice
process as it relates to victims of crime.

The National Archive of Criminal Justice Data
http://www.icpsr.umich.edu/NACJD
Provides information on various international crime victimization surveys.

CRIME AND PROPERTY (CHAPTER 8)

The Home Office: Research Development Statistics – Publications
http://www.homeoffice.gov.uk/rds/pubsintro1.html

The National British Crime Survey provides up-to-date annual information on different types of crime, including property crime, which may or may not be reported to and recorded by the police. Full reports and summaries of BCS findings and many other research studies funded by the Home Office can be found here.

The International Crime Victim Surveys
http://www.unicri.it/icvs/
Information, publications and statistics on international crime victim surveys are available at this site.

CRIME AND SEXUALITY (CHAPTER 9)

The Home Office: The Sexual Offences Bill
http://www.homeoffice.gov.uk/justice/sentencing/sexualoffencesbill/index.html
Information on the Sexual Offences Bill and the White Paper *Protecting the Public*, which was published on 19 November 2000, can be found here.

The National Organisation for the Treatment of Abusers
www.nota.co.uk
NOTA is a growing group comprising practitioners, managers and policymakers for the public, private and voluntary sectors. As a result, NOTA brings a wide variety of perspectives to interventions with sexual aggressors.

The Child and Woman Abuse Unit
http://www.cwasu.org/
The Child and Woman Abuse Unit is based at London Metropolitan University and has a national and international reputation for its research, training and consultancy work. The unit exists to develop feminist research methodologies, theory and practice, especially in relation to connections between forms of sexualised violence.

CRIME AND EMOTION (CHAPTER 10)

American Psychological Association: 'Hate Crimes Today: An Age-Old Foe In Modern Dress'
http://www.apa.org/pubinfo/hate/homepage.html
A question-and-answer site shedding some clarification on the hate crime debate.

Hate Crime.org
http://www.hatecrime.org/
Information and links to related news articles concerning current events, political choices, and victims and further information.

National Gay and Lesbian Task Force: Information on hate crime laws
http://www.ngltf.org/issues/issue.cfm?issueID=12

NGLTF is the national progressive organisation working for the civil rights of gay, lesbian, bisexual and transgender people.

ORGANISATIONAL AND PROFESSIONAL FORMS OF CRIME (CHAPTER 11)

The Web of Justice
http://www.co.pinellas.fl.us/bcc/juscoord/eorganized.htm
The Web of Justice site provides numerous links to other Websites concerned with crime, corruption and power.

The United Nations: Organized Crime
http://www.unodc.org/unodc/en/organized_crime.html
The United Nations site on organised crime provides a source about global developments in crime and control and links to national sites.

The Nathanson Centre: Database
http://www.yorku.ca/nathanson/search.htm
The Nathanson Centre Website provides a searchable bibliographic database to help locate other relevant studies across the whole area of organisational forms of crime.

Criminal Justice Resources: Organised Crime
http://www.lib.msu.edu/harris23/crimjust/orgcrime.htm
The Criminal Justice Resources Website provides links to other sites both official – such as the FBI and Royal Canadian Mounted Police – and unofficial – such as journalist and community sites – concerning various forms of crime.

DRUGS, ALCOHOL, HEALTH AND CRIME (CHAPTER 12)

Drugscope
http://www.drugscope.org.uk/
An invaluable site with access to an online encyclopedia about drugs and to Drugscope's library.

Alcohol Concern
http://www.alcoholconcern.org.uk/
This site provides links to many other useful sites.

Russell Webster: Consultant in Substance Misuse and Crime
http://www.russellwebster.com/
The main purpose of this Website is to signpost UK resources on substance misuse and crime on the Internet.

THINKING ABOUT PUNISHMENT (CHAPTER 13) AND THE CRIMINAL JUSTICE PROCESS (CHAPTER 14)

The Home Office: Publications: A Guide to the Criminal Justice System in England and Wales
http://www.homeoffice.gov.uk/rds/cjspub1.html
Publication available online, on the criminal justice process in England and Wales.

Criminal Justice System
http://www.cjsonline.org/home.html
This is another site that has useful information on the criminal justice process in England and Wales.

Crown Office and Procurator Fiscal Service
http://www.crownoffice.gov.uk/
This site has information on the Scottish criminal justice system plus a selection of other links for reference.

Criminal Justice System Northern Ireland
http://www.cjsni.gov.uk/
A site on the criminal justice process in Northern Ireland.

The Proceedings of the Old Bailey
http://www.oldbaileyonline.org/
A fully searchable online edition of the largest body of texts detailing the lives of non-elite people ever published, containing accounts of over 100,000 criminal trials held at London's central criminal court.

POLICE AND POLICING (CHAPTER 15)

A Web of History: The Peel Web
http://dspace.dial.pipex.com/town/terrace/adw03/peel/laworder/police.htm
An introduction to the formation of the police service.

The Home Office: Police
http://www.homeoffice.gov.uk/crimpol/police/index.html
Provides an insight into the working of the police force.

The Police Complaints Authority
http://www.pca.gov.uk
The PCA is an independent body set up by the government to oversee public complaints against police officers in England and Wales, plus the National Crime Squad, National Criminal Intelligence Service, British Transport, Ministry of Defence, Port of Liverpool, Port of Tilbury, Royal Parks and UKAEA police.

The UK Police Service Portal
http://www.police.uk/
This site provides links to Official Police Forces – both regional and non-regional – and related organisations.

Association of Police Authorities
http://www.apa.police.uk/apa_home.htm
The national voice for police authorities in England, Wales and Northern Ireland. Includes publications and links to other useful sites.

PRISONS AND IMPRISONMENT (CHAPTER 16)

The Home Office
http://www.homeoffice.gov.uk
Provides access to a wide range of information on the CJS generally.

The Home Office: Publications
http://www.homeoffice.gov.uk/rds/pubsintro1.html
Provides access to a wide range of publications.

HM Prison Service
http://www.hmprisonservice.gov.uk/
Contains news, reports, statistics and prison rules for prisons in England and Wales.

The Scottish Prison Service
http://www.sps.gov.uk
Contains news, reports, statistics and prison rules for prisons in Scotland.

The Prison and Probation Ombudsman
http://www.ppo.gov.uk/
The Prisons and Probation Ombudsman provides access to annual reports and publications.

Report of Her Majesty's Chief Inspector of Prisons
http://www.homeoffice.gov.uk/justice/prisons/index.html
A link to a report by the Inspector of Prisons can be found here along with further information on the Inspectorate.

The Howard League for Penal Reform
http://www.howardleague.org/
Information, links and publications on penal reform.

National Association for the Care and Rehabilitation of the Offender (NACRO)
http://www.nacro.org.uk/
This site has information on penal reform and lists relevant publication.

Prison Reform Trust
http://www.prisonreformtrust.org.uk/
Information on the Prison Reform Trust, which aims at creating a just, humane and effective penal system.

Youth Justice Board for England and Wales
www.youth-justice-board.gov.uk.
Contains information on policies, news, press releases and details of youth offending teams.

The Guardian: Prisons
www.guardian.co.uk/prisons
The *Guardian*'s coverage of prison issues is an excellent resource.

The Observer: Special Reports
http://observer.guardian.co.uk/crimedebate
This offers further critical commentary on prison issues.

THE GREENING OF CRIMINOLOGY (CHAPTER 17)

The online environmental community
http://www.envirolink.org/
A major resource for Websites connected to the environment.

Europe and Environmental Crime
http://europa.eu.int/comm/environment/crime/
The pages of the European online site that deals with the environment and crime.

Earthscan
http://www.earthscan.co.uk/
Provides resources and books giving information about the state of the environment.

Friends of the Earth
http://www.foe.org/
Greenpeace
http://www.greenpeace.org/international_en/
The two major activist Websites.

CRIME AND THE MEDIA (CHAPTER 18)

Independent Media Centre
www.indymedia.org
Daily articles produced by a collective of independent media organisations and journalists.

Media Studies.Com
http://www.newmediastudies.com/
A Website for the study of new media, with articles, reviews, guides and other resources.

HUMAN RIGHTS AND CRIMES OF THE STATE (CHAPTER 19)

Amnesty International
http://www.amnesty.org/
A Website on the worldwide movement campaigning for internationally recognised human rights.

Death Penalty Information Centre
http://www.deathpenaltyinfo.org
This Website has information on issues concerning capital punishment.

INDEX

eBooks

eBooks - at www.eBookstore.tandf.co.uk

A library at your fingertips!

eBooks are electronic versions of print books. You can store them onto your PC/laptop or browse them online.

They have advantages for anyone needing rapid access to a wide variety of published, copyright information.

eBooks can help your research by enabling you to bookmark chapters, annotate and use instant searches to find specific words or phrases. Several eBook files would fit on even a small laptop or PDA.

NEW: Save money by eSubscribing: cheap, online acess to any eBook for as long as you need it.

Annual subscription packages

We now offer special low cost bulk subscriptions to packages of eBooks in certain subject areas. These are available to libraries or to individuals.

For more information please contact webmaster.ebooks@tandf.co.uk

We're continually developing the eBook concept, so keep up to date by visiting the website.

www.eBookstore.tandf.co.uk